Ethical Dilemmas in the Global Defense Industry

THE OXFORD SERIES IN ETHICS, NATIONAL SECURITY, AND THE RULE OF LAW

Series Editors: Claire O. Finkelstein and Jens David Ohlin
Oxford University Press

About the Series

The *Oxford Series in Ethics, National Security, and the Rule of Law* is an interdisciplinary book series designed to address abiding questions at the intersection of national security, moral and political philosophy, and the law. It seeks to illuminate both ethical and legal dilemmas that arise in democratic nations as they grapple with contemporary national security challenges. The series also seeks to create a synergy between academic researchers and practitioners as they focus on common problems in national security theory and practice. The aim of the series is ultimately to advance thinking about how to protect and augment the rule of law in the context of contemporary armed conflict and national security.

The book series grew out of the work of the Center for Ethics and the Rule of Law (CERL) at the University of Pennsylvania. CERL is a nonpartisan interdisciplinary institute dedicated to the preservation and promotion of the rule of law in twenty-first century warfare and national security. The only center of its kind housed within a major research university, CERL draws from the study of law, philosophy, and ethics to answer the difficult questions that arise in times of war and contemporary transnational conflicts.

Ethical Dilemmas in the Global Defense Industry

Edited by

DANIEL SCHOENI AND TOBIAS VESTNER

OXFORD
UNIVERSITY PRESS

OXFORD
UNIVERSITY PRESS

Oxford University Press is a department of the University of Oxford. It furthers the University's objective of excellence in research, scholarship, and education by publishing worldwide. Oxford is a registered trade mark of Oxford University Press in the UK and certain other countries.

Published in the United States of America by Oxford University Press
198 Madison Avenue, New York, NY 10016, United States of America.

CIP data is on file at the Library of Congress

ISBN 978–0–19–067581–3

DOI: 10.1093/oso/9780190675813.001.0001

Printed by Integrated Books International, United States of America

Note to Readers

This publication is designed to provide accurate and authoritative information in regard to the subject matter covered. It is based upon sources believed to be accurate and reliable and is intended to be current as of the time it was written. It is sold with the understanding that the publisher is not engaged in rendering legal, accounting, or other professional services. If legal advice or other expert assistance is required, the services of a competent professional person should be sought. Also, to confirm that the information has not been affected or changed by recent developments, traditional legal research techniques should be used, including checking primary sources where appropriate.

(Based on the Declaration of Principles jointly adopted by a Committee of the American Bar Association and a Committee of Publishers and Associations.)

Contents

Foreword

Dr. Leo Mackay, Jr.[*]

The defense industry has much to add to the global discussion on business ethics—both regarding general business ethics and in particular regarding the specific challenges for the defense industry itself. Its contributions have been built on a checkered history with well-publicized failures of integrity in business practices. Out of those ashes, however, has emerged a global industry committed to high ethical standards.

The chapters in this volume grew out of a conference held several years ago at the Center for Ethics and the Rule of Law at the University of Pennsylvania, which brought together defense industry leaders, academics, and lawyers to discuss ethical challenges for the industry. In this book you will find the authors grappling with ongoing challenges. While some of those challenges are common to other industries, many are driven by forces unique to this sector. Such forces include large-scale procurements, complex weapon systems, urgent needs, intense competition, and offset agreements. Defense-specific forces can create a toxic environment where the demons of unethical behavior may rear their ugly heads (about which more later), but I maintain that the worst of such unethical behavior lies in the past, as industry and government have come a long way toward managing such risks.

The Evolution of the Defense Industry's Ethical Standards

The industry's current ethical posture—which is resilient and attuned to the particular challenges related to defense—resulted from decades of growing pains when ethical problems and scandals prevailed. Up until the mid-1970s, the U.S. defense industry and the global defense industry generally were largely unregulated. The absence of oversight and the industry-specific forces mentioned above combined to create an environment in which bribery and corruption, among other ethically questionable practices, were far too common.

[*] I would also like to thank the ethics director for one of our major business areas, Craig Cash, for his contributions to this foreword. His expertise, professionalism, and ardor for our work distinguish him.

Beginning in 1975, the Subcommittee on Multinationals, known as the Church Committee for its chairman, Senator Frank Church, began to shine a light on corruption in the defense industry.[1] As scrutiny intensified, firms began to try to right their own ships. For example, in 1977 Lockheed Aircraft Corporation published the "Lockheed Principles of Business Conduct,"[2] a document that linked right-minded behavior to the success of the company.[3]

In the mid-1980s, the cycle of corruption, public outrage, and attempted self-correction culminated in two important events: the FBI's Operation Ill Wind and the Packard Commission. While Ill Wind uncovered the most blatant graft in the U.S. government since the Teapot Dome scandals of the 1920s, the Packard Commission proposed solutions.[4] In addition to recommending specific procurement controls,[5] it suggested that the solution to the defense industry's corruption problems lay within the industry itself, within its culture.[6] Its report took a strong stance: "To assure that their houses are in order, defense contractors must promulgate and vigilantly enforce codes of ethics that address the unique problems and procedures incident to defense procurement."[7]

In pointing this out, the Commission was acknowledging the difficulties associated with individual firms attempting to self-police. During this time, companies had to decide if, when, and how to make trade-offs between virtue and competitiveness. Their individual efforts enjoyed varying levels of success. Collective efforts were accelerated with the formation of the Defense Industry Initiative on Business Ethics and Conduct (DII) in 1986, wherein General Electric CEO Jack Welch assembled the CEOs of 17 other U.S. defense firms to "up their game" on business ethics.[8]

The DII founders not only agreed to improve their ethical conduct generally but also to adhere to six principles. These principles, while they seem obvious today, were groundbreaking at the time:

1. Have and adhere to written Codes of Conduct;
2. Train employees in those Codes;

[1] *See, e.g.*, Marc B. Langston, *Rediscovering Congressional Intelligence Oversight: Is Another Church Committee Possible Without Frank Church?*, 2 Tex. A&M L. Rev. 433, 453–64 (2015) (summarizing the Church Committee's efforts to investigate wrongdoing by various federal agencies).

[2] *Lockheed Principles of Ethical Conduct*, adopted by the Board of Directors on May 2, 1977.

[3] *Id.*

[4] *See generally* Report of the President's Blue Ribbon Commission on Defense Management, A Question for Excellence (1986).

[5] *Id.* at xxvi–xxxvii, 90–111.

[6] *Id.* at xxix, 80–89.

[7] *Id.* at xxix.

[8] Defense Industry Initiative on Business Ethics and Conduct, *About DII*, https://www.dii.org/about/about-dii (last visited Jan. 8, 2022).

3. Encourage internal reporting of violations of the Codes, within an atmosphere free of fear of retribution;
4. Practice self-governance through the implementation of systems to monitor compliance with federal procurement laws and the adoption of procedures for voluntary disclosure of violations to the appropriate authorities;
5. Share with other firms their best practices in implementing the principles, and participate annually in "Best Practices Forums";
6. Be accountable to the public.[9]

By July 1986, 32 companies had signed onto these principles. DII is still a strong, going concern, having updated the principles in 2013 to reflect the maturation of ethical expectations and practices.[10] The now 75 signatories have signed on the dotted line and agreed to adhere to the principles, thus demonstrating their commitment to establishing high ethical standards. Alas, not everyone in the industry lives by those standards.

The Insidiousness of Corruption

Corruption and other ethical issues are more than a business problem; they are a societal problem. They erode the fundamental trust that is central to stable market transactions. Once people lose trust that their leaders, public or private, are acting for their collective best interests, the very fabric of civil society is threatened.

What is more, corruption begets corruption. Once officials become accustomed to receiving what are euphemistically called "incentives," they come to expect and even demand such incentives. This can extend to the point where otherwise honest companies are "shaken down" in order to participate in the procurement process, especially abroad. And not all companies have the scale, or nonpareil products, of a major defense contractor that would make resisting corruption easier.

Robert Hurley has described the far-reaching impact of (un)trustworthy organizations. Such trust is developed "because all elements of the organization (mission, strategy, leadership, structure, culture, systems, and core processes) work congruently to serve all stakeholders in a trustworthy manner. These stakeholders feel they can place trust—confident reliance—in these firms

[9] Defense Industry Initiative, *DII Principles*, July 1986.
[10] Defense Industry Initiative on Business Ethics and Conduct, https://www.dii.org/dii-principles-pdf (last visited Jan. 12, 2022).

because of their track record."[11] Untrustworthy organizations, by contrast, contribute to the "crisis of trust" felt around the world, across organizations both public and private.[12] Trust is the coin of the realm, and the ramifications of its loss are profound—and not only for the defense industry.

Industry-Specific Problems

As noted above, concerns about corruption and other ethical dilemmas in the defense industry are amplified due to industry-specific factors. First and foremost the industry builds instruments of destruction and lethality, which customers use to defend their nations from threats, both foreign and domestic, and to maintain their way of life, even their very existence. The industry's customers are governments, which creates singular risks because normal market forces do not apply. Product development and procurement decisions can be many years in the making and drive significant long-term impact to the competing organizations. Further, the inherent nature of defense products introduces unique concerns associated with such products falling into the wrong hands.

Beyond the lethal nature of these products, their cost must be factored into the corruption equation. Defense products are costly and burden a nation's finances. With such high stakes, transparency is paramount. Governments must articulate why these expenditures are justified based on societal needs, not the personal gains of the defense industry or of the purchasing authorities.

Corruption in the defense industry is complicated by related factors such as "conflict minerals"[13] and their impact in high-corruption regimes, technological proliferation (including resistance to or ability to facilitate cyberattacks), and the political dynamic of constantly changing regimes. Ethical challenges in this sector abound. My chapter and indeed this whole volume barely scratch the surface. That is why the academic treatment of the subject matter considered here is long overdue. The defense industry's ethical problems merit closer scrutiny.

A Higher Standard

The foregoing industry-specific challenges raise the question of whether the defense industry should be held to a higher standard. I assert, and I believe my

[11] Robert Hurley, *The Trustworthy Leader: The First Step Toward Creating High-Trust Organizations*, 66 Leader to Leader 33, 34 (Fall 2012).

[12] *Id.* at 33–34.

[13] "Conflict resources" are natural resources extracted in a war zone sold to perpetuate the fighting. Currently, this list includes metals tantalum, tin, tungsten, and gold.

industry would agree, that we should be.[14] The erosion of trust in defense procurement is perhaps the most corrosive any nation can suffer. Governments must be part of the solution, by holding the industry to a higher standard. Only by maintaining such standards can the industry establish and maintain the public trust.

In contemplating what higher standards should look like, one significant consideration is differing legal and ethical standards around the globe. For example, it was only in 2000 that France removed foreign bribery as a tax deduction. U.S. companies have been prohibited from bribing foreign officials since passage of the Foreign Corrupt Practices Act in 1977. This cleavage afforded French firms an advantage vis-à-vis American firms for two decades. More generally, if foreign bribery was not illegal in Country A, sales personnel would happily offer bribes to customers in Country B, even if the *receipt* of bribes in Country B was illegal. This was the thrust of the infamous Rokkiedo Jiken incident in 1971 that led to the resignation and subsequent arrest and conviction of Prime Minister Tanaka Kakeui and other top leaders in Japan.[15] Laws and regulations continue to evolve around the globe, accompanied by increasing transparency and public dialogue.[16]

Through the efforts of groups such as Transparency International, the Organization for Economic Cooperation and Development, the aforementioned DII in the United States, and the International Forum on Business Ethical Conduct (IFBEC), national laws and industrial standards are rising and becoming mainstream.

Yet we must do more. As an industry that is composed of a closely networked web of vendors and customers, we should continue to elevate our expectations, commitments, and actions. We do that by continually demanding more from all of the myriad participants in the global arms industry. The age of winking and looking the other way is behind us. How to demand a higher standard boils down to three lines of effort: cooperation, transparency, and mentorship.

A. Cooperation

Cooperation on the ethics front is critical. While we all compete vigorously in the marketplace, our work in ethics should not be antagonistic. By sharing best

[14] In Chapter 9, Philip M. Nichols offers a persuasive argument that the public only allows the defense industry to exist in the first place on the basis of industry's strict adherence to high ethical standards.

[15] *See generally* A. CARL KOTCHIAN, *ROKKIEDO JIKEN* (1978).

[16] Examples include the United Kingdom Bribery Act of 2010, Brazil's Clean Company Act of 2014, and France's Sapin II of 2016.

practices and being open about the standards we maintain, companies can learn from one another and be fully confident that their peer companies are, from an ethical standpoint, competing fairly.

The DII has facilitated such cooperation in the U.S. defense industry. Its annual Best Practices Forum is a valuable source of lessons learned and innovative approaches. Since 2010, IFBEC has been serving a similar role globally. Further, defense companies participate in broader ethics consortia such as the Ethics and Compliance Initiative and the Society of Corporate Compliance and Ethics. These are all valuable enterprises.

I should also address here cooperation with academia, a topic which Steve Schooner and Evan Matsuda discuss in the closing chapter. The conference on which this book is based is an excellent example of such cooperation. Academic study of business ethics has typically included topics such as cheating, ethical decision-making, the impact of leadership on organizational culture, appropriate norms and regulations, and so forth. Such studies inform industry as we shape our ethics and compliance programs. This relationship is reciprocal, with defense companies offering case studies for such research. But our cooperation shouldn't be limited *only* to case studies.

As I write, universities are educating the next generation of professionals. They need to increase their research on the ethical issues and raise their standards in teaching ethics and imparting to these future leaders sound moral judgment. Our view at Lockheed Martin has always been that we hire ethical people and then train and mentor them on applying ethical principles when they face tough decisions. But we hope that new employees come with well-tuned moral compasses. Such lessons must be nurtured in childhood, instilled through the higher education system, and reinforced within industry—and, when all else fails, enforced by governments.

B. Transparency

Transparency can be viewed as the *sine qua non* for business ethics. Transparency in ethics should spread through all stakeholders including customers, employees, investors, and citizens. Further, it should not await a crisis; transparency should be ongoing even if crises do not materialize. Disclosure has been proven the best long-term strategy. Yet, given the defense industry's products and customers, there remains still much to improve regarding transparency. This is primarily the work of government[17] and nongovernmental organization (NGOs)

[17] In Chapter 12, Daniel Schoeni highlights the failure of governments around the world to gather and report data about defense offsets, which makes diagnosing the ethical problems and prescribing solutions a challenging enterprise.

watchdogs.[18] But academia and research institutions can also support the endeavor, notably with data assembly and analysis.[19]

C. Mentorship

Large companies in the global defense industry have the resources—and therefore the ability—to institute comprehensive ethics and compliance programs complete with dedicated ethics officers, helplines, investigation databases, communicators, training, expert legal advice, and so forth. Smaller companies have the same mandate for ethical behavior but much fewer resources. Large companies can and should support smaller companies as well as companies new to the field in their efforts for attaining ethical standards either directly or via industry ethics consortia and cooperation with governments.[20] NGOs and academia also have a valuable role to play in fostering and supporting such collaboration.[21]

Conclusion

Decades of experience in the industry have led me to believe that we have come a long way regarding the most salient ethical challenges in the defense industry. Yet the authors in this volume are not all sanguine about the status quo. I may disagree with many of the particulars of their assessments, but I welcome this dialogue: their work signifies a major contribution to the ethical development of the industry. I am proud of our progress and, by my lights, high level of ethical comportment. But I am not so Pollyannaish to suppose that we cannot improve. I welcome the sunlight, scrutiny, and insight that come with a volume such as this. May we continue this journey together.

[18] Prominent examples of such NGOs include Transparency International and the U.S.-based Project on Government Oversight.

[19] The Stockholm International Peace Research Institute, for instance, is a leading example for maintaining valuable databases about military spending around the world.

[20] In Chapter 15, Jessica Tillipman and Vijaya Surampudi describe the U.S. government's new compliance mentorship program, which provides smaller contractors better access to and awareness of valuable anti-corruption best practices.

[21] The Geneva Centre for Security, for instance, has offered train-the-trainer workshops for defense industry staff on their rights and obligations under international human rights law and international humanitarian law.

References

DEFENSE INDUSTRY INITIATIVE, *DII Principles* (July 1986), https://www.dii.org/dii-principles-pdf.

DEFENSE INDUSTRY INITIATIVE ON BUSINESS ETHICS AND CONDUCT, https://www.dii.org/about/about-dii.

Robert Hurley, *The Trustworthy Leader: The First Step Toward Creating High-Trust Organizations*, 66 LEADER TO LEADER 33 (Fall 2012).

A. CARL KOTCHIAN, *ROKKIEDO JIKEN* (1978).

Marc B. Langston, *Rediscovering Congressional Intelligence Oversight: Is Another Church Committee Possible Without Frank Church?*, 2 TEX. A&M L. REV. 433 (2015).

Lockheed Principles of Ethical Conduct, adopted by the Board of Directors on May 2, 1977.

REPORT OF THE PRESIDENT'S BLUE RIBBON COMMISSION ON DEFENSE MANAGEMENT, A QUESTION FOR EXCELLENCE (1986).

U.S. DEPARTMENT OF COMMERCE, INTERNATIONAL TRADE ADMINISTRATION, ADDRESSING THE CHALLENGES OF INTERNATIONAL BRIBERY AND FAIR COMPETITION: THE THIRD ANNUAL REPORT UNDER SECTION 6 OF THE INTERNATIONAL ANTI-BRIBERY AND FAIR COMPETITION ACT OF 1998 (2001).

Acknowledgments

This volume involved the work of many hands, for which we are very grateful. Thanks go to the Center for Ethics and the Rule (CERL) at the University of Pennsylvania, which initiated and hosted the eponymous conference on April 15–16, 2015. The research presented there forms the core of this work. We are grateful to all participants—and especially to the keynote speaker, Sarah Chayes of the Carnegie Endowment for International Peace—for having made the conference a success and an opportunity for stimulating thinking about a subject that has long been neglected. If not for the ideas sparked there, this book would not have been possible.

We are deeply grateful to Claire Finkelstein for her vision, leadership, and engagement. Her efforts started with organizing the conference and ended with helping to select the cover art—and included everything in between. She not only served this project in her role as editor of Oxford University Press's series in *Ethics, National Security, and the Rule of Law*, but by all rights could have been credited as a coeditor. Her guidance and support were crucial.

We are also grateful to Kevin Govern, who not only conceived of the idea for the conference and invited many of the participants but also coauthored one chapter and was instrumental in converting the substance of the conference into this book.

This effort also benefited from generous support by the University of Pennsylvania Carey Law School, CERL, and the Lockheed Martin Corporation for covering the conference expenses and for funding the costs associated with publishing this volume. Lockheed Martin was respectful of our academic freedom, keeping themselves a safe distance from the writing and editorial process. We are grateful.

Special thanks also go to the Oxford University Press editors for their excellent support, especially to the lead editor David Lipp. We appreciated their diligence and expertise throughout the process.

Last, we thank the authors for their excellent contributions. Some demonstrated great patience, others extraordinary efficiency, and all professionalism of the highest order. It has been an honor to collaborate with such scholars. They have personified the maxim that alone you can go fast but together you can go far.

List of Contributors

Thomas E. Ayres is the Chief Legal Officer and General Counsel at Voyager Space. He served in the U.S. Army from 1984, upon commissioning from the U.S. Military Academy at West Point, until his retirement in 2017. After service in Italy as an airborne rifle platoon leader, executive officer, and personnel officer, he attended the University of Pennsylvania School of Law (J.D. 1991). His JAG Corps assignments included Commander, U.S. Army Legal Services Agency; Chief Judge, U.S. Army Court of Criminal Appeals; Commandant of The Judge Advocate General's Legal Center and School; Deputy Legal Counsel to the Joint Chiefs of Staff; and multiple staff judge advocate tours, including one each in Iraq and Afghanistan. He finished his Army career as the Deputy Judge Advocate General, retiring in the rank of Major General. He then served for three years as the U.S. Air Force General Counsel.

Jeffrey Biller is an Assistant Professor of Cyber Law and Policy in the Department of Law at the U.S. Air Force Academy, Colorado Springs, Colorado. In addition to performing faculty duties with the Department of Law, he is part of Air Force CyberWorx, partnering with government, industry, and academia to develop innovative cyber solutions to the Air Force's most complex problems. He is also the Director of Cyber Programs for the Law, Technology, and Warfare Research Cell. He is a retired Lieutenant Colonel in the U.S. Air Force, where he served over 20 years as a SERE instructor, intelligence officer, and judge advocate. He is a graduate of the University of Washington (B.A. in History 1998), University of Kansas School of Law (J.D. 2007), and the George Washington University Law School (LL.M. National Security Law 2012).

Michael Davis is a Senior Fellow at the Center for the Study of Ethics in the Professions and Emeritus Professor of Philosophy, Illinois Institute of Technology (IIT), Chicago. Before coming to IIT in 1986, he taught at Case Western Reserve, Illinois State, and the University of Illinois at Chicago. His research interests include the integration of ethics into technical courses, promotion of globally responsive research, social contract (especially Locke and Hobbes), engineering ethics, and punishment theory. His books include *To Make the Punishment Fit the Crime* (1992), *Justice in the Shadow of Death* (1996), *Thinking Like an Engineer* (1998), *Ethics and the University* (1999), *Profession, Code, and Ethics* (2002), *Actual Social Contract and Political Obligation* (2002), and *Engineering as a Global Profession* (2021), as well as numerous edited works.

Nicholas G. Evans is an Associate Professor of Philosophy at the University of Massachusetts Lowell, where he conducts research on national security and emerging technologies. His recent work on assessing the risks and benefits of dual-use research of concern has been widely published. In 2017, he was awarded funding from the National Science Foundation to examine the ethics of autonomous vehicles. Prior to his appointment at the University of Massachusetts, he completed postdoctoral work in medical ethics and health policy at the Perelman School of Medicine at the University of Pennsylvania. He has conducted research at the Monash Bioethics Centre, the Centre for Applied Philosophy and Public Ethics, Australian Defence Force Academy, and the University of Exeter. In 2013, he served as a policy officer with the Australian Department of Health and Australian Therapeutic Goods Administration.

Timothy Goines serves as the Senior Military Faculty and an Assistant Professor of Law at the U.S. Air Force Academy, Colorado Springs, Colorado, where he teaches Cyberlaw, Law for Air Force Officers, and the Legal Studies Capstone Course. He also serves as the Director of the Law, Technology, and Warfare Research Cell. He is a Lieutenant Colonel on active in the U.S. Air Force and has served in various roles as a judge advocate—assistant staff judge advocate, an area defense counsel, a deputy staff judge advocate, and as a legal adviser to the Combined Air Operations Center in Qatar. He is a graduate of Creighton University (B.S. Mathematics 2004), Baylor University (J.D. 2009), and the University of Nebraska (LL.M. Cyber, Space, and Telecommunications Law 2016). He regularly presents at conferences on cyber and space law, writes on the same topics, and has been published in various journals.

Kevin Govern is an Associate Professor of Law at Ave Maria School of Law. He began his career as an Army judge advocate, serving 20 years at every echelon during peacetime and war in assignments involving every legal discipline. He has also served as an Assistant Professor of Law at the U.S. Military Academy and taught at California University of Pennsylvania. He has published widely and spoken frequently on international and comparative law, national security and homeland security law, military operations, and professional ethics. He was a contributing author and editor to *Cyber War—Law and Ethics for Virtual Conflicts* and the coauthor of *Illuminating Islamic Jurisprudence* (first and second editions). He has been a founding Executive Board Member of the University of Pennsylvania's Center for Ethics and the Rule of Law.

Brian D. Green has been a judge advocate on active duty in the U.S. Air Force since 2005. He is the Chief of Space and Operations Law and Space Law Instructor for Space Training and Readiness Command at Peterson Space Force Base, Colorado. His previous assignments have included tours as an assistant staff judge advocate, disability counsel, senior medical law consultant, chief of space and international law, and instructor. He has deployed to a detainee operations task force in Iraq and as a legal adviser to the Combined Air Operations Center in Qatar. He is a graduate of the University of Washington (B.A. Political Science 2001; B.A. Interdisciplinary Visual Arts 2001), the University of Virginia School of Law (J.D. 2004), and McGill University (LL.M. Air and Space Law 2015). He is a regular presenter at courses and conferences on air and space law, and published his LL.M. thesis on the same subject in the *Air Force Law Review*.

Blake Hereth is a Postdoctoral Research Associate in the Department of Philosophy at the University of Massachusetts, Lowell. Following graduation from the University of

Washington with their Ph.D. in 2019, they worked as a Visiting Assistant Professor in the Department of Philosophy at the University of Arkansas. Their research interests include applied ethics (war, biology, artificial intelligence, and animal ethics), philosophy of religion, and feminist philosophy, and they have published extensively in all three areas. Their research on self-defense was awarded the 2019 Frank Chapman Sharp Memorial Prize by the American Philosophical Association for the best essay on the ethics of war and peace. Before completing their doctoral work, they earned a B.A. (Philosophy) from Cedarville University and an M.A. (Philosophy) first from the University of Arkansas and then from the University of Washington.

Nancy Hite-Rubin is Affiliated Faculty at the Jonathan M. Tisch College of Civic Life, Tufts University. She received her Ph.D. in Political Science at Yale University in 2012 and served as an Assistant Professor of Political Economy at the Fletcher School from 2012 to 2018. She holds an LL.M. in Law and Economics from the University of Hamburg (earned on a Fulbright Scholarship) and a B.A. in Economics (with distinction) from the University of Texas, Austin. Her research and teaching interests lie at the intersection of comparative political economy and international relations. She focuses mainly on comparative politics in developing and transitional countries and is keenly interested in corruption, informality, clientelism, political psychology, and access to state institutions. Her book manuscript, *Economic Modernization and the Disruption of Patronage Politics: Experimental Evidence from the Philippines*, employs qualitative, field experimental, and quantitative research methodology to investigate how marginalized people respond politically to economic and institutional development. Her work has been published in both policy-focused outlets, such as Brookings Institution for Oxford University Press, and academic journals, such as the *American Journal of Political Science*. She was the Research and Evaluation Lead for Global Development at the Cloudburst Group (2019–20), managing and contributing to dozens of USAID and MCC development projects while maintaining active, academic research as Affiliated Faculty.

Duncan MacIntosh is a Professor of Philosophy at Dalhousie University and serves on the Executive Board of the Center for Ethics and the Rule of Law at the University of Pennsylvania. For much of his career he wrote on traditional philosophical issues in the nature of language, knowledge, rationality, and morality. More recently, he has focused on the themes occupying the aforementioned Center, including the nature of the rule of law, whether secret laws are intelligible and defensible, the ethical use of lethal autonomous weapons, whether it can ever be right to destroy cultural artifacts in war, the use of moral injury as a weapon and as featuring in post-traumatic stress injury, the weaponization of disinformation and incivility, foreign interference with democratic processes, decision-theoretic issues in gray-zone conflict, and ethical issues in the defense industry.

Leo Mackay, Jr. is the Senior Vice President of Ethics and Enterprise Assurance for Lockheed Martin Corporation. In his current role, he serves as his employer's chief audit executive. He previously served as their vice president of Corporate Domestic Business Development and as president of a joint venture between Lockheed Martin and Northrop Grumman for the Coast Guard's modernization. He studied at the U.S. Naval Academy

(Navy Distinguished Midshipman Graduate), spent three years flying the F-14, and later graduated from the Navy's prestigious Fighter Weapons School ("Topgun"). In 2001–03, he served as Deputy Secretary of Veterans Affairs. He is a member of the U.S. Naval Institute and the Council on Foreign Relations. He earned his M.A. and Ph.D. in public policy from Harvard University and was a Kennedy Fellow, Harvard MacArthur Scholar, Graduate Prize Fellow, and Research Fellow at the Center for Science and International Affairs.

Evan Matsuda is a student at the George Washington University Law School and Elliott School of International Affairs. He is pursuing a J.D. with a concentration in Government Procurement Law and an M.A. in International Affairs specializing in International Security Studies. He received a B.A. in International Relations from the University of Southern California with concentrations in Security Studies and International Politics. He is a Managing Editor of *The George Washington Law Review* and a research assistant to Professor Steven L. Schooner.

Michael W. Meier serves as the senior civilian adviser to the Army Judge Advocate General on matters related to the Law of War. Prior to his current position, he served as an Attorney-Adviser with the Office of the Legal Adviser for Political-Military Affairs, U.S. Department of State, where his portfolio included International Humanitarian Law issues on legal and legal policy issues associated with the interpretation and application of the law of war to U.S. military operations; U.S. diplomatic initiatives, including ongoing dialogue with the International Committee of the Red Cross, the United Nations, and other intergovernmental organizations; and international agreements and arms control agreements, such as the Ottawa Convention, the Convention on Cluster Munitions, the Convention on Certain Conventional Weapons, and the Arms Trade Treaty. He served almost 23 years as an Army judge advocate until his retirement in 2009 and served in a variety of roles, including the various deputy staff judge advocate and staff judge advocate positions and as the Principal Deputy Legal Counsel to the Chairman of the Joint Chiefs of Staff. He is an Adjunct Professor at Georgetown Law.

Philip M. Nichols is the Joseph Kolodny Professor of Social Responsibility in Business and Professor of Legal Studies and Business Ethics at the Wharton School of the University of Pennsylvania. He studies the effects of and control of corruption, particularly in emerging economies. He has conducted fieldwork in or worked on projects with dozens of countries and organizations around the world. He recently served as the co-chair of the American Society of International Law's Anti-Corruption Law Interest Group and has also served on the Executive Council and as President of the Academy of Legal Studies in Business. He has been a visiting professor in India, Mongolia, Singapore, South Korea, and Uruguay, and is a Fellow at the GIBS Centre for Business Ethics in South Africa.

Richard W. Painter is the S. Walter Richey Professor of Corporate Law, University of Minnesota Law School, where he has been since 2007. He previously taught at the University of Oregon and the University of Illinois law schools. He has held fellowships and visiting professorships at a number of institutions, including Harvard University's

Safra Center for Ethics and Humboldt University (Berlin). He studied at Harvard College (B.A. History) and Yale Law School, and clerked for Judge John T. Noonan, Jr. of the U.S. Court of Appeals for the Ninth Circuit. In private practice, he worked for Sullivan & Cromwell in New York and Finn Dixon & Herling in Stamford, Connecticut. From 2005 to 2007, he served as Associate Counsel to the President and chief White House ethics lawyer. His teaching and research areas include business ethics, government ethics, professional responsibility, and securities regulations. He is also a reporter for the American Law Institute Principles of Government Ethics.

C. Edward Peartree has held positions in government, public policy research, and the defense and aerospace industry for over 25 years. From 2013 to 2017, he served as Director of the Office of Defense Trade Controls Policy at the U.S. Department of State, where he oversaw the development of regulations and policies governing U.S. arms exports. He also led engagement with foreign partners and allies on bilateral and multilateral defense trade matters, including U.S.-U.K. and U.S.-Australia Defense Trade Cooperation Treaties, and the U.S.-EU COARM dialogue. He began U.S. government service as a Presidential Management Fellow and formerly served as a Research Associate in Political-Military Studies at the Center for Strategic and International Studies in Washington, D.C., and as an analyst in the Office of Net Assessment at the U.S. Department of Defense. He is a distinguished graduate of National Defense University and also holds an M.A. from George Washington University's Elliot School of International Affairs and a B.A. from Johns Hopkins University.

Mark Pyman is the cofounder of Curbing Corruption (together with Professor Paul Heywood). He is an experienced advocate, scholar, and practitioner at the forefront of ways to reduce corruption. Since 2018 he has led Curbing Corruption, a not-for-profit entity that provides sector-specific corruption reform strategies for public officials, politicians, and others. From 2015 to 2017, he was one of three International Commissioners in Afghanistan's National Anti-Corruption Monitoring and Evaluation Committee. From 2004 to 2015, he was the founder and director of Transparency International's global Defence & Security program, pioneering practical corruption-prevention in defense ministries, militaries, and security forces. He led the team's work in over 30 countries, contributed to security policy forums such as the annual Munich Security Conference, and was instrumental in shaping the anti-corruption elements of the UN Arms Trade Treaty (2013) and in changing NATO policy and operations in respect of counter-corruption. He pioneered the quantitative evaluation and comparison of corruption vulnerabilities in the defense sector. The resulting Government Defence Anti-Corruption Index—ranking the corruption vulnerabilities of defense ministries and military forces of some 120 countries—and the Global Companies Index—ranking the world's 130 largest defense companies—have become core sources of reference for the sector. He has authored or supervised over 100 publications on curbing corruption. Prior to 2004, he was Chief Financial Officer for Shell International in China, West Africa, and elsewhere. He holds a Ph.D. from the University of Western Australia, an M.Sc. from the University of Bath, and a B.Sc. from Birmingham University, U.K.

Daniel Schoeni has been with the U.S. Air Force JAG Corps since 2004 and is currently assigned to Air Force Materiel Command at Wright-Patterson Air Force Base, Ohio. He has served as a prosecutor, trial and appellate defense counsel, program counsel, and staff judge advocate. He has deployed twice. As a Language Enabled Airman Program scholar, he has extensive experience in security cooperation. He studied at Brigham Young University (B.A.), the University of Iowa (M.A./J.D.), and George Washington University (LL.M.). Prior to the military, he clerked for the Honorable Jerry Larson of the Iowa Supreme Court. He has published on a variety of subjects related to government contracts. He completed a Ph.D. in public procurement law at the University of Nottingham last summer, is a lecturer at King's College London, and was recently hired as an adjunct professorial lecturer in law at George Washington University.

Steven L. Schooner is the Nash & Cibinic Professor of Government Procurement Law at the George Washington University Law School, where he previously served as Senior Associate Dean for Academic Affairs. Before joining the faculty, he was the Associate Administrator for Procurement Law and Legislation at the Office of Federal Procurement Policy in the Office of Management and Budget in the Executive Office of the President. He previously practiced law at the Department of Justice and with private law firms. He served (on active duty) as a Commissioner at the Armed Services Board of Contract Appeals and (as a reserve officer) as an Adjunct Professor at the Army's Judge Advocate General's School. Outside of the United States, he has advised government officials, either directly or through multigovernment programs, in more than three dozen countries. His dispute resolution experience includes serving as an expert witness, arbitrator, mediator, neutral, and ombudsman. He received his B.A. from Rice University, J.D. from the College of William and Mary, and LL.M. (with highest honors) from the George Washington University. He is a Fellow of the National Contract Management Association (NCMA), a recipient of NCMA's Charles A. Dana Distinguished Service Award, and a Certified Professional Contracts Manager. He is a Director of the Procurement Round Table, a faculty adviser to the American Bar Association's *Public Contract Law Journal*, and a member of the *Government Contractor* Advisory Board. He coauthored *The Government Contracts Reference Book: A Comprehensive Guide to The Language of Procurement* (now in its fifth edition).

Vijaya Surampudi is a trial attorney in the Department of Justice National Courts Division, where she litigates government contracts cases before the U.S. Court of Federal Claims and Court of Appeals for the Federal Circuit. Previously, she was an associate at Holland & Knight, LLP, where she specialized in government contracts and small business issues and litigated before the Boards of Contract Appeals. Previously, she worked as agency counsel at the U.S. Department of Labor (DOL), where she represented the DOL in a wide range of procurement issues and litigated before the General Accountability Office, U.S. Court of Federal Claims, and U.S. Civilian Board of Contract Appeals. She counseled numerous contracting officials throughout all phases of the acquisition process. While in law school, she interned in the procurement divisions of several agencies, including the U.S. General Services Administration, Air Force Office of General Counsel, and U.S. Department of Health and Human Services. She also interned with the White

House Office of Federal Procurement Policy. She also served as an articles editor for the *Public Contract Law Journal* and was vice president of the Moot Court Board.

Jessica Tillipman is the Assistant Dean for Government Procurement Law Studies and Government Contracts Advisory Council Lecturer in Government Contacts Law, Practice, and Policy at the George Washington University Law School. She also teaches Anti-Corruption & Compliance, a course that focuses on anti-corruption, ethics, and compliance issues in government procurement. Prior to joining GW Law, she served as a law clerk to the Honorable Lawrence S. Margolis of the U.S. Court of Federal Claims and was an associate at Jenner & Block, where she specialized in Government Contracts and White Collar Criminal Defense. She is a Senior Editor of the "The FCPA Blog"—a leading Foreign Corrupt Practices Act resource on the internet. She has also published numerous articles that address legal and policy issues involving anti-corruption, government procurement, white-collar crime, and government ethics law. She is also a co-chair of the American Bar Association, International Anti-Corruption Committee. She frequently organizes and presents at domestic and international government procurement and anti-corruption conferences and colloquia, and her legal commentary has been featured in numerous domestic and international media outlets. She is a member of the bars of the U.S. Court of Federal Claims, the state of Virginia, and the District of Columbia. She graduated cum laude from Miami University (Oxford, OH) in 2000 and obtained her J.D., with honors, from the George Washington University Law School in 2003.

Tobias Vestner is the Head of the Research and Policy Advice Department and the Head of the Security and Law Programme at the Geneva Centre for Security Policy (GCSP). He leads the Centre's analysis and advice activities as well as researches and teaches on the intersection between security and law. He regularly advises governments, international organizations, and private firms and has widely published on security and legal issues. He is an Honorary Senior Research Fellow at the University of Exeter, a Fellow at Supreme Headquarters Allied Powers Europe, and a Non-Resident Fellow at the United Nations Institute for Disarmament Research. A former reserve member of the Swiss Special Forces Command, he serves as reserve Legal Advisor at the Swiss Armed Forces Staff. He is a member of the Board of Directors of the International Society for Military Law and the Law of War and a member of the International Institute of Humanitarian Law. Before joining the GCSP, he was Research Affiliate and Global Futures Fellow at Georgetown University. Prior to that, he was Policy Advisor at the Swiss State Secretariat for Economic Affairs, where he managed political processes with regard to the export of conventional weapons and participated in the UN negotiations of the Arms Trade Treaty. Previously, while at the Law of Armed Conflict Section at the Swiss Federal Department of Defence, Civil Protection, and Sports, he contributed to bilateral negotiations on military cooperation and trained military officers in international humanitarian law.

Patricia Werhane is a Professor of Philosophy at the Driehaus College of Business and the Wicklander Chair of Business Ethics and Managing Director, Institute for Business and Professional Ethics at DePaul University. She is a Professor Emerita at the Darden School of Business, University of Virginia, where she was the Peter and Adeline Ruffin

Chair of Business Ethics and Senior Fellow at the Olsson Center for Applied Ethics. She is the author or editor of over 25 books and over 100 published articles, case studies, and book chapters on various business ethics on such topics as employee and employer rights, mergers and acquisitions, responsibilities of multinational corporations, intellectual property, and the intersection between healthcare organizations and business ethics. In 2008, she was listed as one of the 100 most influential people in business ethics by *Ethisphere Magazine*.

Christopher R. Yukins is the Lynn David Research Professor in Government Procurement Law at the George Washington University Law School. He has taught there on contract formations and performance issues in public procurement, bid protests and claims litigation, state and local procurement, anti-corruption issues, foreign contracting, procurement reform, and comparative and international law. He has spoken as a guest lecturer at institutions around the world, and he was a contributing editor to the UN Office on Drugs and Crime manual, *Guidebook on Anti-Corruption in Public Procurement*. He is an active member of the Public Contract Law Section of the American Bar Association and is a member of the Procurement Roundtable. He is a faculty adviser to the *Public Contract Law Journal*, a member of the editorial board of the *European Procurement & Public-Private Partnership Law Review*, and on the advisory board of *The Government Contractor*. He has worked on a wide array of international projects on capacity building in procurement, and he was an adviser to the U.S. delegation to the working group on reform of the UN Commission on International Trade Law Model Procurement Law. Together with his colleagues Jessica Tillipman and Steven Schooner, he runs a colloquium series on procurement reform. In private practice, he has been an associate, partner, and counsel at leading national firms. He is currently counsel to the firm of Arnold & Porter LLP.

Introduction

Engaging Both Horns of the Ethical Dilemma

Daniel Schoeni and Tobias Vestner

1. Setting the Stage

A public official who was new on the job visited an arms manufacturer whose wares were sold around the world. The official asked how he could sleep at night, knowing that his weapons would likely be used to kill someone, somewhere in the world. This didn't worry him in the least. He was merely the producer, making them available for sale abroad subject to government approval. It was the government that bore the responsibility for where the arms would be sold and to whom.

Later, the same official asked a senior official in the arms exports department how he could sleep at night given that people would die based on his decisions. This did not worry him at all. His unit merely assessed and approved exports. The man ultimately responsible for the deaths, he said, was he who produced and sold the weapons.

Who was right? Or are both wrong? It's complicated. In one sense, this is a simple question. To produce weapons is prima facie problematic because in general taking another's life violates our fundamental values. Intuitively, humanity would be better off if we lacked sophisticated tools for killing one another and had no need to defend ourselves. That is not, however, the world that we live in. Here, innocents may need to be protected by force, even if this entails taking the life of another. Already, this question has become more complicated.

So far only two players have been considered. This binary setup oversimplifies a complex world. Apart from the manufacturer and the arms export official who decides what can be sold and where, many others may also bear moral responsibility during the life cycle of a weapon. What of the engineer who designs the weapon? The bureaucrat who purchases it? The statesman who chooses the foreign policy that puts her armed forces in harm's way, whether by attacking, defending, or policing? The officer who orders the attack? Or the soldier, sailor, or airman who pulls the trigger? More abstractly, what of those who benefit from the military's actions, private citizens at home and abroad who may profit from

Daniel Schoeni and Tobias Vestner, *Introduction* In: *Ethical Dilemmas in the Global Defense Industry*. Edited by: Daniel Schoeni and Tobias Vestner, Oxford University Press.
DOI: 10.1093/oso/9780190675813.003.0001

containing a threat? Each of these—and possibly many others—arguably bears *some* share of the blame for the killing. "Use every man after his desert, and who should 'scape whipping?"[1]

As this story illustrates, it is all too human to avoid responsibility, especially for ethically complex actions. But these moral issues are not someone else's problem. Most of us neither build weapons nor approve their sale abroad, yet however attenuated these issues may seem from our daily lives, all of us bear some responsibility for such matters. It behooves us, then, to think about them more carefully. Surprisingly, the literature on this subject is scarce. Much has been written about the defense industry, arms procurement, and international arms trade, but the associated ethical issues have received comparatively little attention.

Both public discourse and academic writing often connect the ethical issues of the defense industry to what U.S. President Dwight D. Eisenhower famously called the "military-industrial complex" (MIC).[2] The literature on the MIC describes how politicians, the armed forces, and the defense industry may exaggerate threats for their personal advantage.[3] Numerous analyses have discussed the MIC's existence, dynamics, and implications.[4] Yet the MIC remains a descriptive rather than analytical concept which is too loosely defined for serving a broad and critical examination of the ethical issues related to the defense industry. Moreover, because this term is associated with ethically problematic behavior, its use tends to be pejorative and this makes it difficult to have objective and unbiased discussions about the ethical dilemmas of the defense industry. For that reason, the term is generally avoided in this volume, with only a few exceptions.

One can only speculate about why ethical issues in this field have generally been neglected. Perhaps some have supposed that the end of history was near,[5] and that soon mankind would lay down its swords and beat them into

[1] William Shakespeare, *The Tragedy of Hamlet, Prince of Denmark*, Act II, Scene ii, *in* THE COMPLETE WORKS OF WILLIAM SHAKESPEARE 751 (William Wright ed., 1936).

[2] *See, e.g.*, THE BUSINESS OF WAR: THEOLOGICAL AND ETHICAL REFLECTIONS ON THE MILITARY-INDUSTRIAL COMPLEX (James McCarty, Matthew Tapie & Justin Bronson Barringer eds., 2020); Edmund F. Byrne, *The U.S. Military-Industrial Complex Is Circumstantially Unethical*, 95 J. BUS. ETHICS 153 (2010).

[3] *See, e.g.*, ALEX ROLAND, DELTA OF POWER: THE MILITARY-INDUSTRIAL COMPLEX (2021); Charles J. Dunlap, *The Military-Industrial Complex*, 140 DAEDALUS 135 (2011); J. Paul Dunne & Elisabeth Sköns, *The Military Industrial Complex*, *in* THE GLOBAL ARMS TRADE, 281 (Andrew T.H. Tan ed., 2010).

[4] *See, e.g.*, William J. Lynn III, *The End of the Military-Industrial Complex*, FOREIGN AFF., Nov./Dec. 2014, at 104; Bruce G. Brunton, *Institutional Origins of the Military-Industrial Complex*, 22(2) J. ECON. ISSUES 599 (1988); PAUL A.C. KOISTINEN, THE MILITARY-INDUSTRIAL COMPLEX: A HISTORICAL PERSPECTIVE 99 (1980); Walter Adams, *The Military-Industrial Complex and the New Industrial State*, 58 AM. ECON. REV. 652 (1968).

[5] *See generally* FRANCIS FUKUYAMA, THE END OF HISTORY AND THE LAST MAN (1992).

plowshares,[6] making the defense industry a vestigial enterprise and studying its ethical standards a quaint anachronism. Others perhaps think that the industry's ethical flaws are irremediable given inherently the gruesome purposes for which its wares are used. Still others may simply accept that the nature of the business—which in furtherance of national security requires secrecy and strong ties with governments[7]—inevitably requires that we make certain ethical compromises. Or do we simply prefer to avoid conversations about hard questions?

Whatever the reason for the scholarly neglect, this book aims to contribute to a field of study whose significance has been underappreciated. Indeed, the ethical questions, challenges, and dilemmas are even more diverse than the simple story related above would suggest. This volume addresses many varieties of ethical issues. To do so, it offers a rare combination of disciplines, including philosophy, economics, law, and political science.

Addressing the defense industry's ethical challenges is not a problem that is to be solved once and done. Given its unique structure and incentives, these challenges are perennial. They are perhaps akin to mowing the grass or taking out the trash. One does not mow the yard or take out the trash once and for all. Some problems require our constant vigilance. One such, surely, is ethical issues in the defense industry. Despite our best efforts to eliminate bribery, corruption, and the like, these are hardy plants that resist permanent solutions. They grow back. The ethical challenges in question require constant vigilance.

Consider how this relates to the law of war, which governs how wars are conducted (*jus in bello*). This volume assumes that wars will continue and that a large share of global wealth will be devoted to the manufacture of arms for the foreseeable future. Though industry is temporally and physically removed from the battlefield, how and in what manner it equips forces are questions of great moral significance, effectively questions about *jus in bello*. Just as soldiers are judged for their conduct in battle, so also can industry be held to account for the acquittal of its duties. *Jus in bello* is designed to limit the suffering caused by war. In a similar fashion, studying the moral questions about the manufacture, sale, and distribution of arms may teach us how to curtail any unnecessary harm that this bloody industry causes. Such an industry must exist, but its ethical shortcomings can be identified, studied, and perhaps even mitigated.

[6] Isaiah 2:4 (King James Bible) ("They will beat their swords into ploughshares and their spears into pruning hooks. Nation will not take up sword against nation, nor will they train for war anymore.").

[7] *See, e.g.*, Glenn R. Fong, *The Political Economy of Pentagon-Industry Collaboration in Technology Development*, *in* The Political Economy of Defense: Issues and Perspectives 68–70 (Andrew L. Ross ed., 1991).

This is the right moment for addressing ethical issues in the defense industry. Laws and regulations have been enacted in recent decades to ensure that industry's activities are conducted in a more ethical and transparent fashion. Industry has enacted its own codes of conduct.[8] Nongovernmental organizations such as Transparency International have helped policymakers and the public to be more sensitive to these issues. Now that an ethical baseline has been established, it is time for the academy to assess that progress, study what can be improved, and point the way forward. The ethical dilemmas of the global defense industry are a subject fitting for a scholar's gimlet eye.

The time is ripe for scholarly input for another reason. Recent technological developments create new challenges. The defense industry used to be one of the major drivers of technical innovation. It developed novel technologies, which were then used for civilian purposes. The Global Positioning System (GPS) is a good example. This has been a reversal. Now the private sector has the lead, and innovation concentrates on civilian use. Only later are technologies adapted to military purposes.[9] This has both transformed the defense sector and expanded the industrial base. Further, new technologies such as cyber tools, human enhancement, and artificial intelligence (AI), raise ethical challenges of their own. Ethical questions should be considered while these weapons are still in development.[10] For those attempting to make sense of moral issues amidst rapidly changing technology, scholarly insights into such novel questions can support their endeavors.

Geopolitical developments also increase the relevance of the defense industry. Revived great-power competition tends to cause states to increase their defense budgets, arms procurement, and investments in domestic defense-industrial capabilities.[11] Perhaps there is no global arms race to date, but rivalry, competition,

[8] *See, e.g.*, Defense Industry Initiative, *DII Principles* (July 1986), https://www.dii.org/dii-principles-pdf (last visited Jan. 12, 2022).

[9] *See, e.g.*, Brummer Matthew, *Innovation and Threats*, 33(5) Def. Peace Econ. 563 (2020); Raska Michael, *The Sixth RMA Wave: Disruption in Military Affairs?*, 44 J. Strateg. Stud. 456 (2021); Elisabeth Sköns, John J. Dunne & Nan Tian, *The Changing Economics of Global Arms Production*, *in* PRISM Working Paper No. 2, 5 (2020); Maaike Verbruggen, *The Role of Civilian Innovation in the Development of Lethal Autonomous Weapon Systems*, 10 Glob. Pol. 338, 341 (2019).

[10] Referring again to the analogy to the laws of war, it is interesting the *jus in bello* obliges states to assess the legality of a new weapon already at its development stage. *See* Article 36 of the 1977 Additional Protocol I to the Geneva Conventions. For the U.S. practice in this regard, *see* Chapter 5.

[11] *See, e.g.*, John J. Mearsheimer, *The Inevitable Rivalry: America, China, and the Tragedy of Great-Power Politics*, Foreign Aff. (2021), https://www.foreignaffairs.com/articles/china/2021-10-19/inevitable-rivalry-cold-war (last visited Jan. 11, 2022); Daniel H. Nexon, *Against Great Power Competition*, Foreign Aff. (2021), https://www.foreignaffairs.com/articles/united-states/2021-02-15/against-great-power-competition (last visited Jan. 11, 2022); Christopher Layne, *The US–Chinese Power Shift and the End of the Pax Americana*, 94 Int'l. Aff. 89–111 (2018); Rush Doshi, The Long Game: China's Grand Strategy to Displace American Order (2021).

and national security concerns may lead in this direction.[12] The major powers are already engaged in competing over certain technologies such as hypersonic missiles, the weaponization of space, and the military applications of AI. In addition to the United States and Russia, which have for some time devoted a large share of their wealth to defense outlays, China and several European countries have increased their efforts.

The war between Russia and Ukraine, which started on February 24, 2022, has accelerated these trends. The hostilities have led to significant military assistance to Ukraine, notably in the form of weapons transfers and many states' decision to increase their military spending.[13] The United States leads the military assistance, having promised arms deliveries worth several billion dollars and re-enacted the lend-lease program that was last used during World War II.[14] Notably, in Europe, the war has led to a new political consciousness regarding the need for hard power as well as major policy changes. The European Union, for instance, has promised to finance and transfer weapons to directly support an attacked country for the first time in its history.[15] Germany, which has traditionally spent less than 2 percent of its GDP on defense as pledged to NATO, has decided to increase its military spending by 100 billion euros and to rapidly purchase F-35 fighter jets.[16] These trends portend more activity in and reliance on

[12] *See, e.g.*, CHRISTIAN BROSE, THE KILL CHAIN: DEFENDING AMERICA IN THE FUTURE OF HIGH-TECH WARFARE (2020); Fiona S. Cunningham & M. Taylor Fravel, *Assuring Assured Retaliation: China's Nuclear Posture and U.S.-China Strategic Stability*, 40 INT'L. SEC. 7–50 (2015).

[13] *See, e.g.*, Brad Howard, *Russia's Invasion of Ukraine Could Spark a NATO Defense Spending Spree*, CNBC (Apr. 7, 2022, 8:41 PM), https://www.cnbc.com/2022/04/01/why-russias-invasion-of-ukraine-could-spark-a-nato-spending-spree.html; Daniel Michaels, *Ukraine War Set to Prompt NATO Countries to Raise Military Spending*, WALL ST. J. (Mar. 31, 2022, 9:16 AM), https://www.wsj.com/articles/ukraine-war-set-to-prompt-nato-countries-to-raise-military-spending-11648732604; Christina Mackenzie, *Seven European Nations Have Increased Defense Budgets in One Month: Who Will Be Next?*, BREAKING DEFENSE (Mar. 22, 2022, 10:54 AM), https://breakingdefense.com/2022/03/seven-european-nations-have-increased-defense-budgets-in-one-month-who-will-be-next/; *Poland Wants to Urgently Buy US Reaper Drones, as Russia Fears Mount*, EURACTIVE (Mar. 17, 2022), https://www.euractiv.com/section/global-europe/news/poland-wants-to-urgently-buy-us-reaper-drones-as-russia-fears-mount/.

[14] *See, e.g.*, Kathryn Watson & Rebecca Kaplan, *Congress Passes Bill Letting U.S. Lend Weapons Systems to Ukraine*, CBS NEWS (Apr. 29, 2022), https://www.cbsnews.com/news/lend-lease-ukraine-weapons-bill-passes-congress/. *See also* Ukraine Supplemental Appropriations Act, 2022, S.3811, 117th Cong (2022).

[15] Brooks Tigner & Nicholas Fiorenza, *Ukraine Conflict: EU Breaks with History to Send Weaponry to Ukraine*, JANES (Mar. 1, 2022), https://www.janes.com/defence-news/news-detail/update-ukraine-conflict-eu-breaks-with-history-to-send-weaponry-to-ukraine.

[16] *See, e.g.*, Federal Chancellor, *Policy Statement by Olaf Scholz, Chancellor of the Federal Republic of Germany and Member of the German Bundestag, 27 February 2022 in Berlin* (2022), https://www.bundesregierung.de/breg-en/news/policy-statement-by-olaf-scholz-chancellor-of-the-federal-republic-of-germany-and-member-of-the-german-bundestag-27-february-2022-in-berlin-2008378; Bastian Giegerich & Ben Schreer, *Germany's New Defence Policy: the 100 Billion Euro Question*, INT'L INST. STRATEGIC STUD. (Mar. 1, 2022), https://www.iiss.org/blogs/military-balance/2022/03/germanys-new-defence-policy-the-100-billion-euro-question; Sylvia Pfeifer, *Germany to Buy US F-35 Jets in First Big Deal Since Defence Budget Boost*, FIN. TIMES (Mar. 14, 2022), https://www.ft.com/content/02a162fc-6482-4fa2-8121-aa1414baf853.

the defense industry and, potentially, increased ethical risks. Against this backdrop, research to further our understanding of the ethical dilemmas of the global defense industry is certainly timely.

Methodologically, this volume concentrates on the U.S. industry and regulations. It does so for several reasons. In particular, the United States is the world leader in terms of arms production, military spending, and arms exports.[17] It is also the home of most of the leading defense firms, such as Raytheon and General Dynamics. Further, it arguably has the most comprehensive and sophisticated regulatory system. This makes the United States an ideal model for the study of and discussion about the global defense industry. A close study of the United States may provide insights about the defense industry generally and may inform future research about the ethical issues confronting defense industries in other countries.

2. The Volume in a Nutshell

This volume is structured in four main parts with an additional concluding part. Part I serves as an overview and introduction to the subject matter—assessing the ethical norms surrounding the defense industry and proposing some analytical perspectives on how to approach the inquiry. Part II considers what ethical dilemmas arise with emerging and disruptive technologies—evaluating such new technologies from the perspectives of the end user as well as delving into specific ethical challenges of outer space, cyber, and AI. Part III turns to concerns about corruption in global markets—assessing a broad range of questions, including why corruption is problematic, what has been done to counter this common practice, and how offsets relate to corruption. Part IV advances original and unconventional solutions to some of the many beguiling problems that are discussed throughout this volume, including the role of engineers and the prevention of silo mentalities and dominant logics. Part V concludes the volume by reflecting on the different arguments advanced throughout as well as considering the appropriate role for the academy's partnership with the defense industry.

As to Part I, in Chapter 1, Tobias Vestner starts by examining the global defense industry's function in light of states' national security. He retraces the global context and dynamics of the defense industry. He identifies, applies, and discusses three mechanisms by which the defense industry serves national security. First,

[17] *See, e.g.*, *SIPRI Arms Industry Database*, Stockholm Int'l Peace Res. Inst., https://www.sipri.org/databases/armsindustry (last visited Jan. 12, 2022); *SIPRI Arms Industry Database*, Stockholm Int'l Peace Res. Inst., https://www.sipri.org/databases/armsindustry (last visited Jan. 12, 2022); *SIPRI Arms Military Expenditure Database*, Stockholm Int'l Peace Res. Inst., https://www.sipri.org/databases/milex (last visited Jan. 12, 2022).

it provides access to military goods, technologies, and services. Second, when exporting weapons, it creates dependencies and interdependencies with the importing states. Third, it can enhance status and national pride. He finds, however, that most states' defense industries struggle to effectively contribute to national security, the U.S. industry being a notable exception. He argues that there is an ethical dimension to this because, even when defense industries do not or only partially contribute to national security, they still profit by producing tools to kill. To address this issue, he calls for a renewed research agenda on how the defense industry contributes to security.

In Chapter 2, Duncan MacIntosh discusses the fundamental question of the defense industry's role and legitimacy for societies. He begins with a parable of a psychopath doing something self-serving that has beneficial moral consequences. Analogously, he argues, the fact that the defense industry profits by selling weapons that can kill people makes it useful in solving moral problems not solvable by people with ordinary moral scruples. Next, he argues that while the defense industry is a business, it is also implicated in the security of its home nations. In addition, its products can be used for good or evil. Thus, it must navigate conflicting values, with the result that the rules often thought to rightly regulate the industry—codes of business ethics, engineering ethics, procurement ethics, plus laws of the land, and dicta of conscience—require supplementation by general moral reflection. MacIntosh argues for a decision principle that tells us when to violate the rules, for a theory of rational choice on which choosing by this principle is rational, and for teaching that theory to defense industry employees to ensure their ethical behavior.

In Chapter 3, Richard W. Painter argues that officers and directors of military contractors have a fiduciary duty to strengthen the national security of the United States. Thus, their fiduciary duty extends beyond maximizing the profits of shareholders. Painter starts by defining fiduciary duty—a core concept in business law. After outlining why the shareholder primacy theory is generally wrong, he argues that this theory is particularly inapt for defense contractors. He proposes instead a "business judgment" as an appropriate performance measure for the fiduciary duties to the United States and to shareholders. He then applies this to four dilemmas that arise in the defense industry: (1) foreign arms sales; (2) spending on lobbying and electioneering; (3) increasing profits versus providing the best possible weapons to the military; and (4) tensions between U.S. national security interests and those of a potential importing state. Painter concludes by suggesting steps that industry and government can take to ensure that defense contractors duly align their conduct with national security interests.

C. Edward Peartree assesses the locus of ethical dilemmas that arise when the U.S. defense industry sells arms abroad in Chapter 4. He argues that for arms exports, industry's ethical dilemmas are few because of the unique level of oversight to which these transactions are subjected. He contends that for an ethical dilemma to exist, a defense firm must have a choice, citing Kant's famous dictum that "ought" implies "can." For the industry itself, then, ethical issues have been reduced to questions of compliance. That the industry is largely compliant with these regulatory burdens is not due to any particular virtue in this sector but because firms find cooperation to be in their best interest. Punishment for deviation from the rules is severe (inability to sell one's wares), and relying on the government to approve foreign sales shields contractors from liability should something go wrong. Peartree retraces modern U.S. arms export control policy and concludes that the government shoulders most of the moral responsibility for foreign weapons sales.

Part II moves on to the discussion of ethical dilemmas related to new technologies. In Chapter 5, Thomas E. Ayres, Kevin Govern, and Michael W. Meier offer a military lawyer's perspective on how soldiers deserve the best weapons possible. Under the law of armed conflict (LOAC, also known as international humanitarian law or IHL), deadly force may be used against an identified enemy as a first option. Service members need not put themselves at risk. LOAC similarly allows for the use of superior weapons that minimize risk to oneself. Therefore, when it comes to a service member's perspective, the authors postulate that there are five reasons that make it ethically permissible and even obligate the development and procurement of the best weapons possible. The authors explain how U.S. laws, regulation, and practice ensure that the best weapons are provided to the armed forces within the international legal framework, including legal reviews of weapons and the implementation of technology-specific ethical principles. When doing so, they consider the ethical and legal particularities of emerging and disruptive technologies, notably AI.

In Chapter 6, Brian D. Green considers some of the ethical challenges facing industry and the U.S. Department of Defense's newest service, the Space Force. He suggests that because many of the "new space" startups are nontraditional contractors, the defense industry's established norms may be unfamiliar to such newcomers. This includes gift rules, restrictions on post-government employment, as well as impartiality and fair dealing standards. These rules have proven essential to preventing, identifying, and punishing misconduct, and they must be inculcated and enforced anew for the many nondefense contractors entering the space sector. Green also offers a broad overview of the concerns that motivate the ethical standards governing relationships between the military and industry. He observes that the government's concern for ethical lapses arises not only from their intrinsic wrongfulness but also from the understanding that such failures can have tertiary consequences potentially harmful to national security interests.

In Chapter 7, Jeffrey Biller and Timothy Goines address one of the most salient yet unresolved issues regarding cyber operations: protecting civilian data during armed conflicts. They illustrate how certain state operations target civilian data in foreign countries, including the United States. They describe the IHL governing cyber operations in armed conflicts. They note that international law is unclear as to whether data qualifies as an "object", which is essential for the proper application of IHL to cyber operations and describe further inadequacies of existing protections of civilian data. After highlighting current initiatives to address this issue, which mostly ignore the role of industry, Biller and Goines present original ideas on how the industry can contribute to the fight: (1) in developing alternative methods of achieving strategic cyber effects without harming civilian data; (2) by enhancing collaborative cybersecurity efforts related to the protection of key sectors of civilian data; and (3) by using economic and social influence to push toward a more protective legal regime.

In Chapter 8, Blake Hereth and Nicholas G. Evans address a notorious ethical issue concerning the military use of AI, which may represent the most disruptive and ethically problematic emerging technology on the horizon. They argue war entails what they call the "moral cost-sharing" of the burden of killing. AI would subvert this burden in unjust ways if applied to lethal autonomous weapon systems (LAWS). Because LAWS lack moral agency, in particular the capacity for moral emotions, moral costs are only borne by the dead and their loved ones. Hereth and Evans argue that it is unjust insofar as those responsible for harm to others ought to share in the associated costs. This presents a dilemma: either autonomous weaponry are designed to be capable of moral emotions, which may be a step too far even for proponents of LAWS, or the use of such weaponry needs to be limited, which may worsen casualties and otherwise undermine the achievement of strategic aims.

Part III turns to corruption in global markets, an activity involving ethical trade-offs all too common in the defense-related business, which tends to persist despite continued efforts against it. In Chapter 9, Philip M. Nichols examines the defense firm's duties to society when presented with an opportunity to pay a bribe. He establishes the moral and economic landscape of the defense industry by summarizing the distortions that beset this industry, explaining that a combination of concentration of both supply and demand sides, secrecy, and close government and industry relationships render this market nearly dysfunctional. Secrecy, high-value (or "high stakes") contracts, complexity, and the political nature of defense make the sector vulnerable to corrupt practices. Nichols then offers a normative argument for the defense firm's status as a responsible moral agent and the nature of its responsibilities both to society at large and to vulnerable persons. Corruption leads firms to concentrate not on price or quality but on crafting bribes, which in turn degrades the quality of weapon systems, endangers the armed forces, and wastes scarce resources. He also warns that it is a short step from paying bribes to win contracts to paying bribes for access so that one can sell to (otherwise) prohibited buyers. He urges that attempts to limit a firm's moral responsibility based on its attenuation from the consequences of its actions ought to be re-examined and that perhaps firms should be held accountable not only for harm that they proximately cause but also for harm that they facilitate.

In Chapter 10, Mark Pyman provides a historical account and reflects on how Transparency International contributed to addressing defense corruption. Retracing two decades of efforts since the beginning of Transparency International's Defence & Security program, Pyman identifies mechanisms for change. Collaborating with, and pressuring, defense ministries, military forces, defense companies, NATO, and nongovernmental organizations is a key to answering the seemingly intractable ethical problems in this industry. Gathering and publishing relevant data, engagement among corporate ethics officers, and the bravery of government officials are further elements of these reform efforts. The progress achieved indicates a "whole sector" approach—embracing companies, governments, regulators, and civil society—can be effective. Pyman concludes by suggesting that this experience contains valuable lessons for how corruption reform can be effectively implemented in other sectors.

Nancy Hite-Rubin conducts an empirical analysis on the complex relationship between arms embargoes, corruption, and foreign direct investment (FDI) in countries importing defense items in Chapter 11. Less-developed countries—many that are at best institutionally weak and at worst corrupt—have become more important markets for defense firms. This, she observes, creates an ethical minefield. She further examines the effectiveness of arms embargoes. The data gathered and analyzed in the chapter demonstrates that there is little evidence that embargoes would stop inflow of illicit weapons into sanctioned states. Apart from offering a preliminary analysis of her original data set, Hite-Rubin raises questions and identifies lines of research, both empirical and normative, that are essential to understanding and addressing the ethical issues related to arms embargoes, corruption, and FDI. Not least of these is the opportunity to explore a potential feedback mechanism, whereby defense spending attracts FDI but also pivots on corruption. She lays the foundation for considering how this mechanism works in practice and for potential future studies on how to ameliorate its effects.

In Chapter 12, Daniel Schoeni examines defense offsets, a widely practiced but understudied element of the international arms trade. Offsets are routinely condemned as an inherently corrupt transaction, or at least one that entails major corruption risks; but he argues that contrary to received opinion, offsets have been presumed guilty without receiving a fair appraisal. He examines the three most common ethical complaints and finds all three require further study. Last, in what is his most original contribution, Schoeni considers a case study of an ethical concern about offsets brought to his attention by an industry insider. This is evocative precisely because it does not fit neatly into one of the three categories, suggesting that although serious ethical issues may exist, research about offsets thus far may concentrate on the wrong problems. Developing better policies requires a deeper understanding of offsets and identifying what the *genuine* ethical perils may be.

Part IV considers innovations for improving ethical standards and compliance across the global defense industry. Michael Davis explores the role of engineers in the ethical development and proliferation of weapons and technology in Chapter 13. He observes that engineers employed by manufacturers have a critical role in foreign military sales that is often unnoticed. These engineers do much more than the design fighter jet, for instance. At an early stage of negotiations, engineers are sent out to work with their foreign counterparts to evaluate the local infrastructure that would support the jets—air bases, maintenance practices, pilot training, local suppliers, and so forth. This involves ongoing discussions and handshake agreements between engineers. Davis describes these relationships between the exporting firm's and purchasing country's engineers as "intimate and enduring." Hence, Davis proposes that ethical standards be embedded in the standards of the engineering profession. This would address arms industry ethical dilemmas in three dimensions. Horizontally, this would broaden the industrial and international ethical standards. Vertically, this would push standards down to the practical level of engineers, where many of the critical ethical decisions are made. Temporally, this would introduce ethical considerations from the very beginning that would endure throughout the life cycle of the weapon system.

Christopher R. Yukins offers a case study in how anti-corruption measures can affect competition in defense markets by focusing on mandatory disclosure in Chapter 14. He observes that the mandatory disclosure regime can have a perverse effect on competition, favoring large incumbents over smaller upstarts. This policy, however well intentioned, exacerbates the divide between large and small contractors, as the latter will often find elaborate compliance systems unaffordable. This not only increased corruption risks but also caused undue reputational risks for the stakeholders with the most to lose: the government and major defense contractors. In response, Yukins proposes a return to the voluntary disclosure system existing for two decades after the "Ill Wind" procurement scandals of the 1980s, which served as a model for the World Bank's voluntary reporting requirements. Making this program voluntary again would allow coverage of a broader array of misconduct, would reduce implementation costs, and, not least, would have a less damaging effect on competition. Counterintuitively, perhaps, lighter-touch anti-corruption measures may yield better results.

In Chapter 15, Jessica Tillipman and Vijaya Surampudi address compliance in small to midsized contractors, answering in part Yukins's concerns about small firms that cannot afford elaborate compliance programs. They contrast the resources and expertise that large firms dedicate to compliance, detailing some of the additional burdens placed on defense contractors, with the limited resources that are available to firms with less capital and smaller profit margins. They also note the strain that this asymmetry places on the entire supply chain: if large contractors depend on small subcontractors for essential components, then the debarment of a small firm for misconduct can have far-reaching ramifications. As a solution, Tillipman and Surampudi commend the mentor-protégé program introduced in 1991. They cite two recent government studies indicating that program is working largely as intended. Accordingly, this program could have wider application abroad. After all, the "critical gap" in internal controls between large and small firms is not only an American problem but a simple question of economics.

Patricia Werhane identifies in Chapter 16 how the tragic loss of life in the space shuttle accidents in 1987 and 2003 as well as the two deadly crashes of 737 MAXes in 2018 could occur despite very high levels of expertise and professionalism both in NASA and Boeing. She argues that corporate cultures may lead to disastrous moral consequences when people—who do not desire to do harm—work as a group. She identifies two phenomena that are particularly to blame: silo mentalities and dominant logics. The former concerns the tendency to overspecialization within large organizations, sometimes resulting in an almost deliberate ignorance of problems for which detection requires a broader awareness. The latter concerns an overriding cultural lens that can obscure what should be obvious. Werhane proposes two possible remedies. First is the adoption of Adam Smith's perspective of an "impartial spectator." Awareness of cognitive framing and bounded awareness are vital steps toward attaining that perspective. Second, she recommends communication, cross-disciplinary training, and improved risk- and system-analyses to counter any divide between engineers and the business side of an organization—especially engineers' tendency to remain silent based on respect for superiors.

Part V closes the volume. Steven L. Schooner and Evan Matsuda offer reflections on the potential for the academy's engagement with the defense industry, which encapsulates the purpose of this entire volume. They ask if the converse in a representative democracy might be "out of sight, out of mind." How did the United States, which was originally conceived as a government that would be responsive to the will of the people, come to be a nation that boasts the world's most powerful military, spends the most resources on defense, and exports the most dangerous weapons? How can such a country not study, research, analyze, think, and talk about the ethical aspects of its defense industry?

Schooner and Matsuda contend that focusing on the underlying policies, and asking the *why* question, rather than simply *how* or *what* questions, is a valuable exercise because the military enterprise, the defense industry, and the market that binds private sector contractors with government customers are a sprawling and confusing mess—impenetrable to the uninitiated, overwhelming to the casual observer, and riddled with inconsistent policies. Not only are the thought-provoking issues endless but the intrinsic ethical dilemmas also do not conform to intellectually lazy categories. Indeed, it is not just that these issues are ripe for debate or that they provide innumerable research opportunities. Rather, they are a critically important component of the kind of practical knowledge that citizenship in a representative democracy requires.

3. Variety and Common Themes

The following 17 chapters identify many salient issues, develop analytical approaches, suggest solutions, and most of all stimulate the discussion about the way forward in the debate about the ethical challenges of the global defense industry. These chapters represent a variety of different disciplines, backgrounds, and perspectives as well as of analytical levels and themes. The aim is not to offer a narrowly focused or rigid treatment of these issues. Rather, it is to reflect on and lay the foundation for further work in this field.

There are, however, some common themes. One is that the industry faces significant challenges in its efforts to both fulfill its purpose and to be perceived as legitimate. Defense firms also have a broader range of stakeholders from an ethical point of view than is generally assumed—ranging from the nation as a whole to the individual warfighter to the victims of armed attacks harmed by the firm's weapons. This complicates the identification of the appropriate locus of moral responsibility. There is no easy solution, or as lawyers tend to say when asked to take a position: "It depends." In this case, it depends on the perspective one takes and how one values different trade-offs. Indeed, just like two lawyers are said to have at least three different views on a matter, so are the approaches, assumptions, and arguments regarding the ethical dilemmas in the global defense industry manifold.

Another recurring theme is that the defense industry is heavily regulated at the domestic level yet still subject to unalterable economic laws. This creates intrinsic tensions and blind spots regarding—or even willful acceptance of—ethical problems. Laws, regulations, and oversight cannot and arguably should not be relied upon to control the sector's activities. That would be tantamount to a state-owned and -controlled industry, and such an industry would be inefficient, inflexible, and less innovative. Even well-intentioned regulations cannot address all ethical issues. More importantly, the sector's purpose makes it susceptible to ethical perils, such as market dysfunctionality or distortions, wasted resources, corruption, or lack of democratic accountability. Addressing such issues in the defense industry is like mowing the grass. They come back again and again.

Further, emerging technologies compound the ethical challenges. New firms are entering the defense field. This poses challenges for the appropriate regulation and governance of the sector. Such newcomers to the field, or developers who may not have considered their inventions' potential military use, are unlikely to know about the existing ethical standards in the defense industry. Further, current initiatives to regulate emerging technologies tend to take a top-down approach. The industry thus has untapped potential both for better self-policing and to shape future norms and standards.

Recent decades have witnessed significant advances in laws and policies addressing ethical challenges in the defense industry. But academia has not much focused on the ethical issues of the global defense industry. Just as the academy needs to engage more in this field, so also does the defense industry need to share experiences, stand ready to answer critics, and engage in collaborative endeavors with researchers. Academia and industry should engage and cooperate with one another to address tough questions whose answers may be unpalatable. The stakes are simply too high for these issues to remain obscure niches, ignored by many and debated by few. This volume aims, therefore, to serve as a catalyst to stimulate discussion about the ethical issues in the global defense industry.

References

Walter Adams, *The Military-Industrial Complex and the New Industrial State*, 58 Am. Econ. Rev. 652–665 (1968).

Christian Brose, The Kill Chain: Defending America in the Future of High-Tech Warfare (2020).

Matthew Brummer, *Innovation and Threats*, 33(5) Def. Peace Econ. 563 (2020).

Bruce G. Brunton, *Institutional Origins of the Military-Industrial Complex*, 22 J. Econ. Issues 599–606 (1988).

The Business of War: Theological and Ethical Reflections on the Military-Industrial Complex (James McCarty, Matthew Tapie & Justin Bronson Barringer eds., 2020).

Edmund F. Byrne, *The U.S. Military-Industrial Complex is Circumstantially Unethical*, 95 J. Bus. Ethics 153–165 (2010).

Fiona S. Cunningham & M. Taylor Fravel, *Assuring Assured Retaliation: China's Nuclear Posture and U.S.-China Strategic Stability*, 40 Int'l. Sec. 7–50 (2015).

Defense Industry Initiative, *DII Principles* (July 1986), https://www.dii.org/dii-principles-pdf.

Rush Doshi, The Long Game: China's Grand Strategy to Displace American Order (2021).

Charles J. Dunlap, *The Military-Industrial Complex*, 140 DAEDALUS 135–47 (2011).

J. Paul Dunne & Elisabeth Sköns, *The Military Industrial Complex*, *in* THE GLOBAL ARMS TRADE 281 (Andrew T.H. Tan ed., 2010).

EURACTIVE, *Poland Wants to Urgently Buy U.S. Reaper Drones, as Russia Fears Mount* (Mar. 17, 2022), https://www.euractiv.com/section/global-europe/news/poland-wants-to-urgently-buy-us-reaper-drones-as-russia-fears-mount/.

Federal Chancellor, *Policy Statement by Olaf Scholz, Chancellor of the Federal Republic of Germany and Member of the German Bundestag, 27 February 2022 in Berlin* (2022), https://www.bundesregierung.de/breg-en/news/policy-statement-by-olaf-scholz-chancellor-of-the-federal-republic-of-germany-and-member-of-the-german-bundestag-27-february-2022-in-berlin-2008378.

Glenn R. Fong, *The Political Economy of Pentagon-Industry Collaboration in Technology Development*, *in* THE POLITICAL ECONOMY OF DEFENSE: ISSUES AND PERSPECTIVES (Andrew L. Ross ed., 1991).

FRANCIS FUKUYAMA, THE END OF HISTORY AND THE LAST MAN (1992).

Bastian Giegerich & Ben Schreer, *Germany's New Defence Policy: The 100 Billion Euro Question*, INT'L INST. STRATEGIC STUD. (Mar. 1 2022), https://www.iiss.org/blogs/military-balance/2022/03/germanys-new-defence-policy-the-100-billion-euro-question.

Brad Howard, *Russia's Invasion of Ukraine Could Spark a NATO Defense Spending Spree*, CNBC (Apr. 7, 2022, 8:41 PM), https://www.cnbc.com/2022/04/01/why-russias-invasion-of-ukraine-could-spark-a-nato-spending-spree.html.

PAUL A.C. KOISTINEN, THE MILITARY-INDUSTRIAL COMPLEX: A HISTORICAL PERSPECTIVE 99 (1980).

Christopher Layne, *The U.S.–Chinese Power Shift and the End of the Pax Americana*, 94 INT. AFF. 89–111 (2018).

William J. Lynn III, *The End of the Military-Industrial Complex*, FOREIGN AFF., Nov./Dec. 2014.

Christina Mackenzie, *Seven European Nations Have Increased Defense Budgets in One Month: Who Will Be Next?*, BREAKING DEFENSE (Mar. 22, 2022, 10:54 AM), https://breakingdefense.com/2022/03/seven-european-nations-have-increased-defense-budgets-in-one-month-who-will-be-next/.

John J. Mearsheimer, *The Inevitable Rivalry: America, China, and the Tragedy of Great-Power Politics*, FOREIGN AFF. (2021), https://www.foreignaffairs.com/articles/china/2021-10-19/inevitable-rivalry-cold-war.

Daniel Michaels, *Ukraine War Set to Prompt NATO Countries to Raise Military Spending*, WALL ST. J. (Mar. 31, 2022, 9:16 AM), https://www.wsj.com/articles/ukraine-war-set-to-prompt-nato-countries-to-raise-military-spending-11648732604.

Daniel H. Nexon, *Against Great Power Competition*, FOREIGN AFF. (2021), https://www.foreignaffairs.com/articles/united-states/2021-02-15/against-great-power-competition.

Sylvia Pfeifer, *Germany to Buy U.S. F-35 Jets in First Big Deal Since Defence Budget Boost*, FIN. TIMES (Mar. 14, 2022), https://www.ft.com/content/02a162fc-6482-4fa2-8121-aa1414baf853.

Michael Raska, *The Sixth RMA Wave: Disruption in Military Affairs?*, 44 J. STRATEGIC STUD. 456 (2021).

ALEX ROLAND, DELTA OF POWER: THE MILITARY-INDUSTRIAL COMPLEX (2021).

William Shakespeare, *The Tragedy of Hamlet, Prince of Denmark*, *in* THE COMPLETE WORKS OF WILLIAM SHAKESPEARE 751 (William Wright ed., 1936).

SIPRI Arms Industry Database, Stockholm Int'l Peace Res. Inst., https://www.sipri.org/databases/armsindustry.

SIPRI Arms Industry Database, Stockholm Int'l Peace Res. Inst., https://www.sipri.org/databases/armsindustry.

SIPRI Arms Military Expenditure Database, Stockholm Int'l Peace Res. Inst., https://www.sipri.org/databases/milex.

Elisabeth Sköns, John J. Dunne & Nan Tian, *The Changing Economics of Global Arms Production*, *in* PRISM Working Paper No. 2 (2020).

Brooks Tigner & Nicholas Fiorenza, *Ukraine Conflict: EU Breaks with History to Send Weaponry to Ukraine*, Janes (Mar. 1, 2022), https://www.janes.com/defence-news/news-detail/update-ukraine-conflict-eu-breaks-with-history-to-send-weaponry-to-ukraine.

Ukraine Supplemental Appropriations Act, 2022, S.3811, 117th Cong (2022).

Maaike Verbruggen, *The Role of Civilian Innovation in the Development of Lethal Autonomous Weapon Systems*, 10 Glob. Pol. 338 (2019).

Kathryn Watson & Rebecca Kaplan, *Congress Passes Bill Letting U.S. Lend Weapons Systems to Ukraine*, CBS News (Apr. 29, 2022), https://www.cbsnews.com/news/lend-lease-ukraine-weapons-bill-passes-congress/.

PART I

ASSESSING ETHICAL NORMS IN THE DEFENSE INDUSTRY

1

The Defense Industry's Contribution to National Security

*Tobias Vestner**

1. Introduction

The defense industry's name reflects its purpose: to serve the state's defense. National security, in turn, is a concept that encompasses the management of threats to nations and their citizens more broadly. Yet how does the defense industry further national security? This question has not received broad attention. The literature examines the defense industry mainly from the perspective of economics or international political economy. In policymaking, the defense industry's contribution to national security is oftentimes assumed, and states and defense firms often act accordingly.

This chapter examines how the global defense industry serves national security in the twenty-first century. It aims to provide the context for further analyses, to offer an overview of issues, to provide conceptual clarity, and to deduce some ethical implications. The chapter starts by outlining the context and dynamics of the global defense industry. This allows to situate the analysis in light of new security challenges, in particular emerging technologies and the revival of great power competition. Then the chapter examines the defense industry's contribution to national security. As a framework for analysis, it identifies three mechanisms by which industry may serve national security. First, the defense industry provides access to military goods, technology, and services. Second, the defense industry creates dependencies and interdependencies between states. Third, the defense industry enhances a nation's international status and national pride. The chapter analyzes these mechanisms by reviewing the literature, recent developments, and informative cases.

* The author thanks Emilian Berutti for various inputs, stimulating discussions, as well as support for this volume and other work related to the defense industry. Much appreciation also goes to Daniel Schoeni for extensive comments on a previous draft and valuable editing. Moreover, the author is indebted to Claire Finkelstein for her inspiration, leadership, and support.

Tobias Vestner, *The Defense Industry's Contribution to National Security* In: *Ethical Dilemmas in the Global Defense Industry.* Edited by: Daniel Schoeni and Tobias Vestner, Oxford University Press.
 DOI: 10.1093/oso/9780190675813.003.0002

When assessing how defense industries contribute to national security, the chapter finds that their contribution tends to be limited. With the possible exception of the U.S. defense industry, domestic industries do not promote national security to a high degree. This is consistent with the features of the global arms production and transfer system, and has been referred to as "limited autarky."[1] The chapter argues that the defense industry's limited contribution to national security has an ethical dimension. Although most defense industries do not significantly further national security, they always generate monetary gains. Hence, the defense industry profits without fully achieving its core purpose. This is ethically problematic because the industry produces deadly weapons. To address this issue, a better understanding of how the defense industry contributes to national security is needed. The chapter thus concludes by proposing a new research agenda.

2. Global Context and Dynamics

2.1. The Emergence of a Global Arms Production and Transfer System

During the Cold War, both the United States and the Soviet Union heavily invested in their defense industries to support their military apparatuses.[2] Their allies as well as nonaligned states also undertook considerable efforts to maintain defense industrial capacities and to acquire foreign military goods. From this arose a "global arms production and transfer system." This system notably emerged when the pace of technological change slowed, and new technologies were diffused in line with the global power structures.[3] It featured a three-tiered structure, whereby states are classified by the level of local arms production, the sophistication of that production, the quality of defense-related research and development, and domestic procurement and export dependence.[4]

The first tier was comprised of the United States and the Soviet Union. Both had the most advanced and productive industrial capacities and, driven by their rivalry, led global weapons development. Both states' industries were nearly self-sufficient, and their exports mostly followed political rather than economic calculations. Yet with the diffusion of new technologies and a narrowing gap

[1] *See* Richard Bitzinger, Towards a Brave New Arms Industry? 81 (2003).

[2] *See generally* J. Paul Dunne & Elizabeth Sköns, *The Military Industrial Complex*, *in* The Global Arms Trade: A Handbook 281 (Andrew T.H. Tan ed., 2010).

[3] *See* Keith Krause, Arms and the State: Patterns of Military Production and Trade 84 (1992).

[4] *Id.* at 212.

between the weapons possessed by first-tier states and others, their priorities shifted away from influencing the global military balance and fostering alliances and instead shifted toward protecting their technological advantages.[5]

The second tier emerged in the 1970s, when France, Japan, and Germany developed enough capacity to supply a large share of their defense needs locally, and other nations such as Sweden, Czechoslovakia, Spain, and Italy acquired some production capabilities.[6] Most of these industries were developed with infusions of military technologies from first-tier states. Although technological innovation continued to be driven by the first tier, the second tier emerged as alternative suppliers, which reduced the first tier's ability to dominate the system and freely use transfers for political ends.[7] Nonetheless, the first-tier producers maintained advantages of scale, which resulted in a stabilization of arms exports by the second tier.[8] In addition, defense firms in many second-tier states became export-oriented to the extent that they struggled to meet domestic military needs.[9]

The remaining states constituted the third and largest tier. These states' fundamental motivation to produce arms was the attempt to improve their subordinate position in the global arms transfer and production system.[10] However, as late entrants, their efforts yielded modest results. As they tried to catch up by technology transfers, this resulted in continued dependence on technology from states in the first and second tiers. Consequently, most did not advance beyond a relatively low level of sophistication in production.[11] Domestic production thereby primarily sought to reduce the dependence on foreign suppliers, in particular when the states were confronted with security threats.[12]

2.2. Developments after the Cold War

After the Cold War, the defense industry was highly influenced by globalization.[13] The global arms production and transfer system with its three-tier structure remained in place. The tiers' composition changed, however. The collapse of the Soviet Union resulted in a consolidation of the United States at the center

[5] *Id.* at 125.
[6] *Id.* at 131.
[7] *Id.* at 208.
[8] *Id.* at 136.
[9] *Id.* at 141.
[10] *Id.* at 153.
[11] *Id.* at 158.
[12] *Id.* at 162.
[13] *See generally* Richard A. Bitzinger, *The Globalization of the Arms Industry: The Next Proliferation Challenge*, 19 INT'L SEC. 170 (1994).

of the global arms industry network.[14] The first tier now consisted of the United States and the aggregation of Western European states.[15] Australia, Sweden, Israel, and a few others represented the second tier, with niche production abilities but not full-scale capacities. Third-tier states continued to produce limited amounts of mostly low-tech weapons.

The global arms production and transfer system was subject to new dynamics, however. The end of the Cold War led to a ten-year decline in military expenditure and demand for weapon systems. As a result, the global defense industry went through a major restructuring process. Originally focusing on downsizing and diversification, the restructuring subsequently involved a surge of mergers and acquisitions that led to an increased concentration of the industry.[16] In the United States, a series of mergers and acquisitions in the early 1990s created four super-companies that controlled a substantial share of the American market, namely, Northrop Grumman, Lockheed Martin, Boeing, and Raytheon.[17] While it was argued that these mergers and acquisitions were intended to protect or increase company profits, this maintained the hierarchy in the global defense industry as the share of the U.S. industry continued to increase.[18]

Alliances also became less important as determinants of arms sales.[19] States formerly part of the Soviet Union started to trade with members of the North Atlantic Treaty Organization (NATO) and sold their stocks to developing countries.[20] Generally, there was less reluctance to trade with politically distant regimes, and strategic considerations became less important.[21] The United States maintained its independence from foreign suppliers. Western Europe, however, was characterized by fragmentation in supply and demand, scant cooperation,[22] and less support for exports than the United States.[23] The growing globalization

[14] Jurgen Brauer, *Economic Aspects of Arms Trade Offsets*, *in* ARMS TRADE AND ECONOMIC DEVELOPMENT: THEORY, POLICY, AND CASES IN ARMS TRADE OFFSETS 58, 67 (Jurgen Brauer & J. Paul Dunne eds., 2011).

[15] BITZINGER, *supra* note 1, at 6–7.

[16] Elisabeth Sköns, J. Paul Dunne & Nan Tian, *The Changing Economics of Global Arms Production*, *in* PRISM, Working Paper No. 2020-2, at 5, 5 (2020).

[17] Saar Golde & Asher Tishler, *Security Needs, Arms Exports, and the Structure of the Defense Industry: Determining the Security Level of Countries*, 48 J. CONFLICT RESOL. 672, 677 (2004).

[18] Stephanie G. Neuman, *Power, Influence, and Hierarchy: Defense Industries in a Unipolar World*, 21 DEF. & PEACE ECON. 105, 120 (2010); Derrick J. Neal & Trevor Taylor, *Globalisation in the Defence Industry: An Exploration of the Paradigm for US and European Defence Firms and the Implications for Being Global Players*, 12 DEF. & PEACE ECON. 337, 342 (2001).

[19] Paul W. Thurner et al., *Network Interdependencies and the Evolution of the International Arms Trade*, 63 J. CONFLICT RESOL. 1736, 1738 (2019); Anders Akerman & Anna Larsson Seim, *The Global Arms Trade Network 1950–2007*, 42 J. COMP. ECON. 535, 541 (2014).

[20] Thurner et al., *supra* note 19, at 1757.

[21] *See generally* Paul W. Thurner et al., *Corrigendum to Network Interdependencies and the Evolution of the International Arms Trade*, 64 J. CONFLICT RESOL. 1548 (2020).

[22] Neuman, *supra* note 18, at 106–07.

[23] Neal & Taylor, *supra* note 18, at 351.

of defense industrial processes were indeed driven mainly by the defense industry rather than by deliberate public policies.[24]

Strategic considerations and military spending increased again with the start of the new millennium, however, in particular after the 9/11 terrorist attacks.[25] The wars in Iraq and Afghanistan significantly accelerated the U.S. military spending, "driving it to historic heights and increasing America's global share of a $1.55 trillion market to 44 percent—more than six times the share of China, the second-leading spender."[26] Yet this development was mostly confined to the United States. Accordingly, defense firms generally maintained their previous strategies, which included international arms sales, business reform, and diversification into other sectors.[27] Arms sales to emerging markets, in particular in the Middle East and less developed countries, continued to be highly relevant. The monopolistic and monopsonistic structure of the defense industry, the strong relationships between the arms industry and governments, and the industry's perceived importance to national security contributed to shielding it from economic downturns throughout this period.[28]

Hence, in general, the post-9/11 era was notably marked by states taking measures, to protect their domestic defense industries from decreases in sales caused by austerity measures, such as support for cost reductions and promotion of arms exports.[29] The early 2000s also witnessed the emergence of new exporters, such as China. Other arms-producing states increased their exports, which further led to increased competition in the global arms market.[30] The decline of arms transfers in the 1990s proved transient, and arms sales started to increase at a constant rate at the beginning of the new millennium.[31] Moreover, starting in 2013, global defense spending accelerated again.[32]

[24] BITZINGER, *supra* note 1, at 68.

[25] Thurner et al., *supra* note 19, at 1761.

[26] Kevin Dehoff, John Dowdy & John Niehaus, *Managing a Downturn: How the US Defense Industry Can Learn from Its Past*, MCKINSEY & CO. 1 (Apr. 1, 2013), https://www.mckinsey.com/industries/aerospace-and-defense/our-insights/managing-a-downturn. It is noteworthy that comparisons based on financial values may not accurately represent states' actual military spending in relation to each other. Nonetheless, for the purpose here, these figures clearly indicate the rise of U.S. defense spending in the given period.

[27] STOCKHOLM INT'L PEACE RES. INST., SIPRI YEARBOOK 2010: ARMAMENTS, DISARMAMENT AND INTERNATIONAL SECURITY 267 (2010) [hereinafter SIPRI YEARBOOK 2010].

[28] *Id.* at 271.

[29] STOCKHOLM INTERNATIONAL PEACE RESEARCH INSTITUTE, SIPRI YEARBOOK 2013: ARMAMENTS, DISARMAMENT AND INTERNATIONAL SECURITY 206 (2013).

[30] Inmaculada Martínez-Zarzoso & Florian Johannsen, *The Gravity of Arms*, 30 DEF. & PEACE ECON. 2, 16 (2019).

[31] Thurner et al., *supra* note 19 at 1740.

[32] Alexandra Marksteiner, Diego Lopes da Silva & Nan Tian, *Trends in World Military Expenditure, 2020*, STOCKHOLM INST. PEACE RES. INST. 1, 1 (2021); STOCKHOLM INST. PEACE RES. INST., SIPRI ARMS TRANSFERS DATABASE, https://www.sipri.org/databases/armstransfers (last visited Dec. 20, 2021).

2.3. New Arms Production Trends and Developments

New trends have manifested in recent years. At the beginning of the last decade, there were continued mergers and acquisitions within the industry and stagnant markets in arms-producing countries.[33] Companies from North America and Western Europe continued to dominate the global market. Yet the concentration of the global arms production in Western countries started to reduce when producer countries outside of North America and Western Europe increased their activity and sales.[34] Brazil, India, South Korea, and Turkey are notable emerging producers which are home to firms that tend to rank among the world's top 100 and seek greater levels of self-sufficiency in arms production and procurement.[35]

This diffusion diversified the global arms suppliers. This increasingly made the arms market a buyer's market. Hence, although emerging suppliers export smaller volumes than established suppliers, the availability of alternative suppliers decreases states' dependence on the latter and can notably affect unstable regions.[36] Nevertheless, the global defense industry and the global arms market remain relatively stable. Several defense companies, notably Lockheed Martin, BAE Systems, Thales, and Rheinmetall, are always among the 100—generally even among the 20—largest defense firms, for instance.[37] Moreover, major changes in rank among the largest firms tend to be caused primarily by mergers, acquisitions, and divestments of companies that were already significant producers.[38]

The most significant change in recent years concerns new technologies, notably in the digital field. Indeed, the "rapid developments in high technology have created an increased supply of technologies that have military applications and have further created demand to develop new capabilities."[39] Network-centric warfare, for instance, emerged from the development of sophisticated technologies but also demanded constant improvement of technologies to prove effective. Significant research and development have also started regarding artificial intelligence (AI) and autonomous systems, leading some analysts to call

[33] Stockholm Int'l Peace Res. Inst., SIPRI Yearbook 2017: Armaments, Disarmament and International Security 404–05 (2017) [hereinafter SIPRI Yearbook 2017].

[34] Stockholm Int'l Peace Res. Inst., SIPRI Yearbook 2014: Armaments, Disarmament and International Security 209 (2014) [hereinafter SIPRI Yearbook 2014].

[35] Lucie Béraud-Sudreau et al., *Emerging Suppliers in the Global Arms Trade*, SIPRI Insights Peace & Sec., No. 2020/13 (Dec. 2020); Stockholm Int'l Peace Res. Inst., SIPRI Yearbook 2018: Armaments, Disarmament and International Security 225 (2018) [hereinafter SIPRI Yearbook 2018]; Stockholm Int'l Peace Res. Inst., SIPRI Arms Industry Database, https://www.sipri.org/databases/armsindustry (last visited Dec 20, 2021).

[36] Béraud-Sudreau et al., *supra* note 35, at 20; David Kinsella, *Arms Transfer Dependence and Foreign Policy Conflict*, 35 J. Peace Res. 7, 20 (1998).

[37] *See, e.g.*, SIPRI Yearbook 2014, *supra* note 34, at 213–17.

[38] SIPRI Yearbook 2018, *supra* note 35, at 224.

[39] Sköns, Dunne & Tian, *supra* note 16, at 12.

this the sixth revolution in military affairs.[40] Most important to this revolution is cyber. Starting in the early 2010s, defense firms sought to compensate for defense cuts by moving into new markets, notably the market on cybersecurity for civilian clients.[41] This resulted, notably in the United States, in a new wave of mergers and acquisitions, including acquisitions of information technology (IT) and other high-tech business units from other defense and civil companies.[42]

Major high-tech companies also started to collaborate with the military. Their primary aim was to win defense-sponsored research and development funding. Technology companies also aimed to become major suppliers of IT, internet, and software components and services. In the United States, such firms included Amazon, Apple, Google, Microsoft, and Oracle.[43] The expansion of the range of business sectors and companies that are relevant to defense industrial activities fostered competitive strategies that continue to shape military innovation.[44] Such new entrants to this sector have assumed roles that are critical to the defense industrial base: critical innovators, adapters and modifiers, and copiers and reproducers.[45]

In sum, certain patterns emerge regarding the global arms production and transfer system. The United States continues to dominate the global arms production, though China and others are increasingly competitive. The biggest arms-producing companies have grown in size and market share. Further, high-tech companies with no previous connection to defense are increasingly important players in this field.[46] Yet despite these new dynamics, the global arms production and transfer system as well as the distribution of states within its tiers is characterized by continuity.[47] The United States, Western Europe, China, and Russia are all increasing defense spending due to revived great power competition and global tensions.[48] So far, however, this has done little to alter the system's general makeup.

The war between Russia and Ukraine, which started on February 24, 2022, has led to considerable military assistance to Ukraine, notably in the form of weapons transfers, and many states' decision to increase their military spending.[49] This

40 *Id.* at 12; Michael Raska, *The Sixth RMA Wave: Disruption in Military Affairs?*, 44 J. Strategic Stud. 456, 457–58 (2021).

41 Stockholm Int'l Peace Res. Inst., SIPRI Yearbook 2012: Armaments, Disarmament and International Security 229 (2012).

42 Sköns, Dunne & Tian, *supra* note 16, at 17.

43 *Id.* at 19.

44 Michael Raska, *Strategic Competition for Emerging Military Technologies: Comparative Paths and Patterns*, 8 PRISM 64, 69 (2019).

45 *Id.* at 78.

46 *See* Sköns, Dunne & Tian, *supra* note 16, at 20.

47 Joanna Spear, *Defence Offsets: A System-Level View*, Strateg. Anal., 439 (2013).

48 Marksteiner, Lopes da Silva & Tian, *supra* note 32, at 2; Stockholm Int'l Peace Res. Inst., SIPRI Arms Military Expenditure Database, https://www.sipri.org/databases/milex (last visited Dec. 20, 2021).

49 For more details and respective sources, *see* the Introduction of this volume.

suggests that national defense industries will become more important to states and will expand their activities due to increased national procurement, investment in research and development (R&D), and international arms trade. This also suggests that arms transfers will increasingly become subject to geopolitical and geostrategic considerations. The next years will tell if such tendencies clearly materialize, subsist, and potentially transform the global arms market.

3. How the Defense Industry Contributes to National Security

This background on the global production and transfer system as well as the historical and current dynamics enables the examination of the defense industry's contribution to national security in the twenty-first century. Such analysis, however, requires first some clarification about the term "national security."

National security can be defined as "the safekeeping of the nation as a whole. Its highest order of business is the protection of the nation and its people from attack and other external dangers."[50] It thus focuses on external threats to the state, which tend to be constructed as military threats.[51] By this logic, when the state protects itself, by extension it protects its population. The definition of the concept's scope and its application in practice remains subject to assorted debates and multitudes of governmental processes, leading some to criticize the concept as self-referential, symbolic, or epiphenomenal.[52] Yet despite the concept's intrinsic challenges and more recent conceptualizations of security as international security and human security, national security—mostly referred to as "country X's [national] security"—remains the predominant logic for states' actions in security affairs.[53]

Three major mechanisms of the defense industry's contribution to national security can be identified. First, it generates access to military goods, technology, and services. Second it creates dependencies and interdependencies among

[50] 2015 Index of U.S. Military Strength: Assessing America's Ability to Provide for the Common Defense 23 (Wood Dakota L. ed., 2015).

[51] Richard H. Ullman, *Redefining Security*, 8 Int'l Sec. 129, 133 (1983); Melvyn P. Leffler, *National Security*, 77 J. Am. Hist. 143 (1990).

[52] Robert Latham, The Liberal Moment: Modernity, Security, and the Making of Postwar International Order 94 (1997); Arnold Wolfers, *"National Security" as an Ambiguous Symbol*, 67 Pol. Sci. Q. 481, 481–83 (1952); Philip Zelikow, *The Transformation of National Security: Five Redefinitions*, 71 Nat'l Int. 17 (2003).

[53] Matthew Sussex, Michael Clarke & Rory Medcalf, *National Security: Between Theory and Practice*, 71 Aust. J. Int'l Aff. 474–78, 475 (2017); Roland Paris, *Human Security: Paradigm Shift or Hot Air?*, 26 Int'l Sec. 87 (2001). Regarding the conceptualization and practice of U.S. national security, *see* Oxford Handbook of U.S. National Security (Derek S. Reveron, Nikolas K. Gvosdev & John A. Cloud eds., 2018).

states. Third, it can contribute to a nation's status abroad and national pride. What follows explores and discusses these three mechanisms in detail.

3.1. Access to Military Goods, Technology, and Services

The defense industry's primary function for national security is to develop, produce, and service military goods, technology, and related services to provide material capabilities for states' armed forces and other security forces. This entails both a qualitative and a quantitative aspect. The former relates to the sophistication of the goods, technology, and services provided and to the industry's general level of expertise and competence. Indeed, the defense industry's expertise can be a strategic asset for states and their armed forces in and of itself. The latter relates to the volume that the industry is able to produce. Even in a business field that is so highly regulated and subsidized as this one, defense firms are still subject to economic laws. So production may implicate conflicting objectives.[54]

A key driver of defense industrial production is a state's threat environment. Higher levels of threats lead to a significant increase in military innovation, and countries with higher threat levels tend to innovate more over time.[55] Israel is a prominent example of maintaining a strong domestic defense industry due to a high-threat environment. Israel has developed several cutting-edge weapon systems, including unmanned aerial vehicles (UAVs), the "Iron Dome" missile defense system, and reconnaissance satellites.[56] South Korea and Japan provide similar examples of states that decided to raise their investments into their defense production capabilities, mainly due to rising tensions with China,[57] ultimately leading to an increase in the industries' sales.[58] Likewise, strategic competition between the United States, China, and Russia also drives defense innovation, in particular regarding emerging technologies.[59]

Yet the defense industry's contribution largely depends on its ability to innovate and access novel technologies. Factors of success are notably firms' R&D activities, interactions with the public science and technology system (including

[54] María D.C. García-Alonso & Paul Levine, *Arms Trade and Arms Races: A Strategic Analysis*, *in* 2 Handbook of Defense Economics 941, 950 (Todd Sandler & Keith Hartley eds., 2007).

[55] Matthew Brummer, *Innovation and Threats*, Def. & Peace Econ. 1, 1, 10, 13 (2020).

[56] *See generally* Marc R. DeVore, *Commentary on the Value of Domestic Arms Industries: Security of Supply or Military Adaptation?*, 17 Def. Stud. 242 (2017).

[57] Chris Hughes, *Japan's Emerging Arms Transfer Strategy: Diversifying to Re-Centre on the US–Japan Alliance*, 31 Pac. Rev. 424, 428 (2018); Stockholm Int'l Peace Res. Inst., SIPRI Yearbook 2015: Armaments, Disarmament and International Security 427 (2015) [hereinafter SIPRI Yearbook 2015].

[58] Stockholm Int'l Peace Res. Inst., SIPRI Yearbook 2011: Armaments, Disarmament and International Security 248 (2011) [hereinafter SIPRI Yearbook 2011].

[59] Raska, *supra* note 40, at 470.

the private sector), as well as the ability to focus on core competencies, identify opportunities, and participate in offset agreements.[60] The defense industry relies on the general technological base where it is located, which includes a well-educated populace and an appropriate infrastructure. Indeed, military and civilian patents diffuse at similar rates.[61] As the base level of technology in the arms industry has risen,[62] so has the importance of the capacity to develop and to produce dual-use technologies which can support the integration of advanced technologies from the civilian sector into military applications.[63] An overreliance on firms acting as such system integrators, however, may undermine innovation.[64]

Most states' domestic arms industries rely on technology transfers and imports of components and subsystems. Indeed, the exploitation of foreign-sourced technologies is a key factor in the development of domestic arms industries.[65] Licensed production is often used to acquire broader technological know-how. Offset agreements are a widely used instrument to build up advanced production techniques.[66] Eventually, they may even enable importing countries to develop niche markets and to become a supplier of a major international arms manufacturer.[67] South Africa is an example where the import of arms arguably contributed more to developing the domestic defense industry than purely national endeavors.[68]

There also are more recent examples. The United Arab Emirates (UAE), for instance, is dependent on the import of technology and components as well as may lack sufficient investment in R&D to build up core competencies for new technologies, such as drones, cyber-defense, and surveillance systems.[69] South Korea continues to depend on foreign sources for novel technologies,[70] despite having sacrificed uncompetitive domestic capabilities.[71] Turkey's progress both

[60] Fulvio Castellacci & Arne Fevolden, *Capable Companies or Changing Markets? Explaining the Export Performance of Firms in the Defence Industry*, 25 DEF. & PEACE ECON. 549, 550 (2014).

[61] Jon Schmid, *The Diffusion of Military Technology*, 29 DEF. & PEACE ECON. 595, 606 (2018).

[62] SIPRI YEARBOOK 2011, *supra* note 58, at 234–35.

[63] Raska, *supra* note 40, at 458. *See also generally* MICHAEL RASKA, MILITARY INNOVATION IN SMALL STATES: CREATING A REVERSE ASYMMETRY (2020).

[64] Vasilis Zervos & G.M. Peter Swann, *The Impact of Defence Integrators and Standards on Vertical and Horizontal Innovation in the Defence Industry*, 20 DEF. & PEACE ECON. 27, 28, 41 (2009).

[65] SIPRI YEARBOOK 2011, *supra* note 8, at 248; Richard A. Bitzinger, *Defense Industries in Asia and the Technonationalist Impulse*, 36 CONTEMP. SEC. POL'Y 453, 453 (2015).

[66] Peter Hall & Stefan Markowski, *On the Normality and Abnormality of Offsets Obligations*, 5 DEF. & PEACE ECON. 173, 178 (1994); Bernard Udis & Keith E. Maskus, *Offsets as Industrial Policy: Lessons from Aerospace*, 2 DEF. ECON. 151, 157–61 (1991).

[67] Sköns, Dunne & Tian, *supra* note 16, at 19.

[68] BITZINGER, *supra* note 1, at 47.

[69] Béraud-Sudreau et al., *supra* note 35, at 7; Michael Brzoska, *Economic Factors Shaping Arms Production in Less Industrialized Countries*, 10 DEF. & PEACE ECON. 139, 150 (1999).

[70] SIPRI YEARBOOK 2011, *supra* note 58, at 243; Béraud-Sudreau et al., *supra* note 35, at 10–11.

[71] Ann Markusen, *Arms Trade as Illiberal Trade*, *in* ARMS TRADE AND ECONOMIC DEVELOPMENT: THEORY, POLICY, AND CASES IN ARMS TRADE OFFSETS 69, 80 (Jurgen Brauer & J. Dunne Paul eds., 2011).

qualitatively and quantitatively has been described as a "military breakthrough," in particular related to the production of modern equipment such as UAVs, the T129 combat helicopter, and the Altay tank.[72] Nonetheless, despite the industry's high level of autarky, it remains highly dependent on imports of components and technology due to a small technological base.[73] Russia, despite being a leading arms manufacturer, has also started to import advanced military items, such as UAVs and naval platforms, and also to acquire foreign technologies and joint ventures to support the modernization of its industry.[74]

Many states export weapons to maintain a competitive defense industrial base capable of satisfying its armed forces' needs. Indeed, most R&D and production of military items require high levels of specialization and are expensive. In addition, most domestic markets are relatively small compared to the investments needed. Exports enable economies of scale and help finance R&D costs. In Israel, for instance, export sales comprise around 70 percent of the sales of its defense industry.[75] Switzerland also perceives arms exports as an instrument to sustain its defense industrial base and exports weapons to maintain domestic access to military goods, technology, and services.[76] An overemphasis on exports, however, can also undercut a domestic producer's capacity to arm its host nation, negating the very purpose of having a domestic defense industry in the first place. Sweden's industry, for instance, prioritized foreign markets to ensure its economic survival to the extent that it could no longer satisfy Sweden's own demands.[77]

In sum, while domestic industries provide access to military items, technology, and services, accomplishing this objective remains difficult. Most states do not achieve high levels of defense industrial autarky. In addition, it is very difficult to both improve quality performance and increase independence simultaneously.[78] Large investments, which are oftentimes not available, and long-term commitments from domestic customers are necessary. Further, the

[72] Béraud-Sudreau et al., *supra* note 35, at 9.

[73] SIPRI YEARBOOK 2011, *supra* note 58, at 245; Béraud-Sudreau et al., *supra* note 35, at 9; Ferhat Gurini, *Turkey's Unpromising Defense Industry*, CARNEGIE ENDOWMENT FOR INTERNATIONAL PEACE (2020), https://carnegieendowment.org/sada/82936 (last visited Dec. 21, 2021).

[74] SIPRI YEARBOOK 2010, *supra* note 27, at 261; SIPRI YEARBOOK 2015, *supra* note 57, at 450–51.

[75] SIPRI YEARBOOK 2011, *supra* note 58, at 238–39.

[76] *Sicherheitsrelevante Technologie- Und Industriebasis (STIB)*, BUNDESAMT FÜR RÜSTUNG ARMASUISSE, https://www.ar.admin.ch/de/beschaffung/ruestungspolitik-des-bundesrates/sicherheitsrelevante-technologie-und-industriebasis-stib.html (last visited Dec. 20, 2021).

[77] *See generally* Barbara Kunz, *Sweden's NATO Workaround: Swedish Security and Defense Policy Against the Backdrop of Russian Revisionism*, 64 INST. FRANCAIS RELAT. INT. 1 (2015); Masako Ikegami, *The End of the "National" Defence Industry?: Impacts of Globalization on the Swedish Defence Industry*, 38 SCANDINAVIAN J. HIST. 436 (2013); BITZINGER, *supra* note 1, at 56; BRYAN MABEE, THE GLOBALIZATION OF SECURITY: STATE POWER, SECURITY PROVISION AND LEGITIMACY 88–112 (2009).

[78] Bitzinger, *supra* note 65, at 467.

lag between R&D and commercialization is typically long, which places a further burden on the industry.[79] For less industrialized countries, a trade-off exists "between the level of technological aspiration, independence of production and costs. Aspirations often have to be adapted to capabilities if arms are to be produced domestically."[80] Misalignments between a state's needs and the domestic industry's production may also hinder the effective provision of domestic access.[81] As a result, most states remain dependent on foreign arms, components, and technologies. Domestic defense production can counter this, but only to a limited extent.

3.2. Creation of Arms-related Dependencies and Interdependencies

Defense industries can also create dependencies that offer their states political leverage over other states, as well as interdependencies that alleviate such leverage. Industry itself may not aim to create dependencies, but this can be a consequence of its international activities, ultimately serving the host state's security interests. Dependency of one state upon another arises under on three conditions. First, the item must be necessary for the importing state's core goals. Second, there must be few alternative suppliers selling identical or interoperable items. Third, the item must not be easily substitutable.[82] Dependencies may notably emerge when arms imports are complemented by technical assistance.[83]

Dependencies make importing states vulnerable because supply shortfalls for critical military items have strategic and tactical consequences for armed forces.[84] This vulnerability provides the exporting state leverage based on its power to withhold access to critical military items—leverage that exceeds only weapons-related cooperation and concerns broader bilateral security relations and security affairs.[85] Accordingly, both a state's limited ability to produce weapons domestically, as discussed earlier, and a state's ability to export weapons

[79] SIPRI YEARBOOK 2017, *supra* note 33, at 408; Castellacci & Fevolden, *supra* note 62 at 573.

[80] Brzoska, *supra* note 69, at 147–48; KRAUSE, *supra* note 3, at 172.

[81] STOCKHOLM INT'L PEACE RES. INST., SIPRI YEARBOOK 2016: ARMAMENTS, DISARMAMENT AND INTERNATIONAL SECURITY 548 (2016) [hereinafter SIPRI YEARBOOK 2016]; Richard A. Bitzinger, *Asian Arms Industries and Impact on Military Capabilities*, 17 DEF. STUD. 295 (2017); Robert Czulda, *Defence Industry in Iran—Between Needs and Real Capabilities*, 36 DEF. & SEC. ANALYSIS 201 (2020).

[82] Richard A.I. Johnson, *Decision-Making in the Arms of a Dependent Relationship: Explaining Shifts in Importer Acquisition Patterns of Major Weapon Systems, 1955–2007*, 31 DEF. & PEACE ECON. 851, 853–54 (2020).

[83] García-Alonso & Levine, *supra* note 54, at 947.

[84] Matthew Moore, *Arming the Embargoed: A Supply-Side Understanding of Arms Embargo Violations*, 54 J. CONFLICT RESOL. 593, 596 (2010).

[85] *Id.* at 597. *See also* CHRISTIAN CATRINA, ARMS TRANSFERS AND DEPENDENCE 149 (1988).

affect relations between the states. Arms-related dependencies are not the only factor determining relations between states; indeed, arms trade is often correlated with political closeness between states.[86] Yet higher levels of dependency decrease the likelihood that buyers will change suppliers, which in turn suggests that such dependencies have an appreciable effect on interstate relationships.[87]

States may also be subject to mutual dependencies. Such interdependence arises when states are reciprocal in their arms trade relationships according to the conditions outlined earlier.[88] Various network analyses emphasize that states are embedded in networks with dyadic and hyper-dyadic relationships which shape the international flow of weapons.[89] Such interdependencies are reassuring as they enable states to alleviate their vulnerability: the leverage that an exporting state has over an importing state as to access of military items is counterbalanced by the latter's reciprocal leverage.[90] Increased cooperation between firms due to the globalization of production furthers interdependencies.[91] Interdependent relationships may also be fostered by Defense Cooperation Agreements (DCAs), which formalize "procurement and acquisition, joint weapons collaborations, and defense industrial cooperation,"[92] among other activities. Indeed, DCAs are strongly correlated with the arms trade relationships.[93]

While interdependencies are a common feature of the global defense industrial landscape, sole dependencies (nonmutual dependencies) are more common. Indeed, almost 80 percent of the actors in the global arms trade network do not export military items on an annual basis.[94] Hence, the international arms trade resembles strong network dependency structures that imply a network typology with pronounced nonreciprocity, strong outdegree centralization, and exporting states frequently sharing the same importing states. Very few exporters deliver to many importers.[95]

Central to this network is the United States. As the largest arms exporter—in particular of modern military technology—and with a high degree of

86 Yang Xiaoxin & Chen Bo, *Defense Burden and the Effect of Others: From Neighbors to Allies*, 32 DEF. & PEACE ECON. 927, 928 (2020).

87 Thurner et al., *supra* note 19, at 1742.

88 Oliver Pamp et al., *Explaining Destinations and Volumes of International Arms Transfers: A Novel Network Heckman Selection Model*, 69 EUR. J. POL. ECON. 1, 4 (2021); CATRINA, *supra* note 85, at 151–52.

89 Pamp et al., *supra* note 88, at 15.

90 DeVore, *supra* note 56, at 245–46; Marc R. DeVore, *Armaments After Autonomy: Military Adaptation and the Drive for Domestic Defence Industries*, 44 J. STRATEGIC STUD. 325, 331–33 (2021).

91 Vincenzo Bove, Claudio Deiana & Roberto Nisticò, *Global Arms Trade and Oil Dependence*, 34 J.L. ECON. & ORG. 272, 273 (2018).

92 Brandon J. Kinne, *The Defense Cooperation Agreement Dataset (DCAD)*, 64 J. CONFLICT RESOL. 729, 732, 735 (2020).

93 *Id.* at 749; Brandon J. Kinne, *Agreeing to Arm: Bilateral Weapons Agreements and the Global Arms Trade*, 53 J. PEACE RES. 359, 375 (2016).

94 Thurner et al., *supra* note 19, at 1742.

95 *Id.* at 1744, 1754.

self-sufficiency, many states are dependent on it for their arms and technology acquisition. Given the rising costs of defense technologies, smaller producers lacking economies of scale struggle to compete and cannot avoid dependence upon the United States.[96] Even Europe's major industrialized countries are in a similar position, which was illustrated by their dependence on technology for UAVs from the United States and Israel following problems with the development of the Eurodrone.[97] The United States' network centrality has proven stable over time and reinforces existing dependencies. Indeed, not only are U.S. suppliers better connected than other suppliers, the United States is also less dependent on foreign exports to sustain its defense sector than other major arms-producing countries. The size of the domestic market provides leverage over states that wish for their defense firms to sell to the United States.[98] The result is that sourcing of weapon systems reflects the patterns of hegemonic relations.[99]

Recent developments, however, have altered the underlying dynamics regarding dependencies and interdependencies. Arms-producing states have reduced their dependency on the import of finished weapon systems yet remain dependent on the import and knowledge transfer of critical technologies and subsystems.[100] High levels of dependency remain as to weapon design, engineering and development assistance, critical components and subsystems, machine tools, and production know-how.[101] In addition, states are increasingly dependent upon certain defense contractors, notably super-companies in the United States and Western Europe.[102] Barriers to entry are high. The capital intensity in production, high R&D costs, and secrecy standards impair the diffusion of know-how and consolidate long-term dependencies from arms suppliers regarding training, maintenance, and reorders.[103] Accordingly, a few large manufacturers dominate the global market, thereby creating and furthering dependencies.[104]

In sum, the defense industry may contribute to national security by creating and maintaining dependencies related to arms procurement. This creates a "hub and spoke" model with a few large firms operating at the center and lines of outsourced production extending to second-tier states on the periphery, which

[96] Neuman, *supra* note 18, at 117.

[97] Dominika Kunertova, *European Drone Clubs Stall Strategic Autonomy*, 9 CENTER SEC. STUD. 1, 4 (2021); Neuman, *supra* note 18, at 117.

[98] Srdjan Vucetic & Atsushi Tago, *Why Buy American? The International Politics of Fighter Jet Transfers*, 48 CAN. J. POL. SCI. 101, 109 (2015); Neuman, *supra* note 18, at 115, 130.

[99] Vucetic & Tago, *supra* note 98, at 102.

[100] BITZINGER, *supra* note 1, at 29; Béraud-Sudreau et al., *supra* note 35, at 1.

[101] BITZINGER, *supra* note 1, at 25, 27.

[102] Vucetic & Tago, *supra* note 98, at 105; Zervos & Swann, *supra* note 64, at 40.

[103] DeVore, *supra* note 90, at 328.

[104] Johannes Blum, *Arms Production, National Defense Spending and Arms Trade: Examining Supply and Demand*, 60 EUR. J. POL. ECON. 1, 2 (2019).

offers leverage to the dominant states and firms.[105] Yet defense industries also create interdependencies. Most states lack the industrial capacity to make major arms-producing nations dependent on their subcomponents in this manner, however. Interdependencies can arguably be more easily achieved among second-tier producers, although such endeavors be hindered by competition from first- and second-tier states. Overall, as states tend to increasingly depend on technology, parts, and components, those that already develop, produce, and service such goods are in the best position to create and sustain dependencies as well as associated leverage that can be used to further their national security interests.

3.3. Enhancement of Status and National Pride

Domestic defense industries can also provide status and national pride. This may have political affects both at the international and national levels, thereby contributing to national security. Indeed, status ambitions are a prominent motive of governmental behavior.[106] States' efforts to maintain a domestic defense industry may even reflect a sort of techno-nationalism, where the aim to enhance status may take precedence over sound strategies for arms production.[107] Most large states in Asia—China, India, Japan, South Korea, and Indonesia—have sought to create indigenous defense industries and have initiated ambitious arms manufacturing to buttress their regional power ambitions.[108]

In essence, domestic production shows that states have military-industrial capabilities and know-how. Even when states are not self-sufficient, the fact that they maintain domestic defense industries signals to other states that they have relevant capabilities and that they take national security seriously. The sort of military goods and technology produced, especially their technical complexities, indicate the levels of military technological expertise available in a state. From this can be deduced, to a certain extent, the capabilities of the state's armed forces. The defense industry's quantitative capabilities further indicate to what degree a state's armed forces can be domestically supported in times of war, thereby providing information on their survivability.[109] Accordingly, domestic defense industries can contribute to signaling levels of military strength. Thus,

[105] BITZINGER, *supra* note 1, at 74–75.

[106] Hans Kammler, *Not for Security Only: The Demand for International Status and Defence Expenditure an Introduction*, 8 DEF. & PEACE ECON. 1, 3 (1997).

[107] Bitzinger, *supra* note 65, at 466.

[108] *Id.* at 458.

[109] *See also* Michael C. Horowitz, Paul Poast & Allan C. Stam, *Domestic Signaling of Commitment Credibility: Military Recruitment and Alliance Formation*, 61 J. CONFLICT RESOL. 1682, 1685 (2017).

the defense industry can strengthen states' deterrence, which relies on appropriate production capacities.[110]

Defense industries' capabilities can also engender respect by other states, which may signify political influence. Possessing industrial capabilities may demonstrate a state's industrial and technological prowess beyond the defense sector, thereby establishing or confirming the status of great or regional power.[111] The United Kingdom and France have traditionally perceived defense production as a symbol of great-power status.[112] Both see defense spending and their defense industry as means to foster their importance in global affairs. Saudi Arabia and the UAE are recent examples of states with defense industrial strategies that seek to increase their regional clout and to deter their adversaries.[113] In Russia, the domestic demand for arms is arguably not only motivated by the perception of foreign threats but also by the idea that the resulting military power is a central component of Russia's great-power status.[114]

Weapon transfers also have political and symbolic value that may serve national security interests. Arms exports support allies and may help to counter common adversaries and rivals. In addition, by authorizing arms exports, a state communicates that it supports the other state's national security interests. This may increase influence and the formation of defense-related relationships.[115] Accordingly, industry enables a state to be perceived as a relevant actor in regional or global defense affairs, and it also enables the development and maintenance of political influence based on concrete relationships. Yet states need to carefully manage their exports, since export approvals may antagonize the importer's rivals and denials may negatively affect foreign relations.[116]

Recent geopolitical developments and tendencies regarding emerging technologies reflect the defense industry's function to enhance status and influence. China, for instance, is among the largest arms suppliers to sub-Saharan Africa, thereby expanding its global influence.[117] In response, Japan now aims to develop a viable defense industry, produce weapon systems, and strengthen partnerships in the Pacific region.[118] More generally, small states and middle powers, such as

[110] Richard A. Bitzinger, *New Ways of Thinking About the Global Arms Industry: Dealing with "Limited Autarky"*, AUST. STRATEGY POL'Y INST. 12, 3 (2015).

[111] BITZINGER, *supra* note 1, at 15.

[112] Trevor Taylor, *Defence Industries in International Relations*, 16 REV. INT'L STUD. 59, 59 (1990).

[113] Heiko Borchert, *The Arab Gulf Defense Pivot: Defense Industrial Policy in a Changing Geostrategic Context*, 37 COMP. STRATEGY 299 (2018).

[114] SIPRI YEARBOOK 2016, *supra* note 81, at 546–47.

[115] There is a generally positive relationship between arms and allies, especially at formative stages. *See* Horowitz, Poast & Stam, *supra* note 109, at 1703; SIPRI YEARBOOK 2016, *supra* note 81, at 551; Bove, Deiana & Nisticò, *supra* note 91, at 291.

[116] Pamp et al., *supra* note 88, at 3.

[117] PIETER D. WEZEMAN, LUCIE BÉRAUD-SUDREAU & SIEMON T. WEZEMAN, ARMS FLOWS TO SUB-SAHARAN AFRICA iv (2011).

[118] Alexandra Sakaki & Sebastian Maslow, *Japan's New Arms Export Policies: Strategic Aspirations and Domestic Constraints*, 74 AUST. J. INT'L AFF. 649, 656 (2020); Hughes, *supra* note 57, at 434, 436.

Australia, Israel, Singapore, and South Korea, try to leverage their production of advanced technologies, such as AI systems, not only for defense purposes but also to advance their influence in international affairs.[119]

In addition to the effects at the international level, domestic defense industries may be a source of national pride, which, in turn, can improve national security by stimulating confidence, willingness to fight, and resilience. Citizens and soldiers can appreciate the fact that the armed forces' weapons were domestically produced based on citizens' preferences for national products in general. Domestically produced weapons may also reinforce the appearance of military competence. This applies notably for certain small states, including smaller states in Asia-Pacific.[120] Being (partially) independent on foreign suppliers also serves as domestic propaganda.[121] In Turkey, for instance, besides underlining that it wishes to be a regional power, having a defense industrial base is politically valuable.[122] Politicians showcase the domestic development and production of modern weaponry, such as UAVs, engendering national pride and support for the government.[123]

Yet citizens may not approve of the production of military goods or arms exports. In Japan, for instance, the decision in 2014 to end the prohibition of arms exports encountered resistance from industry and citizens alike. Companies such as Mitsubishi and Kawasaki were hesitant to engage in foreign arms sales.[124] In the United Kingdom, the fact that British soldiers fighting in Iraq were confronted with U.K.-produced weapons that had been sold to Iraq in the 1980s had significant political consequences.[125] And in Switzerland, citizens launched ballot initiatives that would have limited arms exports and financing of the domestic defense industry. The Swiss rejected these initiatives, indicating that most were not averse to maintaining a domestic defense industry.[126] While having a domestic defense industry may encourage national pride, public opposition may also diminish or even outweigh such sentiment.

In sum, the domestic defense industry may contribute to a state's international status and national pride that serve national security. Notably small states and middle powers invest in their industry to enhance their status, eventually aiming

[119] Raska, *supra* note 40, at 457–60.

[120] SIPRI YEARBOOK 2011, *supra* note 58, at 234; Bitzinger, *supra* note 65, at 466.

[121] Brzoska, *supra* note 69, at 160–161.

[122] Hüseyin Bağcı & Çağlar Kurç, *Turkey's Strategic Choice: Buy or Make Weapons?*, 17 DEF. STUD. 38 (2017).

[123] Umar Farooq, *How Turkey Defied the U.S. and Became a Killer Drone Power*, THE INTERCEPT (May 14, 2019), https://theintercept.com/2019/05/14/turkey-second-drone-age/.

[124] Hughes, *supra* note 57, at 437.

[125] JENNIFER L. ERICKSON, DANGEROUS TRADE: ARMS EXPORTS, HUMAN RIGHTS, AND INTERNATIONAL REPUTATION 114–117 (2015).

[126] GSoA—Gruppe für eine Schweiz ohne Armee, *Geschichte*, GSOA—GRUPPE FÜR EINE SCHWEIZ OHNE ARMEE, https://www.gsoa.ch/geschichte/ (last visited Dec. 20, 2021).

to achieve the status as a regional or great power. The degree to which these states achieve this objective remains difficult to assess, however. Gaining international prestige in this way is an expensive and challenging endeavor. Qualitative and quantitative performance arguably must be remarkable to be taken seriously. Yet the more sophisticated the weaponry and technology produced, the stronger this effect is. Further, the extent to which the defense industry enhances national pride is likely to depend on the state's political regime, threat perceptions, as well as citizens' values and political convictions. While a strong defense industry may contribute to national pride, this is not a given.

4. The Ethical and Analytical Dimensions

Thus far it has been shown that, taken together, the defense industry's provision of access to military goods, technology, and services, its creation of dependencies and interdependencies with foreign states, and its enhancement of international status and national pride serve states' national security interests. Domestic access to military items, technology, and expertise enables a state's armed forces and contributes to autonomy in national security policy. Making other states dependent on the domestically developed and produced items provides leverage over the other states' arms imports and security affairs. Interdependencies alleviate such vulnerability. Status arising from a defense industrial base can foster respect and garner influence in global and regional security matters. Enhanced national pride can lead to confidence, a willingness to fight, and resilience.

States tend to support and invest in domestic defense industries to benefit from their contribution to national security. Yet, as the preceding analysis of the mechanisms showed, most states' domestic defense industries do not contribute much to national security. The United States is arguably the outlier. Besides the United States, no other state has achieved a (near) defense industrial autarky; no other state has created a broad spectrum of salient dependencies related to arms and technology transfers; and no other state maintains a defense industry that unequivocally contributes to the status of a great power. Rather, for a number of reasons, most states' domestic defense industries contribute to national security only to a limited degree.

In the big scheme, most domestic defense industries' contributions to their states' national security are insignificant. They may contribute to various degrees according to the three mechanisms discussed earlier. Yet does it really matter if a state is able to produce some military items, but remains dependent of imports of parts and components, core technologies, and many other items? Does it really matter if a state can create interdependencies with certain states but not with the technologically most advanced one(s)? Even if states enjoy some level of status and national pride from their defense industries, is this enough to change outcomes in political, diplomatic, or military confrontation? The answers to these questions are uncertain.

And yet states continue to support and invest in their defense industries, even when considerable efforts to improve their industrial base may not have much effect on national security. Moreover, states may invest without knowing whether such efforts will yield the intended results. Rather, states may support their domestic industries assuming—hoping—that this will improve their national security prospects in the short and/or long term. Defense firms, on the other hand, may simply develop their business activities without much consideration as to their contribution to national security. This has several implications.

4.1. The Ethical Dimension of Only Partially Achieving the Industry's Purpose

There is an ethical dimension to this because even if the defense industry's contribution to national security is limited, the industry always generates economic benefits. A defense firm's owners, stakeholders, and employees make monetary gains as long as the firm stays in business—independently of whether the firm's contribution to national security is significant, negligible, or nonexistent. States also benefit from the firm's tax revenues. Arguably, however, defense firms that do not contribute to national security should go out of business because the government should not procure items that are not relevant for national security. This may be the case for individual firms. Yet because most states wish to maintain some kind of defense industrial base despite its limited contribution to national security, defense firms may nonetheless continue receiving state support and thus stay in business.

This ethical dimension has several layers. As with any failure or insufficient performance of the public sector or in the production of public goods, not contributing (much) to national security is a waste of public resources. This particularly applies when domestic defense industries are heavily subsidized, or when the government deliberately procures domestically produced military items instead of more competitive foreign goods.[127] In the latter case, notably when

[127] To expand on this, for the argument that corruption practices undermine national security objectives, *see* Philip M. Nichols, "Defense Firms' Duties to Society When Presented with an Opportunity to Pay a Bribe," in Chapter 9 of this volume. Related to this, for a case study of anti-corruption measures' impact on defense markets, *see* Christopher R. Yukins, "Mandatory Disclosure: How Anti-Corruption Measures Can Affect Competition in Defense Markets," in Chapter 14 of this volume.

this implies accepting lower quality standards, this may lower the armed forces' mission success and put soldiers at risk. Exporting weapons to finance and sustain the domestic defense industry may also represent making profits without contributing (much) to national security—notably when the firms' products and expertise are not needed by the armed forces.

Most importantly, industry's insignificant contribution to national security becomes a serious ethical issue because of the product being manufactured: weapons and military technologies are tools to kill people. Making profits from this activity is problematic as a matter of principle when not properly justified by an overarching purpose—in this case, national security. In addition, the production of such tools increases states' and people's ability to kill and destroy. Some may argue that this is not a problem as a state never possesses too much weaponry because such armaments only increase the armed forces' capacity to deter and project national power. Yet such excess capacity may create different risks, encouraging the use of force to advance a nation's foreign policy interests.

This ethical issue—which is intrinsic to the defense industrial activity and arguably concerns the entire sector across the globe—lies at the heart of the industry's purpose. The less the defense industry contributes to national security, the less legitimate it is. Moreover, the less the defense industry fulfills its purpose of advancing national security (while generating economic benefits, including creating jobs and tax revenues), the more its business activities become ethically problematic.

Accordingly, fulfilling its purpose—rather than simply producing military items—should be a core concern of all involved in the defense industry and of every single firm.[128] The responsibility for achieving this is not limited to the defense industry, however, since its activities are strongly regulated and dependent on states.[129] Governments and lawmakers have a duty to enable the defense industry to fulfill its purpose as they are primarily responsible for guaranteeing national security and managing related processes. The means to this end are sound laws, policies, and procedures ensuring that defense industries' activities effectively contribute to national security in the twenty-first century—not just hypothetically or potentially, but actually.

[128] In line with this argumentation, for the development of the argument that officers and directors of defense firms have a fiduciary duty to act in the national security interest of the United States, *see* Richard W. Painter, "Fiduciary Duties of Officers and Directors of Military Contractors: Shareholder Primacy or Loyalty to the United States?," in Chapter 3 of this volume.

[129] For a further discussion on the defense industry's function for society as well as related governance, *see* Duncan MacIntosh, "The Sniper and the Psychopath: A Parable in Defense of the Weapons Industry," in Chapter 2 of this volume.

4.2. The Need for a Renewed Research Agenda

To address this ethical issue, a better understanding of how the defense industry contributes to national security is needed. Solid knowledge exists on how the global arms production and transfer system works. Yet generally applicable and precise knowledge of the industry's role for security does not exist *en abondance*. In policy realms, the industry's contribution to national security is generally assumed as obvious. The academic and applied policy research does not seem to represent a broad enough agenda. A renewed and broader research agenda on how the defense industry contributes to security in the twenty-first century is necessary for orienting states' and the defense industry's actions toward better serving national security. Based on all this, the following presents some avenues for further research and reflection.

Regarding the creation of dependencies and interdependencies, it has been demonstrated that patterns of the international arms trade overlap with alliance patterns. How the arms trade affects broader security cooperation in the context of alliances and outside such a context, however, is not well established. For the United States, which is the world's largest military power engaged in a broad spectrum of alliances and defense cooperation with other states as well as possessing many forms of leverage in global security affairs, this question may not lead to particularly surprising findings since the arms trade is likely to be just one of many instruments at the United States' disposal. Notably for middle powers and smaller states, however, the international arms trade and cooperation on armaments may lead to security ties and influence in regional and global security affairs potentially disproportionate to its usual power.

In this context, it is interesting that by providing access to military goods, technology, and services for other states, a state and its defense industry contribute to the other states' national security. This means that exporting defense firms may be on state A's soil but contribute to state B's national security. The firms' contribution is thus not only to the host state's but to the foreign state's national security, which leads to further unexplored questions regarding the functioning and significance of the defense industry.

Modern development and production processes further affect national security. As the development and production have become globalized, the question arises as to what extent these processes create ties and industry-related (inter)dependencies that are (not) in a state's national security interests. While the United States has the bureaucratic means to control foreign (re)use of domestically developed and/or produced parts, components, and technology,[130] most states

[130] In this regard, *see* C. Edward Peartree, "What Ethical Dilemmas? The U.S. Defense Industry and Foreign Arms Sales," in Chapter 4 of this volume.

do not. This can allow (inter-)dependencies that are contrary to their security interests. Similarly, if the development and production of military technologies is increasingly based on civilian technology development, to what extent does the civilian/nondefense technology sector directly or indirectly form part of the defense industrial base and thus need to be understood as part of the national security architecture? If so, which arguably would imply more governmental oversight, regulations, and public scrutiny, would this help or hinder future technological development? And how would this affect national security?

Overall, while states take action to support the defense industry to attain certain national security goals, the defense industry's role for national security remains poorly theorized. In addition, empirics on whether states achieve their aims via their domestic defense industries are rare. This is particularly striking regarding the defense industry's contribution to international status and national pride. States do invest in their industries to achieve this effect. Yet it is not clear how this concretely affects their security standing and to what extent they actually reach this goal. A particular question in this context is what citizens think about domestic defense industries and how this affects national security, notably regarding the nation's morale, cohesion, resilience, and willingness to fight.

5. Conclusion

The defense industry's contribution to national security is generally assumed. States' policies and actions tend to mirror this assumption. Thus, the defense industry's contribution to national security may even represent a global norm from which actions and expectations arise. Nonetheless, the defense industry's actual role for security remains not well understood. This chapter has examined the defense industry's contribution to national security in the twenty-first century according to three main mechanisms, namely, the domestic provision of access to military goods, technology, and services, the creation of dependencies and interdependencies, and the enhancement of status and national pride.

This chapter found that with the exception of the United States, domestic defense industries tend to struggle to significantly contribute to their states' national security. In theory, domestic defense industries may contribute to national security, yet in practice, they achieve this goal only to a limited degree. While limited performance for the creation of public goods may not be unusual in the public sector, this does contain an ethical dimension: whether the industry significantly contributes to national security or not, its activities always are still profitable. Since the defense industry produces tools to kill, this is a serious ethical issue. Indeed, in general, not achieving a firm's or industry's purpose is not particularly problematic. But this is problematic when the products are tools to kill and destroy.

This problem is different from the classical argument about the military-industrial complex, which claims that the constellation of the military, politicians, and defense industry overemphasizes threats to national security to advance their particular interests to the detriment of society.[131] Indeed this ethical issue may arise even when the threat assessment is done correctly, simply based on the industry's inability to contribute to the overarching goal of national security. Thus, while this issue certainly applies to states with smaller defense industries, it also applies to states with larger defense industries, like that of in the United States, whenever their defense firms do not contribute to national security in a meaningful way and yet they still generate monetary gains. This suggests that the ethical issue is relative: the greater the defense industry's contribution to national security, the lesser the ethical problem, and vice versa.

Is the answer to this ethical issue to simply stop the domestic production of military items and technology, namely dissolve states' domestic defense industry? This is hardly convincing and unrealistic because as long as some states produce weapons, others will see the need to do so. Moreover, the domestic defense industry can contribute to national security in some form or another. From a governmental perspective, a response to this challenge is to support only those projects whose contribution to national security is unquestionable. For the defense industry, a response would be to abstain from projects that do not effectively contribute to national security. Producing and exporting military items solely to maintain defense industrial capacities is problematic, despite the fact that this may be in the defense industry's interest. This hints at the complexities of the question. Accordingly, a first and necessary answer to this ethical issue is a renewed research agenda on how the defense industry contributes to national security.

A renewed research agenda is needed not only for the reasons outlined earlier but also because of the geopolitical and technological developments that characterize the beginning of the twenty-first century. Revived great power competition makes states increasingly invest in national security and military equipment. In addition, new security challenges and modern forms of warfare complicate the provision of national security. Moreover, with the emergence of new technologies, the industry relevant to national security arguably encompasses a broad spectrum of firms working on dual-use technologies. This complicates the research agenda but also increases its relevance. To add further complexity, the

131 For more details and respective sources on the military-industrial complex, *see* the Introduction of this volume.

industry's contribution to other conceptualizations and forms of security, notably international security and human security, should be examined.[132]

Finally, the war between Russia and Ukraine may represent a watershed moment for the global defense industry, military spending and arms procurement, as well as the international arms trade, ultimately leading to new dynamics, trends, and challenges. Serious analysis of these developments, issues, and implications is much needed for enhancing the knowledge and reflections on the global defense industry, the related ethical dilemmas, as well as the quality of states' policies and the defense industries' actions.

Contributing to national security is certainly a challenge for domestic defense industries. Yet it is essential that they do so to fulfill their purpose and be legitimate too. Indeed, the industry's activities are oftentimes described as reflecting "simply business." Some use this characterization to communicate that this is a cynical business based on producing tools to kill and destroy. Others invoke this expression to exempt firms from moral responsibility by claiming that their sole function is to produce weapons. Both are wrong. To be justified, this business activity must have a higher purpose. But to achieve this purpose, industry's contribution to national security needs to be better understood and then made effective. National security should not be used as a false justification for inadequate governance and support of the defense industry, nor for producing or selling weapons that are not needed.

References

2015 INDEX OF U.S. MILITARY STRENGTH: ASSESSING AMERICA'S ABILITY TO PROVIDE FOR THE COMMON DEFENSE (Dakota L. Wood ed., 2015).

Anders Akerman & Anna Larsson Seim, *The Global Arms Trade Network 1950–2007*, 42 J. COMP. ECON. 535 (2014).

Hüseyin Bağcı & Çağlar Kurç, *Turkey's Strategic Choice: Buy or Make Weapons?*, 17 DEF. STUD. 38 (2017).

Lucie Béraud-Sudreau et al., *Emerging Suppliers in the Global Arms Trade*, SIPRI INSIGHTS PEACE & SEC., NO. 2020/13 (Dec. 2020).

Richard A. Bitzinger, *The Globalization of the Arms Industry: The Next Proliferation Challenge*, 19 INT'L SEC. 170 (1994).

RICHARD A. BITZINGER, TOWARDS A BRAVE NEW ARMS INDUSTRY? (2003).

Richard A. Bitzinger, *Defense Industries in Asia and the Technonationalist Impulse*, 36 CONT. SEC. POL'Y 453 (2015).

[132] While the former conceptualization relates to how the industry affects states' interactions in the international system, the latter relates to the effects at the individual level, notably the weapon's end-user and its victim. For a discussion on the point of view of the military end-user, *see* Thomas E. Ayres, Kevin Govern, and Michael W. Meier, "The Ethics of Better Weapons: A Soldier Lawyer's View," in Chapter 5 of this volume.

Richard A. Bitzinger, *New Ways of Thinking About the Global Arms Industry: Dealing with "Limited Autarky"*, AUST. STRATEGIC POL'Y INST. 12 (2015).

Richard A. Bitzinger, *Asian Arms Industries and Impact on Military Capabilities*, 17 DEF. STUD. 295 (2017).

Johannes Blum, *Arms Production, National Defense Spending and Arms Trade: Examining Supply and Demand*, 60 EUR. J. POL. ECON. 101814 (2019).

Heiko Borchert, *The Arab Gulf Defense Pivot: Defense Industrial Policy in a Changing Geostrategic Context*, 37 COMP. STRATEGY 299 (2018).

Vincenzo Bove, Claudio Deiana & Roberto Nisticò, *Global Arms Trade and Oil Dependence*, 34 J.L. ECON. & ORG. 272 (2018).

Jurgen Brauer, *Economic Aspects of Arms Trade Offsets*, *in* ARMS TRADE AND ECONOMIC DEVELOPMENT: THEORY, POLICY, AND CASES IN ARMS TRADE OFFSETS (Jurgen Brauer & J. Dunne Paul eds., 2011).

Matthew Brummer, *Innovation and Threats*, DEF. & PEACE ECON. 1 (2020).

Michael Brzoska, *Economic Factors Shaping Arms Production in Less Industrialized Countries*, 10 DEF. & PEACE ECON. 139 (1999).

Fulvio Castellacci & Arne Fevolden, *Capable Companies or Changing Markets? Explaining the Export Performance of Firms in the Defence Industry*, 25 DEF. & PEACE ECON. 549 (2014).

Center of Excellence STIB, *Sicherheitsrelevante Technologie- und Industriebasis (STIB)*, BUNDESAMT FÜR RÜSTUNG ARMASUISSE, https://www.ar.admin.ch/de/beschaffung/ruestungspolitik-des-bundesrates/sicherheitsrelevante-technologie-und-industriebasis-stib.html.

CATRINA CHRISTIAN, ARMS TRANSFERS AND DEPENDENCE (1988).

Robert Czulda, *Defence Industry in Iran—Between Needs and Real Capabilities*, 36 DEF. & SEC. ANALYSIS 201 (2020).

Kevin Dehoff, John Dowdy & John Niehaus, *Managing a Downturn: How the US Defense Industry Can Learn From its Past*, MCKINSEY & CO. (Apr. 1, 2013), https://www.mckinsey.com/industries/aerospace-and-defense/our-insights/managing-a-downturn.

Marc R. DeVore, *Armaments After Autonomy: Military Adaptation and the Drive for Domestic Defence Industries*, 44 J. STRATEGIC STUD. 325 (2021).

Marc R. DeVore, *Commentary on the Value of Domestic Arms Industries: Security of Supply or Military Adaptation?*, 17 DEF. STUD. 242 (2017).

J. Paul Dunne & Elizabeth Sköns, *The Military Industrial Complex*, *in* THE GLOBAL ARMS TRADE: A HANDBOOK 281 (Andrew T.H. Tan ed., 2010).

JENNIFER L. ERICKSON, DANGEROUS TRADE: ARMS EXPORTS, HUMAN RIGHTS, AND INTERNATIONAL REPUTATION (2015).

Umar Farooq, *How Turkey Defied the U.S. and Became a Killer Drone Power*, THE INTERCEPT (May 14, 2019), https://theintercept.com/2019/05/14/turkey-second-drone-age/.

María D.C. García-Alonso & Paul Levine, *Arms Trade and Arms Races: A Strategic Analysis*, *in* 2 HANDBOOK OF DEFENSE ECONOMICS 941 (Todd Sandler & Keith Hartley eds., 2007).

Saar Golde & Asher Tishler, *Security Needs, Arms Exports, and the Structure of the Defense Industry: Determining the Security Level of Countries*, 48 J. CONFLICT RESOL. 672 (2004).

GsoA—Gruppe für eine Schweiz ohne Armee, *Geschichte*, GSOA—GRUPPE FÜR EINE SCHWEIZ OHNE ARMEE (2017), https://www.gsoa.ch/geschichte/.

Ferhat Gurini, *Turkey's Unpromising Defense Industry*, Carnegie Endowment for Int'l Peace (2020), https://carnegieendowment.org/sada/82936.

Peter Hall & Stefan Markowski, *On the Normality and Abnormality of Offsets Obligations*, 5 Def. & Peace Econ. 173 (1994).

Michael C. Horowitz, Paul Poast & Allan C. Stam, *Domestic Signaling of Commitment Credibility: Military Recruitment and Alliance Formation*, 61 J. Conflict Resol. 1682 (2017).

Chris Hughes, *Japan's Emerging Arms Transfer Strategy: Diversifying to Re-Centre on the US–Japan Alliance*, 31 Pac. Rev. 424 (2018).

Masako Ikegami, *The End of a "National" Defence Industry?: Impacts of Globalization on the Swedish Defence Industry*, 38 Scandinavian J. Hist. 436 (2013).

Richard A.I. Johnson, *Decision-Making in the Arms of a Dependent Relationship: Explaining Shifts in Importer Acquisition Patterns of Major Weapon Systems, 1955–2007*, 31 Def. & Peace Econ. 851 (2020).

Hans Kammler, *Not for Security Only: The Demand for International Status and Defence Expenditure an Introduction*, 8 Def. & Peace Econ. 1 (1997).

Brandon J. Kinne, *Agreeing to Arm: Bilateral Weapons Agreements and the Global Arms Trade*, 53 J. Peace Res. 359 (2016).

Brandon J. Kinne, *The Defense Cooperation Agreement Dataset (DCAD)*, 64 J. Conflict Resol. 729 (2020).

David Kinsella, *Arms Transfer Dependence and Foreign Policy Conflict*, 35 J. Peace Res. 7 (1998).

Keith Krause, Arms and the State: Patterns of Military Production and Trade (1992).

Dominika Kunertova, *European Drone Clubs Stall Strategic Autonomy*, 9 ETH Zurich Center Sec. Stud. 1 (2021).

Barbara Kunz, *Sweden's NATO Workaround: Swedish Security and Defense Policy Against the Backdrop of Russian Revisionism*, 64 Inst. Francais Relat. Int'l 1 (2015).

Robert Latham, The Liberal Moment: Modernity, Security, and the Making of Postwar International Order (1997).

Melvyn P. Leffler, *National Security*, 77 J. Am. Hist. 143 (1990).

Bryan Mabee, The Globalization of Security: State Power, Security Provision and Legitimacy (2009).

Alexandra Marksteiner, Diego Lopes da Silva & Nan Tian, *Trends in World Military Expenditure, 2020*, Stockholm Inst. Peace Res. Inst. 1 (2021).

Ann Markusen, *Arms Trade as Illiberal Trade*, *in* Arms Trade and Economic Development: Theory, Policy, and Cases in Arms Trade Offsets 69 (Jurgen Brauer & J. Dunne Paul eds., 2011).

Inmaculada Martínez-Zarzoso & Florian Johannsen, *The Gravity of Arms*, 30 Def. Peace & Econ. 2 (2019).

Matthew Moore, *Arming the Embargoed: A Supply-Side Understanding of Arms Embargo Violations*, 54 J. Conflict Resol. 593 (2010).

Derrick J. Neal & Trevor Taylor, *Globalisation in the Defence Industry: An Exploration of the Paradigm for US and European Defence Firms and the Implications for Being Global Players*, 12 Def. & Peace Econ. 337 (2001).

Stephanie G. Neuman, *Power, Influence, and Hierarchy: Defense Industries in a Unipolar World*, 21 Def. & Peace Econ. 105 (2010).

OXFORD HANDBOOK OF U.S. NATIONAL SECURITY (Derek S. Reveron, Nikolas K. Gvosdev & John A. Cloud eds., 2018).

Oliver Pamp et al., *Explaining Destinations and Volumes of International Arms Transfers: A Novel Network Heckman Selection Model*, 69 EUR. J. POL. ECON. 102033 (2021).

Roland Paris, *Human Security: Paradigm Shift or Hot Air?*, 26 INT'L SEC. 87 (2001).

MICHAEL RASKA, MILITARY INNOVATION IN SMALL STATES: CREATING A REVERSE ASYMMETRY (2020).

Michael Raska, *Strategic Competition for Emerging Military Technologies: Comparative Paths and Patterns*, 8 PRISM 64 (2019).

Michael Raska, *The Sixth RMA Wave: Disruption in Military Affairs?*, 44 J. STRATEGIC STUD. 456 (2021).

Alexandra Sakaki & Sebastian Maslow, *Japan's New Arms Export Policies: Strategic Aspirations and Domestic Constraints*, 74 AUST. J. INT'L AFF. 649 (2020).

Jon Schmid, *The Diffusion of Military Technology*, 29 DEF. & PEACE ECON. 595 (2018).

Elisabeth Sköns, John J. Dunne & Nan Tian, *The Changing Economics of Global Arms Production*, *in* PRISM, Working Paper No. 2020-2 (2020).

Joanna Spear, *Defence Offsets: A System-Level View*, 37 STRATEGIC ANALYSIS 430 (2013).

STOCKHOLM INT'L PEACE RES. INST., SIPRI ARMS INDUSTRY DATABASE, https://www.sipri.org/databases/armsindustry.

STOCKHOLM INT'L PEACE RES. INST., SIPRI ARMS MILITARY EXPENDITURE DATABASE, https://www.sipri.org/databases/milex.

STOCKHOLM INT'L PEACE RES. INST., SIPRI ARMS TRANSFERS DATABASE, https://www.sipri.org/databases/armstransfers.

STOCKHOLM INT'L PEACE RES. INST., SIPRI YEARBOOK 2010: ARMAMENTS, DISARMAMENT AND INTERNATIONAL SECURITY (2010).

STOCKHOLM INT'L PEACE RES. INST., SIPRI YEARBOOK 2011: ARMAMENTS, DISARMAMENT AND INTERNATIONAL SECURITY (2011).

STOCKHOLM INT'L PEACE RES. INST., SIPRI YEARBOOK 2012: ARMAMENTS, DISARMAMENT AND INTERNATIONAL SECURITY (2012).

STOCKHOLM INT'L PEACE RES. INST., SIPRI YEARBOOK 2013: ARMAMENTS, DISARMAMENT AND INTERNATIONAL SECURITY (2013).

STOCKHOLM INT'L PEACE RES. INST., SIPRI YEARBOOK 2014: ARMAMENTS, DISARMAMENT AND INTERNATIONAL SECURITY (2014).

STOCKHOLM INT'L PEACE RES. INST., SIPRI YEARBOOK 2015: ARMAMENTS, DISARMAMENT AND INTERNATIONAL SECURITY (2015).

STOCKHOLM INT'L PEACE RES. INST., SIPRI YEARBOOK 2016: ARMAMENTS, DISARMAMENT AND INTERNATIONAL SECURITY (2016).

STOCKHOLM INT'L PEACE RES. INST., SIPRI YEARBOOK 2017: ARMAMENTS, DISARMAMENT AND INTERNATIONAL SECURITY (2017).

STOCKHOLM INT'L PEACE RES. INST., SIPRI YEARBOOK 2018: ARMAMENTS, DISARMAMENT AND INTERNATIONAL SECURITY (2018).

Matthew Sussex, Michael Clarke & Rory Medcalf, *National Security: Between Theory and Practice*, 71 AUST. J. INT'L AFF. 474 (2017).

Trevor Taylor, *Defence Industries in International Relations*, 16 REV. INT'L STUD. 59 (1990).

Paul W. Thurner et al., *Network Interdependencies and the Evolution of the International Arms Trade*, 63 J. CONFLICT RESOL. 1736 (2019).

Paul W. Thurner et al., *Corrigendum to Network Interdependencies and the Evolution of the International Arms Trade*, 64 J. Conflict Resol. 1548 (2020).

Bernard Udis & Keith E. Maskus, *Offsets as Industrial Policy: Lessons from Aerospace*, 2 Def. Econ. 151 (1991).

Richard H. Ullman, *Redefining Security*, 8 Int'l Sec. 129 (1983).

Srdjan Vucetic & Atsushi Tago, *Why Buy American? The International Politics of Fighter Jet Transfers*, 48 Can. J. Pol. Sci. 101 (2015).

Pieter D. Wezeman, Lucie Béraud-Sudreau & Siemon T. Wezeman, Arms Flows to Sub-Saharan Africa (2011).

Arnold Wolfers, *"National Security" as an Ambiguous Symbol*, 67 Pol. Sci. Q. 481 (1952).

Yang Xiaoxin & Chen Bo, *Defense Burden and the Effect of Others: From Neighbors to Allies*, 32 Def. & Peace Econ. 927 (2020).

Philip Zelikow, *The Transformation of National Security: Five Redefinitions*, 71 Nat'l Int. 17 (2003).

Vasilis Zervos & G.M. Peter Swann, *The Impact of Defence Integrators and Standards on Vertical and Horizontal Innovation in the Defence Industry*, 20 Def. & Peace Econ. 27 (2009).

2

The Sniper and the Psychopath

A Parable in Defense of the Weapons Industry

*Duncan MacIntosh**

1. Introduction

Two fundamental questions deserve particular attention when considering ethical issues in the global defense industry. First, is it inherently an unethical industry given that it makes its money by producing weapons for killing people? Second, the industry is a business, and as such should conform to the requirements of business ethics, just like any other business. But the industry is also implicated in the national security of its respective embedding nations, and in the advance of causes just and, sometimes, sadly, unjust. How then should the industry deal with the seemingly inevitable conflicts between normal ethical business practices, the needs of national security, and the possibility of its being involved in schemes variously good and evil? In this chapter, I seek to answer both questions.

On the first, is not the very idea of a defense industry ethically problematic given that the industry aims to produce lethal weapons for profit, a morally suspicious, even psychopathic, motive? Some would defend the industry by saying that, really, it has the virtuous motive of providing arms to help us prevail against evil; or at least it has that as a functional effect. But I shall argue that in fact sometimes the industry plays a morally valuable role in part precisely because of its prima facie problematic motive. The industry, so motivated, (1) helps us to make progress in situations where an all-pervading morality of altruism would leave us paralyzed, (2) leaves most of us with morally clean hands when morally problematic

* For helpful discussion, my thanks to the students in my classes at Dalhousie University—Introduction to Philosophy, and Theory of Rational Decision—and to the students who attended other talks I gave at various educational venues around Nova Scotia. For useful conversation thanks also to Sheldon Wein, Bill Barthelemy, Greg Scherkoske, Darren Abramson, and LW. Thanks too to Kevin Govern, Daniel Schoeni and Tobias Vestner for their general editorial efforts. My thanks in particular to Schoeni for his detailed comments on the pre-penultimate draft, which resulted in many improvements to the chapter; and to Vestner for some extremely useful insights on the penultimate draft which helped better organize the order of arguments. Finally, my thanks to my fellow participants at the University of Pennsylvania Law School's Center for Ethics and the Rule of Law's Ethical Issues in the Global Defense Industry Conference, April 16, 2015, to which an earlier version of this chapter was presented.

Duncan MacIntosh, *The Sniper and the Psychopath* In: *Ethical Dilemmas in the Global Defense Industry*. Edited by: Daniel Schoeni and Tobias Vestner, Oxford University Press.
DOI: 10.1093/oso/9780190675813.003.0003

things need doing, (3) helps to resolve conflicts where there are no moral markers for who should prevail, and (4) helps resolve conflicts that are really about what decision theorists call pure and impure coordination problems. More controversially, the industry's profit motive as expressed in selling to those who can afford to pay has the effect of advancing moral progress. For in the long run, being a wealthy enough culture to be able to buy the best, most expensive weapons tend to go hand in hand with being a morally better culture and one that ought therefore to prevail. These issues occupy the next two parts of this chapter. Part 2 comprises a parable that starkly shows the moral usefulness of psychopathy in a hypothetical scenario. Part 3 applies the resulting insights to the operation of the defense industry.

These two parts of the chapter purport moral usefulness in the arguably psychopathic motivation that animates the defense industry as a whole. However there remains the issue of what comprises ethical business conduct in the behavior of individual players within the industry given the complicating fact of the security role the industry plays and the fact that its products can be used for good or for evil. Thus Part 4 of the chapter addresses the following question: Are the rules regulating the weapons industry—rules found in business ethics codes, engineering ethics codes, procurement ethics codes, and laws of the land, as well as the more informal rules provided by dicta of conscience informed by ordinary morality—properly seen as sufficient to guide moral conduct in that industry in all cases and absolutely morally binding? Or are there situations that should be seen as affording exceptions to such supposed duties, and where the codes therefore need supplementing by more general moral reflection? I argue for (1) a limited form of the latter, (2) a principle that tells us how to draw the line, (3) a theory of rational choice on which choosing by this principle rather than cheating is rational (rational even for so-called psychopaths, and in effect supporting cooperative solutions to what I shall identify as defense industry Prisoners' Dilemmas), (4) teaching that theory to defense industry employees, and (5) adjusting oversight policy of the industry accordingly to focus on hiring people of integrity and training them in rational choice theory, rather than policing their actual behavior in their activities in the industry. This will be cheaper and more effective, will encourage better practices in nations with whom the defense industry does business, and, more generally, will help bring more people in the world into that total arrangement which is the best deal for everyone.

We will see that while unbridled selfishness expressed in the profit motive best guides the defense industry in its decisions about to whom to sell weapons, that very selfishness rationally justifies the adoption of dispositions rationally constraining its expression in the day-to-day business practices of the industry. This is because principled business practices recruit ever more people into a circle of trust, something which, again, helps produce a total world arrangement that is best for everyone, defense industry players included.

2. A Moral Argument Justifying Immoral Motivations for Some People in the Division of Moral Labor: The Case for Psychopaths

On the face of it, the defense industry is, well, indefensible. For it has the prima facie amoral aim of producing for profit devices meant to kill people. But I shall argue that an amoral entity such as this is needed to resolve moral dilemmas that cannot be properly resolved by ordinary morality and yet whose proper resolution is essential to producing morally approvable outcomes. Sometimes morally best outcomes will be brought about only if some agents do not have normally morally approvable motives. Moreover, their lack of scruples and their readiness to be purely self-serving will liberate them to do things which happen to benefit all of us but which will leave most of us with morally clean hands. I propose then to make a case for the moral value of some people being in effect psychopathic and sociopathic, defined here nonpejoratively as those being disposed to self-serve, to defy conventional morality, and to test legal boundaries.

The logic in question can be illustrated by a parable, a scenario coincidentally military in nature: a sniper has pinned down a platoon. The sniper has wounded one platoon member. Other members are agonized by his cry for help. Every few minutes one of them dashes over to try to rescue the wounded man. But each time, the sniper kills the would-be rescuer. The platoon has a safe exit route but cannot bring itself to retreat because this would mean leaving their man behind.

The motives of the platoon members in refusing to leave vary: for one man the motive is friendship; for another, empathy; for another, a promise; for another, a sense of military duty; for another, a commitment to a moral principle, for example, the Golden Rule; for yet another, a religious dictate; for another still, a view about dignity; for another, a respect for rights; for another, a view about what is virtuous conduct; for another, enlightened self-interest and the worry that his letting down the wounded member would result in others letting him down later. Each, then, has as a motive for not leaving, one or another of the things that have been thought by one theorist or another of morality to be the basis of all morality, the ground of all duty.

One of the platoon's members is a psychopath. And since such persons cannot be moved by the sorts of considerations that move moral people, he is unmoved by friendship, for this friend (the wounded platoon member) has outlived his usefulness. Empathy is foreign to him because it is in his nature to be able to care intrinsically only for himself. And promises? They are made only for convenience to induce self-advantageous action from another, and they lose their force once compliance with them would have no benefit. Military duty? That is something to which you pay lip service to rise in the ranks, but all duty except duty to self is a myth. Moral principles? Just rules one follows only when there is situational advantage to doing so. For how could following any rule for its own sake be a benefit to the self? Religious dictates? Rights? They do not exist, or they do but there is no reason not to violate them for personal advantage. Virtue? What is virtue talk but the attempt by one man to impose a groundless limitation on the behavior of another? Is there a fear of later consequences? No, for psychopaths do not believe bad consequences will inevitably be imposed on them for bad action; in fact, they are compelled to test boundaries, and they trust their own charisma, which is considerable, since there is nothing they will scruple from doing in order to charm their way out of punishments. So our man believes he has a good chance of evading all bad consequences for selfish action; indeed, he is compelled to try to prove this. And if he is caught for doing a "bad" thing, he thinks, whether caught by man or by God, he will figure out a way to escape the punishment when the time comes.

No, our psychopath quickly assesses the situation: he cannot get home without a team to help him. The team will not let him leave as long as they are bound to stay, for then he would be a mutineer. And the team will not leave as long as the wounded man is alive. Meanwhile, the longer they stay, the fewer of them there will be, because they keep sacrificing themselves trying to rescue the wounded man. So the longer they stay, the fewer of them there will be to help get our psychopath home if they ever decide to leave.

On the other hand, if our psychopath were to kill the wounded man, while the rest of the platoon would be outraged, they would secretly be grateful that there was no longer a basis for a duty to stay, and they would all retreat, grumblingly taking the psychopath along—partly because they would need his help in making their escape, and possibly to punish him later, but that is a bridge the psychopath will cross when the time comes.

So without a pang of conscience, our psychopath rises up quickly and shoots the wounded man dead. "Problem solved," he says, "let's move out" (said in every war movie ever).

What is the lesson? There are a number of possibilities.

First, maybe the psychopath in fact took the morally correct path—it was better that the rest of the platoon survive. But did he take it for morally correct reasons? Arguably not: his only motive was self-preservation. And did he cause the outcome in a morally correct way? Arguably not. He did not consult with his peers, for example. And he did not ask the victim's permission. He knew consultation would only yield the status quo. And why take the risk of the wounded man's pleading for help yet again?

Could not the platoon have come to the decision to do what the psychopath did, but by morally approvable deliberation? Arguably not. For each member would have the same reasons to vote not to kill the wounded soldier and retreat, as each had to try to mount a rescue.

Could not all the members have reasoned together to the conclusion that it would be all-things-considered objectively and morally better that they survive than that they all die trying to save the wounded man? And then could not they figure out a morally right way to bring that about? They could all act together like a kind of firing squad to kill the man, putting him out of his misery in a way that shares out the responsibility and freeing them to leave. Or maybe they would draw straws—short straw takes the shot. Either way, could not they have made the shooting righteous by asking permission of the wounded man?

All of these things might be possible. But as Bernard Williams points out in his discussion of the relationship between utilitarianism and integrity,[1] people who think duty requires only that they bring about the greatest good or happiness for the greatest number—utilitarians—fail to be able to explain why, where bringing about the greatest good requires sacrificing someone, it is appropriate to feel morally bad about what one has done. Each member of the platoon would have to feel some blame and regret about abandoning their man. And each might well have felt, and be expected to feel, that in this case acting on the utilitarian calculation would be self-serving in a way that is morally unseemly.

But if the psychopath solves their problem for them, they have no reason to feel guilt and nothing to regret. Indeed, since the psychopath is immune to these sorts of bad feelings the net result is better even by utilitarian measures—the wounded man is put out of his misery quickly (and he had no chance of surviving in any case); the rest of the men survive, so their happiness is added into the equation; and the psychopath, since he does not suffer any pain of conscience about the killing, does not with such suffering detract from the pleasure added to the equation, and of course he adds in his own happiness at surviving. This outcome is then best by utilitarian measures even if nonpsychopaths could have decided to kill the man. Of course, there is another measure by which this outcome is not the morally best. For surely the psychopath ought to have felt some remorse. It would be indecent not to feel in some way bad after having to do something like what he did. So the outcome is morally deficient for failing to contain guilt. On the other hand, arguably the psychopath has an excuse for not feeling remorse, namely, that because of his psychological condition he cannot feel remorse. And an outcome cannot be morally faulted for failing to include an action or attitude that an excusing condition has made impossible.

Well, suppose the shooter had not been a psychopath but instead what we shall call an "altrupath," someone exclusively motivated by altruistic considerations. Could not he have reasoned that the correct action would be the one bringing about the greatest good for the greatest number, namely, killing the

[1] *See generally* Bernard Williams, *Integrity*, *in* J.J.C. SMART & BERNARD WILLIAMS, UTILITARIANISM: FOR AND AGAINST 108 (1973).

wounded man? And could not he then have taken the shot and done so for morally right reasons? Well, perhaps such a person could make himself take the shot. But in doing so he would have to violate other things we think important in a moral agent, namely, each of the considerations that hypothetically motivate the other men to stay and attempt rescue—duty, promises, a sense of the other man's rights, friendship, empathy, love of his fellow soldier, and so on. Indeed, in this way, our altrupath is like the psychopath: he discounts important moral considerations in driving toward a good outcome. In being motivated only by generalized altruism, arguably he fails any number of other duties. In this regard, he is no better than the psychopath, and so he does not in those respects represent a superior solution to the problem. Furthermore, as an altruist, he would have to feel some pain at what he had to do. He would think it better that no one have had to be killed, for example, while the psychopath would be indifferent to this consideration. Again, advantage psychopathy, at least in terms of the overall balance of total resulting psychological pleasure and pain.

Another possibility: our psychopath did something wrong. But in so doing he made it possible for others to do right—to try to fulfill their duties of friendship, to follow their empathy, and so on. Indeed, maybe this was a better way for there to be the morally approvable outcome of the platoon being saved, namely, for them to be saved by the psychopath, and for each other member of the platoon to have the additional morally good status of trying to be a friend, fulfill a promise, and so on. This is a better way to the outcome than, for example, by each of them having had to vote to violate their various other moral duties. (The same result could have been brought about by the altrupath, but there would still be the disutility of the altrupath's pangs of conscience, making the outcome less good than the one able to be brought about by the psychopath.)

We now have a number of possibilities: maybe our psychopath did something purely wrong. Or maybe while his action was wrong, it was redeemed by its having the consequence of the platoon's survival, and/or by its having provided the occasion for yet additional morally right things from other agents (their good intentions and good efforts toward rescuing the wounded), and/or by it having saved other agents from having to do bad things (e.g., compromise their principles, or commitments, or natures). Maybe too it was redeemed by the fact that, since it was performed by a psychopath—someone incapable of the pangs of conscience that would have been experienced by an ordinary person doing the same thing—the overall high utility of the outcome was not reduced by the disutility that would have been represented by a pained conscience.

To these possibilities we might add that the psychopath did something understandable and forgivable. Or did he? What would be the basis of our forgiveness? That we could imagine ourselves doing something similar in similar circumstances? But we cannot imagine it. That is what distinguishes psychopaths from us. Unlike us, they are not merely an admixture of selfish and generous. Rather, they are nothing but selfish. Would it be that we forgive the psychopath because he could not have done otherwise given his nature? But for that sort of consideration, forgiveness is not appropriate at all. We do not "forgive" lions for eating meat.

At any rate, suppose we like the option that the psychopath did something wrong but redeemed by the good consequence of saving the platoon, the good result that each platoon member was able to be additionally morally good, and the absence of pangs of conscience: Could we have designed the situation to be thus, to feature a psychopath? Could it have been morally required and permissible to put him in the mix?

Not obviously. For who could have made the decision to insert him in good faith? Arguably not any of the persons directly involved who had reasons of duty, empathy, friendship, and so on to attempt a rescue. Their adding a psychopath would be the same as them indirectly pulling the trigger they morally cannot bring themselves to pull directly. And not any other person who might have anticipated having any of those duties. One might think that the commander who selected the troops for the platoon would have a duty to make sure that the outcome would represent a correct utilitarian calculation about what should happen, so he should be sure to include a psychopath. On the other hand, surely the commander too would have difficulty making this decision. For by adding in a psychopath he would in effect be conditionally pulling a trigger that would actually kill a man should the platoon face the foregoing scenario.

Perhaps the commander is in precisely the sort of situation that calls for him to make such choices. He is not supposed to be too close to his troop, precisely so that he can make the more impersonal decisions required to preserve his troop strength and, speaking in more humane terms, to do right by the greatest number of people. Yet if the commander included a psychopath in the platoon, and later learned that a situation arose in which the psychopath did what he was put there to do, the commander would have some degree of understandable regret and guilt, even if his staffing decision was the ultimately right call.

Maybe the commander could have arranged for the psychopath to be in the platoon, but be guilt-free if the psychopath ever has to act. For the commander is morally called upon to make such staffing decisions, and the right decision is to deploy a man who can do what the commander could not make himself do. An analogy: while I could not make myself kill someone who wanted to steal from my safe the medicine my son needs to survive, maybe I could make myself put a spring gun in the safe. And if the spring gun winds up defending my son's medicine, maybe that is not something that would have to be on my conscience.

On the other hand, surely if something is the right thing to arrange be done, then it must be the right thing to do. And if it cannot be done without guilt, then it cannot be arranged for without guilt either. Maybe one can find it rationally and morally obligatory to arrange for the doing of something one cannot find it rationally and morally obligatory actually to do.[2] But it appears that putting that kind of distance between what gets done and one's self does not suffice to separate one from liability for guilt for what gets done.[3]

At any rate, we might think that a better outcome would be one where the commander does not have to make these sorts of decisions. Better that there just *happen* to be a psychopath in the mix. For then the commander too is saved from guilt. Even better, perhaps, would be this: the commander has and acts on a duty to eliminate all psychopaths from the equation but discovers after the fact that luckily enough he has failed in this. Now the commander is even better, morally, and so the outcome is better still. To take another tack, arguably we all have a duty to try to eliminate the inclusion of a psychopath in the platoon. And yet we might be grateful to discover that we had failed. (To return to our commander, in constituting and deploying the platoon, perhaps he has a duty to insert a psychopath. But should he have been playing a different role in his army, serving in someone else's platoon, arguably he would have had a duty to try to discover and neutralize any psychopaths in his unit. The responsibilities one has in this regard may vary with one's circumstances.)

Note that the psychopath can do his job only if he himself is empty of moral motivation. For if he is moved by empathy, friendship, and so on, he will not engage in the incidentally platoon-saving behavior. So we need to be grateful for him having nonmoral, immoral, or amoral motivation.

Now some will say that utilitarian ethics would applaud what the psychopath would do and might even criticize those soldiers who would not do it. For their so-called moral scruples in effect result in needless and morally unjustified deaths. And yet many criticize utilitarianism for using the end to justify the means. Utilitarian arguments, it may be said, are in effect precisely attempts to justify immorality, perhaps to claim that sometimes immorality is necessary, even morally necessary. A paradox.

Either way, it appears to be better if the psychopath does what he does while at the same time the others do not do the kind of thing he does, and perhaps even have a nature precluding them from doing this or follow a moral code precluding such actions. It would seem good to have some people resisting utilitarian calculi while having others impose such calculations. The former in effect desperately treasure a given life while the latter proportion the value of each life

[2] *See generally* Gregory Kavka, *Some Paradoxes of Deterrence*, 75 J. PHIL. 285 (1978); Duncan MacIntosh, *Retaliation Rationalized: Gauthier's Solution to the Deterrence Dilemma*, 72 PAC. PHIL. Q. 9 (1991).

[3] *See also* Lawrence Alexander, *The Doomsday Machine: Proportionality, Punishment and Prevention*, 63 MONIST 199 (1980).

to the total number of lives at risk, and the combination results in us having the net good of lives both saved and having been individually treasured. The result comes about by a fortuitous division of moral labor, with some people doing the job of being utilitarians, while other people do the job of being Kantians, virtue ethicists, sentimentalists, and so on. In recognizing that this ethical diversity is a good thing, we discover that morality may approve of conflicting things from different people. (The one true morality sees it as good for some people to play the role of utilitarians and try to kill the wounded man, while also seeing it as good that other people play the role of Kantians, sentimentalists, or whatnot, trying to prevent this.)

I have said the presence of psychopaths can be a good thing. I want now to give some simpler examples. Suppose you and I are in a slowly burning room with only one exit. There is lots of time for us to escape, but the exit is only big enough for one of us to leave at a time. Suppose we are both moral and altruistic people. Then likely each of us will say, "you first." Then, trying to be helpful, we will both say, "OK, I'll go first." Then, back to "you first." Then maybe I reach into my pocket and say, "let's flip a coin." Unfortunately, you do likewise. Then trying to be helpful I say, "let's use your coin." But of course you are simultaneously saying the same thing to me. No, this could in principle go on forever. But suppose one of us is an ordinarily morally decent person, the other, a psychopath. Then the psychopath's first impulse will be to leave first, and the decent person's first impulse will be to offer the other person first exit. "Me first" says the psychopath; "I was just going to suggest that," says the decent person.[4]

Of course, sometimes it is useful to have an altruist around. Imagine the burning room contains two psychopaths. "Me first," each says, and no one gets out. Then each tries to break the tie by mimicking altruism: "you first." And now we have a repeat of the preceding problem. But suppose we replace one of the psychopaths with a morally decent person. Then she would say, "you first," and the remaining psychopath could say, "thanks." Problem solved.

It appears then that despite the prima facie rightness of making moral evaluations of persons by the objectives given to them by their dispositions and characters—evaluations by whether they are selfish or generous, for example—this does not correlate with whether their presence will be useful to the morally laudable solution of moral problems. Each character can have its place. Note that the burning room problem is not guaranteed to be solvable by two

[4] *See* Duncan MacIntosh, *Buridan and the Circumstances of Justice (On the Implications of the Rational Unsolvability of Certain Co-Ordination Problems)*, 73 Pac. Phil. Q. 150 (1992). About this specific example, one might be inclined to say that the problem is not that we have two altruists but that we have two people who are excessively polite. Maybe so. But the point is that the solution to the problem the agents face requires that at least one of them not be so self-effacing. That is, sometimes putting others first is unhelpful.

altrupaths—they might stumble all over each other trying to figure out whose coin to use. But the problem would certainly be solvable by the presence of a psychopath with an altruist.

Now back to whether there is a morally clean way for a psychopath to be designed into a system. There seems to be no way for this to happen. For if someone arranges for this, for example, the platoon commander, then if the psychopath ever has to act, the person who did the arranging—in this case, the commander—is morally tainted, should feel some remorse about what the psychopath has done, and so on. On the other hand, if the commander does his best to prevent the presence of a psychopath, and if this results in his platoon being wiped out, the commander is obviously in for another sort of remorse. Even if he gets lucky, inserts the psychopath, and the psychopath does not have to be used, or if he does not insert the psychopath, and there proves to be no occasion for his use anyway, the commander is in line for a kind of moral condemnation, in this case, for either failing to make sure the platoon was equipped for a possible eventuality, or failing to make sure it was not infected with someone so cold-blooded.

One might reply that we are presenting a dilemma that cannot be solved without the commander being subject to moral condemnation. But a more reasonable ethical theory would say that, since it is no fault of his own that he faces a situation where no matter what he does some kind of evil or other results, as long as he chooses the lesser evil, he is on balance to be praised. And if the evils are equivalent, since he cannot avoid evil, and since condemning him would imply that he ought to have avoided evil, this in violation of the ought-implies-can rule, our commander ought not to be morally condemned.

This may be right. And yet we might still think that the commander should feel badly for doing an evil. Perhaps he should eventually forgive himself for this, but not right away. And this is a cost. Would not it be nice if there were a way for the commander not to have a duty to feel badly at all?

What is the solution? Well, remember the special moral properties of the psychopath: he will feel no guilt, and he cannot help doing what he does. Then clearly, the person whom it is morally best to have making the decision about whether he should be present or absent in a situation is the psychopath himself! He will feel no guilt either way, and he cannot be faulted either way because he has no choice about what he does given his nature. My point here is not that the psychopath is better equipped to make the morally best decision by virtue of his lack of moral feeling. After all, the commander could make the same decision. Rather, the point is that since the psychopath cannot feel guilt, if he makes the decision, no one has guilt. And since he could not have done otherwise given his psychological condition, there is some sense in which he is blameless for his choice. While this will sound morally perverse, I am suggesting that in this sort of case, and precisely because of the psychopath's moral deficiencies, it really would be a happy eventuality if the psychopath did the moral dirty work for us, leaving us with clean hands.

It might be objected that my overall argument for there being able to be a good deployment of psychopaths presupposes that it is we who decide what situations the psychopath will be in, so we can make sure his nature will result in him doing things that have morally salutary results. But what if the psychopath manages to be in the position of being the social engineer who constructs the scenarios, using us for his purposes? Surely, then, he is not so morally useful.[5]

It is true that if we do not get to define the parameters in which psychopaths operate and instead they define the parameters, then there are moral risks. But what I have just suggested is that, in fact, that might at least sometimes be a good thing. A psychopath's taking over can be the morally best way to solve a moral problem.

What finally to say then about psychopaths? Should we vilify them? Or should we welcome their alternative perspectives and values? Where behaving as a psychopath would cause a morally worse situation, as where there is a consensus on what ought to be done by all moral values but the psychopath's impulses put him at odds with this, the psychopath is unwelcome and must be policed. But where there is no such consensus, and where, paradoxically, someone not bound to conventional morality will afford a morally cleaner result, incapable of guilt, driven exclusively by his own interest, and compelled to test boundaries, the psychopath is a salutary presence.

Remember that I here use the term "psychopath" without judgment or prejudice. I take it merely for a term of art to describe a certain psychological type. I neither condemn nor valorize that type going in. Moreover, a good deal of the moral valuableness in some contexts that I am attributing to psychopaths could be offered by degrees of ordinary selfishness. Not all of it, however. This is be cause, for any merely selfish person, as the suffering of another person rises and as the cost of helping them falls, there is an intersection point where the selfish person would help. Merely selfish people are in principle reachable by considerations of the suffering of others. Psychopaths by definition are not. They are not on the spectrum of selfishness and generosity. They stand in a different relation to those ideas. My purpose here is to see what may be said in defense of such a type. Arguably good managers do not see people as good or bad, just useful for different situations; and as a philosopher, in describing contexts in which psychopathy is morally useful, I am operating as a kind of "manager" of the overall moral scheme in which we live, proposing (or recognizing) a morally laudable use or role for a certain kind of person.

5 My thanks to Scott Edgar for this concern.

This may make *me* a psychopath. For I am proposing to insert psychopaths into the moral mix, the very thing I have been arguing cannot be done in a morally clean way.[6] At any rate, I think it worth exploring the possibility of there being morally commendable purposes for psychopaths.

3. Application of the Argument for Psychopaths as an Apologia for the Weapons Industry

But what exactly does all this have to do with the weapons industry? Weapons are things most cultures need at one time or another. But the motives driving their production by the weapons industry, motives to make a profit by building devices for killing people, are prima facie morally problematic. And yet there is a utilitarian call for such weapons. So it is morally good that they get made. But if they are to get made, we need manufacturers who in effect have motives that are either nonmoral (neither right nor wrong), immoral (wrong), or amoral (had without regard to their rightness or wrongness). Someone has to have these motives in the division of moral labor. Metaphorically speaking, someone has to have psychopathic motives. And because some people have them, others of us get to have nice motives most of the time—we get to have the officially valorized humane motives. We get to "be nice, until it's time to not be nice."[7] And then, when we need weapons for self-defense or some other—hopefully good—cause,

[6] Here is another possibility: maybe we can represent the person proposing the insertion of the psychopath as someone engaged in the design of morality and represent him as therefore standing outside of morality, exempting him from criticism (or at least exempting him from criticism in the terms of the system he is designing). There may be an analogy here with the Löwenheim-Skolem theorem and with the idea that no set of rules for a system can include rules governing its own rules—all systems of norms, whether moral or mathematical, are necessarily non-self-referring, so that no one system can contain all norms. Another possibility here is that we are in the odd position of a moral theory telling us what would be ideal in a scenario but failing to issue moral advice. Some morally salutary outcomes are not such that they can be arranged for; rather, they can come about only by happy accident. In this case, no one is told by the theory to act as a psychopath, nor to arrange for there to be a psychopath. Nor does the theory say that anyone would be praiseworthy for acting as a psychopath or for arranging for there to be a psychopath. At most the theory is saying that we should sometimes feel a bizarre form of gratitude for the presence and actions of such creatures. But of course even this is problematic, since normally, morally required or endorsed attitudes are expected to entrain certain actions, and this is in part why the attitudes are valued. In the present case, however, it appears that the permitted or required attitude is to be one entirely not action-guiding.

A related issue was raised for me by Michael Davis, who asks whether we are morally obliged to prosecute the psychopath. After all, if we do not prosecute him, we are complicit in his immorality and so he hasn't really saved us from it. If we do prosecute him, we are rejecting that he has somehow brought about a morally better state of affairs. My reply would be that we should prosecute him. After all, if we do not, we are complicit. And if we do, all we are doing is punishing a wrongdoer. And there is nothing wrong with that. So on this question, the theory I have proposed does offer a clean guide to action.

[7] This is a line from the Patrick Swayze movie, ROADHOUSE (MGM 1989).

the weapons manufacturer has products ready to sell. Moreover, weapons producers generally tend to select themselves into the business by the profit motive, a motive that is neither here nor there morally speaking; and in so self-selecting they spare others the moral stain of deciding to participate in this industry mix. Further, since those who so self-select do so without pangs of conscience, the overall situation is not worsened by their having painful feelings.

"Problem solved. Let's move out."

Now it might be argued that we do not need to represent, and would be mistaken in representing, the typical player in the defense industry as being psychopathic, or as having psychopathic motives. Fair enough. Most people in the business are just ordinary people, many of whom are no doubt wonderful to their spouses, children, parents, and friends, are good citizens, and so on; indeed, in my experience, the people in the weapons industry, and in the military and the public policy fields that superintend military involvements, are some of the most reflective, conscientious, and morally concerned people I have ever met. They just happen to have unusual jobs. They are not psychopaths. On the other hand, a part of their psychology is a little unusual: it allows them to argue for, build, and use devices for killing people. Even here, however, there is more to say; for many of these people probably do not see themselves as doing this. "I don't build rifles, I just build rifle *barrels*" (and so on for each participant in each part of weapons production). Nevertheless, the collective or group effect of these activities is weapons building, so that, arguably, the psychology of the group entity is psychopathic.[8] (This is something often said of corporations, whose mandate to make profits can incentivize selfish collective behavior, even if individual workers in corporations are not particularly selfish.)

It might also be objected that we can see defense industry players (both individuals and corporate entities) as being perfectly ordinarily moral rather than psychopathic in their motivations if only we see them as people (or collectives) who would not produce weapons except for a good cause—the cause of killing only people who deserve to be killed, for example.

That would certainly morally redeem the players from psychopathic status. But I am saying that the weapons industry can only solve certain of our moral problems if it is prepared to produce weapons not just for those deemed to be on the good side of conflict. The problems I have in mind can be solved only by preparedness to sell weapons to *anybody*, conditional only on them being able to afford them. We need Lords of War (think of the Nicholas Cage movie of that title). And if a given person in the industry is not that kind of person, he is

[8] *See generally* Edmund F. Byrne, *Assessing Arms Makers' Corporate Social Responsibility*, 74 J. Bus. Ethics 201 (2007); Gavin Maitland, *The Ethics of the International Arms Trade*, 7 Bus. Ethics 200 (1998).

not contributing to the solution of the problems I have in mind. (Of course that might be fine. That person might be doing other morally useful things.)

Lords of War? Really? How can it possibly be good for an armorer to be disposed to sell so cynically to whomever can pay? Well, imagine scenarios like the following: there are two small nations endlessly in lethal conflict, their conflict stirring up lethal trouble everywhere for everyone else. The reasons for the conflict are lost to history, and for this reason (or for some other reason) it is unknown or unknowable which side is in the right; or perhaps the reasons for the conflict are known, and it is known that no side in the conflict had very good reasons for going to war; or that in fact both sides had good reason, so much so that there is no decisive moral argument that one side and not the other should win. But in any case, now there is an endless violence cycle, each violent act seeming to justify a retaliation.[9] The conflict would end if only one side acquired a decisive advantage. Perhaps one day it acquires a little more money and so can afford the best weapons. Of course this side can buy these weapons only if the seller is not so scrupled as to sell only to those with demonstrable moral right to victory, since there is no such clarity here. Now the more moneyed side gets to buy its weapons. It then wins the war decisively. The conflict is ended, and everyone can move on. This is good for all parties in the long run, better even for the defeated party than had the war gone on indefinitely. The result is a morally superior outcome. "Problem solved; let's move out."

In the foregoing examples, it was assumed that neither side was demonstrably morally better than the other, and no one was such that they deserved to be killed, but nevertheless, morality would be served by the conflict ending in some side's victory, no matter which side wins; and morality would be served even if the winning requires killing. But there are also more subtle scenarios where selling weapons without regard to moral desert would be salutary. The subtlety derives from the fact that many conflicts are in effect over how to solve coordination problems. Some are what decision theorists call pure coordination problems, situations where we would all be better off living under either of several competing arrangements, but choice of arrangement is difficult because the options are equally good, so that, if we disagree about which arrangement to adopt, we are fighting about nothing and so no factor can be offered as decisive. (Notoriously, political conflict is greater the smaller the stakes.) Some are what decision theorists call impure coordination problems, situations where choice of arrangement is difficult because, while we would all be better living under either of the arrangements available to us, several of us would be slightly better off still under one arrangement, others of us, slightly better off still under the other arrangement, each side therefore slightly incentivized to push for its

[9] Many of the conflicts in the Middle East seem like this.

favored arrangement. The conflicts between the world's major ideologies may well be of this sort, for example, between capitalism and communism (although probably not between capitalism and Stalinist communism). Either might be a workable social arrangement, but each would benefit different people more, and each system would be more workable if everyone would just buy into it. Let us assume that in instances of these general scenarios the sense in which we would be better off is the moral sense: fewer people would die, more people would have thriving lives, and so on. In these scenarios it is morally better that there be some decision than that no decision prevail because it was not going to go in one of the particular ways. And if it costs all the parties something to arrive at one of the arrangements rather than another (costs in lives and in reductions of thriving), costs enough that the further costs to all parties of trying to impose the losing arrangement instead would mean that no party had anything to gain, then the arrangement that has prevailed has in effect become the morally best arrangement. It has become the best because reverting to the alternative would be too morally costly. Interestingly, in these cases it is therefore not determinate which arrangement is the morally best one until one of the arrangements prevails—which arrangement is best is what philosophers call a soft fact, a fact about the present that depends on what happens in the future. It is also true that an armorer selling to whichever of the contesting sides happened to be able to afford to buy the best, and so most expensive weapons, thereby allowing it to win the conflict, can be seen has having a morally salutary effect—again, because of having brought about a morally superior arrangement, one that could not have come to exist unless the agent of its existence was not morally motivated in deciding to help one side rather than the other.

I have just argued that weapons sellers having the profit motive can help resolve conflicts where it would be morally good that they be resolved, but where there is no moral marker to the effect that one side rather than the other deserves to win. This will be true where neither side is morally right, or both sides are morally right, or it is not known which side is right, or where there is no fact of the matter yet which side is right but where one side can in effect be made right by being helped to prevail. Here, something is needed to break the tie, and it must be something nonmoral since, in these special cases, moral factors are not decisive. Of course any number of things could break the tie, for example, selling to the party with the most number of blondes. Why is the profit motive the one that should break the tie? Well for one thing, those who have that motive self-select for the role, a factor we have already seen has moral advantages.

But there is a much more general reason for why the profit motive should at least sometimes be what decides who gets sold to, a reason deriving from the fact that good societies tend on average to be wealthier, and therefore able to pay more for weapons. This is because good societies feature things like human rights, mutual respect, inclusiveness, recognition of the value of diversity, wealth sharing, rule of law, freedom from corruption, security of persons and property within the society, protection of the society from external threat, and so on—characteristics that attract ever more people into the society. All of these factors have the effect of making bigger, more thriving economies. And that, in turn, produces ever greater wealth. The result is that if a society can afford to buy better, more expensive weapons than other societies, it is probably a better society. This means that selling to whomever can afford the best, most expensive weapons has the effect of advancing the best societies by helping them prevail over less good societies, ones less respectful, less inclusive, and so forth. Thus having an industry, like the defense industry, be motivated by profit, has the indirect effect of being a force for moral advance.[10]

But would not selling only to those who are judged morally good be an even better force for moral advance? Well, I am suggesting that, very often, the wealthiest and the morally best are one and the same. So the question wrongly implies that there must be a contrast. But even allowing the logical possibility that these things could come apart, there is the problem that the matter of who is in the right is typically contested, cloudy, or indeterminate. That one morally judges that a side is right is therefore a less reliable correlate of its being right than that it can afford the best weapons. Judgments about who is right are likely to be contaminated by religious prejudices, tribe-based presuppositions, moral codes inherited from ancient times designed for different circumstances, habits of thought, unexamined premises, the vested interest of the person doing the judging in whatever status they have in their own society, and so on. Having an amoral interest only in profit cuts through all of this.

But what if one side in a conflict is *obviously* in fact morally problematic? And what if this bad country is suddenly able to afford the best weapons because it has discovered within its borders tremendously valuable natural resources, resources from whose sale it can buy terrific weapons it will then use to oppress the good culture it is in conflict with? Surely weapons should not be sold to the bad side?

Three replies. First, again, the idea that it is obvious who is morally right in most conflicts, or even in a given conflict, is problematic. Each side thinks it is

[10] In future work, I hope therefore to argue that it is a measure of the goodness of a culture just how good its weapons are—the better the weapons, the better the culture. Thus, it is no coincidence that what is the most well-armed and powerful country on earth—the United States—is also, by some people's lights at least, the country that mostly has the morally right end of the stick, and that most defends individual liberties. Probably too it is no coincidence, then, that it is also a gun culture. For what is true in the large in this case is also true in the manner of fractals right down to the small. This is not to say that being such a culture is without cost. Apparently, the cost is 39,000 lives per year in gun violence. But the cost buys you absolute immunity to invasion from without, and from certain kinds of tyranny within.

the right one, for example. And each side's allies think it is in the right. Moreover, very often the issue in a conflict is not really about right and wrong. Instead, as we discussed earlier, it is about solving coordination problems in which neither side is necessarily inherently right (however much each side would like things to go its own way, and however much each side may find justification for its actions in premises held by its side but not the other).

The second reply involves the concept of moral luck—of being considered to be morally good or bad in spite of having that status by luck rather than intention and effort.[11] In the lives of individuals, an example would be the drunk driver who unluckily hits a child and so is in for more moral blame and punishment than the lucky drunk who does not. In the lives of nations and cultures, some countries are richer in natural resources and so wind up having greater cultures.[12] So if a given country acquires power by luck in resources, and that means it will thrive more fully, have broader influence, attract more people to itself, and so on, this cannot be completely gainsaid—the country is still simply a better country.[13]

Third, in order to be able to continually wield power and so to continuingly advance an evil cause, it is not enough to have resources; one must also have a culture in place sufficiently good that one will be allowed to deploy the profits of those resources. And if you are an evil culture, your grasp on the profits of the resources will be tenuous. Few people will ally with you; and others with a better culture and so a greater ability to attract allegiance will band together to overwhelm you and seize your resources, perhaps by making or buying weapons better and so more expensive than the ones you can afford even with your new wealth! (In one of the preceding examples, we imagined one of the contending countries getting a bit more money. What if they got the extra money by being appealing enough as a society to attract a benefactor?) It may be true that, for a while, pure luck, not justice, can result in one power dominating another. For example, apparently, Germany almost got the A-bomb first. Again, however, it would not be enough for them to get it

[11] *See generally* Thomas Nagel, *Moral Luck*, *in* THOMAS NAGEL, MORTAL QUESTIONS (1979) (providing the classic treatment of this concept).

[12] Such resources are sometimes a mixed blessing, posing the risk of the so-called "Dutch Disease," where the resource sectors in a country strengthen at the expense of other aspects of the country's economy. For a quick overview of this phenomenon and how countries can deal with it, *see* Tejvan Pettinger, *Dutch Disease*, ECON. HELP (Nov. 15, 2017), https://www.economicshelp.org/blog/11977/oil/dutch-disease/.

[13] Of course it is possible to resist the idea of moral luck—maybe the lucky and unlucky drunks should get the same sentences. And so it is possible to resist the application of the concept to conflicts between cultures and nations—maybe greater success in various dimensions does not entail moral superiority or rights to greater sorts of influence. I suspect, however, that it is easier to resist the idea of moral luck for personal morality than for the ethics of relations between nations. It is just very hard to argue with thriving and influence as measures of goodness in cultures.

first; they would also have to keep it, or keep the advantage it affords. And my claim would be that a more virtuous culture would eventually displace the unjust but temporarily powerful country, displace it perhaps by availing itself of weapons available on the rationale offered here.[14] We see this happening over and over. Think of the most monstrous cultures you can, for example, Nazi Germany, Bosnia: all collapsed because they were found too unattractive to be allowed to retain their power; and all were overwhelmed by societies that were individually or collectively wealthier.[15]

It might be objected that I have just committed a contradiction: I have said the best cultures are likely to be the ones with the most money and so should be sold to by armorers making the best and so most expensive weapons; but I have also said that a morally lesser society will not be able to attract allegiance, patrons, and so on. This implies there are two criteria driving which societies achieve domination, namely, wealth and moral appeal, and that because morally unappealing societies will not attract allegiance and patrons, they will not have wealth, and so will not be able to induce armorers to sell the best weapons to them. Indeed, I have in effect suggested that we can feel comfortable selling the best weapons to the wealthiest societies because they will be thwarted if they are evil. But since part of thwarting them is making sure they do not have arms, surely this means armorers must make moral discriminations and refuse to sell to evil regimes?

To this I can think of two possible replies: first, I could simply accept that this is true, grant that there are more values in play in deciding to whom to sell weapons, and grant that, apart from the scenarios I rehearsed above where there is no clear moral entitlement to victory by either side, weapons should only be sold to virtuous buyers, not necessarily to the wealthiest buyers. We might then be grateful for psychopathic weapons dealers in those special scenarios, but resist and regulate the dealers in morally problematic cases to prevent the dealers from arming evil.

But a second reply I could make is to double down on the connection between being a morally worthy society and being a wealthy society: when we say a given society is evil, we are necessarily saying its arrangements are less wealth producing for itself, and for everyone so far as it is wasting resources and people in arrangements not maximally wealth conducive. And I could combine this with an idea from Part 4 of this chapter, following, that wealth is increased by ever enlarging the circle of those included in the best—most wealth producing—deal, recognizing that greater wealth is produced by greater sharing of wealth. And

14 Defining "eventually" here is, of course difficult, and this will need more attention in order to satisfactorily operationalize my claim, something I am not sure how to do.

15 Thanks to Bill Barthelemy and Sheldon Wein for some of the concerns in this paragraph.

now I can say that the ever expanding circle will have a stake in overcoming the pockets of inefficient wealth generation represented by so-called evil cultures. That is, again, the wealthiest will be able to afford better weapons than the poorer societies and so will prevail over them militarily, eventually absorbing the conquered society and its members into the deal. If this is right, then, again, we have an argument for its being good that armorers sell to whomever can pay, on the assumption that those who can afford the best weapons will prevail, thereby best enlarging the circle.

4. The Defense Industry and the Rationality of Complying with Its Rules for Good Conduct—Delimiting Permitted Situational Variation in Compliance with Defense Industry Ethics

We turn now to the question how defense industry practitioners should comport not on the question of to whom to sell their products but in their day-to-day practices in producing the products. How should the demands of self-interest, normal business ethics, national security, and mindfulness about just and unjust possible uses of defense industry products be balanced out? We will see that the profit motive which justifies selling the best and so most expensive weapons to whomever can afford them rationally justifies constraints on its own expression in the internal affairs of businesses within the industry. This lesson will emerge as we review various positions on which sorts of codes and motives are thought to be appropriate guides to conduct in the industry.

The defense industry is regulated by codes of engineering ethics enjoining the manufacture of quality products honestly represented, business ethics codes enjoining good character, procurement ethics codes requiring that purchases be driven by mission needs and the public good, corporate ethics codes requiring company leadership to try to turn a profit for investors, as well as government legislation forbidding various practices, such as bribery. Further, many players in the industry are informally regulated by what their consciences dictate. But it might be thought that a given player should violate these standards in a given situation if this would most benefit the national interest—for example, if bribing a foreign government official would procure the materials needed for a weapon system that would provide a decisive advantage against an enemy state. Relatedly, and speaking now more to competitiveness in business, while many in the domestic defense industry are disposed to behave with integrity, they must interact with cheaters in foreign countries. Is it not then permissible to cheat in turn in order to level the playing field? (An example would be competing in bribing an official in order to get a foreign government to buy a weapon from your company.) In this section, I say the answer is sometimes yes for both sorts of scenario, but surprisingly rarely owing to the fact that both nations and companies may benefit more from its being a known fact that industry players are indisposed to violate policies forbidding such behavior. Here I apply ideas from the philosopher and decision theorist, David Gauthier, arguing that the actions players rationally should perform are those dictated by the policy it most advantages them to adopt under ideal choice conditions, not the actions most advantaging in a given moment.

Much of the substance of the codes, laws, and moral principles I have just discussed involves prohibitions against things like using bribery to secure a contract, to get a raw material needed for a product, or to influence the politics of a region in ways advantageous to one's company or to the company's sponsoring nation state. Other concerns have to do with keeping business promises, providing the best product for the client, and ensuring that the product is accurately represented.

Some people reason as if these requirements were absolutes; others think the question of what to do can be solved by people simply behaving with integrity in the ways their respective professions demand, for example, perhaps we should just encourage individual engineers to do the right thing as understood in their profession.[16] Ditto for, say, procurement officers.[17] The idea is that large moral issues will take care of themselves if all parties obey the codes of ethics of their respective technical fields. More generally, it might be thought that morally correct outcomes would come simply from the unswerving application of technocratic and bureaucratic expertise.

Both views seem doubtful to me given the plurality of moral values we have duties to serve, given that the magnitude of our duty to any such value varies from situation to situation, and given the limited purviews of each of the aforementioned norm sources. This becomes evident when we think about what at least some aspects of the defense industry are for, namely, ensuring justice by force; or, more locally, defending the realm, a presumptively just goal (at least if it is a just realm, or a candidate for such). These seem like the most important goals there could be. And this suggests that, if in a given situation these goals would be best achieved by a company's bribing a potential purchaser, government official, or raw materials supplier, then so be it. This would simply be inducing someone to do right, or at least the bribing would be for a justifying cause.

[16] *See* Michael Davis, Address at the University of Pennsylvania Law School's Center for Ethics and the Rule of Law's Ethical Issues in the Global Defense Industry Conference: Ethical Issues in the Global Arms Industry: A Role for Engineers (Apr. 15, 2015).

[17] *See* Kevin Govern, Address at the University of Pennsylvania Law School's Center for Ethics and the Rule of Law's Ethical Issues in the Global Defense Industry Conference: Acting Astutely in Government Acquisition: Procurement Integrity, Corporate Ethics and Avoiding Fraud in Logistics (Apr. 16, 2015).

Likewise, sometimes the foregoing goals might be best achieved precisely by violating codes of engineering ethics requiring the manufacture of good products accurately represented and instead building an inferior product and lying about its quality. Maybe it would be better to build a weapon that will rust out after five years (and maybe better to keep quiet about this fact), for then it would be unlikely to be of use to any unjust enemy who might confiscate it in battle, or buy it on the black market, or to whom it might be sold when they are a good regime, but who it is feared may transform into a bad one. Selling weapons that have a tendency to expire could confine their usability to the situation for which they are ostensibly being purchased. Or maybe the weapons should be able to be turned off by their manufacturer at the behest of the state in which the manufacturer resides, or at the behest of some bigger political body responsible for supervising global conflicts, for example, the United Nations. So the correct larger moral positions do not so straightforwardly emerge from such lower level expertise as constitutes the normative part of good engineering, or, indeed, of any other profession. Sometimes correct all-things-considered morality may require violating an individual profession's ethical code.

Of course, we might amend, for example, engineering ethics codes to require that engineers demand the foregoing conditions on the sale of the weapons they design—the engineers could take themselves to be obliged to so design weapons as to be operable only by those we have reason to think are good guys, for instance. But this would be to intrude global political matters into engineering ethics codes, so that the codes were no longer just about engineering. That might be a good thing (although see the arguments in Sections 2 and 3 of this chapter), but it would not vindicate the idea that merely obeying codes for technical professions as such will always express all-things-considered moral wisdom.

It might be argued, however, that it is a characteristic of the professions—engineering, medicine, architecture, law—that their practitioners must be well-informed about the state of the world, and must be morally reflective at the highest and most general levels. We see this properly reflected in the codes of ethics in the professions. For example, in engineering ethics codes, the public welfare is the preeminent consideration.[18]

There is something right about this claim. Engineered products are supposed to be safe for the public to use, for example. But there is also something wrong about this idea, as is proved by the fact that we would not think it was decisive on questions like whether we ought to get involved in a given war whether the engineering profession was for or against it. The profession is not expected to have opinions about matters of that level of generality. And to the degree that it does have them—perhaps the members of some engineering society would sign a

[18] Michael Davis made this point to me in a conversation.

petition on the matter—this would just be one more opinion in the mix; it would not necessarily be what all things considered ought to be done. More generally, it is not the business of an engineering code of ethics to stipulate whether or under what conditions the code itself should be violated. But there surely are such conditions. And this shows either that such codes are not all-things-considered guides or that they are unlikely to be guides correct for all circumstances.

There are real-world examples of the sometime appropriateness of violating engineering ethics codes from the software and computer hardware engineering professions. Think of the efforts by the United States' National Security Agency (NSA) to make electronics hardware and software that is supposed to be secure in fact nonsecure so as to be able to monitor terrorist use of it.[19] I am not sure how this played out, whether by the NSA asking manufacturers to put code on newly manufactured hard drives allowing the drives to be accessed by others, by the NSA hiring a private company to introduce the code stealthily, or by the NSA doing this itself. In the first two cases, we have the defense industry producing, arguably morally correctly, a bad product, or at least one that will not work as advertised. While in the third case, arguably it was morally better that the industry's attempts to produce secure products be undermined. Obeying the supposedly absolute correct codes of conduct requiring producing a good product here might have been traitorous or morally evil, since doing so would abet terrorism.[20]

Think, too, of Bernard Williams's famous thought experiment:[21] suppose someone who has just earned his doctorate in chemistry cannot find work, is in ill health, and cannot support his family. But his former doctoral supervisor tells him he can get him a job. Unfortunately, the job is research aimed at making a weapon of mass destruction. The former student, George, objects on moral principle to working toward such a goal. But his supervisor points out that George is not a very good chemist, his involvement would set the project back years, so even as a pacifist he can accept the job in good conscience. This, again, would be a case where arguably someone would be doing right morally precisely by failing the codes and standards presumed to govern the defense industry. And even if one is a good engineer, perhaps one should sometimes sabotage product development, for example, if the product is likely to be used in evil ways.

[19] Scott Shane & Nicole Perlroth, *Legislation Seeks to Bar N.S.A. Tactic in Encryption*, N.Y. Times (Sept. 6, 2013), https://www.nytimes.com/2013/09/07/us/politics/legislation-seeks-to-bar-nsa-tactic-in-encryption.html.

[20] A natural question here is this: When a U.S. electronics company makes a product for public purchase and the NSA insists on a modification to make it serviceable for its purposes, who is the customer? If the customer is really, or in part, the NSA, then arguably the modification is, insofar, a feature, not a bug. That is, from the NSA's point of view, the manufacturer is not failing to make a good product. Other end users might of course have a different point of view.

[21] *See generally* Williams, *supra* note 1.

Maybe sometimes one should leak to the other side trade secrets about weapons one's company or nation is developing (thus perhaps contravening a nondisclosure contract, this, again, in violation of a precept of business ethics), for this might be hoped to produce a parity that will yield a standoff and so minimize the likelihood of the harmful use of the weapons. This is what motivated some people to divulge secrets to our enemies in the Cold War. And sometimes such logic works directly to our advantage—think of defecting German physicists and Nazi scientists during the Second World War.

A related case of its being arguably appropriate to violate standard business ethics codes is that of the whistle-blower, someone who breaks commitments to her company and contravenes supposed best practices because she thinks she has a higher duty to the public welfare. (Edward Snowden is the obvious example, although he may not be a whistle-blower proper since he did not stay to face the verdict of the judicial processes designed to adjudicate ostensibly whistle-blowing allegations.) True, whistle-blowing might not be as good for my point, since arguably the laws enjoining and allowing whistle-blowing mandate the overriding of other codes and laws, so that it is really an expression of defense industry rules—at least taken all together—not a violation of them. Still, the sometime rightness of whistle-blowing proves the point that right conduct may consist in violating some rule, even if this is still at the behest of some other rule.

I just argued that the correctness of the various codes defense companies operate under should be seen as varying with such exigencies as may arise in the defense of the realm or in implementing justice more broadly; or that, even if they are always the right rules, sometimes it is better to break them—however good the rules, there can be exceptions to them. But now let me make the opposing case that one should never violate these rules.

Taking an example from the preceding list, suppose this one time you would get more money for your company and shareholders in a business venture by bribing an official, perhaps bribing him into doing a morally wrong thing, or that this one time your bribing him would be your inducing him to do the morally right thing, advancing the cause of world peace, say. Why refrain?

There are many already well-known general sorts of reasons. For example, it could be that your thinking it is up to you whether you should obey a code in a given context would make it more likely that you will violate it in a context where it should not be violated, or that it will make others lose confidence that you are likely to make correct choices in the future, thus undermining your capacity to have self-advantaging or morally just effects in the future. Or maybe you so behaving will have indirect undermining effects on the likelihood of others behaving in ways advantageous or just. That is, the example of your behavior may induce others into making bad choices, whether because these persons are less morally discerning than you and so you should not set an example to them of autonomous, non-rule-governed decision-making, or because your violating the rules will embolden persons less morally scrupled to violate the rules wrongly.

Or maybe we have excellent reason to think that not even you can wisely make these calls, or that the greater wisdom would be to have these things be settled by rules once for all. For often, better outcomes result from people obeying rules of thumb about how best to act than from trying to figure out which action will have the best outcome in each case. This holds when there is not time for research before acting, or when action is required in a time of panic when one would be better served by good habits of choice than by trying to improvise in a panicked state; and sometimes you may have chosen a rule at a moment of calm and wisdom, chosen it precisely to guide you in situations where these virtues were likely to be absent—you made a plan, and the entire point of plans is to provide clarity about what to do unless circumstances have provably changed.[22] Growing out of such reflections we even have act-utilitarian justifications for adopting rules against deciding how to behave by trying to ascertain the consequences of each action—act-utilitarian justifications against making choices the way an act-utilitarian normally would, namely, by calculating the utility of each action. Or think of contractarian justifications for adopting principles constraining one from making self-advantaging, or even prima facie everyone-advantaging, choices in the moment, justifications according to which you being expected to be ruled by the constraint is likely to have better effects than you being free to do what you want in this individual situation.

Of course there may still be temptations. Perhaps the situation is this: domestically you must follow the rules because here we have the rule of law and these regulations on the defense industry advantage all local parties. Meanwhile, nondomestically, it is the Wild West—everyone's cheating all the time. It may then seem that in nondomestic contexts you should do what advantages you even if it violates a rule prevailing domestically.

But even here the truth may be that, if you behave that way nondomestically, you will make it less likely that the region of what counts as domestic will expand—the region regulated by mutually advantageous deals and so featuring reduced externalities.[23] Yet such expansion would be to everyone's advantage, yours included. Everyone is attracted to codes of conduct requiring honesty, forbidding bribery, and so on, provided they are at least as likely to rule the behaviors of others as of themselves. So you should exemplify the change

[22] *See, e.g.*, Michael Bratman, Intention, Plans and Practical Reason (1987) (providing the classic discussion of this subject).

[23] Here I use "externality" to mean anything outside a deal that interferes with the operation of the deal.

you want to see in the world. At the very least we have here an argument for your following the famous tit-for-tat strategy: be decent in your first interaction with someone, then copy what they do. If they are morally educable, they will follow your good example. If they aren't and they cheat, cheat back until they stop cheating. Under conditions where there are more honest people, as there typically are at the interface between home and abroad, this behavior will reduce the number of cheaters even further, because they will get outcompeted by those who can trust each other in cooperative enterprises.

Meanwhile, it is widely agreed that the world as a whole is better off without corruption than with, and that on the whole companies do less well if they bribe. And yet individuals in companies might in the short term be tempted. What could explain this? And what can stop them from thinking this way? George Ainslie suggests that temporally near but inferior options can look better than temporally far but superior options by the obscuring proximity of the former, much as a short building seen close up can look taller than a tall building seen in the distance.[24] So maybe we need to put the long run more fully in view.

But I suggest an additional strategy: we should teach as part of corporate culture that rationality and rational self-interest are not constituted of choosing the most advantageous action but of choosing the action dictated by the most advantaging policy, which, of course, will forbid bribing. The idea is to recognize that individual company member rationality is really expressed by complying with the principles that on the whole it benefits one's company to be known for following.

Bribery is known to be bad for the systems in which it occurs, since it in effect imposes costs on goods and services without returning extra benefits.[25] It is bad for companies as measured by their balance sheets, bad for individuals in companies as beneficiaries of success in companies, bad for countries as measured by the efficiency of their governments and by the quality of the lives of their citizens. Why then does it exist? The standard answer is because an individual act of bribery can be to the immediate advantage of the immediate participants, as, for instance, where the participants can maneuver in secret. And the standard responses to this are to set up a system of monitoring and punishments and to have company leaders model good character in hopes of providing a compelling example to subordinates.

I suggest, however, that we need a further element in explaining the temptation to bribe and that this element gives us more options in providing an antidote to the problem. First, the advantage to an individual of a given act of bribery can

[24] *See generally* George Ainslie, Breakdown of the Will (2001).

[25] *See generally* Philip M. Nichols, *The Business Case for Complying with Bribery Laws*, 49 Am. Bus. L.J. 325 (2012).

explain its occurrence only if the advantageousness of an action is motivating of an individual, which it will tend to be only if the pursuit of advantage action by action is perceived by them as rational. And here philosophers have something to say. In many situations the truth is that, while if an individual bribes, they will benefit from the act of bribing, had they a character that would indispose them to bribing they would benefit even more, since this character trait would attract other opportunities for profit, attract business dealings from those who demand trustworthiness, for example. And this raises the general question whether it is more rational to perform individually advantaging actions, or to do the actions required by individually advantaging character traits.

The philosopher/decision theorist, David Gauthier has an answer: the correct theory of rationality is the one most to your advantage to follow. The one most to your advantage to follow is the one that recommends you to have the character of a trustworthy person, because this will attract more business opportunities, each one profitable. One might think that the character most advantageous to have will change over one's life. For example, being trustworthy and known to be trustworthy might be to your advantage when exchanging promises of mutually beneficial behavior with other persons, but disadvantageous when it comes time to fulfill your part of the promise. If only you had a more scurrilous character at that moment, you could do even better, benefiting from the other person fulfilling her promise to you while you get the additional benefit of breaking your promise to her. This represents business relations as Prisoners' Dilemmas: all parties are better off if all keep promises not to cheat, but each party does better still by cheating where possible whether or not others cheat. But of course if you are known to be likely to think that way, no one will make sincere promises to you. Therefore if you are to attract advantaging promises from others, it must be that the way you choose your character is once and for all, as if at the beginning of your life; for then you will not alter your character when it would be to your advantage to break a promise, provided the promise has the following properties: it is one you would not have been in a position to break had you not first been the kind of person who would not break it, and so who could attract promise-making from others. But since the correct theory of rationality, arguably, is the one that would afford you entry into the most advantageous arrangements in your life, and since the theory that you should choose the actions dictated by the characters you would find most advantageous to choose as if from the beginning of your life forever is the correct theory, and since the main such character trait in question would be that of a promise keeper, it must be that what it is truly rational for you to do is to keep such promises. With this argument, Gauthier justifies what he calls constrained maximizing behavior, behavior constrained from seeking immediate advantage, and instead seeking to express dispositions advantageous to have, this supporting the idea of cooperating in the keeping of agreements in Prisoners' Dilemmas.[26] The same rationale justifies not only promise-keeping but also not bribing, being honest, building good products, and all the rest of the things in the usual codes, laws, and dicta of conscience. For all of these sorts of actions express characteristics in you essential to magnetizing other persons into profitable relations with you. Or at least these characteristics are essential to that enterprise, provided you having them is something about which people can have evidence before putting themselves in a position to have to trust you. Gauthier assumed this was at least in some degree true. And each of us has reason to take steps to make it impossible for us to cheat, thence to make others more comfortable in trusting us.

There are broadly three ways to do this. First, arrange for transparency in contracting, financial transactions, and so on. One problem with this is that there will be the temptation to cheat by seeming transparent but having real maneuvers be in secret. A solution to this problem, a solution that also constitutes a second possible way to make cheating impossible, is to make the penalties for discovered cheating spectacularly high, so that when individuals do the risk reward calculation, they cannot help but chose the path of honesty. A problem with this is that the people most likely to cheat, those with a psychopathic confidence in their ability to elude detection and punishment, will be unaffected by such threats. Further, the higher the proposed penalty, the more difficult we will find it to make ourselves impose it, since the penalty will seem to vastly exceed the crime. Moreover, the worse the penalty people face, the more they are incentivized to take extreme measures to hide their violations. Additionally, the costs of constantly monitoring for and punishing cheating are high, as are the costs of having to refuse to do business in situations where policing would be difficult.

A third proposal to guarantee there will be no cheating is the one in effect offered by Gauthier: instead of having an enforcement scheme against cheating, put your effort into hiring people whose character indisposes them to cheating and into inculcating the theory of rationality as constrained maximizing according to which an action is rational if it expresses a disposition the cultivation of which is advantaging (e.g., dispositions against cheating), not if the action

[26] This argument moves beyond even Gauthier's most recent work in the rationale it affords for adopting and keeping to a certain character. It represents my attempt to solve what I have called the "Reversion Problem" in Gauthier's terms, using some ideas developed by Preston Greene. *See* Preston Greene, Rationality and Success (Oct. 2013) (unpublished Ph.D. dissertation, Rutgers University). The details need not concern us here. *But see* Duncan MacIntosh, *Assuring, Threatening, a Fully Maximizing Theory of Practical Rationality, and the Practical Duties of Agents*, 123 Ethics 625 (2013). *See also* Duncan MacIntosh, Comment to *Ethics Discussions at PEA Soup: David Gauthier's Twenty-Five On*, Pea Soup (July 19, 2013, 7:04 PM), http://peasoup.typepad.com/peasoup/2013/07/ethics-discussions-at-pea-soup-david-gauthiers-twenty-five-on-with-precis-by-dimock-1.html; David Gauthier, Comment to *Ethics Discussions at PEA Soup: David Gauthier's Twenty-Five On*, Pea Soup (July 24, 2013, 6:08 PM), http://peasoup.typepad.com/pea soup/2013/07/ethics-discussions-at-pea-soup-david-gauthiers-twenty-five-on-with-precis-by-dimock-1.html.

itself is advantaging (e.g., the actions of breaking rules in secret). And then do business only with businesses and cultures with similar policies. One effect of this would be incentivizing other businesses and cultures into similar attitudes and practices in order to attract your business. Another would be the extension of the possibility of doing business into situations where policing is difficult but where mutual trust would make it unnecessary. In general, then, if only the theory of rationality as constrained maximizing were more widely taught we would have less bribery, and less of the various other sorts of practices in business generally thought to be unethical. This suggests inducing a level of philosophical reflection about the nature of rationality into corporate culture.

The issue here is whether it can be rational to make and keep a promise not to bribe when there is little possibility of enforcement.[27] Gauthier says it can be rational. And this is a different way of addressing the temptation to cheat: there is such a temptation only if cheating would be rational, that is, only if it is not rationally obligatory to make and keep promises not to cheat in nonenforceable scenarios. Of course, Gauthier merely pushes the enforcement problem back onto the detection of sincerity in promises not to cheat and on to the identification of persons as rational in his sense, or, at any rate, disposed to do what Gauthier says is rational, perhaps from their character: How can we tell who is like this? Psychological expertise may have promise here, as might lie detectors; and as would only hiring people who proved themselves trustworthy when they did not know they were being monitored for trustworthiness.

What is the takeaway for policy on defense industry regulation? I suggest the foregoing implies that governments should expend more effort and supervision on the hiring and training practices of companies, and therefore on corporate culture, than on policing corporate transactions. The better way to regulate is to demand that companies hire for character, or train the theory of rationality as constrained maximization and test for its uptake, or both, and then release people into situations where, while it is difficult to monitor them, they are unlikely to cheat given their predispositions and training. Likewise, it should expend effort on researching and encouraging similar practices in countries and businesses with which its business are likely to want to do business, making its results available to all parties. Of course this is already a practice—governments create corruption indexes, for example, and restrict with whom companies can

[27] In decision theory, such situations are called One-Shot Prisoners' Dilemmas, situations where there are no reputational consequences for cheating, contrasted with so-called Iterated Prisoners' Dilemmas, where you can be punished for cheating in future interactions and so threatened into not cheating in this one. Gauthier purports to have solved the One-Shot version, even for agents who chose purely by rational self-interest: he claims that rationally self-interested choice consists in choosing from dispositions self-advantaging to adopt, not in choosing actions directly self-advantaging to do.

do business. In this respect, the practical policy issue is only one of emphasis, and of giving more credence to policy options sometimes thought to be implausible.

I have given examples of cases where it would seem good to break the rules that normally regulate the defense industry. I have also given arguments for why this should not happen very much. But what rule should you use to decide whether to violate the normal rules in a given case?

The answer comes from the fact that every participant in the defense industry is animated by the aim to make a better life for themselves however they define its being better—some might define it altruistically, others, not. This is true of the participants of all industries and, for that matter, of all participants in any economic activity whatever. And each participant in any system of economic activity gets more advantage the bigger the system of which she is a part. For that means more trade, fewer costly externalities (in the form of people from outside the system trying to steal from or disrupt the system), and so more profit. But that means each participant should always be aiming to expand the circle, to attract more and more people into arrangements regulated by a deal for mutual advantage. And people are attracted to people, businesses, and countries of good character, and so on up to the largest possible units of social and economic interaction, because they can trust them to do what they say and to share profits.

And this, finally, tells us the right principle, again, applying Gauthier's insight: Gauthier says a choice is rational if dictated by the character or policy by which it is best to be ruled considering the effects on others of one's being known to be disposed to follow it no matter what from the beginning of one's life. And here, one would do best to follow a meta-rule that says to follow the subrules governing the industry provided that by doing so, one does not commit or permit a larger harm to the values in play. It is the latter clause that affords exceptions to the standard codes, but it is the benefit one reaps from the effects on other persons of one's being disposed to follow the standard codes that make the justified exceptions rare. In practice that means you should obey the rules when obeying them expands the circle (for you, your company, your country, your civilization). But you should break them when this is necessary to protect the expansion of the circle. So you get to cheat cheaters who cannot be attracted into the principles inside the circle and whose cheating obstructs the circle's expanding, and you get to bribe those who cannot be attracted into the principles of the circle and who would otherwise obstruct its expansion, and likewise for other sorts of business vice.[28]

[28] The rationale for deviating from standard defense industry ethical norms as outlined above would not justify, for example, two otherwise virtuous American companies in trying to compete against each other by bribery. But it might justify an industry-wide practice of sometimes engaging in what would otherwise count as corrupt practices in dealing with corrupt regimes, provided that the actions are likely to expand the circle.

5. Conclusion

Summarizing, I have argued that immoral, amoral, and nonmoral motivations, things like the pure profit motive—which many would see as a psychopathic motivation in the defense industry—can afford solutions to moral problems not solvable by those with ordinarily laudable moral motives. These problems include how to attain utilitarian results without the loss in utility of a pained conscience, how to allow the expression of different good but conflicting values in the moral division of labor, how to resolve conflicts between peoples where there are no clear moral signals about who should prevail in the conflicts, and how to resolve coordination problems in constructing social arrangements. I suggested that people with such motivations in the defense industry can have this effect by selling the best and so most expensive weapons to whomever can afford them. Indeed, I suggested that, since being able to afford the best weapons is evidence of being a better culture, selling such weapons to those who can afford them has the effect of advancing the best cultures over less just cultures.

Apparently, then, there is moral usefulness in having the defense industry be motivated in the large by what may seem to be a psychopathic willingness to make profit by selling the best weapons to whomever can afford them. But there remained the question of what ethical principles ought to guide individual industry players in their daily activities as they contend with the normal expectations we have of business participants and profession members as such, national security issues, and issues of justice more broadly. In this connection, I first argued that business ethics and professional ethics codes are not comprehensive enough to elucidate moral conduct in the defense industry in all situations—there are exceptions to those rules. Second, I offered a more general rule which explains when to violate the former rules and when to stand by them: you should obey them unless violating them would expand the circle of people included in the best total deal for everyone. Third, I offered a theory of rationality according to which obeying this principle is rational (a theory that should appeal even to those motivated purely by self-interest), and suggested that this theory should be taught to defense industry personnel: what makes an action rational is not that it is advantaging but that it expresses a disposition advantaging to have. That will

A further question is, to whom should all of this advice be given? For example, should we construe it as advice to legislators and law enforcement, advice to the effect that you should not penalize too much otherwise noncorrupt companies for engaging in small corruptions in dealing with corrupt regimes where this is likely to reduce corruption overall and expand the circle of those participating in good business practices? I think this question needs more reflection. A further possibility worth considering is having a government organization which could be authorized to give permissions to companies to bribe upon a successful application demonstrating that, in the instance in question, bribing would have good overall effects.

be a disposition of fidelity to business and professional ethics codes, but modulated by the foregoing principle.

References

GEORGE AINSLIE, BREAKDOWN OF THE WILL (2001).

Lawrence Alexander, *The Doomsday Machine: Proportionality, Punishment and Prevention*, 63 MONIST 199 (1980).

MICHAEL BRATMAN, INTENTION, PLANS AND PRACTICAL REASON (1987).

Edmund F. Byrne, *Assessing Arms Makers' Corporate Social Responsibility*, 74 J. BUS. ETHICS 201 (2007).

Michael Davis, Address at the University of Pennsylvania Law School's Center for Ethics and the Rule of Law's Ethical Issues in the Global Defense Industry Conference: Ethical Issues in the Global Arms Industry: A Role for Engineers (Apr. 15, 2015).

David Gauthier, *Assure and Threaten*, 104 ETHICS 690 (1994).

David Gauthier, *Twenty-Five On*, 123 ETHICS 601 (2013).

David Gauthier, Comment to *Ethics Discussions at PEA Soup: David Gauthier's Twenty-Five On*, PEA SOUP (July 24, 2013, 6:08 PM), http://peasoup.typepad.com/peasoup/2013/07/ethics-discussions-at-pea-soup-david-gauthiers-twenty-five-on-with-precis-by-dimock-1.html.

Kevin Govern, Address at the University of Pennsylvania Law School's Center for Ethics and the Rule of Law's Ethical Issues in the Global Defense Industry Conference: Acting Astutely in Government Acquisition: Procurement Integrity, Corporate Ethics and Avoiding Fraud in Logistics (Apr. 16, 2015).

Preston Greene, Rationality and Success (Oct. 2013) (unpublished Ph.D. dissertation, Rutgers University)

Gregory Kavka, *Some Paradoxes of Deterrence*, 75 J. PHIL. 285 (1978).

Duncan MacIntosh, *Retaliation Rationalized: Gauthier's Solution to the Deterrence Dilemma*, 72 PAC. PHIL. Q. 9 (1991).

Duncan MacIntosh, *Buridan and the Circumstances of Justice (On the Implications of the Rational Unsolvability of Certain Co-Ordination Problems)*, 73 PAC. PHIL. Q. 150 (1992).

Duncan MacIntosh, *Assuring, Threatening, a Fully Maximizing Theory of Practical Rationality, and the Practical Duties of Agents*, 123 ETHICS 625 (2013).

Duncan MacIntosh, Comment to *Ethics Discussions at PEA Soup: David Gauthier's Twenty-Five On*, PEA SOUP (July 19, 2013, 7:04 PM), http://peasoup.typepad.com/peasoup/2013/07/ethics-discussions-at-pea-soup-david-gauthiers-twenty-five-on-with-precis-by-di mock-1.html.

Duncan MacIntosh, Re-drawing the Boundaries of Sovereignty: Permissible and Obligatory Interventions in the Affairs of Sovereign Nations (2017) (unpublished manuscript) (on file with author).

Gavin Maitland, *The Ethics of the International Arms Trade*, 7 BUS. ETHICS 200 (1998).

Thomas Nagel, *Moral Luck*, *in* THOMAS NAGEL, MORTAL QUESTIONS (1979).

Philip M. Nichols, *The Business Case for Complying with Bribery Laws*, 49 AM. BUS. L.J. 325 (2012).

Tejvan Pettinger, *Dutch Disease*, ECON. HELP (Nov. 15, 2017), https://www.economicshelp.org/blog/11977/oil/dutch-disease.

ROADHOUSE (MGM 1989).

Scott Shane & Nicole Perlroth, *Legislation Seeks to Bar N.S.A. Tactic in Encryption*, N.Y. TIMES (Sept. 6, 2013), https://www.nytimes.com/2013/09/07/us/politics/legislation-seeks-to-bar-nsa-tactic-in-encryption.html.

Bernard Williams, *Integrity*, *in* J.J.C. SMART AND BERNARD WILLIAMS, UTILITARIANISM: FOR AND AGAINST (1973).

3

Fiduciary Duties of Officers and Directors of Military Contractors

Shareholder Primacy or Loyalty to the United States?

Richard W. Painter

1. Introduction

Do directors and officers of U.S. military contractors have a fiduciary duty only to maximize the profits of their shareholders, or do they also have a duty to strengthen the national security of the United States?

This chapter explores a specific application to the defense industry of a broader question in corporate law of whether directors' and officers' fiduciary duties run only to shareholders or also to other constituencies such as customers, employees, the environment, and the public interest. The focal point of discussion here will be one non-shareholder constituency: U.S. national security.

Fiduciary duty is a core concept in business law. Justice Cardozo once famously said that business partners owe each other "something stricter than the morals of the marketplace. Not honesty alone, but the punctilio of an honor most sensitive, is then the standard of behavior."[1] This concept is used frequently in corporate law to describe the fiduciary duty of officers and directors to the corporation.[2] But fiduciary relationships exist in other contexts. Professor Tamar Frankel explains:

> [F]iduciary relationships involve a crucial component of entrustment. I name the parties to fiduciary relationships "entrustors." Fiduciaries cannot perform their services unless they are entrusted with property or power. No money manager can effectively manage clients' money unless he has some control over it. No doctor can operate on a patient without acquiring full control of

[1] Meinhard v. Salmon, 164 N.E. 545, 546 (N.Y. 1928).

[2] *See, e.g.*, Deborah A. DeMott, *Beyond Metaphor: An Analysis of Fiduciary Obligation*, 37 Duke L.J. 879 (1988).

Richard W. Painter, *Fiduciary Duties of Officers and Directors of Military Contractors* In: *Ethical Dilemmas in the Global Defense Industry.* Edited by: Daniel Schoeni and Tobias Vestner, Oxford University Press.
 DOI: 10.1093/oso/9780190675813.003.0004

the patient's body. No adviser or lawyer can provide advice without exercising discretion.[3]

The question discussed in this chapter is whether military contractors' directors and officers owe a fiduciary duty not just to shareholders but also to protect the national security of their biggest customer, the United States. Or alternatively, do the directors and officers of military contractors fulfill their fiduciary duty if they focus only on loyalty to the corporation's shareholders while leaving the United States to rely upon the "morals of the marketplace" supplemented by whatever contractual and statutory law the U.S. government uses to protect itself from the profit maximizing military contractor?

Before discussing specifics, it is important to recognize that corporate directors and officers have broad discretion in deciding how to fulfill their fiduciary duties. Absent personal conflicts of interest or other evidence that directors and officers are not adhering to their duty of loyalty, judges will not interfere with business decisions. This "business judgment" rule[4] allows directors and officers to decide *how* to fulfill fiduciary duties while courts focus on whether conflict of interest has interfered with those duties.

2. Four Scenarios

Conflict between corporate profit maximization and U.S. national security can arise in business decisions that arise in the C-suites and boardrooms of defense contractors. Following are four hypothetical scenarios that are representative of dilemmas that have arisen for defense contractors or that may arise in the future. Keeping in mind that directors and officers have broad discretion to decide how to fulfill fiduciary duties, we focus in each scenario on what those fiduciary duties are. Do the officers and directors have a fiduciary duty only to maximize profits of the company for shareholders, or do they also have a fiduciary duty to protect the national security of the United States?

Scenario 1

Company D sells arms to the U.S. military and also abroad subject to approval from the U.S. government. D is contemplating a large sale of military aircraft

[3] Tamar Frankel, *Fiduciary Law in the Twenty-First Century*, 91 B.U. L. Rev. 1289, 1293 (2011).

[4] Joy v. North, 692 F.2d 880 (2d Cir. 1982) (articulating the economic rationale for the business judgment rule in corporate law in which judges do not second-guess business decisions, including corporate risk-taking that may increase expected returns).

to a Middle Eastern country that is supposedly an ally of the United States but that also has known connections with terrorism. Top U.S. Department of Defense (DoD) and Department of State officials, all political appointees, have approved the arms sale, but many former high-ranking officials from previous administrations strongly oppose the arms sale and have publicly said that they are concerned about political stability in the country purchasing the arms. They also worry about the arms falling into the hands of hostile countries or terrorists. Many independent military policy analysists also oppose the arms sale on similar grounds. Furthermore, there is evidence that career U.S. government employees in the DoD and the State Department disagree with their political superiors and oppose the arms sale.

D's board of directors is considering whether to approve the arms sale. The chief financial officer projects that D's profit from the arms sale will be approximately \$1.5 billion. This would increase D's total profits by 20 percent over a period of 10 years. The purchasing country will pay a substantial part of the purchase price up front and has assumed the risk that a future U.S. administration might try to delay or block the arms sale. There is very little financial risk to D from agreeing to the arms sale.

Several directors of D believe that the arms sale is dangerous for national security. Others say that the U.S. government makes decisions about national security and has already approved of the arms sale, and that as directors their fiduciary duty is to maximize D's profits for shareholders.

Should the directors consider national security risks from the arms sale, or are they only required to consider the profits accruing to the company and its shareholders?

Scenario 2

Company E's board of directors is considering a proposal to increase E's budget for "government relations" from \$50 million to \$75 million. Such expenditures include lobbying the executive and legislative branches of the U.S. government, working with Political Action Committees (PACs) to support candidates for national office and coordinating independent electioneering communications.

E's head of government relations and its chief operating officer, tell the board that these political expenditures are necessary for E to expand its share of military contracts and to obtain quicker government approval for arms sales to abroad. It is also clear that E's competitors are increasing their own political spending and that E will be disadvantaged if it does not follow suit.

Several directors believe that political spending of this sort amounts to de facto bribery, that it is a threat to democratic principles generally, and that it endangers national security because defense contractors use political spending to get contracts that they otherwise would not be awarded on the merits. These directors believe as a matter of principle that defense contractors should refrain from political spending as much as possible and instead should devote resources to improving the value of their products for the U.S. military.

Should the directors consider the national security implications of such political spending, or are they required to consider only the profits of the company and its shareholders?

Scenario 3

Company F sells fighter planes to the U.S. Air Force. The Air Force has submitted a request for proposals. If F submits a proposal, F would be the likely awardee and the contract would be very profitable. There are few business risks to the contract.

The U.S. government has approved the contract, but for several reasons it is controversial. Many experts in the defense and national security community believe that the price tag is too high and that the technology will be outmoded within two decades, meaning the equipment will have to be replaced at enormous cost to the DoD. Also, it appears that the contract is politically popular only because an important subcontractor is in a powerful senator's home state.

There is an alternative program being discussed which involves subcontracting out a larger part of the project to other defense contractors that can develop more advanced technology less likely to become outmoded. This program is not more expensive for the government than the current proposal, but it will cut out the subcontractor in the senator's home state and result in a smaller portion of profits being retained by F. The first proposal is clearly the more profitable alternative for F, whereas the second proposal is clearly the best proposal for the interest of national security.

If F honestly advises the DoD that the second program is the better choice for national security, against F's own financial interests, that advice will probably be enough to persuade the DoD and the White House to choose the second program despite strong opposition from the senator and subcontractor who would have profited from the first proposal. But F is not obligated to give this advice; it may say nothing about which technology would be better for national security.

Should the directors consider the national security implications of these two programs, or are they required to consider only the profits of the company and its shareholders?

Scenario 4

Company G is choosing between two alternative contracts. It has resources to commit to one of the contracts but not both.

One contract is with the U.S. government for equipment that is important for the national defense and that the United States will have considerable difficulty finding elsewhere. Funding for this equipment is limited, and so the contract will earn only a modest profit for Company G.

The alternative is with a foreign country that is not an adversary of the United States but also is not an important ally. The contract is for similar equipment, and the foreign country is willing to pay more and is ordering in larger quantities than the DoD would. It is likely to be much more profitable than selling to the U.S. government. In this instance, the United States does not have a contractual or other legal right to priority or first refusal. Company G gets to decide.

DoD officials have asked Company G to prioritize the U.S. contract even though it is less lucrative, but the DoD cannot promise to reward Company G with future business if it chooses to prioritize U.S. national security interests. The DoD has conveyed the importance of the equipment to military personnel.

Should the directors of Company G consider these national security implications of these two contracts, or are the directors required to consider only the profits of the company and its shareholders?

All four of these scenarios involve tensions between corporate profit maximization and the impact of a business decision on the national security of the United States. Other societal interests besides national security are also important—including the ethics of certain weaponry or modes of war or the ethics of war itself. These interests are important, particularly in an industry whose products are used to kill. Shareholders have engaged with these societal issues since the Vietnam War, sometimes suing corporate management for access to corporate records.[5] Some institutional shareholders, such as church pension funds, avoid military contractors altogether.[6] But in the interest of a focused analysis of a more singular problem in this chapter, the issue discussed here is narrower: What should directors and officers of defense contractors do when

[5] *See* Pillsbury v. Honeywell, 191 N.W.2d 406 (Minn. 1971) (denying shareholder petition for access to Honeywell's shareholder ledger and documents concerning Honeywell's production of munitions for the Vietnam War).

[6] For example, the Episcopal Church has portfolio restrictions that generally bar investments in "[s]hares of any company (a) among the top U.S. defense contractors, measured in dollar volume of sales and (b) any company among the top 50 defense contractors that receives more than fifty percent of its revenues from military contracts." Episcopal Church Executive Council Corporate Social Responsibility Committee, *Companies Subject to No-buy Portfolio Restrictions* 1 (Feb. 2020), https://www.episcopalchurch.org/wp-content/uploads/sites/2/2020/07/No-Buy-List-Of-Prohibited-Stocks.pdf.

they believe a business plan that maximizes corporate profits is not in the best interests of U.S. national security?

3. The Shareholder Primacy Theory and Why It's Wrong Generally

Do corporations exist principally to enhance shareholder wealth or alternatively is the corporate purpose to enhance overall wealth of all constituents of the corporation including shareholders, employees, customers, suppliers, and the community? Milton Friedman famously articulated the view that corporations should focus exclusively on profits for shareholders,[7] a "shareholder primacy" view of corporate governance that became popular with adherents to "Chicago School" law and economics.[8] The theory is that directors and officers should focus on shareholder wealth maximization while other bodies of law—contract law, labor law, antitrust law, environmental law, consumer safety law, federal and state procurement law, and so forth—protect the public interest and the interests of non-shareholder constituencies.

The alternative view is that corporate boards of directors have an obligation to act in the best interest of the corporation, which can include serving the interests of its shareholders and also its employees, customers, community, and the country at large.[9]

Many institutional investors favor a broad vision of corporate governance beyond mere profit maximization.[10] For them the choice between shareholder welfare and societal welfare is a false choice if portfolio value and social welfare converge for diversified investors exposed to a wide range of assets. Portfolio assets lose value in the long term if individual firms enhance their own share price by engaging in conduct that is detrimental to the overall economy.[11] This could include, for example, defense contractors compromising national security or causing the government to waste resources on weapons systems that are

[7] Milton Friedman, *A Friedman Doctrine: The Social Responsibility of Business Is to Increase Its Profits*, N.Y. Times Mag. Sept. 13, 1970, at 33.

[8] *See, e.g.*, Frank H. Easterbrook & Daniel R. Fischel, The Economic Structure of Corporate Law (1996).

[9] *See, e.g.*, Lynn Stout, Shareholder Value Myth: How Putting Shareholders First Harms Investors, Corporations, and the Public (2012). This is a very large topic in corporate governance that has engaged a wide range of viewpoints in academia, in the investor community, and with management.

[10] *See, e.g.*, Alexander Dyck et al., *Do Institutional Investors Drive Corporate Social Responsibility? International Evidence*, 131 J. Fin. Econ. 693 (2017).

[11] Madison Condon, *Externalities and the Common Owner*, 95 Wash. U. L. Rev. 1, 1 (2020) ("Due to the embrace of modern portfolio theory, most of the stock market is controlled by institutional investors holding broadly diversified economy-mirroring portfolios. . . . [D]iversified investors should rationally be motivated to internalize intra-portfolio negative externalities.").

dysfunctional or that the military does not need. In sum, diversified investors should want companies not only to maximize their own profits but also to engage in business practices that maximize the value of an entire portfolio. If corporate conduct is bad for the broader economy, the diversified investor suffers. If corporate conduct increases asset values in the broader economy the diversified investor benefits.

An "either/or" approach to shareholder primacy versus stakeholder capitalism also has been rejected by the Business Roundtable, an organization of leading corporate CEOs that at least purports to embrace both objectives.[12] The debate over shareholder primacy is a false dichotomy if investors benefit in the long run when corporations make profits *and* contribute to overall social welfare. At least the CEOs of the Business Roundtable seem to think so.

The case law on corporate governance is largely in agreement, with judges in almost all circumstances refusing to hold directors and officers to the shareholder primacy norm. The seminal case in this area is *Shlensky v. Wrigley*,[13] in which William Wrigley, the owner and controlling shareholder of the Chicago Cubs baseball club, refused to have night baseball games because of traffic, noise, and other adverse impact on the surrounding neighborhood. Other shareholders sued for breach of fiduciary duty, arguing that Wrigley and the directors had a fiduciary obligation to maximize profits. The Court held that

> the directors are chosen to pass upon such questions and their judgment unless shown to be tainted with fraud is accepted as final. The judgment the directors of the corporation enjoys the benefit of a presumption that it was formed in good faith and was designed to promote the best interests of the corporation they serve.[14]

Decades earlier in the 1920s, a Michigan court had ruled differently in a case involving Henry Ford's management of Ford Motor,[15] but on very different facts.

[12] *See Business Roundtable Redefines Purpose of a Corporation to Promote an Economy that Serves All Americans*, BUS. ROUNDTABLE (Aug. 19, 2019), https://www.businessroundtable.org/business-roundtable-redefines-the-purpose-of-a-corporation-to-promote-an-economy-that-serves-all-americans. There are divergent views about how much members of the Roundtable and other business executives prioritize social welfare in management decisions. Regardless, the Roundtable's statement about corporate purpose is consistent with Condon's observations about convergence of some aspects of societal welfare, general economic health, and asset values.

[13] 237 N.E. 2d 776 (Ill. App. 1968). The court explained:

> Plaintiff allege[d] that Wrigley ha[d] refused to install lights, not because of interest in the welfare of the corporation but because of his personal opinions "that baseball is a 'daytime sport' and that installation of lights and night baseball games will have a deteriorating effect upon the surrounding neighborhood." *Id.* at 778.

[14] *Id.* at 779 (quoting Davis v. Louisville Gas & Electric Co., 142 A. 654, 659 (Del. Ch. 1928)).

[15] Dodge v. Ford Motor Co., 170 N.W. 668 (Mich. 1919).

The business decision repudiated by the court was Ford's refusal to pay a dividend to shareholders and his cavalier dismissal of shareholders' interests in his management of the company, which he claimed he was managing in the interest of workers and customers.[16] Ford was hardly a credible spokesperson for corporate social responsibility; his aggressive price-cutting was aimed in part at squeezing out competitors, including the plaintiffs, the Dodge brothers, who were not only his shareholders but also his competitors. Ford also had political ambitions (he ran for U.S. Senate as a Democrat in 1918) and used his "business judgment" as owner of the *Dearborn Independent* newspaper to publish violently anti-Semitic editorials.[17] The Ford Motor case gave the shareholders only limited relief, payment of a dividend but little other judicial interference in Ford's management of the company. Even this limited relief was an outlier in corporate governance case law. Most courts followed *Wrigley* in giving wide discretion to directors to make business decisions under the "business judgment rule."

Since the 1980s, Delaware courts have given corporate directors wide discretion to consider non-shareholder constituencies' interests in a wide range of circumstances, including defending companies against hostile takeovers,[18] although this discretion has been narrowed considerably, and shareholder interests must be prioritized if the directors decide to put the company up for sale.[19] In

[16] *Id.* at 683 (stating, "My ambition . . . is to employ still more men, to spread the benefits of this industrial system to the greatest possible number, to help them build up their lives and their homes. To do this we are putting the greatest share of our profits back in the business.").

[17] *See* Bill McGraw, *Henry Ford and the Jews, the Story Dearborn Didn't Want Told*, Bridge Mich. (Feb. 4, 2019), https://www.bridgemi.com/michigan-government/henry-ford-and-jews-story-dearborn-didnt-want-told. He writes:

> Showing the marketing expertise that had catapulted Ford Motor into one of the world's most famous brands, Henry Ford's lieutenants vastly widened the reach of his attacks by packaging the paper's anti-Semitic content into four books. Experts say "The International Jew" distributed across Europe and North America during the rise of fascism in the 1920s and '30s, influenced some of the future rulers of Nazi Germany.

Id.

[18] Paramount Commc'n, Inc. v. Time, 571 A.2d 1140 (Del. 1989). The court held, "absent a limited set of circumstances as defined under *Revlon*, a board of directors, while always required to act in an informed manner, is not under any per se duty to maximize shareholder value in the short term, even in the context of a takeover." *Id.* at 1150. *See also* Unocal v. Mesa Petroleum Co., 493 A.2d 946 (Del. 1985) (holding that in responding to a tender offer, directors may consider its impact on non-shareholder constituencies). It explained:

> If a defensive measure is to come within the ambit of the business judgment rule, it must be reasonable in relation to the threat posed. This entails an analysis by the directors of the nature of the takeover bid and its effect on the corporate enterprise. Examples of such concerns may include: inadequacy of the price offered, nature and timing of the offer, questions of illegality, the impact on "constituencies" other than shareholders (i.e., creditors, customers, employees, and perhaps even the community generally), the risk of nonconsummation, and the quality of securities being offered in the exchange.

Id. at 955.

[19] *See* Paramount Commc'n, 571 A.2d at 1150–51 (explaining the application of Revlon Inc. v. MacAndrews & Forbes Holdings, Inc., 506 A.2d 173 (Del. 1986)).

2010, the Delaware Chancery Court ruled that corporate directors could not go so far as to operate a company as a public benefit corporation when it had been established as a for-profit corporation and had raised capital from shareholders with that expectation.[20] That, however, is a far cry from directors and officers in a for-profit corporation using their discretion to make business judgments on specific transactions with non-shareholder interests as well as shareholder interests in mind. A corporation that makes quality products for its customers and looks after the interest of its customers is hardly a "public benefit" corporation instead of being a for-profit corporation. Indeed, a corporation that pursues both objectives—which is what almost all for-profit businesses tell the public they do—may stay in business longer than one that does not.

4. Why the Shareholder Primacy Theory Is Particularly Wrong for Defense Contractors

The preceding observations concern companies generally. Whether the Business Roundtable corporate leaders practice what they preach is debatable, but their words conform with courts' understanding of corporate purpose. Corporate directors and officers have discretion not just to maximize shareholder profits but also to consider the best interests of other constituencies. Shareholder interests cannot be abandoned, and directors cannot turn a for-profit enterprise into a public benefit corporation,[21] but non-shareholder interests in a for-profit corporation are important. Many institutional investors agree. Adherents of the competing shareholder primacy theory are largely limited to a subset of academics and some hedge funds and other short-term investors interested only in turning a quick profit.

We turn now to specific characteristics of the defense industry that make it even more imperative that directors and officers of a defense contractor be committed to non-shareholder interests. The non-shareholder interest that stands out is the interest that is the very basis for the company's existence: national security. The United States is not just a customer having a contractual relationship with the defense contractor, but has entrusted the defense contractor with classified information, the lives of U.S. service members, and ultimately the safety of the homeland. This unique relationship should be more than enough to create a

[20] E-Bay v. Newmark, 16 A.3d 1 (Del. Ch. 2010).

[21] *See id.* at 34–35. A public benefit corporation or "B corporation" is a separate form of organization available in some jurisdictions for a for-profit corporation whose primary purpose is to serve the public interest. Investors in B corporations know that earning profits is probably a less important objective than in a conventional corporation. The relatively recent emergence of the B corporation does not affect the business judgment rule that gives officers and directors in a conventional corporation broad discretion in managing the corporation, including taking into consideration the interests of other constituencies.

reasonable expectation of a fiduciary duty to the national security of the United States, not just to shareholders.

First, defense contractors get access to a large amount of classified information. Although criminal penalties apply to anyone who without authorization uses or discloses classified information, criminal cases can be hard to prove. Defense contractors have procedures for protecting classified information and are contractually obligated to follow these procedures, but violations are not always easy to detect. For example, a defense contractor probably would not disclose to a foreign country classified information about a new technology used by the United States, but the contractor might use that information to market competing technology to a foreign country or encourage other defense contractors to do so. The ensuing technological "arms race" among rival countries might increase corporate profits. But the classified information in this instance would have been used against U.S. interests by a company that was entrusted with the information to protect the national security, not to undermine it. The United States might or might not detect the breach. In addition to contractual, civil, and criminal constraints, the United States should be able to rely on the concept of trust that lies at the heart of a fiduciary duty. The United States has entrusted the classified information and is owed a fiduciary duty in return.

It is unwise for the government to entrust classified information to a company whose directors and officers believe their primary fiduciary duty is to maximize profits and that national security is only a secondary concern. A company that has been entrusted by the United States with classified information important for our national defense owes an important fiduciary duty to the United States that goes well beyond technical compliance with laws and contracts on handling of classified information. That fiduciary duty is to carry out business operations in a manner that prioritizes the national security of the United States.

Second, the lives of American service members depend upon defense contractors. This is true of other industries as well, for example, airlines, but there is not likely a group of people exposed to greater risk of death or injury in their daily lives than U.S. service members. The premise behind the theory that corporations should focus exclusively on maximizing profits is a Rational Self-Interest theory—which in an extreme iteration amounts to a theory of selfishness—that some economists assume explains economic behavior.[22]

[22] Rational self-interest theories of different iterations have proliferated in economics since Adam Smith. *See generally* ADAM SMITH, AN INQUIRY INTO THE NATURE AND CAUSES OF THE WEALTH OF NATIONS (1776). There are broader and narrower understandings of what is rational self-interest depending on how much an actor considers factors besides the actor's own material well-being, for example, the interests of fellow citizens. Broader rational self-interest theories include self-esteem, ego, and morality as part of the actor's self-interest. *See generally* DAVID GAUTHIER, MORALITY AND RATIONAL SELF-INTEREST (1970). A theory that includes interests of many other persons, or the interests of an entire country, however, does not resemble what is typically thought of as "self-interest," at least in the narrower sense. The narrowest theories of self-interest describe a set of

Whether or not this is true of the business world generally, it is not true of the military. Millions of U.S. service members have put their lives in danger not for themselves but for their country. Defense contractors need not align their values completely with the military—the CEO need not risk his life by parachuting into a war zone to answer a call about a product malfunction (some defense contractor personnel do put their lives at risk in such situations). But defense contractor officers and directors should keep in mind the values of their military customer and the people who serve in the military when thinking about their own values and priorities.

Imagine an airline pilot who announced to passengers that "while this airline is in compliance with FAA safety regulations, our primary fiduciary responsibility is to increase profits for the benefit of our shareholders." Though the risk of dying in a crash would still be extremely small, many would deplane.[23] Because of flying conditions including combat, military aircraft crashes are comparatively common. The aircrew, the maintainers who service the plane, and the air traffic controllers are typically military personnel who put their lives in danger and whose *only* professional loyalty is to the United States. Each has taken an oath affirming the same. Something more than allegiance to shareholder primacy should be expected from the manufacturer of the plane.

Third, the security of the U.S. homeland ultimately turns on the work of defense contractors. As technology advances, our national defense depends more than ever before on those who design, create, manufacture, and/or service military products. It makes little sense for these contractors not to have a relationship with the United States in which loyalty is expected of them just as much as loyalty is expected from the service member who uses their products on land, in sea, and in air.

For these reasons, officers and directors of defense contractors are probably even less likely than other industry leaders to openly embrace an ideology premised on the shareholder primacy theory. Indeed, shareholders very likely would not want it. The business model of defense contractors depends upon public confidence in their serving the national interests, not just the interests of shareholders. Absent a corporate commitment to the national security, the government could and probably should shift more of its work on defense

personal priorities that laypersons if not economists would call "selfishness." It is a narrow theory of rational self-interest that is aligned with the idea that shareholders only seek profits regardless of the cost to society, and that directors' and officers' only fiduciary duty is to give shareholders those profits regardless of the consequences.

23 The greatest civil aviation calamity since 2000 of course was 9/11, which was due in large part to the government allowing a key national security function, airport screening, to be entrusted to private companies paid by airlines that may have been more worried about maximizing profits than they were about airport security.

contracts to DoD employees, whose loyalty is unquestioned. Political pressure to find alternatives to contracting with private companies will build if defense contractors are perceived as being solely focused on profits. The government could even nationalize defense contractors. Set aside shareholders who may invest in defense contractors for patriotic reasons. The last thing even purely self-interested shareholders of a defense contractor would want is a company that is perceived to be so committed to profit maximization that the government withdraws its business altogether.

Even if specific legal rules are the primary legal mechanisms for resolving disputes between the government and a military contractor, the ex ante expectation in the business relationship is mutually beneficial behavior, not selfish individual wealth-maximizing behavior. Such an expectation is probably necessary for the relationship to succeed. The relationship is in many ways a fiduciary relationship, and a company that is not willing to acknowledge the importance of that relationship probably is not to be trusted.

Defense contracting thus is different from some other industries. It is difficult to articulate the nature of a fiduciary relationship, if any, between a large-volume retailer such as Walmart or Amazon and its customers, although even in that context proponents of the shareholder primacy theory are wrong to argue that the directors and officers have fiduciary obligations that run only to shareholders. We view a corporate healthcare provider differently than the retailer because non-shareholder fiduciary relationships (e.g., doctor-patient) are established in the course of the business. As discussed earlier, we also view an airline differently; an airline that did not at least say that passenger safety was its top priority probably would go out of business or be put out of business by the FAA. On this spectrum, the defense contractor is more like the healthcare provider or the airline than the retailer. A fiduciary relationship—a relationship of trust and confidence—is essential to the business model, and that necessary fiduciary relationship is with the United States.

A more nuanced approach is appropriate when defense contractors also do business with civilian customers, particularly if the military is not their principal customer. A duty to strengthen the defense of the United States should mostly apply to directors' and officers' actions in connection with the company's defense-related functions. A software company that markets similar software to banks and to the U.S. military thus should consider the national security of the United States in designing the software sold to the military and also when marketing the software for military use in other countries or to foreign buyers who might transfer the technology to the military. U.S. national security concerns ordinarily would not pertain to sales of the same software to private businesses or other nonmilitary customers when there is no reasonable likelihood of the product being used for military purposes. Furthermore, companies that sell identical or virtually identical products to the U.S. military and to nonmilitary customers (for example, a general-use software such as a payroll program) should not necessarily prioritize the national security of the United States in designing the product if the majority of sales are to nonmilitary users. Using another example, a company that makes gas masks and sells most of its masks to the U.S. military probably should consider whether U.S. national security interests are jeopardized if the company depends on importing an important part from China instead of making the part in the United States (there is not a cut-and-dried answer to this question, but the national security of the United States is a factor to consider). If, however, the company sells most of its gas masks to nonmilitary customers, the obligation to consider the national security of the United States is less pronounced. The U.S. military of course knows or should know this when buying the gas masks because they likely know if the company's sales are mostly in the defense sector.

The foregoing considerations are sufficiently compelling that the shareholder wealth maximization theory is deeply problematic in the defense industry. Indeed, there is scant if any evidence of any executive or director in the defense industry saying that the corporation's only obligation is to shareholders and not to consider national security. Defense contractors wrap themselves in the flag in their advertising, believing that patriotism and profits come hand in hand. What they do to strengthen national security varies, but openly embracing the shareholder primacy theory is anathema to their business model and they know it.

5. Business Judgment as the Performance Measure for Fiduciary Duties to the United States and to Shareholders

The intent of this chapter it not to create a rigid hierarchy of fiduciary duties or to tell directors and officers how to weigh the interests of national security and the interests of shareholders. The concept of business judgment—the well-known business judgment rule in corporate law[24]—applies. So long as officers and directors acknowledge their fiduciary duty to consider the interests of national security as well as shareholders, and the predicates of the business judgment rule are met, principally avoidance of personal conflicts of interest, and exercise of due care,[25] directors' and officers' business judgment should not be second-guessed by courts. Shareholders and the federal defense contracting agency have

24 *See supra* note 4 and accompanying text (citing Joy v. North, 692 F.2d 880 (2d Cir. 1982)).

25 Shareholder suits successfully alleging breach of the duty of care are exceedingly rare. *See* Smith v. Van Gorkom 488 A.2d 858 (Del. 1985). It should be expected that the government also would bring such duty of fiduciary duty of care cases only in rare circumstances except where the duty of care is grounded in the company's performance on a particular contract, in which case due care is almost certain to be an implied in fact if not express term of the contract.

ample means to evaluate performance of fiduciary duties as well as contractual obligations and to act accordingly. Shareholders can use their proxy to elect new directors, and the government can withhold contracts from a recalcitrant company. Both Congress and the military can undertake investigations as well as proposed contract revisions. In most cases, such tools, not lawsuits, should be used to enforce fiduciary duties.

This chapter does not attempt to articulate a precise method for assessing the quality of information about national security available to corporate officers and directors and the weight to be given to their own views on national security vis-à-vis the government's official views articulated by the military, the intelligence community, or the State Department. This chapter also does not articulate a precise formula for weighing competing interests of the United States and shareholders, except that U.S. national security should be as important a corporate objective as shareholder wealth maximization.

Limited access to classified information and limited subject-matter expertise may put directors and officers of a defense contractor at a disadvantage vis-à-vis government officials in discerning what is in the best interest of national security. Former government officials who sit on corporate boards of defense contractors may have outdated or incomplete information. There usually are good reasons to defer to the judgment of government officials who approve an arms sale or frame the specifications for a contract a particular way. Asymmetric information and expertise are among these reasons. In many instances, the U.S. government officials thus have the final say, but this is not because corporate officers and directors of defense contractors have a fiduciary duty to focus only on profits.

Also, military officials sometimes are wrong. Politics, institutional inertia, groupthink, and other factors can distort better judgment in a government agency as much as pursuit of profits distorts good judgment in a defense contractor. The independent judgment of defense contractors in some situations may be better than that of their government counterparts. The defense contractors at least should raise their concerns about national security with government officials when there are such disagreements and should do so with genuine national security concerns rather than profits in mind. Defense contractors having a duty to look after the interests of the United States, not just shareholders, are a needed check on poor judgment on either side of the contract.

6. Applying a Broader Concept of Corporate Purpose to Military Contractors

The following is a discussion of how each of the four scenarios described earlier could be addressed by a board of directors that acknowledges a fiduciary duty to protect the national security interests. This could be articulated in one of two ways. First, one could say that the officers and directors owe their fiduciary duty to the corporation, which in turn has as its principal corporate purpose protecting and enhancing the national security of the United States in addition to earning profits for shareholders. Alternatively, one could assert that officers and directors of a defense contractor, by virtue of their position, have fiduciary duties to the United States as well as to the corporation. Whichever way the duty is articulated, the assumption for the following discussion is that the directors and officers, and shareholders, all understand that the fiduciary duty owed to U.S. national security is at least as important as maximizing shareholder profits.

Scenario 1

In the first scenario, a controversial arms sale to a foreign country, the defense contractor having accepted a fiduciary duty to the United States would have to put that fiduciary interest at least on par with, and probably above, the interest of its shareholders. The U.S. government, however, has said that it wants the arms sale to be consummated, so perhaps that is the end of it. The DoD and the State Department have spoken and approve the contract.

On the other hand, the facts suggest that the political superiors in the DoD who are acting on behalf of the United States may have erred egregiously. Others who have previously held their positions disagree with them, as do outside experts and many career employees in both the DoD and the State Department. The political superiors have the authority to make these decisions on behalf of the United States, as there is only one president and one administration at a time. But that does not mean that they are correct in deciding that what they are allowing the company to do is in the best interests of the United States.

If the defense contractor's directors and officers strongly believe that the arms sale is harmful to the United States, their fiduciary duty to the United States is perhaps best carried out by not approving the arms sale to the foreign country. That is a decision that they have the right to make on behalf of the company, as they are the persons legally in control of the company just as the public officials are legally in control of the DoD and the State Department. This is also a different situation than one in which the United States has itself ordered the arms from the company or where the DoD and the State Department have told the company that they believe the sale to the other country is vitally important for the security of the United States. In this fact pattern, the DoD and State Department officials have only given permission for the arms sale to proceed because they have determined that it is not against the interests of the United States. And in this fact pattern, the directors and officers of the company believe these officials are wrong. If so, a compelling case can be made that the company should not proceed.

But what about the shareholders? The shareholders know when they buy the stock that the company has entered a fiduciary relationship with the United States and that the company's directors and officers have the right and responsibility to use the same "business judgment" in deciding what is in the national interest as they use to decide what is in the interest of the shareholders. Furthermore, the shareholders know that even if the decision made in this instance is not in the best interest of corporate profits, the fiduciary relationship the company has with the United States is an integral part of the company's business model and its long-term value to shareholders. Shareholders who disagree with the decision might later vote to replace the directors, but they would have no legal, or ethical, claim that their fiduciary relationship with the company's directors and officers was broken.

Scenario 2

In the second scenario, the business decision does not relate to a particular contract but to whether the company should increase political spending on lobbying, electioneering communications, and the PAC organizing with the objective of increasing its chances of receiving defense contracts. This spending is designed to allow defense contractors to obtain contracts that they otherwise might not be awarded on the merits. This is not in the interest of national security.

If competitors also are engaging in political spending, the situation is arguably more complex. It may be in the interest of U.S. national security that they do so equally, to balance each other out. Thus, conceivably an individual company's decision to increase political spending might be consistent with the national interest. Indeed, given the proliferation of defense industry lobbying, some lobbying may be necessary for a meritorious proposal to "make the cut" and advance to a contract. On the other hand, one company's increase in political spending may encourage an escalation of political spending by other companies, meaning all or most of them might get defense contacts they would not have received on the merits, a detriment to national security.

In this scenario, for whatever reason, the company's board of directors has serious reservations about whether the political spending is in the national interest. Assuming most of the directors conclude that the decision to increase political spending will be detrimental to national security, they should probably decline to approve the expenditure.

The shareholders might complain, but once again their recourse is to vote out the directors and replace them with directors who might assess the situation differently. The shareholders already have this advantage in that the U.S. government and the public do not have a role in corporate governance (the shareholders alone elect the directors). But unless the shareholder primacy theory is controlling, the directors who decide not to approve the political spending, because they believed it would be harmful to national security, did the right thing.

Scenario 3

In the third scenario, the directors decide between a highly profitable defense contract that the company can get for political reasons but where the technology could soon become obsolete and need to be replaced, and another contract that is not as profitable for the company but provides the U.S. military with better more advanced technology at the same cost.

Assuming the directors of the company agree that the first contract is more profitable for the company, but the second contract is more advantageous for national security, the shareholder primacy theory suggests that they should propose the first contract and perhaps lobby for it, hoping that political factors will prevail. A repudiation of the shareholder primacy theory and acknowledgment of a corporate purpose that includes safeguarding national security would weigh in favor of the company proposing the second contract even if it brings lower profits.

Changing the facts somewhat, if the second contract not only were less profitable for the company but also ran a high risk of a loss, the directors might come to a different decision, even while repudiating the shareholder primacy theory. The company cannot in all instances prioritize the national security interests of the United States over shareholder value. If the shareholders cannot earn a reasonable profit on a contract considering the risk of loss involved, the company probably should look for alternatives. In such instances the outer limits of the duty to protect national security have been reached; a company that cannot expect to earn a reasonable profit is not likely to stay in business for very long, ultimately harming both shareholders and the nation's security as that company becomes unavailable for future contracts. But here again, facts in some situations might drive a different result. In a national emergency a defense contractor might embark on a contract immediately without knowing whether it will result in a profit or a loss, or even while expecting a loss. If national security is seriously in jeopardy, the directors and officers of the defense contractor have the right and obligation to use their business judgment to decide how best to protect the nation as well as their shareholders.

Scenario 4

In the fourth scenario, there is tension not only between the interests of U.S. national security and corporate profits but also tension between U.S. interests and that of another country that seeks to contract with the same company. Companies in other businesses ordinarily treat customers and clients similarly or give preferred customer status principally for business reasons, such as building a customer relationship. When, however, a U.S. military contractor has a fiduciary duty to the United States, the interests of the United States take precedence over the other country for reasons unrelated to the company's business plan or profit maximization.

The defense contractor having a fiduciary duty to the United States should to some extent at least put the interests of the United States before that of another nation, even if the other nation would pay more for its products. Other nations that buy arms from the U.S. company would understand that the interests of the United States come first. This does not change because a country other than the United States offers the company a more lucrative contract. Once the shareholder primacy theory is rejected in favor of a fiduciary duty to U.S. national security, the United States is a preferred customer. Of course, the U.S. military could negotiate a preferred customer clause into its defense contracts, and in some instances does, but the point here is that even without such a contractual provision, a U.S. company doing substantial business with the U.S. military should be expected to have a fiduciary obligation to prioritize the interests of the United States. Because the directors and officers are afforded the protection of the business judgment rule[26] in deciding how to protect the interests of the United States as well as shareholders, and in balancing those competing interests, it would be difficult for the United States to sue for priority on the contract based on this fiduciary relationship. But the reasonable expectation that the United States is afforded some priority would be an important backdrop for the negotiations.

There are limits to this preference for the United States, defined by the corporation's obligation to shareholders to have a reasonable expected return on investment. In many situations, for example, the company should not be expected to turn down highly profitable contracts with other countries to accept a contract with the United States likely to result in a loss. Still, in a wartime emergency, a defense contractor might be expected to prioritize the national security of the United States, even if a financial loss were anticipated. The company's officers, directors, and shareholders would be expected to understand that risk of loss in extenuating circumstances is the price for the opportunity the company has in more ordinary times to earn profits by contracting with the U.S. military.

[26] *See supra* note 4 and accompanying text (citing Joy v. North, 692 F.2d 880 (2d Cir. 1982)).

Once again, the business judgment rule affords directors and officers wide discretion in making these decisions, so long as they acknowledge that fiduciary duties to the United States and to shareholders exist and are important. Dissatisfied shareholders can vote out the directors, and the United States can always build relationships with other military contractors, and in a true national emergency has other means at its disposal, including invoking the Defense Production Act of 1950.[27]

In all four of these scenarios, a lingering question is whether, in the long run, there is a genuine conflict of interest between shareholder interests and the national security of the United States. There is an immediately apparent conflict between these two priorities in each of these scenarios in that the most profitable choice is not the best choice for U.S. national security. But a longer time frame might point in the other direction. A defense contractor's future business success turns on its credibility in the field of national security. Failing to consider national security in making business decisions undermines credibility and ultimately may lead the government to consider other contracting alternatives. Even if the time value of money suggests weighing short-term profits more heavily than profits further in the future, focusing primarily on profits may be a failed long-term business plan as well as a betrayal of patriotic duty.

7. Is the Law Sufficient to Get Corporate Officers and Directors to Focus on National Security as Well as Profits?

So far, this chapter has discussed what corporate officers and directors should do in these types of scenarios. The conclusion is that when they make business decisions, directors and officers should consider national security interests as being important, and indeed at least as important as corporate profits. Their duty of loyalty to the United States is at least on par with their duty of loyalty to shareholders.

In situations where officers and directors are convinced that they have sufficient information and expertise to conclude that a particular business plan, however profitable, is seriously detrimental to national security, it is their legal and ethical right as fiduciaries to reject it. It is also their patriotic duty as Americans, even if not necessarily their legal duty, to reject it.

What does the law say about this corporate fiduciary duty, and how might the law governing military contractors be improved if it does not give sufficient protection to the national security interests of the United States?

[27] 50 U.S.C. Chapter 55 (implementing regulations in the Defense Priorities and Allocation System (DPAS), codified at 15 C.F.R. § 700 *et seq.*).

First, we examine what the law does not do. It is highly unlikely that a court would impose liability on officers and directors in a shareholder suit simply because they put their informed judgment about national security ahead of corporate profits. As discussed in the second part of this chapter describing the four scenarios, cases in which courts have required corporate directors to prioritize the interests of shareholders over other constancies are extremely few in number outside the context of a corporate merger, hostile takeover defense, or other change of corporate control context, which is irrelevant to our discussion here (we put aside the rare circumstance where a defense contractor seeks to merge into a competitor in a transaction beneficial to shareholders but which may disadvantage the U.S. government as a purchaser of its products, a transaction that should be watched closely, and in some circumstances prevented, by the government for reasons related to excessive market power as well as national security). In just about every other context, the business judgment rule gives corporate directors and officers wide discretion in defining the corporate objectives and obtaining them.

To use a specific example, if Wrigley and his fellow directors have the legal right to decide whether night games for the Cubs are in the best interest of the neighborhood surrounding Wrigley Field,[28] a defense contractor's board of directors can decide that a profitable arms sale abroad is not in the interest of the United States (Scenario 1, as described previously), that political spending by defense contractors undermines national security (Scenario 2), to sell a better product to the DoD even if it means less profit (Scenario 3), or to sell its products to the United States instead of a foreign buyer who pays more (Scenario 4). Under existing interpretations of the business judgment rule, it is very unlikely that a shareholder complaining about such decisions in a breach of a fiduciary suit would prevail; the court would instead tell the shareholder to take concerns about insufficient profits to other shareholders and perhaps elect a new slate of directors.

Nonetheless, there are some worrisome signs on the horizon given the vigor with which academic proponents of the shareholder primacy norm have pursued their argument and a few former judges going further in law review articles than the courts have gone thus far in characterizing case law as an endorsement of at least in part of the shareholder primacy theory in corporate law.[29] Far more worrisome is the constant pressure from stock market analysts and some investors, particularly hedge funds, to maximize profits. For all of the reasons articulated in this chapter, the shareholder primacy norm would be antithetical to the business

[28] *See* Shlensky v. Wrigley, 237 N.E. 2d 776 (Ill. App. 1968); *see also supra* notes 13–14 and accompanying text (discussing this case).

[29] *See, e.g.*, Leo Strine, *Our Continuing Struggle with the Idea That For-Profit Corporations Seek Profit*, 47 WAKE FOREST L. REV. 135 (2012).

model of the defense industry and is probably destructive of long-term shareholder value as well as national security. But that does not necessarily relieve the pressure on officers and directors to prioritize profits.

But what does the law do in the other direction—not only to permit but to encourage directors and officers of military contractors to consider U.S. national security interests? The short answer is probably not enough. The long answer is trickier. It requires delving into the messy amalgam of statutes, regulations, and case law that comprises federal acquisition law.

At present the legal incentives to act in the best interests of national security arise principally from the language of the contract itself[30] and applicable statutes and regulations governing defense contracts, including civil and criminal penalties for defrauding the government,[31] lying to the government,[32] or mishandling of classified information.[33] In some cases, contractors must also certify that their cost or pricing data is accurate, complete, and current.[34] The government can terminate for default[35] and then initiate debt collection procedures,[36] which is the closest equivalent in federal procurement to "suing" for breach of contract.[37] But the government cannot sue for breach of fiduciary duty for not putting the interests of the United States first, particularly if the company adheres to the contract and all other applicable law. Given that executive compensation,

[30] Contracts that involve classified information include a security requirements clause, FAR 52-204-2, which mandates that contractors comply with the *National Industrial Security Program Operating Manual* (32 C.F.R. pt. 117). The Defense Federal Acquisition Regulation Supplement (DFARS) requires a number of clauses concerning national security matters, including: (DFARS) 252.204-7000 (prohibition on releasing even *unclassified* information outside the contractor's organization without the government's prior written approval); DFARS 252.203-7001 (prohibition on contracting with persons convicted of fraud for defense contract-related fraud); DFARS 252.209-7002 (requiring disclosure of foreign ownership and for certain contracts prohibiting awards to foreign entities controlled by a foreign government).

[31] *See* 31 U.S.C. §§ 3729–3733 (civil false claims); 18 U.S.C. § 287 (criminal false claims).

[32] *See* 18 U.S.C. § 1001 (false statements).

[33] *See, e.g.*, 18 U.S.C. § 798 (disclosure of classified information); 18 U.S.C. § 1924 (unauthorized removal and retention of classified information).

[34] *See* 10 U.S.C. § 2306a (Truth in Negotiations Act).

[35] *See* FAR 52.249-9 (default clause for service and supply contracts); FAR 52.249-10 (default clause for construction contracts).

[36] "The process of debt collection by withholding and setoff has been complicated by a number of statutes and regulations that are not well coordinated and contain diverse provisions." JOHN CIBINIC, JR., RALPH C. NASH, JR & JAMES F. NAGLE, ADMINISTRATION OF GOVERNMENT CONTRACTS 1175 (4th ed. 2006). These statutes and regulations include the following: 31 U.S.C. § 3701 *et seq.* (Federal Claims Collection Act of 1966 and the Debt Collection Act of 1982, amending the former); 41 U.S.C. § 601 *et seq.* (the Contracts Disputes Act of 1978); FAR Subpart 32.6 (establishing policies and procedures for collecting the government's assertions of contract debts).

[37] *See* CIBINIC, NASH & NAGLE, *supra* note 36, at 888 (explaining that an "uncured material default" is the common law equivalent of the grounds for a termination for default). A breach of contract is sometimes called a repudiation, to which the government may respond with a termination for default. *See* RALPH C. NASH, JR. ET AL., THE GOVERNMENT CONTRACTS REFERENCE BOOK 55, 409 (5th ed. 2021).

promotions, and other incentives are set by directors elected by shareholders, or by officers appointed by those directors, the incentives may weigh heavily toward profit maximization with insufficient legal or economic incentive to act in the best interest of national security. The principal nonlegal countervailing force may be the reputational concerns of the company or of individual officers and directors, who presumably would want to be known for prioritizing the national security of the United States. But against a backdrop of factual uncertainty about how a particular scenario will play out for national security and the more immediate pressures of profit maximization, these countervailing forces may not suffice.

8. Articulating Defense Contractors' Fiduciary Duties in Corporate Charters and by Federal Statute

Military contractors and the U.S. government can take specific steps to assure that defense contractors adhere more closely to the national security interests of the United States. The government already has significant leverage by being these contractors' main customer. How should the government use this leverage? How should defense contractors respond?

One mechanism is to add to the already abundant array of statutes and regulations governing military contractors' conduct in specific situations. This is the prevailing approach to corporate conduct that adversely affects persons outside the corporation. Regulate it. This chapter does not explore this alternative other than to note that we have already done a lot to regulate military contractors and can do more. The cynical approach is to assume that military contractors will almost always prioritize profits over the national security interests and that we need a great many context-specific statutes and regulations to prevent them from doing so in every possible situation we can think of.

Another related approach is to enhance disclosure requirements. Officers and directors of military contractors could be required to disclose to the government more information about their own views, and the views of experts within their company, concerning the impact on U.S. national security form a particular military contract. This might help in some situations—for example, requiring the company in Scenario 1 to disclose the views of its directors and officers about the impact of the weapon sale abroad on U.S. national security. This could expose the fact that the defense contractor in many respects disagrees with the sanguine assessment of officials at the DoD and the State Department. The downside risk of this approach is that requiring a company to disclose to the government too much information about divergent viewpoints concerning a contract's impact on national security might suppress discussion of those divergent viewpoints to begin with. The company might discourage internal discussion of issues that have not been thoroughly analyzed, so the internal discussion need not be disclosed to the government. A "full disclosure" regime thus might narrow the company's focus even more to the specifications of the contract and prompt the company intentionally to avoid the bigger picture.

There are, however, ways to better articulate corporate purpose at least so it is clear what directors, officers, and employees of the company are supposed to do. Whether they do what they are supposed to do will turn on a wide range of legal and nonlegal incentives, but it is important to eliminate the excuse that it is acceptable for directors and officers of a military contractor to prioritize shareholder profits over the national security of the United States.

A good case can be made that companies should only be allowed to compete for large scale U.S. defense contracts if they certify, in articles of incorporation or bylaws or elsewhere and disclose to shareholders, that a primary purpose of the enterprise is to strengthen the national security. The company could also be required to articulate in writing its objective of earning profits will not be an acceptable rationale for a corporate decision that poses a substantial risk to national security. A company unwilling to make these commitments should not be entrusted with high-value contracts upon which the lives of our service members, our allies, and the safety of our homeland depend.

As pointed out earlier in this chapter, some military contractors also have nonmilitary business operations and nonmilitary customers. For these companies, a primary purpose of their defense sector operations should be to strengthen U.S. national security. Other parts of the enterprise have nonmilitary purposes, and there the fiduciary duty to consider the national security of the United States generally should not apply. A multipurpose company would not have to dedicate all its operations to furthering U.S. national security simply because it contracts with the U.S. military.

This broader concept of corporate purpose is not a substitute for legal, contractual, and other mechanisms to hold defense contractors accountable. It is, however, a signaling mechanism to employees from rank and file to the C-suite that their loyalty to our national security interests is expected and is of paramount importance. This clearly articulated corporate mission can furthermore become the basis for an implied-in-fact contractual covenant between the company and its employees and the company and the government. This makes a difference internally within the company and externally.

Matters investigated and contested internally within the company would be resolved against the backdrop of this more clearly articulated business purpose prioritizing national security. Penalizing employees for prioritizing national security interests over profits, performance evaluation metrics too closely tied or exclusively tied to profits, and other similar practices would be discouraged. In some circumstances, an employee subject to too much pressure on profit maximization might have a cause of action for breach of contract. Conversely, the employee who made poor decisions on a contract that ended disastrously for the military, and perhaps also the company, would no longer have the excuse that they were under immense pressure to generate profits for the company. The employee who too quickly approved a design specification to submit a bid, who did not respond to coworkers' concerns about a product design, or who cut corners compromising quality would be reminded that the corporate charter or bylaws language clearly state that furthering the national security of the United States is an important and unsurpassed business objective.

External matters, such as disputes between the company and the government, or disputes with other contractors working on the same project would be adjudicated against this backdrop of corporate purpose. This might affect the standard of care expected of company employees and subcontractors working on a project or at least the way they meet this standard of care. A dispute over substitute parts or services in a project might be adjudicated differently if the objective of the substitution was cost savings for the company but not the government. This chapter does not explore all of the possibilities for these types of disputes, which are ordinary for many businesses, but they should be adjudicated against the backdrop understanding that military contracting is no ordinary business. Contractors working together on a project also would be expected to prioritize the success of the project, not just their own individual profits. Disputes between contractors and subcontractors would be adjudicated not only based on their legal duties to each other but also against this same fundamental understanding about where each participating company's loyalties were supposed to be. For each of the contractors, those loyalties would be to the national security of the United States not just to their own shareholder profit maximization.

Finally, there is an expressive value of this articulation of business purpose.[38] The expressive value of prioritizing national security over the shareholder primacy norm will in some instances, perhaps many instances, change behavior even where no legal consequences would follow. Defense contractor directors, officers, and employees would see themselves as patriots, not profiteers. Sometimes they would act accordingly.

Despite the substantial profitability of the military contracting sector, some might argue that companies don't have the resources both to make high quality products and to consider the broader national security needs of their most important customer—the United States. If defense contractors incur a legal obligation to take U.S. national security interests into consideration in making business

[38] For general discussion of the expressive value of law, *see* Cass R. Sunstein, *On the Expressive Function of Law*, 144 U. Pa. L. Rev. 2021 (1996).

decisions, would this place too heavy a burden on them that interferes with their work? Likely not. Most businesses take customer interests into account, and businesses such as airlines and hospitals and some financial services firms have legal duties to look out for the well-being of their customers. Would considering the broader purpose of U.S. military contracting divert resources from research and development and other investments necessary to produce the highest quality products for the U.S. military? Very likely not, and in any event, national security depends not only on the quality of military products but whom they are sold to and how they are used. The broader picture is relevant to the long-term success of the defense contractor's business as well as the national security of the United States. A defense contractor that understands this broader picture is likely to be more forward thinking, to make better products, and perhaps even to be more profitable for shareholders in the end.

9. Conclusion

We return to the issue raised in the introduction of this chapter: the duty of loyalty in fiduciary law and the law of business organizations, and the fundamental question of where the duty of loyalty of the officers and directors of a military contactor lies. The proposition advanced here is that this loyalty must include U.S. national security and that a fiduciary duty to shareholders cannot be permitted to surpass this duty of loyalty to the United States. This duty should be carried out pursuant to a business plan that is expected to be profitable for the company, and indeed the long-term profitability of the company is important to assure that it continues to attract investors and invests in new technology to meet the future defense needs of the U.S. military. Shareholder return is important, but it is not the only important thing. Prioritizing profits over national security is unacceptable rendition of corporate purpose. The corporate articles or bylaws should clearly say so, and for companies doing substantial military contracting for the U.S. government, this general statement of corporate purpose should be required.

References

Business Roundtable Redefines Purpose of a Corporation to Promote an Economy that Serves All Americans, Bus. Roundtable (Aug. 19, 2019), https://www.businessroundtable.org/business-roundtable-redefines-the-purpose-of-a-corporation-to-promote-an-economy-that-serves-all-americans.

John Cibinic, Jr., Ralph C. Nash, Jr. & James F. Nagle, Administration of Government Contracts (4th ed. 2006).

Madison Condon, *Externalities and the Common Owner*, 95 WASH. U. L. REV. 1 (2020).

Deborah A. DeMott, *Beyond Metaphor: An Analysis of Fiduciary Obligation*, 37 DUKE L.J. 879 (1988).

Alexander Dyck et al., *Do Institutional Investors Drive Corporate Social Responsibility? International Evidence*, 131 J. FIN. ECON. 693 (2017).

FRANK H. EASTERBROOK & DANIEL R. FISCHEL, THE ECONOMIC STRUCTURE OF CORPORATE LAW (1996).

Episcopal Church Executive Council Corporate Social Responsibility Committee, *Companies Subject to No-buy Portfolio Restrictions* (Feb. 2020), https://www.episcopalchurch.org/wp-content/uploads/sites/2/2020/07/No-Buy-List-Of-Prohibited-Stocks.pdf.

Tamar Frankel, *Fiduciary Law in the 21st Century*, 91 B.U. L. REV. 1289 (2011).

Milton Friedman, *A Friedman Doctrine: The Social Responsibility of Business Is to Increase Its Profits*, N.Y. TIMES MAG., Sept. 13, 1970, at 33.

DAVID GAUTHIER, MORALITY AND RATIONAL SELF-INTEREST (1970).

Bill McGraw, *Henry Ford and the Jews, the Story Dearborn Didn't Want Told*, BRIDGE MICH. (Feb. 4, 2019), https://www.bridgemi.com/michigan-government/henry-ford-and-jews-story-dearborn-didnt-want-told.

RALPH C. NASH, JR. ET AL., THE GOVERNMENT CONTRACTS REFERENCE BOOK (5th ed. 2021).

ADAM SMITH, AN INQUIRY INTO THE NATURE AND CAUSES OF THE WEALTH OF NATIONS (1776).

LYNN STOUT, SHAREHOLDER VALUE MYTH: HOW PUTTING SHAREHOLDERS FIRST HARMS INVESTORS, CORPORATIONS, AND THE PUBLIC (2012).

Leo Strine, *Our Continuing Struggle with the Idea that For-Profit Corporations Seek Profit*, 47 WAKE FOREST L. REV. 135 (2012).

Cass R. Sunstein, *On the Expressive Function of Law*, 144 U. PA. L. REV. 2021 (1996).

4

What Ethical Dilemmas? The U.S. Defense Industry and Foreign Arms Sales

C. Edward Peartree[1]

1. Introduction

Among all U.S. industries, even compared with other heavily regulated industries such as banking, energy, or automobiles, the defense industry has a unique relationship with the U.S. government. For major arms producers, the government serves as their principal customer, and prospective sales to foreign buyers are subject to strict limitations and case-by-case government scrutiny. In fact, it is written into law that exports of arms are, essentially, an instrument of foreign policy, only to be undertaken when they are in the interest of the United States, rather than a part of normal international commerce.

The growth of export controls, which has accelerated since the end of the Cold War with the emergence of both new multilateral regimes such as the Wassenaar Arrangement on Export Controls for Conventional Arms and Dual-Use Goods and Technologies (Wassenaar Arrangement), and new humanitarian arms control movements typified by the International Committee to Ban Landmines (ICBL) and Control Arms,[2] would seem to further shackle the defense industry and limit profit-making opportunities by circumscribing potential markets. Yet despite these constraints, U.S. defense firms still gain undeniable benefits from this arrangement.

As an industry focused on the production of implements of war amidst monopsonistic market conditions and "winner-takes-all" competition for government contracts, the defense industry contends with many ethical dilemmas. Yet in perhaps the most fundamental business decision-making area—what is sold and to whom—ethical dilemmas for the industry are mostly outsourced. Because of their status as commercial entities whose products are used

[1] The views expressed in this chapter are those of the author only.

[2] *See, e.g.*, International Campaign to Ban Mines, *Why the Ban*, ICBL.ORG, http://www.icbl.org/en-gb/problem/why-the-ban.aspx (last visited Nov. 1, 2021). *See also* Control Arms, https://controlarms.org/ (last visited on Nov. 1, 2021).

C. Edward Peartree, *What Ethical Dilemmas? The U.S. Defense Industry and Foreign Arms Sales* In: *Ethical Dilemmas in the Global Defense Industry*. Edited by: Daniel Schoeni and Tobias Vestner, Oxford University Press.
 DOI: 10.1093/oso/9780190675813.003.0005

principally by their host government for national defense or are sold to friends and allies overseas to further foreign policy objectives, defense firms enjoy a unique identity, functioning as virtual agents of the United States. This unique identity shields them both from foreign legal liability claims and, for the most part, from the vicissitudes of negative public opinion that might otherwise be directed at them but is instead directed at the U.S government and its policies.

This chapter examines the evolution of the legal, regulatory, and policy framework for U.S. arms exports. Because of export controls, defense firms' freedom to maximize profits is significantly bounded. Yet, it is argued here, these rules—which arose in the last century to address political, moral, and practical questions about the international arms trade—provide a kind of safe harbor which, on balance, is ultimately beneficial both ethically and commercially to the defense industry. While those inclined to question the basic moral character of the arms producing and exporting business are unlikely to be mollified, and may continue to insist that the industry be subject to liability for the misuse of their products, U.S. laws, regulations, and policies prevent indiscriminate transfers, greatly limiting the humanitarian damage that might otherwise be the result of unfettered commerce in arms. What is required of the defense industry, mainly, is that they comply with these rules.

2. Executive Authority over Arms Exports: Legal and Historical Context

On January 27, 1936, the Curtiss-Wright Export Corporation was indicted for conspiring to sell fifteen machine guns to the government of Bolivia, in violation of President Franklin Roosevelt's Proclamation 2087. Presidential Proclamation 2087, which had been authorized by a Joint Resolution of Congress approved on May 28, 1934, prohibited the sale of 'arms and munitions of war' to Paraguay and Bolivia, then engaged in the Chaco War.[3] Curtiss-Wright challenged the indictment and successfully appealed on grounds that, inter alia, the joint resolution was an invalid delegation of legislative power. The government appealed the Court's ruling, thus laying the groundwork for *U.S. v. Curtiss-Wright Export Corp.*, one of the most influential Supreme Court decisions in the twentieth century on questions of national security and the definition of executive powers.

The ruling in *Curtiss-Wright*—which firmly established the broad powers invested in the president to conduct foreign affairs and the "external sovereignty"[4] of the executive—is widely cited and has stood without serious challenge

[3] United States v. Curtiss-Wright Export Corp., 299 U.S. 304, 313 (1936).
[4] *Id.* at 318.

for over 80 years.[5] It may also mark the last time that an American arms manufacturer challenged the export control authorities of the U.S. government. Most scholarship on *Curtiss-Wright* has focused on constitutional matters related to the scope of executive power,[6] and few if any have remarked on its significance to the development of U.S. arms export controls. This neglected question is taken up here.

While the power of the executive to "lay, regulate and revoke embargoes" dates back to the earliest days of the Republic,[7] the exercise of that power had historically been episodic and irregular, utilized to temporarily prevent exports of war material that could support U.S. enemies during periods of armed conflict. In contrast, President Roosevelt was willing to impose an embargo on the combatants in a small, brutal war in a remote region of South America, where there was no immediate national security interest. This was the first time that such an embargo had been imposed for largely humanitarian reasons. Further, he was willing to indict U.S. arms manufacturers and exporters for violations of the embargo and contest appeals all the way to the Supreme Court. The Court ultimately held that the president's authority in matters of foreign policy superseded commercial rights of the firm to pursue profits.[8]

In addition to clarifying the boundaries of the president's power in conducting matters of foreign policy, *Curtiss-Wright* established the precedent of federal restrictions on arms exports. Never again would U.S. defense contractors enjoy unfettered access to overseas markets. The decision of the Court nearly coincided with the emergence of the U.S. defense industry as the preeminent global manufacturer and exporter of defense materiel, a position it assumed following World War II and has maintained ever since. The significance of this opinion, therefore, cannot be overstated.

2.1. The Evolution of Modern Arms Export Controls

Arms export controls throughout most of human history focused, unsurprisingly, on preventing adversaries from obtaining weapons or strategic materials

[5] Kimberly L. Fletcher, *The Court's Decisive Hand Shapes the Executive's Foreign Affairs Policymaking Power*, 73 MD. L. REV 247, 282 (2013).

[6] There is extensive scholarship on *Curtiss-Wright*, some of it critical of the Court's assertion of presidential authority and Justice Sutherland's theory of "extraconstitutional" power in foreign affairs. *See, e.g.*, Michael D. Ramsey, *The Myth of Extraconstitutional Foreign Affairs Power*, 42(2) WM. & MARY L. REV. 379 (2000). *See also* Brief Amicus Curiae of Louis Fisher in Support of Petitioner, at 3–34, Zivotofsky v. Kerry, 576 U.S. 1 (2014).

[7] Curtiss-Wright, 299 U.S. at 322–27.

[8] *Id.* at 319–20, 325–29 (observing that that portion of the authority over foreign affairs vested alone in the president is "plenary and exclusive" and, therefore, exercise thereof does not depend on the delegation of legislative powers).

that might give them an advantage in armed conflict, not on moral questions about harms caused by the proliferation of arms. Over 1,000 years ago, the Byzantines famously safeguarded the formula for Greek fire, a devastatingly effective naval incendiary, as a state secret known only to the emperor.[9] In the United States, Congress granted the president discretionary authorities to prohibit the export of arms during the Spanish-American War,[10] and during World War I ratified the Trading with the Enemy Act and the Espionage Act, issuing a "contraband list" banning exports of arms, ammunition, and strategic materials to Wilhelmine Germany.[11] At the time that Presidential Proclamation 2087 was issued, however, the United States had no comprehensive law addressing the export of arms—a state of affairs that likely emboldened Curtiss-Wright to challenge the government's control over its exports of machine guns to Bolivia.

In 1935, nearly contemporaneously with *Curtiss-Wright*, Congress, troubled by rising global instability and eager to steer clear of foreign conflicts, passed the Neutrality Act. This imposed embargoes on trade in any "implements of war" to belligerents.[12] The Export Control Act, passed in the aftermath of World War II, significantly broadened the scope of U.S. export controls. Unlike previous legislation adopted during war or international crisis and subsequently allowed to lapse once the crisis passed, the Export Control Act was renewed repeatedly, becoming a permanent fixture of the U.S. Code.[13] The Export Control Act also applied worldwide, without regard to belligerency or any other special status.[14] It established the principle that international trade was an important element of national security and strategy.[15]

The Mutual Security Act of 1954 established an Office of Munitions Control at the State Department and the United States Munitions List.[16] Importantly, the Mutual Security Act established in export law the goal of supporting allies in addition to the traditional goal of denying arms to adversaries. The Coordinating Committee for Multilateral Export Controls (COCOM), also established in 1949 and led by the United States (in cooperation with the United Kingdom and France), built a framework for allied cooperation in controlling strategic trade during the Cold War. Denial of military and strategic capabilities to the Soviet

[9] Alex Roland, The Technological Fix: Weapons and the Cost of War xi–xiii (1995).

[10] Manley O. Hudson, Munitions Industry: International Regulation of the Trade in and Manufacture of Arms and Ammunition 54 (1935).

[11] Richard T. Cupitt, Reluctant Champions: U.S. Presidential Policy and Strategic Export Controls, Truman, Eisenhower, Bush, and Clinton 37–39 (2000).

[12] *Id.* at 43.

[13] *Id.*

[14] Harold J. Berman & John R. Garson, *United States Export Controls—Past, Present, and Future*, 67(5) Colum. L. Rev. 791, 792–94 (1967).

[15] Douglas E. McDaniel, United States Technology Export Controls: An Assessment 5 (1993).

[16] Berman & Garson, *supra* note 14, at 808.

Union and Warsaw Pact was the clear focus during this period, and it would have been hard to fathom a U.S. defense firm challenging the status quo—particularly given their reliance on the Department of Defense as a customer.

The Arms Export Control Act (AECA), enacted in 1976 and implemented by the International Traffic in Arms Regulations (ITAR), put in place the framework for modern U.S. export controls: registration of arms manufacturers and exporters;[17] restrictions on the export of military and related materials that may contribute to armed conflict or violations of human rights;[18] prohibitions on exports to certain destinations (i.e., arms embargoes);[19] military assistance for defensive purposes, including the provision of arms and defense services to allies;[20] extraterritorial jurisdiction (i.e., no retransfer or re-export of arms without U.S. authorization);[21] and transparency through regular public reporting of arms transfers.[22] The AECA also established the regulation of arms exports as a foreign policy function, delegating authority from the president to the secretary of state.[23]

The evolution toward a more comprehensive and permanent export control regime by the late 1970s had a marginal impact on the fortunes of the U.S. defense industry, which still relied on the government as its principal customer. The end of the Cold War, however, signaled a sea change in the structure and market for the defense sector. Gone was the paradigm of the U.S. government as (nearly) the sole customer for many major defense contractors. In the face of shrinking budgets and spurred on by then Secretary of Defense William Perry, many of the major producers and suppliers to the Pentagon embarked on a wave of mergers and consolidations. In search of new markets and with the support of the U.S. government, U.S. defense firms began to focus on exports to make up the shortfall in U.S. defense outlays. The results were dramatic: between the late 1980s and late 1990s, the volume of U.S. defense exports went from approximately 20 percent of domestic defense procurement to nearly 70 percent.[24] Concomitant concerns about the risk of arms proliferation amidst the scramble for new global markets gave rise to new national policies, such as the Conventional Arms Transfer (CAT) Policy, issued by President Bill Clinton in 1996 (and updated by President Barack Obama in 2014 and President Donald Trump in 2018), which notably included protection of human rights and promotion of regional stability among the goals

17 Arms Export Control Act, 22 U.S.C § 2778.

18 *Id.*

19 *Id.*, §§ 2773, 2780, 2781.

20 *Id.*, §§ 2751, 2754.

21 *Id.*, § 2753.

22 *Id.*, § 2776.

23 *Id.*, § 2752.

24 Kenneth Flamm, *Post-Cold War Policy and the U.S. Defense Industrial Base*, 35(1) NAT'L ACAD. ENG'G 8 (2008), https://www.nae.edu/7459/Post-ColdWarPolicyandtheUSDefenseIndustrialBase.

and criteria for arms export decision-making.[25] Although humanitarian considerations in arms export decision-making accelerated in the post–Cold War era with its greater emphasis on export trade, attention to such concerns had originally been introduced nearly a century earlier.

2.2. The Ascendance of "Ethical" Arms Export Controls

Efforts to control the proliferation of arms for moral or humanitarian reasons—as opposed to strictly national security interests—are a modern phenomenon, no doubt related to the creation of a "defense industry" during the industrial revolution and the growth of global commerce in arms. The 1890 Brussels Act, signed by the United States and European powers, sought to regulate the export of firearms and ammunition throughout most of Africa "for the preservation of the African population."[26] The carnage of World War I sparked a public outcry about the undue influence of arms producers and introduced a series of attempts by the international community to manage trade in war materials. A League of Nations commission found a "common belief that wars are promoted by the competitive zeal of private armaments firms" and debated the abolition of the private manufacture of arms.[27] While this proposal was unsuccessful, due in large part to the United States' objections, the League continued to push international efforts to control the import and export of munitions, first with the 1919 St. Germain Treaty and then with its successor the Geneva Convention on Trade in Arms in 1925.[28] The United States, ever leery of foreign entanglements, declined to join the League and thus acceded to neither the St. Germain Treaty nor the Geneva Convention. Still, these early efforts, the Geneva Convention especially, laid the groundwork for a morally driven basis for restricting arms exports that would influence both U.S. laws and policies and future multilateral arms export control efforts.

Global concerns about the catastrophic effects of the weapons of mass destruction led to a succession of legally binding treaties—the Nuclear Non-proliferation

[25] President Barack Obama, Presidential Policy Directive/PPD-27 (Jan. 15, 2014), *United States Conventional Arms Transfer Policy*, https://www.whitehouse.gov/the-press-office/2014/01/15/presidential-policy-directive-united-states-conventional-arms-transfer-p [hereinafter Conventional Arms Transfer Policy]. *See also* Jennifer L. Erickson, *Saint or Sinner? Human Rights and U.S. Support for the Arms Trade Treaty*, 130(3) Pol. Sci. Q. 449, 453 (2015) (explaining that the 1973 amendment to the 1961 Foreign Assistance Act was the first U.S. export control law to establish human rights as a criterion for the receipt of military aid).

[26] Hudson, *supra* note 10, at 5.

[27] *Id.* at 2. *See also* League of Nations, Report of the Temporary Mixed Commission on Armaments 11 (1921). Geneva, September 15, 1921.

[28] Hudson, *supra* note 10, at 72–95.

Treaty (NPT),[29] the Biological Weapons Convention (BWC),[30] the Chemical Weapons Convention (CWC)[31]—to either freeze and/or totally prohibit the use of a class of weapons considered too deadly, inhumane, or indiscriminate to be legitimately used in warfare. Prior to joining international efforts to ban the use of biological and chemical weapons, the United States and many other states had active programs to develop and deploy them. While the United States still has a significant nuclear arsenal, along with other permanent members of the UN Security Council ("Permanent Five"; P5), the NPT, and a number of related agreements, as well as widely observed norms, circumscribe the use, testing, and development of such weapons.[32] As global norms developed against the use of such weapons, affected commercial industries went along. The U.S. Chemical Manufacturers Association, for example, supported the CWC—a significant change in posture from the 1920s, when U.S. industry actively lobbied against Senate ratification of the Geneva Convention protocol banning chemical weapons.[33] The upshot was that these weapons, all of which had once been used in warfare and manufactured and sold around the world, were now effectively off the market—at least among parties to the treaties.

As the U.S. defense sector faced reduced Pentagon budgets and greater reliance on export markets in the post–Cold War era, additional multilateral efforts to further restrict arms sales began to emerge. These multilateral controls took two paths: first, agreements among responsible arms-exporting states to observe common restraints on arms exports in the interest of nonproliferation and the promotion of common goals (e.g., peaceful resolution of conflict, restraint in trade in arms as a general principal, etc.); and, second, humanitarian based arms control movements, driven by individuals, nongovernmental organizations (NGOs), and like-minded governments. Both of these trends, creating a more structured, common international framework for arms transfer controls grew substantially as the Cold War, with its bipolar export control orientation, wound down.

[29] Treaty on the Non-Proliferation of Nuclear Weapons, United Nations, July 1, 1968, 21 U.S.T. 483, 729 U.N.T.S. 168.

[30] Convention on the Prohibition of the Development, Production and Stockpiling of Bacteriological (Biological) and Toxin Weapons and on Their Destruction, United Nations, Apr. 10, 1972, 1015 U.N.T.S. 163.

[31] Convention on the Prohibition of the Development, Production, Stockpiling and Use of Chemical Weapons and on their Destruction, Jan. 13, 1993, 1974 U.N.T.S. 45.

[32] *See* Richard Price & Nina Tannenwald, *Norms and Deterrence: The Nuclear and Chemical Weapons Taboos*, *in* The Culture of National Security: Norms and Identity in World Politics (Peter J. Katzenstein ed., 1996) (examining the evolution of norms prohibiting the use of WMD).

[33] U.S. Congress, Office of Technology Assessment, The Chemical Weapons Convention: Effects on the U.S. Chemical Industry 10 (OTA-BP-ISC-106, 1993).

The United Nations founded a standing body to discuss arms control matters in 1979 with the Conference on Disarmament and in the early 1980s successfully negotiated the Convention on Conventional Weapons (CCW)—the first successful modern effort to limit the manufacture, use, and trade in certain conventional arms for humanitarian purposes. The CCW bans or restricts certain weapons which cause unnecessary or unjustifiable suffering to combatants or to affect civilians indiscriminately.[34] Amended repeatedly since its inception, the CCW includes protocols that ban or restrict booby traps, landmines,[35] incendiary weapons,[36] and blinding lasers.[37] More recently, the CCW has taken up discussion of controls of lethal autonomous weapons, or "killer robots" in the parlance of a leading nongovernmental coalition focused on banning and preventing further development of such weapons systems.[38]

In 1994, COCOM was succeeded by the Wassenaar Arrangement, a politically binding regime to coordinate national export controls of conventional weapons and dual-use items among like-minded states, based on general principles of promoting responsible transfers of conventional arms and international stability and security.[39] Like Wassenaar, the Missile Technology Control Regime (MTCR) is a voluntary arrangement among producers of missile technologies establishing guidelines governing transfer and providing a regular forum for exchanges of information among the 35 participating states. Although all ultimate decisions with respect to transfers of MTCR controlled items belong to the states, the United States, by law, includes the MTCR annex (which identifies controlled items) in the ITAR and also references the guidelines (e.g., "strong presumption of denial" for Category I systems) with respect to U.S. exports of MTCR-controlled items.[40]

The rise of human rights and moral criteria in export control initiatives in the post–Cold War period has been widely observed.[41] A flood of small arms and light weapons, many from former Soviet and Warsaw Pact stockpiles, entering

[34] Convention on Prohibitions or Restrictions on the Use of Certain Conventional Weapons Which May be Deemed to be Excessively Injurious or to Have Indiscriminate Effects, Oct. 10, 1980, 1342 U.N.T.S. 137 (amended Dec. 21, 2001).

[35] *Id.*, Protocol II (prohibiting the use of mines, booby traps, and other devices).

[36] *Id.*, Protocol III (prohibiting the use of incendiary weapons).

[37] *Id.*, Protocol IV (prohibiting the use of blinding laser weapons).

[38] Several NGOs, notably Human Rights Watch and the Campaign to Stop Killer Robots, have fomented growing public interest in the development of lethal autonomous weapons and the potential dangers of weapons systems capable of killing without the intercession of any human decision-making. *See Losing Humanity: The Case Against Killer Robots*, HUM. RTS. WATCH (Nov. 19, 2012), https://www.hrw.org/report/2012/11/19/losing-humanity/case-against-killer-robots; CAMPAIGN TO STOP KILLER ROBOTS, https://www.stopkillerrobots.org (last visited Jan. 4, 2020).

[39] Wassenaar Arrangement on Exp. Controls for Conventional Arms and Dual-use Goods and Techs., *Introduction*, WASSENAAR.ORG, https://www.wassenaar.org/ (last visited Jan. 4, 2020).

[40] Missile Technology Control Regime, 22 C.F.R. § 120.29 (LexisNexis, through Federal Register, Title 3, Dec. 31, 2019).

[41] Erickson, *supra* note 25, at 451–52, 459–60.

global markets and stoking conflict,[42] and the long-term harms to civilian populations caused by antipersonnel landmines inspired a new approach driven by NGOs as well as sympathetic governments. And yet while the approach was new, the motivation for these efforts was much the same as those that gave rise nearly 100 years before to the Brussels Act and the St. Germain Treaty: the moral judgment that the arms trade is inherently harmful and in need of vigilant oversight.

The first and most successful of the nongovernmental arms control movement was the formation of the ICBL, resulting in the Mine Ban Treaty. Like the BWC and the CWC, the Mine Ban Treaty consisted of a total ban on a type of weapon considered so inhumane and indiscriminate in its effect so as to warrant not restraint but a complete prohibition of its use. While the United States was among a handful of countries not to sign the treaty (principally due to security concerns on the Korean Peninsula), it has gradually moved toward near-complete compliance with the landmine ban and unilaterally ceased to export landmines in 1992.[43] Similarly, the 2008 Convention on Cluster Munitions succeeded in rapidly developing an arms control process resulting in a "moral prohibition regime" banning the production, stockpiling, or transfer of cluster munitions with over 100 signatories.[44] The Cluster Munitions Convention in its Article 1 "assistance" clause goes further than even the landmine ban, having been interpreted by some states' implementing legislation to prohibit banks and other financial institutions from any investment or assistance to private firms involved in the manufacture of cluster munitions.[45] While the United States has not signed the convention, it has generally supported its humanitarian goals and its influence on U.S. policy is evident in the development of an independent Department of Defense document outlining standards designed to minimize risks of harm to noncombatants.[46]

[42] The literature on the post–Cold War weapons surplus and dangers of proliferation, particularly in developing nations, is extensive. *See, e.g.*, Michael T. Klare, *The Subterranean Arms Trade: Black Market Sales, Covert Operations, and Ethnic Warfare*, *in* CASCADE OF ARMS: MANAGING CONVENTIONAL WEAPONS PROLIFERATION 3, 44–46 (Andrew J. Pierre ed., 1997).

[43] Dep't of State, U.S. Landmine Policy (Feb. 7, 2004), http://2001-2009.state.gov/t/pm/rls/fs/30047.htm (last visited Jan. 4, 2020); Human Rights Watch, *United States Landmine Policy: Questions and Answers*, HRW.ORG (Oct. 3, 2014, 4:15 PM), https://www.hrw.org/news/2014/10/03/united-states-landmine-policy-questions-and-answers.

[44] Denise Garcia, *Banning Evil: Cluster Munitions and the Successful Formation of a Global Prohibition Regime*, 5(2) CORNELL INT'L AFF. REV. 36, 37 (2012).

[45] *Global Ban*, CLUSTER MUNITION COALITION, http://stopclustermunitions.org/en-gb/the-treaty/global-ban.aspx (last visited Jan. 4, 2020); Charlie Cooper, *UK Banks Step Back from Involvement in Cluster Bombs*, INDEPENDENT (June 15, 2012), http://www.independent.co.uk/news/business/news/uk-banks-step-back-from-involvement-in-cluster-bombs-7852112.html.

[46] U.S. Dep't of Defense, News Release No. 577-08, *Cluster Munitions Policy Released* (July 8, 2008), https://archive.defense.gov/releases/release.aspx?releaseid=12049. *See also* John R. Crook, *United States Opposes Ban on Cluster Munitions, Supports Alternative CCW Negotiations*, 102 A.J.I.L. 889, 892 (2008). For more recent developments in this regard, *see* Jeff Abramson, *U.S. to Revise Landmine Policy*, 50(4) ARMS CONTROL TODAY (2021).

The Arms Trade Treaty (ATT)—which was negotiated at the United Nations and entered into force in December 2014—was in many respects the fruition of multilateral arms export control efforts begun nearly 100 years before in the aftermath of World War I.[47] Global in scope, and citing the UN Charter's call to promote the "establishment and maintenance of international peace and security with the least diversion for armaments of the world's economic and human resources," the ATT seeks to create a common framework for responsible, transparent conventional arms export controls.[48] The United States had signed the ATT in September 2013, but the Trump administration communicated in April 2019 that the U.S. government would no longer seek to adhere to the treaty.[49]

The result of more than a century of evolving national laws, international treaties, politically binding regimes, and norms resulting from arms control movements is a wide-reaching web of constraints on the use, sale, and export of arms. Whether initiated by states, international organizations, or global activists, they have the same effect of limiting market space for the defense industry. Yet even as more constraints were imposed, the defense industry has rarely protested, despite the potential impact on their bottom lines.[50] States which opt out of humanitarian arms control efforts (including the United States) have been subject to considerable pressure and criticism from the international community. Manufacturers of the weapons, however, generally have not been the target of public attacks, as they are perceived to be only doing the bidding of their host governments.

3. Ethical Dilemmas for the Defense Industry

That an industry whose products, when used effectively, result in death and destruction of property should be the subject of robust government regulation should come as no surprise. It should also come as no surprise that business firms acting rationally calculate costs and benefits in order to maximize profits. Curtiss-Wright, acting in its economic self-interest and without any apparent independent ethical considerations, elected to defy a presidential proclamation forbidding the export of arms to South America. The result for Curtiss-Wright

[47] The Arms Trade Treaty, preamble, Dec. 24, 2014, 13 U.N.T.S. 27217, https://unoda-web.s3.amazonaws.com/wp-content/uploads/2013/06/English7.pdf [hereinafter Arms Trade Treaty].

[48] *Id.* (citing U.N. Charter, art. 26).

[49] *See, e.g.*, Tobias Vestner, *The New Geopolitics of the Arms Trade Treaty*, 51(10) Arms Control Today 14 (2020).

[50] The response of U.S. defense firms to all of these multilateral initiatives has been relatively muted. Jennifer Erickson notes that with respect to the ATT, the U.S. defense industry "refrained from coming out either in support or opposition to multilateral export standards." Erickson, *supra* note 25, at 466.

was criminal indictment and the dubious honor of living in perpetuity as the loser in a landmark Supreme Court decision. The more lasting result for the defense industry was establishment of the firm principle of government control over their affairs—even in matters that would not seem to directly affect U.S. national security—and the beginning of an increasingly symbiotic relationship with the federal government.

Today, a manufacturer, exporter, or broker of munitions must register with the Department of State and seek authorization for each export. Depending on the sensitivity of the commodity in question, the end user, and the destination, the export license application may be reviewed by the Department of Defense for reasons of technology security, and various State Department offices for foreign policy considerations, including the suitability of the transfer from a human rights perspective. If missile technology is involved, MTCR experts will review as well, and if the technology is particularly sensitive, the export may be subject to National Disclosure Policy Committee review by the Department of Defense, or a variety of other committees which assess and ultimately approve or disapprove export proposals. Even if approved, the transaction—particularly those involving more sensitive items or destinations—may well include extensive provisos on what may be sold (including the capabilities of the product), the scope of use, and/or routine end-use monitoring by U.S. government officials as a condition of the approval. And any retransfer, re-export, or change in end use requires reauthorization by the U.S. government.

Arms transfers subject to the U.S. Foreign Military Sales (FMS) program—government-to-government transfers as opposed to direct commercial sales from a private firm to a foreign buyer—entail far greater collaboration between the manufacturer and the U.S. government. If you are a defense firm selling your products pursuant to FMS, all aspects of the sale are subject to a legally binding "letter of offer and acceptance" between the United States and the foreign government recipient. The letter of offer and acceptance (or LOA in the FMS parlance) includes cradle-to-grave controls over the technology for the life of the product and end-use monitoring by Security Cooperation Officers at U.S. embassies worldwide. FMS sales, even more than commercial sales, are viewed as a direct extension of U.S. foreign policy and must support foreign policy goals first and foremost, irrespective of commercial benefits to the firm. Both FMS and commercial sales over a certain value threshold (generally between $14 million and $100 million, depending on the type of defense article and destination, but only $1 million for firearms) are additionally subject to congressional notification and review.

In both national laws and policies, and international agreements, a balance is being struck between the goal of reducing the risks of arms proliferation and recognizing the legitimate requirement for arms (including the economic preconditions for the success of the industry on which the state is dependent) for national defense and collective security. This balance is the foundation of modern arms export controls, and the relationship of the regulator and the regulated—the U.S. government and the defense industry. The AECA, the principal law governing arms sales states that "an ultimate goal of the United States continues to be a world that is free from the scourge of war and the dangers and burdens of armaments."[51] The AECA recognizes that "the United States and other free and independent countries continue to have valid requirements for effective and mutually beneficial defense relationships in order to maintain and foster the environment of international peace and security."[52] Similarly, the UN Charter, alongside commitments to international peace and security and the pacific resolution of disputes among nations, in Chapter 7, Article 51 recognizes "the inherent right of individual or collective self-defense."[53] The ATT, the most recent global arms agreement, in its preamble recalls Article 51 and also recognizes "the legitimate political, security, economic, and commercial interests of states in the international trade in conventional arms."[54] And U.S. CAT Policy, focused as it is on criteria for arms exports, cites, along with humanitarian impacts of arms sales, support for allies and the health of the U.S. defense industrial base.[55] In all these cases, both the requirement of self-defense and the need to reduce the risk of harms are twinned.

Ethical dilemmas, like rational choices, depend on *choice*.[56] Where choice or free will is limited, does the ethical dilemma exist? Major U.S. defense firms exist in a near monopsony in which the U.S. government is their principal patron and the decision maker for any additional foreign sales they wish to pursue. While this chapter argues that the legal, regulatory, and normative environment for defense firms profoundly limits their choices and thus mitigates (if not eliminates) many ethical dilemmas for the defense industry, some have posited alternative views. One critic of the defense industry rejects the notion that they should enjoy protections afforded to them as government agents and believes they should be held liable for human rights violations involving for the weapons they manufacture.[57] Another commentator recognizes the legitimacy of arms production and exports (for national defense and supporting allies) but worries that profits and competition for fluctuating global markets crowds out ethical

[51] 22 U.S.C. § 2751.

[52] *Id.*

[53] U.N. Charter, art. 51, http://www.un.org/en/sections/un-charter/chapter-vii/index.html.

[54] Arms Trade Treaty, *supra* note 47.

[55] Conventional Arms Transfer Policy, *supra* note 25.

[56] *See, e.g.*, Immanuel Kant, *Perpetual Peace: A Philosophical Sketch*, *in* KANT: POLITICAL WRITINGS 103, 114 (H.S. Reiss ed., Barry Nisbet trans., 2d ed. 1995) (arguing that "ought implies can").

[57] Edmund F. Byrne, *Assessing Arms Makers' Corporate Social Responsibility*, 74 J. BUS. ETHICS 200, 202, 205–06, 212 (2007).

considerations—despite awareness of knowledge of human rights abuses.[58] The 2011 United Nations' *Guiding Principles on Business and Human Rights* (UNGP) recognizes the important role of states as "trustees" of international human rights, but emphasizes that the principle of respect for human rights is expected of all businesses and "exists over and above compliance with national laws and regulations."[59]

Given the essential role played by defense firms and the legal framework for arms exports outlined here, it is dubious that firms could be held liable for the use of products that are provided pursuant to U.S. foreign policy interests. And, unless one rejects the notion of the state itself,[60] or adopts a wholly pacifist worldview, it is questionable whether this would be desirable. Whether or not one agrees with U.S. policy, the United States' export decisions are guided by national and international rules based on a wide range of considerations, including the impact on national security, foreign policy, and human rights. Proposing that private firms be accountable for the downstream effects of their products might take some out of the defense business altogether and would have a chilling effect on the ability of the United States to defend itself and support allies.

3.1. Ethics and Other Regulated Industries

Virtually every commercial enterprise is subject to some form of government regulation. A corner grocery store is required to file for permits with state and municipal authorities and, depending on its wares, may need to abide by a variety of regulatory controls such as those governing the sale of liquor or tobacco. Car manufacturers must comply with safety and environmental regulations but do not typically face restrictions regarding foreign sales. Consumer electronics manufacturers have to contend with various environmental and product safety standards, but their products can be sold virtually anywhere. Compared to other regulated industries, defense is undoubtedly subject to the highest level of scrutiny and the most restrictions on its ability to vend its wares—rightfully so given the dangers entailed in weapons sales. And yet despite the burden of regulation, compared to some other business sectors which are historically more inclined to bend or break the rules when government mandates clash with the corporate

[58] *See generally* Gavin Maitland, *The Ethics of the International Arms Trade*, 7(4) BUS. ETHICS 200 (1998).

[59] Special Representative of the Secretary-General on the Issue of Human Rights and Transnational Corporations and Other Business Enterprises, *Guiding Principles on Business and Human Rights: Implementing the United Nations "Protect, Respect and Remedy" Framework*, U.N. Doc. A/HRC/17/31 (Mar. 21, 2011).

[60] Part of Edmund Byrne's argument does in fact reject the Westphalian state system. *See* Byrne, *supra* note 56, at 202, 205–06, 212.

profits, the transgressions of defense firms, at least with respect to export sales, are relatively few.

Why do cheaters cheat? A perusal of recent violations of consumer laws and regulatory controls may be illustrative. General Motors withheld information about a faulty ignition switch that has been implicated in over 100 fatal crashes. For years, DuPont's Parkersburg, West Virginia, facility evaded environmental standards and allowed the discharge of toxic perfluorooctanoic acid into the local community's water supply.[61] In these and other similar cases involving companies like Volkswagen, Samsung, and Massey Energy, firms jettisoned regulatory compliance, when compliance interfered with profitability. In short, cheaters cheat when they have financial incentives to do so. While doing business outside of the law ultimately cost them, in each case the firms assessed costs and benefits and decided to violate their legal and ethical obligations. Defense firms' incentives, however, are different. With very few exceptions, they generally find it in their self-interest to comply with export controls. Indeed, violations negatively affect a firm's reputation and tend to make the approval of future exports more difficult.

For decades, the energy industry has lobbied aggressively against environmental regulations that could impose significant compliance costs on their companies. The Supreme Court, ruling that the Environmental Protection Agency failed to consider regulatory costs to affected industries, recently struck down air pollution standards for coal-fired power plants—in spite of estimates that the rule could prevent 11,000 premature deaths and $37 billion to $90 billion in benefits annually.[62] More than 80 years after Curtiss-Wright failed to win its bid to defeat government arms export rules in court, it is inconceivable that a major defense company or consortium of companies would sue the federal government over the ITAR's imposition of undue regulatory burdens or, say, a U.S. arms embargo that prevented their doing business with Iran or North Korea. While defense firms certainly lobby the government, often aggressively, for competitive advantages, their efforts are typically focused on contract awards or approval for major export sales. None has challenged the fundamental principle of governmental power to regulate the conduct of foreign affairs. This speaks, again, to the executive's prerogatives regarding foreign and security policy outlined in *Curtiss-Wright*[63] and upheld in subsequent court rulings, and embedded in over 60 years of national laws, regulations, and policies—a generous prerogative that

[61] Elizabeth Weise, *DuPont Settles Water Pollution Case for $300 Million*, USA Today (Sept. 9, 2004), http://usatoday30.usatoday.com/money/industries/manufacturing/2004-09-09-dupont-teflon-settlement_x.htm.

[62] Timothy Cama & Lydia Wheeler, *Supreme Court Overturns Landmark Air Pollution Rule*, The Hill (June 29, 2015), http://thehill.com/policy/energy-environment/246423-supreme-court-overturns-epa-air-pollution-rule.

[63] Curtiss-Wright, 299 U.S. at 319–20, 325–29.

the executive lacks with respect to environmental regulations, for example, the apparent benefits of saving 11,000 lives per annum notwithstanding.[64]

3.2. Corporate Social Responsibility and the Defense Industry

None of this should suggest that the defense industry has not endured significant ethical lapses. A spate of contracting scandals in the 1980s—the infamous Operation Ill Wind affair—led to fraud convictions of a Navy assistant secretary and a number of prominent defense executives.[65] More recently, Darleen Druyun, a former top Air Force procurement official, and a senior Boeing executive were convicted in a kickback scheme involving a major Air Force contract.[66] The legacy of these scandals lingers and is reflected in the corporate social responsibility (CSR) commitments of the firms and major defense industry trade associations such as the National Defense Industry Association (NDIA), which offers "common ethical principles"[67] for its members, emphasizing integrity, compliance with laws and regulations, and that "economic pursuits do not overtake our responsibility to our soldiers, sailors, marines, and airmen."[68] (Not coincidentally, the NDIA's ethics statement was unveiled in the aftermath of the Druyun affair.)[69] The Defense Industry Initiative (DII), founded in 1986 in the wake of Operation Ill Wind and the Packard Commission findings of widespread waste, fraud, and abuse in defense contracting, commits its nearly 80 member companies to ethical standards of conduct and self-governance.[70] Neither organization, however, includes any consideration of the ethics of foreign sales in its enumeration of principles for ethical conduct.

The need for CSR has frequently been invoked in cases where legal jurisdiction was unclear or absent. Unsafe working conditions and environmental damage have long been byproducts of business decisions to cut costs by moving

[64] *See generally* Michigan v. EPA, 575 U.S. 902 (2015).

[65] *See, e.g.*, Douglas Frantz, *Paisley Gets 4-year Term in Ill Wind Case*, L.A. TIMES (Oct. 19, 1991), https://www.latimes.com/archives/la-xpm-1991-10-19-mn-526-story.html; James Rowley, *Pentagon Purchasing Scandal Ends with Conviction of 10th Contractor*, AP (Jan. 14, 1994), https://apnews.com/1669a58e75638714d12168eeca17d579.

[66] *See, e.g.*, Leslie Wayne, *Former Executive at Boeing Given 4 Month Prison Term*, N.Y. TIMES (Feb. 19, 2005), https: //www.nytimes.com/2005/02/19/business/former-executive-at-boeing-given-4month-prison-term.html; Andy Pasztor & Jonathan Karp, *How an Air Force Official's Help for a Daughter Led to Disgrace*, WALL ST. J. (Dec. 9, 2004), https://www.wsj.com/articles/SB110255501607195187.

[67] *Statement of Defense Industry Ethics*, NDIA.ORG, http://www.ndia.org/resources/Pages/TheEthicsSource.aspx.

[68] *Id.*, *Common Ethical Principles and Practices*.

[69] *See* Joe Reeder, *Association Unveils New Ethics Code for Industry*, NAT'L DEF. (Nov. 2004), https://www.nationaldefensemagazine.org/articles/2004/10/31/2004november-association-unveils-new-ethics-code-for-industry.

[70] *Defense Industry Initiative on Business Ethics and Conduct*, DII.ORG, https://www.dii.org/home (last visited Sep. 3, 2022).

manufacturing or other business activities overseas, generally in countries with lax legal and regulatory frameworks. In such cases, CSR provides a supranational guide to responsible behavior. In the context of U.S. export controls, which not only impose extensive rules on exporters but are extraterritorial in scope, CSR may be less relevant.

3.3. Defense Industry Self-identification with the U.S. Government

Perusal of a random sampling of defense industry publications and public advertisements demonstrates that more than collaborate, many defense firms self-identify with the U.S. government and its policies. Dramatized images of armed forces members using the company's products are accompanied by patriotic messages that extol the virtues of not just the products but also the warfighter and his cause. Unlike iconic global brands like Coca-Cola or Apple, defense firms, while differentiating themselves from competitors principally by name, generally subsume their individual corporate identity to their membership as part of the "U.S. team" and cast their products as instruments of American national security and foreign policy. One major defense contractor famously advertised (and trademarked) its aircraft carrier as "90,000 Tons of Diplomacy," an expression which found its way into popular culture via posters and t-shirts.[71] As profit-maximizing commercial entities, one can only assume that their decision to self-identify with the U.S. government is because it is good for business.

3.4. Evolving International Views of CSR and Arms Exports?

Recent proposals within the NGO community to establish global norms mandating that defense firms practice human rights due diligence on arms sales and accept liability for reparations for harms done by their products continue to stimulate debate about the ethical responsibilities of the global defense industry.[72]

[71] "90,000 Tons of Diplomacy" dates back to 1994, was trademarked in 2001 by Newport News Shipbuilding, transferred to Northrup Grumman Corporation after it acquired Newport News, and is now registered to Huntington-Ingalls Corporation. *See* U.S. Patent and Trademark Office, Trademark Database, U.S. Reg. No. 2435323.

[72] *See* Amnesty Int'l, *Outsourcing Responsibility: Human Rights Policies in the Defence Sector*, AI Index ACT 30/0893/2019 (2019), https://www.amnesty.org/download/Documents/ACT300893 2019ENGLISH.PDF (calling for firms to practice strict human rights due diligence on all arms sales and to accept liability for harms done by their products, above and beyond any legal obligations imposed by states).

Building on the principles outlined in the UNGP, the UN Human Rights Council is currently at work on a treaty proposal that would codify supranational human rights obligations and liabilities incumbent on businesses into international law.[73] Ethical debates on matters of public interest are essential, and the participation of governments, civil society, and the defense industry in this arena is to be encouraged. However, it is an established principle that once a defense firm submits an export application on behalf of a foreign buyer it turns over the decision and any attendant ethical considerations to the government. A firm, for ethical reasons, may elect not to pursue a foreign contract. Yet independent judgments about foreign sales—particularly those that might contradict U.S. policy—could jeopardize the firm's ability to continue to work with its principal customer, posing another type of ethical dilemma. It is also questionable whether a private firm that happens to manufacture armaments should substitute its judgment in matters of national security and foreign policy. After all, firms do not have the authority nor the legitimacy to do so, as this is the duty of governments.

The enmeshment of government and the defense industry poses obvious ethical challenges, most famously embodied by President Dwight D. Eisenhower's 1961 farewell warning about the emerging "military-industrial complex." While there is a voluminous literature debating the perils of the military-industrial complex, it is generally acknowledged that some form of close partnership between government and defense industry is an immutable reality, the alternative would be a government that might not be able to rely on the private sector to provide the basic tools of national defense or support of allies overseas. Indeed, any attempt to alter this dynamic by switching liability for harms to the firms themselves could prove an existential threat to defense industries, which might be unable or unwilling to function in the face of unrestricted risk from criminal or financial penalties imposed by foreign and international courts. For governments, an international treaty or binding principles mandating liability for businesses and superseding its own national laws, regulations, and policies in matters of national defense and support of allies could challenge the sovereignty of the state itself and the obligations of a government to protect its citizens and interests. In the aftermath of a recent referral to the Office of the Prosecutor of the International Criminal Court by a consortium of NGOs calling for an

[73] The Human Rights Council, Open-Ended Intergovernmental Working Group on Transnational Corporations and Other Business Enterprises with respect to Human Rights (OEIGWG) revised a draft of a binding instrument in advance of the OEIGWG's fifth meeting in October 2019, https://www.ohchr.org/Documents/HRBodies/HRCouncil/WGTransCorp/OEIGWG_RevisedDraft_LBI.pdf.

investigation of named major defense firms for war crimes, this threat, at least for European firms, is no longer hypothetical.[74]

4. Conclusion

From 1936 onward, U.S. courts have affirmed the broad latitude afforded to the executive branch to regulate commerce in the interest of foreign affairs and national security.[75] Defense exports are disanalogous to exports of other products, even vigorously regulated products, as their very sale overseas is an extension of the conduct of foreign affairs of the U.S. government. American companies do not have the right to pursue unfettered commerce overseas in this sector. The continuing expansion of export laws, regulations, and policies to which the U.S. subscribes continues to support this fundamental fact.

While the defense industry accepts significant constraints on its market, it also gains distinct advantages by playing by the government's rules. In addition to the obvious benefits of remaining in the good graces of its principal customer, with its generous procurement and research and development spending[76] and the advocacy of senior government officials on their behalf for major contract bids by U.S. allies, the defense industry derives additional benefits, namely avoidance of blame for the foreign policy with which their products are associated, when and if it goes badly. Transnational corporations have faced billions in legal settlements not to mention reputational damage from their regulatory lapses. U.S. firms operating overseas are not immune from the consequences of their actions, as attested by the impact of the Bhopal disaster on Union Carbide (which never recovered from the legal, financial, and reputational fallout from the event and was taken over by Dow Chemical in 2001) and decades of litigation against Chevron for alleged environmental pollution in Ecuador.[77] Defense firms historically have not experienced these legal repercussions overseas, despite the inherent potential for harm in the use of their products. Harm to civilians from

[74] Amnesty Int'l, *ICC Must Investigate Arms Company Executives Linked to Yemen War Crimes Violations* (Dec. 12, 2019), https://www.amnesty.org/en/latest/news/2019/12/icc-investigate-arms-companies-yemen-war-crimes-allegations.

[75] Fletcher, *supra* note 5, at 276–77.

[76] In fiscal year 2020 (FY20), Congress appropriated $133.8 billion for Pentagon procurement. DoD Congressional Budget Data, Def. Tech. Info. Ctr., FY2020 Appropriation Conference Report, Procurement (Dec. 19, 2019), https://budget.dtic.mil/pdfs/FY2020_pdfs/APPROP/PROC_Approp_1158SA.pdf. DoD FY20 research, development, test and evaluation (RDT&E) topped $104.4 billion. *Id.*, RDT&E (Dec. 19, 2019), https://budget.dtic.mil/pdfs/FY2020_pdfs/APPROP/RDTE_Approp_1158SA.pdf.

[77] *See, e.g.*, Ryan Villareal, *Chevron Still Won't Bow to Court Decision in $19 Billion Ecuador Pollution Case*, INT'L BUS. TIMES (Oct. 10, 2012), http://www.ibtimes.com/chevron-still-wont-bow-19b-court-decision-ecuador-pollution-case-844401?rel=rel1.

armed drone strikes, for example, has provoked fierce criticism in certain quarters and an intense international debate about the use of these weapons. Yet aside from some very limited, symbolic protests directed at American manufacturers of these products,[78] most of the opprobrium, both in the United States and abroad, is directed at the U.S. government and its leaders, not the manufacturers of the weapons.

States face continuous ethical dilemmas in their decisions whether or not to transfer arms. What are the implications of developing lethal autonomous weapons and should their use be permitted at all? A failing friend may need arms to support its national defense, but what if those arms fall into the hands of terrorists or insurgents when government forces are overrun? What if arms exported to a state for their national defense are turned against their own citizens? These legitimately hard decisions are properly left to states. What the commercial enterprise forgoes in markets due to its compact with the government, it gains in immunity from the censure that follows a policy failure—because, again, it is a failure of *policy*. Imagine an unrestricted arms market for arms, without any limitations on end use, end user, or type of armament, and it is easy to imagine the backlash in the form of reputational damage, civil and even criminal liability to which a private firm, which, for example, sold a particular indiscriminate and inhumane weapon to an unscrupulous end user resulting in injury and death to innocents, would be subject. Lawsuits faced by the automobile and petroleum industries might seem modest in comparison.

Governments need to be eternally vigilant in their commitment to arms transfers that accord with the highest standards of care with respect to minimizing the risk to abuses of human rights and violations of international humanitarian law, or contributing to regional instability and conflict. The United States is justifiably proud of its reputation as the "gold standard" of export controls.[79] Restraint in trade in arms and commitment to world peace is written into U.S. law, and the United States treats its commitments to multilateral regimes, treaties, and international arms embargoes seriously. For the private firms that produce the arms and whose products, since at least the Cold War, have been very much shaped by the unique partnership with their principal customer, the matter of ethical dilemmas in arms sales is largely negated by that partnership and the unique nature of export laws and policies which make the provision of arms a matter of national policy rather than a commercial choice.

[78] *San Diego Veterans for Peace to Lead Weekly Demonstrations Opposing Use of Predator Drone over U.S. Skies, Including Border Region*, E. County Mag. (Aug. 13, 2012), http://www.eastcountymagazine.org/san-diego-veterans-peace-lead-weekly-demonstrations-opposing-use-predator-drone-over-us-skies-includ.

[79] Erickson, *supra* note 25, at 452.

The fundamental ethical dilemma facing the defense industry then may be personal and individual: whether to participate in an industry that serves the national defense of one's country but that also may contribute to human suffering, even inadvertently, due to the nature of the product and its potential for misuse.

PART II

ETHICAL DILEMMAS RELATING TO NEW MILITARY TECHNOLOGIES

5

The Ethics of Better Weapons

A Soldier Lawyer's View

Thomas E. Ayres, Kevin Govern, and Michael W. Meier

Armed conflict has been with humanity since the dawn of time.[1] From the advent of simple weapons, such as knives, swords, and the bow and arrow, mankind has continually sought to develop more advanced ways to kill each other from greater distances. Advancements in technology really began to take off with World War II, which was the first war in history to use weapons that were significantly different from those when the war began.[2] New technologies and weapons, such as the jet aircraft, guided missiles, microwave radar, and proximity fuses, not to mention the atomic bomb, were all developed during the war.[3] World War II also led to another significant development in the United States. It was during this period that the U.S. military implemented a permanent research and development process for new weapons so that it could continue to maintain a technological advantage over any potential adversary, which President Dwight D. Eisenhower referred to as the "military-industrial complex."[4]

The quest for new technologies continued as part of the conflicts in Afghanistan, Iraq, Syria, and the counterterrorism operations as a result of the attack on September 11, 2001, which ushered in its own significant developments and advancements by the United States and its allies. Today, the United States uses stealth bombers to drop precision guided munitions; unmanned aerial systems (UASs) that operate using precision satellite navigation, such as the MQ-9 Reaper and MQ-1 Predator, now are armed and carry out kinetic attacks in

[1] David Hambling, *Introduction: Weapons Technology*, New Scientist (Sept. 4, 2006), https://www.newscientist.com/article/dn9980-introduction-weapons-technology/.

[2] Alex Roland, *War and Technology*, Foreign Pol'y Res. Inst. (Feb. 27, 2009), https://www.fpri.org/article/2009/02/war-and-technology/.

[3] *Id.*

[4] President Dwight D. Eisenhower, Farewell Address 3 (Jan. 17, 1961), https://www.eisenhowerlibrary.gov/sites/default/files/research/online-documents/farewell-address/1961-01-17-press-release.pdf. In his address, Eisenhower presciently cautioned that "[i]n the councils of government, we must guard against the acquisition of unwarranted influence, whether sought or unsought, by the military-industrial complex. The potential for the disastrous rise of misplaced power exists and will persist." *Id.*

Thomas E. Ayres, Kevin Govern, and Michael W. Meier, *The Ethics of Better Weapons* In: *Ethical Dilemmas in the Global Defense Industry*. Edited by: Daniel Schoeni and Tobias Vestner, Oxford University Press.
 DOI: 10.1093/oso/9780190675813.003.0006

addition to providing intelligence, surveillance, and reconnaissance. States now use or at least must be able to defend against cyber weapons and cyber capabilities.

The advancements over the past two decades are just a prelude to what is coming. The "Battlefield Next"[5] will likely include swarms of UASs or even fully autonomous weapons systems. Soldiers on the ground will be outfitted with exoskeletons to carry more equipment with less stress and operate with robotic logistic vehicles. The U.S. Army is developing artillery that will travel 1,000 miles. States are testing hypersonic weapons, and research is underway on human enhancement capabilities.[6] However, the most important advancement in technology will likely be artificial intelligence (AI).

Russian President Vladimir Putin stated, "Artificial intelligence is the future, not only for Russia, but for all humankind. It comes with colossal opportunities, but also threats that are difficult to predict. Whoever becomes the leader in this sphere will become the ruler of the world."[7] China is seeking to become the global leader in AI research by 2030. Although AI will provide advances in industry and medical research, states are also pursuing military applications, including autonomous weaponry, which is often referred to as the "third revolution in warfare," following gunpowder and nuclear weapons.[8]

Incorporating new technology into weapons and the conduct of warfare has many benefits; there is conclusive evidence that advancements in technology, such as precision guidance and the use of self-destruct or self-deactivation devices, results in reducing civilian casualties and collateral damage in military operations. However, history has also showed that in the hands of malicious actors, new weapons and technology can be misused. Therefore, it is important to ensure that states consider the legal and ethical implications as they develop new weapons or incorporate new technologies into existing weapons systems.

It may seem incongruous that new technologies can make warfare more ethical, but the Just War Theory[9] can help in thinking about the ethical issues raised

[5] *See* Lt. Gen. Charles Pede & Col. Peter Hayden, *The Eighteenth Gap: Preserving the Commander's Legal Maneuver Space on "Battlefield Next"*, MIL. REV. 8 (Mar.–Apr. 2021), https://www.armyupress.army.mil/Journals/Military-Review/English-Edition-Archives/March-April-2021/Pede-The-18th-Gap/.

[6] *See* Roxana Tiron, *Hypersonic Weapons: Who Has Them and Why It Matters*, BLOOMBERG (Oct. 27, 2021), https://www.bloomberg.com/news/articles/2021-10-27/hypersonic-weapons-who-has-them-and-why-it-matters-quicktake; Adam Henschke, *"Supersoldiers": Ethical Concerns in Human Enhancement Technologies*, HUMANITARIAN L. & POL'Y (July 3, 2017), https://blogs.icrc.org/law-and-policy/2017/07/03/supersoldiers-ethical-concerns-human-enhancement-technologies-2/.

[7] James Vincent, *Putin Says the Nation that Leads in AI "Will Be the Ruler of the World"*, VERGE (Sept. 4, 2017), https://www.theverge.com/2017/9/4/16251226/russia-ai-putin-rule-the-world.

[8] Kai-Fu Lee, *The Third Revolution in Warfare*, ATLANTIC (Sept. 11, 2021), https://www.theatlantic.com/technology/archive/2021/09/i-weapons-are-third-revolution-warfare/620013/.

[9] Igor Primoratz, *Michael Walzer's Just War Theory: Some Issues of Responsibility*, 5 ETHICAL THEORY & MORAL PRAC. 222 (Just War Theory deals with the morality of war in two aspects. It

by issue of emerging technology and armed conflict. U.S. domestic law and our legal obligations under the laws of war and various treaties, such as the Geneva Conventions and the UN Charter, require incorporating ethical considerations into the development of weapons.[10] So, how does the United States ensure that it incorporates legal and ethical considerations in new weapons that it develops, uses, and transfers?

This chapter will look at five ways that the United States incorporates legal and ethical considerations into the weapons development process to ensure new weapons that are developed, used, and transferred in accordance with the law of armed conflict (LOAC)[11] and U.S. domestic law. First, it will look at the fundamental principles of LOAC and how they help minimize suffering in war and underpin the weapons development process.[12] Second, this chapter will consider that there is nothing in LOAC that requires adversaries to engage in a "fair fight," nor does it prohibit the use of new technology to develop advanced offensive or protective weaponry by a party to the conflict.[13] Third, this chapter will examine the U.S. weapons review process for the acquisition or development of new weapons to ensure that those weapons are in compliance with the principles of LOAC.[14] Fourth, it will explore how emerging technologies will lead to new weapons. These new weapons can provide better protection of civilians in armed conflict as advanced features may better distinguish between combatants and civilians and military objectives and civilian or protected objects as well as help reduce collateral damage and minimize suffering.[15] Finally, this chapter will review how the United States, through the Arms Export Control Act (AECA)[16]

first looks at the conditions for a morally justified decision to go to war (*jus ad bellum*). Second, it considers what actions can be taken during the course of waging war (*jus in bello*)).

10 Trae Stephens, *The Ethics of Defense Technology Development: An Investor's Perspective*, MEDIUM (Dec. 4, 2019), https://medium.com/@traestephens/the-ethics-of-defense-technology-development-an-investors-perspective-45c71bf6e6af.

11 *See* U.S. DEP'T DEF. DIRECTIVE 2311.01, *DoD Law of War Program* 16 (July 2, 2020) [hereinafter DODD 2311.01] ("Sometimes also called the 'law of armed conflict' [LOAC] or 'international humanitarian law' [IHL], the law of war is specifically intended to address the circumstances of armed conflict.").

12 UN News, *Wars Have Rules: 5 Things the UN Humanitarian Chief Wants Countries to Tackle So Human Suffering in Conflict Can Be Minimized*, UNITED NATIONS, https://news.un.org/en/story/2019/04/1035861.

13 *See* NAT'L SEC. L. DEP'T., THE JUDGE ADVOCATE GEN.'S LEGAL CTR. & SCH., U.S. ARMY, OPERATIONAL LAW HANDBOOK 72 (2021).

14 *Id.* at 72 (citing U.S. Dep't Def. Directive 5000.01, *The Defense Acquisition System*, para. E1.1.15 (Sept. 8, 2020)).

15 *Id.* at 60.

16 International Security Assistance and Arms Export Control Act of 1976, P.L. 94-329; 22 U.S.C. § 2751 *et seq.* (1976) [hereinafter Arms Export Control Act].

and the Foreign Assistance Act (FAA),[17] ensures the weapons it sells or transfers to third parties don't wind up in the hands of irresponsible or malicious actors.[18]

1. LOAC Was Developed with the Intention to Minimize Suffering in War

War has been described as a violent clash of interests characterized by the use of force.[19] However, Article 22 of the Annexed Regulations of Hague IV provides: "The right of belligerents to adopt means of injuring the enemy is not unlimited."[20] LOAC, which is also referred to as the law of war or international humanitarian law (IHL), is the body of international law specially adapted to war.[21] For the United States, LOAC includes those treaties that it has ratified, as well as customary international law.[22] LOAC is composed of international rules that define what is permitted and prohibited during an armed conflict.

The International Committee of the Red Cross (ICRC) notes that the main purpose of LOAC is to "maintain some humanity in armed conflict, save lives and help reduce suffering."[23] It does so by protecting combatants, noncombatants, and civilians from unnecessary suffering; providing certain fundamental protections for persons who fall into the hands of the enemy, particularly prisoners of war, civilians, and military wounded, sick, and shipwrecked;

[17] The Foreign Assistance Act of 1961, P.L. 87-195; 22 U.S.C. § 2151 *et seq.* (1961) [hereinafter Foreign Assistance Act.].

[18] *See, e.g.*, U.S. Office of the Sec'y of Def., Department of Defense Budget Fiscal Year 2019 (Feb. 2018) Counter-Islamic State of Iraq and Syria (ISIS) Train and Equip Fund (CTEF).

[19] For example, Dep't of the Army, Field Manual 3-24, *Counterinsurgency*, 1-1 (para. 1-1) (Dec. 2006) explains:

> Insurgency and counterinsurgency (COIN) are complex subsets of warfare. Globalization, technological advancement, urbanization, and extremists who conduct suicide attacks for their cause have certainly influenced contemporary conflict; however, warfare in the 21st century retains many of the characteristics it has exhibited since ancient times. Warfare remains a violent clash of interests between organized groups characterized by the use of force. Achieving victory still depends on a group's ability to mobilize support for its political interests (often religiously or ethnically based) and to generate enough violence to achieve political consequences. Means to achieve these goals are not limited to conventional forces employed by nation-states.

See also U.S. Marine Corps, Marine Corps Doctrinal Publication 1, *Warfighting*, 3 (June 20, 1997) (explaining that war is "a violent clash of interests between or among organized groups characterized by the use of military force.").

[20] Hague Convention (IV) Respecting the Laws and Customs of War on Land of 18 October 1907 (36 Stat. 2277, TS 539, 1 Bevans 631), art. 22 of the Annexed Regulations.

[21] Office of Gen. Counsel, U.S. Dep't of Defense, Law of War Manual § 1.3.2.1 (rev. ed., Dec. 2016) [hereinafter DoD Law of War Manual].

[22] *Id.* at § 1.3.

[23] Int'l Comm. of the Red Cross, *The Laws of War in a Nutshell* (Oct. 19, 2016), https://www.icrc.org/en/document/what-are-rules-of-war-Geneva-Conventions.

facilitating the restoration of peace; assisting the commander in ensuring the disciplined and efficient use of military force; and preserving the professionalism and humanity of combatants.[24]

Three interdependent principles—military necessity, humanity, and honor—provide the foundation for other derivative LOAC principles—most importantly, distinction and proportionality.[25] The 2019 Army Field Manual 6-27, provides:

> LOAC principles work as interdependent and reinforcing parts of a coherent system. *Military necessity* justifies certain actions necessary to defeat the enemy as quickly and efficiently as possible that are not prohibited by LOAC. Conversely, *humanity* forbids certain actions unnecessary to achieve that object. *Distinction* underpins the parties' responsibility to comport their behavior with military necessity, humanity, and proportionality by requiring parties to a conflict to recognize and respect certain legal categories: principally, the distinctions between combatants and civilians, and between military objectives and civilian objects. *Proportionality* requires that even when actions may be justified by military necessity, such actions cannot result in excessive civilian loss. Lastly, *honor* supports the entire system and gives parties confidence in it, and provides legitimacy to the entire endeavor[26] (emphasis added).

Each of these LOAC principles is explored in further detail in the following.

1.1. Military Necessity

The principle of military necessity guides when certain persons and property may be the object of an attack. Military necessity not only justifies violence and destruction but also permits certain incidental harms that inevitably result from the actions it justifies. Importantly, military necessity permits the use of overwhelming force because the object of war is not simply to defeat the enemy, but to do so as quickly and efficiently as possible. Commanders are not required to use the minimum force necessary in a particular fight; such a limitation would unnecessarily prolong the conflict and increase suffering.[27]

24 DoD Law of War Manual, *supra* note 21, at § 1.3.4.

25 U.S. Dep't of the Army & U.S. Marine Corps FM 6-27/MCTP 11-10C, The Commander's Handbook on the Law of Land Warfare, Change 1, para. 1-19 (Aug. 2019) [hereinafter FM 6-27].

26 *Id.* at para. 1-21.

27 *Id.* at para. 1-24.

1.2. Humanity

Humanity is the principle that forbids the infliction of suffering, injury, or destruction unnecessary to accomplish a legitimate military purpose.[28] Humanity is best viewed as the limitation on military necessity. This principle was first codified in the United States via General Order No. 100, the *Instructions for the Government of Armies of the United States in the Field*, commonly known as the Lieber Code, which was written by Professor Francis Lieber and approved by President Abraham Lincoln during the Civil War in 1863.[29] Article 16 of the Lieber Code exhorted that "[m]ilitary necessity does not admit to cruelty—that is, the infliction of suffering for the sake of suffering or for revenge."[30] Since that time, treaties such as the Hague and Geneva Conventions have been "negotiated with the understanding that suffering and destruction are unavoidably part of war."[31]

[28] *See, e.g.*, CHIEF DEFENCE STAFF (CANADA), B-GJ-005-104/FP-021, LAW OF ARMED CONFLICT AT THE OPERATIONAL AND TACTICAL LEVELS para. 202(6) (2001) (saying humanity "forbids the infliction of suffering, injury or destruction not actually necessary for the accomplishment of legitimate military purposes."); U.K. MINISTRY OF DEFENCE, THE JOINT SERVICE MANUAL OF THE LAW OF ARMED CONFLICT para. 2.4 (2004) (writing, "Humanity forbids the infliction of suffering, injury, or destruction not actually necessary for the accomplishment of legitimate military purposes"); MORRIS GREENSPAN, MODERN LAW OF LAND WARFARE 315 (1959) (explaining that the principle of humanity "forbids the employment of all such kinds and degrees of violence as are not necessary for the purpose of the war"); U.K. WAR OFFICE, MANUAL OF MILITARY LAW, PART III: THE LAW OF WAR ON LAND para. 3 (1958) (defining humanity as the principle "according to which kinds and degrees of violence which are not necessary for the purpose of war are not permitted to a belligerent"); LASSA OPPENHEIM, INTERNATIONAL LAW, VOLUME II: DISPUTES, WAR AND NEUTRALITY 227 (Hersch Lauterpacht ed., 7th ed. 1952) (stating that humanity "postulates that all such kinds and degrees of violence as are not necessary for the overpowering of the opponent should not be permitted to a belligerent"); U.S. WAR DEP'T, FIELD MANUAL 27-10, RULES OF LAND WARFARE para. 4b (1940) (defining the principle of humanity as "prohibiting employment of any such kind or degree of violence as is not actually necessary for the purpose of the war"); U.S. WAR DEP'T, OFFICE OF THE CHIEF OF STAFF, RULES OF LAND WARFARE para. 9 (Apr. 25, 1914) (explaining that the principle of humanity "says that all such kinds and degrees of violence as are not necessary for the purpose of war are not permitted to a belligerent").

[29] FRANCIS LIEBER, INSTRUCTIONS FOR THE GOVERNMENT OF ARMIES OF THE UNITED STATES IN THE FIELD, GENERAL ORDERS NO. 100 (promulgated Apr. 24, 1863) (Washington, Government Printing Office, 1898) [hereinafter Lieber Code]. The *DoD Manual Law of War Manuel* also notes:

> A similar code related to naval warfare titled The Law and Usages of War at Sea: A Naval War Code was prepared by then-Captain Charles H. Stockton and approved by President William McKinley in 1900. The War Department published instructions for the armed land forces of the United States in a 1914 manual titled Rules of Land Warfare, which was updated in 1917, 1934, and 1940.
>
> After World War II, in connection with U.S. ratification of the 1949 Geneva Conventions, various DoD departments subsequently published manuals and publications in international law applicable in peace and war.

DOD LAW OF WAR MANUAL, *supra* note 21, at iii.

[30] *Id.* at art. 16.

[31] *See, e.g.*, Edward R. Cummings, Acting Assistant Legal Adviser for Politico-Military Affairs, Remarks at Symposium at Brooklyn Law School (Sept. 25, 1982), *in* DEP'T OF STATE, 3 CUMULATIVE DIGEST OF UNITED STATES PRACTICE IN INTERNATIONAL LAW 1981–88, at 3421, 3422 (1995).

This avoidance of unnecessary suffering remains important given global trends regarding warfare. The RAND Corporation reflected that from the 1960s through 2014, armed conflicts have generally become less frequent and interstate warfare (i.e., warfare between states) has become almost rare. In 2016, due to the conflicts in Syria and Ukraine, there was an increase in armed conflicts around the world.[32] The United Nations confirms this observation such that

> [g]lobally, the absolute number of war deaths has been declining since 1946 . . . yet, conflict and violence are currently on the rise, with many conflicts today waged between non-state actors such as political militias, criminal, and international terrorist groups. Unresolved regional tensions, a breakdown in the rule of law, absent or co-opted state institutions, illicit economic gain, and the scarcity of resources exacerbated by climate change, have become dominant drivers of conflict. In 2016, more countries experienced violent conflict than at any point in almost 30 years.[33]

Whether of brief duration, as with the air and ground campaigns of Operation Desert Storm,[34] or a much longer conflict, such as the 20-year conflict in Afghanistan,[35] the principle of humanity and the avoidance of unnecessary suffering remains a paramount consideration.

1.3. Honor

Honor demands a certain amount of fairness in warfare and a certain mutual respect between opposing forces. It means carrying out, acting, and living the core values of the U.S. Department of Defense (DoD), such as integrity, ethics, loyalty, and courage.[36] Honor has been a vital part of the development of LOAC and

[32] Thomas Szayna et al., What Are the Trends in Armed Conflicts, and What Do They Mean for U.S. Defense Policy?, RAND 4 (2017), https://www.rand.org/pubs/research_reports/RR1904.html.

[33] *A New Era of Conflict and Violence*, United Nations, https://www.un.org/en/un75/new-era-conflict-and-violence (last visited Jan. 1, 2022).

[34] The air campaign of Operation Desert Storm began on January 16, 1991; the ground assault commenced on February 23, 1991; and coalition attacks against Iraq ended on February 28, 1991. *See Gulf War Fast Facts*, CNN (July 29, 2020), https://www.cnn.com/2013/09/15/world/meast/gulf-war-fast-facts/index.html.

[35] Operation Enduring Freedom began on October 7, 2001; the United States and NATO allies ended their combat mission with Afghanistan on December 28, 2014. *See Operation Enduring Freedom Fast Facts*, CNN (Oct. 4, 2020), https://www.cnn.com/2013/10/28/world/operation-enduring-freedom-fast-facts/index.html.

[36] Military Leadership Diversity Comm'n, Department of Defense Core Values, DoD Issue Paper #6, Definition of Diversity (2009), https://diversity.defense.gov/Portals/51/Documents/Resources/Commission/docs/Issue%20Papers/Paper%2006%20-%20DOD%20Core%20Values.pdf.

continues to give it vitality. Honor also requires adherence to LOAC by parties to a conflict regardless of the enemy's level of compliance.

Honor reflects the idea that parties to a conflict must accept that certain limits exist on their ability to conduct hostilities. Honor does not set out what those limits are, but rather it reflects that those engaged in armed conflict accept that there are legal limits. Honor requires individuals make a good faith effort to comply with LOAC. It also demands a certain mutual respect between opposing military forces. Honor means opposing forces should respect each other outside of the fighting because they share a profession and they fight one another on behalf of their respective parties and not out of a personal hostility.[37]

1.4. Distinction

In 1996, the International Court of Justice counseled:

> The cardinal principles contained in the texts constituting the fabric of humanitarian law are the following. The first is aimed at the protection of the civilian population and civilian objects and establishes the distinction between combatants and non-combatants; States must never make civilians the object of attack and must consequently never use weapons that are incapable of distinguishing between civilian and military targets.[38]

Although the principle of distinction is one of the foundational principles of LOAC, it was not codified in a treaty until the adoption of the 1977 Additional Protocol I (API) to the Geneva Conventions.[39] Article 48 of API, which is titled the Basic Rule, requires that parties to an international armed conflict (IAC) "at all times [to] distinguish between the civilian population and combatants and between civilian objects and military objectives and accordingly . . . direct their operations only against military objectives."[40] With respect to non-international armed conflicts (NIAC), Additional Protocol II (APII) used different language. Article 13 of APII provides that "[t]he civilian population as such, as well as

[37] FM 6-27, *supra* note 25, paras. 1-31, 1-32, 1-33.

[38] *Legality of the Threat or Use of Nuclear Weapons*, Advisory Opinion, 1996 I.C.J. Rep. para. 78 (July 8).

[39] Protocol Additional to the Geneva Conventions of 12 August 1949, and Relating to the Protection of Victims of International Armed Conflicts, 1977, 1125 U.N.T.S. 3 [hereinafter Additional Protocol I].

[40] *Id.* at art. 48. *See also* Geoffrey S. Corn, *Targeting, Distinction and the Long War: Guarding Against Conflation of Cause and Responsibility*, 46 ISR. Y.B. ON HUM. RTS. 146 (2016).

individual civilians, shall not be the object of attack."[41] Although Article 13 of APII imposes an obligation to attack only noncivilian persons, it does not set forth a direct prohibition of attacking civilian objects.

The United States is not a party to the Additional Protocols and therefore not legally bound by the treaty provisions. It addresses the principle of distinction in the *DoD Law of War Manual*, which is that "[p]arties to a conflict must apply a framework of legal classes for persons and objects by: (1) discriminating in conducting attacks against the enemy; and (2) distinguishing a party's own person and objects."[42]

Distinction's principal requirement is to separate combatants from the civilian population. However, it is broader than just distinguishing between combatants and civilians as there are certain military personnel, such as military medical and religious personnel, who may not be made the object of an attack.[43] When engaging in an attack, combatants must discriminate between a military objective and a civilian object in good faith based on the information available to them at the time.[44]

The second part of the distinction principle is the obligation of belligerents to distinguish themselves from the civilian population.[45] For example, military members wear uniforms to set themselves apart from civilians. Parties to the conflict must use their best efforts to distinguish or separate their military forces from the civilian population to the maximum extent feasible.[46]

1.5. Proportionality

In armed conflict, despite best efforts of responsible military decision makers, incidental harm to the civilian population and civilian objects is an unfortunate but inevitable consequence. The principle of proportionality recognizes this but still requires combatants to refrain from attacks in which the expected loss or injury to civilians and damage to civilian objects incidental to such attacks would be excessive in relation to the concrete and direct military advantage expected to be gained. Proportionality incorporates the requirement to take feasible precautions in order to reduce the risk of harm to civilians, other protected persons, and civilian objects.[47] This means that even when a party to the conflict

[41] Protocol Additional to the Geneva Conventions of 12 August 1949, and Relating to the Protection of Victims of Non-International Armed Conflicts, art. 13, adopted June 8, 1977, 1125 U.N.T.S. 609 [hereinafter Additional Protocol II].

[42] DoD Law of War Manual, *supra* note 21, at § 2.5.

[43] *Id.* at § 2.5.1.

[44] *Id.* at § 2.5.2.

[45] Corn, *supra* note 40, at 148.

[46] *Id.* at 152.

[47] FM 6-27, *supra* note 25, at para. 1-44.

may target a particular military objective under LOAC, they are prohibited from causing incidental harm to civilians or to civilian objects excessive in relation to the concrete and direct military advantage expected to be gained from targeting the military objective. The principle of proportionality complements the principle of distinction and both principles derive from military necessity and humanity.[48]

Each of these LOAC principles provide the foundation for the specific LOAC rules found in treaty law. They are used by military practitioners to interpret specific treaty rules and customary international law and to help them understand how LOAC operates as a coherent system to regulate the conduct of hostilities.[49] These principles are incorporated into military doctrine that provides the basis for effective military operations and the ethical standards of the military profession.[50]

2. LOAC Does Not Require a Fair Fight, Nor Does It Prohibit the Use of New Technology to Develop Advanced Offensive or Protective Weaponry

In 2002, one of us served as a judge advocate and legal adviser to U.S. forces in Afghanistan when his unit suffered their first combat casualty. A mother and father had lost their only son, a sister had lost her beloved brother, and the unit felt the sense of guilt, anger, and deep personal grief that comes with the loss of a brother in arms. As with every U.S. combat casualty, an investigation was conducted to learn from this tragic event and, to the extent possible in armed conflict, prevent its recurrence. This investigation brought into focus for this judge advocate that there is nothing in LOAC[51] that requires a military force to subject itself to a "fair fight."

Professor Laurie Blank succinctly and correctly points out that LOAC "does not require a 'fair fight'. Rather, it requires that each side 'fight fairly.'"[52] As Professor Blank notes, this is "not simply a play on words" but an essential component of LOAC.[53] There is no rule or principle of LOAC that requires a party

[48] *Id.*
[49] *Id.* at 1-20.
[50] *Id.* at 1-22.
[51] *See* DoD Directive 2311.01, *supra* note 11, at 16 (stating, "Sometimes also called the 'law of armed conflict' [LOAC] or 'international humanitarian law'[IHL], the law of war is specifically intended to address the circumstances of armed conflict.").
[52] Kenneth Anderson, *Laurie Blank on Mark Mazzetti's "The Drone Zone"—Last in Series from Lewis, Dunlap, Rona, Corn, and Anderson*, Lawfare (July 21, 2012, 10:37 AM), https://www.lawfareblog.com/laurie-blank-mark-mazzettis-drone-zone-last-series-lewis-dunlap-rona-corn-and-anderson.
[53] *Id.*

to a conflict only to fight an adversary using the same set of tactics, manpower, weapons, or other tools available to that adversary. Similarly, nowhere does the law require that one party use only tanks against the other's tanks, for example, rather than air assets. What the law does require is that parties to a conflict adhere to the fundamental obligations the law sets forth—that is, fight fairly.

Throughout history, man has sought to gain an advantage in warfare. The ability to fight from outside the range of the enemy's weapons is a considerable advantage. Given this survival instinct, it is axiomatic that no soldier wants a fair fight. Although this instinct can motivate service members and nations alike, LOAC tempers that inclination—at least for those that adhere to it. The U.S. military punctiliously adheres to LOAC.[54] The United States' Department of Defense Law of War Program, first promulgated in the aftermath of the My Lai massacre in Vietnam, codifies that commitment.[55] The U.S. adherence requires consideration of both the justice in engaging in a given armed conflict (*jus ad bellum*) and of the means and weapons of war (*jus in bellum*).[56] Today, the United States has robust processes to implement LOAC through training of its military forces, the implementation of regulations and procedures that set out how to report of incidents involving alleged violations, conduct investigations and reviews of incidents, and appropriate corrective actions.[57]

For an individual soldier, a fair fight means an equal or better chance that all the individual has pledged to protect, and their own life, will survive. Any soldier who desires to live would rather be in a tank than armed with a rifle, or even better, flying a plane with a maximum effective range of twice or three times the distance of their adversary. Just as long-bowmen decimated knights at Agincourt, or radar made possible the aerial defense of the Battle of Britain, the Taliban in Afghanistan use garage-door-openers or washing-machine-timers to kill while minimizing risk to themselves. More broadly, nations share the same survival instinct and thus favor developing more advanced weapons.

The holy grail of technological efforts is to achieve "overmatch." Overmatch puts the enemy in peril without risking one's own life. LOAC places no limitation on overmatch achieved by means of technological advantage. Although certain weapons may be perceived as cruel, and military necessity cannot justify cruelty or wanton violence,[58] no provision of LOAC prohibits the development of a

[54] *See, e.g.*, Bryan A. Frederick, The Continued Evolution of U.S. Law of Armed Conflict (2015).

[55] *See* DoDD 2311.01, *supra* note 11, at 1.2.

[56] *See generally* DoD Law of War Manual, *supra* note 21.

[57] *See* DoDD 2311.01, *supra* note 11, at 1.2.c.(4).

[58] United States v. List, et al. (The Hostage Case), XI Trials of War Criminals Before the NMT, 1253–54 (explaining that military necessity "does not permit the killing of innocent inhabitants for purposes of revenge or the satisfaction of a lust to kill" and that "[i]t does not admit the wanton devastation of a district or the willful infliction of suffering upon its inhabitants for the sake of suffering

superior weapon. For instance, an 1899 Hague Convention banned bullets that "expand or flatten easily in the human body," on the premise they caused unnecessary and inhumane injury.[59] As will be discussed later, new weapons that are developed receive a legal review,[60] and if it was determined that the weapon or munition caused unnecessary suffering, it would be illegal; however, a weapon with longer range, better protective armament, or better ability to sight a target would certainly not be prohibited *per se* for causing unnecessary suffering. In addition, the ability to better sight a target and other advanced features would likely increase its ability to discriminate between combatants and civilians. To study arms races, or national courting of defense contractors, is to understand the desire to acquire such technological advantage. Nations continually seek such an advantage to ensure their service members are not resigned to a fair fight.

One may counter that such one-upmanship is ludicrous and leads to such illogical results as the nuclear arms race. Yet Leon Trotsky, the Russian revolutionary, said, "You may not be interested in war, but war is interested in you."[61] As a previous National Security Advisor noted, "We have a perfect record in predicting the future: we have been wrong 100% of the time."[62] If one looks at Afghanistan, the length and the focus, and the similarities with the rhythm of invasion, budding insurgency, surge, counterinsurgency, and transition to sovereignty may make it seem as if we have seen what all future conflicts will look like.

alone"); Lieber Code, *supra* note 28, art. 16 (stating, "Military necessity does not admit to cruelty—that is, the infliction of suffering for the sake of suffering or for revenge").

[59] Hague Declaration IV, Declaration III Concerning the Prohibition of the Use of Expanding Bullets, July 29, 1899, 26 Martens Nouveau Recueil (ser. 2) 1002 (entered into force Sept. 4, 1900), https://ihl-databases.icrc.org/ihl/INTRO/170%3FOpenDocument.

[60] *See, e.g., A Guide to the Legal Review of New Weapons: Means and Methods of Warfare, Measures to Implement Article 36 of Additional Protocol I of 1977*, INT'L COMM. OF THE RED CROSS (Nov. 2006) [hereinafter ICRC Guide], https://www.icrc.org/en/publication/0902-guide-legal-review-new-weapons-means-and-methods-warfare-measures-implement-article. The ICRC asserts:

> The requirement that the legality of all new weapons, means and methods of warfare be systematically assessed is arguably one that applies to all States, regardless of whether or not they are party to Additional Protocol I. It flows logically from the truism that States are prohibited from using illegal weapons, means and methods of warfare or from using weapons, means and methods of warfare in an illegal manner. The faithful and responsible application of its international law obligations would require a State to ensure that the new weapons, means and methods of warfare it develops or acquires will not violate these obligations. Carrying out legal reviews of new weapons is of particular importance today in light of the rapid development of new weapons technologies.

Id. at 4.

[61] This was attributed to Leon Trotsky in an epigraph in *Night Soldiers: A Novel* (1988) by Alan Furst, but it may actually be a revision of a statement earlier attributed to Trotsky: "You may not be interested in the dialectic, but the dialectic is interested in you." *See, e.g.*, MICHAEL WALZER, JUST AND UNJUST WARS: A MORAL ARGUMENT WITH HISTORICAL ILLUSTRATIONS (2000).

[62] David Feith, *H.R. McMaster: The Warrior's-Eye View of Afghanistan*, WALL ST. J. (May 11, 2012), https://www.wsj.com/articles/SB10001424052702304451104577392281146871796.

It is often said that generals are always preparing to fight the last war and it may seem that our future wars will—like America's wars in the past two decades—resemble police actions more than high-intensity conflicts. However, in a world that periodically produces menaces such as Adolph Hitler, the Khmer Rouge, the genocide in Rwanda, Osama Bin Laden, and more recently the appearance of the Islamic State, ceding technological advantage to other states or armed groups is not only illogical but perilous.[63] As the late Donald Rumsfeld would say, weakness is provocative.[64]

Certainly service members, and nations for that matter, have attempted to rationalize and justify barbarous behavior by appealing to self-defense. Some equate the development of weapons that deliver "stand-off," killing without risk, as equally barbarous. For the soldier, for the nation, where is the fairness? Where is the honor? Where is the justice in such warfare? Is it ethical or legal? As suggested previously, that compound question can be reduced to two components found in the Just War Theory. First, a soldier relies upon the notion that the nation to which she has subjugated her will, and sworn her oath, will only engage in just wars—*jus ad bellum*. Secondly, the U.S. soldier is trained and required to comport herself during the war justly—*jus in bello*.[65]

It is not the intent of this chapter to plumb the depths of those two concepts. Nor will it examine exhaustively the extent to which the U.S. armed forces educate their service members or train upon and respect the legal and ethical requirements of both concepts. However, what is also fully apparent to the experienced soldier is that credibility is the most paramount resource to ultimate both survival and victory. Individual tactical victories can be attained by overmatch, but to return home for good (without the prospect of a return deployment where the enemy has been given the time to creatively undermine the overmatch or

[63] For another recent example, *see* Steven Lee Meyers & Eric Schmitt, *Russian Military Uses Syria as Proving Ground, and West Takes Notice*, N.Y. Times (Oct. 14, 2015), https://www.nytimes.com/2015/10/15/world/middleeast/russian-military-uses-syria-as-proving-ground-and-west-takes-notice.html.

> Two weeks of air and missile strikes in Syria have given Western intelligence and military officials a deeper appreciation of the transformation that Russia's military has undergone under President Vladimir V. Putin, showcasing its ability to conduct operations beyond its borders and providing a public demonstration of new weaponry, tactics and strategy.
>
> The strikes have involved aircraft never before tested in combat, including the Sukhoi Su-34 strike fighter, which NATO calls the Fullback, and a ship-based cruise missile fired more than 900 miles from the Caspian Sea, which, according to some analysts, surpasses the American equivalent in technological capability.

Id.

[64] Jim Rutenberg, *In Farewell, Rumsfeld Warns Weakness Is "Provocative"*, N.Y. Times (Dec. 16, 2006), https://www.nytimes.com/2006/12/16/washington/16prexy.html.

[65] *See, e.g.*, Igor Primoratz, *Michael Walzer's Just War Theory: Some Issues of Responsibility*, 5 Ethical Theory & Moral Prac. 222.

national will) requires credibility. And, that paramount resource, credibility, is and can only be gained and maintained when fighting a just war and fighting it fairly.

3. The United States Reviews All New Weapons to Ensure Compliance with LOAC

The first two sections dealt with the basic principles of LOAC that service members and commanders must intimately understand and be able to apply armed conflict to ensure that the weapons of war they use are in compliance with the law of armed conflict. This next section will consider how the United States, as well as other states, develop and field weapons.

In his book *Weapons and the Law of Armed Conflict*, Bill Boothby argues that all states are bound by the "customary elements of weapons law," and must ensure that when acquiring or developing new weapons that they comply with a nation's applicable laws and treaty obligations.[66] Additional Protocol I to the Geneva Conventions imposes an explicit obligation in Article 36 on those states that are party to it.[67] It provides:

> In the study, development, acquisition or adoption of a new weapon, means or method of warfare, a High Contracting Party is under an obligation to determine whether its employment would, in some or all circumstances, be prohibited by this Protocol or by any other rule of international law applicable to the High Contracting Party.[68]

Although this requires that a review take place, it is silent on the format for such a review.[69] Article 36 leaves it up to the individual states to review and determine for themselves whether the new weapon or means or method of warfare in question is prohibited by international law.[70]

Boothby also argues that states that are not party to Additional Protocol I, such as the United States, have "an applied obligation" to conduct such review as noted by the practice of certain states prior to the adoption of Additional Protocol I.[71] The ICRC takes the same view. In its 2006 *Guide to the Legal Review of New Weapons, Means and Methods of Warfare*, the ICRC maintains that the

[66] William H. Boothby, Weapons and the Law of Armed Conflict 341 (2d ed. 2016).
[67] *Id.*
[68] Additional Protocol I, *supra* note 39, at art. 36..
[69] Boothby, *supra* note 67, at 343.
[70] *Id.*
[71] *Id.*

requirement to assess the "legality of all new weapons, means and methods of warfare is arguably one that applies to *all* States, regardless of whether or not they are party to Additional Protocol I."[72] However, the United States disagrees and denies that Article 36 creates a customary law requirement that is binding on nonsignatories.

The United States' view is that there is insufficient state practice and *opinio juris* to conclude a customary law obligation to review the legality of weapons for consistency with LOAC exists.[73] First, the provision in the 1977 Additional Protocol I to the 1949 Geneva Conventions relating to the review of the legality of new weapons was a new provision at the time of its adoption. Second, even including parties to the 1977 Additional Protocol I, "relatively few states are believed to have systems for the legal review of weapons."[74] In 2015, the Stockholm International Peace Research Institute (SIPRI) reported "only a limited number of states (12 to 15) are known to have a weapon review mechanism in place,"[75] making this a distinctly minority practice rather than a requirement that should be foisted on nonsignatories under the guise of broadly accepted customary law.

Notwithstanding its nuanced position on the existence of an obligation under customary law, the United States does have practices and procedures by which it largely complies with the obligations set forth in API. It has a long-standing policy, which predates the adoption of API. This policy requires a legal review of the intended acquisition of a weapon system to ensure its development and use is consistent with IHL.[76] Each military service has designated an attorney authorized to conduct such legal reviews on its behalf, and each has issued its own regulation implementing this policy.[77] The legal review of the acquisition or procurement of a weapon system should occur at the earliest stage of the acquisition process to ensure its legality under IHL, domestic law, and international law, including the research and development phase.[78]

[72] ICRC Guide, *supra* note 61, at 4 (emphasis added).

[73] *U.S Department of Defense Response to Stockholm International Peace Research Institute (SIPRI) "Questionnaire on Article 36 Review Process"*, Dep't of Def. Office of Gen. Counsel, Other Official Documents Related to the Law of War 40 (Sept. 1, 2017), https://ogc.osd.mil/Portals/99/sipri_questionnaire_on_article_36_review_process_usa_response_final.pdf [hereinafter DoD SIPRI Response].

[74] *Id.*

[75] Vincent Boulanin, *Implementing Article 36 Weapon Reviews in the Light of Increasing Autonomy in Weapons Systems*, SIPRI Insights on Peace & Security 1, 17 (Nov. 2015), https://www.sipri.org/sites/default/files/files/insight/SIPRIInsight1501.pdf.

[76] DoD Law of War Manual, *supra* note 21, at § 6.2.

[77] *See, e.g.*, U.S. Dep't of Army, Regulation 27-53, Legal Review of Weapons and Weapons Systems (Oct. 23, 2019) [hereinafter AR 27-53]; U.S. Sec'y of the Navy, Instruction 5000.2E, Dep't of Navy Implementation & Operation of the Defense Acquisition System and the Joint Capabilities Integration and Development System (2011); U.S. Dep't of the Air Force Instruction 51-401, Law of War (Aug. 3, 2018) [hereinafter DAFI 51-401].

[78] *See* DoD Law of War Manual, *supra* note 21, at § 6.2.2; DAFI 51-401, *supra* note 78, at § 5; AR 27-53, *supra* note 78, at § 6.e.

The weapons review should consider the following questions to determine whether the weapon system is prohibited:

1. Whether there is a specific rule of law, whether as a treaty obligation or viewed as customary international law, prohibiting or restricting the use of the weapon.[79]
2. If there is no specific prohibition or restriction, then the review should determine whether the weapon's intended use is calculated to cause superfluous injury.[80]
3. Whether the weapon is inherently indiscriminate.[81]

In addition to addressing these questions, it is important for the review to determine if there are legal restrictions on the use specific to that weapon or if there are other practical measures needed, such as training or rules of engagement specific to the weapon.[82] In short, context and the intended use of a weapon system matter.

Turning to each of the three questions, the first question of whether there is a specific rule of law or treaty obligation prohibits or restricts a particular weapon or weapons system, any weapon system would be prohibited if it used poison, poisonous gases, chemical weapons, or biological weapons, in contravention of those treaties. Further, a state must look at its own treaty obligations to determine whether a particular weapon would be prohibited or restricted, such as under the Convention on Certain Conventional Weapons, which prohibits or restricts blinding lasers, certain types of mines, or those weapons that result in nondetectable fragments.[83] Once it has been determined there is no specific prohibition or restriction, the reviewer looks at the next two questions to determine if the weapon is calculated to cause superfluous injury or unnecessary suffering.[84]

The second question looks to determine whether the weapon's use is calculated to cause unnecessary suffering/superfluous injury. The terms "unnecessary suffering" and "superfluous injury" are generally synonymous.[85] This analysis

[79] *See* DoD Law of War Manual, *supra* note 21, at § 6.2.2; DAFI 51-401, *supra* note 78, at § 7.1.1; AR 27-53, *supra* note 78, at § 8.a.(3).

[80] *See* DoD Law of War Manual, *supra* note 21, at § 6.2.2; DAFI 51-401, *supra* note 78, at § 7.1.2.1; AR 27-53, *supra* note 78, at § 8.a.(2).

[81] *See* DoD Law of War Manual, *supra* note 21, at § 6.2.2; DAFI 51-401, *supra* note 78, at § 7.1.2.2; AR 27-53, *supra* note 78, at § 8.a.(3).

[82] DoD Law of War Manual, *supra* note 21, at § 6.2.2.

[83] *Id.* at § 6.4.2.

[84] *Id.* at § 6.2.2.

[85] There is no accepted definition of unnecessary suffering. This language is generally accepted as the most clear and accurate formulation of the superfluous injury/unnecessary suffering test:

> The prohibition of unnecessary suffering constitutes acknowledgment that necessary suffering to combatants is lawful, and may include severe injury or loss of life. There is no agreed international definition of unnecessary suffering. A weapon or munition would be

recognizes that the use of weapons in war causes suffering, including injury and loss of life. A weapon causes superfluous injury only if its normal use has a particular effect and the injury caused thereby is manifestly disproportionate to the military necessity for it. This determination cannot be made in isolation from other weapons. A weapon's effects must be weighed in light of comparable, lawful weapons in use on the battlefield.

To determine whether a weapon causes superfluous injury, a legal review must include an evaluation of the military necessity of the weapon; an analysis of the intended results of its use (including design, that is, what it is designed to do, and intended employment, that is, how it is intended to be used in combat); and a comparison of the weapon with lawful comparable weapons already in use.

As noted in the previous section, distinction is a fundamental principle of LOAC. It requires that military forces direct their attacks against enemy military objectives and distinguish these objectives from the civilian population and civilian objects. Combatants, civilians taking a direct part in hostilities, and other military objectives may be targeted. Distinction in targeting requires that the weapon be capable of being directed against a military objective. Indiscriminate attacks are prohibited. As noted in Article 51(4) of Additional Protocol I, indiscriminate attacks are:

> (a) those which are not directed at a specific military objective;
> (b) those which employ a method or means of combat which cannot be directed at a specific military objective; or
> (c) those which employ a method or means of combat the effects of which cannot be limited as required by this Protocol; and consequently, in each such case, are of a nature to strike military objectives and civilians or civilian objects without distinction.[86]

Article 51(5)(a) of Additional Protocol I also provides that an indiscriminate attack includes "those which employ a method or means of combat that cannot

> deemed to cause unnecessary suffering only if it inevitably or in its normal use has a particular effect and the injury caused is considered by governments as disproportionate to the military necessity for it, that is, the military advantage to be gained from its use. This balancing test cannot be conducted in isolation. A weapon's or munition's effect must be weighed in light of comparable, lawful weapons or munitions in use on the modern battlefield. A weapon is not unlawful merely because it may cause severe suffering or injury. The appropriate determination is whether a weapon's or munitions employment for its normal or expected use would be prohibited under some or all circumstances. The correct criterion is whether the employment of a weapon for its normal or expected use inevitably would cause injury or suffering manifestly disproportionate to its military effectiveness.

W. Hays Parks, *Means and Methods of Warfare*, 38 Geo. Wash. Int'l L. Rev. 511, 517 n.25 (2006).

[86] Additional Protocol I, *supra* note 39, at art. 51(4).

be directed at a specific military objective, such as an attack by bombardment by any methods or means which treats as a single military objective a number of clearly separated and distinct military objectives located in a city, town, village or other area containing a similar concentration of civilians or civilian objects."[87]

The ICRC in its weapons review publication argues that proportionality must be taken into consideration. The ICRC views a weapon as indiscriminate if it an attack may be expected to cause incidental loss of civilian life, injury to civilians, damage to civilian objects, or a combination thereof, which would be excessive in relation to the concrete and direct military advantage anticipated, which is the proportionality rule.[88]

In determining distinction, "capable of being directed" does not require terminal guidance to the target or use of the most precise weapon under all circumstances. It does prohibit "blind weapons," which are those weapons that cannot, with any reasonable assurance, be directed against a military objective. Indiscriminate weapons also include those that are essentially random in their effects and would be as likely to hit civilians as combatants.

The United States disagrees with the ICRC that proportionality has any direct applicability in a weapons review. What is proportionate can only meaningfully be determined in relation to an attack based on the circumstances at the time of the attack. The case-specific nature of these factors means that proportionality is not something that has a direct relevance to a weapons review.[89]

The adoption of new technologies present new challenges for the weapons review process. For example, as research into AI advances, it will be important to consider how AI can be appropriately incorporated into new weapons. There have been rapid advances in AI applications that used to be only theoretical. AI has the potential to transform society and affect the way society interacts socially, conducts business, and, importantly, has the potential to revolutionize armed conflict. Lieutenant General (retired) Jack Shanahan, the former Director of the Joint AI Center, cautioned, "What I don't want to see is a future where our potential adversaries have a fully AI-enabled force and we do not . . . I don't have the time luxury of hours or days to make decisions. It may be seconds and microseconds where A.I. can be used."[90]

The 2018 National Defense Strategy (NDS) calls for greater investments in AI and autonomy to provide the United States with competitive military

[87] *Id.* at art. 51(5)(a).

[88] *Id.* at art. 51(5)(b). *See also* ICRC Guide, *supra* note 61, at 15.

[89] DoD SIPRI Response, *supra* note 74, at 20.

[90] Def. Innovation Bd., U.S. Dep't of Def., AI Principles: Recommendations on the Ethical Use of Artificial Intelligence by the Department of Defense 3 (Oct. 2019), https://media.defense.gov/2019/Oct/31/2002204458/-1/-1/0/DIB_AI_PRINCIPLES_PRIMARY_DOCUMENT.PDF [hereinafter DIB Report].

advantages.[91] The DoD's AI Strategy commits to using AI "in a lawful and ethical manner to promote our values."[92] In May 2021, Deputy Secretary of Defense Kathleen Hicks adopted the DoD AI Ethical Principles, noting that "it is imperative that we adopt responsible behavior, processes and, outcomes that reflect the Department's commitment to its ethical principles, including the protection of privacy and civil liberties."[93] The DoD would also develop tools to implement AI principles throughout the acquisition process. Those AI Ethical Principles are:

1. Responsible: DoD personnel will exercise appropriate levels of judgment and care, while remaining responsible for the development, deployment, and use of AI capabilities.
2. Equitable: The Department will take deliberate steps to minimize unintended bias in AI capabilities.
3. Traceable: The Department's AI capabilities will be developed and deployed such that relevant personnel possess an appropriate understanding of technology, development processes, and operational methods applicable to AI capabilities, including transparent and auditable methodologies, data sources, and design procedure and documentation.
4. Reliable: The Department's AI capabilities will have explicit, well-defined uses, and the safety, security, and effectiveness of such capabilities will be subject to testing and assurance within those defined uses across Al capabilities' entire life-cycle.
5. Governable: The Department will design and engineer AI capabilities to fulfill their intended functions while possessing the ability to detect and avoid unintended consequences, and the ability to disengage or deactivate deployed systems that demonstrate unintended behavior.[94]

Applying and adhering to these principles helps the DoD ensure existing policy frameworks, LOAC, U.S. domestic law, and ethical norms that reflect U.S. values are incorporated into the acquisition process.

In conducting legal reviews of new weapons, the United States is able to ensure that any weapons that are fielded comply with its domestic and international legal obligations. Working with the various weapons developers the acquisition process, the legal, technical, and ethical issues can be assessed and addressed early in the process. The DoD has invested hundreds of billions of dollars in the

[91] *Id.*
[92] *Id.*
[93] Deputy Sec'y of Def., U.S. Dep't of Def., *Implementing Responsible Artificial Intelligence in the Department of Defense* (May 26, 2021), https://media.defense.gov/2021/May/27/2002730593/-1/-1/0/IMPLEMENTING-RESPONSIBLE-ARTIFICIAL-INTELLIGENCE-IN-THE-DEPARTMENT-OF-DEFENSE.PDF [hereinafter Hicks AI Ethics Memo].
[94] *Id.*

last half-century to ensure the safety and reliability of its weapons systems and platforms to create more precise and accurate weapons that reduce civilian casualties and protect civilian infrastructure while still achieving military objectives.[95] Accordingly, service members can be confident that the weapons they are using have undergone a rigorous process and are the best weapons possible to comply with LOAC.

4. Superior Weapons Often Equate to a Better Ability to Distinguish between Military Targets and Civilian Noncombatants

In 2019, reports surfaced about the existence of a new precision weapon. The payload carried a precision warhead equipped missile with "six sword-like blades that allow the missile to cut through buildings or cars with ease."[96] *Military Times* reported that weapon had been in use for some time, "with development dating back as far as 2011 under former President Barack Obama," when in 2019, "over a dozen current and former U.S. officials discussed the vicious attributes of the R9X—also known as 'the flying Ginsu' or 'ninja bomb'—a non-explosive munition that was spawned from the widely used Hellfire missile."[97]

As discussed earlier, the last 20 years has seen the development of weapons with greater ability for creating distinction between legitimate targets and protected persons and objects. A former DoD General Counsel has noted that AI and other autonomy-related emerging technologies are being developed because they can produce greater accuracy, precision, and speed in weapon systems.[98] Further, it has led to new capabilities that would be impossible without the incorporation of such technology.[99] One example is the Counter-Rocket Artillery and Mortar System (C-RAM system), which autonomously fires at incoming projectiles with greater accuracy and at speeds which human operators cannot hope to match. In a similar fashion, "the addition of autonomous or 'smart' capabilities can allow weapons to 'lock on' to targets like enemy tanks, warships, or

[95] DIB Report, *supra* note 91, at 7.

[96] J.D. Simkins, *Photos Show Devastation Unleashed on Terror Leaders by Sword-Carrying "Ninja Bomb"*, MIL. TIMES (June 20, 2020), https://www.militarytimes.com/2020/06/20/photos-show-devastation-unleashed-on-terror-leaders-by-sword-carrying-ninja-bomb/.

[97] *Id.* The R9X carries no explosives, but relies on kinetic energy produced by a 100-pound weapon traveling at a thousand miles an hour to deliver a corona of six sword-like blades that fan out from its body in flight on target to, in theory if not practice, kill a single person without hurting those around them, reducing collateral damage.

[98] Just Security, Remarks by Defense Dept General Counsel Paul C. Ney Jr. on the Law of War, JUST SECURITY (May 28, 2019), https://www.justsecurity.org/64313/remarks-by-defense-dept-general-counsel-paul-c-ney-jr-on-the-law-of-war/.

[99] *Id.*

aircraft, to better effectuate the intent of the commanders and operators, and reduce the risk of harm to civilians."[100]

During the March 2019 Group of Governmental Experts (GGE) meeting at the Convention on Certain Conventional Weapons (CCW), the United States discussed five areas where the incorporation of AI and autonomy in weapons systems could reduce risks to civilians: (1) the incorporation of autonomous self-destruct, self-deactivation, or self-neutralization mechanisms; (2) an increased awareness of civilians and civilian objects on the battlefield; (3) improved assessments of the likely effects of military operations; (4) the automation of target identification, tracking, selection, and engagement; and (5) the reduction of the need for immediate fires in self-defense.[101]

The United States has incorporated self-destruct, self-deactivation, or self-neutralization mechanisms in systems such as landmines and cluster munitions. Pursuant to U.S. policies and, with respect to antipersonnel landmines, and Amended Protocol II to CCW, the United States will not use any land mine or cluster munition that does not incorporate such a mechanism.[102] These self-destruct, self-deactivation, or self-neutralization mechanisms have greatly reduced the risk to civilians.

The Army is reliant on a wide variety of systems for situational awareness. Currently, the U.S. Army has two satellite antennas for every soldier on the battlefield. A nine-member infantry squad can rely on up to 150 satellites. A Brigade Combat Team has approximately 2,500 pieces of space-enabled equipment.[103]

Civilian casualties can result because the commander may not be aware of the presence of civilians on the battlefield due to the "fog of war."[104] Similarly, combatants may misidentify civilians as combatants, especially in a non-international armed conflict against an armed group that hides among the

[100] *Id.*

[101] Charles Trumbull, U.S. Statement on LAWS: Potential Military Applications of Advanced Technology, Group of Governmental Experts on Lethal Autonomous Weapons Systems (LAWS) (Mar. 26, 2019), https://geneva.usmission.gov/2019/03/26/u-s-statement-on-laws-potential-military-applications-of-advanced-technology/ [hereinafter Trumbull Statement].

[102] *See* U.S. Sec'y of Def., U.S. Dep't of Def., *DoD Policy on Landmines* 2 (Jan. 31, 2020), https://media.defense.gov/2020/Jan/31/2002242359/-1/-1/1/DOD-POLICY-ON-LANDMINES.PDF; U.S. Sec'y of Def., U.S. Dep't of Def., *DoD Policy on Cluster Munitions* 2 (Nov. 30, 2017), https://dod.defense.gov/Portals/1/Documents/pubs/DOD-POLICY-ON-CLUSTER-MUNITIONS-OSD071415-17.pdf; Protocol on Prohibitions or Restrictions on the Use of Mines, Booby-Traps and Other Devices, as amended on 3 May 1996, Annexed to the Convention on Prohibitions or Restrictions on the Use of Certain Conventional Weapons Which May be Deemed to be Excessively Injurious or to Have Indiscriminate Effects, May 3, 1996, 2048 U.N.T.S. 93.

[103] William T. Coffey, Jr., Joan Rousseau & LTC Scott Mudge, *Tactical Staff Considerations for Winning in a Denied, Degraded, and Disrupted Space Operational Environment*, News CTC (Feb. 1, 2019), https://usacac.army.mil/organizations/mccoe/call/publication/NFTF-DAGR.

[104] *See* Trumbull Statement, *supra* note 102.

civilian population. Autonomy can increase a commander's awareness to the presence of civilians and civilian objects on the battlefield.[105]

Commanders can have an overwhelming amount of information to consider during military operations, such as hours of video from intelligence, surveillance, and reconnaissance (ISR) platforms. During the conflicts in Iraq and Afghanistan, over 11,000 UASs accumulated hundreds of thousands of hours of video. It was estimated that these UASs captured more high-resolution video per day than the combined video of three NFL seasons. It would take 20 analysts 24 hours to go through less than 10 percent of that video. Humans simply can't keep up with this amount of information.[106]

The DoD, through Project Maven, wants to use AI to improve its analysis of video from ISR platforms. By using AI to identify objects of interest from imagery autonomously, analysts are able to search through larger data sets and focus on more sophisticated and important tasks requiring human judgment.[107] This ensures commanders have accurate intelligence, which would increase their awareness of the presence of civilians and protected objects. This increased awareness could help commanders better assess the totality of the expected incidental loss of civilian life, injury to civilians, and damage to civilian objects from an attack, including incidental harms that otherwise would not have been foreseeable.

The United States has a robust targeting system in place, the Joint Targeting Process.[108] Sophisticated computer modeling software helps military planners predict the likely effects that the weapon would create when striking the military objective. AI and better autonomy can improve this process by improving the assessment of the expected incidental loss of civilian life, injury to civilians, and damage to civilian objects from an attack, including incidental harms that otherwise would not be foreseeable with current technology.[109]

Improvements in target identification will allow weapons to strike military objectives more accurately and with less risk of collateral damage. The United States currently fields many munitions that have "lock-on-after-launch" functions that enable the munition to guide itself autonomously to targets after it has been launched.[110] One such system is the AIM-120 Advanced Medium-Range, Air-to-Air Missile (AMRAAM), which incorporates an active radar in

[105] *See id.*
[106] *See* Jon Harper, *Artificial Intelligence to Sort Through ISR Data Glut*, Nat'l Def. (Jan. 16, 2018), https://www.nationaldefensemagazine.org/articles/2018/1/16/artificial-intelligence-to--sort-through-isr-data-glut.
[107] *Id.*
[108] *See* U.S. Dep't of Def., Joint Chiefs of Staff, JP-3-60, Joint Targeting (Jan. 31. 2013).
[109] Trumbull Statement, *supra* note 102.
[110] *Id.*

connection with an inertial reference unit and microcomputer system. The active radar allows AMRAAM to guide itself to its intended target.[111]

Finally, autonomy and AI would further reduce risk of civilian casualties when military forces act in self-defense. Commanders and soldiers often have to take immediate action to counter a threat from the enemy. This reduced response time also reduces the ability for commanders and operators to take precautions in order reduce the risk of civilian harm.[112] The development of these emerging technologies may offer a way to reduce civilian casualties as a result of such engagements by reducing the number of rounds that would need to be fired in self-defense, lessen the risk of misidentification of the source of the incoming fire, or improved systems, such as C-RAM, can reduce the time needed to respond.[113]

The use of autonomy and AI likely result in better weapons systems that enhance compliance with LOAC by reducing the risk of civilian harm and collateral damage. Better weapons and tools that assist commanders in making life and death decisions should not be feared or stigmatized, but rather recognized as way to mitigate the impact of armed conflict on the most vulnerable.

5. U.S. Laws Provide Protections to Ensure Weapons Are Not Provided to Irresponsible Actors

The previous sections dealt with how the United States incorporates legal and ethical considerations in the development and use of new technologies and weapons systems. However, the United States isn't the only user of its new weapons and has an aggressive program to sell or transfer weapons to allies and partners abroad. Over the past two years, the United States has sold over $300 billion in military equipment. The Biden administration has continued to sell major weapons systems overseas, but it has also stopped selling offensive weapons to Saudi Arabia due to civilian casualties in Yemen and is considering a revision to its weapons export policy that emphasizes human rights when evaluating an arms sale.[114]

111 *Id.*

112 U.S. Working Paper, Human-Machine Interaction in the Development, Deployment, and Use of Emerging Technologies in the Area of Lethal Autonomous Weapons Systems, U.N. Doc. CCW/GGE.2/2018/WP.4, para. 33 (Aug. 28, 2018), https://docs-library.unoda.org/Convention_on_Certain_Conventional_Weapons_-_Group_of_Governmental_Experts_(2018)/2018_GGE%2BLAWS_August_Working%2BPaper_US.pdf.

113 *Id.* at paras. 34–37.

114 Mike Stone, *U.S. Weapons Exports Decreased 21% to $138.2 Billion in Fiscal 2021*, Reuters (Dec. 22, 2021), https://www.reuters.com/world/us/us-weapons-exports-decreased-21-1382-billion-fiscal-2021-2021-12-22/.

The AECA[115] and the FAA[116] set the requirements governing Foreign Military Sales (FMS) and Direct Commercial Sales (DCS) to foreign governments and other foreign buyers. FMS refers to the sale of U.S.-origin defense articles, equipment, services, and training (hereinafter "defense articles") on a government-to-government basis. DCS are those sales of defense articles and services directly from U.S. companies to eligible foreign governments and international organizations.[117] Both the AECA and FAA require that any sales must be for specific authorized military purposes and subject to end-use monitoring (EUM). Each authorizes the termination of future sales and deliveries if a recipient is found to be in substantial violation of a sale-related agreement or the recipient uses those defense articles for unauthorized purposes.[118] The United States ensures the proper use of weapons through end-use monitoring.

Sections 38(g)(7) and 40A(a) of the AECA[119] and Section 505(a)(3) of the FAA[120] provide the statutory requirement that defense articles sold via FMS and DCS are subject to EUM to ensure that recipients use such items solely for their intended purposes. End-use monitoring is an important aspect of ensuring accountability and protecting sensitive U.S. military and intelligence technologies. Those governments, organizations, and other foreign buyers must agree, prior to the export or transfer of defense articles to: (1) not retransfer defense articles to a third party without prior U.S. government authorization; (2) only dispose or use defense articles for the purposes for which they were furnished; and (3) maintain the security of those items as the United States would protect such items.[121] Furthermore, in cases where U.S.-origin defense articles and services are transferred to a foreign government via FMS, those governments agree to make those items available for EUM throughout the operational life of the equipment. The Defense Security Cooperation Agency manages the DoD's end-use monitoring through the Golden Sentry program for items sold through FMS. The Directorate of Defense Trade Controls coordinates the State Department's Blue Lantern program, which is the end-use monitoring program for items sold via DCS.[122]

[115] Arms Export Control Act, *supra* note 16.
[116] Foreign Assistance Act, *supra* note 17.
[117] Paul K. Kerr & Liana W. Rosen, Cong. Res. Serv., IF11197, U.S. Arms Sales and Human Rights: Legislative Basis and Frequently Asked Questions 1 (2021) [hereinafter CRS].
[118] *Id.*
[119] Arms Export Control Act, *supra* note 16, at 22 U.S.C. 2778(g)(7) and 2785(a).
[120] Foreign Assistance Act, *supra* note 17, at 22 U.S.C. 2314(a)(3).
[121] U.S. Dep't of State, End-Use Monitoring of U.S. Origin Defense Articles, Bureau of Political-Military Affairs Fact Sheet (Jan. 20, 2021), https://www.state.gov/end-use-monitoring-of-u-s-origin-defense-articles/ [hereinafter End-Use Monitoring Fact Sheet].
[122] *See* CRS, *supra* note 118, at 2.

5.1. Blue Lantern—EUM for Direct Commercial Sales

Under the Blue Lantern program, the Department of State conducts pre-license, post-license/pre-shipment, and post-shipment checks to ensure that foreign consignees and end users are legitimate and also to confirm the legitimacy of proposed transactions.[123] The Blue Lantern program is not a law enforcement function, but a way to provide reasonable assurance that: (1) the recipient is complying with the requirements imposed by the U.S. government with respect to use, transfers, and security of defense articles and defense services; and (2) such articles and services are being used for the purposes for which they were provided.[124] A Blue Lantern check can include many facts, such as interviewing foreign parties, conducting a visual inspection of the defense articles, and confirming from the foreign governments that the recipients are in good standing.[125] The Department of State provides an annual end-use monitoring report that provides information on the Blue Lantern checks by region.[126]

5.2. Golden Sentry—EUM for Government-to-Government Transfers

The DoD, pursuant to its Golden Sentry program, conducts both routine and enhanced EUM checks. Routine EUM checks are done quarterly based on a "watch list" of significant military equipment (SME). They are performed by department personnel during regular visits to partner nation installations as part of their security cooperation duties, and the results of those checks are detailed electronically.[127] An enhanced EUM check is required based on a list of sensitive items, which are found in Chapter 8 of the Security Assistance Management Manual (SAMM).[128] First, personnel will conduct an initial inventory by verifying the serial number. Next, personnel then perform a physical security and accountability assessment of the storage facilities. Finally, there is an annual 100 percent serial number inventory to verify compliance with applicable transfer agreements. Similar to routine EUM checks, the reports are documented electronically.

[123] End-Use Monitoring Fact Sheet, *supra* note 122.

[124] *Id.*

[125] *Id.*

[126] *See* U.S. Dep't of State, Directorate of Def. Trade Controls, End-Use Monitoring of Defense Articles and Defense Services Commercial Exports FY 2019 (2019), https://www.pmddtc.state.gov/sys_attachment.do?sysparm_referring_url=tear_off&view=true&sys_id=c13d692b1b9154102dc36311f54bcb2b.

[127] End-Use Monitoring Fact Sheet, *supra* note 122.

[128] SAMM, ch. 8.

If the U.S. government is notified of a suspected violation of an underlying agreement, the respective department will promptly gather information to confirm the validity of the report. Personnel will then assess whether the activity constitutes a violation of the agreement and will determine the actions the U.S. government will take to prevent such violations from happening again.[129]

6. Conclusion

The United States incorporates legal and ethical considerations throughout the life cycle of weapons it develops, purchases, and sells to other users. It ensures that the weapons in question comply with LOAC and U.S. domestic law. LOAC was developed to minimize suffering in war, and the use of technology in weapons and weapon systems is accomplished in a way that allows our service members to "fight fairly" with superior weaponry. Advanced weapons, including those with autonomy and AI, will not only protect our soldiers but quite often can also enhance compliance with LOAC. Throughout the life cycle, the United States ensures that systems are developed ethically, used in compliance with LOAC, and won't be sold to irresponsible or malicious actors.

Retired General and later Secretary of Defense James Mattis said, "The experience of combat is difficult to understand intellectually and very difficult to appreciate emotionally."[130] Under LOAC, service members engaged in armed conflict are immune from prosecution for killing an armed enemy combatant. Of course, LOAC also places limits on this protection. Some have termed this protection the right to kill, yet acquiring the soldier's uniform also clearly entails donning the risk of being killed. For this reason, no one longs for peace like the experienced soldier. But, when war comes, no one longs for superior technology and weapons like a soldier. This seems a paradox to some—the "peace-loving" soldier as an ardent supporter of the military-industrial complex. Not so. Service members know that when war ignites, those not deterred must be destroyed. And, while not true for all the world's militaries, U.S. service members can trust that sufficient checks on the military and the military-industrial complex are enshrined in the very legal system and Constitution that they have sworn to protect and defend.

[129] *Id.*

[130] Adam Linehan, *Just Kills: How the Marine Corps Blew the Biggest War Crimes Case Since Vietnam*, Task & Purpose (May 23, 2018), https://taskandpurpose.com/popular/true-story-marine-corps-blew-biggest-war-crimes-case/.

References

Kenneth Anderson, *Laurie Blank on Mark Mazzetti's "The Drone Zone"—Last in Series from Lewis, Dunlap, Rona, Corn, and Anderson*, LAWFARE (July 21, 2012, 10:37 AM), https://www.lawfareblog.com/laurie-blank-mark-mazzettis-drone-zone-last-series-lewis-dunlap-rona-corn-and-anderson.

WILLIAM H. BOOTHBY, WEAPONS AND THE LAW OF ARMED CONFLICT (2d ed. 2016).

Vincent Boulanin, *Implementing Article 36 Weapon Reviews in the Light of Increasing Autonomy in Weapons Systems*, SIPRI INSIGHTS ON PEACE & SECURITY (Nov. 2015), https://www.sipri.org/sites/default/files/files/insight/SIPRIInsight1501.pdf.

CHIEF DEFENCE STAFF (CANADA), B-GJ-005-104/FP-021, LAW OF ARMED CONFLICT AT THE OPERATIONAL AND TACTICAL LEVELS (2001).

William T. Coffey, Jr., Joan Rousseau & LTC Scott Mudge, *Tactical Staff Considerations for Winning in a Denied, Degraded, and Disrupted Space Operational Environment*, NEWS CTC, (Feb. 1, 2019), https://usacac.army.mil/organizations/mccoe/call/publication/NFTF-DAGR.

Geoffrey S. Corn, *Targeting, Distinction and the Long War: Guarding Against Conflation of Cause and Responsibility*, 46 ISR. Y.B. ON HUM. RTS. 146 (2016).

Edward R. Cummings, Acting Assistant Legal Adviser for Politico-Military Affairs, Remarks at Symposium at Brooklyn Law School (Sept. 25, 1982), *in* DEP'T OF STATE, 3 CUMULATIVE DIGEST OF UNITED STATES PRACTICE IN INTERNATIONAL LAW 1981–88, at 3421 (1995).

DEF. INNOVATION BD., U.S. DEP'T OF DEF., AI PRINCIPLES: RECOMMENDATIONS ON THE ETHICAL USE OF ARTIFICIAL INTELLIGENCE BY THE DEPARTMENT OF DEFENSE (Oct. 2019), https://media.defense.gov/2019/Oct/31/2002204458/-1/-1/0/DIB_AI_PRINCIPLES_PRIMARY_DOCUMENT.PDF.

Deputy Sec'y of Def., *Implementing Responsible Artificial Intelligence in the Department of Defense* (May 26, 2021), https://media.defense.gov/2021/May/27/2002730593/-1/-1/0/IMPLEMENTING-RESPONSIBLE-ARTIFICIAL-INTELLIGENCE-IN-THE-DEPARTMENT-OF-DEFENSE.PDF.

President Dwight D. Eisenhower, Farewell Address 3 (Jan. 17, 1961), https://perma.cc/7K9X-Y2H5.

David Feith, *H.R. McMaster: The Warrior's-Eye View of Afghanistan*, WALL ST. J. (May 11, 2012), https://www.wsj.com/articles/SB10001424052702304451104577392281146871796.

BRYAN A. FREDERICK, THE CONTINUED EVOLUTION OF U.S. LAW OF ARMED CONFLICT (2015).

ALAN FURST, NIGHT SOLDIERS: A NOVEL (1988).

MORRIS GREENSPAN, MODERN LAW OF LAND WARFARE (1959).

Gulf War Fast Facts, CNN (July 29, 2020), https://www.cnn.com/2013/09/15/world/meast/gulf-war-fast-facts/index.html.

Hague Declaration IV, Declaration III Concerning the Prohibition of the Use of Expanding Bullets, July 29, 1899, 26 Martens Nouveau Recueil (ser. 2) 1002 (entered into force Sept. 4, 1900).

David Hambling, *Introduction: Weapons Technology*, NEW SCIENTIST (Sept. 4, 2006), https://www.newscientist.com/article/dn9980-introduction-weapons-technology/.

Jon Harper, *Artificial Intelligence to Sort Through ISR Data Glut*, NAT'L DEF. (Jan. 16, 2018), https://www.nationaldefensemagazine.org/articles/2018/1/16/artificial-intelligence-to--sort-through-isr-data-glut.

Adam Henschke, *"Supersoldiers": Ethical Concerns in Human Enhancement Technologies*, Humanitarian L. & Pol'y (July 3, 2017), https://blogs.icrc.org/law-and-policy/2017/07/03/supersoldiers-ethical-concerns-human-enhancement-technologies-2/.

Int'l Comm. of the Red Cross, *The Laws of War in a Nutshell* (Oct. 19, 2016), https://www.icrc.org/en/document/what-are-rules-of-war-Geneva-Conventions.

Paul K. Kerr & Liana W. Rosen, Cong. Res. Serv., IF11197, U.S. Arms Sales and Human Rights: Legislative Basis and Frequently Asked Questions (2021).

Kai-Fu Lee, *The Third Revolution in Warfare*, Atlantic (Sept. 11, 2021), https://www.theatlantic.com/technology/archive/2021/09/i-weapons-are-third-revolution-warfare/620013/.

Legality of the Threat or Use of Nuclear Weapons, Advisory Opinion, 1996 I.C.J. Rep. (July 8).

Francis Lieber, Instructions for the Government of Armies of the United States in the Field, General Orders No. 100 (promulgated Apr. 24, 1863) (Washington, Government Printing Office, 1898).

Adam Linehan, *Just Kills: How the Marine Corps Blew the Biggest War Crimes Case Since Vietnam*, Task & Purpose (May 23, 2018), https://taskandpurpose.com/popular/true-story-marine-corps-blew-biggest-war-crimes-case/.

Steven Lee Meyers & Eric Schmitt, *Russian Military Uses Syria as Proving Ground, and West Takes Notice*, N.Y. Times (Oct. 14, 2015), https://www.nytimes.com/2015/10/15/world/middleeast/russian-military-uses-syria-as-proving-ground-and-west-takes-notice.html.

Nat'l Sec. L. Dep't., The Judge Advocate Gen.'s Legal Ctr. & Sch., U.S. Army, Operational Law Handbook (2021).

Office of Gen. Counsel, U.S. Dep't of Defense, Law of War Manual (rev. ed., Dec. 2016)

Operation Enduring Freedom Fast Facts, CNN (Oct. 4, 2020), https://www.cnn.com/2013/10/28/world/operation-enduring-freedom-fast-facts/index.html.

W. Hays Parks, *Means and Methods of Warfare*, 38 Geo. Wash. Int'l L. Rev. 511 (2006).

Lt. Gen. Charles Pede & Col. Peter Hayden, *The Eighteenth Gap: Preserving the Commander's Legal Maneuver Space on "Battlefield Next"*, Mil. Rev. 8 (Mar.–Apr. 2021), https://www.armyupress.army.mil/Journals/Military-Review/English-Edition-Archives/March-April-2021/Pede-The-18th-Gap/.

Protocol Additional to the Geneva Conventions of 12 August 1949, and Relating to the Protection of Victims of International Armed Conflicts, 1977, 1125 U.N.T.S. 3 (Additional Protocol I).

Protocol Additional to the Geneva Conventions of 12 August 1949, and Relating to the Protection of Victims of Non-International Armed Conflicts, art. 13, adopted June 8, 1977, 1125 U.N.T.S. 609 (Additional Protocol II).

Protocol on Prohibitions or Restrictions on the Use of Mines, Booby-Traps and Other Devices, as amended on 3 May 1996, Annexed to the Convention on Prohibitions or Restrictions on the Use of Certain Conventional Weapons Which May be Deemed to be Excessively Injurious or to Have Indiscriminate Effects, May 3, 1996, 2048 U.N.T.S. 93.

Remarks by Defense Dept General Counsel Paul C. Ney Jr. on the Law of War, Just Security (May 28, 2019), https://www.justsecurity.org/64313/remarks-by-defense-dept-general-counsel-paul-c-ney-jr-on-the-law-of-war/.

Alex Roland, *War and Technology*, Foreign Pol'y Res. Inst. (Feb. 27, 2009), https://www.fpri.org/article/2009/02/war-and-technology/.

Jim Rutenberg, *In Farewell, Rumsfeld Warns Weakness Is "Provocative"*, N.Y. TIMES (Dec. 16, 2006), https://www.nytimes.com/2006/12/16/washington/16prexy.html.

J.D. Simkins, *Photos Show Devastation Unleashed on Terror Leaders by Sword-Carrying "Ninja Bomb"*, MIL. TIMES (June 20, 2020), https://www.militarytimes.com/2020/06/20/photos-show-devastation-unleashed-on-terror-leaders-by-sword-carrying-ninja-bomb/.

Trae Stephens, *The Ethics of Defense Technology Development: An Investor's Perspective*, MEDIUM (Dec. 4, 2019), https://medium.com/@traestephens/the-ethics-of-defense-technology-development-an-investors-perspective-45c71bf6e6af.

Mike Stone, *U.S. Weapons Exports Decreased 21% to $138.2 Billion in Fiscal 2021*, REUTERS (Dec. 22, 2021) https://www.reuters.com/world/us/us-weapons-exports-decreased-21-1382-billion-fiscal-2021-2021-12-22/.

THOMAS SZAYNA ET AL. WHAT ARE THE TRENDS IN ARMED CONFLICTS, AND WHAT DO THEY MEAN FOR U.S. DEFENSE POLICY?, RAND (2017), https://www.rand.org/pubs/research_reports/RR1904.html.

Roxana Tiron, *Hypersonic Weapons: Who Has Them and Why It Matters*, BLOOMBERG (Oct. 27, 2021), https://www.bloomberg.com/news/articles/2021-10-27/hypersonic-weapons-who-has-them-and-why-it-matters-quicktake.

Charles Trumbull, U.S. Statement on LAWS: Potential Military Applications of Advanced Technology, GROUP OF GOVERNMENTAL EXPERTS ON LETHAL AUTONOMOUS WEAPONS SYSTEMS (LAWS) (Mar. 26, 2019), https://geneva.usmission.gov/2019/03/26/u-s-statement-on-laws-potential-military-applications-of-advanced-technology/.

U.K. MINISTRY OF DEFENCE, THE JOINT SERVICE MANUAL OF THE LAW OF ARMED CONFLICT (2004).

U.K. WAR OFFICE, MANUAL OF MILITARY LAW (1958).

UN NEWS, WARS HAVE RULES: 5 THINGS THE UN HUMANITARIAN CHIEF WANTS COUNTRIES TO TACKLE SO HUMAN SUFFERING IN CONFLICT CAN BE MINIMIZED, UNITED NATIONS, https://news.un.org/en/story/2019/04/1035861.

UNITED NATIONS, *A New Era of Conflict and Violence*, https://www.un.org/en/un75/new-era-conflict-and-violence.

U.S. DEP'T OF THE AIR FORCE INSTRUCTION 51-401, LAW OF WAR (Aug. 3, 2018).

U.S. DEP'T OF THE ARMY & U.S. MARINE CORPS FM 6-27/MCTP 11-10C, THE COMMANDER'S HANDBOOK ON THE LAW OF LAND WARFARE, CHANGE 1, para. 1-19 (Aug. 2019).

U.S. DEP'T OF ARMY, REGULATION 27-53, LEGAL REVIEW OF WEAPONS AND WEAPONS SYSTEMS (Oct. 23, 2019).

U.S. DEP'T OF THE ARMY, FIELD MANUAL 3–24 (Dec. 2006).

U.S. DEP'T OF STATE, DIRECTORATE OF DEF. TRADE CONTROLS, END-USE MONITORING OF DEFENSE ARTICLES AND DEFENSE SERVICES COMMERCIAL EXPORTS FY 2019 (2019), https://www.pmddtc.state.gov/sys_attachment.do?sysparm_referring_url=tear_off&view=true&sys_id=c13d692b1b9154102dc36311f54bcb2b.

U.S. DEP'T OF STATE, END-USE MONITORING OF U.S. ORIGIN DEFENSE ARTICLES, BUREAU OF POLITICAL-MILITARY AFFAIRS FACT SHEET (Jan. 20, 2021), https://www.state.gov/end-use-monitoring-of-u-s-origin-defense-articles/.

U.S. MARINE CORPS, MARINE CORPS DOCTRINAL PUBLICATION 1 (June 20, 1997).

U.S. SEC'Y OF THE NAVY, INSTRUCTION 5000.2E, DEP'T OF NAVY IMPLEMENTATION & OPERATION OF THE DEFENSE ACQUISITION SYSTEM AND THE JOINT CAPABILITIES INTEGRATION AND DEVELOPMENT SYSTEM (2011).

U.S. Office of the Sec'y of Def., Department of Defense Budget Fiscal Year 2019 (Feb. 2018) Counter-Islamic State of Iraq and Syria (ISIS) Train and Equip Fund (CTEF).

U.S. War Dep't, Field Manual 27-10, Rules of Land Warfare (1940).

U.S. Working Paper, Human-Machine Interaction in the Development, Deployment, and Use of Emerging Technologies in the Area of Lethal Autonomous Weapons Systems, U.N. Doc. CCW/GGE.2/2018/WP.4, para. 33 (Aug. 28, 2018), https://docs-library.unoda.org/Convention_on_Certain_Conventional_Weapons_-_Group_of_Governmental_Experts_(2018)/2018_GGE%2BLAWS_August_Working%2BPaper_US.pdf.

James Vincent, *Putin Says the Nation that Leads in AI "Will Be the Ruler of the World"*, Verge (Sept. 4, 2017), https://www.theverge.com/2017/9/4/16251226/russia-ai-putin-rule-the-world.

Michael Walzer, Just and Unjust Wars: A Moral Argument with Historical Illustrations (2000).

6

Space Ethics for the Modern Warrior

Brian D. Green[*]

1. Introduction

This is an exciting time to be in the space business. Once dominated by government-run enterprises, the exploration and use of the space domain have grown to fulfill the Outer Space Treaty's promise as "the province of all mankind"[1] as commercial satellite construction, space launch, and on-orbit activities have proliferated.[2] At the same time, new threats have emerged that require ever more vigilant, well-equipped, and ready military forces to defend the vital space capabilities of the United States and its allies.[3] We have recently witnessed

* All opinions expressed in this chapter are the author's and not those of the Department of Defense or any of its components, nor do they constitute legal advice to the reader. The mention of commercial companies and products herein should not be construed to convey governmental endorsement.

[1] Treaty on Principles Governing the Activities of States in the Exploration and Use of Outer Space, including the Moon and Other Celestial Bodies, Jan. 27, 1967, art. IV, 18 U.S.T. 2410, 610 U.N.T.S. 205 [hereinafter Outer Space Treaty or OST].

[2] In 2019, 78 of the 102 space launches worldwide were commercial launches; 45% of satellites launched were commercial communications satellites; and the value of the global space economy totaled $366 billion. Bryce Space & Technology, *2020 State of the Satellite Industry Report* 2–3 (July 28, 2020), https://brycetech.com/reports/report-documents/SIA_SSIR_2020.pdf. In 2021, despite the economic disruption caused by the worldwide COVID-19 pandemic, the worth of the global space economy grew to $386 billion, with the number of operational satellites having grown almost five-fold since 2010. Bryce Space & Technology, *2022 State of the Satellite Industry Report* 2–3 (July 13, 2022), https://brycetech.com/reports/report-documents/SIA_SSIR_2022.pdf; Statista, *Number of Active Satellites from 1957 to 2021*, https://www.statista.com/statistics/897719/number-of-active-satellites-by-year/ (last visited Sept. 12, 2022) (listing 997 active satellites on orbit in 2010 and 4,877 in 2021). Moreover, the first on-orbit satellite life extension operation in geosynchronous Earth orbit took place between commercial space vehicles in February 2020. Elizabeth Howell, *Two Private Satellites Just Docked in Space in Historic First for Orbital Servicing*, Space.com (Feb. 27, 2020), https://www.space.com/private-satellites-docking-success-northrop-grumman-mev-1.html. Further, recent developments in suborbital spaceflight may herald the start of a new era in commercial space tourism. Caitlin O'Kane, *Billionaires Jeff Bezos and Richard Branson Have Now Both Gone to Space. Here's the Difference Between Their Blue Origin and Virgin Galactic Flights*, CBS News (July 20, 2021), https://www.cbsnews.com/news/blue-origin-bezos-launch-richard-branson-space-flight-differences/.

[3] *See, e.g.*, *Fiscal Year 2023 Priorities and Posture of United States Space Command*: Hearing Before the S. Armed Services Comm., 117th Cong. (2022) (statement of General James H. Dickinson, Commander, United States Space Command), https://www.armed-services.senate.gov/imo/media/doc/USSPACECOM%20FY23%20Posture%20Statement%20SASC%20FINAL.pdf (describing numerous Chinese and Russian space and counterspace capabilities including direct-ascent

Brian D. Green, *Space Ethics for the Modern Warrior* In: *Ethical Dilemmas in the Global Defense Industry*. Edited by: Daniel Schoeni and Tobias Vestner, Oxford University Press. © Daniel Schoeni and Tobias Vestner 2023.
DOI: 10.1093/oso/9780190675813.003.0007

both the establishment of United States Space Command[4] and the creation of the United States Space Force (USSF),[5] with France,[6] the United Kingdom,[7] Japan,[8] Germany,[9] and the Republic of Korea[10] announcing plans to create similar institutions.[11] In this environment, there is great value in collaboration between military organizations and the commercial space industry. However, business leaders and government officials alike must be sensitive to the legal and ethical principles that govern the interaction between Department of Defense (DoD) components and commercial entities or their representatives.

anti-satellite missiles and directed-energy, cyber, electronic warfare, and space-based robotics capabilities); *Russia Conducts Space-Based Anti-Satellite Weapons Test*, USSPACECOM Pub. Affairs (July 23, 2020), https://www.spacecom.mil/MEDIA/NEWS-ARTICLES/Article/2285098/russia-conducts-space-based-anti-satellite-weapons-test/; *Russian Direct-Ascent Anti-Satellite Missile Test Creates Significant, Long-Lasting Space Debris*, USSPACECOM Pub. Affairs (Nov. 15, 2021), https://www.spacecom.mil/News/Article-Display/Article/2842957/russian-direct-ascent-anti-satellite-missile-test-creates-significant-long-last/.

[4] U.S. Dep't of Def., *Department of Defense Establishes U.S. Space Command* (Aug. 29, 2019), https://www.defense.gov/Newsroom/Releases/Release/Article/1948288/department-of-defense-establishes-us-space-command/. Previously, a unified combatant command called U.S. Space Command [hereinafter, USSPACECOM] existed from 1985 to 2002. Gary Shugart, *Re-establishing U.S. Space Command*, Purview (Oct. 1, 2018), https://purview.dodlive.mil/2018/10/01/reestablishing-u-s-space-command/ (providing a historical overview of the previous version of USSPACECOM and how its functions and organizational structure continued to evolve within U.S. Strategic Command [hereinafter, USSTRATCOM] throughout most of the 2000s and 2010s).

[5] Nat'l Def. Authorization Act for Fiscal Year 2020, Pub. L. No. 116-92 §§ 951–961 (2019) [hereinafter 2020 NDAA]; Rebecca Kheel, *Trump Signs Defense Bill Creating Space Force*, The Hill (Dec. 20, 2019), https://thehill.com/policy/defense/475505-trump-signs-defense-bill-creating-space-force. Whereas USSPACECOM is a warfighting combatant command, deriving its authority from 10 U.S.C. § 164 (2017), the U.S. Space Force, like the military service departments, has the responsibility to organize, train, and equip forces to keep them ready for use by the combatant commands. *See A Conversation with General Raymond*, Ctr. for Strategic & Int'l Stud. (Nov. 18, 2019), https://www.csis.org/analysis/conversation-general-raymond (explaining the difference between the military services and the combatant commands).

[6] Nicholas Wu, *French President Emmanuel Macron Announces Creation of French Space Force*, USA Today (July 13, 2019), https://www.usatoday.com/story/news/world/2019/07/13/french-space-force-macron-announces-creation-space-force-command/1723998001/; Hanneke Weitering, *France Is Launching a "Space Force" with Weaponized Satellites*, Space.com (Aug. 2, 2019), https://www.space.com/france-military-space-force.html.

[7] Andrew Chuter, *Former Fighter Pilot Picked to Lead British Military's Space Command*, Def. News (Jan. 15, 2020), https://www.defensenews.com/global/europe/2020/01/15/former-fighter-pilot-picked-to-lead-british-militarys-space-command/.

[8] *Japan Joins US by Announcing Space Force in Face of New Threats*, Sky News (Jan. 20, 2020), https://news.sky.com/story/japan-joins-us-by-announcing-space-force-in-face-of-new-threats-11913185.

[9] Vivienne Machi, *Germany Establishes New Military Space Command*, Def. News (July 13, 2021), https://www.defensenews.com/space/2021/07/13/germany-establishes-new-military-space-command/.

[10] Park Si-soo, *South Korea's Air Force Opens Space Ops Center*, SpaceNews (Oct. 4, 2021), https://spacenews.com/south-korean-air-force-opens-space-center/.

[11] As the articles in *supra* notes 6–10 make clear, there are differences in scale and structure of the allies' new military space entities. However, the goal for all is the same: to become more aware of potential threats to our space capabilities and more capable of deterring and overcoming those threats.

This chapter will sketch out a framework that will help readers to adhere to the highest ethical standards of behavior in DoD-industry interactions. While not a comprehensive guide to all ethical issues that may arise between military organizations and the space industry, it will identify key sources of authority and provide some examples from the author's experience and those of his colleagues. Of course, for questions about the ethics of any particular situation, the reader should request an opinion from an ethics counselor in his or her own agency.

2. Ethical Standards and Sources

Within the DoD, the primary compendium of ethical rules is DoD 5500.07-R, *The Joint Ethics Regulation* (JER). In addition to the rules it promulgates directly, the JER supplements and incorporates by reference substantial portions of the Office of Government Ethics regulations found in Title 5 of the Code of Federal Regulations.[12] When it comes to relations with the space industry, some key sections of the JER are those concerning relations with non-federal entities (NFEs),[13] those ensuring impartiality and the appearance thereof,[14] and the gift rules.[15] Statutory ethical requirements are found in provisions of the United States Code dealing with topics such as post-government employment,[16] the criminal prohibition against bribery,[17] and competition in contracting requirements.[18] Federal employees must also avoid incurring unauthorized fiscal obligations in violation of the Antideficiency Act,[19] or running afoul of

[12] *See* U.S. Dep't of Def., Reg. 5500.07-R, Joint Ethics Reg. (JER), § 2-200, Aug. 30, 1993, inc. Change 7, Nov. 17, 2011 [hereinafter JER], *cf.* 5 C.F.R. pt. 2635 (2016) (issuing ethics provisions that apply not only to the DoD but more broadly throughout the executive branch of the federal government).

[13] *See generally* JER, *supra* note 12, ch. 3.

[14] *See, e.g.*, 5 C.F.R. § 2635.501 (1997).

[15] 5 C.F.R. §§ 2635.201–206 (2016).

[16] *See generally* U.S. Dep't of Def., Standards of Conduct Office, Non-Senior Employee Post-Government Employment Restrictions (May 2022), https://dodsoco.ogc.osd.mil/Portals/102/Documents/PGE%20and%20PI/Toolbox%20-%20PGE-PI/2022%20PGE%20Restrictions%20Non%20Senior.pdf [hereinafter SOCO], discussing 18 U.S.C. § 207 (2018) and related statutes.

[17] 18 U.S.C. § 201 (1994).

[18] Competition in Contracting Act of 1984, Pub. L. No. 98-369, 98 Stat. 1175 (codified at 10 U.S.C. § 2302 *et seq.* and 41 U.S.C. § 3101 *et seq.*) [hereinafter CICA]. CICA seeks to reduce costs of government procurement by encouraging multiple bidders to compete to provide the government the products or services it wants, which in theory should permit the government to secure a contract with the optimal ratio of price to performance. Of course, if agents for the government or the contractor engage in favoritism or self-dealing in violation of ethical standards, it can skew the competition and deny the government the benefit of competitive pressures. CICA speaks directly to the need for ethical competition when it defines a "responsible source" to mean a prospective contractor who, inter alia, "has a satisfactory record of integrity and business ethics." CICA § 2731 (recodified and amended at 41 U.S.C. § 113(4) (2012)).

[19] The Antideficiency Act, 31 U.S.C. §§ 1341–1342, 1357 (2019), is a long-standing statute that gives teeth to U.S. Const. art. I § 9, cl. 7, which states in part, "No Money shall be drawn from the

the Federal Acquisition Regulation's (FAR's) provisions on improper business practices and personal conflicts of interest.[20]

Other areas with ethical implications include technology transfer, the rules governing intellectual property rights between government and industry collaborators,[21] and the rules on workforce mix, which define which activities are inherently governmental or inherently military in nature and which may be assigned to civilian employees or contracted out.[22] Some of the workforce mix rules have their roots in the government's international legal obligations under the law of armed conflict, such as the principle of distinction, which requires governments to keep a degree of separation between their military forces and protected civilian persons and objects.[23]

In addition, antitrust law has presented challenges for government-industry interaction in the space domain. Although competition has rapidly expanded in recent years,[24] the great expense and risk involved in space launches and operations, and their concomitant regulatory compliance hurdles, historically have resulted in situations where only a small number of firms can supply certain needs,[25] leading

Treasury, but in Consequence of Appropriations made by Law." This means that government employees shall not obligate funds for a purpose, time, or amount for which the funds were not appropriated, such as buying office furniture with current fiscal-year funds to furnish a military construction project that will not be completed until a subsequent fiscal year.

[20] U.S. Federal Acquisition Regulation [hereinafter FAR], 48 C.F.R. pt. 3 (Improper Business Practices and Personal Conflicts of Interest), *cf.* 18 U.S.C. § 203 (1990) (ban on compensation for representational services); 18 U.S.C. § 205 (2002) (ban on prosecuting claims against the U.S. government).

[21] U.S. DEP'T OF DEF., INSTR. 5535.8, *DoD Technology Transfer (T2) Program*, May 14, 1999, inc. Change 1, Sept. 1, 2018, at para. 6.17.11.

[22] *See generally* U.S. DEP'T OF DEF., INSTR. 1100.22, *Policy and Procedures for Determining Workforce Mix*, Apr. 12, 2010, inc. Change 1, Dec. 1, 2017.

[23] *Id.*, encl. 4, § 1(c). *See also* U.S. DEP'T OF DEF., OFFICE OF GEN. COUNSEL, DEPARTMENT OF DEFENSE LAW OF WAR MANUAL § 2.5 (June 2015, updated Dec. 2016), https://dod.defense.gov/Portals/1/Documents/pubs/DoD%20Law%20 of%20War%20Manual%20-%20June%202015%20Updated%20Dec%202016.pdf?ver=2016-12-13-172036-190 [hereinafter DOD LAW OF WAR MANUAL]. For a fuller exposition of the legal status of civilians with special technical expertise supporting military operations, *see* Matthew T. King, *High Tech Civilians, Participation in Hostilities, and Criminal Liability: Reconciling U.S. Perspectives*, *in* THE IMPACT OF EMERGING TECHNOLOGIES ON THE LAW OF ARMED CONFLICT 175 (Ronald T.P. Alcala & Eric T. Jensen eds., 2019).

[24] One industry observer describes the spacecraft construction market as "highly fragmented, with many players." Mordor Intelligence, *Spacecraft Market—Growth, Trends, and Forecast (2021–2026)*, https://www.mordorintelligence.com/industry-reports/spacecraft-market (last visited Dec. 27, 2021). About two years before, the same observer had pegged the market as being midway between a "consolidated" market dominated by no more than five major players and a highly competitive "fragmented" market without dominant players. Mordor Intelligence, *Spacecraft Market—Growth, Trends, and Forecast (2020–2025)*, https://www.mordorintelligence.com/industry-reports/spacecraft-market (last visited Jan. 27, 2020). While much of the following discussion focuses on space launch, other core elements of the space industrial market include spacecraft construction, satellite services, and ground station construction, as described in the reports at *supra* note 2.

[25] For example, the U.S. Air Force relied exclusively for more than a decade on United Launch Alliance (ULA), a quasi-duopolistic joint venture of aerospace industrial behemoths Boeing and

to potential increases in price or reductions in innovation for the government buyer.[26] If economic pressures lead to industry consolidation, this could become a greater risk again.

At the same time, national security concerns will limit the extent to which foreign entities, particularly those governed by adversaries, can compete in the market.[27] In order to spur domestic industry while reducing reliance on foreign parts, Congress has continued to push for fully U.S.-built launch vehicles.[28]

Lockheed Martin, as its commercial space launch services provider. Irene Klotz, *SpaceX Breaks Boeing-Lockheed Monopoly on Military Space Launches*, REUTERS (Apr. 27, 2016), https://www.reuters.com/article/us-space-spacex-launch-idUSKCN0XO2TC. During that time, however, ULA was not the sole launch services provider to the broader U.S. government: the National Aeronautics and Space Administration (NASA) awarded its first contract to SpaceX in 2006, the year after the formation of ULA was announced. *NASA Selects Crew, Cargo Launch Partners*, SPACEFLIGHT NOW (Aug. 18, 2006), https://spaceflightnow.com/news/n0608/18cots/, *cf.* ULA, *Boeing, Lockheed Martin to Form Launch Services Joint Venture* (May 2, 2005), https://www.ulalaunch.com/all_news_items/2005/05/02/boeing-lockheed-martin-to-form-launch-services-joint-venture.

[26] *See, e.g.*, Mike Gruss, *Responding to Critics, ULA Discloses Pricing Information*, SPACENEWS (May 21, 2014), https://spacenews.com/40637news-from-the-30th-space-symposium-responding-to-critics-ula-discloses/ (reporting on SpaceX's accusation that ULA charged inflated prices to the government, as well as ULA's rejoinder). *See also* Maurice E. Stucke, *Is Competition Always Good?*, 1(1) J. ANTITRUST ENFORCEMENT 162 (2013) (discussing the risks associated with competition and analyzing the economic value of competition to assess when it should and should not be promoted); Daniel E. Schoeni, *Whither Innovation?: Why Open Systems Architecture May Deliver on the False Promise of Public-Private Partnerships*, 70 ADMIN. L. REV. 409, 417–21 (2018) (summarizing the several imperfections of the defense market, including problems of oligopsony, oligopoly, and bilateral monopoly).

[27] For example, after the final space shuttle flight in 2011, the United States became reliant on the Russian Federation and Kazakhstan to transport astronauts to the International Space Station using Soyuz capsules developed by the Soviet Union. *See* Adam Taylor, *Russia's Deputy PM Tells U.S. Astronauts to Go to Space on a Trampoline; The Joke May Be on Him*, WASH. POST (Apr. 30, 2014), https://www.washingtonpost.com/news/worldviews/wp/2014/04/30/russias-deputy-pm-tells-u-s-astronauts-to-go-to-space-on-a-trampoline-the-joke-may-be-on-him/. *See also* Elizabeth Howell, *Atlantis: Last Space Shuttle Launch*, SPACE.COM (Nov. 30, 2017), https://www.space.com/18162-space-shuttle-atlantis.html (describing the last Space Transportation System mission, STS-135, performed by the space shuttle *Atlantis* July 8–21, 2011). Moreover, ULA's Atlas 5 space launch vehicles incorporate the Russian-made RD-180 rocket engine. *See* Sandra Erwin, *Crunch Time: Rocket Companies in All-out Battle for Air Force Award*, SPACENEWS (May 24, 2019), https://spacenews.com/crunch-time-rocket-companies-in-all-out-battle-for-air-force-award/; Sandra Erwin, *Air Force "Hopeful" Congress Will Support New Strategy to Phase Out Russian Rockets*, SPACENEWS (Nov. 3, 2017), https://spacenews.com/air-force-hopeful-congress-will-support-new-strategy-to-phase-out-russian-rocket-engines/. Congress attempted to limit future U.S. use and purchases of the RD-180, but ended up exempting existing stocks from the ban. *See, e.g.*, *Assuring National Security Space: Investing in American Industry to End Reliance on Russian Rocket Engines: Hearing Before the Subcomm. on Strategic Forces of the H. Comm. on Armed Services*, 114th Cong. (2015), https://www.govinfo.gov/content/pkg/CHRG-114hhrg95320/html/CHRG-114hhrg95320.htm. More recently, national security concerns have led the U.S. government to criticize the Chinese telecommunications firm Huawei and to discourage other countries from doing business with it. Sean Keane, *Huawei Ban: Full Timeline as Trump Signs Law to Stop Rural Carriers from Using Its Gear*, CNET (Mar. 13, 2020), https://www.cnet.com/news/huawei-ban-full-timeline-us-government-china-trump-ban-rural-carriers-security-threat/.

[28] Valerie Insinna, *As RD-180 Ban Looms, Space Companies Make Steady Progress on New Launch Technologies*, DEFENSENEWS (Apr. 3, 2017), https://www.defensenews.com/digital-show-dailies/space-symposium/2017/04/03/as-rd-180-ban-looms-space-companies-make-steady-progress-on-new-launch-technologies/.

Responding to these incentives, new domestic technologies such as SpaceX's reusable Falcon rockets have contributed significantly to the reduction in costs and the increasing pace of domestic satellite launch operations.[29] As of this writing, the U.S. government, and the private sector are engaged in multiple lines of effort to transport human crews to the International Space Station (ISS) and beyond. SpaceX made history when it launched the first manned Crew Dragon capsule to the ISS in 2020,[30] and it continues to develop its new "Starship" system for future longer-distance missions.[31] The National Aeronautics and Space Administration (NASA) is testing the Orion crew capsule[32] and has developed a new heavy launch vehicle called the Space Launch System (SLS).[33] NASA conducted the first launch and return of the SLS and Orion in 2022,[34] while SpaceX hopes to send a Starship to the Moon by 2024.[35] Meanwhile, Boeing and Bigelow Aerospace are building the "CST-100 Starliner" as part of NASA's Commercial Crew Program.[36] Congress is also encouraging greater use of allied countries' launch capabilities and space-based navigation services.[37]

Amid all these developments, it is critical for interactions between government and industry to proceed in accordance with the utmost standards

29 *See, e.g.*, Jeff Foust, *SpaceX Wins Contract to Launch NASA Small Astrophysics Mission*, SpaceNews (July 8, 2019), https://spacenews.com/spacex-wins-contract-to-launch-nasa-small-astrophysics-mission/. ULA is also improving its ability to conduct multiple separate launches within days to weeks. *See* Theresa Hitchens, *DoD Rethinks Launch Needs to Counter Russia, China*, Breaking Def. (Oct. 23, 2019), https://breakingdefense.com/2019/10/dod-rethinks-launch-needs-to-counter-russia-china/.

30 Nat'l Aeronautics & Space Admin. [hereinafter NASA], Press Release 20-057, Sean Potter, ed., *NASA Astronauts Launch from America in Historic Test Flight of SpaceX Crew Dragon* (last updated June 4, 2020), https://www.nasa.gov/press-release/nasa-astronauts-launch-from-america-in-historic-test-flight-of-spacex-crew-dragon. The Crew Dragon capsule and its crew, astronauts Douglas Hurley and Robert Behnken, successfully splashed down on August 3, 2020. William Harwood, *SpaceX Crew Dragon Astronauts Describe Thrilling Return to Earth*, CBS News (Aug. 5, 2020), https://www.cbsnews.com/news/spacex-crew-dragon-astronauts-return-to-earth/.

31 Stuart Clark, SpaceX Is Bound for the Moon, but 2024 Goal Is Now a Long Shot, *Guardian*, Apr. 30, 2021, https://www.theguardian.com/science/2021/apr/30/spacex-bound-for-moon-but-2024-goal-now-long-shot .

32 NASA, *Orion Spacecraft* (Nov. 10, 2022), https://www.nasa.gov/exploration/systems/orion/about/index.html.

33 NASA, *Space Launch System* (Dec. 19, 2022), https://www.nasa.gov/exploration/systems/sls/index.html.

34 Michael Dougherty, *Detachment 3, AFSPACE Makes Historic Splash with Artemis Recovery off Baja California Coast*, Def. Visual Info. Distrib. Serv. (Dec. 11, 2022), https://www.dvidshub.net/news/435861/detachment-3-afspace-makes-historic-splash-with-artemis-recovery-off-baja-california-coast.

35 Clark, *supra* note 31. *See also* Tariq Malik, *Elon Musk Unveils SpaceX's New Starship Plans for Private Trips to the Moon, Mars and Beyond*, Space.com (Sept. 29, 2019), https://www.space.com/elon-musk-unveils-spacex-starship-2019-update.html.

36 Elizabeth Howell, *Boeing CST-100 Starliner: Next-Generation Spaceship*, Space.com (Mar. 14, 2019), https://www.space.com/18852-spacex-dragon.html.

37 2020 NDAA, *supra* note 5, §§ 1607, 1610.

of integrity. Ethical violations have derailed significant projects in the past.[38] When officials are compromised and put private gain above their fiduciary duty to their agency and taxpayers, when they fail to properly define and communicate requirements,[39] or when industry partners promise more than they can realistically deliver, programs become afflicted with cost overruns, burdensome political oversight, and cancellations.[40] The programs contribute to the ballooning national debt while failing to deliver the promised national security gains. Conversely, when government-industry interactions are conducted with integrity and competence, success is much more likely. At the very least, the program in question will not end in a failure that not only humiliates the parties involved but is potentially catastrophic to national security.[41]

[38] For example, earlier efforts for the U.S. Air Force to acquire its next-generation tanker suffered numerous delays, partly due to a bribery scandal involving Boeing executives and a senior Air Force civilian official. *See generally* Jeffrey Branstetter, *Darleen Druyun: An Evolving Case Study in Corruption, Power, and Procurement*, 34 PUB. CONT. L.J. 443 (2005).

[39] The Air Force's next attempt at a tanker acquisition following the Darleen Druyun scandal failed because officials changed the terms of the competition midstream, leading to an award of the contract to a consortium consisting of Northrop Grumman and Europe's EADS that was, in turn, also rescinded. Adam J. Hebert, *A Tanker for the Air Force*, AIR FORCE MAG. (Sept. 2010), http://www.airforcemag.com/MagazineArchive/Pages/2010/September%202010/0910issbf.aspx. Eventually, Boeing won the contract and has begun to produce the new tanker, now known as the KC-46 "Pegasus," although the program continues to face criticism. *U.S. Air Force Accepts First Boeing KC-46A Pegasus Tanker Aircraft*, BOEING (Jan. 10, 2019), https://boeing.mediaroom.com/2019-01-10-U-S-Air-Force-Accepts-First-Boeing-KC-46A-Pegasus-Tanker-Aircraft; U.S. GOV'T ACCOUNTABILITY OFFICE, GAO-22-104530, AIR FORCE NEEDS TO MATURE CRITICAL TECHNOLOGIES IN NEW AERIAL REFUELING SYSTEM DESIGN (2022), https://www.gao.gov/assets/gao-22-104530.pdf. Space programs in both the wider DoD and NASA have also suffered from similarly troubled acquisition programs. *See, e.g.*, U.S. GOV'T ACCOUNTABILITY OFFICE, GAO-19-458T, DOD FACES SIGNIFICANT CHALLENGES AS IT SEEKS TO ACCELERATE SPACE PROGRAMS AND ADDRESS THREATS (2019), https://www.gao.gov/assets/700/697998.pdf.

[40] These problems are not unique to open, democratic societies that leverage commercial industry, but also plague centrally run space programs in ideological, authoritarian countries. *See, e.g.*, WILLIAM E. BURROWS, THIS NEW OCEAN: THE STORY OF THE FIRST SPACE AGE 396–404 (Modern Library Paperback ed. 1999) (discussing how selfish ambition and misaligned competitive incentives degraded the progress of the Soviet lunar exploration program, culminating in the death of chief rocket designer Sergei Korolyov at the hands of the Soviet Minister of Health Boris Petrovsky, who insisted on operating on this prestigious patient despite being long past his prime as a surgeon). Similarly, Soviet willingness to cut corners in service of political goals led to the disastrous launch failure of the R-16 intercontinental ballistic missile (ICBM) that killed the head of the Strategic Rocket Forces and 91 others. *Id.* at 309.

[41] *See generally* U.S. DEP'T OF DEF., STANDARDS OF CONDUCT OFFICE, ENCYCLOPEDIA OF ETHICAL FAILURE (2021), https://dodsoco.ogc.osd.mil/Portals/102/Documents/Training%20Materials/Encyclopedia%20of%20Ethical%20Failure%202021.pdf (discussing examples of military members, federal employees, and contractors who have run afoul of the ethics rules and sometimes criminal statutes).

3. Selected Issues in Space Ethics

Legal advisers dealing with military activities in outer space encompass may confront a variety of situations where ethical issues arise.[42] Several of these, notably related to gift rules, post-government employment, impartiality and fair dealing, ethics at war, and litigation risks, will be discussed in detail in the sections following.

3.1. Gift Rules

Among the best-known, yet sometimes misunderstood, federal ethics requirements are the gift rules, which prohibit federal employees from accepting

[42] For example, the author worked and advised on several different issues with ethical implications as the Chief of Space and International Law at 14th Air Force between 2014 and 2017. Also known as Air Forces Strategic, or AFSTRAT, 14th Air Force was a numbered air force (NAF) at the intermediate echelon of command between Air Force Space Command (AFSPC) and the five Space Wings at Vandenberg, Buckley, Peterson, Schriever, and Patrick Air Force Bases (AFBs), and also oversaw the 614th Air Operations Center at Vandenberg AFB. *See* Air Force Space Command, *Fact Sheet: Fourteenth Air Force* (Oct. 2019), https://www.afspc.af.mil/About-Us/Fact-Sheets/Display/Article/1604750/fourteenth-air-force/. While the author worked there, Fourteenth Air Force was run by a three-star general who was dual-hatted (i.e., served in a second position simultaneously) as the commander of USSTRATCOM's Joint Functional Component Command for Space (JFCC SPACE). *See, e.g.*, U.S. Air Force, *Lieutenant General David J. Buck* (Dec. 2019), https://www.af.mil/About-Us/Biographies/Display/Article/108707/lieutenant-general-david-j-buck/. On December 1, 2017, JFCC SPACE was inactivated and its functions transferred to the new Joint Force Space Component Command (JFSCC), which remained aligned with AFSPC just as JFCC SPACE had been with 14 AF. U.S. Air Force Space Command, *Joint Space Forces Restructure, AFSPC Commander Becomes JFSCC* (Dec. 4, 2017), https://www.af.mil/News/Article-Display/Article/1386852/joint-space-forces-restructure-afspc-commander-becomes-jfscc/. The JFSCC lasted for less than two years before being elevated out of USSTRATCOM and rebranded as the new USSPACECOM, which continued to share its commander with AFSPC until August 2020. Rachel S. Cohen, *US Space Command Set to Launch Within Weeks*, Air Force Mag. (July 31, 2019), https://www.airforcemag.com/us-space-command-set-to-launch-within-weeks/; *USSPACECOM Makes History with First Change of Command*, USSPACECOM Pub. Affairs (Aug. 20, 2020), https://www.spacecom.mil/MEDIA/NEWS-ARTICLES/Article/2320283/usspacecom-makes-history-with-first-change-of-command/. As soon as USSPACECOM was re-established, General Raymond ordered the establishment of a subordinate command called the Combined Force Space Component Command, which took over many of the roles previously performed by JFCC SPACE at Vandenberg AFB. Cody Chiles, *Combined Force Space Component Command Established at Vandenberg AFB*, Combined Force Space Component Command Pub. Affairs (Oct. 2, 2019), https://www.spacecom.mil/News/Article-Display/Article/1977714/combined-force-space-component-command-established-at-vandenberg/. On December 20, 2019, shortly after AFSPC transformed into the U.S. Space Force, the Secretary of the Air Force redesignated 14 AF as Space Operations Command (SpOC). Cody Chiles, *14th Air Force Redesignated as Space Operations Command*, Space Operations Command Pub. Affairs (Dec. 27, 2019), https://www.spaceforce.mil/News/Article/2048114/14th-air-force-redesignated-as-space-operations-command. In 2020, the name of SpOC was repurposed for the new Space Force field command operating from the former AFSPC headquarters at Peterson AFB, while the organization at Vandenberg was redesignated as "SpOC West." *About Space Operations Command*, Space Operations Command, https://www.spoc.spaceforce.mil/About-Us/About-Space-Operations-Command (last visited Dec. 27, 2021). By July 2021, all of the former Air Force Bases once under 14th Air Force had been renamed as Space Force Bases. Kasia Kerridge, *Peterson, Schriever, and Cheyenne Mountain Air Force Installations Renamed to Space Force Monday*, KKTV (July 26, 2021), https://www.kktv.com/2021/07/26/peterson-schriever-cheyenne-mountain-air-force-installations-renamed-space-force-monday/.

a gift worth more than $20 per occasion or gifts with an aggregate value over $50 in a calendar year that are offered because of the employee's official position or by someone seeking to do business with the government.[43] As "new space" startups, software vendors, and other nontraditional defense contractors begin to vie for business with the Department of Defense, it is important to keep these long-established rules in mind.

Sometimes space industry participants, like many enterprises, will give away products, often bearing the company's logo, to customers and potential customers to advertise and build goodwill. This may occur at conventions or symposiums, when government personnel visit a contractor facility, or by a contractor to a government facility, among other scenarios. While items of lesser value may be accepted, government personnel should decline such gifts if they have a market value above $20,[44] or if "they believe that a reasonable person with knowledge of the relevant facts would question the employee's integrity or impartiality as a result of accepting the gift."[45] Federal employees are also prohibited from soliciting any gift from a prohibited source or to be given one because of the employee's official position.[46] If an employee is unsure whether a gift's market value exceeds the limit, she should seek to ascertain it or obtain an ethics opinion before doing so.

To avoid impropriety or the appearance thereof, industry members should also be aware of the gift rules and refrain from offering federal employees souvenirs or other gifts that exceed the limits. Industry personnel offering a gift are more likely to know its market value than the government recipient is. The market value is the retail, not the wholesale, cost of the item.[47] Thus, if a government contractor is selling a company-branded shirt on its website for $25 and tries to give one to a federal employee visiting its facility, that gift would violate the gift rule—even if it cost the company only $18 to produce. An employee may not "pay down" the excess value.[48] However, "goodie bags" composed of separate items that exceed $20 in aggregate value, but are individually worth less than $20, may be partially accepted to the extent that the aggregate value of the accepted gift or gifts does not exceed $20.[49] For example, if a gift bag offered

[43] Gifts from Outside Sources, 5 C.F.R. §§ 2635.201–2635.206 (2016).

[44] 5 C.F.R. § 2635.204(a). In addition, employees must not accept a gift of cash or other financial instruments such as a gift card, check, or securities. *Id.*

[45] 5 C.F.R. § 2635.201(b)(1) (for example, even a gift worth $20 or less should be rejected if it appears intended to influence the employee's performance of an official action).

[46] 5 C.F.R. § 2635.202(a). A "prohibited source" is any person who is seeking official action by the federal employee's agency, does or seeks to do business with the agency, conducts activities regulated by the agency, has interests that may be substantially affected by the employee's performance or nonperformance of official duties, or is an organization composed mostly of such people. 5 C.F.R. § 2635.203(d).

[47] 5 C.F.R. § 2635.203(c).

[48] 5 C.F.R. § 2635.204(a).

[49] *Id.*

by a government contractor contains a $12 cap, a $7 mug, and a $3 pen, a government employee may accept any two of the items, but not all three.[50] Such limitations may seem overly cautious, but they have been instituted in order to establish a bright-line rule against conflicts of interest, in recognition of well-recognized principal-agent problems in public procurement.[51] Because their personal interests are not well aligned with the public interest, small personal conveniences or benefits could exercise a disproportionate influence on officials' procurement decisions.[52]

3.2. Post-Government Employment

Government ethics rules affect space force organizations just as they affect many other military bases with pools of highly trained and experienced personnel with in-demand skills and relationships. While space operators do not have nearly as many opportunities as members of certain other military occupational specialties to receive benefits such as training, conference attendance, and off-duty employment provided by private-sector entities while they remain on active duty,[53] their specialized knowledge, expertise, and connections may make them valuable recruits for aerospace firms that do business with the government. Because of this, it is important for officials to obtain a post-government employment opinion from an ethics counselor before they leave service, particularly if they "participated personally and substantially in" an acquisition worth more than $10 million, or if they served in certain positions of senior leadership or program responsibility.[54] In the space domain, even relatively minor acquisitions frequently exceed the $10 million threshold.

To obtain the ethics opinion, employees must provide information about where they have worked in the past and any programs for which they had management, contracting, or other discretionary authority over how the government

[50] Assume, for purposes of this example, that the bag itself has no intrinsic value.

[51] *See, e.g.*, Christopher R. Yukins, *A Versatile Prism: Assessing Procurement Law through the Principal-Agent Model*, 40 PUB. CONT. L.J. 63 (diagnosing various manifestations of the principal-agent problem in government contracts); PETER TREPTE, REGULATING PUBLIC PROCUREMENT: UNDERSTANDING THE ENDS AND MEANS OF PUBLIC PROCUREMENT REGULATION 129–30 (2004) (suggesting that procurement regulations exist in large part to manage agency problems).

[52] *See* Steven L. Schooner, *Contractor Atrocities at Abu Ghraib: Compromised Accountability in a Streamlined, Outsourced Government*, 16 STAN. L. & POL'Y REV. 549, 565 (2005) (observing that all too often "speed, convenience, personal preference, and human nature" are factors in procurement decisions).

[53] For example, in the author's previous work as a medical law consultant, he reviewed many such offers and requests for military medical professionals.

[54] SOCO, *supra* note 16, at 5–6.

did business. To ensure that government employees do not illicitly feather their nests by steering business toward a current or prospective private employer, and that they do not improperly trade on nonpublic information, all employees must avoid seeking employment at places that would present an actual or apparent conflict of interest. The U.S. Office of Government Ethics reports that violations of the post-government employment restrictions in 18 U.S.C. § 207 have resulted in less than one prosecution per year on average since 1990.[55]

Ironically, in one respect the U.S. government imposes a higher barrier for military veterans to remain in the DoD as federal civilian employees than to work at most commercial firms after retirement. Since 1964, there has been a statutory 180-day "cooling off" period that generally prohibits the DoD from hiring military retirees into civil service positions during the first six months of their retirement.[56] The restriction was put in place to avoid self-dealing by departing military members who could write a civilian position description to fit themselves and then apply for the job in a noncompetitive fashion.[57] The Office of Personnel Management (OPM) waived this restriction following the terrorist attacks of September 11, 2001, and kept the emergency waiver in place for over 15 years.[58] However, in December 2016, Congress removed OPM's emergency waiver authority and thereby reinstated the cooling-off period.[59] Unlike the

55 U.S. Office of Gov't Ethics, *Conflict of Interest Prosecution Surveys Index (by Statute)*, https://www.oge.gov/web/oge.nsf/Resources/Conflict+of+Interest+Prosecution+Surveys+Index+(by+Statute) (last visited Sept. 12, 2022).

56 Stacy Hojnowski, *Navigating Changes to the 180-Day Rule for Retiring Military*, Nat'l Career Dev. Ass'n (June 1, 2018), https://www.ncda.org/aws/NCDA/pt/sd/news_article/170427/_PARENT/CC_layout_details/false.

57 U.S. Merit Systems Protection Board, Veteran Hiring in the Civil Service: Practices and Perceptions, at ii (2014), https://www.mspb.gov/studies/Veteran_Hiring_in_the_Civil_Service_Practices_and_Perceptions_1072040.pdf [hereinafter MSPB].

58 Hojnowski, *supra* note 56, *cf.* Jared Serbu, *Navy, Air Force Want Congress to Abolish 180-Day Waiting Period to Hire Military Retirees*, Fed. News Network (June 15, 2018), https://federalnewsnetwork.com/defense-main/2018/06/navy-air-force-want-congress-to-abolish-180-day-waiting-period-to-hire-military-retirees/.

59 Nat'l Def. Authorization Act for Fiscal Year 2017, Pub. L. No. 114-328 § 1111 (2016) [hereinafter 2017 NDAA] (amending 5 U.S.C. § 3326 (2016)). Congress reinstated the cooling-off period after the U.S. Merit Systems Protection Board issued a report finding that people perceived some inappropriate favoritism towards veterans in federal civilian hiring practices, as well as, to a lesser extent, inappropriate denial of veteran hiring preferences where such preferences are legally required. MSPB, *supra* note 57, at i–ii. Congress has resisted subsequent attempts to repeal the cooling-off period entirely, although it has provided limited exemptions in recent National Defense Authorization Acts. *Senate Backs Continued Restriction on Hiring of Military Retirees by DoD*, Fedweek (June 19, 2019), https://www.fedweek.com/fedweek/senate-backs-continued-restriction-on-hiring-of-military-retirees-by-dod/, *cf.* 2020 NDAA, *supra* note 5 (making no amendment to 5 U.S.C. § 3326); *but see* William M. (Mac) Thornberry Nat'l Def. Authorization Act for Fiscal Year 2021, Pub. L. No. 116-283 § 1108 (2021) [hereinafter 2021 NDAA] (providing temporary authority for the DoD to hire newly retired military members into GS-13 and lower positions at defense industrial base facilities with a certified need for more potential applicants), *and* Nat'l Def. Authorization Act for Fiscal Year 2022, Pub. L. No. 117-81 § 1103 (2021) [hereinafter 2022 NDAA] (extending the 2021 NDAA's retiree hiring authority to apply to Major Range and Test Facility Bases as well).

post-government employment restrictions that tend to apply only to officers and civilian employees who exercised significant decision-making authority within the military,[60] the 180-day hiring ban applies to all retired military members, including enlisted members, unless they receive a waiver from their Service Secretary or designee[61] or are applying for a particularly hard-to-fill job.[62] Thus, the government, motivated by a desire to prevent military members from establishing federal civilian sinecures for themselves after retirement, induces its retirees to carry their skills and knowledge of government operations into private industry rather than retaining them within the DoD.

It is no surprise, then, that some former DoD officials will parlay their experience, former rank, and network of contacts into lucrative positions lobbying the government from their new perches in the private sector. They may do so as employees of a DoD contractor, or in a not-so-subtle attempt to skirt conflict-of-interest rules, as independent consultants retained by a DoD contractor to lobby the government on their behalf.[63] Military members may be tempted to accord such former officials the protocol, access, and deference to which they were once entitled by virtue of their rank and position. However, all must remember that when a retired senior officer returns to the base in pursuit of a government contract, he is to be treated like any other contractor's representative and not given any preferential treatment.

3.3. Impartiality and Fair Dealing

Regardless of who is representing a company, the government must treat all those who seek to do business with the government on a fair and impartial basis. Sometimes, this relates to something as simple as meeting with representatives of these companies, who may be former government officials, or even friends

[60] *See generally*, *e.g.*, 18 U.S.C. § 207; SOCO, *supra* note 16; U.S. Dep't of Def., Standards of Conduct Office, 2022 Senior Employee Post-Government Employment Restrictions, https://dodsoco.ogc.osd.mil/Portals/102/Documents/PGE%20and%20PI/Toolbox%20-%20PGE-PI/2022%20PGE%20Restrictions%20Senior.pdf (last visited Sept. 12, 2022).

[61] 5 U.S.C. § 3326(b)(1), (c), *cf.* U.S. Dep't of Def., Admin. Instr. 45, *Employment of Retired Members of the U.S. Armed Forces* (May 19, 2017), https://www.esd.whs.mil/Portals/54/Documents/DD/issuances/ai/a045p.pdf (specifying procedures to obtain a waiver to the 180-day hiring ban).

[62] 5 U.S.C. § 3326(b)(2), *cf.* 5 U.S.C. § 5305 and the 2021 NDAA and 2022 NDAA provisions cited in *supra* note 59.

[63] For a detailed critique of the practice of former senior defense officials representing major defense contractors soon after retirement, *see generally* Project on Government Oversight, Brass Parachutes: Defense Contractors' Capture of Officials Through the Revolving Door (Nov. 5, 2018), https://docs.pogo.org/report/2018/POGO_Brass_Parachutes_DoD_Revolving_Door_Report_2018-11-05.pdf. This report argues that existing law on post-government employment defines prohibited conduct so narrowly that many departing government officials can traipse through the "revolving door" between government and industry with impunity.

or former colleagues of their government hosts. Such meetings can be ethically perilous, particularly if an official enters into contracts that bind the government without following proper procedures.[64] If one company is granted a meeting with a senior leader or a tour of a secure facility, then that company's competitor should not be denied the same treatment, provided the competitor possesses the same level of security clearance.[65] When senior-level meetings are granted, it should be communicated throughout the agency, so that subordinate commanders do not impose a more restrictive policy that would inadvertently result in disparate treatment of industry representatives at other levels of command.

One best practice to facilitate this type of organization-wide ethical situational awareness is to develop a proactive screening process for visit requests. At Vandenberg Space Force Base, the legal office for the Combined Force Space Component Command (CFSCC) recently won a CFSCC team innovation award for its role in designing such a process, called the Industry Engagement Program. In this planned program, the commander will designate particular offices within the organization to assess all requests for meetings from NFEs that may do or seek to do business with the DoD. Those who request meetings must submit a questionnaire that supplies relevant information about potential conflicts of interest. The lead military office must then consult with the appropriate contracting officer, technical director, and servicing judge advocate (JA). If a meeting request is granted, the lead military office and JA will provide a guidance paper that outlines the ethical rules and the appropriate scope of the discussions, along with any tailored advice that may be necessary, to the officials who may meet with the NFE. The lead military offices maintain auditable electronic records of the program.[66] By formalizing the process and maintaining records in this way, the organization can ensure that its leaders stay within the proper ethical bounds and that contractors do not receive disparate treatment from their similarly situated competitors.

[64] *See, e.g.*, Craig Whitlock, *Key Army Commander Accused of Steering a Contract to Ex-classmates*, WASH. POST (June 21, 2015), https://www.washingtonpost.com/world/national-security/key-us-commander-leaves-middle-east-after-reprimand-for-misconduct/2015/06/21/7c3e8d7a-155a-11e5-9518-f9e0a8959f32_story.html; Sam LaGrone, *Paying the Price: The Hidden Cost of the "Fat Leonard" Investigation*, USNI NEWS (Jan. 24, 2019, updated Jan. 25, 2019), https://news.usni.org/2019/01/24/paying-price-hidden-cost-fat-leonard-investigation.

[65] As General Raymond, then-Commander, Air Force Space Command, and subsequently the Space Force's first Chief of Space Operations, observed, classification barriers made it harder for him to communicate with as many industry members as he would like; however, his team was "working very hard to reduce the classification on issues that allow . . . more conversation back and forth." *A Conversation with General Raymond*, *supra* note 5, *cf. General John W. "Jay" Raymond*, U.S. DEP'T OF DEF., https://www.defense.gov/About/Biographies/Biography/Article/1996612/commander-us-space-command-and-commander-air-force-space-command/ (last visited Dec. 27, 2021).

[66] Telephone conversation with Major Matthew G. Zellner, Legal Advisor for Combined Space Operations Center (CSpOC) and Space Delta 5, Sept. 2, 2020.

A government agency may often benefit when its leaders meet with industry representatives in order to learn about new products and services—as long as no improper commitments are made. In some cases, such as when the government itself needs to conduct market research (in contrast to contractor-initiated meeting requests), meeting with contractors to learn about their offerings is actually required by agency policy or regulation.[67] The Air Force and Space Force have lately touted the virtues of "Space Pitch Days," in which numerous companies with promising technologies, many of them small businesses, come together to make their case to the military service and are awarded on-the-spot contracts and payments in exchange for commitments to produce prototype systems within two years.[68] On the first Space Pitch Day in November 2019, for example, the Air Force heard pitches from 30 prescreened small businesses, granted Small Business Innovation Research awards to 12 of them, and listened to the winners' proposals for what they could do with double or quadruple the amount of total funding.[69] A contracting officer was on hand, as required, to sign the deals,[70] which were for the maximum $750,000 value permitted under the FAR's Simplified Acquisition Threshold.[71] These types of industry days give a diverse range of companies an opportunity to compete on a level playing field in an open and transparent fashion. Of course, for acquisitions with millions or billions of dollars at stake, the traditional process with its greater degree of formal procedures may work better, and indeed is generally required by law. Even so, Congress continues to admonish the DoD to "achieve faster [Space Systems] acquisition, improve synchronization and more rapid fielding of critical end-to-end capabilities (including by using new commercial capabilities and services), while maintaining accountability for effective programs that are delivered on time and on budget."[72]

[67] *See, e.g.*, FAR, *supra* note 20, §§ 7.102(a) ("Agencies shall . . . conduct market research . . . for all acquisitions"); 10.001(a)(2) ("Agencies shall . . . [c]onduct market research appropriate to the circumstances"); and 2.101 (defining market research as "collecting and analyzing information about capabilities within the market to satisfy agency needs") (Jan. 15, 2020). One of the most natural ways to collect information about capabilities is to meet with, listen to, and ask questions of representatives of firms that may wish to provide those capabilities to the government.

[68] Secretary of the Air Force Public Affairs, *"Space Pitch Day" Yields Innovative Technologies and New Partners for the Air Force* (Nov. 8, 2019), https://www.af.mil/News/Article-Display/Article/2012708/space-pitch-day-yields-innovative-technologies-and-new-partners-for-the-air-for/; Space and Missile Systems Center, *Space Force Pitch Day*, https://www.losangeles.spaceforce.mil/About-Us/Space-Force-Pitch-Day/ (last visited Dec. 27, 2021).

[69] Debra Werner, *Air Force Awards $9 Million on First Space Pitch Day San Francisco*, SpaceNews (Nov. 5, 2019), https://spacenews.com/air-force-awards-9-million-on-first-space-pitch-day-san-francisco/; Video by Airman 1st Class Amy Younger, *Air Force Hosts Space Pitch Day*, Def. Visual Info. Distrib. Serv. (Nov. 6, 2019), https://www.dvidshub.net/video/720900/air-force-hosts-space-pitch-day.

[70] Werner, *supra* note 69, *Air Force Hosts Space Pitch Day*, *supra* note 69.

[71] FAR, *supra* note 20, § 2.101 & pt. 13.

[72] 2021 NDAA, *supra* note 59, § 807(c)(1).

Another good example of how a government agency engaged equitably with commercial partners was in the formation of the Commercial Integration Cell (CIC) at the organization then known as 14th Air Force.[73] The CIC concept originated from the Commercial Operator Talks, which were a forum for military space leaders to engage with a broad swath of space industry participants.[74] In the CIC, the government entered into a series of cooperative research and development agreements (CRADAs)[75] with commercial operators of satellite communications and remote sensing systems, in order to research and develop new techniques to optimize space domain awareness (SDA),[76] electromagnetic interference resolution, and overall resiliency of satellite systems.[77] CRADAs require participants to be screened for conflicts of interest[78] and do not permit the government to provide funds to the collaborating party.[79]

When the CIC was first being formed, the 14th Air Force and partner agencies conducted an evaluation as to which companies should be part of the pilot program "based on the scope of their contributions to DOD operations."[80] To be

[73] *See supra* note 42 for a discussion of the evolution of 14 AF and related organizations since 2017.

[74] Nicholas Mercurio, *Commercial Integration Cell Pilot Program Underway*, U.S. AIR FORCE (June 5, 2015), https://www.af.mil/News/Article-Display/Article/590721/commercial-integration-cell-pilot-program-underway/, *cf.* Stacie N. Shafran, *JFCC SPACE Hosts Inaugural Operator Talks*, U.S. AIR FORCE SPACE COMMAND (July 23, 2013), https://www.afspc.af.mil/News/Article-Display/Article/731530/jfcc-space-hosts-inaugural-operator-talks/.

[75] *See* 15 U.S.C. § 3701 (1986), *et seq.* "Such an agreement combines the resources of the private sector, state and local governments, and university, or consortia with the federal government." RALPH C. NASH, JR., KAREN R. O'BRIEN-DEBAKEY & STEVEN L. SCHOONER, THE GOVERNMENT CONTRACTS REFERENCE BOOK 131 (4th ed. 2013). CRADAs are "a means of federal technology transfer whereby the government may share its research resources but may not use appropriated funds to conduct joint research products." *Id.*

[76] Existing law, joint doctrine, and many bilateral agreements use the term "space situational awareness" (SSA). *See, e.g.*, 10 U.S.C. § 2274 (2018), *and* U.S. CHAIRMAN OF THE JOINT CHIEFS OF STAFF, JOINT PUBL'N 3-14, *Space Operations* (Apr. 10, 2018, Change 1, Oct. 26, 2020), https://www.jcs.mil/Portals/36/Documents/Doctrine/pubs/jp3_14.pdf [hereinafter JP 3-14]. JP 3-14 defines SSA as "the requisite foundational, current, and predictive knowledge and characterization of space objects and the [operational environment] upon which space operations depend—including physical, virtual, information and human dimensions—as well as all factors, activities, and events of all entities conducting, or preparing to conduct, space operations." However, in 2019 AFSPC issued a memorandum directing personnel to use the term "SDA" instead, defining it as the "identification, characterization and understanding of any factor, passive or active, associated with the space domain that could affect space operations and thereby impact the security, safety, economy or environment of our nation." Sandra Erwin, *Air Force: SSA Is No More; It's "Space Domain Awareness"*, SPACENEWS (Nov. 14, 2019), https://spacenews.com/air-force-ssa-is-no-more-its-space-domain-awareness/. The new term "SDA" is both more concise and more focused on national security implications of what is happening in space. This chapter will still use "SSA" where appropriate, but will use "SDA" where possible.

[77] Caleb Henry, *Air Force to Make Long Term Commercial Integration Cell at JSpOC*, VIA SATELLITE (June 9, 2016), https://www.satellitetoday.com/innovation/2016/06/09/air-force-make-long-term-commercial-integration-cell-jspoc/.

[78] *See* 15 U.S.C. § 3710a(c)(3)(A) (2000).

[79] *Id.* § 3710a(b)(3)(A).

[80] Mercurio, *supra* note 74.

eligible for the CIC, prospective partners needed to have a preexisting contractual relationship with the DoD, as well as a space situational awareness (SSA) sharing agreement.[81] No cap was imposed on the number of potential members, enabling other companies that met the criteria for entry to subsequently sign CRADAs and join the CIC's original six industry members.[82] By setting reasonable threshold requirements, coordinated with multiple agencies, while also encouraging participation from a variety of firms on equal terms, the Air Force and Space Force both upheld their ethical obligations and advanced U.S. national security interests. Discussions with a broad range of industry partners, not limited to those in the CIC, continue to provide important opportunities for military and commercial space leaders to develop a shared understanding of how to address space threats together.[83]

3.4. Ethics at War

As alluded to earlier, the law of war contains some interesting conundrums for space forces and their commercial partners. Motivated by desires to reduce costs, increase resiliency, speed acquisitions of capabilities, and support the national defense industrial base, the United States has increasingly sought commercial space service providers to perform vital national security functions.[84] For example, a 2013 AFSPC white paper argued, "Hosting a government payload on a commercial satellite may lower program costs while complicating an adversary's decision calculus regarding attacking a commercial system,"[85] noting

[81] SSA sharing agreements, entered into under the authority of 10 U.S.C. § 2274, enable much of the information-sharing that takes place under the CRADAs.

[82] The first six CIC members were U.S.-registered corporate entities of Intelsat, Inmarsat, SES Government Solutions, Eutelsat, Iridium, and DigitalGlobe. Mercurio, *supra* note 74. XTAR, Viasat, Hughes Network Systems, and SpaceX joined later. Combined Force Space Component Command, *Commercial Integration Cell Fact Sheet* (June 2021), https://www.vandenberg.spaceforce.mil/Portals/18/documents/CFSCC/CIC-FactSheet-June2021.pdf; *see also* Sandra Erwin, *Space Command to Expand Network of Allies that Help Monitor Orbital Traffic*, SpaceNews (Jan. 29, 2021), https://spacenews.com/space-command-to-expand-network-of-allies-that-help-monitor-orbital-traffic/. In addition, DigitalGlobe, one of the original members, was acquired and rebranded as Maxar, but remains in the CIC in its new form. *History*, Maxar, https://www.maxar.com/history (last visited Dec. 27, 2021); Stephen Clark, *Canada's MDA Buys DigitalGlobe, Reveals Next-generation WorldView Satellite Fleet*, Spaceflight Now (Feb. 27, 2017), https://spaceflightnow.com/2017/02/27/canadas-mda-buys-digitalglobe-reveals-next-generation-worldview-satellite-fleet/.

[83] Sandra Erwin, *Satcom Conundrum: Air Force Contemplating Right Mix of Commercial, Military Satellites*, SpaceNews (May 6, 2019), https://spacenews.com/satcom-conumdrum-air-force-contemplating-right-mix-of-commercial-military-satellites/.

[84] *See, e.g.*, U.S. Air Force Space Command, *Resiliency and Disaggregated Space Architectures* (2013), https://www.afspc.af.mil/Portals/3/documents/AFD-130821-034.pdf (advocating for greater resiliency through disaggregation of space capabilities, including by placing military "hosted payloads" on commercial satellite buses, while acknowledging the legal concerns and potential conflicts of interest in doing so) [hereinafter AFSPC White Paper].

[85] *Id.* at 12.

that "[a]ttacking a commercial communications satellite . . . may instill a much different perception in the public eye than interference with a purely military space asset."[86]

The problem is, however, that military use of a commercial space system or service may make that commercial system or service targetable under the law of war. Under the principles of military necessity and distinction, the law of war permits attacks on objects "which by their nature, location, purpose or use make an effective contribution to enemy military action and whose total or partial destruction, capture or neutralization, in the circumstances ruling at the time, offers a definite military advantage."[87] It has been common practice in previous wars for countries to attack and defend commercial and economic targets such as factories, fuel production, and communications and transportation networks, even when they were privately owned, because of their contributions to the sustainment of the war effort.[88] In a future space war, the same principles could apply to orbital assets, ground stations, or the signals that link them. If the U.S. military is using a commercial satellite, a hostile power might seek to neutralize it in order to gain military advantage. Indeed, adversaries already seek to jam satellite signals in both peacetime and conflict, whether military or commercial.[89] Moreover, because the UN Charter characterizes interruption of communications such as

[86] *Id.* at n.17.

[87] Protocol Additional to the Geneva Conventions of 1949, and Relating to the Protection of Victims of International Armed Conflicts, art. 52(2), *opened for signature* Dec. 12, 1977, 1125 U.N.T.S. 3 (entered into force on July 12, 1978) [hereinafter Additional Protocol I, or AP I]. The United States has not ratified AP I, but considers some of its provisions, including this definition of a military objective, to accurately state customary international law. DoD Law of War Manual, *supra* note 23, § 5.6.3; *see also* W. Hays Parks et al., Memorandum for Mr. John H. McNeill, Assistant General Counsel (International), OSD, *1977 Protocols Additional to the Geneva Conventions: Customary International Law Implications* (May 9, 1986), *and* Theodore T. Richard, Unofficial United States Guide to the First Additional Protocol to the Geneva Conventions of 12 August 1949, at 98–106 (2019), https://www.airuniversity.af.edu/Portals/10/AUPress/Books/B_0157_UNOFFICIAL_UNITED_STATES_GUIDE_TO_THE_FIRST_ADDITIONAL_PROTOCOL_TO_THE_GENEVA_CONVENTIONS_OF_12_AUGUST_1949.PDF. In addition to military necessity and distinction, lawful targeting decisions must also comply with principles such as proportionality and humanity.

[88] For example, the U.S. Army Air Corps targeted German aircraft factories, ball bearing plants, and fuel production facilities during World War II. Williamson Murray, Strategy for Defeat: The Luftwaffe 1933–1945, at 170 (1983), https://www.airuniversity.af.edu/Portals/10/AUPress/Books/B_0012_MURRAY_STRATEGY_FOR_DEFEAT.pdf.

[89] *See, e.g.*, Sarah M. Mountin, *The Legality and Implications of Intentional Interference with Commercial Communication Satellite Signals*, 90 Int'l L. Stud. 101, 104 (2014); Peter B. de Selding, *France Seeks ITU Help to Halt Satellite Signal Jamming by Iran*, SpaceNews (Jan. 8, 2010), http://www.spacenews.com/article/france-seeks-itu-help-halt-satellite-signal-jamming-iran; Choe Sang-Hun, *North Korea Tried to Jam GPS Signals Across Border, South Korea Says*, N.Y. Times (Apr. 1, 2016), https://www.nytimes.com/2016/04/02/world/asia/north-korea-jams-gps-signals.html; Julia Siegel, *Commercial Satellites Are on the Front Lines of War Today. Here's What This Means for the Future of Warfare*, Atl. Council (Aug. 30, 2022), https://www.atlanticcouncil.org/content-series/airpower-after-ukraine/commercial-satellites-are-on-the-front-lines-of-war-today-heres-what-this-means-for-the-future-of-warfare/.

radio transmissions as a measure "not involving the use of armed force,"[90] disruption of satellite signals may be an alluring option for a hostile power looking to diminish U.S. and allied space power without triggering an armed response.

Recognizing these risks, U.S. Air Force Lieutenant Colonel Joseph Iungerman warned in 2014 that adversaries could threaten commercial satellite systems in ways that made it unprofitable for them to continue participating in U.S. military contracts.[91] As if to drive the point home, Russia deployed a satellite to perform close approaches to geosynchronous Intelsat communications satellites on multiple occasions between 2015 and 2019—in 2015, potentially coming as close as 5–10 kilometers,[92] and significantly worrying Intelsat, a commercial space operator that does business with the U.S. military.[93] Although no interference or collision occurred, the incident raises questions about Russia's intentions in conducting such close approaches to a U.S.-aligned commercial satellite.

To plan against such potential threats, AFSPC (now USSF) in recent years included representatives of commercial space operators in its annual wargames and other activities to ensure a full-spectrum approach to space defense.[94] Thus, if commercial space operators are threatened with attack or disruption because of their support for U.S. and allied warfighters, they may have the benefit of close coordination with the military for threat assessment and interference resolution, and the military may gain similar insights from them.[95]

[90] U.N. Charter art. 41.

[91] Joseph Iungerman, *What Happens If They Say No? Preserving Access to Critical Commercial Space Capabilities during Future Crises*, Air & Space Power J. 103–16 (Nov.–Dec. 2014), https://www.afspc.af.mil/Portals/3/documents/Schreiver%20Essay%202019/2014_SEW-Iungerman.pdf. Air Force Space Command recognized this article as a winner in its annual General Bernard A. Schriever Memorial Essay Contest.

[92] Mike Gruss, *Russian Satellite Maneuvers, Silence Worry Intelsat*, SpaceNews (Oct. 9, 2015), https://spacenews.com/russian-satellite-maneuvers-silence-worry-intelsat/; Nathan Strout, *Russian Satellite Creeps Up to Intelsat Satellite—Again*, C4ISRNET (Sept. 3, 2019), https://www.c4isrnet.com/battlefield-tech/2019/09/03/russian-satellite-creeps-up-to-intelsat-satellite-again/.

[93] Peter B. de Selding, *U.S. Military Rebounding as a Satellite Customer*, SpaceNews (Nov. 8, 2016), https://spacenews.com/u-s-military-rebounding-as-a-commercial-satellite-customer/.

[94] *See, e.g.*, Lauren Hill, *Schriever Wargame Concludes*, AFSPC Pub. Affairs (Sept. 13, 2019), https://www.afspc.af.mil/News/Article-Display/Article/1960610/schriever-wargame-concludes/ (describing an objective to "[e]xplore opportunities and challenges of national, commercial, and coalition architectures to synchronize effects that protect and defend the space enterprise"); Tracy Cozzens, *Schriever Wargame 2018 Concludes*, GPS World (Oct. 19, 2018), https://www.gpsworld.com/schriever-wargame-2018-concludes/ (describing an objective of "exploring partnerships framed by a whole of governments approach (International, Civil, Commercial) to combined space and cyberspace operations"); U.S. Air Force Space Command, *Schriever Wargame Concludes* (Oct. 20, 2017), https://www.afspc.af.mil/News/Article-Display/Article/1349906/schriever-wargame-concludes/ (describing an objective of "investigating partnerships framed by a whole of governments approach (allied, civil, commercial) to joint and combined operations").

[95] *Fiscal Year 2018 Priorities and Posture of the National Security Space Enterprise*: Hearing Before the Subcomm. on Strategic Forces of the H. Comm. on Armed Services, 115th Cong. 4–5 (2017) (statement of Lt. Gen. David J. Buck, Commander, Joint Functional Component Command for Space), https://docs.house.gov/meetings/AS/AS29/20170519/105974/HHRG-115-AS29-Wstate-BuckD-20170519.pdf; Rebecca Cowen-Hirsch, *Optimal Space Protection*, Milsat Mag. (Apr. 2016), http://www.milsatmagazine.com/story.php?number=1770700025.

One other potential area for ethical challenges to arise could be in what defensive services, if any, the military may provide to privately owned space assets in orbit. If commercial space objects are to be defended by military space forces, it should be for reasons of national security and military necessity, not out of favoritism for one commercial operator over another. While it is certainly possible for commercial space objects to be designated to receive military protection as a matter of national or collective self-defense,[96] states and their military forces may not always have the resources or will to defend such assets. Therefore, it is also conceivable that commercial space objects could be equipped with defensive capabilities in the future, which could raise a host of issues for their launching states under the outer space treaties and the international law of state responsibility.[97] Some commentators have even discussed licensing space "privateers" to conduct *offensive* operations in space, although the legal and ethical implications of doing so are beyond the scope of this chapter.[98]

Whether one is defending a commercial asset or a military asset in space, one may also turn to ethics to help determine what one *should* do as opposed to merely what one is *allowed* to do under the law of war. The inherent right of self-defense, including national and collective self-defense where authorized, permits the use of force if it is necessary and proportionate to defeat a given threat, and when de-escalatory measures fail or are not feasible.[99] That said, the risk calculus for self-defensive measures in space is different from that for defense against terrestrial threats.

[96] The U.S. Standing Rules of Engagement [hereinafter SROE] define U.S. commercial assets, in certain circumstances, to be covered by national self-defense, and even foreign property can be designated for protection when collective self-defense is authorized by the President or Secretary of Defense. CHAIRMAN OF THE JOINT CHIEFS OF STAFF INSTR. (CJCSI) 3121.01B, *Standing Rules of Engagement/Standing Rules for the Use of Force for U.S. Forces*, Encl. A, paras. 3.b–c (June 13, 2005), *reprinted in* INTERNATIONAL AND OPERATIONAL LAW DEPARTMENT, THE JUDGE ADVOCATE GENERAL'S LEGAL CENTER & SCHOOL, U.S. ARMY, OPERATIONAL LAW HANDBOOK 97 (2015).

[97] OST, *supra* note 1, arts. VI–VII (providing that launching states shall be internationally responsible for national activities in space, including those of their private entities, and shall be internationally liable for damages caused by their space objects).

[98] James D. Rendleman & Robert E. Ryals, *Private Defense of Space Systems & Letters of Marque and Reprisal*, AM. INST. OF AERONAUTICS & ASTRONAUTICS (Aug. 28, 2015), https://arc.aiaa.org/doi/abs/10.2514/6.2015-4571 (paper first presented at the AIAA Space Conference & Exposition, Pasadena, CA, Aug. 31–Sept. 2, 2015). For a fictional treatment of this idea, *see* P.W. SINGER & AUGUST COLE, GHOST FLEET: A NOVEL OF THE THIRD WORLD WAR 141–43 (Kindle ed. 2015).

[99] U.N. Charter art. 51 affirms states' inherent right to engage in national and collective self-defense if an armed attack occurs. The United States and the United Kingdom, among others, take the position that force may also be used to ward off an imminent armed attack or hostile use of force. DOD LAW OF WAR MANUAL, *supra* note 23, § 1.11.5. *See also* Aurel Sari, *The Mutual Assistance Clauses of the North Atlantic and EU Treaties: The Challenge of Hybrid Threats*, 10 HARV. NAT'L SEC. J. 405, 454 (2019) (describing the U.S. position that "any use of force against a state, regardless of its gravity, gives rise to the right to use necessary and proportionate force in self-defense"). *See also* SROE, *supra* note 96, Encl. A, para. 4.a (describing the need to apply principles of necessity, proportionality, and de-escalation in self-defense).

On Earth, when you shoot back at an enemy who is threatening or attacking you, the collateral effects are often relatively narrow in scope and duration. Bullets embed themselves in the target, or in some object or person along a discrete and finite trajectory. Bomb blast effects dissipate quickly. Fires burn out. Shrapnel falls to the ground. But similar kinetic actions in space could transform the targeted satellite and its kill vehicle into deadly clouds of shrapnel, zooming around the Earth for decades or centuries at speeds 10 times as fast as a speeding bullet.[100] Thus, defending a satellite by destroying a space object that's threatening it may mitigate the immediate threat but produce a higher degree of long-term risk to all spacefaring countries for generations to come. Although the law of war and the inherent right of self-defense, as *lex specialis*, would logically trump the Outer Space Treaty's due regard obligation as between the belligerents,[101] destructive self-defensive actions could potentially result in liability to third parties for damage caused by the space debris,[102] and could present serious risks to one's own space objects and astronauts.

For this reason, the U.S. military has prioritized counterspace capabilities with nondestructive, reversible effects,[103] and no country is known to have authorized

[100] For example, the Chinese anti-satellite (ASAT) test in January 2007 produced over 3,000 pieces of trackable debris, thousands of which remain in orbit—more than any accidental collision or explosion in orbit to date. Brian Weeden, *2007 Chinese Anti-Satellite Test Fact Sheet*, Secure World Foundation (Nov. 23, 2010), http://swfound.org/media/205391/chinese_asat_fact_sheet_updated_2012.pdf; P.D. Anz-Meador, *Debris by the Numbers*, 23(1–2) ORBITAL DEBRIS Q. NEWS 6 (May 2019), https://orbitaldebris.jsc.nasa.gov/quarterly-news/pdfs/odqnv23i1.pdf; John V. Lambert, Paper Presented at Advanced Maui Optical and Space Surveillance Technologies Conference: *Fengyun-1C Debris Cloud Evolution over One Decade* (Sept. 2018), https://amostech.com/TechnicalPapers/2018/Poster/Lambert.pdf; Peter Zimmer, John T. McGraw & Mark R. Ackermann, Paper Presented at Advanced Maui Optical and Space Surveillance Technologies Conference, Sept. 2019: Optical Measurements of Faint LEO RSOs: Cubesats and Fengyun 1C Debris, https://amostech.com/TechnicalPapers/2019/Orbital-Debris/Zimmer.pdf. *See also* Alex Brown, *How to Dodge a Space Bullet in Three (Not So Easy) Steps*, ATLANTIC (Apr. 3, 2014), https://www.theatlantic.com/politics/archive/2014/04/how-to-dodge-a-space-bullet-in-three-not-so-easy-steps/441348/.

[101] *Compare* OST, *supra* note 1, art. IX, *with* discussion at *supra* notes 96 and 99. While it is beyond the scope of this chapter to perform a detailed analysis of how certain principles of outer space law might be superseded in wartime, the International Law Commission has provided a useful framework for such analysis. Int'l Law Comm'n, Draft Articles on the Effects of Armed Conflicts on Treaties, with Commentaries, UNITED NATIONS (2011), https://legal.un.org/ilc/texts/instruments/english/commentaries/1_10_2011.pdf.

[102] *Id.* art. VII, *cf.* Convention on International Liability for Damage Caused by Space Objects art. III, Mar. 29, 1972, 24 U.S.T. 2389, 961 U.N.T.S. 187 (entered into force Sept. 1, 1972) [hereinafter Liability Convention]. Note, however, that under the Liability Convention, a launching state accused of causing damage to a space object as a result of its self-defensive actions in outer space could presumably disclaim legal liability by arguing that the damage is not "due to its fault."

[103] Joseph Trevithick, *Space Force Just Received Its First New Offensive Weapon*, THE DRIVE (Mar. 13, 2020), https://www.thedrive.com/the-war-zone/32570/space-force-just-received-its-first-new-offensive-weapon (describing how the Air Force and now the Space Force operate the Counter Communications System, a ground-based jammer, to neutralize hostile space assets without physically destroying them), *cf.* SECRETARY OF DEFENSE LLOYD AUSTIN, TENETS OF RESPONSIBLE BEHAVIOR IN SPACE (July 7, 2021), https://media.defense.gov/2021/Jul/23/2002809598/-1/-1/0/TENETS-OF-RESPONSIBLE-BEHAVIOR-IN-SPACE.PDF.

private entities to use space weapons in offense or defense.[104] Nevertheless, it is troubling that other countries have continued to develop and demonstrate destructive military counterspace capabilities.[105] As the barriers to entry for having a military presence in space have lowered over time and more countries therefore enter this domain,[106] a policy of self-restraint may not serve to resolve all ethical dilemmas that are international in nature. Political, military, and diplomatic officials will need to exercise sound judgment to determine how best to deter threats to space assets, and how and when to respond if deterrence fails.

Finally, commercial space operators may face hard choices in the event of a conflict between two or more of their state customers. If two opposing belligerents both lease satellite communications bandwidth from a commercial operator, and both request the operator to cease providing service to the other side, what should the operator do? What standards will the operator apply to decide which request to grant? Will the operator deny both requests, grant both, or grant one and deny the other? What if one of the belligerents threatens to take action against the satellite, its signal, or its ground control stations, or to arrest the operator's personnel and suspend its business license, if operator fails to comply with the belligerent's demands? As the potential for a conflict in space grows, commercial operators will increasingly face legal, contractual, ethical, and operational risks associated with providing services to one or more potential belligerents involved.

3.5. Litigation Risk

Sometimes, an existing or prospective contractor may challenge the propriety of the government's decisions. In such cases, it pays to be prepared from an ethical

[104] Interestingly, in recent years Japan seems to have led the way in building "space cannons" for peaceful purposes, such as a spring-loaded satellite launcher aboard the International Space Station and its asteroid-thumping Hayabusa2 spacecraft. Elizabeth Tasker, *Creating a Crater to Constrain the Age of an Asteroid's Surface*, Japanese Aerospace Exploration Agency (JAXA) (Mar. 23, 2020), http://www.hayabusa2.jaxa.jp/en/topics/20200320_science/; *JEM Small Satellite Orbital Deployer (J SSOD)*, JAXA, https://iss.jaxa.jp/en/kiboexp/jssod/ (last visited Dec. 27, 2021).

[105] Sandra Erwin, *U.S. Space Command Blasts Russia for Anti-Satellite Missile Test*, SpaceNews (Apr. 15, 2020), https://spacenews.com/u-s-space-command-blasts-russia-for-anti-satellite-missile-test/ (describing U.S. criticism of Russia for a recent test launch of an anti-satellite missile, as well as Russian maneuvers with a potential orbital weapon in the vicinity of a National Reconnaissance Office satellite); Jeff Foust, *NASA Warns Indian Anti-Satellite Test Increased Debris Risk to ISS*, SpaceNews (Apr. 2, 2019), https://spacenews.com/nasa-warns-indian-anti-satellite-test-increased-debris-risk-to-iss/; *Russia Conducts Space-Based Anti-Satellite Weapons Test*, *supra* note 3 (describing Russian testing of a projectile-firing satellite in orbit); Secretary of State Anthony J. Blinken, *Russia Conducts Destructive Anti-Satellite Missile Test* (Nov. 15, 2021), https://www.state.gov/russia-conducts-destructive-anti-satellite-missile-test/.

[106] *See, e.g.*, Stephen Clark, *Iran Places Military Satellite in Orbit*, Spaceflight Now (Apr. 22, 2020), https://spaceflightnow.com/2020/04/22/iran-places-military-satellite-in-orbit/.

standpoint, as well as clearly defining what one's requirements are. When the government was seeking to acquire new SDA software,[107] one business that sought to compete for the contract was Analytical Graphics, Inc. (AGI), which produced commercial SSA products that it believed would satisfy the government's needs. Indeed, both the Joint Space Operations Center (JSpOC)[108] and the Joint Interagency Combined Space Operations Center (JICSpOC)[109] employed some AGI software under other agreements.[110] Prior to the challenged competition, AGI had repeatedly sought to gain additional access to the JSpOC, offering to embed personnel as "technical support," but with a broader scope than the Air Force considered to fall under a traditional understanding of technical support. These requests were denied, partly in order to avoid giving AGI an unfair competitive advantage through an overly generous reading of its contract.

Later, when the Air Force awarded a contract for the SDA software to a different bidder, AGI filed a protest with the Government Accountability Office (GAO).[111] When denied, AGI followed up with a protest in the Court of Federal Claims (COFC).[112] Both the GAO and the COFC held in the Air Force's favor,

[107] The software was intended to enhance SDA and battle management, command, and control (BMC2) at the Joint Interagency Combined Space Operations Center (JICSpOC), which has since been renamed as the National Space Defense Center (NSDC). Analytical Graphics, Inc. v. United States, 135 Ct. Fed. Cl. 378, 381 (2017) [hereinafter AGI]; Shellie-Anne Espinosa, *National Space Defense Center Transitions to 24/7 Operations*, U.S. Air Force Space Command (Jan. 26, 2018), https://www.afspc.af.mil/News/Article-Display/Article/1423932/national-space-defense-center-transitions-to-247-operations/.

[108] The JSpOC, collocated with the 614th Air Operations Center (614 AOC) at Vandenberg Air Force Base, California, was renamed the CSpOC in 2018. *Combined Space Operations Center Established at Vandenberg AFB*, U.S. Strategic Command (July 19, 2018), https://www.stratcom.mil/Media/News/News-Article-View/Article/1579497/combined-space-operations-center-established-at-vandenberg-afb/. In July 2020, 614 AOC was inactivated and redesignated as Space Delta 5. Blythe Goya, *CSpOC and 614th AOC Change of Command, Space Delta 5 Activation*, CSpOC Pub. Affairs (July 24, 2020), https://www.vandenberg.spaceforce.mil/News/Article-Display/Article/2282681/cspoc-and-614th-aoc-change-of-command-space-delta-5-activation/.

[109] The JICSpOC, established in 2015 at Schriever Air Force Base, Colorado, was renamed the NSDC in 2017. Espinosa, *supra* note 107; Philip Swarts, *The JICSpOC Is Dead; Long Live the National Space Defense Center*, SpaceNews (Apr. 4, 2017), https://spacenews.com/the-jicspoc-is-dead-long-live-the-national-space-defense-center/. In military parlance, "joint" refers to activities or organizations in which multiple U.S. military services (e.g., the Army, Navy, and Air Force) work together, whereas "interagency" refers to multiple federal government agencies working together and "combined" refers to multinational coalition operations. Office of the Chairman of the Joint Chiefs of Staff, *DOD Dictionary of Military and Associated Terms* 38, 102, 107 (Aug. 2022), https://jdeis.js.mil/jdeis/new_pubs/dictionary.pdf (restricted access).

[110] Marketwire, *AGI Software Selected for Joint Space Operations Center (JSpOC) Mission System (JMS)*, Yahoo! Finance (Dec. 17, 2012), https://finance.yahoo.com/news/agi-software-selected-joint-space-145445283.html; AGI, 135 Ct. Fed. Cl. at 383. AGI remains a government-approved software vendor. Gen. Services Admin. Fed. Supply Service, Authorized Federal Supply Schedule Price List, GS-35F-056DA, https://www.gsaadvantage.gov/ref_text/GS35F056DA/0WMX7A.3SDA61_GS-35F-056DA_GS35F056DA.PDF.

[111] Analytical Graphics, Inc., B-413385, 2016 WL 6212299 (Comp. Gen. Oct. 17, 2016).

[112] Among other things, AGI alleged that the Air Force arbitrarily and capriciously chose to conduct the solicitation as a small business set-aside with a noncommercial solution. The court ruled against AGI on all counts. AGI, 135 Ct. Fed. Cl. at 381, 436.

finding that the Air Force had conducted a sufficiently fair bidding process and was within its authority to set and modify its requirements for the contract.[113] The COFC recognized, for example, that the Air Force had held an "industry day" for all potentially qualified applicants to learn about its proposal and discuss their interest and capabilities in meeting the project's requirements, which allowed the Air Force to refine its proposal and gain an adequate understanding of what options were available.[114]

In this case the Air Force prevailed, but often the incentive for officials will be to develop relationships with incumbents that are too cozy, thus discouraging new entrants, raising costs, and stifling innovation.[115] The Air Force resisted the natural inertia of an ongoing contractual relationship and AGI's apparent efforts to leverage its insider advantage through the overbroad construction of "technical support." By doing so, the Air Force protected itself from additional ethical and legal risk and won this bid protest.

4. Conclusion

Even as commercial space products and services have become increasingly essential contributors to U.S. national security,[116] government employees remain responsible to comply with the law and ethics rules when dealing with industry representatives. The foregoing discussion has outlined what many of these rules are, the consequences for breaking them, and proactive measures that people can take to avoid ethical compromise. By keeping the rules in mind, following them in practice, and seeking advice from an ethics counselor when there is doubt, decision makers can maintain the ethical high ground that enables them to better secure and exploit the "ultimate high ground" of outer space.

References

P.D. Anz-Meador, *Debris by the Numbers*, 23(1–2) ORBITAL DEBRIS Q. NEWS 6 (May 2019), https://orbitaldebris.jsc.nasa.gov/quarterly-news/pdfs/odqnv23i1.pdf.

113 *Id.* at 436.

114 *See id.* at 409, 416–18.

115 *See, e.g.*, Michele Estrin Gilman, *Legal Accountability in an Era of Privatized Welfare*, 89 CAL. L. REV. 569, 599–600 (2001) (arguing that incumbents soon become entrenched due to close relationships with government officials).

116 2020 NDAA, *supra* note 5, §§ 1608 (including requirements for the DoD to use more commercial SSA services), 1612 (also including requirement to incorporate remote sensing services). *See also* U.S. NAT'L SEC. STRATEGY 31 (2017), https://www.acq.osd.mil/ncbdp/docs/NSS-Final-12-18-2017-0905.pdf; U.S. NAT'L SPACE POL'Y 5, 29–31 (2020), https://trumpwhitehouse.archives.gov/wp-content/uploads/2020/12/National-Space-Policy.pdf.

Assuring National Security Space: Investing in American Industry to End Reliance on Russian Rocket Engines: Hearing Before the Subcomm. on Strategic Forces of the H. Comm. on Armed Services, 114th Cong. (2015), https://www.govinfo.gov/content/pkg/CHRG-114hhrg95320/html/CHRG-114hhrg95320.htm.

Boeing, *U.S. Air Force Accepts First Boeing KC-46A Pegasus Tanker Aircraft* (Jan. 10, 2019), https://boeing.mediaroom.com/2019-01-10-U-S-Air-Force-Accepts-First-Boeing-KC-46A-Pegasus-Tanker-Aircraft.

Jeffrey Branstetter, *Darleen Druyun: An Evolving Case Study in Corruption, Power, and Procurement*, 34 Pub. Cont. L.J. 443 (2005).

Alex Brown, *How to Dodge a Space Bullet in Three (Not So Easy) Steps*, Atlantic (Apr. 3, 2014), https://www.theatlantic.com/politics/archive/2014/04/how-to-dodge-a-space-bullet-in-three-not-so-easy-steps/441348/.

Bryce Space & Technology, *2020 State of the Satellite Industry Report* (July 28, 2020), https://brycetech.com/reports/report-documents/SIA_SSIR_2020.pdf.

Bryce Space & Technology, *2022 State of the Satellite Industry Report* 2–3 (July 13, 2022), https://brycetech.com/reports/report-documents/SIA_SSIR_2022.pdf.

William E. Burrows, This New Ocean: The Story of the First Space Age (Modern Library Paperback ed., 1999).

Ctr. for Strategic & Int'l Stud., *A Conversation with General Raymond* (Nov. 18, 2019), https://www.csis.org/analysis/conversation-general-raymond.

Chairman of the Joint Chiefs of Staff Instr. (CJCSI) 3121.01B, *Standing Rules of Engagement/Standing Rules for the Use of Force for U.S. Forces* (June 13, 2005), *reprinted in* International and Operational Law Department, The Judge Advocate General's Legal Center & School, U.S. Army, Operational Law Handbook 97 (2015).

Cody Chiles, *Combined Force Space Component Command Established at Vandenberg AFB*, Combined Force Space Component Command Pub. Affairs (Oct. 2, 2019), https://www.spacecom.mil/News/Article-Display/Article/1977714/combined-force-space-component-command-established-at-vandenberg/.

Cody Chiles, *14th Air Force Redesignated as Space Operations Command*, Space Operations Command (Dec. 27, 2019), https://www.spaceforce.mil/News/Article/2048114/14th-air-force-redesignated-as-space-operations-command.

Andrew Chuter, *Former Fighter Pilot Picked to Lead British Military's Space Command*, Def. News (Jan. 15, 2020), https://www.defensenews.com/global/europe/2020/01/15/former-fighter-pilot-picked-to-lead-british-militarys-space-command/.

Stephen Clark, *Canada's MDA Buys DigitalGlobe, Reveals Next-generation WorldView Satellite Fleet*, Spaceflight Now (Feb. 27, 2017), https://spaceflightnow.com/2017/02/27/canadas-mda-buys-digitalglobe-reveals-next-generation-worldview-satellite-fleet/.

Stephen Clark, *Iran Places Military Satellite in Orbit*, Spaceflight Now (Apr. 22, 2020), https://spaceflightnow.com/2020/04/22/iran-places-military-satellite-in-orbit/.

Stuart Clark, *SpaceX Is Bound for the Moon, but 2024 Goal Is Now a Long Shot*, Guardian (Apr. 30, 2021), https://www.theguardian.com/science/2021/apr/30/spacex-bound-for-moon-but-2024-goal-now-long-shot.

Rachel S. Cohen, *US Space Command Set to Launch Within Weeks*, Air Force Mag. (July 31, 2019), https://www.airforcemag.com/us-space-command-set-to-launch-within-weeks/.

Combined Force Space Component Command, *Commercial Integration Cell Fact Sheet* (Feb. 2021), https://www.vandenberg.spaceforce.mil/Portals/18/documents/CFSCC/CIC-FactSheet-Feb21.pdf.

Convention on International Liability for Damage Caused by Space Objects, Mar. 29 1972, 24 U.S.T. 2389, 961 U.N.T.S. 187.

Rebecca Cowen-Hirsch, *Optimal Space Protection*, MILSAT MAG. (Apr. 2016), http://www.milsatmagazine.com/story.php?number=1770700025.

Tracy Cozzens, *Schriever Wargame 2018 Concludes*, GPS WORLD (Oct. 19, 2018), https://www.gpsworld.com/schriever-wargame-2018-concludes/.

Peter B. de Selding, *France Seeks ITU Help to Halt Satellite Signal Jamming by Iran*, SPACENEWS (Jan. 8, 2010), http://www.spacenews.com/article/france-seeks-itu-help-halt-satellite-signal-jamming-iran.

Peter B. de Selding, *U.S. Military Rebounding as a Satellite Customer*, SPACENEWS (Nov. 8, 2016), https://spacenews.com/u-s-military-rebounding-as-a-commercial-satellite-customer/.

Marcia Dunn, *NASA to Potentially Reattempt Artemis 1 Launch in Late September*, PBS (Sept. 9, 2022), https://www.pbs.org/newshour/science/nasa-to-potentially-reattempt-artemis-1-launch-in-late-september.

Sandra Erwin, *Air Force "Hopeful" Congress Will Support New Strategy to Phase Out Russian Rockets*, SPACENEWS (Nov. 3, 2017), https://spacenews.com/air-force-hopeful-congress-will-support-new-strategy-to-phase-out-russian-rocket-engines/.

Sandra Erwin, *Satcom Conundrum: Air Force Contemplating Right Mix of Commercial, Military Satellites*, SPACENEWS (May 6, 2019), https://spacenews.com/satcom-conumdrum-air-force-contemplating-right-mix-of-commercial-military-satellites/.

Sandra Erwin, *Crunch Time: Rocket Companies in All-out Battle for Air Force Award*, SPACENEWS (May 24, 2019), https://spacenews.com/crunch-time-rocket-companies-in-all-out-battle-for-air-force-award/.

Sandra Erwin, *Air Force: SSA Is No More; It's "Space Domain Awareness"*, SPACENEWS (Nov. 14, 2019), https://spacenews.com/air-force-ssa-is-no-more-its-space-domain-awareness/.

Sandra Erwin, *U.S. Space Command Blasts Russia for Anti-Satellite Missile Test*, SPACENEWS (Apr. 15, 2020), https://spacenews.com/u-s-space-command-blasts-russia-for-anti-satellite-missile-test/.

Sandra Erwin, *Space Command to Expand Network of Allies that Help Monitor Orbital Traffic*, SPACENEWS (Jan. 29, 2021), https://spacenews.com/space-command-to-expand-network-of-allies-that-help-monitor-orbital-traffic/.

Shellie-Anne Espinosa, *National Space Defense Center Transitions to 24/7 Operations*, U.S. AIR FORCE SPACE COMMAND (Jan. 26, 2018), https://www.afspc.af.mil/News/Article-Display/Article/1423932/national-space-defense-center-transitions-to-247-operations.

Fiscal Year 2018 Priorities and Posture of the National Security Space Enterprise: Hearing Before the Subcomm. on Strategic Forces of the H. Comm. on Armed Servs., 115th Cong. (2017) (statement of Lt. Gen. David J. Buck, Commander, Joint Functional Component Command for Space), https://docs.house.gov/meetings/AS/AS29/20170519/105974/HHRG-115-AS29-Wstate-BuckD-20170519.pdf.

Fiscal Year 2023 Priorities and Posture of United States Space Command: Hearing Before the S. Armed Services Comm., 117th Cong. (2022) (statement of General James H. Dickinson, Commander, United States Space Command), https://www.armed-services.senate.gov/imo/media/doc/USSPACECOM%20FY23%20Posture%20Statement%20SASC%20FINAL.pdf.

Jeff Foust, *NASA Warns Indian Anti-Satellite Test Increased Debris Risk to ISS*, SPACENEWS (Apr. 2, 2019), https://spacenews.com/nasa-warns-indian-anti-satellite-test-increased-debris-risk-to-iss/.

Jeff Foust, *SpaceX Wins Contract to Launch NASA Small Astrophysics Mission*, SpaceNews (July 8, 2019), https://spacenews.com/spacex-wins-contract-to-launch-nasa-small-astrophysics-mission/.

Gen. Services Admin. Fed. Supply Service, Authorized Federal Supply Schedule Price List, GS-35F-056DA, https://www.gsaadvantage.gov/ref_text/GS35F056DA/0WMX7A.3SDA61_GS-35F-056DA_GS35F056DA.PDF.

Michele Estrin Gilman, *Legal Accountability in an Era of Privatized Welfare*, 89 Cal. L. Rev. 569 (2001).

Blythe Goya, *CSpOC and 614th AOC Change of Command, Space Delta 5 Activation*, CSpOC Pub. Affairs (July 24, 2020), https://www.vandenberg.spaceforce.mil/News/Article-Display/Article/2282681/cspoc-and-614th-aoc-change-of-command-space-delta-5-activation/.

Mike Gruss, *Responding to Critics, ULA Discloses Pricing Information*, SpaceNews (May 21, 2014), https://spacenews.com/40637news-from-the-30th-space-symposium-responding-to-critics-ula-discloses/.

Mike Gruss, *Russian Satellite Maneuvers, Silence Worry Intelsat*, SpaceNews (Oct. 9, 2015), https://spacenews.com/russian-satellite-maneuvers-silence-worry-intelsat/.

William Harwood, *SpaceX Crew Dragon Astronauts Describe Thrilling Return to Earth*, CBS News (Aug. 5, 2020), https://www.cbsnews.com/news/spacex-crew-dragon-astronauts-return-to-earth/.

Adam J. Hebert, *A Tanker for the Air Force*, Air Force Mag. (Sept. 2010), http://www.airforcemag.com/MagazineArchive/Pages/2010/September%202010/0910issbf.aspx.

Caleb Henry, *Air Force to Make Long Term Commercial Integration Cell at JSpOC*, Via Satellite (June 9, 2016), https://www.satellitetoday.com/innovation/2016/06/09/air-force-make-long-term-commercial-integration-cell-jspoc/.

Lauren Hill, *Schriever Wargame Concludes*, U.S. Air Force Space Command (Sept. 13, 2019), https://www.afspc.af.mil/News/Article-Display/Article/1960610/schriever-wargame-concludes/.

Theresa Hitchens, *DoD Rethinks Launch Needs to Counter Russia, China*, Breaking Def. (Oct. 23, 2019), https://breakingdefense.com/2019/10/dod-rethinks-launch-needs-to-counter-russia-china/.

Stacy Hojnowski, *Navigating Changes to the 180-Day Rule for Retiring Military*, Nat'l Career Dev. Ass'n (June 1, 2018), https://www.ncda.org/aws/NCDA/pt/sd/newsarticle/170427/_PARENT/CC_layout_details/false.

Elizabeth Howell, *Atlantis: Last Space Shuttle Launch*, Space.com (Nov. 30, 2017), https://www.space.com/18162-space-shuttle-atlantis.html.

Elizabeth Howell, *Boeing CST-100 Starliner: Next-Generation Spaceship*, Space.com (Mar. 14, 2019), https://www.space.com/18852-spacex-dragon.html.

Elizabeth Howell, *Two Private Satellites Just Docked in Space in Historic First for Orbital Servicing*, Space.com (Feb. 27, 2020), https://www.space.com/private-satellites-docking-success-northrop-grumman-mev-1.html.

Valerie Insinna, *As RD-180 Ban Looms, Space Companies Make Steady Progress on New Launch Technologies*, DefenseNews (Apr. 3, 2017), https://www.defensenews.com/digital-show-dailies/space-symposium/2017/04/03/as-rd-180-ban-looms-space-companies-make-steady-progress-on-new-launch-technologies/.

Int'l Law Comm'n, Draft Articles on the Effects of Armed Conflicts on Treaties, with Commentaries, United Nations (2011), https://legal.un.org/ilc/texts/instruments/english/commentaries/1_10_2011.pdf.

Joseph Iungerman, *What Happens If They Say No? Preserving Access to Critical Commercial Space Capabilities during Future Crises*, Air & Space Power J. 103–16 (Nov.–Dec. 2014), https://www.afspc.af.mil/Portals/3/documents/Schreiver%20Essay%202019/2014_SEW-Iungerman.pdf.

Japan Joins US by Announcing Space Force in Face of New Threats, Sky News (Jan. 20, 2020), https://news.sky.com/story/japan-joins-us-by-announcing-space-force-in-face-of-new-threats-11913185.

JEM Small Satellite Orbital Deployer (J-SSOD), JAXA, https://iss.jaxa.jp/en/kiboexp/jssod/.

Sean Keane, *Huawei Ban: Full Timeline as Trump Signs Law to Stop Rural Carriers from Using Its Gear*, CNET (Mar. 13, 2020), https://www.cnet.com/news/huawei-ban-full-timeline-us-government-china-trump-ban-rural-carriers-security-threat/.

Kasia Kerridge, *Peterson, Schriever, and Cheyenne Mountain Air Force Installations Renamed to Space Force Monday*, KKTV (July 26, 2021), https://www.kktv.com/2021/07/26/peterson-schriever-cheyenne-mountain-air-force-installations-renamed-space-force-monday/.

Rebecca Kheel, *Trump Signs Defense Bill Creating Space Force*, The Hill (Dec. 20, 2019), https://thehill.com/policy/defense/475505-trump-signs-defense-bill-creating-space-force.

Matthew T. King, *High Tech Civilians, Participation in Hostilities, and Criminal Liability: Reconciling U.S. Perspectives*, *in* The Impact of Emerging Technologies on the Law of Armed Conflict 175 (Ronald T.P. Alcala & Eric T. Jensen eds., 2019).

Lynn Kirby, *USSF Field Command Structure Reduces Command Layers, Focuses on Space Warfighter Needs*, U.S. Space Force Pub. Affairs (June 30, 2020), https://www.spaceforce.mil/News/Article/2242267/ussf-field-command-structure-reduces-command-layers-focuses-on-space-warfighter.

Irene Klotz, *SpaceX Breaks Boeing-Lockheed Monopoly on Military Space Launches*, Reuters (Apr. 27, 2016), https://www.reuters.com/article/us-space-spacex-launch-idUSKCN0XO2TC.

Sam LaGrone, *Paying the Price: The Hidden Cost of the "Fat Leonard" Investigation*, USNI News (Jan. 24, 2019, updated Jan. 25, 2019), https://news.usni.org/2019/01/24/paying-price-hidden-cost-fat-leonard-investigation.

John V. Lambert, Paper Presented at Advanced Maui Optical and Space Surveillance Technologies Conference: Fengyun-1C Debris Cloud Evolution Over One Decade (Sept. 2018), https://amostech.com/TechnicalPapers/2018/Poster/Lambert.pdf.

Vivienne Machi, *Germany Establishes New Military Space Command*, Def. News (July 13, 2021), https://www.defensenews.com/space/2021/07/13/germany-establishes-new-military-space-command/.

Tariq Malik, *Elon Musk Unveils SpaceX's New Starship Plans for Private Trips to the Moon, Mars and Beyond*, Space.com (Sept. 29, 2019), https://www.space.com/elon-musk-unveils-spacex-starship-2019-update.html.

Marketwire, *AGI Software Selected for Joint Space Operations Center (JSpOC) Mission System (JMS)*, Yahoo! Finance (Dec. 17, 2012), https://finance.yahoo.com/news/agi-software-selected-joint-space-145445283.html.

Maxar, *History*, https://www.maxar.com/history.

Nicholas Mercurio, *Commercial Integration Cell Pilot Program Underway*, U.S. Air Force (June 5, 2015), https://www.af.mil/News/Article-Display/Article/590721/commercial-integration-cell-pilot-program-underway/.

Mordor Intelligence, *Spacecraft Market—Growth, Trends, and Forecast (2020–2025)*, https://www.mordorintelligence.com/industry-reports/spacecraft-market.

Mordor Intelligence, *Spacecraft Market—Growth, Trends, and Forecast (2021–2026)*, https://www.mordorintelligence.com/industry-reports/spacecraft-market.

Sarah M. Mountin, *The Legality and Implications of Intentional Interference with Commercial Communication Satellite Signals*, 90 INT'L L. STUD. 101, 104 (2014).

WILLIAMSON MURRAY, STRATEGY FOR DEFEAT: THE LUFTWAFFE 1933–1945 (1983), https://www.airuniversity.af.edu/Portals/10/AUPress/Books/B_0012_MURRAY_STRATEGY_FOR_DEFEAT.pdf.

Nat'l Def. Authorization Act for Fiscal Year 2020, Pub. L. No. 116-92 (2019).

Nat'l Def. Authorization Act for Fiscal Year 2022, Pub. L. No. 117-81 (2021).

NASA, *Orion Spacecraft* (Aug. 22, 2022), https://www.nasa.gov/exploration/systems/orion/about/index.html.

NASA, *Space Launch System* (Sept. 12, 2022), https://www.nasa.gov/exploration/systems/sls/index.html.

NASA Press Release 20-057, Sean Potter, ed., *NASA Astronauts Launch from America in Historic Test Flight of SpaceX Crew Dragon*, https://www.nasa.gov/press-release/nasa-astronauts-launch-from-america-in-historic-test-flight-of-spacex-crew-dragon.

RALPH C. NASH, JR., KAREN R. O'BRIEN-DEBAKEY & STEVEN L. SCHOONER, THE GOVERNMENT CONTRACTS REFERENCE BOOK (4th ed. 2013).

OFFICE OF THE CHAIRMAN OF THE JOINT CHIEFS OF STAFF, *DOD Dictionary of Military and Associated Terms* (Aug. 2022), https://jdeis.js.mil/jdeis/new_pubs/dictionary.pdf (restricted access).

OFFICE OF THE CHAIRMAN OF THE JOINT CHIEFS OF STAFF, JOINT PUBL'N 3-14, *Space Operations* (Apr. 10, 2018, Change 1, Oct. 26, 2020), https://www.jcs.mil/Portals/36/Documents/Doctrine/pubs/jp3_14.pdf.

Caitlin O'Kane, *Billionaires Jeff Bezos and Richard Branson Have Now Both Gone to Space. Here's the Difference Between Their Blue Origin and Virgin Galactic Flights*, CBS NEWS (July 20, 2021), https://www.cbsnews.com/news/blue-origin-bezos-launch-richard-branson-space-flight-differences/.

W. Hays Parks et al., Memorandum for Mr. John H. McNeill, Assistant General Counsel (International), OSD, *1977 Protocols Additional to the Geneva Conventions: Customary International Law Implications* (May 9, 1986).

PROJECT ON GOVERNMENT OVERSIGHT, BRASS PARACHUTES: DEFENSE CONTRACTORS' CAPTURE OF OFFICIALS THROUGH THE REVOLVING DOOR (Nov. 5, 2018), https://docs.pogo.org/report/2018/POGO_Brass_Parachutes_DoD_Revolving_Door_Report_2018-11-05.pdf.

Protocol Additional to the Geneva Conventions of 1949, and Relating to the Protection of Victims of International Armed Conflicts, *opened for signature* Dec. 12, 1977, 1125 U.N.T.S. 3 (entered into force on July 12, 1978).

James D. Rendleman & Robert E. Ryals, *Private Defense of Space Systems & Letters of Marque and Reprisal*, AM. INST. OF AERONAUTICS & ASTRONAUTICS (Aug. 28, 2015).

THEODORE T. RICHARD, UNOFFICIAL UNITED STATES GUIDE TO THE FIRST ADDITIONAL PROTOCOL TO THE GENEVA CONVENTIONS OF 12 AUGUST 1949 (2019), https://www.airuniversity.af.edu/Portals/10/AUPress/Books/B_0157_UNOFFICIAL_UNITED_STATES_GUIDE_TO_THE_FIRST_ADDITIONAL_PROTOCOL_TO_THE_GENEVA_CONVENTIONS_OF_12_AUGUST_1949.PDF.

Choe Sang-Hun, *North Korea Tried to Jam GPS Signals Across Border, South Korea Says*, N.Y. Times (Apr. 1, 2016), https://www.nytimes.com/2016/04/02/world/asia/north-korea-jams-gps-signals.html.

Aurel Sari, *The Mutual Assistance Clauses of the North Atlantic and EU Treaties: The Challenge of Hybrid Threats*, 10 Harv. Nat'l Sec. J. 405 (2019).

Daniel E. Schoeni, *Whither Innovation?: Why Open Systems Architecture May Deliver on the False Promise of Public-Private Partnerships*, 70 Admin. L. Rev. 409 (2018).

Steven L. Schooner, *Contractor Atrocities at Abu Ghraib: Compromised Accountability in a Streamlined, Outsourced Government*, 16 Stan. L. & Pol'y Rev. 549 (2005).

Secretary of the Air Force Public Affairs, *"Space Pitch Day" Yields Innovative Technologies and New Partners for the Air Force* (Nov. 8, 2019), https://www.af.mil/News/Article-Display/Article/2012708/space-pitch-day-yields-innovative-technologies-and-new-partners-for-the-air-for/.

Secretary of Defense Lloyd Austin, Tenets of Responsible Behavior in Space (July 7, 2021), https://media.defense.gov/2021/Jul/23/2002809598/-1/-1/0/TENETS-OF-RESPONSIBLE-BEHAVIOR-IN-SPACE.PDF.

Julia Siegel, *Commercial Satellites Are on the Front Lines of War Today. Here's What This Means for the Future of Warfare*, Atl. Council (Aug. 30, 2022), https://www.atlanticcouncil.org/content-series/airpower-after-ukraine/commercial-satellites-are-on-the-front-lines-of-war-today-heres-what-this-means-for-the-future-of-warfare/.

Secretary of State Anthony J. Blinken, *Russia Conducts Destructive Anti-Satellite Missile Test* (Nov. 15, 2021), https://www.state.gov/russia-conducts-destructive-anti-satellite-missile-test/.

Senate Backs Continued Restriction on Hiring of Military Retirees by DoD, Fedweek (June 19, 2019), https://www.fedweek.com/fedweek/senate-backs-continued-restriction-on-hiring-of-military-retirees-by-dod/.

Jared Serbu, *Navy, Air Force Want Congress to Abolish 180-day Waiting Period to Hire Military Retirees*, Fed. News Network (June 15, 2018), https://federalnewsnetwork.com/defense-main/2018/06/navy-air-force-want-congress-to-abolish-180-day-waiting-period-to-hire-military-retirees/.

Stacie N. Shafran, *JFCC SPACE Hosts Inaugural Operator Talks*, U.S. Air Force Space Command (July 23, 2013), https://www.afspc.af.mil/News/Article-Display/Article/731530/jfcc-space-hosts-inaugural-operator-talks/.

Gary Shugart, *Re-establishing U.S. Space Command*, Purview (Oct. 1, 2018), https://purview.dodlive.mil/2018/10/01/reestablishing-u-s-space-command/.

P.W. Singer & August Cole, Ghost Fleet: A Novel of the Third World War (Kindle ed. 2015).

Park Si-soo, *South Korea's Air Force Opens Space Ops Center*, SpaceNews (Oct. 4, 2021), https://spacenews.com/south-korean-air-force-opens-space-center/.

Space and Missile Systems Center, *Space Force Pitch Day*, https://www.losangeles.spaceforce.mil/About-Us/Space-Force-Pitch-Day/.

Space Operations Command, *About Space Operations Command*, https://www.spoc.spaceforce.mil/About-Us/About-Space-Operations-Command.

Spaceflight Now, *NASA Selects Crew, Cargo Launch Partners* (Aug. 18, 2006), https://spaceflightnow.com/news/n0608/18cots/.

Statista, *Number of Active Satellites from 1957 to 2021*, https://www.statista.com/statistics/897719/number-of-active-satellites-by-year/ (last visited Sept. 12, 2022) (listing 997 active satellites on orbit in 2010 and 4,877 in 2021).

Nathan Strout, *Russian Satellite Creeps Up to Intelsat Satellite—Again*, C4ISRNET (Sept. 3, 2019), https://www.c4isrnet.com/battlefield-tech/2019/09/03/russian-satellite-creeps-up-to-intelsat-satellite-again/.

Maurice E. Stucke, *Is Competition Always Good?*, 1(1) J. ANTITRUST ENFORCEMENT 162 (2013).

Philip Swarts, *The JICSpOC Is Dead; Long Live the National Space Defense Center*, SPACENEWS (Apr. 4, 2017), https://spacenews.com/the-jicspoc-is-dead-long-live-the-national-space-defense-center/.

Elizabeth Tasker, *Creating a Crater to Constrain the Age of an Asteroid's Surface*, JAXA (Mar. 23, 2020), http://www.hayabusa2.jaxa.jp/en/topics/20200320_science/.

Adam Taylor, *Russia's Deputy PM Tells U.S. Astronauts to Go to Space on a Trampoline; The Joke May Be on Him*, WASH. POST (Apr. 30, 2014), https://www.washingtonpost.com/news/worldviews/wp/2014/04/30/russias-deputy-pm-tells-u-s-astronauts-to-go-to-space-on-a-trampoline-the-joke-may-be-on-him/.

Treaty on Principles Governing the Activities of States in the Exploration and Use of Outer Space, including the Moon and Other Celestial Bodies, Jan. 27, 1967, 18 U.S.T. 2410, 610 U.N.T.S. 205.

PETER TREPTE, REGULATING PUBLIC PROCUREMENT: UNDERSTANDING THE ENDS AND MEANS OF PUBLIC PROCUREMENT REGULATION (2004).

Joseph Trevithick, *Space Force Just Received Its First New Offensive Weapon*, THE DRIVE (Mar. 13, 2020), https://www.thedrive.com/the-war-zone/32570/space-force-just-received-its-first-new-offensive-weapon.

ULA, *Boeing, Lockheed Martin to Form Launch Services Joint Venture* (May 2, 2005), https://www.ulalaunch.com/all_news_items/2005/05/02/boeing-lockheed-martin-to-form-launch-services-joint-venture.

U.S. AIR FORCE, *Lieutenant General David J. Buck* (Dec. 2019), https://www.af.mil/About-Us/Biographies/Display/Article/108707/lieutenant-general-david-j-buck/.

U.S. AIR FORCE SPACE COMMAND, *Fact Sheet: Fourteenth Air Force* (Oct. 2019), https://www.afspc.af.mil/About-Us/Fact-Sheets/Display/Article/1604750/fourteenth-air-force/.

U.S. AIR FORCE SPACE COMMAND, *Resiliency and Disaggregated Space Architectures* (2013), https://www.afspc.af.mil/Portals/3/documents/AFD-130821-034.pdf.

U.S. AIR FORCE SPACE COMMAND, *Schriever Wargame Concludes* (Oct. 20, 2017), https://www.afspc.af.mil/News/Article-Display/Article/1349906/schriever-wargame-concludes/.

U.S. AIR FORCE SPACE COMMAND, *Joint Space Forces Restructure, AFSPC Commander Becomes JFSCC* (Dec. 4, 2017), https://www.af.mil/News/Article-Display/Article/1386852/joint-space-forces-restructure-afspc-commander-becomes-jfscc/.

U.S. AIR FORCE SPACE COMMAND, *Fact Sheet: Fourteenth Air Force* (Oct. 2019), https://www.afspc.af.mil/About-Us/Fact-Sheets/Display/Article/1604750/fourteenth-air-force/.

U.S. DEP'T OF DEF., ADMIN. INSTR. 45, *Employment of Retired Members of the U.S. Armed Forces* (May 19, 2017), https://www.esd.whs.mil/Portals/54/Documents/DD/issuances/ai/a045p.pdf.

U.S. DEP'T OF DEF., *Department of Defense Establishes U.S. Space Command* (Aug. 29, 2019), https://www.defense.gov/Newsroom/Releases/Release/Article/1948288/department-of-defense-establishes-us-space-command/.

U.S. DEP'T OF DEF., INSTR. 5535.8, *DoD Technology Transfer (T2) Program*, May 14, 1999, inc. Change 1, Sept. 1, 2018.

U.S. DEP'T OF DEF., INSTR. 1100.22, *Policy and Procedures for Determining Workforce Mix*, Apr. 12, 2010, inc. Change 1, Dec. 1, 2017.

U.S. DEP'T OF DEF., REG. 5500.07-R, JOINT ETHICS REG., Aug. 30, 1993, inc. Change 7, Nov. 17, 2011.

U.S. DEP'T OF DEF., OFFICE OF GEN. COUNSEL, DEPARTMENT OF DEFENSE LAW OF WAR MANUAL (Dec. 2016), https://dod.defense.gov/Portals/1/Documents/pubs/DoD%20Law%20of%20War%20Manual%20-%20June%202015%20.

U.S. DEP'T OF DEF., STANDARDS OF CONDUCT OFFICE, ENCYCLOPEDIA OF ETHICAL FAILURE (2021), https://dodsoco.ogc.osd.mil/Portals/102/Documents/Training%20Materials/Encyclopedia%20of%20Ethical%20Failure%202021.pdf.

U.S. DEP'T OF DEF., STANDARDS OF CONDUCT OFFICE, NON-SENIOR EMPLOYEE POST-GOVERNMENT EMPLOYMENT RESTRICTIONS (May 2022), https://dodsoco.ogc.osd.mil/Portals/102/Documents/PGE%20and%20PI/Toolbox%20-%20PGE-PI/2022%20PGE%20Restrictions%20Non%20Senior.pdf.

U.S. DEP'T OF DEF., STANDARDS OF CONDUCT OFFICE, SENIOR EMPLOYEE POST-GOVERNMENT EMPLOYMENT RESTRICTIONS (2022), https://dodsoco.ogc.osd.mil/Portals/102/Documents/PGE%20and%20PI/Toolbox%20-%20PGE-PI/2022%20PGE%20Restrictions%20Senior.pdf(last visited Sept. 12, 2022).

U.S. GOV'T ACCOUNTABILITY OFFICE, GAO-19-458T, DOD FACES SIGNIFICANT CHALLENGES AS IT SEEKS TO ACCELERATE SPACE PROGRAMS AND ADDRESS THREATS (2019), https://www.gao.gov/assets/700/697998.pdf.

U.S. MERIT SYSTEMS PROTECTION BOARD, VETERAN HIRING IN THE CIVIL SERVICE: PRACTICES AND PERCEPTIONS (2014), https://www.mspb.gov/studies/Veteran_Hiring_in_the_Civil_Service_Practices_and_Perceptions_1072040.pdf.

U.S. NAT'L SEC. STRATEGY (2017), https://www.acq.osd.mil/ncbdp/docs/NSS-Final-12-18-2017-0905.pdf.

U.S. NAT'L SPACE POL'Y (2020), https://trumpwhitehouse.archives.gov/wp-content/uploads/2020/12/National-Space-Policy.pdf.

U.S. OFFICE OF GOV'T ETHICS, *Conflict of Interest Prosecution Surveys Index (by Statute)*, https://www.oge.gov/web/oge.nsf/Resources/Conflict+of+Interest+Prosecution+Surveys+Index+(by+Statute).

USSPACECOM PUB. AFFAIRS, *USSPACECOM Makes History with First Change of Command* (Aug. 20, 2020), https://www.spacecom.mil/MEDIA/NEWS-ARTICLES/Article/2320283/usspacecom-makes-history-with-first-change-of-command/.

USSPACECOM PUB. AFFAIRS, *Russia Conducts Space-Based Anti-Satellite Weapons Test* (July 23, 2020), https://www.spacecom.mil/MEDIA/NEWS-ARTICLES/Article/2285098/russia-conducts-space-based-anti-satellite-weapons-test/.

USSPACECOM PUB. AFFAIRS, *Russian Direct-Ascent Anti-Satellite Missile Test Creates Significant, Long-Lasting Space Debris* (Nov. 15, 2021), https://www.spacecom.mil/News/Article-Display/Article/2842957/russian-direct-ascent-anti-satellite-missile-test-creates-significant-long-last/.

U.S. STRATEGIC COMMAND, *Combined Space Operations Center Established at Vandenberg AFB* (July 19, 2018), https://www.stratcom.mil/Media/News/News-Article-View/Article/1579497/combined-space-operations-center-established-at-vandenberg-afb/.

Brian Weeden, *2007 Chinese Anti-Satellite Test Fact Sheet*, Secure World Foundation (Nov. 23, 2010), http://swfound.org/media/205391/chinese_asat_fact_sheet_updated_2012.pdf.

Hanneke Weitering, *France Is Launching a "Space Force" with Weaponized Satellites*, SPACE.COM (Aug. 2, 2019), https://www.space.com/france-military-space-force.html.

Debra Werner, *Air Force Awards $9 Million on First Space Pitch Day San Francisco*, SPACENEWS (Nov. 5, 2019), https://spacenews.com/air-force-awards-9-million-on-first-space-pitch-day-san-francisco/.

Craig Whitlock, *Key Army Commander Accused of Steering a Contract to Ex-classmates*, WASH. POST (June 21, 2015), https://www.washingtonpost.com/world/national-security/key-us-commander-leaves-middle-east-after-reprimand-for-misconduct/2015/06/21/7c3e8d7a-155a-11e5-9518-f9e0a8959f32story.html.

William M. (Mac) Thornberry Nat'l Def. Authorization Act for Fiscal Year 2021, Pub. L. No. 116-283 (2021).

Nicholas Wu, *French President Emmanuel Macron Announces Creation of French Space Force*, USA TODAY (July 13, 2019), https://www.usatoday.com/story/news/world/2019/07/13/french-space-force-macron-announces-creation-space-force-command/1723998001/.

Airman 1st Class Amy Younger, Video, *Air Force Hosts Space Pitch Day*, DEF. VISUAL INFO. DISTRIB. SERV. (Nov. 6, 2019), https://www.dvidshub.net/video/720900/air-force-hosts-space-pitch-day.

Christopher R. Yukins, *A Versatile Prism: Assessing Procurement Law through the Principal-Agent Model*, 40 PUB. CONT. L.J. 63 (2010).

Peter Zimmer, John T. McGraw & Mark R. Ackermann, Paper Presented at Advanced Maui Optical and Space Surveillance Technologies Conference, Sept. 2019: Optical Measurements of Faint LEO RSOs: Cubesats and Fengyun 1C Debris, https://amostech.com/TechnicalPapers/2019/Orbital-Debris/Zimmer.pdf.

7

Protecting Civilian Data in Armed Conflicts

The Need for an Ethical Foundation

Jeffrey Biller and Timothy Goines[1]

1. Introduction

The laws governing armed conflict have progressed steadily, if unevenly, over the past two centuries. This change results from a mixture of evolving values driven by governments and industry alike, to include the development of emerging technologies, revolutions in warfighting tactics and strategy, and shifting societal values. One consistent characteristic, however, is that law generally lags behind these driving factors. This reality is no less true with the advent of warfighting's newest domain: cyberspace. While the law's challenge of keeping pace with a changing warfighting landscape will never be fully solved, cyber operations present new challenges that have proven particularly complex. The fact that information technologies are largely driven by commercial, not military, requirements only enhances this complexity.

Two features of the cyber domain make the application of the law of armed conflict challenging. States developed the law governing warfare for a domain of visible and tangible things, where people and objects were subjected to violent, physical forces. The purpose-built machinery of warfare could generally be located separately and distinctly away from valuable civilian infrastructure. Neither of these characteristics is true for cyberspace, which largely shares its infrastructure with commercial entities. This physical reality has challenged traditional theories of what should be protected in warfare. This challenge is particularly vexing regarding the protection of civilian data.

The rise in importance of networked information systems and the data housed therein has been meteoric over the past quarter-century. Modern economic systems depend upon massive amounts of digital data transiting worldwide

[1] The views expressed in this chapter are the authors' and do not reflect an official position of the U.S. Air Force, the Department of Defense, or any other U.S. government agency.

Jeffrey Biller and Timothy Goines, *Protecting Civilian Data in Armed Conflicts* In: *Ethical Dilemmas in the Global Defense Industry*. Edited by: Daniel Schoeni and Tobias Vestner, Oxford University Press.
 DOI: 10.1093/oso/9780190675813.003.0008

networks, often at the speed of light. Military operations are no different. Readily available data are vital to the operation of modern weapon systems, making cyber infrastructure a valuable target. However, it is not only military or national security-related data that hostile states seek to manipulate. Whether in peacetime or in war, states utilize adversary civilian data for a variety of purposes. From propaganda and political pressure to outright theft, states are increasingly targeting civilian digital data to achieve national objectives. Despite the importance of this data to the civilian populace, it is unclear what, if any, wartime legal protections exist.

The laws governing armed conflicts seek to balance the necessity of conducting necessary and effective military operations against the protection of civilians from the worst effects in wartime. Hence, states and the industrial sectors responsible for developing the next generation of military equipment are frequently wary of rapid developments of the law that are driven solely by humanitarian considerations. Development of both military strategy and equipment require significant developmental lead time, even in the rapidly developing world of cyberspace. This chapter argues that current international law provides limited protection to civilian data for two primary reasons: cyber operations do not generally meet the definition of violent activities upon which much of the law depends, and digital data does not meet the definition of an object that could then be protected under the law. Therefore, there is a significant gap in protection between an important aspect of modern life and that law intended to protect in wartime. Furthermore, given that many international powers, including Russia and China, are unlikely to extend traditional legal protections of objects to civilian data, rapid development in international law to cover this gap is unlikely. Therefore, this chapter argues that the difficult task of creating a shared foundation for the protection of civilian data must be undertaken by a combination of ethical scholars, industry, and states.

This chapter starts by confronting the reality that foreign states are already targeting civilian data, including during the course of armed conflicts. Examples are provided of three prominent states conducting such operations: North Korea, China, and Russia. Next, potential areas of protection for civilian data under international law are analyzed. In particular, laws governing the targeting of objects and special categories of protection are considered. The significant legal issues of defining "attacks" and "objects" take center stage, demonstrating the paucity of coverage for civilian data. Given this lack of coverage, the need and methodology for producing such protections under the law are discussed. Ultimately, this chapter recommends that the solution to this problem begins with developing a shared ethical foundation for protecting civilian data in armed conflicts. The ethical foundation should drive the development of future cyber capabilities and strategy. Ideally, these efforts will result from a collaboration between industry, scholars, and states. Only then can normative practices and international law develop in a manner that is accepted and followed. Finally, potential lines of effort are suggested for industry that can help achieve both commercial and ethical ends.

2. State Operations against Civilian Data

The targeting of civilian data through cyber operations is not unprecedented. The majority of such operations are characterized as espionage or intelligence-gathering operations, where states conduct cyber operations to gather large amounts of civilian data for analysis and likely later exploitation. However, while most operations against civilian data take place outside the context of armed conflicts, there are recent examples of states targeting civilian data in concert with an international armed conflict. This section reviews the aforementioned three examples: North Korea, China, and Russia. These conflicts highlight the importance of determining what legal protections exist under international law during armed conflicts.

2.1. North Korea

Perhaps the most infamous example of a state-based cyber operation that targeted civilian data is the 2014 malicious cyber operation against Sony Pictures Entertainment. This operation is widely attributed to the Guardians of Peace, likely working for the government of North Korea to suppress *The Interview*, a movie produced by Sony depicting the assassination of North Korean leader Kim Jong-un. North Korean operatives infiltrated Sony Pictures Entertainment in November 2014 by utilizing multiple lines of effort, including sending spear-phishing messages to individuals and entities associated with the production of *The Interview* and posting links on social media pages associated with *The Interview*. These efforts led users to links containing malware, giving the operators unauthorized access to the Sony network. Once inside the network, they extracted movies, confidential information, and many internal emails. Hackers then left thousands of Sony computers inoperable.[2]

After the data extraction, the North Korean operators used this information for coercive purposes, purportedly to prevent the release of *The Interview*.[3] In

[2] Indictment, United States v. Park Jin Hyok, Case No. MJ-18-1479 (C.D. Cal. June 8, 2018), at 23–49.

[3] The Interview (Sony Pictures Entertainment 2014).

the course of this cyber operation, they posted financial data and unreleased movies online for public download before sending emails to Sony executives and employees. Later, the operators released emails from Sony executives that contained embarrassing comments and trade secrets. At first, their strategic intent was unclear. However, a few weeks later, the operation's goal materialized, with communications specifically citing *The Interview* and threatening actions upon its release. At the same time, the operation expanded to include AMC Theatres, a U.S.-based civilian-owned theater chain.[4] While the operation was ultimately unsuccessful in preventing the movie's release, the operation remains a prime example of a state deliberately targeting civilian data. The operation was a large-scale assault on two civilian-owned companies to achieve political ends.

The Sony Pictures cyber operation is not North Korea's only attempt at targeting civilian data—the same group targeted multiple financial institutions to steal money. In February 2016, the same North Korean group targeted the Bangladesh Bank, using similar tactics, techniques, and procedures—spear-phishing, targeted emails, and malware. Specifically, it targeted employees to access the SWIFT system, a global communication network used to facilitate international payment instructions between banks and other financial institutions. Once they gained access, they submitted fraudulent messages to send money from the Bangladesh Bank to accounts in the Philippines and Sri Lanka. Operators then concealed their activities within the system and laundered the stolen money through multiple accounts, including other financial institutions. While the operation attempted to steal the equivalent of $1 billion, the group ultimately was only able to obtain around $81 million.[5]

The Bangladesh Bank operation is just one example of North Korea's targeting of financial institutions; others include operations targeting the African Bank, the Polish banking sector, and two Central American casinos. Furthermore, North Korea has recently focused on stealing cryptocurrencies from civilian-owned companies, with victims in Slovenia, Indonesia, and New York. As John Demers, the former head of the Justice Department's National Security Division, said, North Korea's cyber operatives "have become the world's leading bank robbers."[6]

In addition to these targeted operations, a larger U.S. indictment from early 2021 included evidence that North Korean operatives were behind the global

[4] *Id.* at 50–53; *see also* Tatiana Siegel, *Five Years Later, Who Really Hacked Sony?*, HOLLYWOOD REP. (Nov. 25, 2019), https://www.hollywoodreporter.com/movies/movie-features/five-years-who-hacked-sony-1257591.

[5] *Park Jin Hyok*, MJ-18-1479, at 56.

[6] Kartikay Mehrotra & David Voreacos, *U.S. Calls North Korean Hackers "World's Leading Bank Robbers"*, BLOOMBERG (Feb. 17, 2021, 8:15 PM), https://www.bloomberg.com/news/articles/2021-02-17/u-s-charges-3-north-koreans-linked-to-sony-hack-in-new-scheme.

WannaCry ransomware operation. The indictment cited strong similarities between this operation and those against Sony Pictures and the Bangladesh Bank. Much like the previous examples, the WannaCry ransomware targeted civilian data; however, its propagation was more random—it did not appear to be targeted at any one group—and spread through self-propagation. As a result, affected parties included both civilian and government-owned companies.[7]

2.2. China

Like North Korea, China has a history of targeting civilian networks through cyber operations to exploit civilian data. In late 2018, Marriott disclosed that an intrusion exposed the data of 500 million customers of their Starwood hotel brand, including names, passport numbers, birthdates, and credit card information. Later reports linked the data breach to Chinese operatives working for the Ministry of State Security. While many details of the cyber operation remain undisclosed, there are indications that the infiltration began with phishing emails that provided a link to malware designed to find username and password combinations within the system memory. Once in the reservation system, the operator took over an administrator's account and queried the database for the exfiltrated data.[8]

Similarly, intelligence linked China to the Equifax data breach in 2017, which resulted in the disclosure of records containing personally identifiable information (PII) of at least 145.5 million U.S. customers and nearly one million from outside the United States. The operation began in March 2017 when hackers discovered a vulnerability on the Apache Struts web framework, which hosted Equifax's online dispute portal. The vulnerability, reported two days earlier by the U.S. Computer Emergency Readiness Team (CERT), allowed an intruder to execute commands on Equifax's system. Two months later, the intruder used the vulnerability to gain access to the online dispute portal, potentially to send queries and commands to other systems within the Equifax network. Once inside the network, the intruder found a repository of PII and a cache of usernames and passwords, which they used to access a trove of other databases beyond the online dispute portal. Over the next 76 days, the operation slowly extracted PII, disguising the extraction as normal network traffic.[9]

[7] *Park Jin Hyok*, MJ-18-1479, at 78–81.

[8] Josh Fruhlinger, *Marriott Data Breach FAQ: How Did It Happen and What Was the Impact?*, CSO ONLINE (Feb. 12, 2020), https://www.csoonline.com/article/3441220/marriott-data-breach-faq-how-did-it-happen-and-what-was-the-impact.html.

[9] U.S. GOV'T ACCOUNTABILITY OFFICE, GAO-18-559, DATA PROTECTION: ACTIONS TAKEN BY EQUIFAX AND FEDERAL AGENCIES IN RESPONSE TO THE 2017 BREACH (2018).

While North Korea's cyber operations targeted civilian data for either political or financial gain, Chinese intentions are less clear. However, both operations appear focused on gathering intelligence information for later exploitation. Analyzed in conjunction with the Chinese operation against the U.S. Office of Personnel Management, which targeted the PII of 21.5 million current, former, and prospective government employees and contractors, it appears that China primarily targets civilian data for intelligence, and possibly counterintelligence, purposes.[10] If that is the case, it is worth noting that collecting information for intelligence purposes, even if that information is civilian data, would qualify as an intelligence operation akin to espionage and should be treated as such under international law.[11] That being the case, it is important to distinguish between intelligence gathering and targeting (e.g., destroying or corrupting) civilian data. The former is a practice engaged in by many states and is not considered per se illegal.[12] The latter, as discussed later, has legal and ethical challenges that should be explored further. In any event, the collection of data can still be concerning. More specifically, as artificial intelligence technology develops, the exploitation of large data sets may result in innovative uses, and exploitation, of civilian data.

While the preceding examples demonstrate the willingness of state actors to conduct operations on civilian data, they were conducted outside the context of an armed conflict. Therefore, the laws applicable to such conflicts do not apply. That is not to say international law does not govern—peacetime laws, such as international human rights law and the principles of sovereignty and nonintervention, may be violated by state operations against civilian data. However, they demonstrate that many states view civilian data differently from tangible civilian objects, in particular as these states generally do not kinetically target civilian objects to the same extent they do in the cyber realm. That said, the targeting of civilian data within armed conflict is not without precedent.

2.3. Russia

Since 2014, Russia has been in a protracted armed conflict with Ukraine, primarily in the Crimea and Donbas regions. As part of its overall campaign, Russia has extensively used cyber operations, including those targeting civilian infrastructure. One noteworthy aspect is how Russia employed cyber operations to weaken their adversary and lower resistance to conventional armed operations.

[10] Michelle D. Christensen, *OPM Data Breach: Personnel Security Background Investigation Data*, CRS Insights (July 24, 2015), https://sgp.fas.org/crs/natsec/IN10327.pdf.

[11] Law of War Manual, *supra* note 34, at para. 16.3.2.

[12] The United States, for example, readily admits conducting cyber operations for intelligence purposes. *Id.*

For example, prior to 2014 and as early as 2009, Russian hackers employed cyber operations to wreak havoc on the Crimean region, undermining confidence in the Ukrainian government and sowing discord among the populace. Operations included distributed denial-of-service (DDoS) operations[13] and defacements of websites, disabling Crimea's one Internet Exchange Point, and cutting off access to first-aid, fire, and rescue services. When Russian forces invaded the region in March 2014, hackers disabled Ukrainian government, news, and social media websites, in addition to their mobile phone infrastructure. Russian operational goals included cutting off Crimean officials and civilians from the rest of the world as their conventional forces invaded. The Ukrainian government's inability to communicate resulted both in internal confusion and delayed responses by the international community. These delays allowed Russian military forces to enter Crimea with little resistance and to consolidate their gains.[14] This tactic mirrored Russian operations against civilian cyber infrastructure in the 2008 Russian military campaign against Georgia.

Following the 2014 invasion, Russia has continued to conduct cyber operations against civilian data sets in support of the Russian-backed separatist forces in Ukraine. For example, shortly before Christmas in 2015, Russian operators infiltrated the computer systems of three civilian-owned Ukrainian energy distribution companies. Russians accessed the system using credentials acquired through spear-phishing emails sent to employees earlier that spring. Once inside, they moved laterally and disrupted the supply of electricity to more than 225,000 customers. Then, as they concluded the operation, operators used destructive malware (KillDisk) to delete all the files on the computers, rendering them inoperable. Similarly, a year later, cyber operators infiltrated a state-owned electric company and deleted key system files using a similar procedure, resulting in a loss of system functionality.[15]

Perhaps most notably, in June 2017, Russian operatives launched an extensive cyber campaign targeting civilian data that has been called the "most destructive and costly cyber-attack in history."[16] Named NotPetya, this malware appeared to be ransomware, encrypting a victim's computer files until payment of a ransom, similar to its precursor and namesake, Petya. However, unlike Petya, even if the ransom was paid, NotPetya would never decrypt the files, rendering the files

[13] A DDoS operation typically utilizes a large number of compromised devices, sometimes referred to as a botnet to overwhelm a target computing service with requests, thus making the service unavailable to users.

[14] Inst. for Nat'l Sec. Stud., *The Ukrainian Crisis—A Cyber Warfare Battlefield*, DEFENSE UPDATE (Apr. 5, 2014), https://defense-update.com/20140405_ukrainian-crisis-cyber-warfare-battlefield.html.

[15] Indictment, United States v. Yuriy Sergeyevich Andrienko, et al., Crim No. 20-316 (W.D. Pa. Oct. 15, 2020), at 9–10.

[16] Press Release, White House, Statement from the Press Secretary (Feb. 15, 2018), https://trumpwhitehouse.archives.gov/briefings-statements/statement-press-secretary-25/.

unrecoverable. While initially directed at Ukrainian civilian-owned banks, newspapers, and electricity companies, the malware fulfilled its intended design to spread from computer to computer. This self-propagation resulted in the malware spreading to more than 60 countries, ultimately costing more than an estimated $10 billion in damage. Within Ukraine, the primary target of the operation, NotPetya infected "four hospitals in Kiev alone, six power companies, two airports, more than 22 Ukrainian banks, ATMs, and card payment systems in retailers and transport, and practically every federal agency."[17] It is estimated that 10 percent of all computers in the affected companies—both civilian and government-owned—were wiped of their contents.[18]

Given their success, Russia's use of cyber in military operations is a harbinger of future campaigns, and not just for Russia. Using cyber operations in concert with conventional forces creates compound effects too valuable to go unused. More specifically, employing cyber effects against civilian data can severely weaken an adversary's war-sustaining abilities, affecting a state's ability to maintain an effective fighting force and eroding public support. Possible targets include: (1) critical war-sustaining infrastructure (power grids, factories, warehouses, etc.), upsetting the logistical supply chain; (2) communications services (mobile phone infrastructure, internet access, etc.), affecting command and control; (3) transportation services (planes, trains, automobiles, etc.); (4) the healthcare industry (hospitals, emergency services, etc.); and (5) the financial sector (banks, stock exchanges, etc.).[19]

In most cases, states can use existing cyber capabilities to create these effects in wartime. Ransomware (e.g., Petya, NotPetya) would be an effective tool to disable factory control systems, reducing output. It could also be used to encrypt mobile phone communications, cutting off critical communication capacity. Alternatively, a state could use malware such as KillDisk to delete retirement accounts of a large percentage of the population, affecting civilian morale. Or, a state could infiltrate and collect data on transportation services, enabling the tracking of civilians. Each of these tactics is readily available, having already been used to target civilian data over the last 10 years. However, operations targeting civilian data also seem to violate fundamental notions of warfighting that have evolved over the last century. The total wars of the mid-twentieth century led to the formulation and codification of extensive wartime protections for civilians. However, these laws developed in a predigital age. Therefore, they

[17] Andy Greenberg, *The Untold Story of NotPetya, the Most Devastating Cyberattack in History*, Wired (Aug. 22, 2018), https://www.wired.com/story/notpetya-cyberattack-ukraine-russia-code-crashed-the-world/.

[18] *Id.*

[19] It is noteworthy that in armed conflicts if civilian items are used for military purposes, the items are considered as military objectives for legal purposes. For more on this, *see* Section 3.1.1 *infra*.

must be examined closely to determine their applicability in the context of cyber operations.

3. Laws Governing Military Cyber Operations

The previous section revealed the clear intention by states to utilize cyber operations against civilian data targets. When states conduct military operations against adversaries as part of an armed conflict, a body of law known as international humanitarian law (IHL) applies. This body of law is considered a *lex specialis*, a term indicating that a body of law takes precedence over more general or conflicting rules in a given circumstance.[20] Thus, this section examines what, if any, protections the existing IHL may provide to civilian data within the context of an armed conflict.

A common misconception concerning cyber operations is that a "Wild West" type of legal regime exists, where anything goes. As will be demonstrated, the cyber domain is not lawless by. However, cyber operations are a relatively new operational domain of warfighting. It would therefore be surprising if the applicable laws were already agreed upon and well defined. To begin, there is broad agreement that as a general matter international law applies to cyberspace. The 2015 report of the UN Group of Governmental Experts in the Field of Information and Telecommunications in the Context of International Security (UN Cyber GGE) affirmed "the established international legal principles, including, where applicable, the principles of humanity, necessity, proportionality and distinction."[21] Moreover, there is a majority of states that agree as to how the law applies in several essential areas. For example, cyber operations resulting in violent effects are covered under the same analysis as traditional methods of warfare, such as aerial bombardment.[22]

An example at this point is instructive. Suppose a state's military during an armed conflict wanted to shut down an adversary airfield currently used solely by civilian aircraft. Should they conduct a cyber operation tampering with air traffic control data, with the foreseeable consequence that several civilian aircraft are damaged or destroyed, the civilian protection provisions of the targeting laws within IHL would apply to the cyber operation. Such laws include a prohibition

[20] D. Fleck, The Handbook on International Humanitarian Law 37 (2013).

[21] U.N. General Assembly, Group of Governmental Experts on Developments in the Field of Information and Telecommunications in the Context of International Security: Note by the Secretary-General, U.N. Doc. A/70/174, 22 July 2015, paras. 24, 28(d).

[22] For an in-depth discussion of the views as to the application of the law of armed conflict to cyber operations, *see* Tallinn Manual 2.0 on the International Law Applicable to Cyber Warfare (Michael N. Schmitt ed., 2017) [hereinafter Tallinn Manual 2.0].

on intentionally targeting civilian aircraft unless currently in use for military purposes.[23]

Despite several important advances, however, significant gaps or disagreements remain regarding the applicability of specific IHL rules to cyber operations. One particular gap is the protection of civilian data. For example, what protections exist for economic data related to prominent but nonmilitary industries? A review of the general IHL scheme will aid in revealing where those gaps exist. Yet several factors to be discussed later complicate the application of the following rules to civilian data.

3.1. Laws Governing the Targeting of Objects in Armed Conflicts

The civilian protections contained in IHL can be subdivided in many ways, but for this discussion, it is helpful to break them into two categories: targeting law and special protections. The primary treaty governing protections of civilians in armed conflicts is the Protocol Additional to the Geneva Conventions of 12 August 1949, and relating to the Protection of Victims of International Armed Conflicts (Protocol I), of 8 June 1977 (AP I). Although several states, including the United States, are not a party to this treaty,[24] most of its provisions are considered customary international law (CIL).[25] Therefore, we use AP I to highlight and discuss those protections.

Targeting laws are those that cover the use of violence in armed conflicts. These laws serve to balance the necessary use of force by state militaries with the protection of civilians. It should be emphasized from the outset that targeting laws do not exist to spare civilians from *all* harm or inconveniences, but rather from the most severe effects associated with armed conflicts. For example, there is a long tradition of deliberately affecting the civilian populace through nonviolent means, such as the use of propaganda to erode public support for the conflict. However, the bulk of targeting law would not apply to propaganda operations because they are nonviolent.[26] For purposes of discussing civilian data,

[23] Protocol Additional to the Geneva Conventions of 12 August 1949, and Relating to the Protection of Victims of International Armed Conflicts art. 52(1), June 8, 1977, 1125 U.N.T.S. 3 [hereinafter Additional Protocol I]; JEAN-MARIE HENCKAERTS & LOUISE DOSWALD-BECK, 1 CUSTOMARY INTERNATIONAL HUMANITARIAN LAW (2005), r. 7 [hereinafter CUSTOMARY IHL].

[24] Other states not party to Additional Protocol I include Andorra, Azerbaijan, Bhutan, Eritrea, India, Indonesia, Iran, Israel, Kiribati, Malaysia, the Marshall Islands, Myanmar, Nepal, Pakistan, Papua New Guinea, Singapore, Somalia, South Sudan, Sri Lanka, Thailand, Turkey, and Tuvalu. *Id.*

[25] *See, e.g.*, Michael J. Matheson, *Session One: The United States Position on the Relation of Customary International Law to the 1977 Protocols Additional to the 1949 Geneva Conventions*, 2 AM. U. J. INT'L L. & POL'Y 419 (1987).

[26] TALLINN MANUAL 2.0, *supra* note 22, at r. 92, at para. 2.

this chapter focuses on the provisions of AP I covering civilian objects, as opposed to individuals.

Whether and to what extent targeting laws apply to nonviolent cyber operations is a matter of some controversy. Military operations might affect civilian data through several different means, both violent and nonviolent. For example, a state could use kinetic weapons such as explosive ordinance to physically destroy cyber infrastructure, affecting any civilian data housed on such infrastructure. Conversely, a state could use malicious but nonviolent techniques to access cyber infrastructure and alter or delete a similar data set. Both operations would have a similar result but through very different means. Hence, it is vital to give a close reading to targeting law and to understand the meaning of the relevant terms of art.

3.1.1. Distinction

Distinction is a cardinal principle of IHL.[27] Promulgated initially in the 1868 St. Petersburg Declaration, it finds current and most clear expression relating to objects in Article 52(1) of AP I, requiring that "[c]ivilian objects shall not be the object of attack or reprisals." Civilian objects are defined negatively; they encompass all objects that do not meet the definition of a military objective.[28] Military objectives are "those objects which by their nature, location, purpose or use make an effective contribution to military action and whose partial or total destruction, capture or neutralization, in the circumstances ruling at the time, offers a definite military advantage."[29] Thus, previously civilian objects, such as a vehicle, bridge, or building, can become military objectives if their nature, location, purpose, or use changes during an armed conflict.

A frequently raised concern in the context of cyber is dual-use objects, which are objects that serve both military and civilian purposes. Most states do not have a purely military cyber infrastructure. Instead, they use existing civilian infrastructure. AP I states that objects "normally dedicated to civilian purposes, such as a place of worship, a house or other dwelling, or a school" should carry a presumption that they remain civilian objects when questions arise as to whether they are being used for military purposes.[30] However, if evidence indicates a definite military use, the military objective criterion applies during the period of military use, and the object would be subject to attack. Consequently, any cyber infrastructure definitively used for military purposes during an armed conflict

[27] Legality of the Threat of Use of Nuclear Weapons, Advisory Opinion, 1996 I.C.J. 226, para. 78 (July 8).

[28] Additional Protocol I, art. 52(1)

[29] *Id.*, art. 52(2).

[30] *Id.*, art. 52(3).

becomes a military object by its purpose or use and, therefore, can be targeted by the opposing force.[31]

This targetable status clearly has implications for civilian uses of shared network infrastructure. For example, an undersea internet cable utilized by a military to communicate with its forces overseas becomes a military object. Rendering that cable useless through any means could have significant consequences for the transfer of civilian data as well. Currently, undersea cables carry nearly the entirety of internet data that crosses an ocean. Military forces are no exception to this reality and rely heavily on undersea cables to communicate overseas.

Although the intentional targeting of dual-use objects, such as cyber infrastructure, does not violate the rule of distinction because those objects qualify as military objectives, the dual-use nature of the object would necessitate application of the rules of proportionality and precautions. These rules may also apply to the targeting of purely military objectives when the operation will likely result in severe damage to a separate civilian object.

3.1.2. Proportionality and Precautions in Attack

Once an object is determined to meet the qualification of a military objective, the operation must additionally comply with the rules of proportionality and precautions in attack. There is disagreement as to which rule should be considered first in a legal review, but it is undisputed that both must be considered if damage to civilian objects is foreseeable. Here, we consider proportionality first.

The rule of proportionality prohibits "an attack which may be expected to cause incidental loss of civilian life, injury to civilians, damage to civilian objects, or a combination thereof, which would be excessive in relation to the concrete and direct military advantage anticipated."[32] It is important to state at the outset that this rule does not prohibit damage to civilian objects, labeled "collateral damage," but rather precludes attack when the damage would be "excessive" in comparison to the military advantage expected to be gained. The proportionality analysis can be challenging in the cyber context, given the complexity of network operations.[33] Additionally, target values vary widely depending on the conflict and the context at the time of the attack.

The proportionality evaluation hinges mainly on two factors: first, the amount of military advantage to be gained, and second, the level of incidental injury or collateral damage expected to be caused. Given the complexity of the factors involved, the standard here is a reasonable evaluation based on available evidence

[31] *See* Tallinn Manual 2.0, *supra* note 22, at r. 100, at para. 10.
[32] *Id.*, art. 51(5)(b); *see also* Customary IHL, *supra* note 23, r. 14.
[33] Tallinn Manual 2.0, *supra* note 22, at r. 113, at para. 6.

known to the actor at the time of the operation. Unlike the binary calculus in the distinction rule, military advantage for a proportionality calculation is a sliding scale based on the amount of advantage expected to be gained. The military advantage, however, must be foreseeable, not relying on potential but unanticipated effects. There is no temporal restriction on when the effects occur. Thus, the effects may be considered in the analysis even if they will not be realized until a later time.

The second portion of the proportionality evaluation concerns the amount of collateral damage or incidental injury. Here, the effects can be either direct or indirect.[34] Direct effects are "the immediate, first-order consequences, unaltered by intervening events or mechanisms," whereas indirect effects are "the delayed and/or displaced second-, third-, and higher-order consequences of action, created through intermediate events or mechanisms."[35] Most military operations against data will almost certainly contain indirect and potentially cascading effects. However, this is an ex ante assessment based solely on what is known or should have been known at the time of the operation. Like many calculations made in the proportionality analysis, this standard is highly dependent on context. This may be partly the reason that violations of the rule of proportionality have never been considered a war crime in the technical sense.[36]

In addition to the proportionality analysis, violent military operations likely to affect civilian objects must also comply with the rule of "precautions in attack." The rule, as laid down in AP I, requires taking "feasible" precautions to minimize the damage to civilian objects.[37] Specifically, operational planners and commanders must "do everything feasible to verify that the objectives to be attacked are neither civilians nor civilian objects . . . [or] subject to special protection."[38] Thus, even if an operation otherwise complied with the rules of distinction and proportionality, armed forces would still need to consider how to minimize damage to civilian objects.

The obligation to take precautions in attack also requires that military forces conducting attacks warn civilians when civilian objects will be affected.[39] However, this requirement is only levied when circumstances permit.[40] Providing advance warning to the civilian populace carries the risk that enemy

[34] U.S. DEP'T OF DEF., OFFICE OF THE GEN. COUNSEL, LAW OF WAR MANUAL (2016), at para. 16.5.1.1 [hereinafter LAW OF WAR MANUAL].

[35] JOINT CHIEFS OF STAFF, JOINT PUBLICATION 3-60, JOINT TARGETING (Jan. 31, 2013), at II-36.

[36] "War crimes" are those IHL violations carrying individual, as opposed to state, responsibility. The most broadly applicable war crimes include all grave breaches of the 1949 Geneva Conventions. *See* Hersch Lauterpact, *The Law of Nations and the Punishment of War Crimes*, 21 BRIT. Y.B. INT'L L. 77 (1944).

[37] Additional Protocol I, art. 57(2)(a); *see also* CUSTOMARY IHL, *supra* note 23, at ch. 5.

[38] Additional Protocol I, art. 57(2)(a)(i).

[39] *Id.*, art. 57(2)(c); *see also* Customary IHL, *supra* note 23, r. 20.

[40] *Id.*

forces will learn of the operation and degrade mission effectiveness. Particularly in the cyber context, this may render an operation ineffective, eliminating the requirement for warnings. It bears repeating that the law only requires such precautions when there is an *attack* on a civilian *object*. Exactly what those terms means and their import in the cyber context is discussed as follows.

3.2. "Attacks" as a Legal Term of Art

As stated previously, civilian objects are legally protected from attacks during armed conflicts. In fact, most prohibitions in armed conflicts are expressed in terms of "attacks."[41] Colloquially, the term "cyberattacks" is often used to describe any malicious cyber operation both during and outside of armed conflicts. Anything from a DDoS operation, which temporarily prevents access to a remote server, to a ransomware operation against critical infrastructure is called a cyberattack. However, under IHL, the word "attack" is a term of art. AP I provides the standard definition: "acts of violence against the adversary, whether in offence or in defence."[42] This notion of violence plays a key role in determining when civilian data is protected.[43]

It is uncontroversial that cyber operations resulting in physical damage qualify as attacks. This also encompasses attacks that affect civilian data. For example, operations against supervisory control and data acquisition (SCADA) systems have a high potential to qualify as an attack. A SCADA system enables both manual and automated supervision of machines and processes. Should an operation during an armed conflict intentionally corrupt or delete data causing a system, such as an electric generator, to malfunction with physically damaging consequences, then it would clearly qualify as an attack.

On the other hand, significant controversy exists as to whether cyber operations that do not clearly result in visibly apparent damage might qualify as attacks. Some states, such as France, have issued statements identifying loss of system functionality as an attack.[44] Israel, on the other hand, has stated that physical damage is required, excluding mere loss of functionality.[45] However, the vast majority of states, including the United States, have failed to take a clear position on the issue. Thus, there is no common international standard for an attack

[41] *See, e.g.*, Additional Protocol I, arts. 51, 52.

[42] *Id.*, art. 49(1).

[43] Tallinn Manual 2.0, *supra* note 22, at r. 92, at para. 6.

[44] Ministère des Armées, International Law Applied to Cyberspace § 2.2.1 (2019), https://www.defense.gouv.fr/content/download/567648/9770527/file/international+law+applied+to+operations+in+cyberspace.pdf.

[45] Roy Schöndorf, *Israel's Perspective on Key Legal and Practical Issues Concerning the Application of International Law to Cyber Operations*, 97 Int'l L. Stud. 395, 400 (2021).

54(2) prohibits operations "to attack, destroy, remove or render useless objects indispensable to the survival of the civilian population, such as foodstuffs, agricultural areas for the production of foodstuffs, crops, livestock, drinking water installations and supplies and irrigation works, for the specific purpose of denying them for their sustenance value to the civilian population or to the adverse Party, whatever the motive, whether in order to starve out civilians, to cause them to move away, or for any other motive." Should the availability of civilian data be indispensable to survival, then such data would receive the additional protections. An example here might be the data necessary to operate the only facility capable of providing safe drinking water to a large municipality. If that data were corrupted so that it rendered the plant "useless," it would undoubtedly violate this protection.

The final special protection to be discussed is that of protection of civil defense organizations. AP I, Article 62 states that "[c]ivilian civil defence organizations and their personnel shall be respected and protected" and that "[t]hey shall be entitled to perform their civil defence tasks except in case of imperative military necessity." This section has broad applicability, covering operations from warning and evacuation to firefighting and rescue operations. Suppose, for example, that a state's civil defense organization developed a phone application that provided civil defense information to the public. A cyber operation that prevented the application from working as intended would violate this protection, except in cases of "imperative military necessity."[52]

As noted earlier, several other special protections are contained in IHL that could theoretically protect specific categories of civilian data. This section is not exhaustive and serves to provide some of the more likely examples. However, when viewed together with the lack of coverage in targeting law, these limited special protections demonstrate the minimal protections for civilian data under IHL.

Before closing this section, it must be recognized that many scholars disagree with the current state of the law. They seek to redefine "attack" and "object," thereby broadening protections under targeting law.[53] Although opinions diverge widely on what types of data receive protection and under what circumstances, there is a near consensus in the desire to read legal protections for what many consider the engine of modern society: digital information. Thus, while we have shown that such protections are absent in current law, we also recognize that the existing protections are inadequate.

52 Additional Protocol I, art. 62.

53 *See, e.g.*, Kubo Mačak, *Military Objectives 2.0: The Case for Interpreting Computer Data as Objects under International Humanitarian Law*, 48 Isr. L. Rev. 39 (2015).

4. Inadequacy of Existing Protections

The desire to close the coverage gap for civilian data during armed conflicts is understandable. For many states, digital data undergirds economic, cultural, and social structures. Data also contain the most private and sensitive aspects of individual lives. Digital information systems now house the majority of this data. Hence, societies worldwide are actively debating digital data privacy. Reflective of this need for privacy, the UN Declaration of Human Rights states that "[n]o one shall be subjected to arbitrary interference with his privacy, family, home or correspondence."[54] Increasingly, the data contained in information systems are more valuable than the system itself. Thus, while a physical attack against an information system may cause temporary disruption to one of these structures, recovery will often occur in short order with a replacement of the affected hardware. However, a complete data loss is likely to generate long-term harm even if it is not accompanied by damage to the physical information infrastructure. In short, digital data is a crucial component of most aspects of modern life and worthy of the highest levels of protection that IHL can provide. However, as previously detailed, these protections do not yet exist. Therefore, the mechanisms for advancing IHL toward a place where this data is protected must be analyzed.

That analysis must begin with an understanding that IHL is both a limiting and a permissive regime. Protections for civilians must always be weighed against the principle of military necessity. The U.S. Department of Defense defines military necessity as "the principle that justifies the use of all measures needed to defeat the enemy as quickly and efficiently as possible that are not prohibited by the law of war."[55] Thus, if a military finds a cyber operation against civilian data necessary to accomplish its military objectives, and it is not otherwise prohibited under the law, then it is permitted. How broadly states should be permitted to understand military necessity is a fair question, but it is also difficult to second-guess. As detailed in the preceding sections, several states have found it in their interest to conduct such operations as part of an overall military strategy. Therefore, it is unlikely that a high number of states would support the amendment of IHL treaties to cover civilian data. It should also be noted that military necessity is often tied to the development of military capabilities. As industry develops new capabilities, military leaders will seek to utilize those capabilities in a manner that best achieves tactical and strategic objectives. Historically, necessity and the advent of new capabilities have directly driven major changes in the laws of war.[56]

[54] Universal Declaration of Human Rights, G.A. Res. 217A (III), U.N. Doc. A/810, art. 12 (Dec. 12, 1948).

[55] Law of War Manual, *supra* note 34, at para. 2.2.

[56] *See* Jon Jacobson, *The Law of Submarine Warfare Today*, 64 Int'l L. Stud. 205 (1991).

Beyond formulation of new treaties or the amendment of existing ones, IHL can also evolve to provide greater protections through the development of CIL. CIL consists of rules wholly outside of treaty law, but in some circumstances it may also serve to interpret or clarify existing treaty law. CIL develops through a combination of state practice and evidence of a state's belief that a given practice is mandatory, known as *opinio juris*.[57] Importantly, there are many reasons why states choose to follow a particular practice, only one of which is the belief that they are required to do so under international law. For example, practice may also result from perceived norms of ethical behavior, fear of offending powerful states, or pure self-interest, to name a few. Therefore, it is significant when states recognize a particular practice as a legal requirement.

Given these requirements, it can be difficult to determine when a norm of behavior has ripened into CIL, requiring scholars to closely examine state behavior and, more importantly, their reasons for behavior. In doing so, scholars and practitioners look to statements by central authorities within a government. These statements are typically preceded with an acknowledgment that the official is offering the state's understanding of international legal obligations. Additionally, publications such as a military manual on IHL may also serve as a source of *opinio juris*.[58]

Although states are beginning to make formal expressions about how IHL applies in the context of cyber operations, relatively few have offered direct opinions regarding the protection of civilian data. This is not surprising given the complexity of the issue and the potential military value of targeting civilian data in armed conflicts. States will likely want to deliberate over the legal, operational, and strategic implications of their positions, making it highly unlikely in the near future that states will close the coverage gap regarding the protection of civilian data.

5. The Development of Norms Relating to Civilian Data

As detailed by the preceding arguments, there is a coverage gap under the law regarding the protection of civilian data. While this topic is not the only subject of disagreement regarding military cyber operations and the law, scholars have agreed on many open questions.[59] However, no issue better represents the

[57] *See* Statute of the International Court of Justice, art. 38(1)(b), June 26, 1945, 33 U.N.T.S. 993; Case Concerning the Continental Shelf (Libyan Arab Jamahiriya v. Malta), 1985 I.C.J. 13, paras. 27, 34 (June 3). *See also* ANDREW CLAPHAM, BRIERLY'S LAW OF NATIONS: AN INTRODUCTION TO THE ROLE OF INTERNATIONAL LAW IN INTERNATIONAL RELATIONS 57–63 (2012).

[58] *See, e.g.*, LAW OF WAR MANUAL, *supra* note 34.

[59] *See, e.g.*, TALLINN 2.0, *supra* note 22.

split between perceived ethical obligations and IHL than the protection of civilian data. As a result, scholars and practitioners are actively advocating for an extension of legal protections; however, such an advancement is currently unrealistic. Case in point, in 2017, both Russia and China refused to confirm that international humanitarian law applies to cyber operations expressly in apparent contradiction to the 2015 GGE conclusion.[60] If both China and Russia refuse to recognize that cyber operations are constrained by existing IHL, they are even less likely to be willing to constrain their operations through the development of new obligations. This is likely due to the perceived necessity of such operations and their relative advantages over other states in the cyber domain, an advantage that is unlikely to change soon.

Understanding the roadblocks to formal legal protections, some scholars have instead advocated for new policies that protect civilian data.[61] The international community listened. In December 2018, the United Nations established an Open-Ended Working Group on developments in the field of information and telecommunications in the context of international security (hereinafter, OEWG).[62] Over the course of three meetings and a final report, the OEWG emphasized the importance of building consensus regarding voluntary, non-binding norms on the responsible use of information and communications technologies.[63] While a step in the right direction, it is too early to determine whether this effort will be successful. However, given the history of consternation with similar endeavors, we are not optimistic. Simply put, forming broadly agreed-upon normative policies, seen as quasi or "soft" law, is equally unlikely for the same reasons they are unlikely to agree to "hard" law. Perhaps equally likely, in the event a consensus is reached, states may agree to new norms but recognize their unenforceable nature, disregarding them when convenient. In either case, we believe the gap will remain, and it will remain, in large part, due to incongruities between states in the perceived need to protect civilian data.

As a more productive alternative, we promote a course of action where the international community and the information technologies industry work together to promote a shared set of values relating to civilian data. Both play key roles in driving changes to the law. The most expeditious path toward developing normative agreements and, ultimately, hard law is when states and industry

[60] Michael N. Schmitt & Liis Vihul, *International Cyber Law Politicized: The UN GGE's Failure to Advance Cyber Norms*, Just Security (June 30, 2017), https://www.justsecurity.org/42768/international-cyber-law-politicized-gges-failure-advance-cyber-norms/.

[61] *See, e.g.*, Michael N. Schmitt, *Wired Warfare 3.0*, 910 Int'l Rev. Red Cross 333 (2019).

[62] United Nations, General Assembly, Open-ended working group on developments in the field of information and telecommunications in the context of international security: Final Substantive Report, A/AC.290/2021/CRP.2 (Mar. 10, 2021), https://front.un-arm.org/wp-content/uploads/2021/03/Final-report-A-AC.290-2021-CRP.2.pdf.

[63] *Id.*

share a common set of values. States will benefit from the resulting increase in security, while industry will benefit from the increased stability and predictability shred norms provide. Our proposal will be frustrating to many who advocate for immediate protections. Working toward common values is a slow process. However, this process is not new; in fact, it tracks the successful development of many of the principles of international humanitarian law.[64] In general, societies must first recognize a particular value and then identify actions that violate such values. This is the process by which norms develop. Once a norm has existed for a sufficient period of time, laws are adopted that codify broadly accepted norms and make them binding. Though it is tempting to skip over this process, to assert that consensus exists, and to declare a new principle by fiat, customary international laws must develop slowly and organically if they are to be accepted and followed.

The fundamental flaw with shortcutting this developmental process, and jumping straight to the establishment of new laws, is that it assumes that values, and the weight we afford them, are universal. That is simply not the case with civilian data. As outlined previously, states such as North Korea and Russia have consistently shown a disregard for the primary values that would protect personal digital data over and above intelligence collection. This disregard will undoubtedly be magnified in light of potential military advantage. When states enjoy a potential strategic or military advantage, they are loathe to relinquish that advantage. To the extent that ethical considerations may encourage them to lay down their swords, casuistry and other forms of motivated reasoning may lead them to discount the significance of such values.

Additionally, balancing tests are inherently subjective; one state's assessment will invariably differ from another's. Therefore, to convince a state to forgo a potential military advantage, other states must first seek out a common ethical foundation that demonstrates how the moral costs outweigh the military benefits. Only then will it be possible to convince states to create and adopt norms and eventually laws that are more protective of civilian data. Ideally, that would entail a categorical prohibition (e.g., all operations against civilian data should be prohibited). The creation of such prohibitions has proven very difficult, even for more universal values, absent a catastrophic event.

One example of a catastrophic event that can help effectuate the acceptance of a universal value is the bedrock principle of modern IHL, that an innocent civilian should not suffer the worst consequences of war needlessly. Thus, the principle of distinction (the prohibition on making civilians the object of attack)

64 *Id.* at 345 (providing that "most [international humanitarian law] norms were either adopted in treaty form or crystallized into customary law *only after* the international community found the actions to which they apply unacceptable or inappropriate in the circumstances" (emphasis added)).

is cemented within international law. While there are exceptions to this rule (e.g., the proportionality analysis explained earlier), it is clear that the international community places great value on human life, particularly of those not engaged in the conflict. Consequently, the principle of distinction, formally articulated in Additional Protocol I of the Geneva Convention, has been ratified by 174 countries, with near-universal recognition of distinction as customary international law.[65]

However, this bedrock principle took over a century to find footing within the international community. It is worth noting that the advancement of the principle of distinction started with ineffective legal prohibitions over the course of a hundred years before being widely accepted and followed. One of the first known articulations of the special protection of civilians is found in the Lieber Code, Article 22, developed during the American Civil War.[66] Versions of distinction were later included in the preamble of the St. Petersburg Declaration of 1868, The Hague Peace Conference of 1907, The Hague Rules of Air Warfare of 1923, and a nonbinding resolution by the League of Nations in 1938.[67]

Despite these prohibitions (some laws, some norms), civilians were still made the object of attack through the American Civil War, both world wars, the Korean War, and the Vietnam War.[68] It was not until 1978, when Additional Protocol I entered into force, that distinction was widely recognized and states began to constrain their operations to comply with the principle. Importantly, this recognition only occurred after states had the opportunity to reflect on industrial war, widespread civilian casualties, and the value of human life. Equally important, the latter half of the twentieth century also witnessed the development of increasingly precise weapon systems. Although these systems provided increased tactical capability, an equally important advantage was the ability to reduce civilian casualties through precision strike.

Advancement of new laws to constrain cyber operations from targeting civilian data, even if achieved, would likely suffer a similar fate—they would largely be ignored until states recognize the detriments of those operations and come closer together on related values or acceptable alternatives that achieve the same strategic outcomes without harm to civilian data. Although this path may prove more difficult, it offers greater promise for an effective prohibition.

[65] ICRC, *State Parties to the Following International Humanitarian Law and Other Related Treaties as of 18-Oct-2021* (Oct. 18, 2021), http://ihl-databases.icrc.org/applic/ihl/ihl.nsf/xsp/.ibmmodres/domino/OpenAttachment/applic/ihl/ihl.nsf/40BAD58D71673B1CC125861400334BC4/%24File/IHL_and_other_related_Treaties.pdf?Open; Law of War Manual, *supra* note 34.

[66] Francis Lieber, Instructions for the Government of Armies of the United States in the Field, General Orders No. 100 (promulgated Apr. 24, 1863) (Washington, Government Printing Office, 1898), art. 22.

[67] Gabriel Swiney, *Saving Lives: The Principle of Distinction and the Realities of Modern War*, 39(3) Int'l Law. 733 (2005).

[68] *Id.* at 737–41.

6. The Role of Industry

As suggested in the previous section, industry plays a key role in the resolution of this issue. "Industry" here refers not only the core defense industrial base, whose business is mainly in the defense sector, but also to the broader technology sector. From the abundant collection and long-term storage of civilian data to the often insufficient cybersecurity practices and standards, the broader technology industry is a tempting target. For example, new media companies, such as Meta (Facebook/Instagram), Alphabet (Google/YouTube), and Twitter collect terabytes of data on their users, ranging from what videos they watch, to who their "friends" are, to what stories they read, to what products they look at.[69] More traditional consumer companies have also increased their collection of civilian data.[70] These companies suffer regular breaches targeting civilian data; some of them multiple times, resulting in significant effects on their business interests.[71] These are all potential targets for strategic adversary cyber operations during an armed conflict.

Given the scope of this potential target and their own financial interests, technology companies should be motivated to collaborate in finding a realistic and viable solution to this legal gap. This section proposes three interlocking lines of effort: (1) cooperate in developing alternative methods of achieving strategic cyber effects without harming civilian data; (2) enhance collaborative cybersecurity efforts related to the protection of key sectors of civilian data; and (3) utilize economic and social influence to push toward a more protective legal regime.

The first line of effort leverages industry's key role in the development of military capabilities, particularly the defense industrial base. While this role may not be a pronounced in the cyber domain as it is, say, in the development of space capabilities, it is nevertheless vital. By placing an ethical focus on research and development related to military cyber targets, industry can push strategic thinking away from targeting civilian data. Obviously, certain regimes will certainly continue to push internal development of military cyber capabilities toward focus on civilian targets. However, industry should maintain their ethical focus by refraining from developing capabilities and refusing to work with states that target civilian data. While industry cannot prevent the independent

[69] Klara Lee & Mack Willett, *How Do Social Media Companies Collect and Use Your Personal Data?*, RIGHTLY (Feb. 18, 2021), https://www.rightly.co.uk/your-personal-data-explained/blog/the-privacy-policies-of-social-media-companies-how-do-they-use-your-data/.

[70] Louise Matsakis, *The WIRED Guide to Your Personal Data (and Who Is Using It)*, WIRED (Feb. 15, 2019), https://www.wired.com/story/wired-guide-personal-data-collection/.

[71] *See, e.g.*, Kevin McCoy, *Target to Pay $18.5M for 2013 Data Breach That Affected 41 Million Consumers*, USA TODAY (May 23, 2017), https://www.usatoday.com/story/money/2017/05/23/target-pay-185m-2013-data-breach-affected-consumers/102063932/.

development of these capabilities and covert employment by state-based operations, their development should not be aided and abetted by the careless development of technology that furthers nefarious aims. On the contrary, solutions to the problems presented may come not from laws or treaties but from directed and humane technological innovation. That is largely industry's domain.

The prospect of success for the second effort, improved collaborative cybersecurity, is difficult to evaluate. That is because success of cybersecurity practices has been variable. However, it remains true that the information technology industry is largely driving the widespread collection of civilian data. This creates an ethical obligation to protect such data, even from adversary states in armed conflicts. After all, if a consumer is required to provide information as an inflexible condition of service in furtherance of a for-profit enterprise, isn't it incumbent on that company to safeguard that information? This is particularly true for information that is in excess of what is actually required for the service or product.[72]

Furthermore, efforts toward increased cybersecurity largely align with commercial incentives. Recent malicious operations focused on consumer data have had widespread economic impacts.[73] Admittedly, there is a trade-off: every dollar spent on cybersecurity means one dollar less spent on the improvement of the product or service. As a result, many executives are unwilling to allocate sufficient resources to cybersecurity.[74] However, the return on investment is only the beginning of the challenge, and there are many steps that could be taken from a procedural standpoint.

Cybersecurity is a cooperative endeavor—once a vulnerability is detected, distribution of that vulnerability is critical to its containment and protection of similarly situated companies. Therefore, immediate notification of any breach and the tactics used are beneficial to industry, the state, and society at large. Unfortunately, given the potential negative consequences of public acknowledgment of a breach, many companies are weary of providing widespread notice. This creates an ethical dilemma for industry: either provide notification and suffer the impacts of the breach, or remain silent and allow other companies to also become victims. For the company's valuation, the answer may be clear, but for the ethical executive, the choice is rather difficult.

[72] For example, if Facebook asks for one's zip code, purely for the purposes of curating advertisements and not for facilitating connections to those in one's local area, Facebook should be obligated to protect the excessive personal information they choose to monetize.

[73] *See, e.g.*, William Turton & Kartikay Mehrotra, *Hackers Breached Colonial Pipeline Using Compromised Password*, Bloomberg (June 4, 2021), https://www.bloomberg.com/news/articles/2021-06-04/hackers-breached-colonial-pipeline-using-compromised-password.

[74] Alex Blau, *The Behavioral Economics of Why Executives Underinvest in Cybersecurity*, Harv. Bus. Rev. (June 7, 2017), https://hbr.org/2017/06/the-behavioral-economics-of-why-executives-underinvest-in-cybersecurity.

The final effort is for the technology industry to use its reach and influence to create a legal regime that is protective. This would require industry to throw its weight behind the development of shared values related to the protection of civilian data in armed conflicts that can be formed into norms, and then into enforceable laws. This approach may put industry in confrontation with regimes that have control over lucrative markets, particularly China. However, it may also be a key factor to long-term stability in the cyber domain, something that should be attractive to industry. This approach should focus on bringing cyber in line with other warfighting.

In pursuing this option, industry could play three important roles. First, industry should work with the academy to identify the ethical value of civilian data. As noted earlier, the international community places great value on civilian life; this value is universal. The value of civilian data is less obvious and less universal. By articulating the type of data collected, the importance of it, the potential consequences of its exposure, and how the lives of civilians will be impacted, industry can be the leader in starting the conversation toward identifying the values of civilian data. Then, in collaboration with academics and other researchers, industry leaders can promote a better understanding of how valuations of civilian data should align with other values represented in traditional principles governing the conduct of warfare.

Second, industry leaders should act as an intermediary with like-minded leaders around the world. While the preceding case studies focused on civilian industry within the United States and Europe, companies from all parts of the globe have been the victims of malicious actors targeting civilian data. Industry leaders should work with these companies to demonstrate how the value of civilian data and the impact of its exposure is shared throughout the nations of the world. In so doing, these leaders present a united front to world governments, convincing those states that do not see the need for the protection of civilian data and communicating the importance of closing this legal gap.

Third, and vitally important, industry must be willing to serve as an accountability mechanism, communicating when actors target civilian data. As the shared values start to develop into norms, political leaders need to know when the norms are being violated. By informing political leaders of any violations, industry is enabling the government to address the issues and help develop consensus or momentum for more enforceable regimes. It is worth noting that this would not require full breach notification, which could result in impacts to a company's valuation. Rather, this is a confidential notification of a malicious act and nothing more. This would allow the government to be equipped with greater information as it seeks to advance the ethical argument on the protection of civilian data.

The value and abundance of the collection of civilian data by the defense industrial base and the broader technology sector makes it a tempting target. This, along with the fact that their financial interests would benefit, these sectors play a key role in resolving this legal gap. By pursuing these three interlocking lines of effort, industry can help bring about realistic and viable solutions.

7. Conclusion

The advent of cyber operations has created many new military advantages and opportunities. It has also created several legal challenges. The modern iteration of IHL was drafted over the last 75 years; however, it is a world away from the realities of today's geopolitical landscape. The current legal regime was written for the domains of visible and tangible things, while current operations skew toward virtual "objects." Consequently, a coverage gap exists within IHL for the protection of civilian data.

This would be of little consequence if civilian data had not been or would not be targeted by cyber operations. However, many international powers, including North Korea, China, and Russia, have demonstrated their willingness to engage in cyber operations directed at civilian data. While many of these operations have occurred outside the context of armed conflicts, Russian cyber operations against Ukraine provide an example of the state use of cyber operations in concert with conventional forces during an armed conflict. Moreover, given the overwhelming success of these operations, the targeting of civilian data is likely an indication of future campaigns; the compound effects are too valuable to go unused.

Conversely, civilian data is too important in our digital age to leave largely unprotected during armed conflict. As a result, some scholars and practitioners have sought an expanded interpretation of IHL, enabling greater protections for civilian data. However, such interpretations have failed to receive widespread acceptance. Other scholars and practitioners have advocated for an extension of legal protections through binding or normative agreements; however, such agreements are currently unrealistic. A more realistic and productive alternative is to follow the natural formation of international law: begin by promoting a shared set of values relating to civilian data, which will lead the international community to create normative practices and, ultimately, binding international law. Importantly, it is not the lawyers nor the statesmen who can best promote a solution for the protection of civilian data. Rather, it is industry leaders partnered with the academy who are perhaps best suited to begin this conversation, build consensus, and start the process to eliminate the coverage gap.

References

Alex Blau, *The Behavioral Economics of Why Executives Underinvest in Cybersecurity*, HARV. BUS. REV. (June 7, 2017), https://hbr.org/2017/06/the-behavioral-economics-of-why-executives-underinvest-in-cybersecurity.

Michelle D. Christensen, *OPM Data Breach: Personnel Security Background Investigation Data*, CRS INSIGHTS (July 24, 2015), https://sgp.fas.org/crs/natsec/IN10327.pdf.

ANDREW CLAPHAM, BRIERLY'S LAW OF NATIONS: AN INTRODUCTION TO THE ROLE OF INTERNATIONAL LAW IN INTERNATIONAL RELATIONS (2012).

COMMENTARY ON THE ADDITIONAL PROTOCOLS OF 8 JUNE 1977 TO THE GENEVA CONVENTIONS OF 12 AUGUST 1949 (Yves Sandoz, Christophe Swinarski & Bruno Zimmermann eds., 1987).

DIETER FLECK, THE HANDBOOK ON INTERNATIONAL HUMANITARIAN LAW (2013).

Josh Fruhlinger, *Marriott Data Breach FAQ: How Did It Happen and What Was the Impact?*, CSO ONLINE (Feb. 12, 2020), https://www.csoonline.com/article/3441220/marriott-data-breach-faq-how-did-it-happen-and-what-was-the-impact.html.

Andy Greenberg, *The Untold Story of NotPetya, the Most Devastating Cyberattack in History*, WIRED (Aug. 22, 2018), https://www.wired.com/story/notpetya-cyberattack-ukraine-russia-code-crashed-the-world/.

JEAN-MARIE HENCKAERTS & LOUISE DOSWALD-BECK, 1 CUSTOMARY INTERNATIONAL HUMANITARIAN LAW (2005).

Inst. for Nat'l Sec. Stud., *The Ukrainian Crisis—A Cyber Warfare Battlefield*, DEF. UPDATE (Apr. 5, 2014), https://defense-update.com/20140405_ukrainian-crisis-cyber-warfare-battlefield.html.

Int'l Comm. of the Red Cross Legality of the Threat of Use of Nuclear Weapons, *State Parties to the Following International Humanitarian Law and Other Related Treaties as of 18-Oct-2021* (Oct. 18, 2021), http://ihl-databases.icrc.org/applic/ihl/ihl.nsf/xsp/.ibmmodres/domino/OpenAttachment/applic/ihl/ihl.nsf/40BAD58D71673B1CC125861400334BC4/%24File/IHL_and_other_related_Treaties.pdf?Open.

THE INTERVIEW (Sony Pictures Entertainment 2014).

Jon Jacobson, *The Law of Submarine Warfare Today*, 64 INT'L L. STUD. 205 (1991).

JOINT CHIEFS OF STAFF, JOINT PUBLICATION 3-60, JOINT TARGETING (Jan. 31, 2013).

Hersch Lauterpact, *The Law of Nations and the Punishment of War Crimes*, 21 BRIT. Y.B. INT'L L. 77 (1944).

Klara Lee & Mack Willett, *How Do Social Media Companies Collect and Use Your Personal Data?*, RIGHTLY (Feb. 18, 2021), https://www.rightly.co.uk/your-personal-data-explained/blog/the-privacy-policies-of-social-media-companies-how-do-they-use-your-data/.

Legality of the Threat of Use of Nuclear Weapons, Advisory Opinion, 1996 I.C.J. 226, para. 78 (July 8).

FRANCIS LIEBER, INSTRUCTIONS FOR THE GOVERNMENT OF ARMIES OF THE UNITED STATES IN THE FIELD, GENERAL ORDERS NO. 100 (promulgated Apr. 24, 1863) (Washington, Government Printing Office, 1898).

Kubo Mačak, *Military Objectives 2.0: The Case for Interpreting Computer Data as Objects under International Humanitarian Law*, 48 ISR. L. REV. 39 (2015).

Michael J. Matheson, *Session One: The United States' Position on the Relation of Customary International Law to the 1977 Protocols Additional to the 1949 Geneva Conventions*, *in* 2 AM. U. J. INT'L L. & POL'Y 419 (1987).

Louise Matsakis, *The WIRED Guide to Your Personal Data (and Who Is Using It)*, WIRED (Feb. 15, 2019), https://www.wired.com/story/wired-guide-personal-data-collection/.

Kevin McCoy, *Target to Pay $18.5M for 2013 Data Breach that Affected 41 Million Consumers*, USA TODAY (May 23, 2017), https://www.usatoday.com/story/money/2017/05/23/target-pay-185m-2013-data-breach-affected-consumers/102063932/.

Kartikay Mehrotra & David Voreacos, *U.S. Calls North Korean Hackers "World's Leading Bank Robbers"*, BLOOMBERG (Feb. 17, 2021, 8:15 PM), https://www.bloomberg.com/news/articles/2021-02-17/u-s-charges-3-north-koreans-linked-to-sony-hack-in-new-scheme.

MINISTÈRE DES ARMÉES, INTERNATIONAL LAW APPLIED TO CYBERSPACE (2019), https://www.defense.gouv.fr/content/download/567648/9770527/file/international+law+applied+to+operations+in+cyberspace.pdf.

Press Release, White House, Statement from the Press Secretary (Feb. 15, 2018), https://trumpwhitehouse.archives.gov/briefings-statements/statement-press-secretary-25/.

Protocol Additional to the Geneva Conventions of 12 August 1949, and Relating to the Protection of Victims of International Armed Conflicts (Protocol I), adopted June 8, 1977, 1125 U.N.T.S. 3.

Michael N. Schmitt, *Wired Warfare 3.0*, 910 INT'L REV. RED CROSS 333 (2019).

Michael N. Schmitt & Liis Vihul, *International Cyber Law Politicized: The UN GGE's Failure to Advance Cyber Norms*, JUST SECURITY (June 30, 2017), https://www.justsecurity.org/42768/international-cyber-law-politicized-gges-failure-advance-cyber-norms/.

Roy Schöndorf, *Israel's Perspective on Key Legal and Practical Issues Concerning the Application of International Law to Cyber Operations*, 97 INT'L L. STUD. 395 (2021).

Tatiana Siegel, *Five Years Later, Who Really Hacked Sony?*, HOLLYWOOD REP. (Nov. 25, 2019), https://www.hollywoodreporter.com/movies/movie-features/five-years-who-hacked-sony-1257591/.

Gabriel Swiney, *Saving Lives: The Principle of Distinction and the Realities of Modern War*, 39 INT'L LAW. 733 (2005).

TALLINN MANUAL 2.0 ON THE INTERNATIONAL LAW APPLICABLE TO CYBER WARFARE (Michael N. Schmitt ed., 2017).

William Turton & Kartikay Mehrotra, *Hackers Breached Colonial Pipeline Using Compromised Password*, BLOOMBERG (June 4, 2021), https://www.bloomberg.com/news/articles/2021-06-04/hackers-breached-colonial-pipeline-using-compromised-password.

U.N. General Assembly, Group of Governmental Experts on Developments in the Field of Information and Telecommunications in the Context of International Security: Note by the Secretary-General, U.N. Doc. A/70/174, 22 July 2015, paras. 24, 28(d).

U.S. DEP'T OF DEF., OFFICE OF GEN. COUNSEL, LAW OF WAR MANUAL (2016), https://dod.defense.gov/Portals/1/Documents/pubs/DoD%20Law%20of%20War%20Manual%20-%20June%202015%20Updated%20Dec%202016.pdf?ver=2016-12-13-172036-190.

U.S. GOV'T ACCOUNTABILITY OFFICE, GAO-18-559, DATA PROTECTION: ACTIONS TAKEN BY EQUIFAX AND FEDERAL AGENCIES IN RESPONSE TO THE 2017 BREACH (2018).

Universal Declaration of Human Rights, G.A. Res. 217A (III), U.N. Doc. A/810 (Dec. 10, 1948).

Vienna Convention on the Law of Treaties, *opened for signature* May 23, 1969, 1155 U.N.T.S. 331 (entered into force Jan. 27, 1980).

8

Make Them Rare or Make Them Care

Artificial Intelligence and Moral Cost-Sharing

Blake Hereth and Nicholas G. Evans[*]

1. Introduction

Artificial intelligence (AI) describes a set of computational tools in which machines can evaluate, act on, and modify future behavior based on their own calculations and behaviors. AI comes in a broad range of formats, from basic personal assistants such as Apple's Siri that recognizes natural language to potential future "artificial *general* intelligence" that can make decisions over an exceptionally large range of domains and may even possess its own mental states. The military has long expressed interest in AI's processing power over very large and multimodal data sets. This power could be leveraged in areas as diverse as intelligence collection; educating soldiers or calculating precise nutrition and training regimens; and deploying AI in combat either through the use of unmanned vehicles or defending against cyberattackers or other AI.

A central component of the broader debate about military AI is lethal autonomous weapon systems (LAWS). LAWS, in brief, are armed weapon systems capable of learning, adapting, and decision-making capacities and thus in principle to make better *ethical* decisions about which targets to kill.[1] Critics such as Robert Sparrow, however, argue that moral responsibility (and attendant liability) for illegal or immoral killings by LAWS rests neither with the programmer, nor the commanding officer, nor LAWS themselves.[2] This, Sparrow contends, violates the *jus in bello* principle that someone can be held responsible for illegal or immoral killing.[3] More recently, Michael Skerker, Duncan Purves,

[*] We are grateful to Tobias Vestner and Daniel Schoeni for comments on an earlier draft. Special thanks to Claire Finkelstein for inviting us to contribute to this volume.

[1] *See generally* Ronald C. Arkin, Governing Lethal Behavior in Autonomous Robots (2009).

[2] *See generally* Robert Sparrow, *Killer Robots*, 24(1) J. Applied Phil. 62 (2007).

[3] *Id.* at 67. As Sparrow explains, "The least we owe our enemies is allowing that their lives are of sufficient worth that someone should accept responsibility for their deaths. Similarly, their grieving relatives are entitled to an answer as to why they died, which includes both knowing who is responsible and what their reasons were. Ensuring that someone can be held responsible for each death caused in war is therefore an important requirement of *jus in bello*."

Blake Hereth and Nicholas G. Evans, *Make Them Rare or Make Them Care* In: *Ethical Dilemmas in the Global Defense Industry*. Edited by: Daniel Schoeni and Tobias Vestner, Oxford University Press.
 DOI: 10.1093/oso/9780190675813.003.0009

and Ryan Jenkins defended a novel explanation for widespread unease about LAWS, namely, that human agents forfeit their right against harm *exclusively* to fellow humans who comprehend their value[4] and their "functioning in response to changing circumstances in the environment in which they are deployed," as well as being capable of making firing decisions on their own.[5] LAWS have generated a rigorous debate in ethics.[6] Advocates of LAWS such as Ronald Arkin will claim we can expect LAWS to eventually surpass humans in their capacity for information processing.[7]

A question arises, then, as to how we should *develop* LAWS and other military AI. According to one analysis, the market capture for military AI will exceed $11.6 billion by 2025.[8] The debate around LAWS and other AI applications have largely focused on when or if it is permissible to use AI, but has largely (with the exception of Sparrow) avoided the question of what kinds of AI it is permissible to *develop*. Development offers an interesting ethical quandary because, much like the pharmaceutical industry, it asks less which kinds of weapon are permissible to use and more what kinds of properties a useable weapon should have.[9] And while there may be some kinds of weapon it is simply impermissible to develop (e.g., biological weapons), for most others the question is how we should develop LAWS and what they should be developed to do. Here we defend a novel conception of moral cost-sharing when it comes to AI and military decision-making and tie it to questions of AI development in the defense industry. Drawing from recent work on compensation in the ethics of war, we argue that the moral costs of unjust harming should be equitably distributed across responsible parties. We then argue that as some of the deepest moral costs are *psychological* in nature (e.g., the grief experienced by families of civilian "collateral damage"), justice requires that these costs be shared. In Section 2, we argue that widespread substitution of AI in critical military decisions, using LAWS as the paradigmatic example, undermines a requirement of justice in virtue of lacking moral emotions and thus being unable to share in the psychological costs of war. Then,

[4] By this, Skerker et al. maintain that human agents can't forfeit their rights against non-agents, since that would require them to have had rights against those non-agents—a view that in turns requires non-agents to have had moral obligations, *per impossibile*. *See generally* Michael Skerker, Duncan Purves & Ryan Jenkins, *Autonomous Weapons Systems and the Moral Equality of Combatants*, 22 Ethics & Info. Tech. 197 (2020).

[5] Heather M. Roff, *Lethal Autonomous Weapons and Jus Ad Bellum Proportionality*, 47 Case W. Res. J. Int'l L., 37, 37 (2015).

[6] *See, e.g.*, *id*.

[7] Arkin *supra note* 1.

[8] *Artificial Intelligence in Military Market Worth $11.6 Billion by 2025*, MarketsandMarkets (Mar. 15, 2021), https://www.prnewswire.com/news-releases/artificial-intelligence-in-military-market-worth-11-6-billion-by-2025--exclusive-report-by-marketsandmarkets-301247146.html.

[9] Aaron Fichtelberg, *Applying the Rules of Just War Theory to Engineers in the Arms Industry*, 12(4) Sci. & Eng'g Ethics (2006).

in Section 3, we consider arguments from Bradley Strawser and others claiming that because LAWS enhance the safety of justified combatants, their use is morally obligatory. In response, we raise the possibility of *sentient LAWS* (SLAWS) with the capacity for moral emotion.[10] Our conciliatory contention, which weds our argument against non-emotive LAWS with Strawser's argument for LAWS, is that the development of SLAWS is itself morally obligatory. Our second contention is less conciliatory: where the choice is exclusively between deploying LAWS or deploying humans in warfare, this entails a choice between prioritizing the interests of justified combatants who cause unjust harm to civilians or prioritizing the interests of the civilians whose interests they unjustly threaten. Absent a lesser-evil obligation on the part of justified combatants, justice requires prioritizing the psychological interests of civilians. We then consider what this argument might look like, abstracted to military AI in more general terms.

Unlike other arguments against LAWS, our argument doesn't conclude that the use of LAWS is all-things-considered morally impermissible to use or develop. Rather, our argument holds that the use of LAWS is pro tanto impermissible, that there are competing considerations to using LAWS (i.e., facilitating the safety of justified combatants), and that a moral dilemma emerges: either we should design LAWS capable of moral emotions, or we should limit the use of (non-emotive) LAWS. We then chart what this might look like for the defense industry to navigate this space and develop AI applications that are permissible to deploy in the use of lethal force.

2. Moral Cost-Sharing and Psychological Costs

In general, *moral cost-sharing* refers to a fair distribution of burdens between interested parties, where the moral burdens in question can be wide-ranging *financial cost-sharing*, that is, how to equitably balance economic burdens across relevant parties. For example, cost-sharing elements of the Patient Protection and Affordable Care Act caused extensive debate over the fairness of requiring healthy, responsible taxpayers to foot the bill for unhealthy, less responsible patients while often acknowledging that cost-sharing between healthy, responsible parties was equitable.[11] Or, to take another example, Avia Pasternak argues that citizens ought to share in the costs of injustices committed by

[10] Our view is that sentience is necessary but insufficient for moral emotion. Psychopaths, for instance, are sentient, but lack moral emotion.

[11] *See generally* John P. Geyman, *Cost-Sharing Under Consumer-Driven Health Care Will Not Reform U.S. Health Care*, 40(3) J.L., Med. & Ethics 574 (2012); Allison K. Hoffman, *Cost-Sharing Reductions, Technocrat Tinkering, and Market-Based Health Policy*, 46(4) J.L., Med. & Ethics 873 (2018).

their state because they benefit from the intrinsically good civic bond that allows citizens to pursue, through their elected officials, morally worthy social outcomes.[12]

Ethicists and political philosophers have more recently expanded the application of moral cost-sharing to nonfinancial burdens. Sara Van Goozen, for instance, claims that insofar as noncombatants benefit from their compatriots fighting just wars that endanger foreign noncombatants, the former noncombatants ought to share in these costs.[13] A relatively uncontroversial example of this is President Woodrow Wilson's "Meatless Mondays" campaign during the First World War, intended to limit civilian consumption of meat to conserve food for both American troops abroad and foreign civilians whose livelihoods were disrupted by global warfare. However, questions remain about the extent to which noncombatants are obligated to shoulder these costs. Had Wilson instituted "Starving Solstices" and required the American Midwest to forgo food for the duration of the winter in order to feed war-displaced foreign civilians, his humanitarian-motivated austerity would have been opposed as transparently unjust.

Against views like Van Goozen's, Helen Frowe sketches an argument intended to limit the liability of justified combatants—that is, combatants whose wartime involvement is morally justified—and, by extension, innocent (i.e., nonliable) noncombatants. Frowe's argument is meant to solve a problem raised by Jeff McMahan: Can combatants who cause collateral harm to civilians as a side effect of attacks on lawful targets be morally liable to defensive harm on that basis?[14] To see the problem, imagine a case where an aerial bomber is morally justified in dropping a bomb that will (as intended) kill mostly unjust combatants—that is, combatants whose wartime involvement is morally unjustified—and merely foreseeably kill a few civilians.[15] The bomber poses a justified but unjust harm to the civilians, and we typically think it is permissible to defend oneself against unjust harm. McMahan's solution is to claim that justification defeats liability,

[12] *See generally* Avia Pasternak, *Sharing the Costs of Political Injustices*, 10(2) Pol., Phil. & Econ. 188 (2011).

[13] *See generally* Sara Van Goozen, "Sharing the Costs of Fighting Justly," 2 Critical Rev. Int'l Soc. & Pol. Phil. 1 (2018).

[14] Persons are liable to *defensive harm* just in case they forfeit their right against others harming them in self-defense or defense of others. In such cases, persons are liable to a specific kind of instrumental harming (i.e., harm that averts an unjustified threat) that is distinct from liability to other kinds of harming, such as desert-based harming which is non-instrumental. *See generally* Jeff McMahan, *Self-Defense Against Justified Threateners*, *in* How We Fight: Ethics in War 104 (Helen Frowe & Gerald Lang eds., 2014).

[15] We prefer the just/unjust combatant distinction to the lawful/unlawful combatant distinction for two reasons: first, because ours is an *ethical* critique of AI-enabled LAWS that tracks primarily the morality rather than the law of war, and second, because McMahan and Frowe represent revisionist views of the Just War Theory tradition for whom the lawful/unlawful combatant distinction has no intrinsic moral importance.

such that justified threateners cannot be liable to defensive harm for the justified harms they pose.[16] In short, this means that posing a *justified* threat to someone immunizes you against their justifiably harming you in self-defense.[17] However, McMahan's view has been vigorously challenged.[18]

In clever fashion, Frowe sidesteps McMahan's solution and instead contends that whether or not lesser-evil justifications are sufficient to block moral liability, lesser-evil *obligations* are.[19] Returning to the scenario, suppose the bomber was not merely justified but obligated to drop their bomb and that the obligation in question was an agent-neutral (that is, an obligation applying to all agents, irrespective of partisanship), lesser-evil (that is, an obligation to prevent the greater evil) obligation. In that case, were the civilians to kill the bomber and prevent the bombing, they would violate *their own* lesser-evil obligation to permit the bombing. As Frowe puts it:

> It seems generally implausible that one might forfeit basic rights by doing one's duty, since this entails that morality might leave one with no morally permissible options for retaining one's rights. [. . .] Moreover, it seems straightforwardly incoherent that morality might pronounce Pedestrian liable to be harmed to prevent her from doing the very thing that morality requires her to do.[20]

Accounts like Van Goozen's and Frowe's are illustrative of the more general phenomenon of moral cost-sharing. In all the aforementioned cases, cost-sharing is *zero-sum*: a finite, definite moral burden is distributed equitably.[21] We "subtract" burdens (e.g., the civilians') from one party and "add" to another (e.g., the bomber's). Like matter itself, the costs are neither created nor destroyed, only redistributed. Call the thesis that moral cost-sharing is necessarily restricted to reallocation or redirection the *Non-Additive Thesis*.[22] Having now illustrated

16 *Id.* at 118.

17 In practice, this means that insofar as the threat you pose is justified, no one can justifiably harm you to prevent you from posing that threat.

18 *See generally* Adam Hosein, *Are Justified Aggressors a Threat to the Rights Theory of Self-Defense?*, *in* HOW WE FIGHT 87 (Helen Frowe & Gerald Lang eds., 2014).

19 Helen Frowe, *Lesser-Evil Justifications for Harming: Why We're Required to Turn the Trolley*, 68(272) PHIL. Q. 460, 476–77 (2018).

20 *Id.* at 476.

21 The standard conception of *zero-sum* is, in short, that whatever benefits one party harms the other and vice versa.

22 Our discussion of the Non-Additive Thesis resembles discussions within political philosophy of the so-called *leveling-down objection*. According to this objection, egalitarian views requiring strict equality of goods imply that justice can be satisfied merely by *removing* goods from parties with more goods than others. *See generally* Derek Parfit, *Equality or Priority?*, *in* THE IDEAL OF EQUALITY (Matthew Clayton & Andrew Williams eds., 2002). The Non-Additive Thesis raises a similar objection: just as it seems impermissible to remove goods from parties to achieve equality, so also it seems impermissible to *add evils* (in this case, harms) to achieve equality.

non-additive moral cost-sharing, we will defend the possibility and moral equity of *additive* moral cost-sharing.[23] Specifically, we offer a hearty defense of *solidarity-based* moral cost-sharing that, while additive in nature, explains our moral intuitions in ways the Non-Additive Thesis cannot. Said differently, we contend that moral cost-sharing concerns not simply *who suffers* or *how much someone suffers*, but also *who suffers alone*. So we will argue that the Non-Additive Thesis should be rejected.

Before examining the Non-Additive Thesis more directly, consider a powerful argument in its favor. The premises of this argument could be drawn from a number of ethical theories:

The Less Harm Argument

P1. We should not cause nonconsensual harm unless it is practically necessary to avert a worse nonconsensual harm. [Assumption]

P2. If P1, then the Non-Additive Thesis is true. [By definition]

C. So the Non-Additive Thesis is true. [From P1 to P2]

The argument relies primarily on the plausibility of P1, which we hold to be extremely plausible. Once we leave room for causing consensual and lesser-evil harms, we are left with only nonconsensual harms that *do not* prevent worse harms.[24] Surely, it is impermissible to cause *those* harms. If so, then permissible moral cost-sharing is restricted to extant harm and prohibits the creation of new harm. So P1 by definition entails the Non-Additive Thesis, just as P 2 claims. So, as P3 follows from P1 and P2, P3 is true.

The *Less Harm Argument* fails, and with it the Non-Additive Thesis, as shown by a real-life event that serves as the central case for our essay. It's July 12, 2007, in Iraq. Crazy Horse 1-8, an American Apache helicopter, mows down 11

[23] Here's an example designed to explain the Non-Additive Thesis:

Abdul and Cleo live in a community where flashfloods are common. Abdul, who controls the emergency levies that determine where surplus water is redirected, is one day forced to decide whether to redirect flashflood waters to Cleo's home (thereby saving Abdul's home) or redirect it to his own home (thereby saving Cleo's home). If Abdul does nothing, both homes will be destroyed. There's no way to save both homes. Not wanting his home destroyed, Abdul chooses the emergency levy that preserves his home but destroys Cleo's. Later, and without Cleo ever knowing, Abdul burns his own home to the ground to alleviate his guilt.

In this example, there's something perverse about Abdul's destruction of his home. Cleo isn't helped by it, and nor is Abdul. When Abdul razes his home, he neither reallocates nor redirects any harm suffered by Cleo; rather, he merely adds new harm, which is forbidden as a form of moral cost-sharing under the Non-Additive Thesis. By contrast, imagine Abdul had another option at his disposal: to choose an emergency levy that would redirect *most* of the flood waters away from both homes but still cause *mild* damage to both homes. In the revised case, Abdul effectively minimizes the amount of harm suffered by all parties, as neither he nor Cleo must shoulder *all* the flash flood damage by having their respective homes destroyed. Thus, Abdul *reallocates* the harms posed by the flash flood—a permissible form of moral cost-sharing under the Non-Additive Thesis.

[24] For an example, see the case of Abdul in the previous footnote.

civilians. As the American gunner, known only as "Kyle," fires, he exclaims, "All right! Haha! I hit 'em." Among the dead are two Reuters reporters, both of whom tried to escape the gunfire and were killed as they took shelter. Later, an ambulance arrived to transport the wounded to a nearby hospital. Crazy Horse 1-8 destroyed it and killed both medics. The war crimes of Crazy Horse 1-8 were initially documented in 2010 by Chris McGreal at *The Guardian*.[25] Footage of the crimes, including audio, was later released by Wikileaks under the title "Collateral Murder."[26]

This incident was indisputably a war crime. But let us examine Kyle's emotional reaction to killing 11 civilians. As is made transparent both from the video and our reconstruction of the event, Kyle is downright *gleeful* about his lethal work. He laughs as he pumps hot lead through the bodies of his targets, demonstrating no sadness or remorse. Even without video, an attentive listener might mistakenly assume Kyle was not engaging *people* but rather simulated or inanimate targets. But he wasn't, and they weren't. Kyle killed human beings—people with feelings, who feared death, who suffered as they were cut down—people with families, friends, and communities who would come to miss them. And Kyle *enjoyed* cutting them down. Because he was destroying not inanimate objects but human beings, his affects were *morally ill-suited* to his behavior. Indeed, Kyle's reaction to killing human beings—whether permissible targets or not—is morally perverse. He ought not delight in others' suffering, death, or misfortune.

Let us assume, contrary to fact, that Kyle's targets *were* enemy combatants and that his killing them was morally justified. Even so, Kyle should not react gleefully to gunning them down. One reason for this concerns the fact that Kyle's targets do not exist in a moral vacuum; they are connected to others who care for them and who are adversely impacted by their demise. More relevantly, these others—partners, children, parents, friends, neighbors, imams—are not liable to the harms Kyle imposes on them. That is, they don't forfeit their rights against Kyle that he does not harm them. Whatever they lose, they lose unjustly—even if justifiably. Like civilians harmed in tactical bombings, those who harm them act unjustly in the sense that they harm people who are not liable to be harmed. An action is *morally justified* if it is permissible to perform it, but an action is *morally just* only if all harmed parties are liable to be harmed. Indeed, civilians harmed as unavoidable side effects of military action are entitled to compensation in

[25] Chris McGreal, *Wikileaks Reveals Video Showing US Air Crew Shooting Down Iraqi Civilians*, The Guardian (Apr. 5, 2010), http://www.guardian.co.uk/world/2010/apr/05/wikileaks-us-army-iraq-attack.

[26] *Collateral Murder*, WikiLeaks (Apr. 5, 2010), https://wikileaks.org/wiki/Collateral_Murder,_5_Apr_2010.

war.[27] Indifference toward their suffering (or, worse, *enjoyment* of it) is a moral failing, an improper response to causing others' pain.[28] Thus, Kyle experiences a deficiency in moral affect for the unjust harm he causes to nonliable parties with vested interests in the welfare of Kyle's victims.

We propose to explain normatively permissible moral affect in terms of cost-sharing. In cases like Kyle's, most theorists agree it is intrinsically better for *Kyle* to shoulder the costs of war than for *nonliable civilians* to suffer them, as Kyle bears greater responsibility than civilians for their endangerment. But this is often infeasible and counterproductive: if justified combatants are injured or killed, they are far less likely to achieve their justified tactical aims and thus less likely to satisfy the reasonable chance of success criterion for permissible warfare.[29] What, then, is the next best thing justified combatants can do? If they cannot *relieve* the suffering of nonliable parties, they can at least *share in them*. This requires, minimally, that justified combatants *care* about their innocent victims, that they avoid apathy or cruel delight. To be sure, this requirement is partially instrumental: the obligation to *act* cautiously with respect to nonliable civilian interests tends to lead to *caring* about their interests, and thus a deficiency in the latter is evidence of a deficiency in the former. Said differently, combatants who *care little* about civilians are more likely to *mistreat* them. But the obligation to care has a further, noninstrumental underpinning: we *should* care about others, *including* feeling remorseful when they suffer unjustly, *irrespective* of whether our caring about them improves their plight, and *especially* when we have wronged them.

Call this principle the *Moral Affect Principle* (MAP). So stated, MAP approaches moral bedrock: we should feel remorseful when we have wronged others.[30] To feel otherwise, or to feel nothing at all, divorces wrongdoing from caring and expresses to those we have wronged that we will cause them to suffer at no cost to us. In the next section, we explain the ways in which an expansive use of LAWS threatens MAP.

[27] *See generally* Saba Bazargan-Forward, *Compensation and Proportionality in War*, *in* WEIGHING LIVES IN WAR 173 (Jens David Ohlin, Larry May & Claire Finkelstein eds., 2017); Saba Bazargan-Forward, *Defensive Wars and the Reprisal Dilemma*, 93(3) AUSTRALASIAN J. PHIL. 583 (2015). *Cf.* Jessica Flanigan & Christopher Freiman, *Drug War Reparations*, 97(2) RES PHILOSOPHICA 141 (2020).

[28] *See generally* Kristján Kristjánsson, *Fortunes-of-Others Emotions and Justice*, 28(105) J. PHIL. RES. (2003).

[29] *See generally* Ned Dobos, *Idealism, Realism, and Success in Armed Humanitarian Intervention*, 44(2) PHILOSOPHIA 497 (2016); Suzanne Uniacke, *Self-Defense, Just War, and a Reasonable Prospect of Success*, *in* HOW WE FIGHT: ETHICS IN WAR (Helen Frowe & Gerald Lang eds., 2014).

[30] *See* SETH LAZAR, SPARING CIVILIANS 108 (2015).

3. How LAWS Threaten Moral Cost-Sharing

LAWS are still some way off, and early systems will mimic sentience, mirroring human cognitive processes rather than possessing mental states.[31] They are autonomous only in the sense that they can act without real-time direction from human operators. Autonomous drones, for instance, will run on algorithms that cause them to terminate specific targets on-sight without further human approval. Setting aside the question of whether AI weapons like LAWS might ever *become* sentient, it's clear that any near-future LAWS will be nonsentient.

Their lack of sentience, moreover, implies that they lack the full range of mental properties for which sentience is necessary. LAWS lack beliefs and other doxastic attitudes, possess neither desires nor other feelings, and are not "subjects" in the sense that there is something-it-is-like to be them.[32] By implication, LAWS also lack moral affects (i.e., moral feelings) and moral responsibility generally. They are neither happy nor sad, relieved nor frustrated when they achieve their objectives. They are indifferent to human flourishing or floundering. As James Cameron's *Terminator* character Kyle Reese memorably describes Arnold Schwarzenegger's iconic Model 101 Series 800 killing machine, "It can't be bargained with. It can't be reasoned with. It doesn't feel pity, or remorse, or fear. And it absolutely will not stop until you are dead."[33]

Returning to the real-life Kyle in Iraq, imagine his entire aerial unit—pilot and gunner—had been replaced with autonomous AI, that the AI had autonomously chosen a patrol route, identified the 11 targets, and without explicit human approval eliminated them. In this counterfactual, we know at least two things. First, we know the AI did not care about the victims or those unjustly harmed by their deaths.[34] Their widespread replacement of human soldiers with LAWS, then, would result in far less caring—or, as we detail later, a kind of perverse concentration of care—for civilian casualties.[35] Second, given the argument in the previous section, we know we *should* care about others, including feeling remorseful when

[31] *See* Nicholas G. Evans, *Blind Brains and Autonomous Weapon Systems*, *in* LETHAL AUTONOMOUS WEAPONS 203, 215 (Jai Galliott, Duncan MacIntosh & Jens David Ohlin eds., 2021).

[32] *Cf.* Daniel Stoljar, *The Semantics of "What It's Like" and the Nature of Consciousness*, 125(500) MIND 1161 (2016).

[33] THE TERMINATOR (Orion Pictures 1984).

[34] Tobias Vestner asks how our argument works when human soldiers don't care about the civilians they harm. Our answer is unambiguous: it strengthens our argument against LAWS, since as the number of human soldiers who care about the civilians they harm decreases (despite being obligated to care), the number of persons who should be cared for—and the strength of the obligation to care for them—increases, and with it the number of permissible LAWS (which are incapable of caring) decreases. Private correspondence on file with the authors.

[35] Dan Schoeni asks whether the person who switches on a LAWS might feel some remorse about the civilian casualties that will later result. Perhaps they would, but this "secondary" form of caring is less likely than the "primary" form of caring soldiers experience when they are more directly responsible for civilian casualties.

they suffer unjustly, *irrespective* of whether our caring about them improves their plight, and *especially* when we have wronged them (i.e., MAP). Thus, we have an initial argument against the use of LAWS in warfare:

> *The Simple MAP Argument Against LAWS*
>
> P1. We should care about others, including feeling remorseful when they suffer unjustly, irrespective of whether our caring about them improves their plight, and especially when we have wronged them. [MAP]
>
> P2. The widespread replacement of human soldiers with LAWS would lessen the extent to which we care about others, including feeling remorseful when nonliable civilians suffer unjustly, would not improve the plight of nonliable civilians, and would constitute a wrong.[36]
>
> C. So the widespread replacement of human soldiers with LAWS is morally wrong. [From P1 to P2]

The Simple MAP Argument, while simple enough, contains some shortcomings. A major worry is the responsibility problem developed by Robert Sparrow:

> Firstly, the possibility that the machine may attack the wrong targets may be an acknowledged limitation of the system. If the manufacturers have made this clear to those who purchase or deploy the system, then it seems they can no longer be held responsible, should this occur. . . . Secondly, and more importantly, the possibility that an autonomous system will make choices other than those predicted and encouraged by its programmers is inherent in the claim that it is autonomous. If it has sufficient autonomy that it learns from its experience and surroundings that may make decisions which reflect these as much, or more than, its initial programming. . . . At some point then, it will no longer be possible [sic] hold the programmers/designers responsible for outcomes that they could neither control nor predict.[37]

Nor can commanding officers be held morally responsible, Sparrow argues, if "machines are really choosing their own targets."[38] Nor can we hold LAWS

[36] Daniel Schoeni objects that widespread replacement and deployment of LAWS might redistribute human remorse to, for example, all 330 million Americans, each of whom feels .001% of the remorse that a single bomber pilot would feel if they pulled the trigger. In that case, the *aggregate* remorse would equal (if not rival) the single bomber's remorse. We concede this possibility but reply that, in this scenario, *each person cares too little*. That is, each of us, or at least some of us, should be deeply remorseful about civilian casualties, yet no one does under the aggregate remorse scenario Schoeni describes.

[37] *See* Sparrow, *supra* note 2, at 69, 70.

[38] *Id.* at 71. By extension, although commanding officers might feel remorse when LAWS cause civilian casualties, the success of Sparrow's argument (if it succeeds) entails they aren't morally *required* to feel remorse as a result of being morally responsible for LAWS' behavior.

themselves morally responsible, as LAWS lack moral agency.[39] Sparrow's arguments can be adapted to construct a new trilemma:

Sparrow's Trilemma

P1. If nonliable civilians are wronged when harmed by LAWS, they are wronged either by (a) the LAWS' programmers, (2) the LAWS' commanding officers, or (3) the LAWS themselves. [Sparrow's Assumption]

P2. Harms caused by LAWS are ones for which neither the LAWS' programmers, nor the LAWS' commanding officers, nor the LAWS themselves are morally responsible. [Sparrow's Argument]

C. So nonliable civilians are not wronged when harmed by LAWS. [From P1 to P2]

However, applied to LAWS, premise 2 is false. Sparrow concedes that when people send killer robots into war knowing the potential risks, they bear responsibility for the anticipated risks. A commonly anticipated risk of war, as it occurs in all wars, is that nonliable civilians will be harmed during the war. That's true in wars fought with or without LAWS. When commanding officers accept the risk of harming nonliable civilians by deploying LAWS, they bear responsibility for the expected unjust harm to civilians caused by LAWS. Those who bear responsibility for unjust harm are, themselves, the ones *wronging* victims of those unjust harms.

Furthermore, we have reason to reject 1: Moral responsibility is not a precondition for moral wrongdoing. Suppose I am driving around Boston and paying exceptional attention to my surroundings, local laws, and the presence (or absence) of pedestrians or other vehicles.[40] Suppose further that, despite my conscientious best intentions, I hit a motorcyclist because my brakes, which I have otherwise maintained, fail due to a manufacturing defect. Plausibly, the auto manufacturer has still *wronged* the motorcyclist despite its total lack of moral responsibility for harming them, given that both the car and the motorcyclist arguably share the road as part of a system of risk-sharing.[41] Indeed, torts concerning strict liability reflect this moral principle in law: financial liability does not require willful or negligent action on behalf of a manufacturer. In auto manufacturing this is further codified in a highly regulated recall process for systemic manufacturing issues, in which the government ensures that manufacturers not only bear financial responsibility for harms done but also bears responsibility for preventing future harms that may foreseeably arise from similar causes. All

[39] *Id.*

[40] Because I am driving conscientiously, it follows that I am not driving negligently.

[41] *See generally* SVEN OVE HANSSON, THE ETHICS OF RISK: ETHICAL ANALYSIS IN AN UNCERTAIN WORLD (2013).

that is required for this wrongdoing is that the motorcyclist has a right against which someone trespasses, and it is difficult to see why the manufacturer's ignorance undermines the motorcyclist's right that I not harm them. Here, the manufacturer's excuse would be nonculpable ignorance: they did not know the brakes would fail nor did they know they would fail in front of the motorcyclist, so the manufacturer should not be held responsible for hitting them. But others' rights against us persist despite our moral excuses. So although we wrong the motorcyclist, we are not morally responsible for doing so.

Another worry for the Simple MAP Argument is that the nonsentience of LAWS notwithstanding, human monitors are aware of LAWS-caused collateral damages and capable of moral affect. So although LAWS cannot feel remorse when they kill, their human monitors can. Maybe that is enough to rebuff the apparent impermissibility of widely deploying LAWS. However, despite recent evidence showing that remote killing *enhances* empathetic affects from controllers,[42] the psychological disparities between *causing* remote killings and (merely) *observing* remote killings are stark.[43] For instance, drone operators are less prone to post-traumatic stress disorder (PTSD) than soldiers who kill face to face.[44] Our current, best evidence tells us that physical distance is inversely correlated with empathy: the farther apart people are or perceive themselves to be, the less they care.[45] Thus, a reasonable expectation of widespread deployment of LAWS, at least insofar as they replace neurotypical human soldiers, is that nonliable civilians will be cared for less.

In addition to the preceding, proponents of LAWS maintain that with sufficiently advanced weapon platforms, human soldiers may be replaced with LAWS.[46] But this would, if it came to pass, likely overburden human monitors. As the number of human soldiers declines, the burden of moral affect goes up for remote human monitors. Soldiers are no longer physically present on the battlefield or encountering civilians eye to eye, but instead are huddled inside a warehouse for remote operations. And there are fewer of them. The shift from physically present warfighters to remote operators/monitors would increase the number of remote operators/monitors. However, we could still reasonably

[42] *See generally* LT. COL. WAYNE PHELPS, ON KILLING REMOTELY: THE PSYCHOLOGY OF KILLING WITH DRONES (2021).

[43] *See generally* Annie Brookman-Byrne, *There Is a Spectrum of Responses to Killing Far-Off Enemies*, 4(2) PSYCHOL. 40 (2020); Abraham M. Rutchick et al., *Technologically Facilitated Remoteness Increases Killing Behavior*, 73 J. EXPERIMENTAL SOC. PSYCHOL. 147 (2017).

[44] *See* Rutchick et al., *supra* note 43, at 147.

[45] Arianna Schiano Lomoriello et al., *Out of Sight Out of Mind: Perceived Physical Distance Between the Observer and Someone in Pain Shapes Observer's Neural Empathic Reactions*, 9 FRONTIERS PSYCHOL. 1824 (2018).

[46] *See generally* Arkin, *supra* note 1. *Cf.* Evans, *supra* note 30; Nicholas Greig Evans, *Emerging Military Technologies: A Case Study in Neurowarfare*, *in* NEW WARS AND NEW SOLDIERS: MILITARY ETHICS IN THE CONTEMPORARY WORLD 105 (Paolo Tripodi & Jessica Wolfendale eds., 2011).

expect a considerably smaller number of soldiers bearing roughly the same psychological burden initially borne by hundreds of thousands more.[47] This is not unique to LAWS—famously, Joanna Bourke's study of killing in war noted that artillerymen experience what is arguably a form of moral cost-sharing through their concern and suffering at distant casualties they cannot see[48]—but given advances in human-machine interfaces and the possibility of controlling multiple LAWS simultaneously,[49] there is reason to fear that the toll may become extraordinary.

4. The Cost-Sharing Dilemma

MAP prima facie rejects the use of LAWS. After all, without the ability to engage in plausible or defensible moral cost-sharing, it seems that there is—another—pro tanto reason to abandon the use of "killer robots" in favor of humans. This would then place us in conflict with, for example, Ronald Arkin and Bradley Strawser who have both argued for a strong moral duty to deploy LAWS.[50]

But things need not be that simple. Nothing in our argument rides on LAWS, and indeed in the following we extend the argument to moral cost-sharing in other AI defense systems. Rather, the argument here is only against LAWS that are incapable of engaging in moral cost-sharing. All near-future LAWS fall into this category, by virtue of lacking mental states.

But it is plausible that future LAWS could be developed to have some kind of sentience, and thus be in principle capable of experiencing moral sympathies in a way that allows for MAP to be satisfied. Over the last 10 years significant advances have been made that suggest that while current AI applications may not be sentient, there may be some artificial *general* intelligence (AGI) that could possess the capacity for mental states. This may be in virtue of sufficiently broad and deep computing power to generate mental states or the capacity for sentience through novel computing methods that allow computers to perform abductive and other human-like cognition.[51] While disagreements remain as to

[47] Tobias Vestner makes the critical observation that this concern also holds for other groups, including aerial bombers whose targets are invisible to the naked eye. Fortunately, our argument against the use of LAWS to replace human soldiers doesn't require that LAWS be the *only* technology indicted. Correspondence on file with the authors.

[48] *See generally* JOANNA BOURKE, AN INTIMATE HISTORY OF KILLING: FACE TO FACE KILLING IN TWENTIETH CENTURY WARFARE (2000).

[49] *See* NICHOLAS G. EVANS, THE ETHICS OF NEUROSCIENCE AND NATIONAL SECURITY 72–85 (2021).

[50] *See generally* ARKIN, *supra* note 1; Bradley Jay Strawser, *Moral Predators: The Duty to Employ Uninhabited Aerial Vehicles*, 9(4) J. MIL. ETHICS 342 (2010).

[51] *See generally* ERIK J. LARSON, THE MYTH OF ARTIFICIAL INTELLIGENCE: WHY COMPUTERS CAN'T THINK THE WAY WE DO (2021). We note there are some difficulties here about knowing

exactly what form moral agency for machines might take, there is general agreement that if sentience is possible, moral status is also possible.[52] For those skeptical of the likelihood or possibility of sentient LAWS, our position (developed below) is that nonsentient LAWS ought not replace human soldiers.

If proponents such as Arkin and Strawser are to be believed *and* LAWS can be designed that satisfy the MAP, then they would be obligatory to design and deploy. That is, agents that are capable of executing the acts of armed conflict with greater attention to avoiding noncombatant deaths *and* are capable in engaging in moral cost-sharing are in principle better than human agents who fail to achieve the former but satisfy the latter. So here we can act in a conciliatory manner toward advocates for LAWS, by claiming that LAWS are obligatory—if they are sentient. It may be that opponents of AI engaged in lethal decision-making retain some simple, emotive concern to AI killing—but in this case, so do the AI applications!

This possibility raises a number of interesting empirical questions that we sketch but set aside here. There will first be questions of what kinds of sentience, and how much, will be required to engage in MAP. Surely human levels of sentience are excessive for this purpose—Corvids and other animals display sufficient levels of sentience to allow for this. The precise architecture of sentient LAWS (SLAWS) will also have to be determined, and what counts as sympathies will need to be understood to a much higher degree to *know* or have appropriate confidence that sentience is in fact achieved.[53]

The normative questions, on the other hand, are deeper. The first is whether creating sentient machines *specifically* to place them in harm's way, of the kind we describe previously, is morally permissible.[54] An objection here might be that there is a perversity to creating a sentient creature, as far as an AI application is a creature, solely so that we can conscript it to undertake our risky aims. But creating SLAWS does just that. The argument against this is simple: if we believe (with Immanuel Kant) that we should not treat self-governing agents as a mere means (since they are self-governing, rational agents with the capacity and right to self-determination), and if the sole reason we are creating a self-governing, sentient agent is to deploy it in combat and thereby expose it to risks to which it neither consented nor is liable, then we have treated that agent as a mere means.

whether AGI is "really" sentient, but point out that this is, on a number of accounts of philosophy of mind, also a challenge with other humans.

[52] Steve Torrance, *Machine Ethics and the Idea of a More-Than-Human Moral World*, *in* MACHINE ETHICS 115 (Michael Anderson & Susan Leigh Anderson eds., 2011).

[53] *See* EVANS, *supra* note 49, at 37–47.

[54] *See* Alexander A. Guerrero, *Appropriately Using People Merely as a Means*, CRIM. L. & PHIL. 777, 785 (2016).

Worse, the *way* in which we have treated them as a mere means is exposing them to unjust harm—a practice that hardly seems justified.

As an analogy, consider recent work on the ethics of using sex robots. On the view defended by Lily Frank and Sven Nyholm,[55] there are moral reasons favoring consent-capable sex robots. Sparrow, by contrast, holds that consent-capable sex robots carries a risk of enabling rape fantasies: if sex robots can give consent, they can also withhold it, and if they can withhold it, then they can be (at least expressively) raped.[56] Imagine a sentient sex robot created for the express purpose of sex with humans. Absent an opportunity to withhold consent, humans using those robots sexually would be *sexually assaulting* them. By analogy, humans using SLAWS as mere means, where those same SLAWS are then destroyed in combat, are liable to a similar moral charge: murder.

A more compelling concern, and one in which we are less conciliatory, is what we do in the meantime. SLAWS are not yet possible. It is not clear they will *ever* be possible, as experts disagree about whether sentient robots are in principle achievable, or in practice achievable given the current trajectory of modern computer science. So, for now (and potentially forever), our choice is between deploying LAWS and humans in warfare.[57]

What this entails is a choice between prioritizing the interests of justified combatants who cause unjust harm to civilians, on the one hand, and prioritizing the interests of civilians whose interests they unjustly threaten, on the other. For the reasons outlined earlier, most would favor the former disjunct of this set of choices. This is because while just combatants are permitted to engage in acts of lethal force, they are not permitted to wrong noncombatants unjustly. This, we have argued, includes the psychological costs of war.

We concede that there may be a lesser-evil justification for *not* prioritizing the interests of civilian psychological integrity over justified combatant psychological integrity. For instance, we can imagine a case wherein severe psychological harm to justified combatants makes them less likely to achieve their justified aims, such as the humanitarian rescue of endangered civilians. For a more detailed case, imagine that justified combatants have placed enormous side-effect burdens on the civilian population up to a certain point in the war and, if the justified combatants do not preserve their own mental health at the cost of additional

[55] *See generally* Lily Frank & Sven Nyholm, *Robot Sex and Consent: Is Consent to Sex Between a Robot and a Human Conceivable, Possible, and Desirable?*, 25(3) ARTIFICIAL INTELLIGENCE & L. 305 (2017).

[56] By "expressively," we mean only that the nonconsensual use of robots for sex *looks* like rape and risks reinforcing the immoral message that consent is unnecessary for permissible sex. *See generally* Sparrow, *supra* note 1.

[57] A third option, suggested to us by Daniel Schoeni, is the creation of LAWS that *behave as if* they have moral affect. However, our position is that this is morally unsatisfactory for the same reason it's unsatisfactory for soldiers merely to behave as if they care about civilian casualties, namely, because *actually caring* is what's required by MAP.

civilians' mental health, then past side-effect harms suffered by civilians will have been in vain. In such a case, what McMahan calls "wide proportionality" requires that the goods secured by prior civilian suffering outweigh that prior suffering.[58] Where the securement of such goods is threatened by declining mental health among justified combatants, it follows that justified combatants ought to prioritize their mental health over others' (including civilians') mental health to satisfy wide proportionality.

We might, finally, extend this to the development and deployment of other AI systems that replace human functions in ways that ought to be meaningfully cost-shared. Consider the analyst who sifts through intelligence signals in search of a target. When they find that potential target, there is often a significant margin of error around whether that target is (1) the person the analyst thinks they are, and (2) occupying the role in a military or terrorist group they are said to occupy. Even if they are right in whom they target, however, we might think they ought to engage in the moral cost-sharing involved in the knowledge that the person targeted is a sibling, parent, spouse, and so on. They may also live knowing they never really know, *for sure*, that they killed the right person.

The trend of AI-substituted judgments for human actors has been a long time coming. AI has been suggested, since the mid-90s, as a replacement for these kinds of analytic processes. This effort began with the Total Information Awareness program that preceded 2001, became infamous immediately after it, and was shut down—but whose central functions were taken up by the National Security Agency in what would become the U.S. mass surveillance apparatus revealed by Edward Snowden.[58]

All these AI enterprises fall victim to analogous concerns as LAWS in terms of MAP. Through these innovations, the defense industry is engaged in a process of rearranging, through the evolution of technologies, national security decision-making, and moral cost-sharing. The process by which an individual is targeted and eliminated by a state is now rarely an individual process of defensive action in a conventional setting of armed conflict. It is an institutional decision, made through a collaboration of discrete actors who determine separately which targets exist, which ought to be subject to lethal force, the timing and structure of that force, its authorization, and its ultimate execution. The military calls this a "kill chain." By developing novel AI, and especially broad general intelligences that are capable of synthesizing complex information and making decisions on the use of lethal force, the defense industry is engaged in—indeed, may always have been—an active, knowing, and responsible participant in the kill chain.[59]

[58] *See* Jeff McMahan, Killing in War 21 (2009). Some harmful act is proportionate in the wide sense just in case it doesn't cause more harm to nonliable parties than it prevents.

[59] Evans, *supra* note 49, at 11–24. We concur with Helen Frowe that agents (individual or group) are morally liable in proportion of the size of the threat to which they contribute and *not* in proportion

Given this, the moral cost-sharing of AI automation of lethal action in armed conflict should be treated with the same care as we suggest earlier. Incorporating sentience would allow AI to engage in obligatory moral cost-sharing and would relieve individuals from becoming increasingly focused sites of (justified) psychological load in the decision to kill others.

We suspect some will find this conclusion repugnant. After all, we are positing that "basic" AI is not sufficient, and instead are suggesting that we *intentionally* push further into the AI that is the stuff of science fiction nightmares. Why would we forgo ED-209 of *RoboCop*[60] and jump straight to the Skynet of *Terminator*? And why does that sound so horrific?

This is partly an empirical question, but we want to suggest one possible answer. What makes LAWS and other AI weapons so attractive to military decision makers and proponents is *precisely* that it portrays a cooler, less morally costly form of war. Christian Enemark, who notes this is a key attraction of drones and LAWS in turn, writes that "political leaders, having less cause to contemplate the prospect of deaths, injuries and grieving families, might accordingly feel less anxious about the using force to solve political problems."[61] While Enemark was primarily referring to *allied* casualties, we think this likely applies to our feelings of enemy or noncombatant casualties as well. The defense industry can market the use of sentient AI precisely because it obviates our need for moral cost-sharing. It relieves us of a burden in weighty moral decision-making and renders it impersonal and algorithmic.

Our argument is quite simply that the moral weight of these decisions ought not be obviated. We do not need to deny that AI may make certain kinds of acts safer or less costly in terms of human lives. But we note that obviating moral cost-sharing is impermissible in the use of AI for lethal force. And if the defense industry will not stop making AI applications that make these decisions, then they ought to make AI applications that are capable of bearing that cost-sharing with us, rather than creating a sink in which we can hide the moral weight of, to borrow a phrase from Michael Walzer, the "crime of war." Moreover, insofar as the defense industry bears causal and moral responsibility for its position in the "kill chain," they too must share some of the costs of war.

to the size of their contribution to a threat. So the defense industry (*qua* group-agent) is liable in proportion to the size of the SLAWS threat to which it contributes, which is potentially significant. *See generally* Helen Frowe, Defensive Killing 175–77 (2014).

60 RoboCop (Orion Pictures 1987).

61 Christian Enemark, Armed Drones and the Ethics of War: Military Virtue in a Post-Heroic Age 22 (2015).

6. Conclusion

Interest in the use of AI in warfare has increased substantially over the last 20 years and continues to expand in quantity and application. Our chapter raised a novel objection to the implementation of autonomous weapons, namely, that their replacement of human soldiers severely curtails moral cost-sharing. The debate about the use of AI in defense typically focuses on the accuracy with which those AI applications can inflict harm on combatants and spare civilians. However, as we noted at the outset, civilians are never *spared* in war. At the absolute minimum, no one belongs to no one,[62] and all persons—even those justly killed—are part of a web of social support that means that when a combatant it killed, civilians are wronged. Part of the process of war is the moral cost-sharing of this burden for killing. AI subverts this burden in unjust ways.

To grasp the basics of our argument, consider the case of uninhabited aerial vehicles that act autonomously (i.e., LAWS). Imagine that a LAWS terminates a military target and that five civilians die as a side effect of the LAWS bombing. Because LAWS lack *moral* agency, and in particular the capacity for moral emotions, moral cost-sharing is limited to dead civilians and their loved ones. We argue that's unjust insofar as those responsible for unjust harm to others *ought* to share in those costs. Our worry expands to other strategic uses of AI, for example, cyber warfare. Here we contribute to this debate by outlining the Moral Affect Principle and putting it through its paces. Along the way, we provide a way for proponents of military AI to have their way: simply make AI sentient and capable of moral affect. However, we note that this is a bridge too far even for proponents of military AI, who increasingly are reticent to admit to this developmental and technological possibility.

This presents a dilemma: either we design autonomous weaponry capable of moral emotions, or we limit the use of autonomous weaponry. We then consider the more general case for any AI. The former undermines the risk-mitigation purpose of creating autonomous weaponry and expands the number of sentient individuals whose welfare is risked in war. The latter risks worsening combatant casualties and achieving strategic aims.

References

RONALD C. ARKIN, GOVERNING LETHAL BEHAVIOR IN AUTONOMOUS ROBOTS (2009).

Saba Bazargan-Forward, *Defensive Wars and the Reprisal Dilemma*, 93(3) AUSTRALASIAN J. PHIL. 583 (2015).

[62] *See generally* EVA FEDER KITTAY, LOVE'S LABOR: ESSAYS ON WOMEN, EQUALITY, AND DEPENDENCY (1999).

Saba Bazargan-Forward, *Compensation and Proportionality in War*, *in* WEIGHING LIVES IN WAR 173 (Jens David Ohlin, Larry May & Claire Finkelstein eds., 2017).

JOANNA BOURKE, AN INTIMATE HISTORY OF KILLING: FACE TO FACE KILLING IN TWENTIETH CENTURY WARFARE (2000).

Annie Brookman-Byrne, *There Is a Spectrum of Responses to Killing Far-Off Enemies*, 4(2) PSYCHOL. 40 (2020).

Ned Dobos, *Idealism, Realism, and Success in Armed Humanitarian Intervention*, 44(2) PHILOSOPHIA 497 (2016).

CHRISTIAN ENEMARK, ARMED DRONES AND THE ETHICS OF WAR: MILITARY VIRTUE IN A POST-HEROIC AGE (2015).

Nicholas Greig Evans, *Emerging Military Technologies: A Case Study in Neurowarfare*, *in* NEW WARS AND NEW SOLDIERS: MILITARY ETHICS IN THE CONTEMPORARY WORLD 105 (Paolo Tripodi & Jessica Wolfendale eds., 2011).

NICHOLAS G. EVANS, THE ETHICS OF NEUROSCIENCE AND NATIONAL SECURITY (2021).

Nicholas G. Evans, *Blind Brains and Moral Machines: Neuroscience and Autonomous Weapon Systems*, *in* LETHAL AUTONOMOUS WEAPONS: RE-EXAMINING THE LAW AND ETHICS OF ROBOTIC WARFARE 2013 (Duncan MacIntosh, Jai Galliott & Jens David Ohlin eds., 2021).

Nicholas G. Evans, *Blind Brains and Moral Machines: Neuroscience and Autonomous Weapon Systems*, *in* LETHAL AUTONOMOUS WEAPONS 203 (Jai Galliott, Duncan MacIntosh & Jens David Ohlin eds., 2021).

Aaron Fichtelberg, *Applying the Rules of Just War Theory to Engineers in the Arms Industry*, 12(4) SCI. & ENG'G ETHICS 685–700 (2006).

Jessica Flanigan & Christopher Freiman, *Drug War Reparations*, 97(2) RES PHILOSOPHICA 141 (2020).

Lily Frank & Sven Nyholm, *Robot Sex and Consent: Is Consent to Sex Between a Robot and a Human Conceivable, Possible, and Desirable?*, 25(3) ARTIFICIAL INTELLIGENCE & L. 305 (2017).

Helen Frowe, *Lesser-Evil Justifications for Harming: Why We're Required to Turn the Trolley*, 68(272) PHIL. Q. 460 (2018).

HELEN FROWE, DEFENSIVE KILLING (2014).

John P. Geyman, *Cost-Sharing Under Consumer-Driven Health Care Will Not Reform U.S. Health Care* 40(3) J.L., MED. & ETHICS 574 (2012).

Alexander A. Guerrero, *Appropriately Using People Merely as a Means*, CRIM. L. & PHIL. 777 (2016).

SVEN OVE HANSSON, THE ETHICS OF RISK: ETHICAL ANALYSIS IN AN UNCERTAIN WORLD (2013).

Allison K. Hoffman, *Cost-Sharing Reductions, Technocrat Tinkering, and Market-Based Health Policy*, 46(4) J.L., MED. & ETHICS 873 (2018).

Adam Hosein, *Are Justified Aggressors a Threat to the Rights Theory of Self-Defense?*, *in* HOW WE FIGHT 87 (Helen Frowe & Gerald Lang eds., 2014).

EVA FEDER KITTAY, LOVE'S LABOR: ESSAYS ON WOMEN, EQUALITY, AND DEPENDENCY (1999).

Kristján Kristjánsson, *Fortunes-of-Others Emotions and Justice*, 28(105) J. PHIL. RES. 105–128 (2003).

ERIK J. LARSON, THE MYTH OF ARTIFICIAL INTELLIGENCE: WHY COMPUTERS CAN'T THINK THE WAY WE DO (2021).

SETH LAZAR, SPARING CIVILIANS (2015).

Arianna Schiano Lomoriello et al., *Out of Sight Out of Mind: Perceived Physical Distance Between the Observer and Someone in Pain Shapes Observer's Neural Empathic Reactions*, 9 Frontiers Psychol. 1824 (2018).

MarketsandMarkets, *Artificial Intelligence in Military Market Worth $11.6 Billion by 2025* (Mar. 15, 2021), https://www.prnewswire.com/news-releases/artificial-intelligence-in-military-market-worth-11-6-billion-by-2025--exclusive-report-by-marketsandmarkets-301247146.html.

Chris McGreal, *Wikileaks Reveals Video Showing US Air Crew Shooting Down Iraqi Civilians*, The Guardian (Apr. 5, 2010), http://www.guardian.co.uk/world/2010/apr/05/wikileaks-us-army-iraq-attack.

Jeff McMahan, Killing in War (2009).

Jeff McMahan, *Self-Defense Against Justified Threateners*, *in* How We Fight: Ethics in War 104 (Helen Frowe & Gerald Lang eds., 2014).

Derek Parfit, *Equality or Priority?*, *in* The Ideal of Equality (Matthew Clayton & Andrew Williams eds., 2002).

Avia Pasternak, *Sharing the Costs of Political Injustices*, 10(2) Pol., Phil. & Econ. 188 (2011).

Lt. Col. Wayne Phelps, On Killing Remotely: The Psychology of Killing with Drones (2021).

RoboCop (Orion Picture 1987).

Heather M. Roff, *Lethal Autonomous Weapons and* Jus Ad Bellum *Proportionality*, 47 Case W. Res. J. Int'l L. 37 (2015).

Abraham M. Rutchick et al., *Technologically Facilitated Remoteness Increases Killing Behavior*, 73 J. Experimental Soc. Psychol. 147 (2017).

Michael Skerker, Duncan Purves & Ryan Jenkins, *Autonomous Weapons Systems and the Moral Equality of Combatants*, 22 Ethics & Info. Tech. 197 (2020).

Robert Sparrow, *Killer Robots*, 24(1) J. Applied Phil. 62 (2007).

Daniel Stoljar, *The Semantics of "What It's Like" and the Nature of Consciousness*, 125(500) Mind 1161 (2016).

Bradley Jay Strawser, *Moral Predators: The Duty to Employ Uninhabited Aerial Vehicles*, 9(4) J. Mil. Ethics 342 (2010).

The Terminator (Orion Picture 1987).

Steve Torrance, *Machine Ethics and the Idea of a More-Than-Human Moral World*, *in* Machine Ethics 115 (Michael Anderson & Susan Leigh Anderson eds., 2011).

Suzanne Uniacke, *Self-Defense, Just War, and a Reasonable Prospect of Success*, *in* How We Fight: Ethics in War (Helen Frowe & Gerald Lang eds., 2014).

U.S. Dep't of Def., *Unmanned Aircraft Systems (UAS): DoD Purpose and Operational Use*, https://dod.defense.gov/UAS/.

Sara Van Goozen, "Sharing the Costs of Fighting Justly," 2 Critical Rev. Int'l Soc. & Pol. Phil. 1 (2018).

WikiLeaks, *Collateral Murder* (Apr. 5, 2010), https://wikileaks.org/wiki/Collateral_Murder,_5_Apr_2010.

PART III
ADDRESSING CORRUPTION IN GLOBAL MARKETS

9

Defense Firms' Duties to Society When Presented with an Opportunity to Pay a Bribe

Philip M. Nichols

1. Introduction

Defense industry firms frequently encounter circumstances in which they are either tempted or invited to pay bribes. Historically, these firms have often yielded to temptation. The disclosure of bribes paid by defense industry firms played a highly visible role in the congressional investigations and debates that culminated in the passage of the United States' Foreign Corrupt Practices Act.[1] Decades later, the revelation of defense industry bribes played a highly visible role in undermining the credibility of the Serious Fraud Office's claims that it would vigorously enforce the United Kingdom's new Bribery Act. In between, and since, scarcely a year has passed without revelations of bribery in connection with a defense industry firm.

When presented with the opportunity to pay a bribe, the legal responsibilities of defense industry firms are clear. The aforementioned laws, and many others, prohibit the payment of bribes. Legal responsibility, however, differs from moral duty. This chapter examines the moral duties of defense firms when faced with demands to pay bribes or situations in which they could offer a bribe, and in particular to whom those duties are owed. This is not a frivolous exercise. Exploring the moral responsibility of defense firms provides insights into the relationship between those firms and the rest of society, into the nature of defense markets, and into justifications for anti-corruption legal regimes. Moreover, opportunities to pay bribes often occur in the shadows, with little chance of detection, or in polities in which legal enforcement is feeble. In such circumstances, business firms may find normative guidance more compelling than legal compliance.

[1] *See* Frank Badua, *Laying Down the Law on Lockheed: How an Aviation and Defense Giant Inspired the Promulgation of the Foreign Corrupt Practices Act of 1977*, 42(1) Acct. Historians J. 105, 112–17 (2015).

Philip M. Nichols, *Defense Firms' Duties to Society When Presented with an Opportunity to Pay a Bribe* In: *Ethical Dilemmas in the Global Defense Industry*. Edited by: Daniel Schoeni and Tobias Vestner, Oxford University Press.
 DOI: 10.1093/oso/9780190675813.003.0010

This chapter finds that firms owe primary duties to society at large and to potential victims of harm caused by the weapons and weapon systems that they sell. This chapter begins by observing that the defense industry operates within a distorted marketplace. Society allows defense industry firms to accrue revenue for investors within this distorted market, but in exchange for society's forbearance, these firms must respect the basic human right to be safe. The distortions in the defense industry market create opportunities for corruption; corruption in turn vitiates the right to be safe. Therefore, this chapter concludes that when presented with an opportunity to pay a bribe, defense firms owe a duty to society and to potential victims of harm that supersedes any duty that the firms might have to investors.

2. Market Distortion

Markets are social constructs. Amartya Sen divides the moral justifications for these social constructs into two types: those that examine consequences and those that emphasize rights.[2] At the risk of oversimplifying complex schools of thought, those who emphasize consequences tend to view markets as places through which resources are transformed into the goods and services needed or desired by society. Such consequentialists recognize that unfettered markets may act in unjust or inimical ways, and thus posit that society has an interest in regulating or even replacing markets.[3] Rights-based justifications for markets tend to justify markets as places in which people can exercise rights to freely associate and liberties to use their property as they choose. Even those who justify markets on grounds of individual freedom, however, recognize that society has a duty to intervene when markets operate in ways that are unjust or inimical to society.[4]

Resolving, or even fully explicating, the tensions between rights perspectives and consequence perspectives of markets is well beyond the scope of this chapter. The ideas salient to a discussion of the responsibilities of defense firms operating in markets, however, can be easily summarized. Markets are social constructs, in which society has many interests. When markets act against society's interests, society has the right to intervene. Defense firms, therefore, do not have an inviolate right to operate within the context of a market. If a meaningful public interest is at issue, and if markets operate in a way contrary to that interest, then the defense industry could justifiably be mandated to operate in ways other than

[2] *See generally* Amartya Sen, *The Moral Standing of the Market*, 2(2) Soc. Phil. & Pol'y 1 (1985).
[3] *See* John Rawls, Political Liberalism 5–6 (1993).
[4] *See, e.g.*, John Tomasi, Free Market Fairness (2012).

through markets. As the next two subsections discuss, both of these conditions are in fact satisfied.

2.1. The Public Interest in the Defense Industry

Other chapters in this volume undoubtedly describe the public interest in the weapons industry; this chapter will not belabor the discussion. In the interest of completeness, however, two aspects of the public's interest should be mentioned. First, the public has an interest in the deterrence of violent attack by other polities. Indeed, "[n]ational defense is *the* textbook example of a public good presented to undergraduate students throughout their education, from introductory courses to advanced theory to elective courses."[5]

Second, the public has an interest in weapons not being transferred to those who would use those weapons to commit harm. This has become particularly profound as the public becomes more aware of and perhaps vulnerable to phenomena such as terrorism and weapons that can inflict destruction on a massive scale. "Perhaps never in the history of human conflict have so few people with so few actual means and capabilities frightened so many."[6]

These public interests are related to a fundamental right, the "basic right to be safe."[7] The right to be safe exists at the level of individual persons, as recognized in Article 3 of the Universal Declaration of Human Rights.[8] The right also exists at the level of community, as acknowledged in the United Nations Charter.[9] The latter, in particular, has been interpreted as memorializing jus cogens, a principal of international law that is so fundamental that its breach is inconceivable.[10]

The arms market affects profound social interests. These interests include very basic rights different from rights of association or property, and potentially involve existential consequences. Society would, therefore, be justified in interfering in this market were it to act in inimical ways.

[5] Christopher Coyne & David S. Lucas, *Economists Have No Defense: A Critical Review of National Defense in Economics Textbooks*, 31(4) J. PRIVATE ENTERPRISE 65, 65 (2016).

[6] SCOTT ATRAN, TALKING TO THE ENEMY: FAITH, BROTHERHOOD, AND THE (UN)MAKING OF TERRORISTS xiv (2010).

[7] Michael D. Pendleton, *A New Human Right—The Right to Globalization*, 22(5) FORDHAM INT'L L.J. 2052, 2080 (1999).

[8] Universal Declaration of Human Rights, G.A. Res. 217A (III), art. 3, U.N. Doc. A/810 (Dec. 10, 1948) (establishing: "Everyone has the right to life, liberty and security of person.").

[9] U.N. Charter, art. 2(4) (establishing: "All Members shall refrain in their international relations from the threat or use of force against the territorial integrity or political independence of any state, or in any other manner inconsistent with the Purposes of the United Nations.").

[10] Military and Paramilitary Activities in and against Nicaragua (Nicar. v. U.S.), Judgment, 1986 I.C.J. Rep. 100–01, para. 190 (June 27).

2.2. The Weapons Market Is Distorted

Goods or services that significantly affect the general public are often created and distributed through nonmarket mechanisms. Weapons, however, are created and distributed through markets. In the case of weapons, this market is severely distorted. It should be noted that in some cases these distortions work to inhibit outside observation, rendering the study of market mechanisms difficult. Robert Leonard laments, "Why has the economics of defense not become as developed as, say, health or education economics?"[11] Nonetheless, it is possible to outline distortions in the weapons industry, albeit with a broad brush.

Concentration distorts the defense market. Depending on the scale, arms markets present monopsonies or at best oligopsonies. At the national level, weapons markets almost always consist of monopsonies—the only real purchaser is the national government. Similarly, the supply side consists of oligopolists, a situation compounded by the fact that at the level of individual weapon systems the supplier is usually a monopolist.[12] At the transnational level, more actors participate on the demand side, but the market still consists of oligopsonists and oligopolists, often with a single supplier for particular weapon systems.[13]

Secrecy also distorts weapons markets. Against the current background of whistleblowing and revelations of scandals, "state secrets are increasingly viewed with suspicion."[14] Nonetheless, within the context of defense and deterrence, secrecy has an accepted role. Secrecy manifests itself in at least two forms. First, the technical specifications, capabilities, or even existences of weapons and weapon systems are often kept secret. Second, largely in support of the first form of secrecy, military budgets, or specific spending or deployment within military budgets, are often kept secret or partially secret. Secrecy facilitates the deception of other polities, which can have a powerful deterrent effect.[15] Secrecy also preserves the viability of weapons as a means of defense. The release, for example, of technical specifications of cyberwarfare systems could render those systems easily hackable and thus of little deterrent value.[16] Similarly, making public the

[11] Robert J. Leonard, *War as a "Simple Economic Problem": The Rise of an Economic of Defense*, *in* Economics and National Security: A History of Their Interaction 261 (C.D. Goodwin ed., 1991).

[12] Andrew L. Ross, *The International Arms Market: A Structural and Behavioral Analysis*, *in* The Political Economy of Defense: Issues and Perspectives 114 (Andrew L. Ross ed., 1991).

[13] *Id.* at 114–15.

[14] Dennis Broeders, *The Secret in the Information Society*, 29(3) Phil. & Tech. 293, 297 (2016).

[15] Sam R. Bell & Carla Martinez Machain, *Democracy, Transparency, and Secrecy in Crisis*, 14(4) Foreign Pol'y Analysis 592, 593 (2018); Michael Colaresi, *A Boom with Review: How Retrospective Oversight Increases the Foreign Policy Ability of Democracies*, 56(3) Am. J. Pol. Sci. 671, 673 (2014).

[16] Jeppe T. Jacobsen & Jens Ringsmose, *Cyber-Bombing ISIS: Why Disclose What Is Better Kept Secret?*, 3(2) Global Aff. 126 (2017).

budgeted-for number and deployment of missile defense batteries could render those batteries into nothing more than an easily evaded Maginot Line.[17]

The most intricate, yet perhaps most foundational, market distortion in the defense industry stems from the complex relationship between governance and armament. The relationship is inherently political in a policymaking sense. There is no single "correct" answer to questions regarding how resources should be allocated so that they will have the greatest deterrent effect (nor probably, although unstudied, so that they will have the greatest offensive capacity).[18] Different weapon systems might deter different threats in differing degrees. Resources available for defense are not infinite, and their allocation must be weighed against other needs. Constituencies might not agree on the nature or existence of threats, or even agree on the level of security needed or the amount of risk that is tolerable. National defense is not a crisp, scientific formulation with parameters that can be easily communicated;[19] rather, it is a kaleidoscope of needs, context, and objectives that are only obliquely related to anything approaching supply and demand.

The defense industry is also political in a relational sense. With respect to individual weapon systems, buyers, which are usually national governments, often present a specific need or objective. Weapons suppliers must work closely with buyers, cooperatively developing new technologies, and often, as discussed, working in secrecy.[20] This relationship resonates closely with a market distortion called "regulatory capture." Lobbying and outright bribery leads to regulatory capture, but so too can frequent and focused interactions, as well as a shared worldview.[21] Regulatory capture results in the concerns of a small, deeply interested group being given more consideration than the wider general public.[22] By unintentionally skewing the creation and enforcement of regulations, this process distorts markets.[23] Weapons development may foster close relationships in a similar manner.

[17] *See generally* Roy C. Macridis, *The New French Maginot Line: A Note on French Strategy*, 2(1) J. POL. & MIL. SOC. 105 (1974).

[18] *See* WILLIAM J. WEIDA & FRANKLIN L. GERTCHNER, THE POLITICAL ECONOMY OF NATIONAL DEFENSE 8 (1987).

[19] *See* William K. Domke, *Fiscal Constraints and Defense Planning in Advanced Industrial Democracies*, *in* THE POLITICAL ECONOMY OF DEFENSE: ISSUES AND PERSPECTIVES 24 (Andrew L. Ross ed., 1991).

[20] Glenn R. Fong, *The Political Economy of Pentagon-Industry Collaboration in Technology Development*, *in* THE POLITICAL ECONOMY OF DEFENSE: ISSUES AND PERSPECTIVES 68–70 (Andrew L. Ross ed., 1991).

[21] Melissa F. Wasserman, *Deference Asymmetries: Distortions in the Evolution of Regulatory Law*, 93(3) TEX. L. REV. 625, 629–30 (2015).

[22] *See generally* George J. Stigler, *The Economic Theory of Regulation*, 2(1) BELL J. ECON. & MGMT. SCI. 3 (1971).

[23] Jean-Jacques Laffont & Jean Tirole, *The Politics of Government Decision-Making: A Theory of Regulatory Capture*, 106(4) Q.J. ECON. 1089, 1109–10 (1991).

The market in which society allows the defense industry to operate is very distorted. One could argue that *all* markets are distorted, that a perfect market exists only in the imaginary realms of textbooks and abstract theories, and that some imperfections must be accommodated in the translation of theory to the real world. Even so, the distortions in defense are truly significant. Such imperfections have consequences, especially in terms of the potential for corruption in the defense industry.

3. Market Distortions Open a Door for Bribery

Transparency International has studied bribery within the arms industry for almost a decade.[24] As part of this program, the global anticorruption organization occasionally publishes evaluations of the vulnerabilities of both large and small weapons firms.[25] Transparency International has identified at least four factors that render "the defence sector especially vulnerable to corruption: secrecy, high value contracts, the complexity of those contracts, and the political nature of the sector.[26] Each of these factors is closely related to market distortions. This analysis illuminates the relationship between such distortions and bribery in the arms market.

Secrecy is "a major facilitator of defence corruption."[27] Though sometimes necessary in this sector, secrecy is in general the antithesis of honest business. "One of the best tools to combat corruption is transparency."[28] Transparency enables a society to hold those in power accountable, while secrecy facilitates nefarious behavior.[29] Secrecy within the defense industry is compounded by the fact that defense firms often interact with some of the most endemically corrupt and opaque governments in the world.[30]

Transparency International uses the phrase "high value contracts"[31] to designate a second factor that contributes to corruption in the defense industry, but "high stakes" might more accurately describe the nature of their relationship

[24] *Defence Companies Anti-Corruption Index*, TRANSPARENCY INTERNATIONAL, http://ti-defence.org/dci/ (describing Transparency International's ongoing research into corruption in the defense industry) (last visited June 6, 2020).

[25] Katie Fish et al., *Defence Companies Anti-Corruption Index 2015*, TRANSPARENCY INTERNATIONAL (2015), http://companies.defenceindex.org/.

[26] KATHERINE DIXON ET AL., OUT OF THE SHADOWS: PROMOTING OPENNESS AND ACCOUNTABILITY IN THE GLOBAL DEFENCE INDUSTRY 4 (2018), https://ti-defence.org/publications/out-of-the-shadows/.

[27] *Id.*

[28] Roger P. Alford, *A Broken Windows Theory of International Corruption*, 73(5) OHIO ST. L.J. 1253, 1269 (2012).

[29] Lynn M. LoPucki, *Court-System Transparency*, 94(2) IOWA L. REV. 494 (2009).

[30] DIXON ET AL., *supra* note 26, at 17.

[31] *Id.* at 4.

to corruption. Many defense contracts do involve large contract prices, but these contracts are valuable because there are so few of them. Transparency International notes that even wealthy countries do not regularly place orders for large or complex weapon systems, and therefore each contract represents a substantial portion of the sales opportunities for any given defense firm.[32] The scarcity of potential sales is attributable to the relative paucity of buyers and creates an environment in which firms feel they cannot afford to lose the next contract.

These monopsonistic or oligopsonistic conditions contribute to another avenue for corruption. Demand-side market concentration confers asymmetrical power on buyers' agents. Agents may, particularly under the cover of secrecy, ask for illicit personal benefits.[33] Such benefits may be called kickbacks or bribes, but in all cases they are corrupt. Transparency International finds that the corrupting effect of such demand-side market concentration is particularly acute in defense.[34]

Transparency International identifies the complexity of defense contracting as a third factor contributing to corruption in defense.[35] The complexity of this market is closely related to the political nature of the defense sector. There are no decisions in defense policy that ex ante are clearly right or wrong. Most decisions involve political consensus and compromise. Lobbying, cronyism, and bribery can therefore affect these decisions.[36] Indeed, cronyism, particularly through the offer of high-paying private sector jobs to government officers, occurs frequently in the defense industry.[37] Defense industries spend billions of dollars each year lobbying governments around the world.[38] Interestingly, lobbying by defense firms not only affects purchasing decisions; it also significantly affects the content of defense policy.[39] If nothing else, large-scale lobbying demonstrates the complexity and political nature of this industry.

The complexity and political uncertainty of defense policy also make it difficult to hold decision makers accountable. Outside observers cannot easily discern whether a government official or bureaucrat who favors one defense firm over another is doing so for corrupt reasons or as part of the political process.

32 *Id.*

33 Rajeev K. Goel, Jelena Budak & Edo Rajh, *Private Sector Bribery and Effectiveness of Anti-Corruption Policies*, 22(10) App. Econ. Letters 759, 760 (2015).

34 Dixon et al., *supra* note 26, at 15.

35 *Id* at 4.

36 *See* Jin H. Kim, *Is Your Playing Field Unleveled? US Defense Contracts and Foreign Firm Lobbying*, 40(12) Strategic Mgmt. J. 1911, 1931–33 (2019) (describing the means through which lobbying helps foreign firms achieve nonmarket results).

37 Henry Walter, *The Defense Industrial Base: How Idiosyncratic and Historical Influences Dictate Its Future*, 95(1) Int'l Soc. Sci. Rev 14–15 (2019).

38 Dixon et al., *supra* note 26, at 4.

39 Jordi C. Rufanges, *The Arms Industry Lobby in Europe*, 60(3) Am. Behav. Sci. 305, 317–18 (2016).

Negotiations for defense contracts often occur over periods of several years and involve dozens of agreements and complicated financing networks. When woven into the inherently political nature of defense policy, the complexity of these transactions creates an opacity that stymies even seasoned investigators.[40] Genuine oversight by the general public is unlikely.

Finally, Transparency International identifies the political nature of the defense industry as a contributor to corruption.[41] By "political nature," Transparency International means the close relationships between weapon producers and purchasers. These relationships are compounded by the use of third-party intermediaries, often used specifically because they already have close relationships with government, a practice that Transparency International considers "one of the most significant and pervasive bribery and corruption risks in defence."[42] As discussed earlier, close relationships are inevitable when the purchaser and developer must work together to develop complex weapon systems. Those relationships, however, open the door for corruption.

4. Corruption in the Defense Industry Inflicts Social Harms

At this point, one might concede that the defense market is distorted and that those distortions open the door for corruption but still ask whether relevant social interests are damaged sufficiently to justify intervention in that market.

Corruption inflicts tremendous damage on society. Corruption weakens the relationship between the governed and the governing, diminishes both the length and the quality of life, exacerbates the plight of the poor, and contributes to the degradation of the social and physical environment.[43] Its effects are so pernicious that some scholars suggest that corruption itself constitutes a violation of basic human rights.[44]

Even if one narrows one's focus only to business, corruption imposes costs.[45] In the past, some people thought that corruption only moved rents from one

[40] Sam Perlo-Freeman, *Arms, Corruption, and the State: Understanding the Role of Arms Trade Corruption in Power Politics*, 13(2) Econ. Peace & Security J. 37, 40 (2018).

[41] Dixon et al., *supra* note 26, at 4.

[42] *Id.* at 15.

[43] Philip M. Nichols, *The Mercantilist Fallacy and the Contextual Reality of the Foreign Corrupt Practices Act*, 53(1) Harv. J. Legis. 203, 210–11 (2016).

[44] *See generally* Martine Boersma, Corruption: A Violation of Human Rights and a Crime under International Law? (2012). *But see* Cecil Rose, *The Limits of a Human Rights Approach to Corruption*, 65(2) Int'l & Comp. L.Q. 422, 430–37 (2016) (vigorously opposing the consideration of corruption as a human rights violation and arguing that treating corruption as a violation of human rights would actually circumscribe responses to corruption, for example, by limiting responses to governments rather than to all economic actors).

[45] Philip M. Nichols, *The Business Case for Complying with Bribery Laws*, 49(2) Am. Bus. L.J. 325, 335–41 (2012).

party to another and had no net effect on economies. People also suggested that bribery was useful in overcoming regulatory barriers and facilitating entry into various economies.[46] Those who study corruption now have a much deeper understanding of the phenomenon and use finer tools and techniques to study it. Johann Lambsdorff and others have shown that the notion that corruption merely transfers rent is erroneous because corruption affects the size of the rent and unproductively distorts allocations.[47] Daniel Kaufmann and Shang-Jin Wei, in turn, have demonstrated that bribery does not reduce barriers to entry but instead increases the time and money a business firm spends interacting with government.[48]

Narrowing the focus to the defense industry reveals more specific harms. There are at least two types of harms that could be caused by corruption in the defense industry. One is harms caused by general failures in the market process. The other is harms caused by failures in the regulatory process. Each negatively affects the right to be safe.

With respect to understanding the potential harms associated with market failures, it is important to understand how corruption affects decision-making by a government purchaser. In the simplest conceptualization, a buyer in an uncorrupt market makes consumption decisions based on the price and the quality of a good or service. A "rational" producer therefore uses its resources to bring the quality of a good or service as close as possible to that desired by the purchaser and to bring its price as close as possible to the price that the purchaser will pay.[49] In an endemically corrupt system, the purchaser makes a decision based on the quality of the bribe. A high-quality bribe is one that a purchaser wants and can use. A "rational" producer therefore uses its resources to craft high-quality bribes.[50] In a market that is functioning properly, a producer that uses its resources to craft a bribe rather than to improve quality and lower prices will not be able to compete with a producer that uses its resources to produce low-cost, high-quality products. In an endemically corrupt system, however, the reverse occurs. A producer who devotes resources to the quality of goods or services cannot compete with a producer who uses its resources to craft high-quality bribes. The world outside of defense offers many examples of the

46 David Hess & Thomas W. Dunfee, *Fighting Corruption: A Principled Approach: The C² Principles (Combating Corruption)*, 33(3) CORNELL INT'L L.J. 593, 595 (2000) (identifying and addressing the argument that bribery can serve a useful purpose in overcoming regulatory barriers and facilitating entry into closed economies).

47 Johann G. Lambsdorff, *Corruption and Rent-Seeking*, 113(1–2) PUBLIC CHOICE 97, 120 (2002).

48 *See generally* Daniel Kaufmann & Shang-Jin Wei, *Does "Grease Money" Speed Up the Wheels of Commerce?* (Nat'l Bureau of Econ. Research Working Paper No. 7093, 1999).

49 Mark B. Bader & Bill Shaw, *Amendment of the Foreign Corrupt Practices Act*, 15(3) N.Y.U. J. INT'L L. & POL. 627, 627–52 (1983).

50 *Id.* at 627; Shouyoung Shi & Ted Temzelides, *A Model of Bureaucracy and Corruption*, 45(3) INT'L ECON. REV. 873–908 (2004).

results of corrupt procurement processes, in the forms of unwanted infrastructure that has no function, shopping centers and housing projects that collapse, substandard education and health facilities, and more.[51]

Unfortunately, the defense industry also offers examples. Given the difficulties in finding usable data when analyzing a market as opaque as the defense industry, Tetsuro Mizoguchi and Nguyen Van Quyen analyze the effects of corruption on the quality of the Japanese military using tools of game theoretics.[52] Noting the oligopsonist nature of the defense industry in Japan, and extrapolating from data on corruption in Japanese industry and government, they find that corruption significantly degrades the quality of weapon systems and diverts funding from effective deterrence.[53] This in turn leaves Japan less secure and less capable of defending its people.

Less speculative examples exist, although the surreptitious nature of corruption makes their effect difficult to quantify. One study found that corruption was a "prime factor" in the Nigerian military's inability to arm itself sufficiently to provide security against Boko Haram, leading to the deaths of 20,000 civilians and displacement of 1.3 million people in Nigeria.[54] Corruption in Russia results in the purchase of weapon systems that do not meet standards, substantially delayed deliveries, and 20 to 50 percent of the defense budget being used to buy nothing at all.[55] Corruption seems to have motivated India's purchase of 7,000 substandard military trucks at inflated prices, which delayed its ability to purchase effective weapon systems for a quarter of a century.[56] Through corrupted transactions, Afghanistan purchased hundreds of millions of rounds of faulty, aging ammunition, hampering its efforts to control brutal insurgent movements.[57] Afghanistan was also the site of a still controversial failure of weapons that may have been caused by corruption. When a forward post of U.S. soldiers charged with protecting local villages in the Wanat Valley was attacked by overwhelming insurgent forces, soldiers reported that their weapons

[51] Philip M. Nichols, *Corruption as an Assurance Problem*, 19(6) AM. U. INT'L L. REV. 1307, 1318 (2004).

[52] *See generally* Tetsuro Mizoguchi & Nguyen Van Quyen, *Corruption in Japanese Defense Procurement: A Game Theoretic Analysis* (Keio/Kyoto Global COE Discussion Paper Series No. DP2008-007, 2009), https://ideas.repec.org/p/kei/dpaper/2008-007.html.

[53] *Id.* at 12, 17–18.

[54] Otu O. Duke, Dickson D. Agbaji & Okon Bassey, *Corruption and the Challenge of Boko Haram Terrorism in Nigeria: A Case of the Nigerian Armed Forces*, 4(2) ASIAN RES. J. ARTS & SOC. SCI. 1, 2 (2017).

[55] Susanne Oxenstierna & Fredrik Westerlund, *Arms Procurement and the Russian Defense Industry: Challenges up to 2020*, 26(1) J. SLAVIC MIL. STUD. 1, 10 (2013).

[56] Pramit P. Chaudhuri, *Why India Is Poor at Making Its Own Weapons*, RHODIUM GROUP (Apr. 9, 2012), https://rhg.com/research/why-india-is-poor-at-making-its-own-weapons/.

[57] Christopher J. Chivers, *Supplier Under Scrutiny on Arms for Afghans*, N.Y. TIMES (Mar. 27, 2008), https://www.nytimes.com/2008/03/27/world/asia/27ammo.html.

failed.[58] Although unproven after an investigation that some people considered flawed, corruption is alleged to have driven the decision to purchase those weapons.[59]

The second type of harms inflicted by corruption in the defense industry is those that could be ascribed to regulatory failures. The defense industry faces numerous regulations around the world, defying an easy, comprehensive typology. This chapter discusses types of regulation, not for the purpose of creating a typology but instead to attempt to more finely parse possible harms.

Some regulations are designed to keep technologies developed in a polity out of the hands of potential threats. Large polities, such as the European Union or the United States, have created complex regulatory regimes intended to keep numerous potentially threatening polities from obtaining weapons.[60] Smaller polities might create a legal regime aimed at a specific threat, as the case of numerous regulations created by South Korea to keep weapons and technology out of the hands of North Korea.[61] Corruption undermines the effectiveness of these regulations. Brian Patrick Regan, for example, a civilian contracted to the U.S. National Reconnaissance Office, solicited $13 million in bribes from the governments of China, Iran, Iraq, and Libya in exchange for technical details about missile delivery systems used by the United States.[62]

Some regulations function to keep dangerous weapons out of the hands of violent organizations or rogue states that embrace mayhem. The United Nations Security Council has called on members to "eliminat[e] the supply of weapons to terrorists."[63] Numerous treaties and international regimes create regulatory networks intended to prevent violent organizations and rogue polities from obtaining weapons.[64] Most members of the North American Treaty Alliance

[58] *M4 Rifles Causing Problems for U.S. Troops*, CBSNEWS.COM (Oct. 12, 2009), https://www.cbsnews.com/news/m4-rifles-causing-problems-for-us-troops/.

[59] Marie H. Larsen & Susann Øvretveit, Corruption in the Arms- and Defense Industry: A Comparative Study of the Largest American and European Arms Dealers 27 (Spring 2019) (unpublished master's thesis, Norwegian School of Economics), https://openaccess.nhh.no/nhh-xmlui/handle/11250/2609971.

[60] Hamed Alavi & Tatsiana Khamichonak, *EU and US Export Control Regimes for Dual Use Goods: An Overview of Existing Frameworks* 17(1) ROMANIAN J. EURO. AFF. 59, 60–71 (2017); Christopher M. Tipler, *Defining "National Security": Resolving Ambiguity in the CFIUS Regulations*, 35(4) U. PENN. J. INT'L L. 1223, 1299–31 (2014).

[61] Jaewon Lee, *South Korea's Export Control System*, Stockholm International Peace Research Institute Background Paper (Nov. 2013), https://www.sipri.org/sites/default/files/files/misc/SIPRIBP1311.pdf.

[62] Sarah F. Cable, Note, *An Unanswered Question in* Kennedy v. Louisiana: *How Should the Supreme Court Determine the Constitutionality of the Death Penalty for Espionage?*, 70(3) LA. L. REV. 995, 996 (2010).

[63] U.N. Security Council, Threats to International Peace and Security Caused by Terrorist Acts—Preventing Terrorists from Acquiring Weapons, S/RES/2370, at 3 (Aug. 2, 2017).

[64] Thomas Graham, Jr., *Nuclear Nonproliferation and Nuclear Terrorism*, 17(1) TRANSNAT'L LAW. 89, 90 (2004); BARRY KELLMAN, BIOVIOLENCE: PREVENTING BIOLOGICAL TERROR AND CRIME (2007); Gro Nystuen & Kjølv Egeland, *The Potential of the Arms Trade Treaty to Reduce*

have enacted laws that prohibit the transfer of technology and of weapons or military-oriented materials to groups deemed as terrorist organizations.[65]

Corruption undermines these regulations as well. After analyzing aggregate information on individual terrorist attacks, Kate Ivanova and Todd Sandler find corruption a "prime determinant" of terrorist attacks, because corruption enables the acquisition of weapons and other means of committing mayhem.[66] Violent organizations and rogue states inflict appalling harm on innocent people. While the misery generated by the activities of these organizations escapes quantification, the number of forced immigrants can be counted. The United Nations High Commissioner for Refugees reports that "thousands of people are fleeing their homes every day in search of safety" and that tens of millions have been displaced by this type of violence.[67]

Two distinct groups of people, therefore, might be harmed by corrupt circumvention of the rules. One consists of persons resident in a polity threatened by another polity. The other consists of innocent people anywhere who are vulnerable to the violence inflicted by organizations or rogue states that embrace mayhem.

This chapter carefully avoids identifying specific business firms within the defense industry as malfeasors, and violations of these regulations occurs out of the spotlight of public scrutiny or reporting. The case that bribes are paid for such a purpose, however, is easily made. The military industry has a troubled history with the payment of bribes for the purpose of obtaining contracts from or making sales to governments. The payment of bribes to a government official for purposes of self-enrichment by definition involves a violation of rules. Numerous studies have found that the payment—or even merely the observation of the payment—of bribes by members of a firm erodes the "ethical climate" within that firm.[68] Persons within such firms tend to be more opportunistic and to violate other rules.[69] It takes only a small step to move from paying bribes for the purpose of selling products to paying bribes for the purpose of *being*

Violations of International Humanitarian Law and Human Rights Law, *in* Research Handbook on International Law and Peace 267–83 (Cecilia M. Bailliet ed., 2019); Damien Rogers, Postinternationalism and Small Arms Control: Theory, Politics, Security (2009).

[65] Michael D. Beck & Seema Gahlout, *Introduction to Nonproliferation Export Controls*, *in* To Supply or To Deny: Comparing Nonproliferation Export Controls in Five Key Countries 2 (Michael D. Beck et al. eds., 2003).

[66] Kate Ivanova & Todd Sandler, *CBRN Attack Perpetrators: An Empirical Study*, 1(3) Foreign Pol'y Analysis 273, 292 (2007).

[67] U.N. High Commissioner for Refugees, *Global Appeal 2018–2019*, at 7 (2018), https://www.unhcr.org/en-us/publications/fundraising/5a0c05027/unhcr-global-appeal-2018-2019-full-report.html.

[68] Nichols, *supra* note 43, at 342.

[69] Willa Bruce, *Ethical People Are Productive People*, 17(3) Pub. Productivity & Mgmt. Rev. 241, 248 (1994); William A. Weeks et al., *The Role of Mere Exposure Effect on Ethical Tolerance: A Two-Study Approach*, 58(4) J. Bus. Ethics 281, 282 (2005).

allowed to sell products. It seems likely, therefore, that bribes are paid to evade regulations that control the sale and transfer of weapons, thus endangering the safety and well-being of hundreds of millions of people throughout the world.

5. To Whom Does the Defense Industry Owe Duties?

This chapter does not consider whether defense industry firms are required to obey the law, because that is easily answered. Defense firms are of course required to obey the myriad laws and regulations that prohibit the offering or payment of bribes. Rather, this chapter explores a purely normative question: To whom does a defense firm owe a moral duty when that firm is in a position to offer or pay a bribe? That question exists because each firm has multiple stakeholders, which include the general public, defense forces, and potential victims of violence and mayhem, but which also include shareholders, managers, and salaried employees who anticipate earnings from the activities of that firm.[70]

A preliminary question is the extent to which defense firms, as businesses, are moral agents with a fulsome set of duties. The majority of business ethicists argue that at a minimum firms are in fact moral agents to whom moral responsibility and blame can be assigned. Tom Donaldson, for example, notes that firms are "capable of controlling the structure of [their] policies and rules" and thus bear moral responsibility for the decisions made through them.[71] Eric Posner and Adrian Vermeule suggest two broad arguments for thinking of business firms as moral agents: one set of arguments de-emphasizes strict individualism and allows for the assignment of blame to collections of individuals; the other simply treats business firms as individual actors for moral purposes, much the same way that blame is assigned to business firms (and many other entities, such as nations, or unions, or sports teams) in everyday language.[72]

A defense firm might argue that as a moral agent, its primary normative responsibility is to its shareholders, if it is a corporation, or to those with an investment interest in the firm in general.[73] This is a weak argument. Far too many ethicists take issue with the notion of investor primacy for the argument to be

70 Weida & Gertchner, *supra* note 18, at 8–9.

71 Thomas Donaldson, Corporations and Morality 30 (1982). *See also* Patricia H. Werhane, Persons, Rights, and Corporations 59 (1985) (arguing that because business firms structure the rules and processes for the "secondary actions" taken by their agents, those firms "are and should be held morally responsible for actions within their control when . . . they could have acted otherwise").

72 Eric A. Posner & Adrian Vermeule, *Reparations for Slavery and Other Historical Injustices*, 103(3) Colum. L. Rev. 689, 703–04 (2003).

73 *See* Robert J. Rhee, *A Legal Theory of Shareholder Primacy*, 102(5) Minn. L. Rev. 1951, 1951–52 (2018).

considered universally accepted.[74] Business leaders have renounced the notion of investor primacy.[75] Moreover, even a commitment to investor primacy would of necessity be bounded by stronger normative rules. Few people would have sympathy for a business firm that argued, for example, that it should be allowed to enslave humans simply because it had a responsibility to generate wealth to distribute to others.[76]

The weakness of this argument, however, does not in itself mean that defense firms have duties to other parties. A weak argument is, after all, more persuasive than no argument at all. There are, however, strong arguments that defense firms owe duties to society in general and to vulnerable people in specific.

With respect to society in general, the fact that defense firms have investors points to the direction in which their duties lie. Markets are not inevitable. Society allows them to exist and allows discrete industries to operate within those markets. In the absence of distortions, markets generally are effective at finding optimal means of production and distribution, but in the face of distortions and externalities society often chooses other means of production and distribution to better serve the public. This is particularly true when, as with the defense industry, difficult social choices are involved.[77] In the case of the defense industry, however, society tolerates a distorted market and allows defense firms to organize themselves as regular firms and to operate within that market. The defense industry is not as lucrative as some sectors but nonetheless generates substantial income and other benefits for investors and managers.[78] In turn, society asks that defense firms produce goods and services that actually contribute to the fundamental right of that society to be safe. Whether through operation of a specific social contract, or through a more general principle of reciprocity, defense firms owe a duty to society to perform in that way.

Bribery within the defense industry reduces the safety of society. Bribery ineluctably diminishes the quality and viability of weapons and of defense systems

[74] *See, e.g.*, MARTIN SANDBU, JUST BUSINESS: ARGUMENTS IN BUSINESS ETHICS 15–23 (2012); Lynn A. Stout, *Bad and Not-so-Bad Arguments for Shareholder Primacy*, 75(5) S. CAL. L. REV. 1189, 1204 (2002).

[75] BUSINESS ROUNDTABLE, *Business Roundtable Redefines the Purpose of a Corporation to Promote "An Economy That Serves All Americans"* (Aug. 19, 2019), https://www.businessroundtable.org/business-roundtable-redefines-the-purpose-of-a-corporation-to-promote-an-economy-that-serves-all-americans.

[76] *See* Matthew Lippman, *War Crimes Trials of German Industrialists: The "Other Schindlers"*, 9(2) TEMP. INT'L & COMP. L.J. 173, 229–49 (1995) (discussing the failed uses of arguments by corporations that shareholder primacy allowed them to engage in slavery).

[77] Jonathan Anomaly, *Public Goods and Government Action*, 14(2) POL. PHIL. & ECON. 109, 109–10 (2015).

[78] Charles W. Mahoney, *Acquire or Expire: Publicly Traded Defense Contractors, Financial Markets, and Consolidation in the U.S. Defense Industry*, DEF. & PEACE ECON. (Sept. 19, 2019), DOI:10.1080/10242694.2019.1667216.

and causes misallocation of resources and misspending of limited budgets. It also opens backdoors through which violent organizations and rogue states can obtain weapons with which to commit mayhem. When presented with a request for or an opportunity to pay a bribe, therefore, a defense firm must first consider its duty to respect the fundamental right to safety. Respect for that duty would preclude the offering or payment of bribes.

Respect for the right to be safe also imposes on defense industry firms a duty not to participate in the harming of others. In the case of combatants, the duties of defense industry firms are clear. Bribery diminishes the quality of weapons, thus reducing the defensive capacity of those weapons and increasing the likelihood of harm to combatants. Defense firms owe a duty to combatants, particularly those engaged in legitimate policing of violent organizations or rogue polities. The duty to not endanger combatants and to respect their right to safety trumps any duty to enhance the material wellbeing of investors.

With respect to innocent persons in general, defense firms might argue that they cannot be found to violate this duty because defense firms themselves do not directly harm those people, nor do they even make the decision to inflict harm on those people. Both legal and moral theories of complicity, however, undercut this argument.

As a legal matter, international law assigns culpability to firms that work with malfeasant international actors if three conditions are satisfied:

> (1) there is a strong and interdependent business relationship between the [firm] and the host government [or organization] (i.e., the [firm] hires the security forces or contracts for their services); (2) the [firm] is aware of the human rights violations; and (3) the [firm] . . . continues to perform under contractual arrangements, particularly in furtherance of a collaborative project or endeavor.[79]

Relying on this doctrine, Human Rights Watch has encouraged litigation against defense firms that provide devices to malfeasant polities, stating that a firm "facilitates or participates in government human rights violations. Facilitation includes the company's provision of material or financial support for states' security forces which then commit human rights violations that benefit the company."[80]

[79] Anita Ramasastry, *Corporate Complicity: From Nuremberg to Rangoon: An Examination of Forced Labor Cases and Their Impact on the Liability of Multinational Corporations*, 20(1) Berkeley J. Int'l L. 91, 103 (2002).

[80] Human Rights Watch, *The Enron Corporation: Corporate Complicity in Human Rights Violations* (1999), http://www.hrw.org/reports/1999/enron/.

As a moral concept, theories of complicity tend to examine the degree of proximity between the actively wrong actor and the putatively complicit actor.[81] Complexity theory teaches that many actions have many effects: a butterfly flapping its wings in New York affects the weather in Tokyo.[82] The butterfly, however, is hardly either spatially or temporally proximate to the effects in Tokyo and as a moral matter would bear little culpability in any harms caused by inclement weather. A difficult question, and one lacking an algorithmic answer, is the degree of proximity at which moral responsibility ceases to exist.

Notwithstanding the lack of a clear line, the degree of proximity between defense firms that pay bribes to escape regulation and the infliction of harm by organizations or rogue states that embrace mayhem would clearly be close enough to warrant blame. Violent organizations and rogue polities are not entities that engage in deliberation or choice; constitutionally, these entities use weapons to inflict harm. The Clarion Project, a nonaligned organization dedicated to the promotion of dialogue, describes Boko Haram as "follow[ing] a doctrine of unrestrained warfare, making no distinction between non-combatants and combatants; civilians and soldier; females or males," and notes that its leader has proclaimed that when its followers meet people of other ideologies "there is no[t] any talk except hitting of the neck."[83] To provide weapons to Boko Haram, Ansaru, Epanastatikos Agonas, Kach Chai, Kahane Chai, Lashkar-e-Jhangvi, Lashkar-e-Taiba, or any of the dozens of similar organizations, is to know that those weapons will be used to hurt innocents. Defense firms cannot claim otherwise. In both a legal and a moral sense, firms that provide weapons to violent organizations and rogue polities are complicit in the harms inflicted on innocents. Defense firms, therefore, have a duty to not engage in bribery for the purposes of circumventing regulations intended to keep weapons away from those entities.

6. Conclusion

As a legal matter, defense firms *may* not pay bribes. Just as importantly, as a moral matter, defense firms *should* not pay bribes. A duty owed to society in general and to potential victims of violence prohibits them from doing so.

[81] Amy J. Sepinwall, *Conscience and Complicity: Assessing Pleas for Religious Exemptions in* Hobby Lobby's *Wake*, 82(4) U. Chi. L. Rev. 1897, 1945–48 (2015). Sepinwall argues that when individuals contemplate their own fears of complicity, rules of proximity should be relaxed rather than requiring close proximity because expression of self is different than assignment of moral blame. Amy J. Sepinwall, *Conscientious Objection, Complicity and Accommodation*, *in* Law, Religion and Health in the United States 203, 207 (I. Glenn Cohen et al. eds., 2016).

[82] Steven M. Manson, *Simplifying Complexity: A Review of Complexity Theory*, 32(3) Geoforum 405, 407 (2001).

[83] Ryan Mauro, The Clarion Project, *Boko Haram: Nigerian Islamist Group* 7 (2017), http://clarionproject.org/wp-content/uploads/ClarionProject_FactSheet%20-%20BOKO%20HARAM.pdf.

Defense firms are members of society, and like any member of society owe duties to more than one party. They do have duties to investors. When presented with opportunities to pay bribes, defense firms continue to have duties to investors. When presented with opportunities to pay bribes, however such firms also have duties to society in general and to potential victims of violence in particular. Society allows defense firms to generate revenue for managers and investors in a distorted market; in exchange for this tolerance, defense firms must respect the fundamental human right to be safe. This duty takes precedence over any duty to investors. Corruption vitiates safety. The duties owed by defense firms, therefore, bar the payment of bribes.

References

Hamed Alavi & Tatsiana Khamichonak, *EU and US Export Control Regimes for Dual Use Goods: An Overview of Existing Frameworks* 17(1) ROMANIAN J. EURO. AFF. 59 (2017).

Roger P. Alford, *A Broken Windows Theory of International Corruption*, 73(5) OHIO ST. L.J. 1253 (2012).

Jonathan Anomaly, *Public Goods and Government Action*, 14(2) POL. PHIL. & ECON. 109 (2015).

SCOTT ATRAN, TALKING TO THE ENEMY: FAITH, BROTHERHOOD, AND THE (UN)MAKING OF TERRORISTS (2010).

Mark B. Bader & Bill Shaw, *Amendment of the Foreign Corrupt Practices Act*, 15(3) N.Y.U. J. INT'L L. & POL. 627 (1983).

Frank Badua, *Laying Down the Law on Lockheed: How an Aviation and Defense Giant Inspired the Promulgation of the Foreign Corrupt Practices Act of 1977*, 42(1) ACCT. HISTORIANS J. 105 (2015).

Michael D. Beck & Seema Gahlout, *Introduction to Nonproliferation Export Controls*, *in* TO SUPPLY OR TO DENY: COMPARING NONPROLIFERATION EXPORT CONTROLS IN FIVE KEY COUNTRIES (Michael D. Beck et al., eds., 2003).

Sam R. Bell & Carla Martinez Machain, *Democracy, Transparency, and Secrecy in Crisis*, 14(4) FOREIGN POL'Y ANALYSIS 592 (2018).

MARTINE BOERSMA, CORRUPTION: A VIOLATION OF HUMAN RIGHTS AND A CRIME UNDER INTERNATIONAL LAW? (2012).

Dennis Broeders, *The Secret in the Information Society*, 29(3) PHIL. & TECH. 293 (2016).

Willa Bruce, *Ethical People Are Productive People*, 17(3) PUB. PRODUCTIVITY & MGMT. REV. 241 (1994).

BUSINESS ROUNDTABLE, *Business Roundtable Redefines the Purpose of a Corporation to Promote "An Economy That Serves All Americans"* (Aug. 19 2019), https://www.businessroundtable.org/business-roundtable-redefines-the-purpose-of-a-corporation-to-promote-an-economy-that-serves-all-americans.

Sarah F. Cable, Note, *An Unanswered Question in* Kennedy v. Louisiana: *How Should the Supreme Court Determine the Constitutionality of the Death Penalty for Espionage?*, 70(3) LA. L. REV. 995 (2010).

Pramit P. Chaudhuri, *Why India Is Poor at Making Its Own Weapons*, RHODIUM GROUP (Apr. 9, 2012), https://rhg.com/research/why-india-is-poor-at-making-its-own-weapons/.

Christopher J. Chivers, *Supplier Under Scrutiny on Arms for Afghans*, N.Y. TIMES (Mar. 27, 2008), https://www.nytimes.com/2008/03/27/world/asia/27ammo.html.

Michael Colaresi, *A Boom with Review: How Retrospective Oversight Increases the Foreign Policy Ability of Democracies*, 56(3) AM. J. POL. SCI. 671 (2014).

Christopher Coyne & David S. Lucas, *Economists Have No Defense: A Critical Review of National Defense in Economics Textbooks*, 31(4) J. PRIVATE ENTERPRISE 65 (2016).

KATHERINE DIXON ET AL., OUT OF THE SHADOWS: PROMOTING OPENNESS AND ACCOUNTABILITY IN THE GLOBAL DEFENCE INDUSTRY (2018), https://ti-defence.org/publications/out-of-the-shadows/.

William K. Domke, *Fiscal Constraints and Defense Planning in Advanced Industrial Democracies*, *in* THE POLITICAL ECONOMY OF DEFENSE: ISSUES AND PERSPECTIVES (Andrew L. Ross ed., 1991).

THOMAS DONALDSON, CORPORATIONS AND MORALITY (1982).

Otu O. Duke, Dickson D. Agbaji & Okon Bassey, *Corruption and the Challenge of Boko Haram Terrorism in Nigeria: A Case of the Nigerian Armed Forces*, 4(2) ASIAN RES. J. ARTS & SOC. SCI. 1 (2017).

Katie Fish et al., *Defence Companies Anti-Corruption Index 2015*, TRANSPARENCY INTERNATIONAL (2015), http://companies.defenceindex.org/.

Glenn R. Fong, *The Political Economy of Pentagon-Industry Collaboration in Technology Development*, *in* THE POLITICAL ECONOMY OF DEFENSE: ISSUES AND PERSPECTIVES (Andrew L. Ross ed., 1991).

Rajeev K. Goel, Jelena Budak & Edo Rajh, *Private Sector Bribery and Effectiveness of Anti-Corruption Policies*, 22(10) APP. ECON. LETTERS 759 (2015).

Thomas Graham, Jr., *Nuclear Nonproliferation and Nuclear Terrorism*, 17(1) TRANSNAT'L LAW. 89 (2004).

David Hess & Thomas W. Dunfee, *Fighting Corruption: A Principled Approach: The C^2 Principles (Combating Corruption)*, 33(3) CORNELL INT'L L.J. 593 (2000).

Human Rights Watch, *The Enron Corporation: Corporate Complicity in Human Rights Violations*, http://www.hrw.org/reports/1999/enron/ (1999).

Kate Ivanova & Todd Sandler, *CBRN Attack Perpetrators: An Empirical Study*, 1(3) FOREIGN POL'Y ANALYSIS 273 (2007).

Jeppe T. Jacobsen & Jens Ringsmose, *Cyber-Bombing ISIS: Why Disclose What Is Better Kept Secret?*, 3(2) GLOBAL AFF. 126 (2017).

Daniel Kaufmann & Shang-Jin Wei, *Does "Grease Money" Speed Up the Wheels of Commerce?* (Nat'l Bureau of Econ. Research Working Paper No. 7093, 1999).

BARRY KELLMAN, BIOVIOLENCE: PREVENTING BIOLOGICAL TERROR AND CRIME (2007).

Jin H. Kim, *Is Your Playing Field Unleveled? US Defense Contracts and Foreign Firm Lobbying*, 40(12) STRATEGIC MGMT. J. 1911 (2019).

Jean-Jacques Laffont & Jean Tirole, *The Politics of Government Decision-Making: A Theory of Regulatory Capture*, 106(4) Q.J. ECON. 1089 (1991).

Johann G. Lambsdorff, *Corruption and Rent-Seeking*, 113(1–2) PUBLIC CHOICE 97 (2002).

Marie H. Larsen & Susann Øvretveit, *Corruption in the Arms- and Defense Industry: A Comparative Study of the Largest American and European Arms Dealers* 27 (Spring 2019).

Jaewon Lee, *South Korea's Export Control System*, Stockholm International Peace Research Institute Background Paper (Nov. 2013), https://www.sipri.org/sites/default/files/files/misc/SIPRIBP1311.pdf.

Robert J. Leonard, *War as a "Simple Economic Problem": The Rise of an Economic of Defense*, *in* ECONOMICS AND NATIONAL SECURITY: A HISTORY OF THEIR INTERACTION (C.D. Goodwin ed., 1991).

Matthew Lippman, *War Crimes Trials of German Industrialists: The "Other Schindlers"*, 9(2) TEMP. INT'L & COMP. L.J. 173 (1995).

Lynn M. LoPucki, *Court-System Transparency*, 94(2) IOWA L. REV. 494 (2009).

M4 Rifles Causing Problems for U.S. Troops, CBSNEWS.COM (Oct. 12, 2009), https://www.cbsnews.com/news/m4-rifles-causing-problems-for-us-troops/

Roy C. Macridis, *The New French Maginot Line: A Note on French Strategy*, 2(1) J. POL. & MIL. SOC. 105 (1974).

Charles W. Mahoney, *Acquire or Expire: Publicly Traded Defense Contractors, Financial Markets, and Consolidation in the U.S. Defense Industry*, DEF. & PEACE ECON. (Sept. 19, 2019), DOI:10.1080/10242694.2019.1667216.

Steven M. Manson, *Simplifying Complexity: A Review of Complexity Theory*, 32(3) GEOFORUM 405 (2001).

Ryan Mauro, The Clarion Project, *Boko Haram: Nigerian Islamist Group* (2017), http://clarionproject.org/wp-content/uploads/ClarionProject_FactSheet%20-%20BOKO%20HARAM.pdf.

Tetsuro Mizoguchi & Nguyen Van Quyen, Corruption in Japanese Defense Procurement: A Game Theoretic Analysis (Keio/Kyoto Global COE Discussion Paper Series No. DP2008-007, 2009), https://ideas.repec.org/p/kei/dpaper/2008-007.html.

Philip M. Nichols, *Corruption as an Assurance Problem*, 19(6) AM. U. INT'L L. REV. 1307 (2004).

Philip M. Nichols, *The Business Case for Complying with Bribery Laws*, 49(2) AM. BUS. L.J. 325 (2012).

Philip M. Nichols, *The Mercantilist Fallacy and the Contextual Reality of the Foreign Corrupt Practices Act*, 53(1) HARV. J. LEGIS. 203 (2016).

Gro Nystuen & Kjølv Egeland, *The Potential of the Arms Trade Treaty to Reduce Violations of International Humanitarian Law and Human Rights Law*, *in* RESEARCH HANDBOOK ON INTERNATIONAL LAW AND PEACE 267 (Cecilia M. Bailliet ed., 2019).

Susanne Oxenstierna & Fredrik Westerlund, *Arms Procurement and the Russian Defense Industry: Challenges Up to 2020*, 26(1) J. SLAVIC MIL. STUD. 1 (2013).

Michael D. Pendleton, *A New Human Right—The Right to Globalization*, 22(5) FORDHAM INT'L L.J. 2052 (1999).

Sam Perlo-Freeman, *Arms, Corruption, and the State: Understanding the Role of Arms Trade Corruption in Power Politics*, 13(2) ECON. PEACE & SECURITY J. 37 (2018).

Eric A. Posner & Adrian Vermeule, *Reparations for Slavery and Other Historical Injustices*, 103(3) COLUM. L. REV. 689 (2003).

Anita Ramasastry, *Corporate Complicity: From Nuremberg to Rangoon: An Examination of Forced Labor Cases and Their Impact on the Liability of Multinational Corporations*, 20(1) BERKELEY J. INT'L L. 91 (2002).

JOHN RAWLS, POLITICAL LIBERALISM (1993).

Robert J. Rhee, *A Legal Theory of Shareholder Primacy*, 102(5) MINN. L. REV. 1951 (2018).

DAMIEN ROGERS, POSTINTERNATIONALISM AND SMALL ARMS CONTROL: THEORY, POLITICS, SECURITY (2009).

Cecil Rose, *The Limits of a Human Rights Approach to Corruption*, 65(2) INT'L & COMP. L.Q. 422 (2016).

Andrew L. Ross, *The International Arms Market: A Structural and Behavioral Analysis*, *in* The Political Economy of Defense: Issues and Perspectives (Andrew L. Ross ed., 1991).

Jordi C. Rufanges, *The Arms Industry Lobby in Europe*, 60(3) Am. Behav. Sci. 305 (2016).

Martin Sandbu, Just Business: Arguments in Business Ethics (2012).

Amartya Sen, *The Moral Standing of the Market*, 2(2) Soc. Phil. & Pol'y 1 (1985).

Amy J. Sepinwall, *Conscience and Complicity: Assessing Pleas for Religious Exemptions in* Hobby Lobby's *Wake*, 82(4) U. Chi. L. Rev. 1897 (2015).

Amy J. Sepinwall, *Conscientious Objection, Complicity and Accommodation*, *in* Law, Religion and Health in the United States (I. Glenn Cohen et al. eds., 2016).

Shouyoung Shi & Ted Temzelides, *A Model of Bureaucracy and Corruption*, 45(3) Int'l Econ. Rev. 873 (2004).

George J. Stigler, *The Economic Theory of Regulation*, 2(1) Bell J. Econ. & Mgmt. Sci. 3 (1971).

Lynn A. Stout, *Bad and Not-so-Bad Arguments for Shareholder Primacy*, 75(5) S. Cal. L. Rev. 1189 (2002).

Christopher M. Tipler, *Defining "National Security": Resolving Ambiguity in the CFIUS Regulations*, 35(4) U. Penn. J. Int'l L. 1223 (2014).

John Tomasi, Free Market Fairness (2012).

Transparency International, *Defence Companies Anti-Corruption Index*, http://ti-defence.org/dci/.

Henry Walter, *The Defense Industrial Base: How Idiosyncratic and Historical Influences Dictate Its Future*, 95(1) Int'l Soc. Sci. Rev 14 (2019).

Melissa F. Wasserman, *Deference Asymmetries: Distortions in the Evolution of Regulatory Law*, 93(3) Tex. L. Rev. 625 (2015).

William J. Weida & Franklin L. Gertchner, The Political Economy of National Defense (1987).

Patricia H. Werhane, Persons, Rights, and Corporations (1985).

10

Tackling Defense Corruption

A "Whole Sector" Approach

Mark Pyman

1. Introduction

Tackling defense corruption is about much more than stopping dodgy commissions on arms sales. Civilians and soldiers die because of corruption in defense, insecurity rises, peace is compromised, and wars are extended.

This chapter describes the progress over more than two decades since 1995, and especially since the formation of TI's Defence & Security Program in 2004, across the whole defense sector: collaborating with, and pressuring, defense ministries, military forces, defense companies, NATO, nongovernmental organizations (NGOs), and others. The sector is showing the way in several respects—defense-specific corruption issues, comparative corruption vulnerability indexes, the professional communities of ethics officers in the defense companies, collaborative efforts by the national and global industry associations, the roles of the offices of suspension and debarment and the inspectors general, the bravery of many government officials, and the readiness of ministers to lead defense reform. The progress achieved suggests that a "whole sector" approach—embracing companies, governments, regulators, international organizations, and civil society—can be effective. The experience holds lessons for how corruption reform in other sectors can be conceived and implemented.

2. Mechanisms for Change

The defense sector is not an obvious candidate for change. It combines the "normal" problems of corruption together with other tough issues: the secrecy surrounding military technology, the closed nature of the military, and the inherently political nature of most defense decisions. The idea that an NGO could have an impact was described by the senior anti-corruption adviser in the

Mark Pyman, *Tackling Defense Corruption* In: *Ethical Dilemmas in the Global Defense Industry*. Edited by: Daniel Schoeni and Tobias Vestner, Oxford University Press. © Daniel Schoeni and Tobias Vestner 2023. DOI: 10.1093/oso/9780190675813.003.0011

U.K. government as "trying to penetrate the impenetrable."[1] Nonetheless, in these first two decades of the twenty-first century, preventing corruption in the defense sector has moved from being a taboo subject to a mainstream and acceptable subject for discussion and analysis, partly due to broad trends on greater worldwide awareness of the harm done by corruption, but also due to the effort of many committed individuals and initiatives *within* the sector.

Within this trend, the Transparency International Defence & Security program (TI-DS) has had considerable influence: taking a global perspective from the outset and engaging robustly with defense companies, Ministries of Defense, military leaders, diplomats, journalists, civil society, and whistle-blowers. TI-DS' engagement encompasses 11 angles of approach. Each contributed to the overall sector-wide changes in defense and offers lessons for other sectors:

1. **A Sector-focused NGO.** The presence throughout the two decades of TI-DS, a "sector-specific" anti-corruption NGO, was critical in both catalyzing and monitoring change.
2. **Defense Companies Worldwide.** The corporate ethics and compliance systems of defense companies were of very variable quality in 2004, the U.S. company programs generally better than the European, the European in turn better than those from other nations. The defense companies as a whole have dramatically improved their compliance programs since then. This also benefited from a wider private sector trend, the growing profession of ethics and compliance officers. National and regional defense industry associations also established new collective groupings for strengthening anti-corruption practices. The narrow-but-deep defense industry structure was, unexpectedly, a positive factor in enabling change.
3. **NATO.** NATO established a distinct voice on the topic from 2007, through its "Building Integrity" program (NATO BI). This was developed in an unusual cooperation between NATO and TI-DS. NATO BI has gone on to jointly develop tools and guidance for nations, leading to integrity becoming a formal NATO policy. This was a lesson in how multilateral bodies within a sector, which can easily be a passive lowest common denominator on corruption, can become a force for system-wide improvement.
4. **National Ministries of Defense (MODs).** MODs in Western European countries were initially dismissive of the need to improve, but MODs

[1] Tobias Bock, Mark Pyman & Ida Höckerfelt, *MEKANIC: Making Sense of Progress in the Defense and Security Sector—Implementing Lessons Learned*, Praxis Note No. 66, INTRAC 1, 2 (Jan. 2014), https://www.intrac.org/wpcms/wp-content/uploads/2017/07/Praxis-Note-66.-MEKANIC-1.pdf.

in countries such as Bulgaria, Colombia, and Poland took action to strengthen measures against defense corruption through strong leadership commitments. Other MODs started to change following participating in NATO assessments, and many more started to take action after TI-DS published a report in 2013 that made both good and bad practices publicly available.[2] The strong focus on the particularities of defense meant that reformers in ministries felt that their problems were understood and that they were not alone.

5. **Defense Procurement.** National and EU rules have gradually tightened up during the last three decades. In the United States, it became the norm for companies to have compliance program after the introduction of the Foreign Corrupt Practices Act (FCPA) and related legislation. In Europe, defense procurement increased greatly in rigor and competitiveness from 2009 through implementation of the EU Defense Procurement Directive[3] and following parallel reforms by European defense ministries. Major scandals in the United States (such as the Boeing tanker refueling contract) and in Europe (such as BAE-Al Yamamah) also led to strengthened national defense procurement practices. Despite the importance of procurement, the broader sector lesson was that there were many other, equally important, corruption issues in the defense sector.
6. **Research.** Defense corruption prevention was almost a research-free zone in 2004. The lesson from TI-DS's experience was that even the smallest research projects could have a disproportionate impact in raising and awareness deepening understanding of corruption issues.
7. **Independent Analyses and Indexes.** The development of detailed comparative analyses of the corruption vulnerability of both defense companies and national defense establishments by TI-DS, first published in 2012 and 2013, made the defense corruption vulnerability of each nation more visible, more comparable, and more addressable. This was perhaps the single biggest contributor to change. The national "score" and the quantitative basis for detailed improvement appealed both to the competitiveness and to the pride of those involved.
8. **Military Forces.** The recognition from about 2009 that corruption was the principal obstacle to progress of the international military mission in Afghanistan accelerated the need for military forces to pay attention to corruption issues in fragile and conflict countries. Western militaries also

[2] Transparency Int'l Def. & Sec., *Government Defence Anti-Corruption Index 2013* (Jan. 29, 2013), http://ti-defence.org/wp-content/uploads/2016/03/gi-2013-mainreportphase04.pdf.

[3] Council Directive 2009/81/EC, 2009 O.J. (L 216/76) (EC).

increasingly recognized the corruption issues connected with giving security assistance to nations. The work of the Special Inspector General for Afghanistan Reconstruction (SIGAR) in independently analyzing U.S. support for reconstruction was also significant in raising awareness of the presence of corruption and changing behavior. Such a strong external monitor could surely be applied in other sectors and contexts.

9. **Fragile States, Peacekeeping, and Security Policymaking.** Those concerned with national and international security policy had not previously considered corruption as a significant factor, but this changed from about 2008, driven by developments in Afghanistan and in Ukraine and the rise of insurgencies. Since about 2014, the relevance of corruption to security policy has become mainstream. For example, it is now a regular feature at the Munich Security Conference, a development catalysed by TI-DS.
10. **Building Expertise and Networks.** Specialist groups with expertise in tackling defense corruption have emerged: besides groups at NATO, TI-DS, and SIGAR, there are also anti-corruption teams at the UK, Norwegian and Ukrainian military academies. Networks have been crucial behind the scenes, such as defense industry associations working cooperatively across borders on anti-corruption standards, the ethics and compliance communities in defense companies sharing good practices, and among smaller groupings of reformers.
11. **Budgets and Donors.** Companies have to allocate budget to compliance staff and to integrity programs, governments have to fund integrity units and oversight functions, and NGOs need donors. Behind the scenes, the decisions leading to positive funding are crucial for progress. Defense companies, largely, already had funding for such staff, driven by the support for compliance programs by their largest customer, the U.S. Department of Defense (DoD). The main donor supporting the TI-DS team, the U.K. Department for International Development, provided core funding for the team, rather than project funding.

The role played by each of these mechanisms in defense sector reform is analyzed in the following in light of the TI-DS's work over the years.

3. Early Years

Between 1995 and 2002, Transparency International UK (TI-UK), the British arm of the nonprofit organization Transparency International, had been challenging corrupt defense sales to developing countries, such as for a radar system sale to Tanzania by Siemens/Plessey, including the explicit support being given by the British government through providing financing credit. TI-UK's leadership—development economist Laurence Cockcroft, businessman David Murray and former *Financial Times* journalist Joe Roeber—developed this into a wider mandate for action by organizing conferences in 2000 and 2001 on corruption in the arms trade in Stockholm[4] and Cambridge,[5] with the support of governments such as Sweden, companies such as Lockheed Martin, and defense-specific NGOs such as Saferworld and Corner House.[6] The conference participants stressed the need for reforms to the importing and exporting of weapons, as summarized in a TI-UK paper by Catherine Courtney.[7]

This early work led to TI-UK being awarded a small grant from the U.K. Department for International Development (DFID) in 2003 to work on "Corruption in the Official Arms Trade." The award funded two to three people for six months, plus the hosting of a small conference. TI-UK planned three rather ambitious lines of collaboration: (1) working with a group of major defense companies to develop industry standards against bribery and corruption in arms contracts; (2) working with governments to extend the use of "integrity pacts" to the defense sector; and (3) engaging with governments that may be ready to collaborate to improve the integrity of defense procurement. The objective was whole-sector reform, rather grandly stated in the proposal as being "to reverse the prevalence of corruption in the official arms trade in order to create a corruption free defense sector."[8] The team comprised a part-time project leader, a research assistant, and two part-time ex-senior military officers. The work on promoting integrity pacts made some progress, with pacts established for defense procurements in Colombia and Poland (see Section 8) but the engagement with European governments, mostly with the national defense procurement chiefs, led nowhere. On the other hand, the defense companies, initially the U.S. company Lockheed Martin and the French company Thales, responded more productively.

[4] *See* Ikram Sehgal, *Corruption in the Arms Trade*, DEF. J. (2000), http://www.defencejournal.com/2000/mar/arms-trade.htm (describing the Transparency International's Stockholm Colloquium on Corruption in the Arms Trade, Feb. 4–6, 2000).

[5] Transparency Int'l, Proceedings of the TI(UK) Conference on Corruption in the Official Arms Trade, Cambridge (Apr. 5, 2001), https://curbingcorruption.com/wp-content/uploads/2020/10/Transparency-International-UK-2001-Report-on-the-Conference-Corruption-in-the-Official-Arms-Trade.pdf.

[6] Susan Hawley, *Turning a Blind Eye: Corruption and the UK Export Credits Guarantee Department*, CORNER HOUSE (2003), http://www.thecornerhouse.org.uk/sites/thecornerhouse.org.uk/files/correcgd.pdf.

[7] Catherine Courtney, *Corruption in the Official Arms Trade*, TRANSPARENCY INT'L (2003), https://curbingcorruption.com/wp-content/uploads/2019/10/191008-Catherine-Courtney-TI-paper-2002.pdf.

[8] Mark Pyman, Address at the Transparency International Collaborative Programme: Preventing Corruption in the Official Arms Trade (July 14, 2004), https://curbingcorruption.com/wp-content/uploads/2018/07/Transparency-International-UK-2004-Project-summary-Preventing-corruption-in-the-official-arms-trade-Phase-1.pdf.

4. Working with Defense Companies

The global defense industry has a distinct structure. The companies that are the "platform makers"—builders of military planes, vehicles, defensive shields, ships, command and control systems—are at the top of the pyramid, with a high level of power in the industry. Everyone below them, in supply chains that go down dozens of layers, is strongly influenced by them, on ethics as much as on technical and commercial matters.

For any change program to succeed, it is necessary that these top-level companies feel they want to improve and that they will encourage improvement down the supply chain. National initiatives are likely to have limited broader impact, because so many of the supply chains are international. The major exception is the United States because of its dominant position, representing approximately 50 percent of the global defense market. Having U.S. regulators on board in any global change initiative is also essential, because the foreign defense companies all know that they have to line up with U.S. companies and with U.S. laws because of their extraterritoriality.

In 2004, the only part of the corporate defense sector where there was active anti-corruption effort was in the U.S. defense companies, driven by legislation introduced in the late 1970s following a slew of defense corruption scandals. Further to the FCPA legislation, the U.S. DoD had implicitly accepted the introduction and costs of ethics and compliance systems in U.S. companies. Over the subsequent two decades, these ethics and compliance systems had become quite sophisticated, and the Pentagon was also energetic in chasing down non-compliant companies via the Office of Suspension and Debarment (S&D). The S&D mechanism is available in all executive agencies, but it was only the military that energetically enforced it, particularly the U.S. Air Force.[9] This did not mean that everything was clean—far from it; scandals continued. But it meant that there was institutional corruption-prevention machinery in place that could be improved.

When TI-DS made contact with some of the first-tier U.S. companies (e.g., Boeing, Lockheed Martin, Raytheon, United Technologies, Northrop Grumman, Honeywell), explaining that they wanted to catalyze a worldwide association of defense companies ready to act together against corruption, most of them were supportive, at least "in principle." Meanwhile, U.K. and European defense companies had less by way of ethics or compliance systems and were defensive about any engagement with TI-DS, or even with the U.S. companies. The

[9] Steven A. Shaw & Jade C. Totman, *Suspension and Debarment: Strengthening Integrity in International Defence Contracting*, Transparency Int'l Def. & Sec. (2015), http://ti-defence.org/wp-content/uploads/2016/03/150507-Suspension-and-Debarment.pdf.

major U.K. defense company, BAE, was actively suspicious of TI-DS at the time. The catalyst for change in the U.K. came with the growing corruption scandal over the BAE–Saudi Arabia giant "Al Yamamah" contract. Though some of the bribery prosecutions were stopped by the U.K. government, fearful of the impact this might have on U.K. relations with Saudi Arabia, the aftershocks were profound for BAE. The company changed its chairman, and the new team instituted a major review of all operating practices across the company headed by the former Lord Chief Justice.[10] Over the following few years this led to large-scale change across the company.[11]

This overhaul of corporate behavior of BAE following the Saudi scandal was also a factor in changing behavior of the industry because the United Kingdom was one of the major national arms exporters. While the other major European arms exporters (France, Germany, Italy, and pan-European entities like airplane manufacturer Airbus and missile manufacturer MBDA) did not have any equivalent crisis, they were nonetheless prepared to go along with improved industry standards and actively cooperate with TI-DS.

These factors—a narrow but deep industry structure, supportive top-tier companies, an energetic regulator in the primary market, and major scandals—together with the constructive way that TI-DS engaged, were crucial to defense sector progress.

5. Bringing the Global Defense Companies Together

Transparency International's founder, Peter Eigen, believed that the way to achieve action against corruption was always to engage government *and* industry *and* civil society, bringing people together in multiple forms of collaboration. The same approach was followed for the defense program, bringing together a community that would be ready to support good anti-corruption actions and practices. TI-DS' first conference at Arundel, England, in July 2004, brought together six defense companies (Thales of France, Lockheed Martin of the United States, and four U.K. companies, BAE amongst them), the U.S. Air Force S&D General officer, the U.K. military, representatives from other governments and civil society groups from many countries, to debate how the defense sector could improve.[12] Bilateral meetings with many more defense companies followed.

10 Woolf Committee, *Ethical Business Conduct in BAE PLC, The Way Forward* (2008), https://www.icaew.com/~/media/corporate/files/technical/ethics/woolf report 2008.ashx.

11 Dick Olver, Address at Tomorrow's Values Lecture Series: Tomorrow's Company (Mar. 13, 2013), http://www.tomorrowscompany.com/wp-content/uploads/2013/03/dick_olver_tomorrows_company_speech-3.pdf.

12 Mark Pyman, Address at Transparency International conference in Arendel, UK: Preventing Corruption in the Official Arms Trade (June 8, 2004), https://curbingcorruption.com/wp-content/

Through these discussions, some of the tensions hindering defense company cooperation became better understood. The main tension was the divide between the United States and the European companies, with the U.S. companies seeing the Europeans as still being supportive of corrupt practices, such as acceptance of facilitation payments, and the Europeans seeing the U.S. companies' adherence to FCPA and compliance programs as being something of a public show rather than substance. The U.S.-European divide had been evident in the failure of an earlier attempt at enabling industry collaboration led by Mark Pieth at the Basel Institute a few years earlier[13] (the "Clovis" principles). It was also the reason why there was cooperative working among the U.S. defense companies on integrity and anti-corruption topics, but none with companies outside the United States. There was also distrust on corruption matters between the European companies, despite considerable cooperation on technical projects.

TI-DS nonetheless felt that the desire of the companies to cooperate was sincere, and that there was potential for a global defense industry integrity grouping to develop. Being a small player among such large companies, TI-DS sought someone of stature who could act as a neutral "node" around which the U.S. companies, the European companies, and TI-DS could convene. TI-DS was fortunate to find and engage the help of Lord George Robertson, a former NATO Secretary General and former UK Defence Minister, highly respected across the sector. With his energetic involvement and chairing, TI-DS was able to convene a series of four formal meetings between senior industry representatives, at which trust was built and possible forms of industry collaboration examined. This gradually bore fruit, initially with a common integrity standard across all European defense companies in 2008—called, somewhat unimaginatively, the Common Industry Standard,[14] which then led into a global forum in 2010 of the major defense companies, called the International Forum for Business and Ethical Conduct of Defense and Aerospace Companies (IFBEC).[15] There are currently 30 IFBEC members, all large global defense companies.

Building such a collaboration requires an immense amount of discussion between the participants. In this case, there were 14 people principally involved

uploads/2018/07/Transparency-International-UK-2004-Arundel-Conference-Proceedings-for-preventing-corruption-in-the-official-arms-trade.pdf.

[13] Mark Pieth, *Aeronautics and Defence*, *in* Confronting Corruption: Past Concerns, Present Strategies and Future Challenges 149, 150–55 (Fritz Heimann & Mark Pieth eds., 2018).

[14] *Common Industry Standards: European Common Industry Standards for the Prevention of Corruption in the Aerospace and Defence Sector*, Aerospace & Def. Indus. Ass'n of Eur. (June 2012), https://www.asd-europe.org/sites/default/files/atoms/files/ASD_Common_Industry_Standards.pdf.

[15] *What Is IFBCEC?*, Int'l F. on Bus. Ethical Conduct for Aerospace & Def. Indus., https://ifbec.info/about/ (last visited June 12, 2021).

between 2005 and 2010: four from U.S. companies (Lockheed Martin, Raytheon, Northrop Grumman, and Honeywell), five from European companies (Thales, BAE, Rolls Royce, Airbus, and Saab), four from defense industry associations (U.K., Europe, two from U.S. associations), and TI-DS.

An insight into how this evolved is available because a research student made a detailed analysis of the network, speaking at length with the people involved and mapping the interactions. Elize Sakamoto, then a Ph.D. student at the London School of Economics, tracked who met with whom and how the collaboration developed into industry-wide collaboration and the writing of formal codes. Her recording of the network is shown in Figure 10.1. Each of the representatives of the European defense companies are shown as blue squares, European defense industry association representatives as blue triangles, U.K. defense company representatives as yellow squares, U.K. industry associations as yellow triangles, U.S. company representatives as red squares, U.S. industry associations as one red and one black triangle, and TI-DS as a green circle.[16]

This analysis shows up the critical role of small groups of people who are ready to go well beyond their formal roles in order to achieve a goal. Despite the different backgrounds—NGO/major company, U.S./European, U.K./French, Sales/Legal—and initial distrust, the 14 people built up trust in each other and in the desirability of the objective. They did this through regular contact, demonstrable additional effort, continuing the discussions through each setback, and meeting several times per year.

Why did the participants engage so energetically? On the company side, such engagement rarely happens without being sanctioned at a senior level. The senior influencer behind the scenes was the "American Industries Association" (AIA), a defense forum where the industry leaders can discuss and agree on taking actions as a group tackling various issues. Most U.S. companies were receptive to an anti-corruption initiative because of their own international experience of losing tenders to competitors suspected of corruption. They also had prior positive experience of creating and sustaining a good ethical practice forum for U.S. defense companies, called the Defense Industries Initiative.[17] This had been created after the scandals of the 1970s and, rather surprisingly, had evolved to be the focal point through which industry good practices on ethics and compliance were presented, discussed, and disseminated. The chair of the AIA at the

[16] Eiko Elize Sakamoto, Changing the Rules of the Game: A Voluntary Code of Conduct by the Defence and Arms Industry and Transparency International's Defence Against Corruption (Dec. 2010) (unpublished doctoral research, London School of Economics), https://curbingcorruption.com/sakamoto-2010-changing-the-rules-of-the-game-a-voluntary-code-of-conduct-by-the-defence-and-arms-industry-and-transparency-international/.

[17] *See* Def. Indus. Initiative on Bus. Ethics & Conduct, *About DII*, https://www.dii.org/about/about-dii (last visited June 12, 2021).

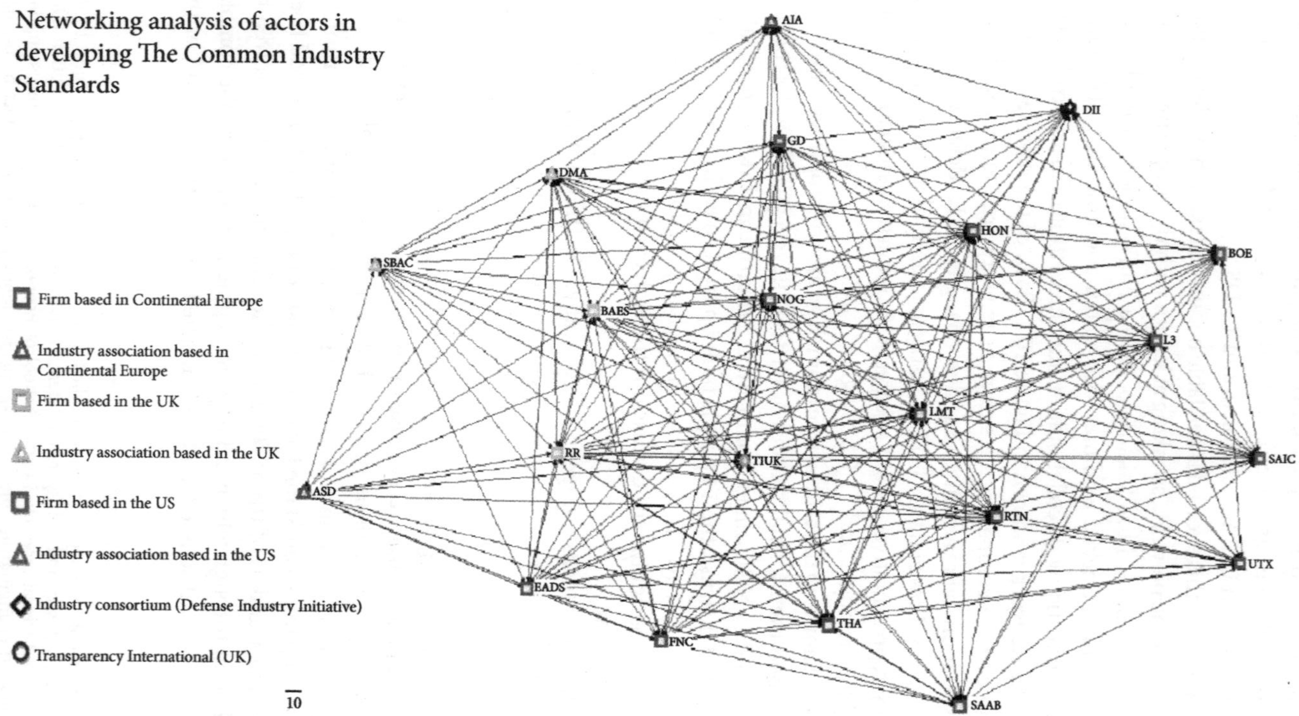

Figure 10.1 Network analysis of the actors developing the defense industry anti-corruption standards.

Id. at 37.

time, the CEO of Raytheon, was enthusiastic about this possible forum and actively encouraged participation. There were AIA linkages with the equivalent defense associations in the United Kingdom (ADS Group) and on the continent (ASD, representing the Aeronautics, Space, Defense and Security Industries in Europe), which were also helpful in giving additional momentum to closing the U.S.-European divide.

Whether the outcome would be worthwhile, or effective, was something the participants were all ready to leave to a later time, believing that "getting something started" was a valuable deliverable in its own right. That question, of whether it was worth it, is still with us. Some from that original group felt that it was a lot of effort for a modest outcome; but we don't know that, and structures once in place can be bent to all sorts of unexpectedly useful new functions.

6. Linking with NATO

TI-DS realized by 2006 that working with the defense companies could only ever be half of the solution and that it would be necessary to try again to influence governments and MODs, despite the negative results of the earlier meetings with West European defense procurement chiefs. Progress in doing this was achieved via two routes. First, working through TI national chapters round the world to identify MODs ready to work on corruption, which led to TI-DS working with Colombia, Latvia, and Poland (see Section 8). Second, TI-DS reached out to NATO headquarters, through links developed by one of its senior military advisers, Rear Admiral Hugh Edleston. NATO was unexpectedly receptive, thanks to two supportive ambassadors to NATO, from the United Kingdom and Switzerland, and to support among key officials. As a result, a strong relationship developed that led to a collaboration agreement between TI-DS and NATO in 2006, and to a formal NATO initiative in November 2007. TI-DS led in developing two "products" for NATO countries—an integrity self-assessment process for national defense establishments[18] and a five-day training module for military staff and officers.[19] A Swiss think tank led in developing a compendium of

[18] TI-DS, NATO & DCAF, *Building Integrity and Reducing Corruption Risk in Defence Establishments: An Integrity Self-assessment Process for National Defense Establishments* 2009, EAPC(PC)N(2010)0004, Enclos. 1 (2010), https://www.nato.int/nato_static/assets/pdf/pdf_2010_05/20100603_EAPC_PFP-joint_EAPC-0004-Encl1.pdf.

[19] *See, e.g.*, Moldova Ministry of Def., *Building Integrity Self-Assessment Peer Review Report* (Oct. 2014), http://www.army.md/img/userfiles/anticoruptie/bisaprr.pdf; Mark Pyman, Transparency Int'l Def. & Sec., *Building Integrity and Countering Corruption in Defense and Security: 20 Practical Reforms* (2016), https://ti-defence.org/wp-content/uploads/2016/03/1102_Handbook_IntegrityReducingCorruption.pdf.

guidance on integrity building and anti-corruption for nations, which is now available in 14 languages.[20]

NATO developed the Building Integrity (BI) initiative in ways that were intended to bring integrity/anti-corruption thinking "into the DNA of NATO operations," to use the memorable phrase of Susan Pond, the senior NATO official leading the program. TI-DS gradually stepped out of the cooperation after about 2011 as the NATO-BI initiative gained institutional traction. At the Chicago Summit in 2012, Building Integrity was established as a NATO Education and Training Discipline within the framework of the Allied Command Transformation Global Programming. The 2014 Wales Summit reaffirmed BI as an integral part of NATO's Defense and Related Security Capacity Building Initiative. NATO's BI Policy was endorsed at the NATO Summit in Warsaw in July 2016. Taking part in the 2017 BI Conference, the European Union announced its intentions to contribute to the BI Trust Fund, referring to NATO BI as the partner of choice. The chronology of the development within NATO can be found on the NATO BI website.[21]

7. Regulatory Influences

Through this period, much work was also underway in the European Union to strengthen defense procurement. National defense procurement regulations, which had been largely outside EU procurement rules, increased greatly in rigor and competitiveness from about 2009 through implementation of the Defence Directive. This had come about because of the multiple exemptions from competitive bidding of the defense sector from procurement regulations and the desire for a more Europe-wide defense market (for an evaluation of the directive, see the European Commission 2016 report).[22] Separate efforts to set up an electronic defense procurement forum for defense tenders also came to fruition.

Another regulatory structure that had a major impact was the Office for Suspension and Debarment (OSD) in the United States. The OSD in the U.S. Air Force was especially active due to the strong drive and long tenure of Steven Shaw, the U.S. Air Force's senior S&D official. The impact of the OSD went

[20] DCAF, *Building Integrity and Reducing Corruption in Defense: A Compendium of Best Practices* (2010), https://www.dcaf.ch/sites/default/files/publications/documents/Compendium_Building_Integrity_and_Reducing_Corruption_in_Defence.pdf.

[21] NATO, *Ten Years of NATO's Building Integrity Programme* (2019), https://buildingintegrity.hq.nato.int/?AspxAutoDetectCookieSupport=1.

[22] European Commission, Report from the Commission to the European Parliament and the Council on the Implementation of Directive 2009/81/EC on Public Procurement in the Fields of Defence and Security, to Comply with Article 73(2) of that Directive, COM(2016) 762 final (Nov. 30, 2016), https://ec.europa.eu/docsroom/documents/20376.

beyond the United States: because of the extraterritorial reach of the FCPA and the massive U.S. defense market, defense companies from many other countries wished to do business in the United States and as a consequence were exposed to the OSD. Such OSDs also exist in other countries but have less influence.[23] Here the change-driver was not just the legal structure but the personal commitment of Steven Shaw in support of the larger-scale change initiative from TI-DS.

8. Working with Defense Ministries and Militaries

As well as working with defense companies, TI-DS started working with defense ministries. The initial connections came through the national chapters of TI, seeking to connect the mission of TI-DS with possible reform in their own MODs and militaries. Two countries, Colombia and Poland, were ready to engage on defense reform.

In 2005, Colombia's military and security forces lacked credibility with citizens, being seen—with much justification—as complicit in both the drugs war and the long-running Colombian conflicts with FARC (Revolutionary Armed Forces of Colombia—People's Army) and others. Those in charge of the army and the policy recognized that unless they tackled corruption in the military, and were seen to do so, they had no chance either of winning the two wars or of convincing the public that they were going to make progress. As part of a new strategy, they sought assistance from TI Colombia to review strategy, to monitor progress, to train senior officers, and to implement various other measures. TI Colombia in turn sought assistance from TI-DS. The planned purchase of airplanes that would improve drug interdiction went ahead,[24] but the integrity-pact did not lead to much change.

Nonetheless, the Colombian military made substantive, sustained change in the following years. One example from 2005 showed how to make progress. At the time, almost all defense acquisition was secret, even obviously nonsecret items like food and fuel. This was not necessarily for corruption reasons, more probably

[23] Shaw & Totman, *supra* note 9.

[24] Mark Pyman & Alan Waldron, *Practical Application of Defence Integrity Pacts: Experience in Colombia*, Transparency Int'l (Mar. 20, 2006), https://curbingcorruption.com/wp-content/uploads/2018/07/Pyman-Waldron-and-Avelia-2006-Practical-application-of-defense-integrity-pacts-Experience-in-Colombia.pdf; Mark Pyman & Alan Waldron, *An Independent Review of the Procurement of Military Items and the Use of Integrity Pacts in Those Contracts: Lessons that Can Be Applied in the International Use of Procurement Reviews and Integrity Pacts in Defence Based on work done for the Ministry of Defense of the Republic of Colombia*, Transparency Int'l (May 2006), https://curbingcorruption.com/wp-content/uploads/2018/07/TI-Defence-and-Transparencia-Colombia-2006-Defense-procurement-and-integrity-pacts-in-Colombia-Report-1.pdf; Mark Pyman & Alan Waldron, *Experience with Implementing a Defence Integrity Pact in Respect of the Procurement of Combat Aircraft for the Republic of Colombia*, Report 2, Transparency Int'l (2006), https://curbingcorruption.com/wp-content/uploads/2018/07/TI-defence-and-Transparencia-Colombia-2006-Defence-procurement-and-integrity-pacts-in-Colombia-Report-2-copy.pdf.

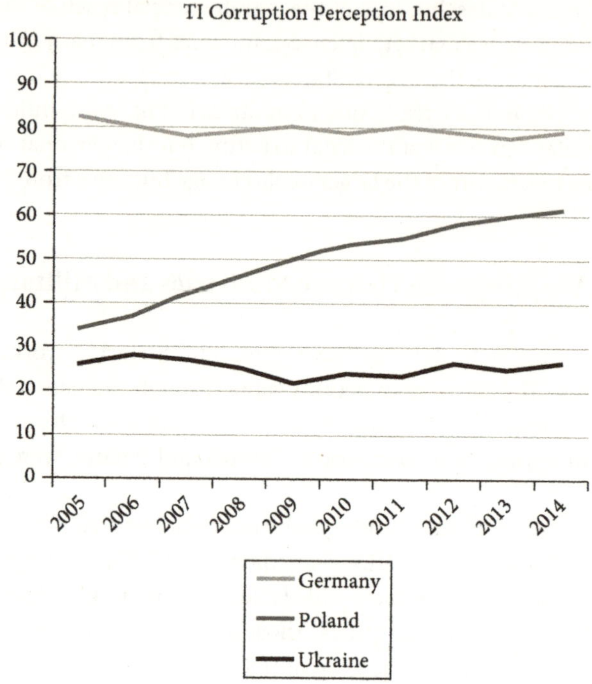

Figure 10.2 Improvement in Poland's CPI score between 2005 and 2014.

for bureaucratic convenience. But such nonaccountability quickly becomes corruption. The then-secretary-general made an administrative order changing this. From the next month, all defense procurement would be public, unless the secretary-general personally signed the requisition request to say otherwise. This change in practice had an immediate effect and over time contributed to changing the culture. Clearly, some things rightly stayed secret. But it was suddenly more perilous for your career to go to the chief of the MOD and argue that an order for one million pairs of trousers just had to be done on a secret basis to one supplier. The percentage of secret procurement dropped dramatically in the following three years. Since then, the Colombian military has made many changes, such as through their 2015 "Plan to Ensure Integrity and Prevention of Corruption."[25]

In 2005, TI's Corruption Perceptions Index (CPI) found Poland to be the most corrupt country in the European Union, yet by 2014 it had risen to fifteenth out of 28 EU member states (see Figure 10.2). This improvement was the result of a significant endeavor by the whole Polish government, but, interestingly, the

[25] Transparency Int'l Def. & Sec., *Regional Results Colombia: Government Defence Anti-Corruption Index* (Sept. 28, 2016), http://ti-defence.org/wp-content/uploads/2016/09/GI-Colombia-2016.pdf.

Polish Defense Ministry, with an energetic minister in charge, was at the forefront of change. TI-DS first worked with Poland on an integrity pact for small logistics aircraft for the Polish military. Like the Colombian example, it did not go smoothly, leading to the cancellation of the contract. At the same time Poland was undertaking many other defense reforms, notably through establishing an Integrity Unit within the MOD to provide independent oversight on all purchases.[26] That unit recently celebrated 10 years of operation.

Between 2006 and 2010, the number of national MODs working with TI-DS expanded as TI-DS joint working with NATO led to cooperation with additional NATO partner countries. After 2012, the number of countries expanded again as TI-DS's Government Defense Anti-Corruption Index (GI) raised the prominence of national defense corruption vulnerabilities. By 2015, some 60 countries were cooperating with TI-DS in the preparation of the country analyses that underpinned the GI.

9. Defense Corruption Issues—More than Procurement

TI-DS recognized early that public concern about defense corruption was not translating into detailed analysis of the defense corruption issues and efforts to solve them. To most people, inside and outside the defense sector worldwide, defense corruption meant dodgy defense procurement and little else. But, though corruption in defense procurement is always a relevant issue, it is often only one corruption problem among many.

TI-DS's early engagement with national MODs in the period 2006 to 2010 led to a broader and yet more granular understanding of what "defense corruption issues" were. Multiple conversations with MODs, militaries, and defense think tanks led to a set of 29 issues being defined, and a categorization of them under five headings: political corruption issues, finance-related issues, personnel-related issues, procurement-related issues, and corruption issues encountered on operations.[27]

Figure 10.3 shows the 29 issues and the five categories. Each issue is expressed in an abbreviated form for a very practical reason: an easy-to-digest one-page table of the issues found immediate popularity as the core discussion tool among groups of military officers or MOD officials. The issues reflect a full range of corruption problems likely to be found in a national defense establishment. Some,

[26] Mark Pyman & Maciej Wnuk, Reducing Corruption: Building Integrity in Defence and Security Institutions, unpublished paper presented at the Twelfth International Anti-Corruption Conference, Guatemala (Nov. 2006), https://curbingcorruption.com/wp-content/uploads/2018/07/Pyman-and-Wnuk-2006-IACC-Conference-Guatemala-Reducing-corruption-and-bulding-integrity-in-defense-and-security.pdf.

[27] Pyman, *supra* note 20.

ANALYSIS – 29 CORRUPTION RISKS

POLITICAL		PERSONNEL		PROCUREMENT	
Defense and Security Policy	10	Leadership Behavior	4	Technical Requirements / Specifications	7
Defense Budgets	7	Payroll, Promotions, Appointments, Rewards	5	Single Sourcing	2
Nexus of Defense & National Assets	1	Conscription	2	Agents/Brokers	1
Organized Crime	2	Salary Chain	2	Collusive Bidders	1
Control of Intelligence Services	2	Values & Standards	4	Financing Packages	1
Export Controls	1	Small Bribes	1	Offsets	3
FINANCE		**OPERATIONS**		Contract Award, Delivery	3
Asset Disposals	2	Disregard of Corruption in Country	2	Subcontractors	1
Secret Budgets	6	Corruption Within Mission	1	Seller Influence	1
Military - owned businesses	2	Contracts	1		
Illegal Private Enterprises	1	Private Security Companies	1		

Figure 10.3 One-page typology of defense sector corruption issues. The figures in each black box show the number of questions associated with that issue in the GI.

Id. at 10.

like corruption in defense policy, are broad; some are very particular, like corruption in financing packages supporting defense procurement. The typology table evolved and improved over the course of discussions in the first four or five countries but then stabilized. It has since been used by numerous countries as the basis for analysis of the issues in that country. The table forms the starting point for the GI questionnaire, in which the broader issues are explored in greater depth through more questions being asked; the number of questions is given by the numbers in the black boxes in Figure 10.3.

With the benefit of hindsight, this easy-to-read "typology" of issues was a critical step in developing the GI, in structuring the detailed country analyses, and in targeting more practical reform strategies. Equivalent typologies for other sectors will hopefully become equally common and useful.

10. Highlighting Corruption Issues through Research

There was limited analysis of defense corruption issues in 2004. Small research projects could have a disproportionate impact in raising understanding, and TI-DS found that that this was a constructive and evidence-based way to raise defense corruption issues with governments and companies in a constructive manner. Three examples are given here: exposure of the extent of noncompetitive procurement, the use of "offsets" in defense, and the opacity in defense budgets.

10.1. Noncompetitive Defense Procurement by MODs

Purchasing goods and services without competition, also known as noncompetitive or single-source procurement, can be done for good reasons: there may be a monopoly (such as buying Microsoft licenses) or there may be only one national state-owned enterprise, such as a shipyard. However, it can also be an excuse for corruption or at least become the start of a corrupt practice. The large extent of noncompetitive procurements in defense was not an issue in 2006, though some defense establishments knew about it. Early TI-DS research in 2006 revealed the remarkably large percentage of noncompetitive defense procurement in some countries, approximately 80 percent in Japan and the Czech Republic, for example, and 50 percent or more in the United Kingdom and the United States.[28] Such research made the scale of the problem

[28] Mark Pyman, Regina Wilson & Dominic Scott, *The Extent of Single sourcing in Defense Procurement and its Relevance as a Corruption Risk: A First Look*, 20(3) DEF. & PEACE ECON. 215 (2009).

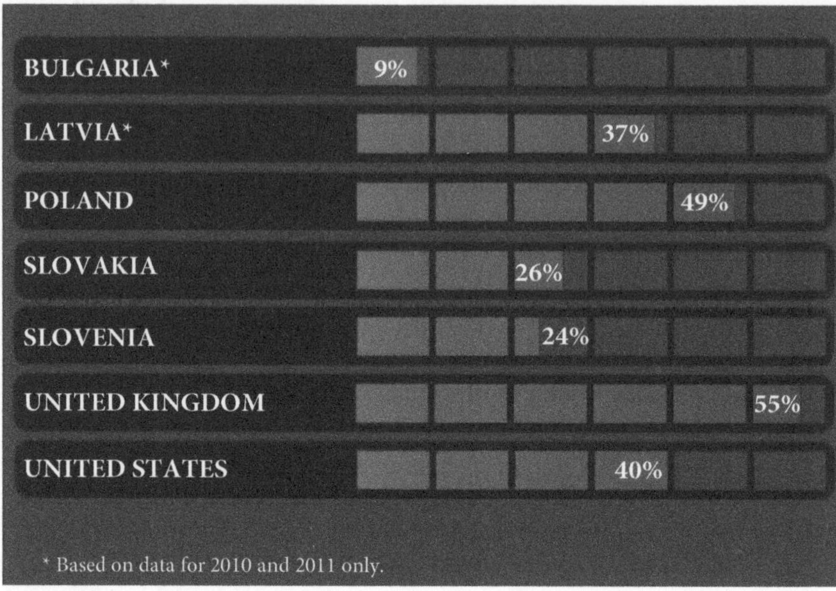

Figure 10.4 Single-source defense procurement as a percentage of total defense procurement 2010–2012.
Mustafa et al., *supra* note 31, at 4.

evident and stimulated discussion with MODs of the appropriate circumstances for single sourcing and how better to control it. By 2012, when TI-DS carried out a second round of similar research, national MODs were more aware of the problem. Figure 10.4, nonetheless, shows for defense procurement in seven countries during the period 2010–2012, how normal it was for at least a quarter of all defense procurement to be single source.[29] The low result in Bulgaria, only 9 percent single source, showed the effect of government action: it was a consequence of a new defense regulation prohibiting single-source procurement in defense except in narrowly defined circumstances.[30] The still-high figure for the United Kingdom (55%) galvanized a change of practice by the U.K. MOD for transparent open-book accounting by the winning company.

[29] Saad Mustafa et al., *Single Sourcing: A Multi-country Analysis of Non-competitive Defence Procurement*, Transparency Int'l Def. & Sec. (2014), https://ti-defence.org/wp-content/uploads/2016/03/140910-Single-Sourcing.pdf.

[30] Mark Pyman, *Monitoring, Evaluation and Learning about Defence Corruption Prevention, Avgustina Tzvetkova: An Interview with the former Deputy Defense Minister of Bulgaria 2009–2013*, Transparency Int'l (2015), https://curbingcorruption.com/wp-content/uploads/2018/07/Pyman-2013-An-interview-with-the-former-Deputy-Defence-Minister-of-Bulgaria-2009-to-2013.pdf.

10.2. The Dubious Use of "Offsets" in Defense Procurement

A second defense corruption issue that TI-DS publicized was the use of offsets. Offsets are a countertrade mechanism agreed between purchasing governments and supplying companies, requiring the latter to make additional investments, often unconnected to the main contract, as a condition of undertaking it. Offset programs consist of a package of contracts valued to a percentage of the main acquisition contract. These are not "marginal" additional investments. The value of offsets as a percentage of the main contract can exceed 100 percent of the value of the main contract. The large size of offset programs is one reason for concerns about corruption. The other reason was that MODs and contractors had between them kept the visibility of offsets very low. Largely unknown outside of the defense sector, offsets had been growing 40 percent or so per annum outside of Europe and the United States; outstanding offsets represented about $500 billion as of 2012.[31] TI-DS identified this problem, made it public, and has been active in campaigning against their use since 2008.[32]

10.3. Increasing the Transparency of Defense and Police Budgets

National military and police budgets are not only large, they are also usually hidden from public scrutiny and therefore easily diverted, subverted, or stolen. TI-DS published analyses of defense budget transparency,[33] and again used this research to press for change within MODs. The chart shown in Figure 10.5 is from an analysis in Burundi, a small, fragile state in Southeast Africa. It suffered a smaller version of the genocide that affected Rwanda in the 1990s and is still unstable. The data shows the different budgets of four ministries (agriculture, industry, interior, and justice) plus the police and the military in blue. The red and the green bars show the number of budget headings and the number of budget

[31] Avascent & Fleishman Hillard, *The Half Trillion Dollar Challenge. Designing Offset Strategies to Build Reputation, Promote Development* (2012), https://www.avascent.com/wp-content/uploads/2013/02/Avascent-Offsets-2-White-Paper.pdf.

[32] Ben Magahy, Francisco Vilhena da Cunha & Mark Pyman, *Defense Offsets: Addressing the Risks of Corruption and Raising Transparency*, Transparency Int'l Def. & Sec. (2012), https://ti-defence.org/wp-content/uploads/2016/03/1004_corruption_risk_offsets.pdf; Louise Fluker, Julia Muravska & Mark Pyman, *Due Diligence and Corruption Risk in Defence Industry Offset Programmes*, Transparency Int'l Def. & Sec. (2012), https://ti-defence.org/wp-content/uploads/2016/03/2012-02_DueDiligenceAndCorruptionRiskInOffsets.pdf.

[33] Mariya Gorbanova & Leah Wawro, *The Transparency of National Defence Budgets*, Transparency Int'l Def. & Sec. (2011), http://ti-defence.org/wp-content/uploads/2016/03/2011-10_Defence_Budgets_Transparency.pdf; Oliver Cover & Sazan Meran, *Watchdogs? The Quality of Legislative Oversight of Defence in 82 Countries*, Transparency Int'l Def. & Sec. (Sept. 2013), http://ti-defence.org/wp-content/uploads/2016/03/Watchdogs-low.pdf.

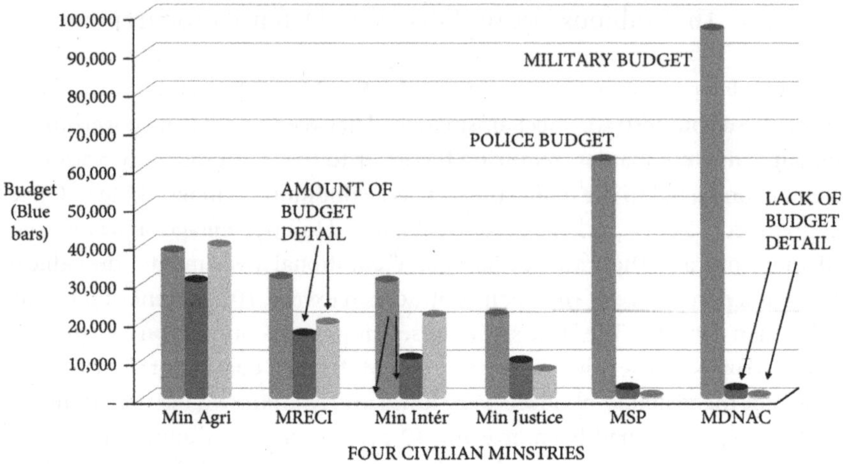

Figure 10.5 Burundi: National budget comparison for military, police, and four other ministries 2013 (blue). Plus number of budget headings (red) and number of budget line items (green).

Mark Pyman, *Addressing Corruption in Military Institutions*, 19(5) PUB. INTEGRITY 513 (2017)

lines, respectively for each ministry's budget (axis heading not shown). The extent to which the police and military budgets are way above the other four ministries depicted, yet have almost zero budget detail, is striking.[34] Working through details of this sort in meetings with the MOD and military in individual countries such as Burundi was a substantive way of proposing reforms to the presentation of that country's defense budget.[35]

10.4. Research on Other Defense Corruption Issues

TI-DS investigated current practice and potential reforms in numerous other corruption risk areas. Examples include performance and powers of Parliamentary Defense Committees,[36] military codes of conduct,[37] access to

[34] *Id.*

[35] Mark Pyman et al., *Études sur les Aspects de l'Intégrité de la Force de Défense Nationale du Burundi*, TRANSPARENCY INT'L DEF. & SEC. (2013), http://ti-defence.org/publications/etude-sur-les-aspects-de-lintegrite-de-la-force-de-defense-nationale-du-burundi/.

[36] Cover & Meran, *supra* note 36.

[37] Thomas Shipley, Anne-Christine Wegener & Mark Pyman, *Codes of Conduct in Defence Ministries and Armed Forces, What Makes a Good Code? A Multi-Country Study*, TRANSPARENCY INT'L DEF. & SEC. (2011), http://ti-defence.org/wp-content/uploads/2016/03/1106_CodesofCond uct.pdf.

information laws relating to defense,[38] peacekeeping,[39] defense higher education academies,[40] military-owned businesses,[41] and defense housing.[42] As always, the purpose was to examine the way that the problem manifested itself, put forward evidence, and propose possible reforms in ways that defense officials and military officers could recognize and respond to.

11. Creation of the Two Global Defense Indexes

The TI-DS strategy of "constructive engagement" with companies and governments was successful in opening many doors that might otherwise have stayed closed. TI-DS collaboration with global defense companies had led to the creation of the European Common Industry Standards for the prevention of corruption in the Aerospace and Defence sector (CIS) and to the creation of the global defense anti-corruption forum IFBEC. TI-DS was actively working with multiple national MODs on reforms, such as in Afghanistan, Bulgaria, Colombia, Georgia, Latvia, Lebanon, Norway, Saudi Arabia, and Ukraine.[43] However, TI-DS came to think that these actions, while positive, would probably not lead to large-scale change, because they were too friendly, focusing only on countries and companies that were willing to engage. Some way to identify the corruption vulnerabilities in countries and companies and to enable comparison between them was needed, if a suitably robust campaign or approach could be conceived and developed.

The team experimented with various approaches,[44] recruited an expert in technical index construction, and finally developed two methodologies. One enabled detailed analyses of corruption vulnerabilities in national defense establishments, using evidence-based answers to 77 questions, plus a system

[38] Ádám Földes, *Classified Information: A Review of Current Legislation Across 15 Countries and the EU*, Transparency Int'l Def. & Sec. (2014), https://ti-defence.org/wp-content/uploads/2016/03/140911-Classified-Information.pdf.

[39] Mark Pyman et al., *Corruption and Peacekeeping: Strengthening Peacekeeping and the United Nations*, Transparency Int'l Def. & Sec. (2013), https://ti-defence.org/wp-content/uploads/2016/03/2013-10_-Corruption-PK-report.pdf.

[40] Yuri Repilo & Serhiy Tarasov, *Corruption Treat assessments in Higher Military Education*, Transparency Int'l (2013), https://curbingcorruption.com/wp-content/uploads/2018/07/Repilo-and-Tarasov-2013-Corruption-threats-assessment-in-higher-military-education-in-Ukraine.pdf.

[41] Kevin Goh & Julia Muravska, *Military-owned Businesses: Corruption and Risk Reform*, Transparency Int'l Def. & Sec. (2012), https://ti-defence.org/wp-content/uploads/2016/03/2012-01_MilitaryOwnedBusinesses.pdf.

[42] NAKO, *The Independent Defence Anti-Corruption Committee of Ukraine, Poor Governance and Corruption in Ukraine's Defence Housing System: Risks and Recommendations*, Transparency Int'l Def. & Sec. (2018), http://ti-defence.org/wp-content/uploads/2018/10/NAKO_Housing_ENG_web-compressed.pdf.

[43] Pyman, *supra* note 38.

[44] Kirby Reiling, How to Assess Corruption in Defence: A Framework for Designing, Comparing and Interpreting Corruption Measurement Tools (2009) (unpublished M.A. thesis, Tufts University), https://dl.tufts.edu/concern/pdfs/k930c7919.

of peer review and checking. This led to detailed, quantified analyses for each country, plus the capability to compare in a "*Government* Defense Corruption Vulnerabilities Index" (GI). In parallel, TI-DS developed a way to analyze each defense company, using a similar semi-quantified methodology, reviewing the theory and practice of each company's ethics and compliance programs. This too led to quantification of the vulnerabilities for each company and a comparative ranking, entitled the "Defense *Companies* Corruption Vulnerability Index" (CI). Both methodologies were based not on subjective perceptions but on evidential answers to a set of questions.

11.1. The TI-DS Government Defense Anti-Corruption Index (GI)

In the GI methodology, each country is researched by an independent assessor using a standard set of 77 questions. These are not subjective questions but technical ones, such as "What percentage of the defense acquisition budget is secret?" or "What percentage of defense procurement is done single-source, without competition?" In each case, the extent of the government measures in place are compared against "model answers," with scores from 0 to 4. The question scores are first aggregated in the five risk areas: political risk, financial risk, personnel risk, operations risk, and procurement risk.

Each country assessment is independently reviewed by up to three peer reviewers. TI-DS also invites the government to conduct a review of the assessment and submit additional information and also invites the input of the Transparency International national chapter. Finally, the GI team reviews all of the answers for consistency and standardization. (See Figure 10.6.[45]) The result is a detailed report for each country, typically 50 pages long, containing the evidence in response to each question, the scores, the input from the peer reviewers, and any input from the government.

The overall score for the country varies from A (best) to F (worst), which is the score that is shown in the GI. The index was first produced for 82 countries in January 2013 and done again in 2015 for 132 countries. The results for 2015 are summarized in Figure 10.7.[46]

When the GI country analyses and index came out, they had an immediate impact. The first time, in 2013, there was much media coverage and protests

[45] Transparency Int'l Def. & Sec., *Government Defence Anti-Corruption Index, Methodology* (2019), https://government.defenceindex.org/methodology/ (last visited July 22, 2021).

[46] Tehmina Abbas et al., *NATO Members and Partner States: Government Defence Anti-Corruption Index*, Transparency Int'l Def. & Sec. 5 (2015), https://government.defenceindex.org/downloads/docs/GI-NATO-Results-web.pdf.

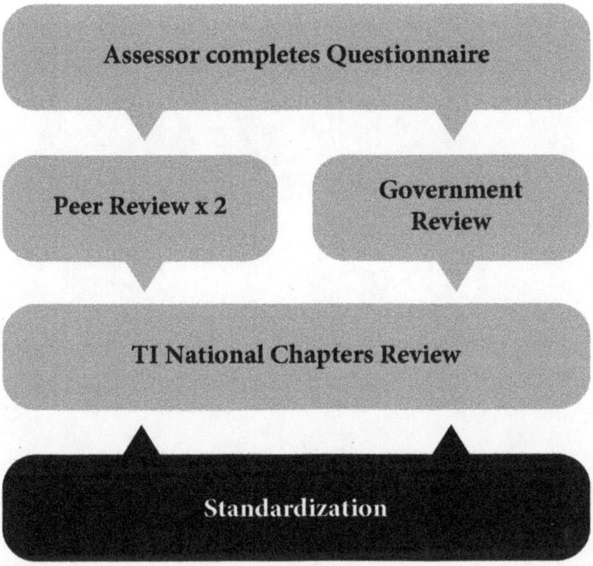

Figure 10.6 Process for assuring evidence gathered for the GI.
TRANSPARENCY INT'L DEF. & SEC., *An Assessment of Corruption Risks in Peacekeeping Operations* (2019), http://ti-defence.org/wp-content/uploads/2019/07/TIDS-CorruptionRisksinUNPeacekeeping.pdf.

from defense ministers, after rather little involvement by the MODs of the countries concerned; only eight countries had responded when asked for their input. The second time around, in 2015, most countries provided detailed responses and additional evidence. Not all responses were positive. TI-DS deemed that in some countries it was not possible to do any assessment without endangering the analysts. Other countries were vehement in their objections to the analysis without providing additional evidence. In some cases, TI-DS's analysis was shown to be flawed, despite the efforts at independent peer review.

This is a tool that is changing the way that defense ministries analyze and address their own corruption risks. TI-DS experience is that most MODs and the military, given a credible tool, are prepared to focus on how they can become more operationally effective, become less wasteful, and operate with higher integrity in defense procurement. Even if their motivation is to prove TI-DS wrong—and this certainly occurs—the country analysis and the index have the effect of focusing senior military attention on a subject that was previously taboo.

The tool can also be used to guide reform in individual MODs. Figure 10.8, for example, shows a sub-set of the results for Georgia in 2013. They asked to see only the "worst" results, where they had been scored 0, 1, or 2. The questions where

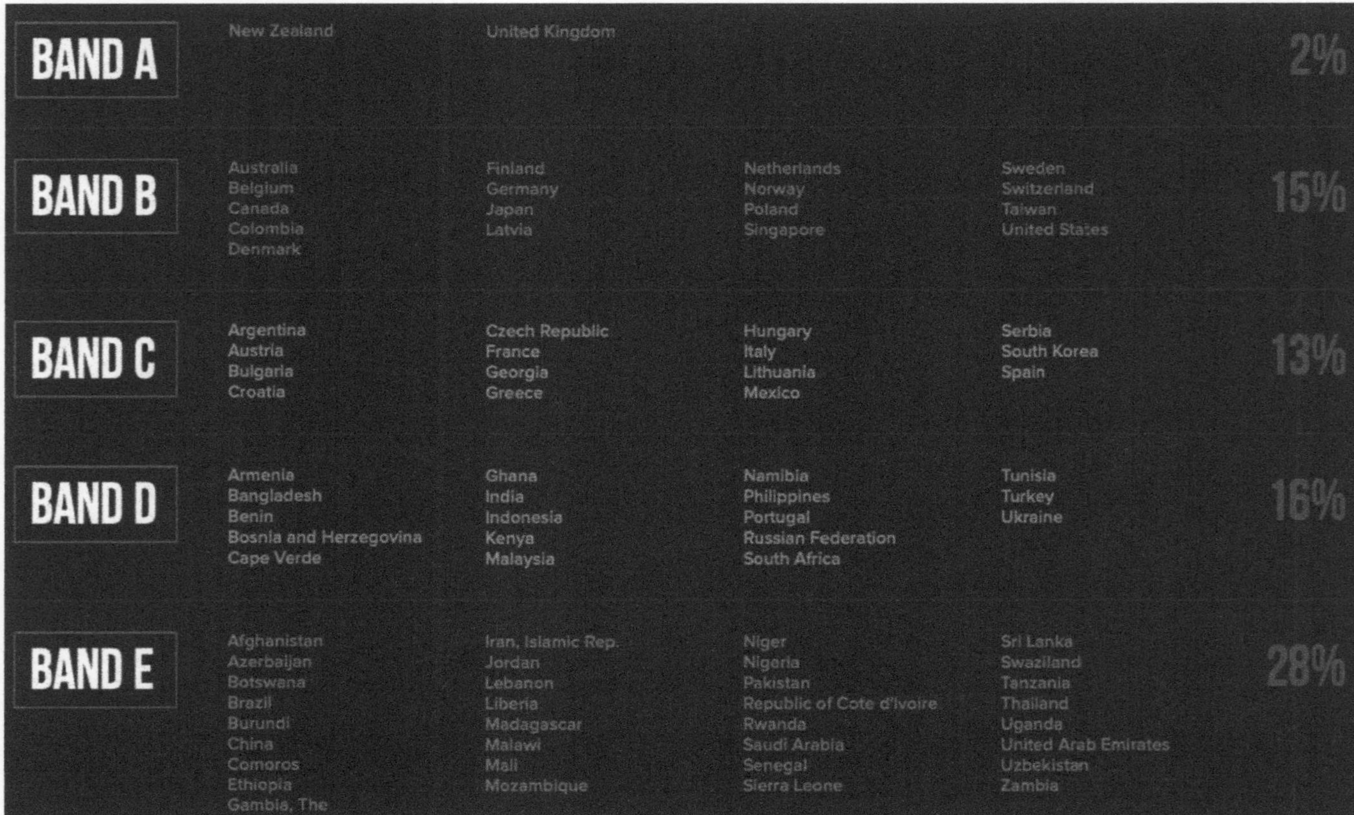

Figure 10.7 Summary of the Government Anti-Corruption Index results for 2015.
Id.

Georgia scored higher (i.e., 3 or 4) were omitted. The Georgians then worked through this list, together with TI-DS, to assess which issues merited action and which would be left for another time. The tool can also be used to compare categories and questions across countries, such as comparing across North African nations[47] or highlighting features such as the relative strength of parliamentary defense committees[48] or of NATO nations.[49]

With this country analysis methodology and index, TI-DS felt confident that they had the sort of benchmarks that could assist and catalyze progress, all the way from specific features of one defense ministry or defense company up to broader national or regional trends. The detailed reports, for each of the individual defense establishments, often 50 pages or more of detail, formed national defense leadership to review the corruption issues and discuss possible reform measures, whether with TI-DS, on their own or with others.

The GI is standing the test of time. Now renamed the Government Defence Integrity Index (GDI), data was most recently updated on a rolling basis between October 2019 and late 2021.[50]

11.2. Defense Companies Anti-Corruption Index (CI)

Having worked with the defense companies from 2004 to 2010, it was clear to TI-DS that some companies were largely sincere, with good programs in place. On the other hand, there were still thousands of companies with minimal programs and many who had sophisticated-looking programs but little substance or intent behind them. The question was how to provide credible public evidence of which were which. There were a few company corruption vulnerability indexes that had been done, notably by TI.[51] However, these had major disadvantages for the defense sector.

First, they weren't detailed enough, being closed yes/no questions rather than the sort of objective questions about the extent to which a measure was being applied. TI-DS held that in terms of methodology, it was essential to apply the same level of objective questions and answers for each company analysis. Second, there were various issues that were particular to defense that were not covered by general index questions (e.g., offsets, secrecy). Third, the defense companies

47 Pyman, *supra* note 38.

48 Cover & Meran, *supra* note 36.

49 Abbas et al., *supra* note 51.

50 Transparency Int'l, *Government Defence Integrity Index 2020*, https://ti-defence.org/gdi/ (last visited Nov. 16, 2021).

51 Transparency Int'l, *Transparency in Corporate Reporting: Assessing the World's Largest Companies* (2012), https://www.transparency.org/whatwedo/publication/transparency_in_corporate_reporting_assessing_the_worlds_largest_companies.

DETAILED RESULTS - GEORGIA 0,1, AND 2 SCORES

POLITICAL	
Defence Committee	2
Defence Policy Debated	2
CSO Engagement	1
Public Debate	1
AC Policy	2
AC Institutions	1
Risk Assessments	0
Acquisition Planning	0
Budget Transparency & Detail	2
Budget Scrutiny	2
Budget Publicly Available	1
Defence Income	1
Internal Audit	2
External Audit	2
Intelligence Services Recruitment	1
Export Controls	2

FINANCE	
Asset Disposal Controls	2
Asset Disposal Scrutiny	1
Percentage Secret Spending	0
Legislative Access to Information	2
Secret Program Auditing	0
Information Classification	1
Mil. Owned Businesses Exist	2
Mil. Owned Business Scrutiny	2

PERSONNEL	
Public Commitment	0
Measures for Corrupt Personnel	2
Whistleblowing	1
Special Attention to Sensitive Personnel	1
Objective Appointments	2
Objective Promotions	0
Bribery to Avoid Compulsory Conscription	2
Bribery for Preferred Postings	1
Code of Conduct Coverage	2
Code of Conduct Breaches Addressed	0
AC Training	1
Prosecution Outcomes Transparent	1

OPERATIONS	
Military Doctrine	1
Operational Training	1
AC Moniotring	1
Controls on Contracting	0
Private Military Contractors	2

PROCUREMENT	
Legislation	1
Transparent Procurement Cycle	1
Oversight Mechanisms	1
Purchases Disclosed	1
Standards Expected of Companies	0
Strategy Drives Requirements	1
Requirements Quantified	0
Open Competition v. Single-Sourcing	1
Tender Board Controls	1
Anti-Collusion Controls	1
Procurement Staff Training	1
Complaint Mechanisms for Firms	2
Sanctions for Corruption	2
Controls of Agents	0
Transparency of Financing Packages	0
Subsidiaries / Sub-Contractors	0
Political Influence	1

Figure 10.8 Follow-up of the GI 2013 results for Georgia. This working table shows those issues with greatest corruption vulnerability, defined as being those with a low index score of 0, 1, or 2.

argued vigorously that there were policies and procedures that were not public and that TI-DS would miss the inside knowledge if its analyses were limited to published information. Restrictions on the release of certain information raised the most controversial issue: Could an NGO access and evaluate this information without having to agree to restrictive, and therefore unacceptable, confidentiality clauses?

TI-DS developed its methodology in a way that answered thoroughly all three questions, and the "private" information—which was used to create a sort of shadow index—was the most important of all in persuading the defense companies to work with the index and to support its methodology (though starting in 2019, TI-DS discontinued such "internal knowledge" part of the methodology).

There are 41 questions in the CI, covering what TI-DS regards as the basic capabilities that a global defense company should have in place, divided into five categories: leadership, governance, and organization; risk management; company policies and codes; training; and personnel and helplines. For every question, TI-DS provides guidance notes and detailed scoring criteria on what evidence is required to achieve a particular score. The results are shown for each question, then aggregated for each of the five categories. The results for the whole company are ranked into one of six bands—from A (the best) to F (the worst), based on their total scores. Figure 10.9 shows the results in each category for an alphabetical sample of the companies.[52]

For example, as shown in Figure 10.9, an extract from the defense company results list, Patria Oyj, a Finnish armored vehicle company, scored very poorly in 2012 (Band F), but had improved significantly on substance and transparency by 2015 (to Band C, based on public information and to Band B if internal information is also considered).

It was clear from comparing the 2015 analysis with the 2012 analysis that many companies in the industry were paying closer attention to corruption risks. Despite increasing the rigor of the questionnaire—five questions were more rigorous, the scoring criteria for 14 questions were tougher, and detailed modeling indicated that the 2015 CI was up to 7 percent more demanding than 2012—there was significant net improvement in the results of the second CI.[53] This improvement occurred both among the companies that already had substantive

[52] Katie Fish et al., *Defense Companies Anti-Corruption Index 2015*, Transparency Int'l Def. & Sec. (2015), http://companies.defenceindex.org/docs/2015%20Defence%20Companies%20Anti-Corruption%20Index.pdf.

[53] Mark Pyman, Katherine Dixon & Katie Fish, Address at Transparency International's Launch of Defence Companies Anti-Corruption Index 2015, London (May 2015), https://curbingcorruption.com/wp-content/uploads/2018/10/150430-Pyman-Dixon-and-Fish-Defence-Companies-Index-2015-launch-London.pdf.

COMPANY	COUNTRY	2012	2015	LEADERSHIP, GOVERNANCE, & ORGANIZATION	RISK MANAGEMENT	COMPANY POLICIES & CODES	TRAINING	PERSONNEL & HELPLINES
Navantia, S.A.	Spain (Europe & Central Asia)	F	E	0%	0%	58%	0%	36%
Navistar International Corporation	USA (North America)	D	D	30%	10%	63%	0%	50%
NEC Corporation	Japan (Asia Pacific)	D	C	60%	40%	42%	60%	64%
incl. internal information		-	B	65%	90%	79%	70%	86%
Nexter Group	France (Europe & Central Asia)	F	F	10%	0%	0%	0%	0%
Northrop Grumman Corporation	USA (North America)	B	B	75%	43%	92%	80%	86%
Oshkosh Corporation	USA (North America)	C	C	35%	29%	63%	40%	79%
incl. internal information		-	C	40%	50%	75%	80%	79%
Otokar Otomotiv ve Savunma Sanayi A.Ş	Turkey (Europe & Central Asia)	F	D	30%	10%	54%	0%	50%
Pakistan Ordnance Factories	Pakistan (Asia Pacific)	F	F	0%	0%	0%	0%	0%
Patria Oyj	Finland (Europe & Central Asia)	F	C	50%	14%	63%	60%	57%
incl. internal information		-	B	65%	79%	79%	70%	71%
Polish Defence Holding	Poland (Europe & Central Asia)	F	F	0%	0%	0%	0%	0%
Poongsan Corporation	South Korea (Asia Pacific)	F	F	0%	0%	0%	0%	0%
Precision Castparts Corp.	USA (North America)	-	D	25%	10%	63%	10%	79%
PT Dirgantara Indonesia (Indonesian Aerospace)	Indonesia (Asia Pacific)	-	F	0%	0%	0%	0%	0%
QinetiQ Group Plc	UK (Europe & Central Asia)	C	B	60%	60%	63%	90%	93%
incl. internal information		-	A	95%	100%	83%	90%	93%

Figure 10.9 Extract from the Defense Companies Anti-Corruption Index results for defense companies 2015. *Id.*

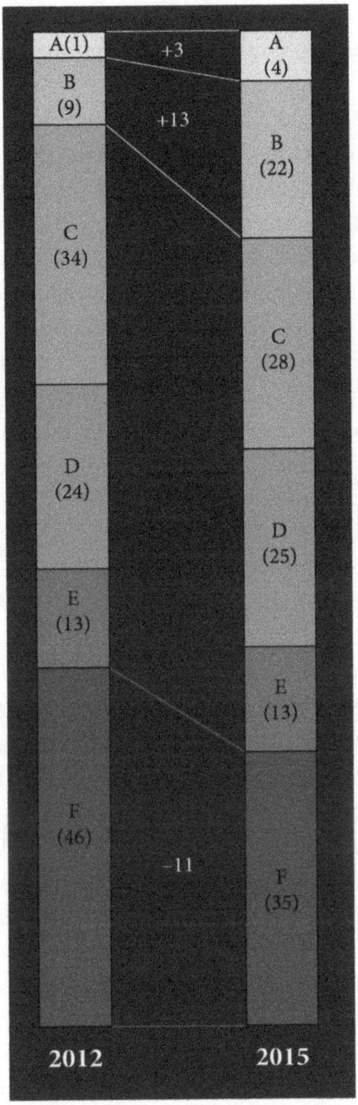

Figure 10.10 Comparison of companies results 2015 versus 2012.
Fish et al., *supra* note 56, at 14.

anti-corruption programs in place in 2012 and those that showed almost no evidence of anti-corruption programs. Figure 10.10 shows the improvement. Such a metric, being able to compare the relative quality of compliance programs over time, is a powerful tool to drive and encourage sector improvement among the corporates in the sector.

TI-DS developed the analysis further by noting the best practices in each of the five categories[54] and producing a detailed guide to 104 examples across the industry.[55]

Does the CI have a significant impact? Anecdotally, there has been much feedback from numerous companies on the beneficial effect of the index. It encouraged the dissemination and application of best practices. Sometimes it enabled the integrity unit at the company to have more influence, usually through presenting credible evidence to their board that others view the company poorly. It is also evident that some companies were visibly trying to game the index, changing the wording of their policies and procedures to match that of better-ranked companies while not noticeably changing actual behavior. Ministries and regulators have also appreciated the CI, both where it identifies deficiencies and through giving feedback where TI-DS has overstated the case for a company. Overall, independent analyses and indexes, like this one, have a powerful effect in "moving the dial" of acceptable behavior.

12. The Case of the Engagement with Afghanistan

In the defense sector, tackling corruption on "operations" means addressing corruption either during war or during military deployments overseas. The wars in Iraq and Afghanistan created multiple corruption challenges, both inside the military forces, whether of the nation concerned or of the supporting deployed nations, and also in the way that military forces reacted to and were affected by endemic corruption. The challenges showed up in that the Western forces were quite unprepared for such high-corruption environments. Today, for example, there is a consensus that corruption significantly damaged the International Security Assistance Force (ISAF) mission. But almost no one believed this until about 2009.

By 2009, ISAF and the U.S. military were sufficiently concerned about the impact of corruption on the war that they developed various task forces for tackling corruption issues. The principal task force, named Shafafiyat (which means "transparency" in Dari), was instrumental in placing countercorruption more at the center of ISAF's mission than it had been before under the early leadership of General H.R. McMaster. From then on, ISAF commanders such as Generals

[54] Tiffany Clark & Mark Pyman, *Raising the Bar: Good Anti-Corruption Practices in Defence Companies, Part I: Seven Practices that Distinguish the Best*, Transparency Int'l Def. & Sec. (June 2013), https://curbingcorruption.com/wp-content/uploads/2018/07/Clarke-and-Pyman-2013-Raising-the-bar-Good-anti-corruption-practices-in-defence-companies-Part-I.pdf.

[55] Tiffany Clark & Mark Pyman, *Raising the Bar: Good Anti-corruption Practices in Defence Companies, Part II: 104 Examples of Good Defense Company Practice*, Transparency Int'l Def. & Sec. (June 2013), https://curbingcorruption.com/wp-content/uploads/2018/07/Clarke-and-Pyman-2013-Raising-the-Bar-Part-II-104-examples-of-good-defence-company-practice.pdf.

John Allen and David Petraeus and others were increasingly frank about the effect of corruption on the mission and spoke publicly about the issue.

TI-DS developed guidance in these areas, training militaries and publishing various guidance documents and assisting in developing military doctrine. The TI-DS report "Corruption Threats and International (military) Missions—Practical Guidance for Leaders" outlined the 10 corrupt pathways that would be encountered and gave guidance on how national military forces preparing for international missions should be organized and trained to be prepared for them.[56] The NATO Joint Analysis and Lessons Learned Centre also evaluated the NATO approach to tackling corruption.[57] TI-DS also carried out reviews of ISAF's effectiveness in relation to tackling corruption.[58]

TI-DS also engaged with the Afghanistan Security and Defense Forces, facilitating a "leadership day" in 2009 on corruption priorities with the Afghan military leadership,[59] and gradually expanding to encompass corruption-prevention training courses for the Afghan military,[60] organizing conferences on how to better deal with corruption in fragile states,[61] researching corruption issues in war zones,[62] and analyzing the reasons why ISAF was so slow to recognize the corruption threat to the mission.[63] However, while such inputs were well

[56] Mark Pyman et al., *Corruption Threats and International Missions: Practical Guidance for Leaders*, Transparency Int'l Def. & Sec. (Sept. 2014), https://ti-defence.org/wp-content/uploads/2016/03/140930-Corruption-Threats-International-Missions.pdf.

[57] NATO Joint Analysis & Lessons Learned Centre, *Counter- and Anti-Corruption: Theory and Practice from NATO Operations* (May 10, 2013), https://www.jallc.nato.int/application/files/7816/0261/3252/factsheet_corruption.pdf.

[58] Mark Pyman & Alan Waldron, *Improving Transparency Accountability and Counter-Corruption (TACC) in the ANSF, MoD and MOI*, Transparency Int'l Def. & Sec. (Oct. 2, 2013), https://curbingcorruption.com/wp-content/uploads/2018/07/Pyman-and-Waldron-2013-Afghanistan-Improving-transparency-accountability-and-counter-corruption-TACC-in-the-Afghan-ANSF-MOD-and-MOI.pdf.

[59] Pyman, *supra* note 38.

[60] James Cohen, Mark Pyman & Alan Waldron, *Training the Military and Defence Security Officials in Understanding and Preventing Corruption*, Transparency Int'l Def. & Sec. (Feb. 2013), https://ti-defence.org/wp-content/uploads/2016/03/2013-02_TrainingMilitaryandDefence.pdf; James Cohen, Mohammad Isaqzadeh & Alan Waldron, *Anti-Corruption Training Course in Kabul for Afghan MOD and MOI Senior Officers*, Transparency Int'l (Feb. 2013), https://ti-defence.org/wp-content/uploads/2016/03/2013-02_AfghanTraining_Report.pdf.

[61] Transparency Int'l Def. & Sec., *Afghanistan in Transition: Governance, Counter-Corruption and Reshaping Priorities* (2011), https://curbingcorruption.com/wp-content/uploads/2018/07/TI-Defence-with-RUSI-and-KAF-2011-Afghanistan-in-Transition-Governance-Counter-Corruption-and-Development-Re-Shaping-Priorities-for-2015-and-Beyond-copy.pdf.

[62] Kyle Alexander et al., *Overview of Political Economy, Contracting and Corruption in Afghanistan: A Case Study in Kandahar*, Transparency Int'l Def. & Sec. (Dec. 2012), https://ti-defence.org/wp-content/uploads/2018/03/Overview-of-political-economy-contracting-and-corruption-in-Afghanistan-A-case-study-in-Kandahar.pdf; Mark Pyman et al., *Corruption as a Threat to Stability and Peace*, Transparency Int'l Def. & Sec. (2014), https://ti-defence.org/wp-content/uploads/2016/03/2014-01_CorruptionThreatStabilityPeace.pdf.

[63] Mark Pyman, *Corruption: Lessons from the International Experience in Afghanistan*, Transparency Int'l Def. & Sec. (2015), http://ti-defence.org/wp-content/uploads/2016/03/150217-Corruption-Lessons-from-the-international-mission-in-Afghanistan.pdf.

received, they were not at a large enough scale to have more than a small impact. For obvious reasons, it was hard for TI-DS researchers to gain access to a war zone. Even when international forces were supportive of the TI initiatives, finding seats for a civilian NGO on military flights was a low priority.

The other major influence in the way that the international community tackled corruption in Afghanistan was the organization of the Special Inspector General for Afghanistan.[64] After a hesitant start in 2009–2011, this office became a powerful independent voice under Inspector General John Sopko, seeking out corruption in the way that funds were used for the reconstruction of Afghanistan and being ready to hold the government and the military accountable, as well as pursuing corruption by U.S. companies.[65]

In terms of the whole defense sector, these setbacks in Iraq and Afghanistan led to broader agreement that corruption issues in fragile states and during military operations were central to military strategy and security policymaking. But such recognition has yet to be incorporated into changes to military doctrine or training.

13. Fragile States, Peacekeeping, and Security Policy

As corruption-related experience from Afghanistan grew, so the importance of recognizing corruption in other fragile states grew. TI-DS had been involved with the Ukrainian military and the Ukrainian security services since 2009. Together they trained hundreds of Ukrainian colonels in corruption prevention. TI-DS also took ten Ukrainian colonels and civilians on three-month secondments to the TI-DS offices in London, so that they can form the core of an anti-corruption unit in the Ukrainian MOD, subsequently established as BITEC. One Ukrainian who worked for the NATO Liaison Office in Kiev and was on one of the three-month secondment to the TI-DS offices in London put it well: "Corruption can be just as deadly as bullets." He had received his call-up papers and immediately faced a dilemma. He could either pay $2,500 to get a medical certificate saying that he was unfit to fight. Or he could pay $2,500 to buy a functioning AK-47, body armor, night sights, and a first-aid kit. He needed to do this because all the money for the "official" equipment from the MOD had been stolen by the Ukrainian military hierarchy.

In countries like Ukraine, corruption is not a pathology or some sort of deviant behavior from the normal: it has been the norm. For the armed forces, who

[64] Special Inspector Gen. for Afghanistan Reconstruction, https://www.sigar.mil.

[65] John F. Sopko, Special Inspector for Afghanistan Reconstruction, Address at the U.S. Naval Academy: Lessons from Afghanistan's Reconstruction: 2001–2019 (Jan. 17, 2019), https://www.sigar.mil/pdf/speeches/SIGAR_USNA_Speech_2019-01-17.pdf.

have been no more and no less corrupt than the rest of the state, this sets up tough issues. The Ukraine MOD and military have put much effort into tackling this, and the performance of the Ukrainian military in the current war with Russia suggests that these efforts have been effective.

Defense assistance to fragile states, a core element of the security policy of numerous countries and organizations, is a second challenging area.[66] Such assistance is easily diverted or stolen on the ground. In a study of security assistance to Mali between 2001 and 2011, when there was a coup, TI-DS found that people on the ground knew full well the weakness of the Malian army, while those providing the assistance, despite good intentions, were absolutely not focused on the corruption threat. Andrew Lebovich said in *Foreign Policy* that "[t]he weakness of the Malian army . . . came as little surprise to anyone who had been watching the steady erosion of state institutions, largely as a result of widespread corruption."[67] The international training missions were no match for those wishing to divert—and indeed subvert—the assistance and use it to support the 2012 coup. Former U.S. Africa Command Commanding General Carter Ham observed that "[w]e were focusing our training almost exclusively on tactical or technical matters. . . . We didn't spend probably the requisite time focusing on values, ethics and a military ethos."[68]

Peacekeeping was a related area where corruption was little examined and routinely passed over. TI-DS's first report on the subject in 2013 led to a very defensive reaction from the UN Department of Peacekeeping Operations (UNDPKO).[69] Since then, UNDPKO and the United Nations more generally are more engaged and attentive to addressing the corruption issues that arise during peacekeeping missions.[70]

On the other hand, all is not negative. The core purpose of the anti-corruption community is to give hope to reformers and to help solve the problems in fragile states, not simply to list the endless difficulties. Figure 10.11 shows the "Control of Corruption" metric from the World Bank for a number of fragile and conflict countries.[71] For this particular group of countries, the graph shows that control

[66] Pyman et al., *supra* note 68.

[67] Andrew Lebovich, *Mali's Bad Trip: Field Notes from the West African Drug Trade*, Foreign Pol'y (Mar. 15, 2013), https://foreignpolicy.com/2013/03/15/malis-bad-trip/.

[68] *Mali Crisis: US Admits Mistakes in Training Local Troops*, BBC News (Jan. 25, 2013), https://www.bbc.com/news/world-africa-21195371.

[69] Pyman et al., *supra* note 43.

[70] Transparency Int'l Def. & Sec., *An Assessment of Corruption Risks in Peacekeeping Operations* (2019), http://ti-defence.org/wp-content/uploads/2019/07/TIDS-CorruptionRisksinUNPeacekeeping.pdf.

[71] RUSI, Transparency Int'l Def. & Sec. & Konrad Adenauer Found., *Afghanistan in Transition: Governance, Counter-Corruption, and Reshaping Priorities for 2015 and Beyond*, Transparency Int'l (May 13, 2011), https://www.transparency.org/files/content/pressrelease/20110513_UK_Afghanistan_in_transition_EN.pdf.

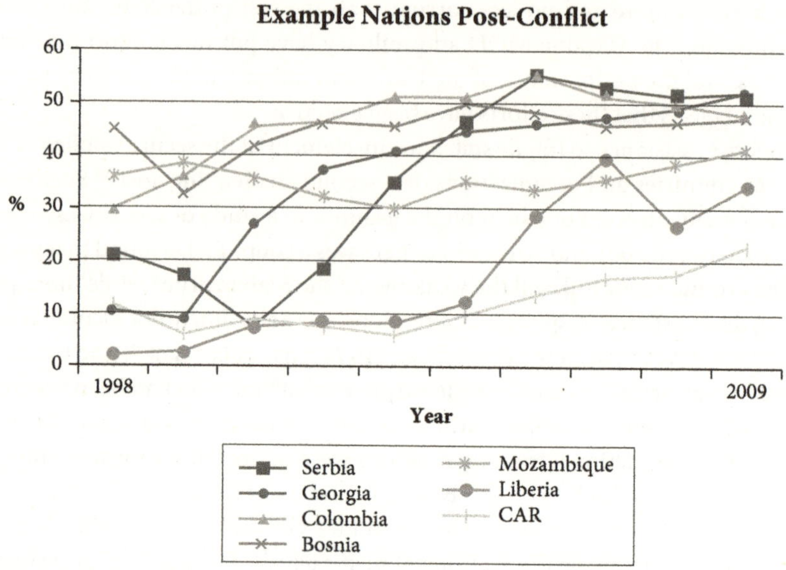

Figure 10.11 "Control of Corruption" metric from the World Bank for post-conflict countries in the 10-year period 1998–2008. Figure shows only those companies that improved on this metric.

of corruption was improving in the 10-year period of 1998–2008. This figure does not claim to be objective—the same data source shows the worsening control of corruption for another group of fragile states—but it does nonetheless indicate that progress is possible.

Finally, TI-DS, working together with DFID, was active in the multicountry efforts to develop and implement the Arms Trade Treaty (ATT), whose purpose is to promote responsibility in the international transfers of conventional arms and which entered into force in 2014. TI-DS worked with representatives of 75 states to influence their views and to ensure that attention to corruption was included in the treaty. As the external evaluation of TI-DS points out: "The single most important is expertise. Many—perhaps most—of the diplomats taking part in the conference were generalists. . . . Rob Wright, one of the two TI-DS representatives at the conference, had long professional experience precisely in the field of export controls."[72] Despite the efforts of TI-DS and some state delegations, most

[72] Jups Kluyskens et al., *Independent Progress Review (IPR) of the DFID Programme Partnership Arrangement (PPA), 2011–2012*, Channel Research 19–22 (Oct. 13, 2012), http://kluyskensconsulting.com/wp-content/uploads/2018/07/121015-Channel-Research-TI-DSP-CHASE-PPA-IPR-Final-Report.pdf (study conducted on behalf of Transparency International).

notably the Dutch delegation, the ATT does not contain an explicit provision on corruption. The ATT indeed has many weaknesses. Nonetheless, perhaps like the industry ethics forums, even modest collective efforts help to change international norms and build platforms for change.

14. Budgets and Donors

The U.S. DoD and the Pentagon had accepted the introduction (and costs) of ethics and compliance systems in U.S. companies after the U.S. scandals of the 1970s and 1980s. This meant that there was institutional corruption prevention machinery in place in the companies that could be built on. However, there was no such incentive for the MODs in other countries. They tended to have few anti-corruption mechanisms in place and rarely did they have an integrity unit. Those that did have such units, such as in the MODs of Poland and Colombia, initially tended to have only a small staff (though in Poland and Colombia they were remarkably effective). For TI-DS, the funding came largely from DFID in the form of core funding. Though this was subject to competitive rebidding at the end of each contract (variously of 6, 12, 18, and 36 months duration) and periodic evaluation, it funded the team and their chosen priorities. Crucially, the funding for these TI-DS reviews was not project-based. The external evaluation done on TI-DS in 2012 summarized the benefits of this form of funding:

- The PPA [DFID funding mechanism] has allowed TI-DS to work systematically on all four designated outcomes[.]
- TI-DS has been able to conduct research, publish papers and develop practical tools which constitute an important source for building concrete reforms in the defence and security sectors.
- Training is a key activity that can be adapted and introduced in stable, conflict affected and fragile states. It has the potential to raise the scope and impact of the programme.
- TI-DS is going through an extended process of consolidating and disseminating learning experience of defence and security reforms that are and are not effective.
- In MEKANIC, TI-DS has developed an innovative learning tool that is unique to the organisation and that other NGOs do not have.

The first particular advantage of the DFID-funding mechanism, as distinct from other funding mechanisms, is that it has provided TI-DS with a financial basis from which to conduct strategic development work, notably the work on the GI and CI indexes. These provide a structured basis for comparison between different government entities and companies and, in doing so, establish an agenda for reform.[73]

15. Estimating the Impact

In the last 20 years, considerable time and effort have been invested in addressing corruption in the defense sector, and TI-DS has played a significant role in this. But has there been an appreciable improvement? Or is this defense sector story yet another saga of "great expectations and humble results," to quote one expert on initiatives to tackle corruption.[74]

Evidence is available that the improvement in the defense sector has been significant. The data comes from one of TI's more general anti-corruption indexes, rather than from the two defense indexes. In the "Bribe Payers Index (BPI)" operated by TI from 1999 to 2011 (though not since), the BPI asks a sample of businessmen around the world about their experience of bribery in different national markets and different industry sectors. In 2002, the arms and defense sector scored as the second worst, with only the public works/construction sector being worse.[75] However, by 2008, though public works/construction was still ranked the worst, arms and defense was being rated more highly—13 sectors higher than public works, with sectors like oil and gas, pharmaceuticals, forestry, and telecoms being seen as more prone to bribery by businessmen.[76] In 2011, public works was once again the worst sector; this time the arms and defense sector were 10 sectors better (though the list of sectors covered was not the same), with a similar score as in 2008.[77]

There is also evidence from the GI and CI of variations over time. For defense companies, the aggregate improvement across all 127 companies in the CI is shown in Figure 10.10. That improvement can be seen company by company in Figure 10.12, along with the companies whose compliance programs appeared to have diminished in quality over the period. A new 2020 iteration of the index, now renamed the Defence Companies Index on Anti-Corruption and Corporate Transparency (CDI), was published in 2021 (delayed due to COVID).[78]

[73] *Id.* at 45–46.

[74] Alina Mungiu-Pippidi, The Quest for Good Governance: How Societies Develop Control of Corruption 207 (2015).

[75] Transparency Int'l, *Bribe Payers Index 2002* (May 13, 2002), https://www.transparency.org/news/pressrelease/transparency_international_releases_new_bribe_payers_index_bpi_2002.

[76] Transparency Int'l, *Bribe Payers Index 2008*, at 11 (Dec. 2008), https://images.transparencycdn.org/images/2008_BPI_EN.pdf.

[77] Transparency Int'l, *Bribe Payers Index 2011*, at 15 (Oct. 2011), https://issuu.com/transparencyinternational/docs/bribe_payers_index_2011?mode=window&backgroundColor=%23222222.

[78] Transparency Int'l Def. & Sec., *Defence Companies Index 2020* (2021), https://ti-defence.org/what-we-do/industry-integrity/defence-companies-index/.

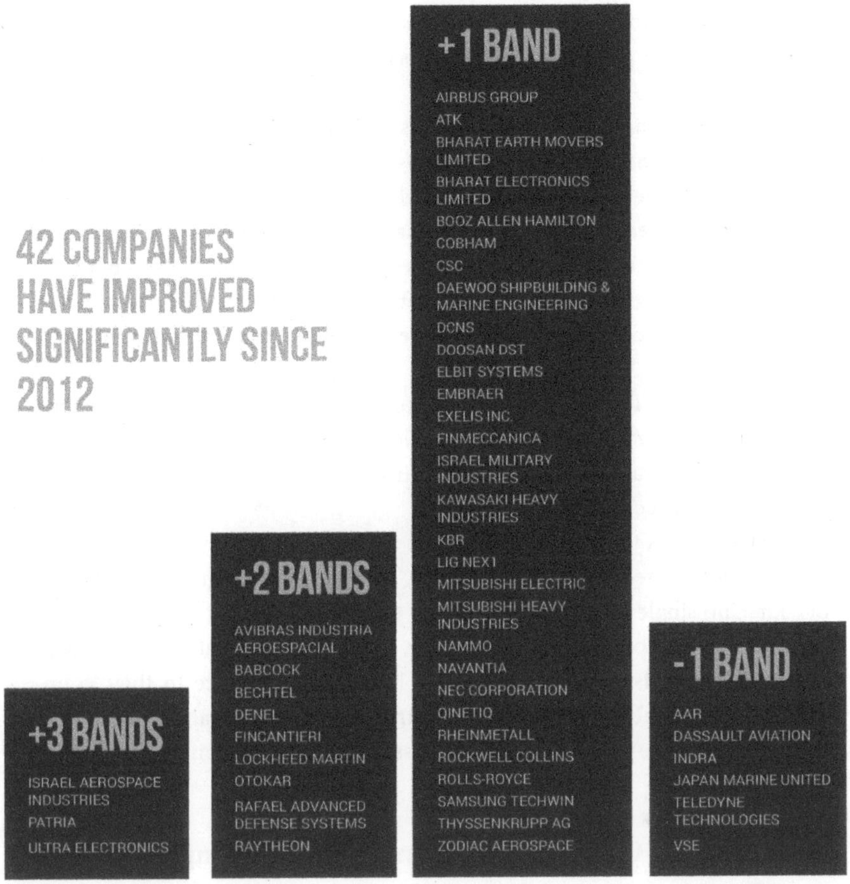

Figure 10.12 Defense companies' change in CI score between 2012 and 2015.
Fish et al., *supra* note 56, at 14.

One of the original defense company executives who worked to set up European Common Industry Standards for the Prevention of Corruption in the Aerospace and Defence Sector (CIS) and IFBEC, when asked to comment on this chapter, added that some of the defense companies used the CI as a basis for discussions with other defense companies to get additional information on anti-corruption commitment before working with them as partners.

Another source of evidence comes from the external evaluations carried out on TI-DS by DFID. DFID commissioned independent evaluations from time to time, thus providing insights into both the impact of TI-DS and the opinions of multiple stakeholders. The review team in the 2012 evaluation point to three themes of the TI-DS program that led to its impact:

> The first, and perhaps most important, is its holistic nature. . . . The defence sector—and defence sector corruption—is quintessentially interconnected, nationally and internationally. TI-DS addresses the different ingredients that make up these interconnections, individually and as part of a wider picture. In particular, it engages with both companies and governments, and in both developed and emerging economies. It is hard to think of any other organisation in any sector that can draw together these different ingredients with the same authority.
>
> The second is TI-DS's approach of constructive but critical engagement. As one of our interviewees put it, some NGOs simply issue criticism from the sidelines. By contrast, TI-DS is seen as being much more constructive. It offers solutions, not just criticism.
>
> The third is its technical expertise. At the outset of the evaluation, one of the interviewees requested us to identify TI-DS's "magic ingredient". There is of course no single ingredient, but one of the program's most distinctive characteristics is the combination of younger, highly talented staff members with older professionals who can draw on a lifetime's experience in their countries' defence establishments and ministries. Again and again, interviewees commented on the power and effectiveness of this combination.[79]

16. Conclusion: Making Sense of Change

There are numerous changes going on every day in the defense sector, both positive and negative, in relation to corruption reform. There are positive efforts by well-intended individuals in companies, governments, NATO, militaries, regulators, and NGOs; collective peer pressure, such as the support of the industry associations; and larger macro-scale pressures, such as the tougher climate of public opinion toward wrongdoing by defense companies, huge arms scandals, and the rise in insecurity and fragility in many countries. How do we make sense of the corruption improvements, and identify which elements were the most significant? Can we construct a plausible narrative of how positive change took place, which could in turn point the way to further reform in defense and perhaps inspire reforms in other sectors? From my perspective as the former leader of the principal NGO involved in this effort, there have been five sets of change-inducing factors.

[79] Kluyskens et al., *supra* note 80.

The first factor is the most obvious one: scandals. There have been numerous defense corruption scandals, involving not just the companies but their governments too. Besides the U.S. examples already mentioned that led to the FCPA, the early involvement of the Swedish government in this reform effort was at least partly driven by the aftermath of the Bofors corruption scandal. Similarly, France was impacted by the long drawn-out follow-up to the sale of frigates to Taiwan by CSF-Thomson (now Thales). They are a reminder of the mantra of the former White House Chief of Staff, Emanuel Rahm, "Never let a good crisis go to waste when it's an opportunity to do things you had never considered or you didn't think were possible."[80]

Second, groups of committed individuals, collaborating over a sustained period, make a huge difference. This was exemplified by the network of senior executives working inside defense companies but also regulators, officials, and civil society, who between them catalyzed the creation of the CIS, the global industry forum IFBEC, and improvements in the individual standards and practices of the companies. Making it as easy as possible for such groups to collaborate is also part of the mix. In the case of the defense industry collaboration, we can identify the creation of a convening body for the early industry meetings (like the early meetings convened by Lord Robertson), the fact that many of the industry interlocuteurs were experienced and respected within the defense industry, the active support for reform from the CEOs of at least some of the defense companies, and the sustained engagement with the industry by TI-DS over many years. A similar effect of collaborating individuals could be seen in relation to reform in some MODs, which have seen the drive and leadership of key individuals, usually the minister and a group of senior military/MOD officials. For example, the efforts throughout the Colombian military[81] in instilling professional pride about integrity among their forces.

Other groups of committed individuals include those responsible for military staff development, who insist on corruption awareness in all officer training. Such mandatory courses are critical for developing a common mindset about the threats from corruption across each layer of seniority—for example, the training of 1,200 colonels from the Ukraine security and defense forces in the period 2010–2016.[82] In the private sector, energetic groups of ethics professionals have built up a common, cooperative approach across the sector.

[80] Merrill Matthews, *Never Let a Good Scandal Go to Waste, As Conservatives Push Their Agenda*, Forbes (May 16, 2019, 12:09 PM), https://www.forbes.com/sites/merrillmatthews/2013/05/16/never-let-a-good-scandal-go-to-waste-as-conservatives-push-their-agenda/.

[81] OECD, *The OECD Water Governance Initiative*, https://www.oecd.org/water/regional/ (last visited July 24, 2021).

[82] Pyman, *supra* note 38.

Third, the economic structure of the sector is important. The defense industry has a narrow-but-deep structure, with many, many layers of subcontracting. The effect of this is a kind of oligopoly, in which a small number of the larger players have a high degree of leverage. This has been a positive factor for change in this narrative. The importance of defense similarly means that the state has strong influence at the top of that hierarchy in each country. While that influence may be negative, it also means that efforts to change that point of view can be concentrated. The preponderance of the United States as a buyer in the defense sector means that companies from all countries that hope to do business with the U.S. DoD must pay attention to the U.S. standards of compliance. The presence of active reformers within the DOD, as was the case with the U.S. offices of Suspension and Debarment in the Armed Forces, amplifies this effect.

Fourth, comparative international indexes can really catalyze change. The catalytic effect in the defense sector was partly the result of peer pressure—generals, ministers and defense officials comparing themselves to their neighbors and competitors—and partly the fact that the GI and the CI could be used for prioritizing and monitoring incremental improvement. This use as an improvement tool is a powerful argument for such technical indexes, because the underlying reasons for poor scores can be examined and addressed, in contrast with indexes based on perceptions. A similar peer pressure effect came from the gentler integrity self-assessments promoted by NATO, gradually changing the rules of the game to one where integrity becomes one of the accepted values of a defense establishment, which could be scrutinized and followed up in routine NATO processes.

Fifth and finally, change is rarely random or accidental. New ideas, new groups, new reactions to old stimuli are encouraged through influential individuals, novel coalitions, by stimulating friction that irritates until solutions start to emerge. TI-DS was an active change-agent. This was a difficult position for TI-DS, pressing for corruption reform, being neither a "consultant" to industry nor taking sides against industry. One defense company interviewee from the external evaluation expressed this ambiguity well: "[I]s TI-DS . . . a collegial source of helpful advice or a potentially problematic external critic"?[83]

This analysis shows in detail what it means to work on reducing corruption through a "whole sector" approach: using sector-specific disaggregation of the corruption problems; embracing action by the industry, the public sector, and the regulators equally; taking an international approach; and using a thorough understanding of the sector to create detailed comparative indexes of corruption vulnerabilities. The more that practitioners and researchers utilize such mechanisms, the more that they can catalyze whole sector change.

[83] Kluyskens et al., *supra* note 78, at 12.

References

Tehmina Abbas et al., *NATO Members and Partner States: Government Defence Anti-Corruption Index*, Transparency Int'l Def. & Sec. (2015), https://government.defenceindex.org/downloads/docs/GI-NATO-Results-web.pdf.

Aerospace & Def. Indus. Ass'n of Eur., *Common Industry Standards: European Common Industry Standards for the Prevention of Corruption in the Aerospace and Defence Sector* (June 2012), https://www.asd-europe.org/sites/default/files/atoms/files/ASD_Common_Industry_Standards.pdf.

Kyle Alexander et al., *Overview of Political Economy, Contracting and Corruption in Afghanistan: A Case Study in Kandahar*, Transparency Int'l Def. & Sec. (Dec. 2012), https://ti-defence.org/wp-content/uploads/2018/03/Overview-of-political-economy-contracting-and-corruption-in-Afghanistan-A-case-study-in-Kandahar.pdf.

Avascent & Fleishman Hillard, *The Half-Trillion Dollar Challenge: Designing Offset Strategies to Build Reputation, Promote Development* (2012), https://www.avascent.com/wp-content/uploads/2013/02/Avascent-Offsets-2-White-Paper.pdf.

BBC News, *Mali Crisis: US Admits Mistakes in Training Local Troops* (Jan. 25, 2013), https://www.bbc.com/news/world-africa-21195371.

Tobias Bock, Mark Pyman & Ida Höckerfelt, *MEKANIC: Making Sense of Progress in the Defense and Security Sector—Implementing Lessons Learned*, Praxis Note No. 66, INTRAC 1, 2 (Jan. 2014), https://www.intrac.org/wpcms/wp-content/uploads/2017/07/Praxis-Note-66.-MEKANIC-1.pdf.

Tiffany Clark & Mark Pyman, *Raising the Bar: Good Anti-Corruption Practices in Defence Companies, Part I: Seven Practices that Distinguish the Best*, Transparency Int'l Def. & Sec. (June 2013), https://curbingcorruption.com/wp-content/uploads/2018/07/Clarke-and-Pyman-2013-Raising-the-bar-Good-anti-corruption-practices-in-defence-companies-Part-I.pdf.

Tiffany Clark & Mark Pyman, *Raising the Bar: Good Anti-corruption Practices in Defence Companies, Part II: 104 Examples of Good Defense Company Practice*, Transparency Int'l Def. & Sec. (June 2013), https://curbingcorruption.com/wp-content/uploads/2018/07/Clarke-and-Pyman-2013-Raising-the-Bar-Part-II-104-examples-of-good-defence-company-practice.pdf.

James Cohen, Mark Pyman & Alan Waldron, *Training the Military and Defence Security Officials in Understanding and Preventing Corruption*, Transparency Int'l Def. & Sec. (Feb. 2013), https://ti-defence.org/wp-content/uploads/2016/03/2013-02_TrainingMilitaryandDefence.pdf.

James Cohen, Mohammad Isaqzadeh & Alan Waldron, *Anti-Corruption Training Course in Kabul for Afghan MOD and MOI Senior Officers*, Transparency Int'l (Feb. 2013), https://ti-defence.org/wp-content/uploads/2016/03/2013-02_AfghanTraining_Report.pdf.

Catherine Courtney, *Corruption in the Official Arms Trade*, Transparency Int'l (2003), https://curbingcorruption.com/wp-content/uploads/2019/10/191008-Catherine-Courtney-TI-paper-2002.pdf.

Oliver Cover & Sazan Meran, *Watchdogs? The Quality of Legislative Oversight of Defence in 82 Countries*, Transparency Int'l Def. & Sec. (Sept. 2013), http://ti-defence.org/wp-content/uploads/2016/03/Watchdogs-low.pdf.

DCAF, *Building Integrity and Reducing Corruption in Defense: A Compendium of Best Practices* (2010), https://www.dcaf.ch/sites/default/files/publications/documents/Compendium_Building_Integrity_and_Reducing_Corruption_in_Defence.pdf.

Def. Indus. Initiative on Bus. Ethics & Conduct, *About DII*, https://www.dii.org/about/about-dii.

European Commission, Report from the Commission to the European Parliament and the Council on the Implementation of Directive 2009/81/EC on Public Procurement in the Fields of Defence and Security, to Comply with Article 73(2) of that Directive, COM (2016) 762 final (Nov. 30, 2016), https://ec.europa.eu/docsroom/documents/20376.

Katie Fish et al., *Defense Companies Anti-Corruption Index 2015*, Transparency Int'l Def. & Sec. (2015), http://companies.defenceindex.org/docs/2015%20Defence%20Companies%20Anti-Corruption%20Index.pdf.

Louise Fluker, Julia Muravska & Mark Pyman, *Due Diligence and Corruption Risk in Defence Industry Offset Programmes*, Transparency Int'l Def. & Sec. (2012), https://ti-defence.org/wp-content/uploads/2016/03/2012-02_DueDiligenceAndCorruptionRiskInOffsets.pdf.

Ádám Földes, *Classified Information: A Review of Current Legislation Across 15 Countries and the EU*, Transparency Int'l Def. & Sec. (2014), https://ti-defence.org/wp-content/uploads/2016/03/140911-Classified-Information.pdf.

Kevin Goh & Julia Muravska, *Military-owned Businesses: Corruption and Risk Reform*, Transparency Int'l Def. & Sec. (2012), https://ti-defence.org/wp-content/uploads/2016/03/2012-01_MilitaryOwnedBusinesses.pdf.

Mariya Gorbanova & Leah Wawro, *The Transparency of National Defence Budgets*, Transparency Int'l Def. & Sec. (2011), http://ti-defence.org/wp-content/uploads/2016/03/2011-10_Defence_Budgets_Transparency.pdf.

Susan Hawley, *Turning a Blind Eye: Corruption and the UK Export Credits Guarantee Department*, Corner House (2003), http://www.thecornerhouse.org.uk/sites/thecornerhouse.org.uk/files/correcgd.pdf.

Int'l F. on Bus. Ethical Conduct for Aerospace & Def. Indus., *What Is IFBCEC?*, https://ifbec.info/about/.

Jups Kluyskens et al., *Independent Progress Review (IPR) of the DFID Programme Partnership Arrangement (PPA), 2011–2012*, Channel Research, 19–22 (Oct. 13, 2012), http://kluyskensconsulting.com/wp-content/uploads/2018/07/121015-Channel-Research-TI-DSP-CHASE-PPA-IPR-Final-Report.pdf.

Andrew Lebovich, *Mali's Bad Trip: Field Notes from the West African Drug Trade*, Foreign Pol'y, Mar. 15, 2013, https://foreignpolicy.com/2013/03/15/malis-bad-trip/.

Ben Magahy, Francisco Vilhena da Cunha & Mark Pyman, *Defense Offsets: Addressing the Risks of Corruption and Raising Transparency*, Transparency Int'l Def. & Sec. (2012), https://ti-defence.org/wp-content/uploads/2016/03/1004_corruption_risk_offsets.pdf.

Merrill Matthews, *Never Let a Good Scandal Go to Waste, As Conservatives Push Their Agenda*, Forbes (May 16, 2019, 12:09 PM), https://www.forbes.com/sites/merrillmatthews/2013/05/16/never-let-a-good-scandal-go-to-waste-as-conservatives-push-their-agenda/.

Moldova Ministry of Def., *Building Integrity Self-Assessment Peer Review Report* (Oct. 2014), http://www.army.md/img/userfiles/anticoruptie/bisaprr.pdf.

Alina Mungiu-Pippidi, The Quest for Good Governance: How Societies Develop Control of Corruption 207 (2015).

Saad Mustafa et al., *Single Sourcing: A Multi-country Analysis of Non-competitive Defence Procurement*, Transparency Int'l Def. & Sec. (2014), https://ti-defence.org/wp-content/uploads/2016/03/140910-Single-Sourcing.pdf.

NAKO, *The Independent Defence Anti-Corruption Committee of Ukraine, Poor Governance and Corruption in Ukraine's Defence Housing System: Risks and Recommendations*, Transparency Int'l Def. & Sec. (2018), http://ti-defence.org/wp-content/uploads/2018/10/NAKO_Housing_ENG_web-compressed.pdf.

NATO, *Ten Years of NATO's Building Integrity Programme* (2019), https://buildingintegrity.hq.nato.int/?AspxAutoDetectCookieSupport=1.

NATO Joint Analysis & Lessons Learned Centre, *Counter- and Anti-Corruption: Theory and Practice from NATO Operations* (May 10, 2013), https://www.jallc.nato.int/application/files/7816/0261/3252/factsheet_corruption.pdf.

Dick Olver, Address at Tomorrow's Values Lecture Series: Tomorrow's Company (Mar. 13, 2013), http://www.tomorrowscompany.com/wp-content/uploads/2013/03/dick_olver_tomorrows_company_speech-3.pdf.

Mark Pieth, *Aeronautics and Defence*, *in* Confronting Corruption: Past Concerns, Present Strategies and Future Challenges 149, 150–155 (Fritz Heimann & Mark Pieth eds., 2018).

Mark Pyman, Address at Transparency International conference in Arendel, UK: Preventing Corruption in the Official Arms Trade (June 8, 2004), https://curbingcorruption.com/wp-content/uploads/2018/07/Transparency-International-UK-2004-Arundel-Conference-Proceedings-for-preventing-corruption-in-the-official-arms-trade.pdf.

Mark Pyman, Address at the Transparency International Collaborative Programme: Preventing Corruption in the Official Arms Trade (July 14, 2004), https://curbingcorruption.com/wp-content/uploads/2018/07/Transparency-International-UK-2004-Project-summary-Preventing-corruption-in-the-official-arms-trade-Phase-1.pdf.

Mark Pyman, *Corruption: Lessons from the International Experience in Afghanistan*, Transparency Int'l Def. & Sec. (2015), http://ti-defence.org/wp-content/uploads/2016/03/150217-Corruption-Lessons-from-the-international-mission-in-Afghanistan.pdf.

Mark Pyman, *Monitoring, Evaluation and Learning about Defence Corruption Prevention, Avgustina Tzvetkova: An Interview with the former Deputy Defense Minister of Bulgaria 2009–2013*, Transparency Int'l (2015), https://curbingcorruption.com/wp-content/uploads/2018/07/Pyman-2013-An-interview-with-the-former-Deputy-Defence-Minister-of-Bulgaria-2009-to-2013.pdf.

Mark Pyman, *Building Integrity and Countering Corruption in Defense and Security: 20 Practical Reforms*, Transparency Int'l Def. & Sec. (2016), https://ti-defence.org/wp-content/uploads/2016/03/1102_Handbook_IntegrityReducingCorruption.pdf.

Mark Pyman, *Addressing Corruption in Military Institutions*, 19(5) Pub. Integrity 513 (2017).

Mark Pyman et al., *Corruption as a Threat to Stability and Peace*, Transparency Int'l Def. & Sec. (2014), https://ti-defence.org/wp-content/uploads/2016/03/2014-01_CorruptionThreatStabilityPeace.pdf.

Mark Pyman et al., *Études sur les Aspects de l'Intégrité de la Force de Défense Nationale du Burundi*, Transparency Int'l Def. & Sec. (2013), http://ti-defence.org/publications/etude-sur-les-aspects-de-lintegrite-de-la-force-de-defense-nationale-du-burundi/.

Mark Pyman, Katherine Dixon & Katie Fish, Address at Transparency International's Launch of Defence Companies Anti-Corruption Index 2015, London (May 2015), https://curbingcorruption.com/wp-content/uploads/2018/10/150430-Pyman-Dixon-and-Fish-Defence-Companies-Index-2015-launch-London.pdf.

Mark Pyman et al., *Corruption and Peacekeeping: Strengthening Peacekeeping and the United Nations*, TRANSPARENCY INT'L DEF. & SEC. (2013), https://ti-defence.org/wp-content/uploads/2016/03/2013-10_-Corruption-PK-report.pdf.

Mark Pyman et al., *Corruption Threats and International Missions: Practical Guidance for Leaders*, TRANSPARENCY INT'L DEF. & SEC. (2014), https://ti-defence.org/wp-content/uploads/2016/03/140930-Corruption-Threats-International-Missions.pdf.

Mark Pyman & Alan Waldron, *Practical Application of Defence Integrity Pacts: Experience in Colombia*, TRANSPARENCY INT'L (Mar. 20, 2006), https://curbingcorruption.com/wp-content/uploads/2018/07/Pyman-Waldron-and-Avelia-2006-Practical-application-of-defense-integrity-pacts-Experience-in-Colombia.pdf.

Mark Pyman & Alan Waldron, *Experience with Implementing a Defence Integrity Pact in Respect of the Procurement of Combat Aircraft for the Republic of Colombia*, Report 2, TRANSPARENCY INT'L (2006), https://curbingcorruption.com/wp-content/uploads/2018/07/TI-defence-and-Transparencia-Colombia-2006-Defence-procurement-and-integrity-pacts-in-Colombia-Report-2-copy.pdf.

Mark Pyman & Alan Waldron, *Improving Transparency Accountability and Counter-Corruption (TACC) in the ANSF, MoD and MOI*, TRANSPARENCY INT'L DEF. & SEC. (Oct. 2, 2013), https://curbingcorruption.com/wp-content/uploads/2018/07/Pyman-and-Waldron-2013-Afghanistan-Improving-transparency-accountability-and-counter-corruption-TACC-in-the-Afghan-ANSF-MOD-and-MOI.pdf.

Mark Pyman, Regina Wilson & Dominic Scott, *The Extent of Single sourcing in Defense Procurement and its Relevance as a Corruption Risk: A First Look*, 20(3) DEF. & PEACE ECON. 215 (2009).

Mark Pyman & Maciej Wnuk, Reducing Corruption: Building Integrity in Defence and Security Institutions, unpublished paper presented at the Twelfth International Anti-Corruption Conference, Guatemala (Nov. 2006), https://curbingcorruption.com/wp-content/uploads/2018/07/Pyman-and-Wnuk-2006-IACC-Conference-Guatemala-Reducing-corruption-and-bulding-integrity-in-defense-and-security.pdf.

Mark Pyman, *Addressing Corruption in Military Institutions*, 19(5) PUB. INTEGRITY 513 (2017).

Kirby Reiling, How to Assess Corruption in Defence: A Framework for Designing, Comparing and Interpreting Corruption Measurement Tools (2009) (unpublished M.A. thesis, Tufts University), https://dl.tufts.edu/concern/pdfs/k930c7919.

Yuri Repilo & Serhiy Tarasov, *Corruption Treat assessments in Higher Military Education*, TRANSPARENCY INT'L (2013), https://curbingcorruption.com/wp-content/uploads/2018/07/Repilo-and-Tarasov-2013-Corruption-threats-assessment-in-higher-military-education-in-Ukraine.pdf.

RUSI, TRANSPARENCY INT'L DEF. & SEC. & KONRAD ADENAUER FOUND., *Afghanistan in Transition: Governance, Counter-Corruption, and Reshaping Priorities for 2015 and Beyond*, TRANSPARENCY INT'L (May 13, 2011), https://www.transparency.org/files/content/pressrelease/20110513_UK_Afghanistan_in_transition_EN.pdf.

Eiko Elize Sakamoto, Changing the Rules of the Game: A Voluntary Code of Conduct by the Defence and Arms Industry and Transparency International's Defence Against Corruption (Dec. 2010) (unpublished doctoral research, London School of Economics), https://curbingcorruption.com/sakamoto-2010-changing-the-rules-of-the-game-a-voluntary-code-of-conduct-by-the-defence-and-arms-industry-and-transparency-international/.

Ikram Sehgal, *Corruption in the Arms Trade*, DEF. J. (2000), http://www.defencejournal.com/2000/mar/arms-trade.htm (describing the Transparency International's Stockholm Colloquium on Corruption in the Arms Trade, Feb. 4–6, 2000).

Steven A. Shaw & Jade C. Totman, *Suspension and Debarment: Strengthening Integrity in International Defence Contracting*, TRANSPARENCY INT'L DEF. & SEC. (2015), http://ti-defence.org/wp-content/uploads/2016/03/150507-Suspension-and-Debarment.pdf.

Thomas Shipley, Anne-Christine Wegener & Mark Pyman, *Codes of Conduct in Defence Ministries and Armed Forces, What Makes a Good Code? A Multi-Country Study*, TRANSPARENCY INT'L DEF. & SEC. (2011), http://ti-defence.org/wp-content/uploads/2016/03/1106_CodesofConduct.pdf.

John F. Sopko, Special Inspector for Afghanistan Reconstruction, Address at the U.S. Naval Academy: Lessons from Afghanistan's Reconstruction: 2001–2019 (Jan. 17, 2019), https://www.sigar.mil/pdf/speeches/SIGAR_USNA_Speech_2019-01-17.pdf.

SPECIAL INSPECTOR GEN. FOR AFGHANISTAN RECONSTRUCTION, https://www.sigar.mil.

TI-DS, NATO & DCAF, *Building Integrity and Reducing Corruption Risk in Defence Establishments: An Integrity Self-assessment Process for National Defense Establishments* 2009, Enclos. 1 (2010), https://www.nato.int/nato_static/assets/pdf/pdf_2010_05/20100603_EAPC_PFP-joint_EAPC-0004-Encl1.pdf.

TRANSPARENCY INT'L, *Bribe Payers Index 1999* (1999), https://www.transparency.org/news/pressrelease/transparency_international_releases_new_bribe_payers_index_bpi_2002.

TRANSPARENCY INT'L, Proceedings of the TI(UK) Conference on Corruption in the Official Arms Trade, Cambridge (Apr. 5, 2001), https://curbingcorruption.com/wp-content/uploads/2020/10/Transparency-International-UK-2001-Report-on-the-Conference-Corruption-in-the-Official-Arms-Trade.pdf.

TRANSPARENCY INT'L, *Bribe Payers Index 2008*, at 11 (Dec. 2008), https://images.transparencycdn.org/images/2008_BPI_EN.pdf.

TRANSPARENCY INT'L, *Bribe Payers Index 2011*, at 15 (Oct. 2011), https://issuu.com/transparencyinternational/docs/bribe_payers_index_2011?mode=window&backgroundColor=%23222222.

TRANSPARENCY INT'L, *Transparency in Corporate Reporting: Assessing the World's Largest Companies* (2012), https://www.transparency.org/whatwedo/publication/transparency_in_corporate_reporting_assessing_the_worlds_largest_companies.

TRANSPARENCY INT'L DEF. & SEC., *Afghanistan in Transition: Governance, Counter-Corruption and Reshaping Priorities* (2011), https://curbingcorruption.com/wp-content/uploads/2018/07/TI-DS-with-RUSI-and-KAF-2011-Afghanistan-in-Transition-Governance-Counter-Corruption-and-Development-Re-Shaping-Priorities-for-2015-and-Beyond-copy.pdf.

TRANSPARENCY INT'L DEF. & SEC., *Government Defence Anti-Corruption Index 2013* (Jan. 29, 2013), http://ti-defence.org/wp-content/uploads/2016/03/gi-2013-mainreportphase04.pdf.

TRANSPARENCY INT'L DEF. & SEC., *Regional Results Colombia: Government Defence Anti-Corruption Index* (Sept. 28, 2016), http://ti-defence.org/wp-content/uploads/2016/09/GI-Colombia-2016.pdf.

TRANSPARENCY INT'L DEF. & SEC., *Government Defence Anti-Corruption Index, Methodology* (2019), https://government.defenceindex.org/methodology/.

Transparency Int'l Def. & Sec., *An Assessment of Corruption Risks in Peacekeeping Operations* (2019), http://ti-defence.org/wp-content/uploads/2019/07/TIDS-CorruptionRisksinUNPeacekeeping.pdf.

Woolf Committee, *Ethical Business Conduct in BAE PLC, The Way Forward* (2008), https://www.icaew.com/~/media/corporate/files/technical/ethics/woolfreport 2008.ashx.

11

The Nexus of Arms Embargoes, Corruption, and Foreign Investment

Nancy Hite-Rubin

1. Introduction

Defense is big business.[1] According to the Stockholm International Peace Research Institute (SIPRI), world military spending reached $1.981 trillion in 2020, up from $1.686 trillion in 2016.[2] Given the advanced technology needed for major weapon systems and the scope of military industrial complex, a significant portion of foreign military budgets are spent in the international arms market. Beyond drivers of cost and production, both the supply of and demand for global defense items are highly contingent upon geopolitics. International defense contracts for arms and services total billions of dollars annually[3] and involve complex contractual arrangements that span decades. The global defense industry continues to do well, and the high levels of international expenditures on arms are driven by the strategic interplay of security and foreign policy with domestic economic interests.

Ultimately, some of the same factors that make defense such a lucrative business and motivate international demand also present major corruption and security risks. Defense suppliers almost always contract directly with government institutions, and—given the nature and specificity of defense contracts—are often in a position to negotiate million-dollar contracts without

[1] *See, e.g.*, Rich Smith, *As the Air War Heats Up, Defense Contractors Rake in Profits*, The Motley Fool (Nov. 22, 2016, 12:13 PM), http://www.fool.com/investing/general/2015/11/22/air-war-heats-up-defense-contractors-rake-profits.aspx; Robert Latiff, *Ethical Issues in Defense Systems Acquisitions*, *in* Routledge Handbook of Military Ethics 209–219 (George Lucas ed., 2015).

[2] Diego Lopes da Silva et al., Stockholm Int'l Peace Research Inst. [hereinafter SIPRI], *Trends in World Military Expenditure, 2020* (2021), https://sipri.org/sites/default/files/2021-04/fs_2104_milex_0.pdf; Press Release, SIPRI, *World Military Spending: Increases in the USA and Europe, Decreases in Oil-exporting Countries* (Apr. 24, 2017), https://www.sipri.org/media/press-release/2017/world-military-spending-increases-usa-and-europe.

[3] Aude Fleurant et al., SIPRI, *The SIPRI Top 100 Arms-Producing and Military Services Companies, 2018* (2019), https://www.sipri.org/sites/default/files/2019-12/1912_fs_top_100_2018.pdf; Richard Grimmett, Cong. Research Serv., R42017, Conventional Arms Transfers to Developing Nations, 2003–2010, at 2 (2011).

Nancy Hite-Rubin, *The Nexus of Arms Embargoes, Corruption, and Foreign Investment* In: *Ethical Dilemmas in the Global Defense Industry*. Edited by: Daniel Schoeni and Tobias Vestner, Oxford University Press.
 DOI: 10.1093/oso/9780190675813.003.0012

the transparency offered by an open and competitive bidding process.[4] As Transparency International's Defence & Security program has explained, "The military, security, and intelligence bodies possess not only a monopoly on the means of violence, as protectors of national security and enforcers of order, but also have privileged access to classified information, arms stocks, natural and financial resources, and high-placed contacts."[5] This unique power and access also implies that officials in the defense realm are in a privileged position to demand bribes. Furthermore, since the end of the Cold War, less developed countries have become important importers of military equipment. These countries are often institutionally weak, consequently creating the perfect environment for corruption and political unrest to thrive. It is for these reasons that the defense sector has been found to be "one of the most prone to corruption worldwide."[6]

The transfer of major arms into such politically risky markets creates major security concerns,[7] as well as development concerns.[8] Accordingly, since the end of the Cold War, a number of states—including the United States and the European Union member states—as well as the United Nations, have begun to vigorously use arms embargoes as a means of controlling the export and re-export of military equipment into certain countries—either to contain the security threats presented by the countries or to dissuade leaders from engaging in human rights abuses.[9] In fact, prior to 1990, the United Nations had only initiated two mandatory arms trade embargoes, compared to at least 27 implemented since that

[4] Steven L. Schooner & Nathaniel E. Castellano, *Review Essay: Reading the Dream Machine: The Untold Story of the Notorious V-22 Osprey, by Richard Whittle, in Light of the Defense Acquisition Performance Study*, 43 PUB. CONT. L.J. 391 (2014); TRANSPARENCY INTERNATIONAL, BUILDING INTEGRITY AND COUNTERING CORRUPTION IN DEFENCE AND SECURITY: 20 PRACTICAL REFORMS (2011). Mark Pyman, Regina Wilson & Dominic Scott, *The Extent of Single Sourcing in Defense Procurement and Its Relevance as a Corruption Risk: A First Look*, 20(3) DEF. & PEACE ECON. 215 (2009). *But see* Barton H. Halpern & Keith F. Snider, *Products that Kill and Corporate Social Responsibility: The Case of U.S. Defense Firms*, 38(4) ARMED FORCES & SOC. 604 (2012), finding that managers of defense firms are no less oriented toward corporate social responsibility than other firms. *Cf.* Edmund F. Byrne, *Assessing Arms Makers' Corporate Social Responsibility*, 74 J. BUSINESS ETHICS 201 (2007), making the opposite finding.

[5] TRANSPARENCY INTERNATIONAL, ORGANISED CRIME, CORRUPTION, AND THE VULNERABILITY OF DEFENCE AND SECURITY FORCES, DEFENCE AND SECURITY PROGRAMME BACKGROUND PAPER 14 (2011).

[6] TRANSPARENCY INTERNATIONAL, BUILDING INTEGRITY, *supra* note 4, at 36.

[7] Cassady Craft & Joseph P. Smaldone, *The Arms Trade and the Incidence of Political Violence in Sub-Saharan Africa, 1967–97*, 39(6) J. PEACE RES. 693 (2002). *See also* Charles H. Anderton, *Economics of Arms Trade*, *in* HANDBOOK OF DEFENSE ECONOMICS: Volume 1, at 547 (Keith Hartley & Todd Sandler eds., 1995); TRANSPARENCY INTERNATIONAL, ORGANISED CRIME, *supra* note 5.

[8] Philip M. Nichols, *The Business Case for Complying with Bribery Laws*, 49(2) AM. BUS. J. 325 (2012).

[9] *See* David Cortright, George A. Lopez & Linda Gerber, *Sanctions Sans Commitment: An Assessment of UN Arms Embargoes* (Project Ploughshares, Working Paper No. 02-2, 2002), http://ploughshares.ca/wp-content/uploads/2012/08/WP2.2.pdf.

time.[10] Arms trade embargoes have been viewed as a "'smart' alternative to comprehensive economic sanctions."[11]

Given low institutional strength and high corruption in many arms importing countries, the myriad laws and regulations implementing arms trade embargoes against many of these politically unstable countries, and the complex public procurement laws that accompany nearly all major government contracts, defense contractors face an ethical minefield when they seek lucrative contracts from less developed countries. Nonetheless, such countries are an important market that defense contractors must target to stay competitive.[12] In fact, Wezeman and Wezeman found that arms transfers into "corrupt" countries were progressively increasing.[13] And even more curiously, empirical scholarship demonstrates that the transfer of major arms into countries that are institutionally weak is robustly correlated with higher foreign direct investment (FDI) flows into those countries.[14]

The empirical research to date has established the existence of a significant and worrisome empirical trend—namely, that the global defense industry is propelled by demand from institutionally weak, developing nations. The security risks and ethical dilemmas related to the sale of military equipment have led a number of states—notably the United States and EU member states—to attempt to control the export and re-export of military equipment into certain countries. This begs the question of what role, if any, international arms trade restrictions play in mitigating the security and corruption risks inherent in this industry.

This study contributes to the broader canon of empirical research on the effectiveness of arms embargoes. A number of scholars have focused on the effect arms embargoes have on changing the target country's conduct, finding

[10] Damien Fruchart et al., United Nations Arms Embargoes: Their Impact on Arms Flows and Target Behaviour (2007), https://www.sipri.org/publications/2007/united-nations-arms-embargoes-their-impact-arms-flows-and-target-behaviour. *See also* Peter Wallensteen, *Save the Arms Embargo* (Joan B. Kroc Institute for International Peace Studies, Policy Brief No. 14, Jan. 2008), https://kroc.nd.edu/assets/227134/save_the_arms_embargo.pdf.

[11] Matthew Moore, *Arming the Embargoed: A Supply-side Understanding of Arms Embargo Violations*, 54(4) J. Conflict Resolution 593 (2010). *See also* Fruchart et al., *supra* note 10.

[12] Press Release, SIPRI, *US Military Spending Falls, Increases in Eastern Europe, Middle East, Africa and Asia Says SIPRI* (Apr. 13, 2015), http://www.sipri.org/media/pressreleases/2015/milex-april-2015; Benjamin Braun et al., *Global Defense Outlook 2015: Defense and Development*, Deloitte (2015), https://www2.deloitte.com/content/dam/Deloitte/global/Documents/Public-Sector/gx-2015-deloitte-global-defense-outlook.pdf.

[13] Siemon T. Wezeman & Pieter D. Wezeman, *SIPRI Fact Sheet: Trends in International Arms Transfers, 2013* (2014), https://www.sipri.org/publications/2014/sipri-fact-sheets/trends-international-arms-transfers-2013.

[14] Nancy Hite-Rubin, *A Corruption, Military Procurement and FDI Nexus?*, *in* Greed, Corruption, and the Modern State: Essays in Political Economy 224–251 (Susan Rose-Ackerman, Henry R. Luce & Paul Lagunes eds., 2015); Daniel W. Drezner & Nancy Hite-Rubin, Paper Presented at the American Political Science Association, Washington, DC: *Does Military Spending Attract (Corrupt) Foreign Investment?: An Empirical Investigation* (Aug. 2014).

less than ideal results.[15] In a historical analysis of 74 cases between 1990 and 2005, Brzoska argues that embargoes do not completely end weapons flows into targeted countries but that longer term and multilateral embargoes may be more effective at curtailing such transfers.[16] Building on this, Moore employs a data set of 872 sender-recipient arms flow dyads and finds 89 violations of UN arms embargoes.[17] Moore employs this database to test predictors of violations and finds that "arms import dependence," that is, the share of arms sales coming from the embargo-imposing country ex ante best predicts whether a violation occurs. Moore also contends that the magnitude of the violation is best predicted by alliance similarity between the recipient and sending state. In a similar dyadic analysis of arms flows under UN embargoes, Erickson argues that, on average, UN embargoes restrain but do not completely eliminate sending states from exporting arms to states under embargo.[18] Taken together, Moore's and Erickson's work points in the direction of cautious optimism, at least as regards the behavior of the sending state that imposes an embargo.

Many outstanding questions remain unanswered regarding whether, and how, arms embargoes influence the political economy of the international defense industry. Historical and case studies have largely mixed results, while recent empirical analysis of exporting state behavior leans in favor of indicating some efficacy, in that sending states are tentatively compliant with their own arms embargoes. Given that the center of gravity for the global defense industry sales has shifted to less developed and institutionally stable markets, it is particularly important to understand more about the role of the global defense industry in its interface with both international law and domestic legal systems. This chapter aims to contribute to that understanding by introducing an original data set of international arms embargo regimes (the United States, the United Nations, and the European Union) and exploring empirical trends in the transfer of major arms in light of the existence of these dynamic embargo regimes.

The purpose of building a dedicated database on international arms embargo regimes is to unlock critical information regarding the role of corruption, military procurement, and FDI. This empirical project is distinguished from existing literature in that it employs data on *global* arms transfers and focuses on the behavior of *receiving*, rather than sending, states. This data set enables scholars to test for relationships across arms embargoes, international arms

[15] *See, e.g.*, FRUCHART ET AL., *supra* note 10; Michael Brzoska, *Measuring the Effectiveness of Arms Embargoes*, 14(2) PEACE ECON, PEACE SCI. & PUB. POL'Y. 1 (2008); Jennifer L. Erickson, *Stopping the Legal Flow of Weapons: Compliance with Arms Embargoes, 1981–2004*, 50(2) J. PEACE RES. 159 (2013).

[16] Brzoska, *supra* note 15.

[17] Moore, *supra* note 11.

[18] Erickson, *supra* note 15.

flows, and FDI flows into institutionally weak countries. By clarifying and empirically codifying a new data set, this chapter opens exciting new avenues for global-level analysis.

This chapter builds the foundation for an exciting research agenda by laying out the basis for rigorous hypothesis testing. The chapter has three remaining sections. The following section begins with a discussion of the global arms trade as a major driver of foreign investment, features international data on arms transfers, and posits ethical challenges that arise as countries challenged by corruption are increasingly incentivized to import major weapons. The third section focuses on the role of international arms embargoes and their potential for curtailing the supply of arms to specific states. After outlining summary information on arms embargoes, the section describes the construction of the global data set for the arms embargo regimes of the United States, the European Union, and the United Nations. Section 3, on arms trade embargoes probes the veracity of scholarship positing that hard law, in the form of unilateral or multilateral export restrictions, influences state behavior.[19] The chapter concludes with a discussion of features and limitations of its preliminary findings, as well as, outlining next steps for quantitative hypothesis testing. By combining this new database with prior empirical research,[20] one can investigate whether restrictions on international arms trade correspond to a reduced amount of flows of major weapons into restricted countries. This work sheds light on important trends in arms acquisition, particularly in emerging markets, and the role of international law in regulating these trends.

2. The Global Arms Trade

International arms trade has increased dramatically over the past twenty years, according to the Stockholm International Peace Research Institute (SIPRI).[21] Global military expenditure reached its peak in 2020 since SIPRI's first measurement in 1998, currently cumulating to an estimated total expenditure of $1.981 trillion.[22] Perhaps even more interesting, defense spending in many middle-income countries had more than doubled between 2004 and 2013, when more developed countries (such as the United States and EU member states) had

19 Brzoska, *supra* note 15; FRUCHART ET AL., *supra* note 10.

20 Hite-Rubin, *supra* note 14; Drezner & Hite-Rubin, *supra* note 14.

21 *See* SIPRI reports, *infra* notes 23–24. *See also* Wallensteen, *supra* note 10.

22 Colin Archer & Annette Willi, *Opportunity Costs: Military Spending and the UN's Development Agenda*, INT'L PEACE BUREAU (2012), https://sustainabledevelopment.un.org/getWSDoc.php?id=3260. *See also* Frank Slijper, *Guns, Debt and Corruption: Military Spending and the EU Crisis*, TRANSNAT'L INST. (Apr. 2013), https://www.tni.org/files/download/eu_milspending_crisis.pdf.

decreased their spending.[23] In the period between 2016 and 2020, the world's top five importers of major weapons were Saudi Arabia, India, Egypt, Australia, and China.[24]

2.1. The Global Arms Trade and Conflict

Transfers of major arms are fraught with security concerns. The world's largest exporters of major conventional weapons between 2016 and 2020 were the United States, Russia, France, Germany, and China,[25] all of whom are members of the United Nations and subject to both domestic and international law that is intended to mitigate security concerns. While there is a strong profit incentive to export major arms, home governments are often cautious about providing arms to less developed countries, especially in view of the threat of terrorism and political unrest in many parts of the world.[26]

The first step of this empirical investigation is to acquire systematic data on the global arms trade. SIPRI has created an arms transfers database that includes an annual estimate of the volume of military weapons purchased or transferred to a particular country from the international market.[27] It only covers "major weapons," such as new and used aircraft, ships, missiles, satellites, and large artillery.[28] It does not cover transfers of small arms and light weapons (other than portable guided missiles), trucks, light ammunition, and certain support equipment.[29] It covers any transfer from one country, rebel force, or international organization to another country, rebel force, or international organization if the equipment has a military purpose.[30] SIPRI collects its arms transfer information from open sources, including the media, industry, and government publications (such as defense white papers, the UN Register of Conventional Arms, and reports to the U.S. Congress).[31] It asserts that it receives information about the

[23] Sam Perlo-Freeman & Carina Solmirano, *SIPRI Fact Sheet: Trends in World Military Expenditure, 2013*, at 6 (Apr. 2014), https://www.sipri.org/sites/default/files/files/FS/SIPRIFS1404.pdf.

[24] Pieter D. Wezeman et al., SIPRI, *Trends in International Arms Transfers, 2020*, at 6 (2021), https://sipri.org/sites/default/files/2021-03/fs_2103_at_2020.pdf.

[25] *Id.* at 2; Keith Hartley, *The Arms Industry, Procurement and Industrial Policies*, *in* HANDBOOK OF DEFENSE ECONOMICS: DEFENSE IN A GLOBALIZED WORLD: Volume 2, at 1139 (Todd Sandler & Keith Hartley eds., 2007).

[26] *Id.*; David Cortright & George A. Lopez, *Bombs, Carrots, and Sticks: The Use of Incentives and Sanctions*, *Arms Control Today* (Mar. 1, 2005), https://www.armscontrol.org/act/2005_03/Cortright.

[27] SIPRI, *Arms Embargoes*, *supra* note 2.

[28] SIPRI, *Coverage*, http://www.sipri.org/databases/armstransfers/background/coverage/ (last visited Jan. 2, 2020).

[29] *Id.*

[30] *Id.*

[31] *Id.*

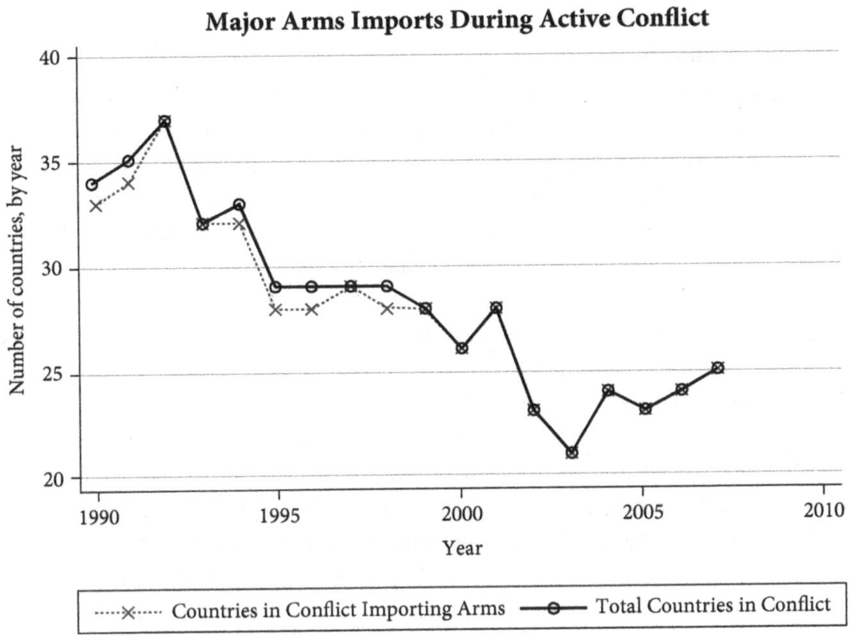

Figure 11.1 The line plot depicts the sum total of countries on the y-axis and year (between 2000 and 2008) on the x-axis. The overlap of the two lines indicates that most countries in active conflict continue to acquire major arms.

transfer of major arms from non-U.S. countries from reports to the U.S. Congress as well.[32] However, because information about arms transfers is often classified, this information may not be complete.[33]

The analysis presented in Figure 11.1 uses SIPRI's non-monetary estimates for country-year-level arms transfers.[34] The trend indicator variable (TIV) is meant to account for the fact that the same arms may be bought for very different prices—or even donated from one country to another. Thus, the value is meant to show relative comparisons of the *amount* of arms moved into a given country in a given year rather than the *cost* of such arms. To generate this figure, the SIPRI

[32] Paul Holtom, Mark Bromley & Verena Simmel, *SIPRI Fact Sheet: Measuring International Arms Transfers* (Dec. 2012), https://www.sipri.org/sites/default/files/files/FS/SIPRIFS1212.pdf.

[33] *See, e.g.*, *id.* at 4, relying on unclassified information and estimated data; Richard F. Grimmett & Paul K. Kerr, Cong. Research Serv., R42678, Conventional Arms Transfers to Developing Nations, 2004–2011, at 69–75 (2012), also relying on unclassified reports; Federation of American Scientists, *Literature Review: CRS' Conventional Arms Transfers to the Third World*, 6 Arms Sales Monitor 1 (Aug. 1991), same.

[34] Wezeman & Wezeman, *supra* note 13, at 1.

data is converted to a binary to indicate whether a country received any known arms in a given year.

Not surprisingly, major arms transfers go hand in hand with active conflict.[35] As Figure 11.1 shows, from 1990 to 2008, the number of countries in conflict that imported major arms in a given year closely tracks the number of countries in conflict in any given year.[36] The figure displays two trend lines, first for the sum of countries that are engaged in active conflict, and then for the sum of countries that are known to be importing arms. What the correlative graph demonstrates is that, with few exceptions, major arms importation is not disrupted by active conflict within the receiving country. This shows that in the majority of cases where countries are in conflict, arms are still flowing. Certainly, we would not expect that the demand for weaponry to evaporate when countries engage in conflict. Yet it is concerning that cross-border flows of arms continue unabated into conflict areas, wherein they may exacerbate conflict and suffering. The primary intention of international arms embargoes is to reduce such flows, and thereby mitigate human rights abuses and security risks, and it appears that they have little effect. To shed light upon this, this chapter presents a new database on international arms embargoes and refers back to these data on major arms imports to help assess the effectiveness of arms embargoes.

2.2. The Global Arms Trade and Corruption

In addition to tracking closely with conflict, arms procurement has also been positively associated with corruption.[37] This is in large part due to the noncompetitive and largely opaque nature of military procurements. In addition, "major arms are difficult to price fairly because of product complexity, uniqueness, and variation in size."[38] These factors make it possible for officials overseeing the procurement process to abuse their position and engage in rent-seeking with arms manufacturers both on the demand and supply side of the transaction.

[35] Craft & Smaldone, *supra* note 7.

[36] The definition of "conflict" comes from the Uppsala Conflict Data Program (UCDP) and the Peace Research Institute Oslo (PRIO) in constructing the UCDP/PRIO data set. *See* Nils Petter Gleditsch et al., *UCDP/PRIO Armed Conflicts Dataset* (2002), https://www.prio.org/Data/Armed-Conflict/UCDP-PRIO/. For a explanation of the source data for this data set, *see* Hite-Rubin, *supra* note 14; Drezner & Hite-Rubin, *supra* note 14.

[37] Sanjeev Gupta, Luiz de Mello & Raju Sharan, *Corruption and Military Spending*, 17(4) Eur. J. Pol. Econ. 749 (2001); Emmanuelle Auriol, *Corruption in Procurement and Public Purchase*, 24(5) Int'l J. Indus. Org. 867 (2006); Susan Willett, *Defence Expenditures, Arms Procurement and Corruption in Sub-Saharan Africa*, 36(121) Rev. Afr. Pol. Econ. 335 (2009); Giorgio D'Agostino, John Paul Dunne & Luca Pieroni, *Corruption, Military Spending and Growth*, 23(6) Def. & Peace Econ. 591 (2012).

[38] Hite-Rubin, *supra* note 14, at 232. *See also* Catherine Courtney, *Corruption in the Official Arms Trade* (Transparency International, Policy Research Paper No. 001, Apr. 22, 2002).

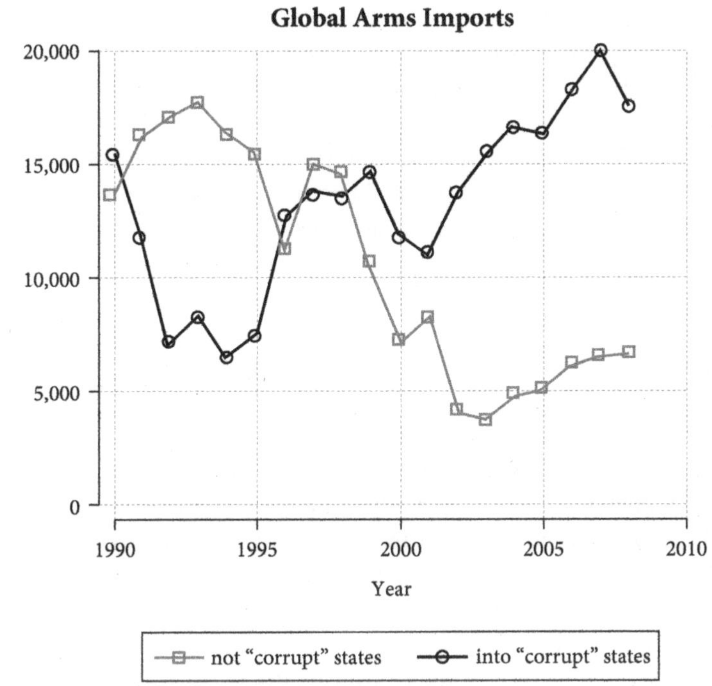

Figure 11.2 The line plot depicts the global aggregate of military weapons purchased (or transferred) into "corrupt" or not "corrupt" states on the y-axis and year (between 1990 and 2008) on the x-axis.

As demonstrated in the empirical analysis presented in Figure 11.1, it is indeed a worrying trend that international arms are flowing to politically fragile countries.[39]

The historical pattern analysis depicted in Figure 11.2 illustrates that the center of gravity for the global arms trade has shifted into states with low institutional capacity. The y-axis depicts the global volume of military weapons purchased (or transferred) on the international market for "corrupt" states verses "not corrupt" states for each year from 1990 through 2008. To measure "corruption" I use the annual International Country Risk Guide (ICRG) measure of "corruption within the political system that is a threat to foreign investment,"[40] measured on a 0–6 scale,

[39] State "fragility" is operationalized into a cross-country comparative measure by the Fund for Peace, *Fragile States Index*, https://fragilestatesindex.org/ (last accessed Oct. 7, 2020). Countries that are actively engaged in conflict are considered to be politically "fragile." As the analysis in Figure 11.1 demonstrates, major arms have been transferred into the majority of countries that experienced active conflict between 1990 and 2008.

[40] The International Country Risk Guide defines this as "a measure of corruption within the political system that is a threat to foreign investment by distorting the economic and financial environment, reducing the efficiency of government and business by enabling people to assume positions of

wherein countries scoring at 4.0 or higher are perceived not to pose a corruption risk, and scoring below 3.99 and lower are considered to have significant corruption risks. Notably, the trend line for major arms transfers to corrupt states crosses over the line for less corrupt states in the late 1990s. In other words, the majority of global arms are flowing to states with high corruption risk. This is significant and comports with the finding that military spending and arms acquisition are rising significantly in less developed countries. Certainly, such a notable shift in the global defense industry poses ethical, economic, and security concerns.

2.3. The Global Defense as Investment into Fragile States?

The correlative analyses of the prior two sections establish two interrelated facts. First, that major arms flow into countries engaged in major conflict, and that the volume of global defense trade is shifting markedly to more corrupt states. The geopolitical considerations of these trends are paramount when juxtaposed with research finding that such countries attract greater FDI when they increase defense spending and import more arms.

A central task of this book chapter is to provide targeted analyses and data collection that builds towards questions laid bare in prior research. These previous studies uncover an empirical triangulation across military spending, global defense trade, corruption, and FDI. First, research finds that when corrupt countries spend more on their military they tend to also receive higher levels of incoming FDI.[41] Furthermore, the feedback mechanism across military spending, arms procurement, and attracting FDI, pivots critically upon corruption. Only countries with low-quality institutional environments deemed to be "corrupt" exhibit this correlative trend that spending more and/or acquiring more arms correspond(s) to a boost in FDI.[42] By evaluating military spending within a macroeconomic regression model of global investment flows, between 1990 and 2008, they find that FDI flows into more corrupt countries are strongly and positively correlated with the amount of military spending by those countries.[43] In a previous essay, I find that this nonlinear relationship also holds when

power through patronage rather than ability, and introducing inherent instability into the political process." PRS Guide, *Guide to Variables*, https://www.ucy.ac.cy/fem/documents/Marios/Countrydata_3.pdf (last accessed Jan. 2, 2020).

[41] Drezner & Hite-Rubin, *supra* note 14; Hite-Rubin, *supra* note 14.

[42] Drezner & Hite-Rubin, *supra* note 14.

[43] On the other hand, the relationship between military spending and/or arms transfers and FDI does *not* hold in countries viewed as less corrupt. *See* Hite-Rubin, *supra* note 14. In short, "the more corrupt a country is perceived to be, the higher the likelihood that an increase in arms imports corresponds to an increase in FDI inflows." *Id.* at 245.

arms transfers (that is, the volume of arms moving into a country) are employed in place of military spending.[44] Thus, that essay shows that it is not just military spending but more specifically importation of military goods that corresponds to statistically significant FDI benefits for countries with poor institutional quality.

The research finding that FDI follows military spending and arms acquisition is particularly concerning in light of recent trends in the global defense industry. This is significant in context with the finding that military spending and arms acquisition spurs FDI in corrupt countries.[45] Essentially, this exposes the threat of incentivizing an arms race in the developing world, particularly among less stable countries, suggesting the need for further consideration of the role of the international arms embargo regime in curtailing the flow of arms into bellicose and unstable countries, wherein security risks are highest.

The finding that arms spending corresponds to higher FDI, but only for corrupt countries seems to conflict with conventional wisdom. Ample studies indicate that corruption stifles FDI (and, consequently, economic growth).[46] However, it is an empirical fact that as more corrupt countries build up their militaries and/or acquire additional arms from the global defense industry an increase in FDI follows.[47] One explanation for this puzzling trend is that FDI tracks military offset agreements. Indeed, my previous essay posits that as large military offsets become increasingly associated with the purchase of major arms, these purchases act as a springboard for broader foreign investment into corrupt markets.[48] First, this can happen directly because the offset agreements often contain provisions that tie the purchase of military goods to specific foreign investments. Second, global defense purchases can lead to increases in FDI indirectly, since they open access to "corrupt" markets. Beyond FDI directly stipulated in military offset agreements, defense purchases may act as a springboard into the broader market by creating first-entry to difficult investment climates, establishing and promoting business channels and exposing these countries to broader networks of international investors. In short, military spending can spur FDI in corrupt countries through the military offset channel.

[44] *Id.* at 14.

[45] Drezner & Hite-Rubin, *supra* note 14; Hite-Rubin, *supra* note 14.

[46] Paolo Mauro, *Corruption and Growth*, 110(3) Q.J. ECON. 681 (1995); Philip Keefer & Stephen Knack, *Why Don't Poor Countries Catch Up? A Cross-national Test of an Institutional Explanation*, 35(3) ECON. INQUIRY 602 (1997); Shang-Jin Wei, *Local Corruption and Global Capital Flows*, 2 BROOKINGS PAPERS ON ECON. ACTIVITY 303 (2000); Mohsin Habib & Leon Zurawicki, *Corruption and Foreign Direct Investment*, 33 J. INT'L BUS. STUD. 291 (2002); Axel Dreher & Thomas Herzfeld, *The Economic Costs of Corruption: A Survey and New Evidence* (Soc. Sci. Res. Network Working Paper, June 2, 2005), https://papers.ssrn.com/sol3/papers.cfm?abstract_id=734184; YUAN-HO HSU, IS CORRUPTION A GRABBING HAND? A PANEL DATA STUDY OF FDI (Program for Encouraging Academic Research, Taiwan, 2008); Conceição Castro & Pedro Nunes, *Does Corruption Inhibit Foreign Direct Investment?*, 51(1) POLÍTICA 61 (2013).

[47] Drezner & Hite-Rubin, *supra* note 14; Hite-Rubin, *supra* note 14.

[48] Hite-Rubin, *supra* note 14.

The feedback loop across military acquisition and FDI for primarily corrupt countries demand attention. If there were systemic global data on offsets, one could test whether offsets explain the FDI boost into corrupt countries. Unfortunately, systemic data on offset arrangements and explicit military sales do not exist.[49] Nevertheless, it is possible to learn more about the way military acquisition corresponds to FDI through arms trade embargo data by looking at the degree to which arms flow into countries that are under embargo. The rationale for acquiring arms embargo information, in lieu of military offsets, is that the practice of military offsets only occurs when the receiving country is not under an arms embargo. Therefore, the arms trade embargoes database, constructed uniquely for this chapter, is essential to empirically unlocking the corruption, global defense, and FDI feedback loop.

3. Arms Trade Embargoes

To investigate the implications of an FDI feedback loop into corrupt countries, this chapter provides a robust database of arms embargoes imposed by major world powers. The goal is to introduce this new database along with its purchase in enabling several exciting research avenues. In particular, the database can be utilized to test the dynamics of arms flows into corrupt regimes and to examine whether arms embargoes act as a mediating mechanism for the military spending-FDI feedback loop. While that analysis is beyond the scope of this chapter, the following sections outline the extensive work in developing the database, verify its accuracy and applicability for large-n analysis, analyze descriptive trends in the arms regimes, and test the hard-null hypothesis that arms embargoes stop the flow of arms.

This section describes the U.S., UN, and EU arms embargoes before detailing the sources of information used to construct the database. The database on arms embargoes imposed by the United Nations, United States, and the European Union for the 1990–2008 time frame was built using publicly available archives. This is followed by a description of the coding rules used to encode embargoes in

[49] *See, e.g.*, Carola Hoyos, *Defence Groups Agree to $75bn of Sweeteners to Win Big Contracts*, Fin. Times, Oct. 10, 2013, at 16; Adel Ben Youssef & Gueorgui Ianakiev, *Intégration du Marché Européen de la Défense et Politiques d'Offsets: Une Analyse en Termes de Coûts de Changement et d'Externalités Technologiques*, 12/13 Economie et Institutions 113, 119 (2008–09); Ron Matthews, *Defense Offsets: Policy Versus Pragmatism*, *in* Arms Trade and Economic Development Theory, Policy, and Cases in Arms Trade Offsets 89, 95 (Jurgen Brauer & J. Paul Dunne eds., 2004); Mark A. Lorell et al., Going Global, U.S. Government Policy and the Defense Aerospace Industry 49–50 (2002); *Foreign Military Sales and Offsets, Hearing Before the H. Comm. on Energy & Commerce Subcomm. on Oversight & Investigations*, 99th Cong. 9 (1985) (statement of Frank C. Conahan, Government Accounting Office); U.S. Gen. Accounting Office, GAO-01-278T, Defense Trade: Observations on Issues Concerning Offsets 107 (2000).

a manner that is applicable as a state-based and comprehensive data source that can be used for future replication and further research purposes. After detailing coding decisions, the chapter turns to descriptive trends in arms embargoes imposed by these three regimes over the period studied. Here the general takeaway is that unilateral embargoes are becoming less common, whereas parallel embargoes, applied to the same states but independently by the U.S., EU, and/or UN regime, are becoming increasingly common. This analysis is followed with a preliminary test of the hard-null hypothesis that arms flows completely stop when a country is under any embargo.

3.1. The Arms Embargo Regimes of the United Nations, the United States, and the European Union

International sanctions are comprised of a variety of forms, such as asset freezes, travel bans, arms embargoes, foreign aid reductions, and capital restraints, as well as specific and general trade restrictions. An arms embargo is "a prohibition or sanction against the export of weaponry and dual-use items—goods which have both a civil and military use."[50] An arms embargo is just one sanction that can help compel states as well as nongovernmental actors to change their behavior.[51] A country may unilaterally impose an arms embargo: for example, in the United States the president or the Department of State may issue an embargo under authority of the Trading with the Enemy Act of 1917, and the embargo will later be codified as part of the federal regulations. The European Commission issues arms embargoes under authority of article 215 of the Treaty on the Functioning of the European Union, which allows the European Union to interrupt or reduce, "in part or completely," its "economic and financial relations," in order to "achieve the objectives of the Common Foreign and Security Policy (CFSP)."[52] The United Nations imposes arms embargoes via resolutions adopted under the authority of Chapter VII, Article 41, of the UN Charter, by a vote at least nine of the 15 members of Security Council, which must include all five permanent members.

Arms embargoes are a type of trade sanction that is distinct from an economic sanction. Economic sanctions relate to *all* types of trade and financial relations

[50] Department for International Trade and Export Control Joint Unit, *Current Arms Embargoes and Other Restrictions*, UK.GOV (Aug. 3, 2012), https://www.gov.uk/guidance/current-arms-embargoes-and-other-restrictions (last updated Oct. 28, 2019) [hereinafter DIT & ECJU].

[51] SIPRI, *Arms Embargoes*, *supra* note 2.

[52] European Commission, *European Union: Restrictive Measures (Sanctions) in Force* (July 31, 2013), http://eeas.europa.eu/cfsp/sanctions/docs/measures_en.pdf (last updated July 7, 2016), listing countries currently under EU sanctions, including those subject to arms trade embargoes.

and can encompass far more areas than the procurement of military equipment.[53] For purposes of this chapter's analysis, the term "embargo" is used to refer to prohibitions against arms transfers and the term "sanction" to refer to the broader area of economic sanctions. Arms embargoes have been viewed in recent years as "smart" sanctions, since they seek to target the human security risk presented by a particular country, rather than the country's economy as a whole.[54] In some instances, broader economic sanctions may precede or follow the imposition of an arms embargo, but in other cases one or the other may be employed based on the unique policy considerations relevant to a particular country.

UN embargoes. UN embargoes tend to be the most widely applied among countries because nearly all countries are members of the United Nations. Between 1990 and 2008, the United Nations imposed 27 mandatory arms embargoes.[55] Another three countries were subject to nonmandatory (or voluntary) embargoes. A mandatory embargo occurs when the UN Security Council (UNSC) resolution setting the embargo "decides that all States shall" prohibit the sale or supply of defense items or establish an embargo on the sale or supply of these items.[56] Chapter VII of the UN Charter obliges member states (including the United States and EU member states) to adhere to any mandatory embargo.[57] Although this does not guarantee that this will always occur in practice,[58] Scholars find that, in general, major arms exporters do comply with these embargoes.[59] A voluntary embargo occurs when the UNSC resolution "calls upon all States" to stop supplying these items.[60]

UN embargoes also vary in terms of their coverage and may be classified as "blanket" (covering transfers to the entire country), "selective" (covering transfers to certain areas or to nongovernmental forces (NGF)), or "global" (prohibiting transfers to certain individuals or terrorist movements anywhere in the world).[61] This distinction is critical for the database, as it only covers

[53] Jonathan Masters, *What Are Economic Sanctions?*, COUNCIL ON FOREIGN REL. https://www.cfr.org/backgrounder/what-are-economic-sanctions (last updated Aug. 12, 2019). For example, American economic sanctions against Cuba have encompassed practically all exports and imports between the two countries.

[54] Moore, *supra* note 11; FRUCHART ET AL., *supra* note 10.

[55] FRUCHART ET AL., *supra* note 10, at xiii. Twenty-seven arms embargoes were a significant increase from the number imposed between 1945 and 2006: only two (against Rhodesia and South Africa). *See* FRUCHART ET AL., *supra* note 10, at xiii. This may be due in part to the end of the Cold War, which allowed for easier agreement on such decisions. *See id.* at 4.

[56] FRUCHART ET AL., *supra* note 10, at 1.

[57] Charter of the United Nations (1945), https://www.un.org/en/charter-united-nations/.

[58] Brian Wood, *Strengthening Compliance with UN Arms Embargoes: Key Challenges for Monitoring and Verification*, Index IOR 40/005/2006, AMNESTY INTERNATIONAL (Mar. 2006), https://www.amnesty.org/download/Documents/76000/ior400052006en.pdf; Erickson, *supra* note 15.

[59] Moore, *supra* note 11.

[60] FRUCHART ET AL., *supra* note 10.

[61] *Id.* at 2–3.

embargoes that target countries that can be encoded in an interstate data set. Thus, global embargoes such as those imposed on the Taliban, Al-Qaeda, and associated individuals and entities, beginning in 2002 are not applicable to the database. This is also the case for selective embargoes, as there is no way to determine a violation of a selective embargo with state-level data. The following are examples of countries that have been subject to selective embargoes and are thus not encoded as being under an arms embargo for that time:

- Democratic Republic of the Congo (during the 2003–2008 time period, the embargo applied only to armed groups in North and South Kivu and Ituri in eastern DRC, as well as to others not party to the 2002 peace agreement))[62]
- Sudan (the embargo only applies in the Darfur region)
- Afghanistan (only applies to arms provided to the Taliban, Al-Qaeda, or related entities)
- Lebanon (only applies to NGF)
- Iraq (since 2004 has only applied to NGF)
- Rwanda (since 1995 has only applied to NGF)
- Sierra Leone (since 1998 has only applied to NGF)
- Liberia (since 2009 has only applied to NGF)

U.S. embargoes. The Arms Export Control Act of 1976 gives the president authority to control the sale and lease of defense articles and services outside the United States.[63] Defense articles and services may only be provided to "friendly countries" and then only

> for internal security, for legitimate self-defense, for preventing or hindering the proliferation of weapons of mass destruction and of the means of delivering such weapons, to permit the recipient country to participate in regional or collective arrangements or measures consistent with the Charter of the United Nations, or otherwise to permit the recipient country to participate in collective measures requested by the United Nations for the purpose of maintaining or restoring international peace and security, or for the purpose of enabling foreign military forces in less developed friendly countries to construct public

[62] A complete listing of all contemporary arms embargoes is available at https://www.sipri.org/databases/embargoes. The following NGF embargoes were established by comparing that database with the following documents: S.C. Res. 1493, U.N. Doc. S/RES/1493 (July 28, 2003) (Democratic Republic of the Congo); S.C. Res. 1333, U.N. Doc. S/RES/1333 (Dec. 19, 2000) (Afghanistan); S.C. Res. 1390, U.N. Doc. S/RES/1390 (Jan. 16, 2002) (Taliban); S.C. Res. 1701, U.N. Doc. S/RES/1701 (Aug. 11, 2006) (Lebanon); S.C. Res. 661, U.N. Doc. S/Res/661 (Aug. 6, 1990) (Iraq); S.C. Res. 918, U.N. Doc. S/RES/918 (May 17, 1994) (Rwanda); S.C. Res. 1132, U.N. Doc. S/RES/1132 (Oct. 8, 1997) (Sierra Leone); S.C. Res. 788, U.N. Doc. S/RES/788 (Nov. 19, 1992) (Liberia).

[63] 22 U.S.C. § 2753(a) (2020).

works and to engage in other activities helpful to the economic and social development of such friendly countries.[64]

A U.S. embargo becomes effective (or is terminated) immediately when the Department of State issues a Federal Register notice. The embargo is later codified in the International Traffic in Arms Regulations (ITAR). These regulations set forth stringent rules regarding the conditions under which defense articles may leave the United States. The defense articles covered by these rules are set forth in the U.S. Munitions List (USML), which is updated regularly to include new technologies and defense items.[65] There are 21 categories of articles on the USML, covering everything from firearms to ground vehicles to military electronics to chemical agents to technical data and "defense services not otherwise enumerated." The USML is written to prohibit the exportation of any item or act that one could loosely interpret to be a "defense article and/or service." In short, the USML encompasses a broader category of arms than the SIPRI database. Thus, all of the materials tracked by SIPRI fall under the USML and would therefore be in violation of Arms Export Control Act if sent to a country under U.S. embargo.

Any person who manufactures, exports, or temporarily imports defense articles, or who furnishes defense services, must register with the Directorate of Defense Trade Controls, an entity in the Department of Defense. Thereafter, the extent to which exports of defense articles are regulated depends on the relationship of the United States to the country where they are going. As a general rule, a license must be acquired before exporting or temporarily importing any defense article. The exact licensing requirements depend on where the item is going and the relationship of the United States with that country; shipments to a NATO ally, for example, would not require the same level of controls as shipments to a non-ally.

For some countries, "[i]t is the policy of the United States to deny licenses and other approvals for exports and imports of defense articles and defense services, destined for or originating in" that country or region.[66] This applies to any country where "an export of defense articles would not otherwise be in furtherance of world peace and the security and foreign policy of the United States," for example, countries that support terrorism or are subject to a UN arms trade embargo.[67] During the 1990–2008 time period, the United States had an arms embargo on over 50 different countries at some point in time (including those it imposed solely to implement a mandatory UN embargo). Given the time period, many of these countries had alliances with the Soviet Union (e.g., Cuba,

[64] 22 U.S.C. § 2754 (2020).
[65] 22 C.F.R. 121.1. *See also* 22 U.S.C. §§ 2778, 2794(7) (2020).
[66] 22 C.F.R. 126.1(a) (2020).
[67] 22 C.F.R. 126.1(c)(3) (2020).

Vietnam, former Soviet states). Others were seen as supporting terrorism (e.g., Libya, several Middle Eastern countries). In some cases, an embargo was imposed because of human rights issues or internal conflict (e.g., South Africa, Ivory Coast, Venezuela, Rwanda). Importantly, U.S. law mandates compliance with UN embargoes, even if the country is not included on the U.S. arms embargo list.[68] Thus, any UN embargo during this period was also enforced by the United States. In the cases where the United States was simply following the UN embargo by default, and not expressly listed in the Federal Register, this was not counted as a U.S. embargo. However, when the United States expressly listed its enforcement of an embargo that coincided with the United Nations' embargoes, this was included and was counted as a "parallel" embargo.

In most cases, these embargoes were comprehensive. However, in some countries the embargo was targeted toward nongovernmental groups and thus did not apply to defense articles provided to the government itself or to international organizations assisting the government. This was the case at some point during the time period for the following countries: Afghanistan, Haiti, Iraq, Rwanda, Somalia, and Zaire/Democratic Republic of the Congo. Here, these cases of embargoes that did not target entire countries but only an NGF were not encoded as embargoes in the database. The embargoes are encoded as a binary variable at the state level, where the presence of a U.S. embargo indicates that any "defense article or service" is restricted from being transferred to any entity within the entire country.

EU embargoes. The Council of the European Union is the body responsible for imposing arms embargoes and other sanctions against states.[69] It does so in furtherance of its Common Foreign and Security Policy (CFSP) objectives.[70] The European Union likewise complies with mandatory UN arms embargoes.[71] Information on all EU embargoes in the sample frame came from SIPRI.[72] Over the time period in question, the European Union placed embargoes on anywhere from two to 11 states (including those implementing a UN-mandatory embargo). Again, only embargoes that are comprehensive for the entire target country are included in the database. EU embargoes and other sanctions are regularly reviewed "to ensure they are contributing towards their stated objectives."[73]

[68] 22 C.F.R. 126.1(c)(1) (2020).

[69] *See* European Commission, *Sanctions in Force*, *supra* note 52.

[70] European External Action Service, *Common Foreign and Security Policy (CFSP)*, https://eeas.europa.eu/topics/common-foreign-security-policy-cfsp/420/common-foreign-and-security-policy-cfsp_en (last updated Nov. 11, 2019).

[71] *See, e.g.*, DIT & ECJU, *supra* note 50, explaining that in the United Kingdom, "[a]n arms embargo might be imposed via various routes such as by the UN, EU or OSCE and where the UK has imposed regulations as a result."

[72] SIPRI, *Arms Embargoes*, *supra* note 2.

[73] Council of the European Union, *Basic Principles on the Use of Restrictive Measures (Sanctions)*, Doc. 10198/1/04 REV 3 (June 7, 2004), http://register.consilium.europa.eu/doc/srv?l=EN&f=

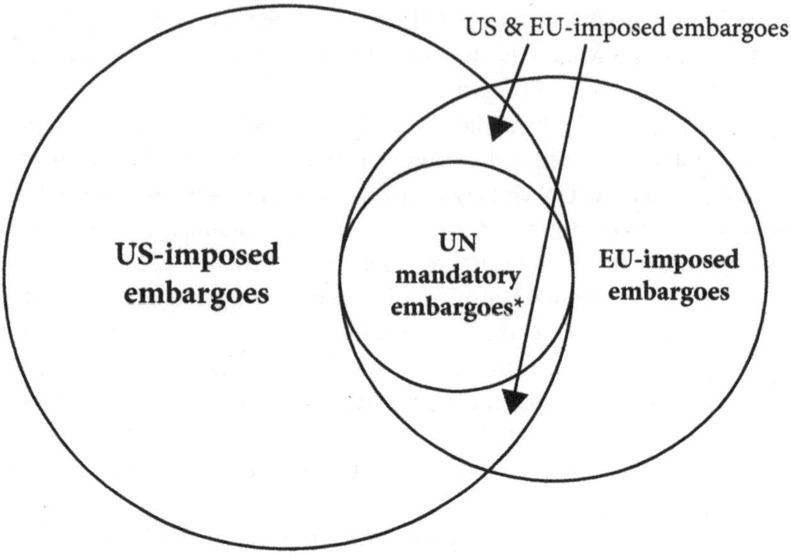

Figure 11.3 The Venn diagram represents the relationships across U.S., UN, and EU arms embargo regimes; as imposing legal obligations under international law. *The UN mandatory embargos set are contained within the intersection of the U.S. and EU sets (EU ∩ US), since implementation of UN embargoes is required of all UN member states.

Figure 11.3 shows the relationship of the three arms embargo regimes and how they sometimes overlap. For example, as already noted, both the United States and the European Union enforce UN arms embargoes; thus, the circle representing UN embargoes is entirely enclosed within the EU and U.S. regimes. However, each jurisdiction also imposes its own *unitary* embargoes. During the 1990–2008 time period, the U.S.-imposed unitary embargoes on more than 20 countries, most of which were Soviet allies. The European Union imposed unitary embargoes on eight countries, three of which were part of the Balkan conflict (Bosnia and Herzegovina, Croatia, and Slovenia).[74]

The United Nations imposed embargoes that restricted arms flows to entire countries ranging from two to 10 instances per year.[75] In some cases, the United

ST%2010198%202004%20REV%201. *See also* European Union External Action, *Sanctions Policy*, https://eeas.europa.eu/topics/sanctions-policy/423/sanctions-policy_en (Aug. 3, 2015).

[74] In addition to Balkan conflict countries, the European Union acted alone in imposing unilateral arms embargoes upon Nigeria (1998), Eritrea (2000), Ethiopia (2000), Uzbekistan (2006–2008), and Zimbabwe (2005–2008).

[75] The minimum UN mandatory and full state-level embargoes occurred 1990 with only Chile and South Africa. The maximal year of UN embargoes was in 1994: Slovenia, Liberia, Angola, Bosnia and

States and/or the European Union imposed a simultaneous embargo on the same country as the United Nations,[76] while in other cases the United States and the European Union merely complied with the UN embargo.[77] Notably, the U.S.-imposed embargo portion is depicted with the largest area given that the United States imposing unitary embargoes without parallel UN or EU embargoes is the most common form of arms embargo. The most rare combination is when the United Nations and the European Union imposed embargoes and the United States did not, with only five cases.[78]

In short, the United States, the European Union, and the United Nations impose arms embargoes for a variety of security- and morality-related reasons. Often these reasons are aligned, and in those cases the UN Security Council may issue an embargo that all UN members are obliged to comply with, including the United States and the European Union. However, at other times, the United States and the European Union may have slightly differing security or political interests, such as divergent conceptions about what constitutes a serious enough violation of human rights and international humanitarian law, leading them to impose unitary embargoes. The next section explains how information about these three types of legal embargoes is drawn upon to create a database for statistical research.

3.2. Developing the Arms Embargoes Database

The purpose of codifying information on arms embargoes imposed by the United Nations, United States, and the European Union is to allow for empirical testing of the efficacy of embargoes. As a collateral benefit, this research enables numerous avenues of inquiry in the fields of international law, international relations, and international political economy. These data cover global arms embargoes during the 1990–2008 time frame and are formatted to be compatible with all other international data series that employ the "ccode" convention.[79] The

Herzegovina, South Africa, Macedonia, Somalia, Iraq, Croatia, and Libya. Note that Yugoslavia is not included as it does not have a code for the international database.

[76] The United States, the United Nations, and the European Union imposed simultaneous embargoes in Iraq, Libya, Somalia, Liberia, North Korea, and Iran.

[77] The European Union and United States were subject to UN embargoes but did not independently levy embargoes: Chile 1991, Macedonia 1991–1995, Angola 1994–2002, and Lebanon 2007–2008.

[78] In the following cases, the United States followed the UN embargo but did not expressly list an independent embargo on the federal registrar: Bosnia and Herzegovina, Slovenia, Croatia, Somalia, and Ivory Coast. In such cases, the embargo may have been listed in the federal register as being applied subject to UN mandatory embargo.

[79] "ccode"—Numeric Country Code. Each country in the data set is defined by this three-digit numeric code, which originated from the Correlates of War's listing of members of the interstate system.

SIPRI Arms Embargo Archive[80] provides extensive information on EU and UN arms embargoes. This section discusses the data sources and coding decisions for the construction of the arms embargo database, which covers U.S., EU, and UN arms embargo regimes.

There are two key attributes of the data that must be explained at the outset. First, the database only includes embargoes that are levied upon an entire country. For example, the United States shifted its embargo on Afghanistan from being a blanket embargo to only targeting the Taliban in May 2001. Therefore, Afghanistan is coded as having "0" embargo from 2001 onward. The decision to exclude non-state-level embargoes is in keeping with the required state-level unit of analysis. Otherwise, there would be no way to discern whether flows of arms, which are measured by SIPRI at the state level, were indeed violations of the U.S. embargo post 2001. The second, critical aspect of data coding regards the timing of embargoes. The data are organized by country-year observations, and thus partial year embargoes are not included. This reduces the number of embargoes observed by the data set as some did not span over a full year. For example, the European Union placed an arms embargo on Indonesia on September 17, 1999, through January 17, 2000. This embargo unfortunately cannot be included since there is no way to determine if 1999 or 2000 transfers occurred during the prohibited period.

UN embargoes. The primary data on UN embargoes comes from SIPRI's arms embargoes archive. The data set applies only to those embargoes that were mandatory during the time period (*un_man*). A UN arms embargo is encoded as a binary variable to indicate whether a particular country was subject to a blanket UN arms embargo (*un_man* = 1) at any time in a given year (*un_man* = 0). In building the database for interstate, annual comparison two forms of exceptions had to be accounted for: (1) if the embargo was a selective embargo that did not apply to the country as a whole, or (2) if the embargo only covered limited arms transfers. In either case, this would be coded as a zero. For example, Rwanda was made subject to a blanket embargo in 1994, but in 1995 the embargo was altered to apply only to nongovernmental forces. Thus, Rwanda is coded as a mandatory UN embargo starting in 1994, but starting in 1995; the country is coded with "0" since the embargo was not state level.

Similarly, the United Nations' 2006 partial embargo against Iran primarily related to nuclear and missile technology, but in 2007 it expanded the embargo to arms more generally.[81] Therefore, Iran is not coded as subject to an embargo for 2006 and 2007 but then is coded starting in 2008.

[80] SIPRI, *Arms Embargoes, supra* note 2.

[81] S.C. Res. 1737, S/RES/1737 (Dec. 27, 2006); S.C. Res. 1747, S/RES/1747 (Mar. 24, 2007). *See also* Permanent Representative of France to the United Nations, Letter dated 13 October 2006 from the Permanent Representative of France to the United Nations Addressed to the President of the Security

U.S. embargoes. Information regarding U.S. embargoes (*itar*) is obtained by reviewing the U.S. Code of Federal Regulations and Federal Register for the years 1990 to 2008. Again, binary variables are used to indicate whether a country was subject to a U.S. embargo in a particular year. Again, cases where the embargo was targeted toward nongovernmental group were noted but not included in the database. Since the data are coded as standardized international data set, the unit of analysis is country-level and thus nongovernmental groups cannot be included. To ensure accuracy in coding the U.S. embargoes data were compared to a publicly available data source on country specific arms embargoes that covers sending country embargoes through 2004.[82]

EU embargoes. Information on EU embargoes (*eu*) was obtained from SIPRI's arms embargoes archive and supplemented this with a review of the EU resolutions setting the embargoes. Again, embargoes are coded as binary variables and exceptions are noted for cases where the embargo was targeted at nongovernmental groups. Again, only cases where the embargo was imposed on the entire state for an entire year are encoded as 1s in the database.

3.3. Historical Comparison of International Embargo Regimes

Initial assessment of the data set on arms embargoes yields two conclusions. First, over time, the landscape of international arms embargoes has shifted from unilateral embargoes imposed by a single regime to parallel embargoes imposed by at least two regimes. Near the beginning of the time period, the majority of arms embargoes were imposed by the United States, acting alone. However, by the end of the period, parallel embargoes, wherein the United States, the European Union, and/or the United Nations separately imposed mirroring embargos, became more common. Second, the overall number of countries subject to arms embargoes has decreased over time.

Although the United Nations, the United States, and the European Union have had different motivations and security concerns when they have imposed arms trade embargoes, the regimes imposed by these three jurisdictions have become more intertwined over time. Figure 11.4 shows the percentage of world countries under embargo by (1) the United States; (2) the European Union; (3) the United Nations; (4) or some combination of U.S., EU, and/or UN embargoes[83]

Council, U.N. Doc. S/2006/815 (Oct. 13, 2006); SIPRI, *UN Arms Embargoes on Iran*, https://www.sipri.org/databases/embargoes/un_arms_embargoes/iran (last updated Jan. 20, 2016).

82 U.S. embargoes were checked against Erickson's database. Erickson, *supra* note 15.

83 Possible permutations of EU, U.S., and/or UN embargoes are as follows: the United States and the United Nations (excluding the European Union); the United States, the United Nations, and the

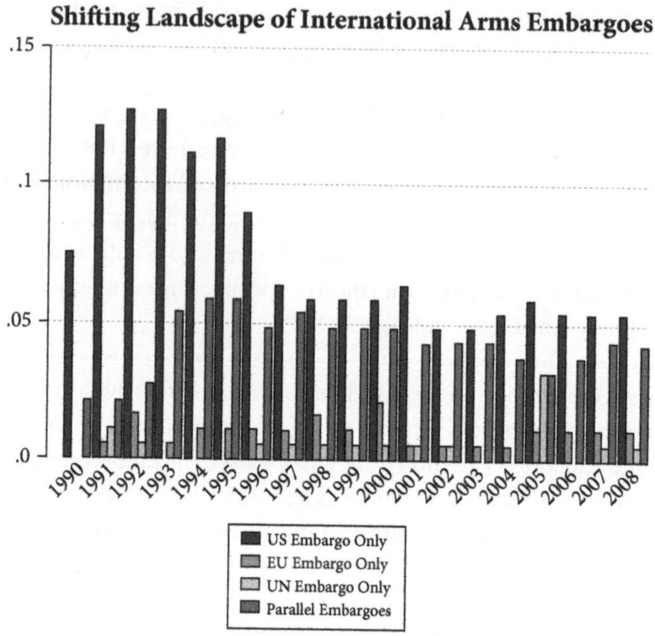

Figure 11.4 The plot depicts the percentage of countries under varying embargo constellations (U.S. embargo only; EU embargo only; UN embargo only; and some combination thereof for each year between 1990 and 2008). "Parallel embargoes" refer to the same country-year mandatory arms embargoes that are issued separately by more than one embargo regime; simultaneous (U.S.-EU-UN) or combination (U.S.-EU; U.S.-UN; EU-UN).

during the 1990–2008 time period. The graph reveals that in the early part of this period, the United States imposed unitary embargoes on a higher percentage of the world's countries; many of these were against communist states. As time progressed, however, it imposed unitary embargoes on a smaller percentage of countries.

The "Shifting Landscape of International Arms Embargoes" depicted in Figure 11.4 shows that the portion of multilateral to unilateral embargoes is rising over time. In essence, the landscape of international arms embargoes is shifting away from unilateral embargoes imposed by the United States toward cooperation. By the end of the time period, it became more common for a given country to be placed under parallel embargoes, which are either three simultaneous (U.S.-EU-UN) or combination (U.S.-EU; U.S.-UN; EU-UN) embargoes.

European Union; the United States and the European Union (excluding the United Nations); the United Nations and the European Union (excluding the United States).

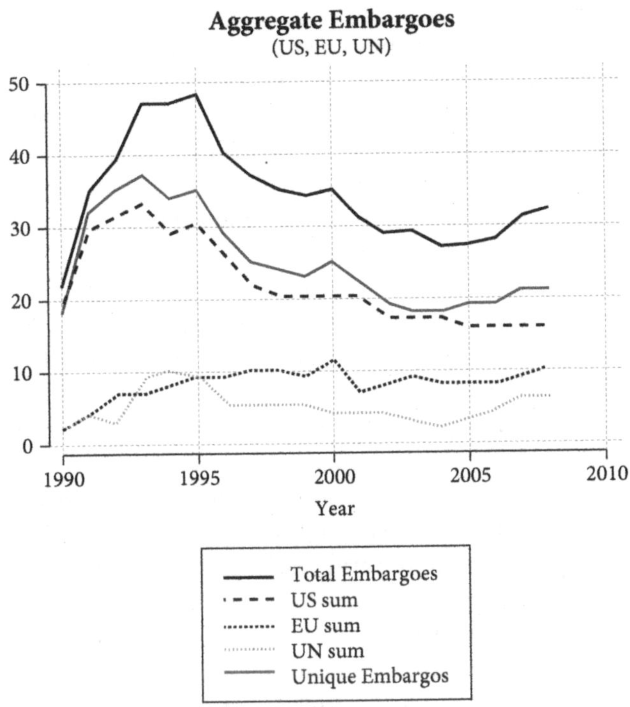

Figure 11.5 The plot depicts the sum total of countries (y-axis) under embargoes for the U.S., EU, and U.N. embargo regimes in each year between 1990 and 2008.

Also notable is the fact that overall, the number of countries subject to *any* arms embargo has decreased since the early 1990s—from a peak of 37 countries in 1994, down to 18 countries in 2003–2004. This may be due to a variety of reasons, including an increase in trust between Western powers and former Soviet states and the fact that international security concerns today tend to focus on transnational and non-state actors rather than opposing governments or blocs of governments.[84]

Figure 11.5 illustrates the change in aggregate embargoes from 1990 to 2008 for the United States, the United Nations, and the European Union. The solid bold lines, "Total Embargoes" and "Unique Embargoes," depict the sum of country-level embargoes levied each year and all unique embargoes levied each year. The fact that the trend lines for "Total" to "Unique" embargoes have been

[84] Note that the United Nations' arms embargoes are increasingly levied against nongovernmental forces or even specific persons, and such embargoes which are not included in this interstate database. *See* SIPRI, *Arms Embargoes*, *supra* note 2.

diverging since the 1990s is indicative of the fact that parallel embargoes are increasingly common. As the graph shows, EU embargoes have increased modestly during the time period. Countries subject to UN embargoes saw an early rise, followed by a leveling off. At the same time, U.S. embargoes have decreased. Eighteen countries were subject to U.S. embargoes in 1990.[85] This number rose to 33 at the peak in 1993, although much of this increase was due to the dissolution of the Soviet Union, leading to separate embargoes on many of the former Soviet states.

The data illustrate an important trend in that arms embargo are becoming more unified over time. The construction of a joint database for the arms embargo regimes of the United States, the European Union, and the United Nations offers myriad opportunities for inquiry. The initial analysis of the shifting landscape of international arms embargoes, presented here as a preliminary analysis of this chapter's newly introduced data, invites contextual interpretation, historical analysis, and theoretical discussion. An immediate question is whether this increased consensus, that is more regime overlap and targeting fewer states, has led to greater effectiveness of the arms embargo regimes. Thus, in addition to laying a foundation for empirical hypothesis testing for the FDI feedback loop, the arms embargo database will hopefully advance other investigations into international law and international political economy.

This chapter builds off of three interrelated research studies that uncover the empirical fact that military spending and arms imports lead to higher FDI, but only for "corrupt" countries. My 2015 book chapter, "A Corruption, Military Procurement and FDI Nexus?," hypothesized that this military spending–FDI feedback loop into "corrupt" countries results from the nature of global defense industry transactions within those institutional environments.[86] I noted the increasing prevalence of military offset agreements in the sale of defense equipment and services, particularly by U.S. suppliers[87] and posited that this may drive the feedback loop. Yet up to this point, this conjecture could not be tested given the absence of systematic data on military offset provisions. Now, through provision of a dedicated data set on arms embargoes, this chapter lays the foundation

[85] The eighteen countries subject to U.S. embargoes were Albania, Bulgaria, Cambodia, Chile, China, Cuba, (Czechoslovakia), Estonia, (East Germany), Hungary, Iran, North Korea, [Latvia], Libya, [Lithuania], Mongolia, Poland, Romania, the Soviet Union, Syria, Vietnam, and (South Yemen). Countries in parentheses were not included as they do not have codes. Bracketed countries were not included as the embargoes were for partial years.

[86] *See generally* Hite-Rubin, *supra* note 14.

[87] The U.S. Department of Commerce Bureau of Industry and Security (BIS) reports that American defense firms entered into defense export sales contracts worth $122.67 billion from 1993 to 2011. Of these contracts, associated offset agreements were valued at $83.73 billion (approximately 68 percent of all contract value); BIS. 2013. "Offsets in Defense Trade: Seventeenth Study." Conducted pursuant to Section 723 of the Defense Production Act of 1950, as amended (Feb. 2013), bis.doc.gov/index.php/documents/sies/687-seventeenth-report-to-congress/file.

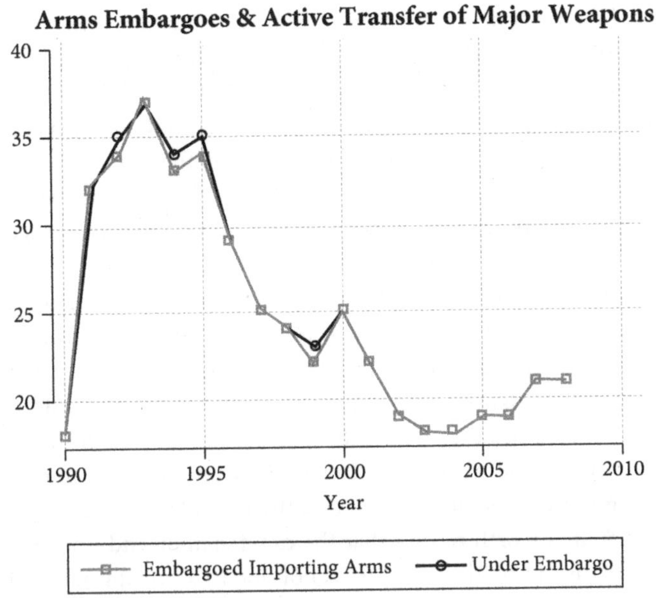

Figure 11.6 *Notes*: The plot compares two trend lines: The total number of countries under any form of arms embargo versus the total number of countries that are under any form of arms embargo and are known to receive arms transfers, for each year between 1990 and 2008.

necessary for testing and ultimately unmasking a causal explanation for this important, and ethically concerning correlation. The purchase of building this arms embargo database is to provide an indirect channel for testing the hypothesis that military offsets drive the FDI–military spending–corruption nexus.

3.4. Correlations across Arms Embargoes and Arms Transfers

The new data set on international arms embargoes opens several promising research avenues. The immediate question that comes to mind is whether having an embargo levied on a state causes the complete cessation, if not a reduction, of arms flows into that country. Insight on this research question is offered through a preliminary empirical test. The new data set is used to consider whether arms embargoes correspond to a cessation of arms transfers into the restricted country, in aggregate.

Figure 11.6 demonstrates that the hard-null hypothesis that arms embargoes lead to a complete cessation of arms transfers into embargoed states cannot be rejected. The figure's analyses are generated by first merging the SIPRI's annual arms transfer data (Section 2) with the newly created database for arms embargo regimes (Section 3). The darker trend line "under embargo" represents the frequency of states that are under any embargo in that year. States are tabulated in this trend line if they are under single or parallel (simultaneous (U.S.-EU-UN) or combination (U.S.-EU; U.S.-UN; EU-UN)) embargoes. The "embargoed importing arms" trend line represents the union of embargoed states (Section 3) and the corresponding state's status as having transferred arms (Section 2), in a given year.

The previous section illustrated the shifting landscape of arms embargoes. Namely, there has been a major shift in post–Cold War time frame from unilateral to multilateral and parallel embargoes.[88] Figure 11.6 also shows that the number of countries that are under an arms embargo of any kind has dropped considerably since a peak in 1993 with nearly 40 countries under embargo to dropping to roughly half that in the 2000s. The trend line for "under embargo" in Figure 11.6 represents the same data as the trend line for "unique embargo" in Figure 11.5. It is worth noting that the exact same trend line appears more dramatic in Figure 11.6. This contrast is not due to a precipitous decline in the frequency of embargoes. Rather, the international embargo regimes have been coalescing to set relatively frequent embargoes upon fewer states.

These fewer countries, targeted for parallel arms embargoes, do not stop receiving transfers of major arms once the embargo is in place. Figure 11.6, we can see by mapping country-year binary status for arms embargoes (U.S., EU, UN) to country-year estimates of arms flows that a high portion (nearly 100 percent) of countries that are under an embargo in any given year are receiving transfers of at least some arms in that year. Rather, most countries embargoed during the 1990–2008 time period continued to receive arms from somewhere.

Not all flows into embargoed countries are necessarily illicit. We can be confident that flows in violation of UN embargoes are illegal. UN embargoes make up about one-third of the cases depicted, so caution is due in assuming illegality for the remaining cases. To illustrate, in 1995, there were 35 countries under an arms embargo from the European Union, the United States, and/or the United Nations. It is not a given that the arms flowing into the 34 or 35 countries in 1995 were in violation of embargoes. For example, the United States imposed an arms embargo on Armenia, whereas neither the European Union nor the United Nations had specified embargoes at that time. Therefore, only flows coming from U.S. suppliers

[88] To clarify, unilateral embargoes are levied by a single state, "multilateral" embargoes are levied by two or more states cooperating with one another, whereas "parallel" embargoes are those levied by individual states upon the same entity but not necessarily in concert with other sanctioning states. For further discussion of the role of international cooperation in economic sanctions, *see* Daniel Drezner, *Bargaining, Enforcement, and Multilateral Sanctions: When Is Cooperation Counterproductive*, 54 INT'L ORG. 73–102 (2000).

would be in violation. Since the SIPRI data are total flows of arms coming into a country, this case cannot be inferred from Figure 11.6 analysis alone.

Scholars have attempted to conclusively determine whether arms embargoes indeed reduce the flow of arms into embargoed countries, with mixed results.[89] The preliminary analysis, conducted with the newly constructed database, cannot definitively answer whether arms embargoes never work but can reject the null hypothesis that they are fully effective.

This initial analysis is not a repudiation of the efficacy of international arms embargoes, but rather an acknowledgment that arms do indeed flow into embargoed states. During the 1990–2008 time frame, nearly all states under major weapons embargoes imported at least some major weapons according to the SIPRI arms transfer data. However, this does not mean that the particular embargo was fully ineffective. It seems likely that other states step in to fill in the gap that when an embargoed state cannot get arms from the state imposing the embargo. In a study on dyadic flows of sending state compliance, Erickson found that on the whole, arms-exporting countries that initiate embargoes tend to follow their own embargo.[90]

In light of these initial tests on arms embargoes, depicted in Figure 11. 6, the cases that stand out are the rare instances wherein a state stopped transferring arms when under an embargo. Over the 1990–2008 time frame there are exactly three cases wherein a country was known to completely stop receiving international arms at some point while under an embargo:

- **Latvia:** Latvia was under a U.S. arms embargo from 1990 to 1994. In 1992, arms transfers to Latvia were zero. However, it did receive arms transfers in 1993 and 1994, while it was still under U.S. embargo, suggesting that it eventually found an alternative weapons source.
- **Croatia:** The United Nations placed Croatia under an arms embargo from 1991 to 1995, and the European Union placed Croatia under embargo from 1991 to 2000. Croatia had no arms transfers in 1994 and 1995. Interestingly, however, the United States placed an embargo on Croatia in 1996, at which point Croatia began to receive arms again from the foreign market. This does not necessarily indicate noncompliance with U.S. ITAR, since the UN embargo had been lifted and thus states outside of the European Union and the United States could have sent arms without violating international law.
- **Somalia:** Somalia was placed under embargo by both the United States and the United Nations in 1992, followed by an EU embargo that began in 2002.

[89] Erickson, *supra* note 15; Moore, *supra* note 11; Brzoska, *supra* note 15; FRUCHART ET AL., *supra* note 10.

[90] Erickson, *supra* note 15.

> According to SIPRI data, there were no arms transfers to Somalia in 1999. Unfortunately, there is little to be learned from this case study since SIPRI has only furnished transfer data for Somalia for 1990 and 1999. The arms data are missing for all other years, most likely because SIPRI was unable to produce an accurate assessment of arms flows for this country.

The analysis presented in Figure 11.6 recognizes that arms *do* flow into embargoed countries—one way or another. This is not by itself a surprising result, but these data and analysis hold the key to unlocking why military spending, particularly arms importation, results in higher FDI only for "corrupt" states. In the absence of systematic data on military offsets, the presence of an arms embargo can be used to proxy whether these offset agreements are in place. The intuition is that states under embargoes will not import arms from major defense companies (such as Lockheed or BAE) when they are under embargo by the sending state. The expectation is that when a country is under a U.S. embargo, for instance, high-profile U.S. defense companies are unlikely to compete to sell major weapons there. In doing so, this turns off the supply of military offsets and other lucrative benefits, which in turn dampens FDI. Therefore, if the military offset explanation for how the global defense sales actually stimulate FDI is true, then the military spending–FDI feedback loop could only be present for non-embargoed states.

Thus, the critical next step for this research would be to test the following conditional hypotheses: H1 (non-embargoed states): *ceteris paribus*, arms inflows are significantly and positively correlated with inflows of foreign direct investment. H1: (embargoed states): *ceteris paribus*, arms inflows are not significantly correlated, possibly negatively correlated, with inflows of foreign direct investment.

The arms embargo data set created for this chapter presents a major opportunity for understanding how the global defense industry influences foreign markets. Prior work has established that military spending and arms imports correspond significantly to higher FDI only in "corrupt" countries. The next step is to explain the mechanism underlying this empirical fact. This chapter advances this research. However, more empirical legwork is necessary for establishing the empirical results of these hypotheses tests and their interpretation.

4. Conclusion

The International Arms Embargo Regimes have arisen as a response to security risks posed by the flow of military equipment into states facing instability or known to be committing humanitarian or human rights abuses. Since the

Cold War, these regimes have evolved and in many ways converged. Until the early 1990s, the majority of arms embargoes were unilaterally by the United States and by the late 2000s the United States, the European Union, and the United Nations tended to mirror each other's decisions on arms embargoes. This suggests not only the changing nature of relations between the countries exporting major arms but also a change in the nature of geopolitical and human-security concerns at the international level. Indeed, the exploratory analysis of the new U.S., EU, and UN embargo database demonstrates the contemporary trend of increased international focus concentrating parallel embargoes against fewer nation-states.

This chapter outlines the framework of three major arms embargo regimes—those of the United Nations, the United States, and the European Union—and systematizes information about the embargoes imposed by these regimes to set forth a new arms embargo database. The initial analysis of the data serves as a springboard for future research. First, the landscape of arms embargoes has changed significantly over time. In the early 1990s, immediately following the Cold War, the United States aggressively imposed arms embargoes against former Soviet bloc countries. However, as the international security situation changed, the approach of the United States toward arms embargoes became more in sync with that of the European Union and the United Nations. Importantly, within the assessed time frame, the portion of parallel arms embargoes has risen and the number of countries under embargoes has decreased. This suggests a trend toward increasing harmonization of international arms embargoes.

Upon the construction of a new database on arms embargoes, this chapter engages in a preliminary test of the null hypothesis that arms embargoes lead to a cessation of arms imports by countries under embargo. The analysis presented in Figure 11.6 very clearly fails to reject the null hypothesis that arms embargoes are fully effective. In fact, as this chapter's original data and analysis reveal that most countries that are under arms embargoes *do* continue to import major arms. This finding is not a refutation of the state of literature on arms embargoes, which has thus far focuses on sending country behavior and argues for tempered optimism. Rather, this empirical project is complementary to the existing inquiry by systematizing state-level data on arms embargoes and focusing on the transfer of major weapons to receiving states.

The results present many questions to address in future research on the effectiveness of arms embargoes. First, preliminary regression analysis on the relationship between arms embargo and receiving state behavior are excluded as they are beyond the scope and word count for this chapter. At this point, there is no known source for arms flows data and thus sender compliance cannot be tested empirically. A significant path forward should include constructing a new database that reconstructs SIPRI's Arms Industry Database on Company level sales to pooled, time-series cross-sectional format.

The arms embargo database and initial findings open up a number of new opportunities for research at the intersection of arms trade, FDI, and corruption. This chapter shows that being subject to an arms embargo (whether by the United Nations, the United States, and/or the European Union) does not preclude the country from importing arms from abroad. Given the security and development concerns arising from the transfer of arms into risky markets,[91] this finding invites further analysis. There is much to explore at the intersection of this research and previous findings by Drezner and Hite-Rubin (2014) and Hite-Rubin (2015) that when "corrupt" countries import *more* arms, it leads to *higher* levels of FDI.[92] This chapter lays the groundwork for the rigorous empirical testing needed to explain why this robust correlation exists. Testing the conditional hypotheses presented herein will shed light on how the imposition of an arms embargo influences the relationship between corruption and FDI flows. Moreover, do arms embargoes have some teeth by providing a secondary impact upon targeted states? Is it the case that the presence of arms embargoes precludes FDI from military offset agreements and the diffuse economic benefits of access to international markets? Are arms embargoes a more powerful tool of influence in international relations than is heretofore realized? Ultimately, such research can assist policymakers in developing more effective mechanisms for maintaining international security and reducing human rights abuses for some of the world's most vulnerable populations.

References

Charles H. Anderton, *Economics of Arms Trade*, *in* HANDBOOK OF DEFENSE ECONOMICS: Volume 1 (Keith Hartley & Todd Sandler eds., 1995).

Colin Archer & Annette Willi, *Opportunity Costs: Military Spending and the UN's Development Agenda* (Int'l Peace Bureau, 2012), https://sustainabledevelopment.un.org/getWSDoc.php?id=3260.

Emmanuelle Auriol, *Corruption in Procurement and Public Purchase*, 24(5) INT'L J. INDUS. ORG. 867 (2006).

Benjamin Braun et al., *Global Defense Outlook 2015: Defense and Development*, DELOITTE (2015), https://www2.deloitte.com/content/dam/Deloitte/global/Documents/Public-Sector/gx-2015-deloitte-global-defense-outlook.pdf.

Michael Brzoska, *Measuring the Effectiveness of Arms Embargoes*, 14(2) PEACE ECON, PEACE SCI. & PUB. POL'Y. 1 (2008).

[91] Craft & Smaldone, *supra* note 7; TRANSPARENCY INTERNATIONAL, ORGANISED CRIME, *supra* note 5, *supra* note 7; Nichols, *supra* note 8.

[92] Drezner & Hite-Rubin, *supra* note 14; Hite-Rubin, *supra* note 14.

Edmund F. Byrne. *Assessing Arms Makers' Corporate Social Responsibility*, 74 J. Business Ethics 201 (2007).

Conceição Castro & Pedro Nunes, *Does Corruption Inhibit Foreign Direct Investment?*, 51(1) Política 61 (2013).

David Cortright & George A. Lopez, *Bombs, Carrots, and Sticks: The Use of Incentives and Sanctions, Arms Control Today* (Mar. 1, 2005), https://www.armscontrol.org/act/2005_03/Cortright.

Catherine Courtney, Corruption in the Official Arms Trade (Transparency International, Policy Research Paper No. 001, Apr. 22, 2002).

Cassady Craft & Joseph P. Smaldone, *The Arms Trade and the Incidence of Political Violence in Sub-Saharan Africa, 1967–97*, 39(6) J. Peace Res. 693 (2002).

Giorgio D'Agostino, John Paul Dunne & Luca Pieroni, *Corruption, Military Spending and Growth*, 23(6) Def. & Peace Econ. 591 (2012).

Axel Dreher & Thomas Herzfeld, The Economic Costs of Corruption: A Survey and New Evidence (Soc. Sci. Res. Network Working Paper, June 2, 2005), https://papers.ssrn.com/sol3/papers.cfm?abstract_id=734184.

Daniel W. Drezner & Nancy Hite-Rubin, Paper Presented at the American Political Science Association, Washington, DC: *Does Military Spending Attract (Corrupt) Foreign Investment?: An Empirical Investigation* (Aug. 2014).

Daniel Drezner, *Bargaining, Enforcement, and Multilateral Sanctions: When Is Cooperation Counterproductive*, 54 Int'l Org. 73 (2000).

Jennifer L. Erickson, *Stopping the Legal Flow of Weapons: Compliance with Arms Embargoes, 1981–2004*, 50(2) J. Peace Res. 159 (2013).

Federation of American Scientists, *Literature Review: CRS' Conventional Arms Transfers to the Third World*, 6 Arms Sales Monitor 1 (Aug. 1991).

Aude Fleurant et al., *SIPRI Fact Sheet: The SIPRI Top 100 Arms-producing and Military Services Companies, 2016* (2017), https://www.sipri.org/sites/default/files/2017-12/fs_arms_industry_2016.pdf.

Foreign Military Sales and Offsets, Hearing Before the H. Comm. on Energy & Commerce Subcomm. on Oversight & Investigations, 99th Cong. 9 (1985) (statement of Frank C. Conahan, Government Accounting Office).

Damien Fruchart et al., United Nations Arms Embargoes: Their Impact on Arms Flows and Target Behaviour (2007), https://www.sipri.org/publications/2007/united-nations-arms-embargoes-their-impact-arms-flows-and-target-behaviour.

Nils Petter Gleditsch et al., *UCDP/PRIO Armed Conflicts Dataset* (2002), https://www.prio.org/Data/Armed-Conflict/UCDP-PRIO/.

Richard Grimmett, Cong. Research Serv., R42017, Conventional Arms Transfers to Developing Nations, 2003–2010 (2011).

Richard F. Grimmett & Paul K. Kerr, Cong. Research Serv., R42678, Conventional Arms Transfers to Developing Nations, 2004–2011 (2012).

Sanjeev Gupta, Luiz de Mello, & Raju Sharan, *Corruption and Military Spending*, 17(4) Eur. J. Pol. Econ. 749 (2001).

Mohsin Habib & Leon Zurawicki, *Corruption and Foreign Direct Investment*, 33 J. Int'l Bus. Stud. 291 (2002).

Barton H. Halpern & Keith F. Snider, *Products that Kill and Corporate Social Responsibility: The Case of U.S. Defense Firms*, 38(4) Armed Forces & Soc. 604 (2012).

Keith Hartley, *The Arms Industry, Procurement and Industrial Policies*, *in* Handbook of Defense Economics: Defense in a Globalized World: Volume 2 (Todd Sandler & Keith Hartley eds., 2007).

Nancy Hite-Rubin, *A Corruption, Military Procurement and FDI Nexus?*, *in* GREED, CORRUPTION, AND THE MODERN STATE: ESSAYS IN POLITICAL ECONOMY (Susan Rose-Ackerman, Henry R. Luce & Paul Lagunes eds., 2015).

Paul Holtom, Mark Bromley & Verena Simmel, *SIPRI Fact Sheet: Measuring International Arms Transfers* (Dec. 2012), https://www.sipri.org/sites/default/files/files/FS/SIPRIFS1212.pdf.

Carola Hoyos, *Defence Groups Agree to $75bn of Sweeteners to Win Big Contracts*, FIN. TIMES, Oct. 10, 2013, at 16.

Yuan-Ho Hsu, *Is Corruption a Grabbing Hand? A Panel Data Study of FDI* (Program for Encouraging Academic Research, Taiwan, 2008).

Philip Keefer & Stephen Knack, *Why Don't Poor Countries Catch Up? A Cross-national Test of an Institutional Explanation*, 35(3) ECON. INQUIRY 602 (1997).

Robert Latiff, *Ethical Issues in Defense Systems Acquisitions*, *in* ROUTLEDGE HANDBOOK OF MILITARY ETHICS (George Lucas ed., 2015).

Diego Lopes da Silva et al., Stockholm Int'l Peace Research Inst., SIPRI Fact Sheet, *Trends in World Military Expenditure, 2020* (2021), https://sipri.org/sites/default/files/2021-04/fs_2104_milex_0.pdf.

MARK A. LORELL ET AL., GOING GLOBAL, U.S. GOVERNMENT POLICY AND THE DEFENSE AEROSPACE INDUSTRY (2002).

Ron Matthews, *Defense Offsets: Policy Versus Pragmatism*, *in* ARMS TRADE AND ECONOMIC DEVELOPMENT THEORY, POLICY, AND CASES IN ARMS TRADE OFFSETS (Jurgen Brauer & J. Paul Dunne eds., 2004).

Paolo Mauro, *Corruption and Growth*, 110(3) Q.J. ECON. 681 (1995).

Matthew Moore, *Arming the Embargoed: A Supply-side Understanding .of Arms Embargo Violations*, 54(4) J. CONFLICT RESOLUTION 593 (2010).

Philip M. Nichols, *The Business Case for Complying with Bribery Laws*, 49(2) AM. BUS. J. 325 (2012).

Sam Perlo-Freeman & Carina Solmirano, *SIPRI Fact Sheet: Trends in World Military Expenditure, 2013* (Apr. 2014), https://www.sipri.org/sites/default/files/files/FS/SIPRIFS1404.pdf.

Press Release, SIPRI, *US Military Spending Falls, Increases in Eastern Europe, Middle East, Africa and Asia Says SIPRI* (Apr. 13, 2015), http://www.sipri.org/media/pressreleases/2015/milex-april-2015.

Press Release, SIPRI, *World Military Spending: Increases in the USA and Europe, Decreases in Oil-exporting Countries* (Apr. 24, 2017), https://www.sipri.org/media/press-release/2017/world-military-spending-increases-usa-and-europe.

PRS Guide, *Guide to Variables*, https://www.ucy.ac.cy/fem/documents/Marios/Countrydata_3.pdf.

Mark Pyman, Regina Wilson & Dominic Scott, *The Extent of Single Sourcing in Defense Procurement and Its Relevance as a Corruption Risk: A First Look*, 20(3) DEF. & PEACE ECON. 215 (2009).

Steven L. Schooner & Nathaniel E. Castellano, *Review Essay: Reading the Dream Machine: The Untold Story of the Notorious V-22 Osprey, by Richard Whittle, in Light of the Defense Acquisition Performance Study*, 43 PUB. CONT. L.J. 391 (2014).

Frank Slijper, *Guns, Debt and Corruption: Military Spending and the EU Crisis*, TRANSNAT'L INST. (Apr. 2013), https://www.tni.org/files/download/eu_milspending_crisis.pdf.

Rich Smith, *As the Air War Heats Up, Defense Contractors Rake in Profits*, THE MOTLEY FOOL (Nov. 22, 2016, 12:13 PM), http://www.fool.com/investing/general/2015/11/22/air-war-heats-up-defense-contractors-rake-profits.aspx.

SIPRI, *Arms Embargoes*, http://www.sipri.org/databases/embargoes.

TRANSPARENCY INTERNATIONAL, BUILDING INTEGRITY AND COUNTERING CORRUPTION IN DEFENCE AND SECURITY: PRACTICAL REFORMS (2011).

TRANSPARENCY INTERNATIONAL, ORGANISED CRIME, CORRUPTION, AND THE VULNERABILITY OF DEFENCE AND SECURITY FORCES, DEFENCE AND SECURITY PROGRAMME BACKGROUND PAPER (2011).

U.S. GEN. ACCOUNTING OFFICE, GAO-01-278T, DEFENSE TRADE: OBSERVATIONS ON ISSUES CONCERNING OFFSETS (2000).

Peter Wallensteen, Save the Arms Embargo (Joan B. Kroc Institute for International Peace Studies, Policy Brief No. 14, Jan. 2008), https://kroc.nd.edu/assets/227134/save_the_arms_embargo.pdf.

Shang-Jin Wei, *Local Corruption and Global Capital Flows*, 2 BROOKINGS PAPERS ON ECON. ACTIVITY (2000).

Pieter D. Wezeman et al., SIPRI, *Trends in International Arms Transfers, 2020* (2021), https://sipri.org/sites/default/files/2021-03/fs_2103_at_2020.pdf.

Susan Willett, *Defence Expenditures, Arms Procurement and Corruption in Sub-Saharan Africa*, 36(121) REV. AFR. POL. ECON. 335 (2009).

Adel Ben Youssef & Gueorgui Ianakiev, *Intégration du Marché Européen de la Défense et Politiques d'Offsets: Une Analyse en Termes de Coûts de Changement et d'Externalités Technologiques*, 12/13 ECONOMIE ET INSTITUTIONS (2008–2009).

12

Some Ethical Dimensions of Defense Offsets

Daniel Schoeni[*]

1. Introduction

A volume on the ethical dilemmas in the defense industry would be incomplete without a chapter on defense offsets. Offsets are a prominent feature of an industry whose character is increasingly defined by its dependence on exports.[1] In the post–Cold War business environment, which is definitely a buyer's market, offsets are here to stay.[2] Understanding them better is thus an essential task. Such an understanding would enable policymakers to identify or perhaps to mitigate the associated dangers, including the corruption risks and other ethical perils outlined in this chapter.

This chapter considers a subject that has been presumed guilty without first receiving a fair appraisal; before offsets are condemned, they should be understood. It seeks to improve our appreciation of the ethical questions related to offsets, a subject that has been sorely neglected.[3] This chapter's contribution is

[*] The views expressed in this chapter are the author's and do not reflect an official position of the Department of the Air Force, the Department of Defense, or any other U.S. government agency. The author is grateful for comments by Kogila Balakrishnan, Luke Butler, Baudouin Heuninckx, Helge Hveem, Peter Platzgummer, Martin Trybus, and Tobias Vestner.

[1] *See, e.g.*, Marjorie Censer, *Contractors Refocus on Offsets as International Market Heats Up*, Inside Def. (June 3, 2015), https://insidedefense.com/daily-news/contractors-refocus-offsets-international-market-heats (reporting that the industry is increasingly pursuing international sales); Richard A. Bitzinger, The Modern Defense Industry: Political, Economic, and Technological Issues 5 (2009) (noting the industry's growing dependence on exports).

[2] *See, e.g.*, Aude-Emmanuelle Fleurant & Yannick Quéau, *Defense Spending, Arms Production, and Transfers: The Political Economy of Defense in a Transitional Phase*, *in* Peace and Conflict 2016, at 79, 86–87 (David Backer, Ravinder Bhavani & Paul Huth eds., 2016); Charles H. Anderton, *Economics of Arms Trade*, *in* 1 Handbook of Defense Economics: Defense in Globalized World 558 (Keith Hartley & Todd Sandler eds., 1995) (calling the industry a buyer's market); Ethan B. Kapstein, The Political Economy of National Security 168 (1992) (observing that market is so competitive that buyers are able to demand offsets; Ron Matthews, *Defense Offsets: Policy versus Pragmatism*, *in* Arms Trade and Economic Development: Theory, Policy, and Cases in Arms Trade Offsets 89, 90 (Jurgen Brauer & J. Paul Dunne eds., 2004) [hereinafter Arms Trade and Economic Development] (recounting buyers' increasing market power since the 1980s).

[3] *See* Peter Platzgummer, *Arms Trade Offsets and Cases of Corruption: The Usage of Anti-Corruption Tools in Special Forms of Arms Acquisitions*, 14(2) Int'l Pub. Mgmt. Rev. 17, 21 (2013)

Daniel Schoeni, *Some Ethical Dimensions of Defense Offsets* In: *Ethical Dilemmas in the Global Defense Industry*.
Edited by: Daniel Schoeni and Tobias Vestner, Oxford University Press.
DOI: 10.1093/oso/9780190675813.003.0013

inconclusive, both descriptively and normatively.[4] But this indeterminacy is a feature not a bug. Clearly identifying the gaps in our knowledge is still a valuable exercise; this chapter thereby identifies the extant ethical issues and where further research is needed.

To lay the foundation for understanding offsets from an ethical perspective, this chapter proceeds in three parts. It first defines and describes offsets; next it considers the three main charges laid against them; and third, it relates a case study of a new ethical issue faced by U.S. offset suppliers. Notably, this case study identifies a problem that does not fit neatly into any of the three common ethical complaints about offsets. Nor to the author's knowledge has it been discussed elsewhere. It is neither fish nor fowl, but truly a novel issue. By demonstrating the problems with the principal ethical complaints against offsets and then describing a fourth previously unknown ethical issue, a compelling argument is made that the case against offsets is not so straightforward as supposed. The ethical objections made thus far lack force. That is not to say that ethical hazards do not exist, but the case study suggests that the literature might have been fixating on the wrong problems. And as noted, what has been written has often been too dismissive. To isolate what ethical hazards may be fairly attributable to offsets, we must first attempt a more careful examination of the evidence. Only then can we triage, mitigate, and perhaps eliminate such hazards.

2. Defining and Describing Defense Offsets

Offsets are notoriously hard to define.[5] Indeed, whole essays have been devoted to that effort.[6] This is in part because offsets have developed not by preordained design but by accident,[7] in part because "offset" is a hypernym,

[hereinafter *Arms Trades Offsets and Cases of Corruption*] (noting that while the literature has discussed the economics of offsets extensively, questions about corruption have not received similar treatment).

[4] *See* Ron Matthews & Irfan Ansari, *Economic Orthodoxy v. Market Pragmatism: A Case Study of Europe's "Abandonment" of Defense Offset*, 15(4) Pub. Fin. & Mgmt. 378, 387 (2015) (observing that "intellectual ambiguity" is clearly unhelpful to policymakers but that such ambiguity is unavoidable because we know so little about offsets).

[5] *See* Jurgen Brauer, *Economic Aspects of the Arms Trade Offsets*, *in* Arms Trade and Economic Development, *supra* note 2, at 54 (lamenting the cluttered "babel of terms" in the literature).

[6] For lengthy summaries of the scholarship on the definition of offsets see Daniel E. Schoeni, *Second-Best Markets: On the Hidden Efficiency of Defense Offsets*, 44 Pub. Cont. L.J. 369, 374–78 (2015) [hereinafter *Second-Best Markets*]; and Daniel E. Schoeni, *Defense Offsets and Public Policy: Beyond Economic Efficiency*, 76 A.F. L. Rev. 96, 100–06 (2016) [hereinafter *Beyond Economic Efficiency*].

[7] Luke R.A. Butler, Transatlantic Defence Procurement: EU and US Defence Procurement Regulation in the Transatlantic Defence Market 430 (2017) (suggesting

which encompasses a wide variety of heterogenous trade practices that are only loosely related to one another.[8] Yet while it has been said that the variety of offsets is only limited by the parties' ingenuity,[9] about 80 percent fit into three familiar categories: purchasing agreements, subcontracting, and technology transfer.[10] So as commentators have often observed, offsets are to arms-importing nations what the Buy American Act is to the United States:[11] their purpose is, quite often,

U.S. offset policies and practices are a product of circumstance rather than design); CHARLES W. WESSNER ed., TRENDS AND CHALLENGES IN AEROSPACE OFFSETS (1999) 71 (summarizing comments by MIT's Albert Kelley, who remarked during a panel that this "[t]his mechanism was not devised as a complete set of activities" but rather offsets "grew out of a series of unique individual deals"); Bernard Udis & Keith E. Maskus, *U.S. Offset Policy* [hereinafter *U.S. Offset Policy*], *in* THE ECONOMICS OF OFFSETS: DEFENCE PROCUREMENT AND COUNTERTRADE 357, 372 (Stephen Martin ed., 1996) [hereinafter ECONOMICS OF OFFSETS] (noting that U.S. offsets policy has been developed through benign neglect and substantial uncertainty about how offsets affect American interests).

[8] Among the various forms of offsets are coproduction, subcontracting, licensing, overseas investment, countertrade, technology transfer, and barter. *See* Stephanie G. Neuman, *Coproduction, Barter, and Countertrade: Offsets in the International Arms Market*, 29 ORBIS 183, 187–89 (1985).

[9] *See* Baudouin Heuninckx, *Security of Supply and Offsets in Defence Procurement: What's New in the EU?*, 23 PUB. PROCUREMENT L. REV. 33, 36 (2014) (suggesting that "the types of offsets are only limited by the imagination of the parties concerned"). *See also Guns and Sugar: The Defence Industry*, ECONOMIST, May 25, 2013, at 63 (observing that satisfying buyers' demands requires increasing creativity) [hereinafter *Guns and Sugar*]; Jurgen Brauer, *Arms Industries, Arms Trade, and Developing Countries*, *in* 2 HANDBOOK OF DEFENSE ECONOMICS 988 (Todd Sandler & Keith Hartley eds., 2007) (calling offsets' practical arrangements inventive); Björn Hagelin et al., *International Arms Transfers*, *in* SIPRI YEARBOOK 2002: ARMAMENTS, DISARMAMENT, AND INTERNATIONAL SECURITY 392 (2002) (listing some of buyers' creative approaches to offsets).

[10] BUREAU OF INDUS. & SEC., U.S. DEP'T OF COMMERCE, OFFSETS IN DEFENSE TRADE: TWENTY-FIFTH STUDY 9 (2021) [hereinafter BIS REPORT]. Dominance of these three categories has been steady for more than a decade. *Compare id. with* ALLEN B. GREEN, INTERNATIONAL GOVERNMENT CONTRACT LAW 279 (2011).

[11] *See, e.g.*, *U.S. Offset Policy*, *supra* note 7, at 371 (observing that for years it has been U.S. policy to mandate a North American supplier for major systems and that foreign observers agree that this is indistinguishable from an offset requirement). Examples of foreign and domestic commentators making this very observation include BUTLER, *supra* note 7, at 417 (stating that U.S. domestic preference legislation is a close analog to offsets); ROBERT B. DURHAM, SUPPLYING THE ENEMY: THE MODERN ARMS INDUSTRY & THE MILITARY–INDUSTRIAL COMPLEX 40 (2015) (noting that many consider the Buy American Act the equivalent of offsets); *Arms Trade Offsets and Cases of Corruption*, *supra* note 3, at 31 (claiming that America's opposition to offsets is not taken seriously because the Buy American Act entails mostly the same goals and principles); JEFFREY P. BIALOS ET AL., FORTRESSES AND ICEBERGS: THE EVOLUTION OF THE TRANSATLANTIC DEFENSE MARKET AND THE IMPLICATIONS FOR THE U.S. NATIONAL SECURITY POLICY 19–20, 90–99 (2009) (explaining that American domestic content rules and European offset requirement serve basically the same purpose); Neil Davies, *Reducing Corruption Risks in Defence Contracts: The Challenge of Offset Agreements*, *in* NATO CONFERENCE: BUILDING INTEGRITY AND DEFENCE INSTITUTION BUILDING, DRAFT CONFERENCE REPORT 93, 93 (2009) (saying that the United States denounces offsets while having a domestic preference policy); Keith Hartley, *Arms Industry, Procurement, and Industrial Policies*, *in* 2 HANDBOOK OF DEFENSE ECONOMICS, *supra* note 9, at 1139, 1171–72 (suggesting that Buy American supports the defense industrial base and constitutes an industrial policy that functions much like offsets); Bernard Udis & Keith E. Maskus, *Offsets as Industrial Policy: Lessons from Aerospace*, 2 DEF. ECON. 151, 162, n.7 (1991) [hereinafter *Offsets as Industrial Policy*] (saying that the requirement for a North American source is interpreted abroad as a 100% offset requirement). *See also* Kogila Balakrishnan, *Generating Value Through Offsets in International Defence Procurement*, *in* MANAGING SECURITY: CONCEPTS AND CHALLENGES 177 (Laura R. Cleary & Roger Darby eds., 2021).

to maintain domestic production capabilities by means of joint ventures, production by local subsidiaries, subcontracting, and similar arrangements.[12] The debate tends to concentrate on whether they deliver the promised benefits.[13] Offsets' goals have generally proven elusive,[14] but this may disguise their true purpose, which is usually political[15] and often concerns genuine worries about security of supply[16] or technology transfers to that end.[17] In such cases, offsets are not so much about illicit payoffs that encourage overspending on defense (sometimes pejoratively called "sweeteners")[18] but rather about garnering support for an undervalued public good.[19] That is, the false promise of the benefits of offsets may be used, sometimes—like Plato's noble lie—to win support for necessary but unpopular spending on defense. This sort of duplicity is perhaps less

[12] Offsets can be a mechanism for local market integration akin to entering into joint ventures with local businesses or establishing subsidiaries. Susan R. Sandler, *Cross-Border Competition in the European Union: Public Procurement and the European Defence Equipment Market*, 7 WASH. U. GLOB. STUD. L. REV. 373, 402 (2008). This is also what U.S. domestic preferences rules do, effectively forcing foreign competitors to move production to North America with some form of subsidiary or local partner. *See Offsets as Industrial Policy*, *supra* note 11, at 162, n.7 (explaining that U.S. domestic sourcing requirements effectively require that foreign defense firms team with an American partner). An informal or implicit domestic content requirement is far more important than any particular statute or regulation, and foreign firms so that savvy firms feel themselves compelled to establish work onshore in order to win the contract. *See* BIALOS ET AL., *supra* note 11, at 92; BUTLER, *supra* note 7, at 68.

[13] *See, e.g.*, *Second-Best Markets*, *supra* note 6 at 391–95 (summarizing the failure of offsets as an industrial policy).

[14] *Guns and Sugar*, *supra* note 9, at 63. In their seminal collection on the economics of offsets, Brauer and Dunne observe that among the authors, "there is near unanimous consensus that arms trade offsets do not work as advertised." ARMS TRADE AND ECONOMIC DEVELOPMENT, *supra* note 2, at 1. They conclude, "while positive economic development effects from arms trade offsets are not impossible, they are theoretically implausible and empirically improbable." *Id.* at 5. Yet because offsets are shrouded in secrecy, perhaps good news stories are sometimes buried. *See* KOGILA BALAKRISHNAN, TECHNOLOGY OFFSETS IN INTERNATIONAL DEFENCE PROCUREMENT 120 (2019); Matthews, *supra* note 2, at 95–96.

[15] GRANT T. HAMMOND, COUNTERTRADE, OFFSETS, AND BARTER IN INTERNATIONAL POLITICAL ECONOMY 86 (1990) (saying, "perhaps the most important insight into offsets is that they occur for political rather than economic reasons").

[16] Keith Hartley, *Industrial Policies in the Defense Sector*, *in* 1 HANDBOOK OF DEFENSE ECONOMICS, *supra* note 2, at 460, 479, 481 (explaining that offsets can be used to sustain the defense industrial base without paying the premium for production licensing agreements or attempting even costlier independent national ventures); Baudouin Heuninckx, *The EU Defence and Security Procurement Directive: Trick or Treat?*, 20 PUB. PROCUREMENT L. REV. 9, 23 (2011) (saying that offsets are used for security of supply reasons, to build or consolidate defense production capabilities on national soil). *But see* MARTIN TRYBUS, BUYING DEFENCE AND SECURITY IN EUROPE 409 (2014) (warning that offsets are rarely motivated by national security concerns and that their purpose is usually real or perceived economic benefit).

[17] Peter Platzgummer, *The EDA and Defence Offsets: Trailing After the Commission*, *in* THE EUROPEAN DEFENCE AGENCY: ARMING EUROPE 225, 226–27 (Nikolaos Karampekios & Iraklis Oikonomou eds., 2015) [hereinafter *EDA and Defence Offsets*] (arguing that offsets are often aimed at supporting the defense industrial base by maintaining or advancing domestic technical capabilities).

[18] *See* Carola Hoyos, *Defence Groups Agree to $75bn of Sweeteners to Win Big Contracts*, FIN. TIMES., Oct. 10, 2013, at 1; MATT SCHAFFER, WINNING THE COUNTERTRADE WAR: NEW EXPORT STRATEGIES FOR AMERICA 188 (1989).

[19] *See Offsets as Industrial Policy*, *supra* note 11, at 159 (observing that in many countries offsets are considered a "convenient means of achieving certain political objectives").

worrisome than officials spending more on defense because they themselves are induced by illicit payments.

Many economists consider offsets suspect because they are a nonstandard form of transaction.[20] That is, they are not the typical cash-for-goods exchanges by which modern economies function; rather, they resemble outdated bartering systems. Perhaps so, but offsets may still serve valuable ends.[21] The mere fact that a transaction is unconventional is insufficient to settle the debate. Once novel contractual arrangements that orthodox economists considered suspect have later proven useful innovations.[22]

No attempt is made to redefine offsets to resolve the lingering confusion about this term, but here is a provisional definition: offsets are reciprocal trade agreements that are a condition of sale for the defense exports.[23] They are, in other words, a form of countertrade in the defense industry. Countertrade, in turn, signifies purchases that are not conducted solely on a cash basis.[24] Offsets are sometimes characterized as "side deals" or "side agreements" that are collateral to the primary transaction.[25] That is a useful heuristic, yet for complex

[20] *Compare* Travis K. Taylor, *Modeling Offset Policy in Government Procurement*, 25 J. POL'Y MODELING 985, 985 (2003) ("Offsets are non-standard contracts that governments use to extract rent from multinational corporations."), *with* Peter Hall & Stefan Markowski, *On the Normality and Abnormality of Offsets Obligations*, 5 DEF. & PEACE ECON. 173, 177–78 (1993) (challenging the assertion that offsets are somehow abnormal or nonstandard transactions).

[21] *See, e.g.*, *Offsets as Industrial Policy*, *supra* note 11, at 159–61 (suggesting that offsets may serve a number of political objectives with varying degrees of legitimacy, such as achieving economies of scale, establishing local defense production capabilities, promotion of exports, and rewarding favored interest groups); Matthews, *supra* note 2, at 39–41 (arguing that despite the anti-offsets rhetoric and lack of data, there are clearly some tangible benefits). *But see* Ann Markusen, *Arms Trade as Illiberal Trade*, *in* ARMS TRADE AND ECONOMIC DEVELOPMENT, *supra* note 5, at 66, 80 (observing that defense ministries make dubious pitch to electorates and politicians that offsets produce long-term economic benefits).

[22] *See Offsets as Industrial Policy*, *supra* note 11, at 162 (citing OLIVER E. WILLIAMSON, THE ECONOMIC INSTITUTIONS OF CAPITALISM (1985)) (giving the example of Williamson's work showing that bundled contracts were used not for monopolistic aims as thought but rather to reduce transactions costs)); Taylor, *supra* note 20, at 993 (also citing Williamson and arguing that offsets may be an efficient, private-ordered solution to problems with the inordinate expense of maintenance and repair associated with high technology systems sold across borders). *Cf.* Jean-François Hennart & Erin Anderson, *Countertrade and the Minimization of Transaction Costs: An Empirical Examination*, 9 J.L., ECON. & ORG. 290, 308 (1993) (observing a striking parallel exists between Williamson's work on antitrust authorities contempt for nonstandard forms of contracting in the 1960s and countertrade).

[23] *See* Grant T. Hammond, *The Role of Offsets in Arms Collaboration*, *in* GLOBAL ARMS PRODUCTION: POLICY DILEMMAS FOR THE 1990S, 205 (Ethan B. Kapstein ed., 1992) [hereinafter Hammond, *Role of Offsets*].

[24] *Id. See also Offsets as Industrial Policy*, *supra* note 11, at 155 (arguing offsets may be a form of "reciprocal bargaining" beyond that normally found in the exchange of goods or services for monetary compensation).

[25] *See, e.g.*, Grant T. Hammond, *Offsets, Arms, and Innovation*, 10 WASH. Q. 173, 175 (1987) [hereinafter Hammond, *Offsets, Arms, and Innovation*] (stating that offsets are usually a side agreement to a [defense] contract"); TRYBUS, *supra* note 16, at 44 (defining an offset arrangement as a contract that is separate from the primary contract but which is also a condition for that primary contract).

transactions it is sometimes hard to distinguish the primary and secondary transactions.[26]

Offsets originated with U.S. efforts in the 1950s to rearm its allies, especially Germany and Japan, by rebuilding their industrial capacity and encouraging production of interoperable arms.[27] Offsets were at first, then, not about the recovery of U.S. spending in defense of its allies but about supporting and equipping those allies.[28] Only later did America mandate offsets to recover its expenses.[29] Other countries soon adopted and demanded offsets of their own.[30] In the 1970s, the end of the Vietnam conflict made exports essential to sustaining U.S. arms manufacturers,[31] so defense offsets became even more important. After the 1980s' defense build-up came the end of the Cold War, supply surpassed demand, and defense became a buyer's market.[32] Buyers demanded offsets, and thus offsets became the norm.[33] Today, more than 130 countries have offset policies.[34]

With the proliferation of offsets, opposition has grown. Much of that opposition, unsurprisingly, centers in the United States, the world's largest arms exporter. Since 1990, the U.S. government has maintained that offsets are inefficient and trade distorting.[35] It is not alone. Members of the World Trade Organization's Agreement on Government Procurement have banned *civil* offsets.[36] And until recently, efforts were afoot to also prohibit *defense* offsets within the European Union.[37] So far, such efforts have come to naught; even advocates of such bans

[26] *See* Hall & Markowski, *supra* note 20, 178–79 (observing that sometime the defense equipment itself is "window dressing" and what the country *really* wants is something else entirely, such as developing domestic technical skills).

[27] Joel L. Johnson, *The United States: Partnerships with Europe*, *in* GLOBAL ARMS PRODUCTION: POLICY DILEMMAS FOR THE 1990S, at 105, 107–08 (Ethan B. Kapstein ed., 1992).

[28] *Id.*

[29] *See* Hammond, *Offsets, Arms, and Innovation*, *supra* note 25, at 177.

[30] *See U.S. Offset Policy*, *supra* note 7, at 358 (observing that America's offset demands in the 1950s had significant and long-lived implications for U.S. defense exports).

[31] *See* JAMES F. NAGLE, HISTORY OF GOVERNMENT CONTRACTING 478 (2d ed. 1999).

[32] *See, e.g.*, *EDA and Defence Offsets*, *supra* note 17, at 228 (explaining reasons for the rapid growth offsets during the 1990s); Christopher Layne & Robert S. Metzger, *Reforming Post-Cold War US Arms Sales Policy: The Crucial Link Between Exports and the Defence Industrial Base*, 18(4) J. STRATEGIC STUD. 1, 14 (1995) (recounting that because the market was saturated, producers were competing for fewer sales and competition became cutthroat).

[33] *See* Johnson, *supra* note 27, at 108–09.

[34] Murat Sumer & Jason Chuah, *Emerging Legal Challenges for Countertrade Techniques in International Trade*, 13(6) INT'L TRADE 111, 121 (2007).

[35] Presidential Policy on Offsets in Military Exports (Apr. 16, 1990), *reprinted in* DISAM J. INT'L SEC. COOPERATION MGMT. 46 (Summer 1990) [hereinafter Presidential Policy Statement].

[36] *See* Agreement on Government Procurement, Apr. 15, 1994, Marrakesh Agreement Establishing the World Trade Organization, 1867 U.N.T.S. 154, annex 4(b), art. XVI.

[37] *See generally* Aris Georgopoulos, *Revisiting Offset Practices in European Defence Procurement: The European Defence Agency's Code of Conduct on Offsets*, 20 PUB. PROCUREMENT L. REV. 29 (2011) (describing efforts to curb offsets first by the Commission and then by the European Defence Agency, including the introduction of the Code of Conduct on Offsets, whose "ultimate aim"

would concede that they will likely fail.[38] Some stalwarts, however, still favor prohibition.[39]

Scarce data make it hard to study offsets.[40] Besides the United States, it does not appear that any other arms-exporting country publishes detailed statistics.[41] Offset sellers are notoriously secretive about the details because how offsets demands are satisfied has become a valuable trade secret. This is because, often, it is the offset that determines who wins the main contract.[42] Given the data shortage, studies often suffer from two common weaknesses. Either they study mere anecdotes, sometimes leading to hasty conclusions. Or they rely too much on theory, not enough on evidence. For both, the root cause of the weakness is insufficient data. For now, researchers should be circumspect in their conclusions and modest in their proposals. For a clearer understanding and better policy prescriptions, more data must come first.

Three broad categories of alleged ethical issues are identified in the literature. First, defense offsets pose corruption risks.[43] Second, offsets may create false hopes of economic gains and thus may be used to "exploit the masses."[44]

was to create market conditions and a defense industrial base wherein offsets would no longer be needed). Passage of the defense directive made the EDA's Code of Conduct on Offsets "practically obsolete." *EDA and Defence Offsets*, *supra* note 17, at 237. In private correspondence, Trybus noted that it would be inaccurate to say that the European Union is *only* seeking to ban offsets. In fact, its policy is messier. The 2009 Defence Directive banned offsets, at least by implication. Yet Member States still do offsets by invoking the Treaty on the Functioning of the European Union (TFEU), Article 346. Alternately, he suggests that the Defence Directive provides for an underutilized subcontracting regime. Directive 2009/81/EC, art. 21; Trybus, *supra* note 16, at 452–54. Correspondence is on file with the author.

38 *See, e.g.*, Trybus, *supra* note 16, at 424 (conceding that it will not be possible to eliminate offsets in the near term and perhaps a gradual phasing out is best scenario).

39 *See, e.g.*, Andrew Feinstein, Paul Holden & Barnaby Pace, *Corruption and the Arms Trade: Sins of Commission*, *in* SIPRI Yearbook 2011: Armaments, Disarmaments, and International Security 13, 32 (2011).

40 *See, e.g.*, *Second-Best Markets*, *supra* note 6, at 386–88; *Beyond Economic Efficiency*, *supra* note 6, at 116–19.

41 *See* Economics of Offsets, *supra* note 7, at 15. Though Martin's assertion is dated, the author is unaware of improvements in reporting about offsets since then. *Cf.* Matthews & Ansari, *supra* note 4, at 396 (recommending a European equivalent of the Department of Commerce's annual report on offset agreements; Jurgen Brauer & John Paul Dunne, *Arms Trade Offsets: What Do We Know?*, *in* The Handbook on the Political Economy of War 243, 243, 259 (Christopher J. Coyne & Rachel L. Mathers eds., 2011) [hereinafter, *Arms Trade Offsets*] (reporting from a literature review of 2004–09, there were no new empirical papers on defense offsets and that there remained a "crying need" for governments to gather more data about offsets).

42 *See* Kevin Dehoff et al., *Defense Offsets: From "Contractual Burden" to Competitive Weapon*, McKinsey & Co. (July 1, 2014), at 2–3, https://www.mckinsey.com/industries/public-and-social-sector/our-insights/defense-offsets-from-contractual-burden-to-competitive-weapon (saying that buyers often give offsets more weight than the main contract); Layne & Metzger, *supra* note 32, at 19 (stating that offsets are increasingly the key to winning procurement contracts).

43 *See Beyond Economic Efficiency*, *supra* note 6, at 126–32.

44 *See id.* at 119–22 (discussing the economics of offsets, including the opportunity costs); *Second-Best Markets*, *supra* note 6, at 391–95 (listing the various failed offset policies of the past).

Third, if offsets cause arms proliferation, they may also create instability and security challenges.[45] The next section discusses these dilemmas. The penultimate section considers the import of a new problem brought to the author's attention. Broadly, the following analysis suggests that the treatment of offsets has been too melodramatic, often assuming without proving that they present serious ethical problems. However, the tendency to overstate the problem does not mean that ethical issues do not exist. To the extent that there are ethical challenges with defense offsets, they should be identified, studied, and addressed.

3. Three Alleged Ethical Problems

This section explores the three most notorious allegations of ethical shortcomings made about offsets. It is not a comprehensive list. Insofar as defense offsets constitute an essential element in the sale of dangerous weapons to governments who use them to intimidate, coerce, injure, and kill, it takes little imagination to conjure up other ethical dilemmas.[46] However, the purpose is not to enumerate all of the possible ethical complaints. Rather, this piece attempts to scrutinize only the problems most commonly discussed in the literature and which seem to be the most weighty ethical issues raised. But discussing them here is not a tacit endorsement of their merit. Rather, when subjected to closer scrutiny, the ethical charges made thus far seem somewhat flimsy.

3.1. Offsets and Corruption Risks

As noted, the literature has generally neglected ethical questions related to offsets.[47] Corruption has been especially neglected.[48] In 2010, Transparency International (TI) issued a landmark report on the corruption risks associated

[45] *See Beyond Economic Efficiency*, *supra* note 6, at 133–39.

[46] The author is indebted to Trybus for suggesting one example of such a problem that will not be considered here, except for this summary: pursuing offsets sometime leads to disingenuous circumvention of the law. As he has argued elsewhere, *see* TRYBUS, *supra* note 16, at 411–21, offsets clearly violate both TFEU and the Defence Directive. Yet member states routinely invoke TFEU, Article 346 to do offsets. To make offsets fit under this narrow exemption for national security requires motivated reasoning, at least. In private correspondence on file with the author, Trybus suggests that this too constitutes a troubling ethical question.

[47] *See Arms Trade Offsets and Cases of Corruption*, *supra* note 3, at 21.

[48] *See id.* at 24 (contrasting the extensive work done on the economics of offsets with the comparative neglect of corruption). Further, corruption during the contract administration phase has been mostly ignored. *Id.* at 24.

with offsets.[49] It was the first of its kind, and has been widely cited in the decade since.[50] The report explained why offsets are especially susceptible to corruption[51] and provided useful guidance as to risk mitigation.[52] Its contribution was tremendous.[53] Until the publication of this report, the magnitude of corruption risks in this area had been unexplored.[54]

Corruption is a serious allegation. Further, because objections on the basis of economic efficiency cannot be resolved without more data,[55] the question of corruption becomes even more important.[56] Yet there is a concern that the corruption risks are exaggerated. Perhaps a better case can be made as more evidence becomes available, but for now the allegations seem too polemical, relying more on zealotry than hard evidence or sound analysis. Consider three problems with these allegations.

First, allegations of offset corruption tend to rhetorical excess.[57] Indeed, they are so pejorative that one cannot help questioning whether the arguments, to the extent logic is employed, are circular. Offsets are *assumed* to be a corruption risk.[58] Cases of bribery or various forms of corruption are adduced in procurements that involve offsets.[59] Q.E.D. However, such polemical arguments fail to prove a

49 The latest version of that TI report was published in 2016, BEN MAGAHY ET AL., TRANSPARENCY INT'L, DEFENSE OFFSETS: ADDRESSING THE RISKS OF CORRUPTION & RAISING TRANSPARENCY (2016), https://ti-defence.org/publications/defence-offsets-addressing-the-risks-of-corruption-raising-transparency/ [hereinafter TI REPORT].

50 *See* BALAKRISHNAN, *supra* note 14, at 121–22 (noting that the TI report was the first research devoted to carefully studying the question of corruption risks associated with offsets).

51 TI REPORT, *supra* note 49, at 15–19.

52 *Id.* at 31–42.

53 *See* BALAKRISHNAN, *supra* note 14, at 121 (claiming that the report's corruption mitigation recommendations were especially valuable).

54 TI REPORT, *supra* note 49, at 6.

55 *See Second-Best Markets*, *supra* note 6, at 404–05.

56 "[I]f efficiency is to play a less decisive role in this debate, noneconomic considerations will come to the fore." *Id.* at 374. Chief among these is corruption, the most serious remaining charge leveled against defense offsets. *Id.* at 411–12; *Beyond Economic Efficiency*, *supra* note 6, at 126.

57 One favorite labeled offsets the "Holy Grail of graft." Shana Marshall, *The Modernization of Bribery: The Arms Trade in the Arab Gulf*, JADALIYYA (Dec. 22, 2010), https://www.jadaliyya.com/Details/23603/The-Modernization-of-Bribery-The-Arms-Trade-in-the-Arab-Gulf. Offsets are seldom mentioned except with similarly derisive terms. *See Guns and Sugar*, *supra* note 9, at 63 (calling offsets a "dark art"); ANDREW FEINSTEIN, THE SHADOW WORLD: INSIDE THE GLOBAL ARMS TRADE 180, 530 (2012) (decrying their "inherently suspect" nature and calling the practice "systemic legal bribery"); Leslie Wayne, *A Well-Kept Military Secret*, N.Y. TIMES (Feb. 16, 2003), https://www.nytimes.co m/2003/02/16/business/a-well-kept-military-secret.html (claiming that offsets are at best a necessary evil and at worst a race to the bottom). Shanson mocks this tendency toward hyperbole, observing the one report on about offsets by Transparency International reads "as if approaching the climax of a disaster movie." Shanson, *Behind the Shadows*, *supra* note 67, at 1.

58 *See* BALAKRISHNAN, *supra* note 14, at 120; Matthews & Ansari, *supra* note 4, at 383.

59 *See, e.g.*, FEINSTEIN, *supra* note 57, at 179–83, 201, 208, 218–19, 291 (making sweeping generalizations about offsets based on a few examples in a volume on corruption in the arms market spanning 696 pages); TI REPORT, *supra* note 49, at 23, 26–34 (acknowledging that the evidence has been anecdotal, but later presenting choice anecdotes to make its case against offsets); Ryan J. Lambrecht, *The Big Payback: How Corruption Taints Agreements in International Trade*, 70 A.F. L. REV. 73, 74, 100–04 (2013) (discussing anecdotes in South Africa and Saudi Arabia).

causal relationship between offsets and corruption.[60] This mechanism by which offsets *cause* corruption—assuming one exists—merits further study.[61]

Second, a compelling argument has been made that the prevalence of corruption may be overstated. Platzgummer searched in English-language periodicals from 1980 to 2012 for offset corruption. This yielded 990 hits, and on closer examination only 250 of these concerned the subject matter in question.[62] He also added an unspecified number of academic papers from that time frame.[63] More than half (153) concerned a single episode in South Africa.[64] Fifty-seven originated from three countries. Twenty alleged corruption without citing specific examples.[65] After reviewing the evidence, he observed that 100 corruption cases for a practice spread over 30 years and 130 countries belied allegations of pervasive corruption.[66] He also questioned whether all of the allegations constituted corruption, noting that many did not result in prosecutions, and some were dubbed "corrupt" only because the large figures were thought suspiciously high.[67] Platzgummer demonstrated that complaints about corruption often rely on anecdotal evidence.[68] That limits the inferences that can be drawn. He is not alone. Others have also noticed a tendency to overgeneralize.[69] Histrionic

[60] In private correspondence with the author, Platzgummer suggested that the real problem may not be offsets per se but preexisting corruption risks in certain countries. The problem is not the medium (offsets) but the business partner. If so, then perhaps the solution would not be to regulate offsets generally but rather to prohibit doing offsets with, or even selling arms to, certain countries where corruption is rampant. Private correspondence is on file with the author.

[61] *But see* TI Report, *supra* note 49, at 18–19 (briefly outlining the pathways by which offsets may cause corruption).

[62] *Arms Trade Offsets and Cases of Corruption*, *supra* note 3, at 22.

[63] Platzgummer lists three academic reports, *id.* at 22, 33, n.6, but does not state how many were added. From this author's survey, the number would be perhaps a few dozen. He also does not say if he limited his survey of academic reports to those in English. Since the three examples cited were in English, one could reasonably infer that he did so.

[64] *Id.* at 23.

[65] India received 30 hits, Saudi Arabia 15, and Australia 12. *Id.*

[66] Lindsey Shanson, *A Hundred Cases of Corruption Involving Corruption Are Not a Lot*, 6 Countertrade & Offsets 3, 3–4 (Mar. 24, 2014) (explaining that he found overall he found about 100 cases spread across 200 countries and concluding that "the number of cases correctly alleging corruption in relation to offsets is relatively low").

[67] *Arms Trade Offsets and Cases of Corruption*, *supra* note 3, at 26. Further, he notes that many such allegations involve a "legal gray area," which may involve questionable practices but are not technically illegal. *Id. See also* Lindsey Shanson, *Behind the Shadows of Transparency International's Attack on Defence Offsets*, 33(9) Countertrade & Offset 1, 2 (May 11, 2015) [hereinafter *Behind the Shadows*] (quoting Platzgummer, "More than once we have seen allegations of corruption that in the end were not true.").

[68] To be clear, the TI Report acknowledges this dependency of the economics literature on anecdotal evidence rather than cross-sectional studies. TI Report, *supra* note 49, at 23. Further, additional evidence of offset-related corruption later emerged when Austria's Eurofighter scandal became public, which was not included in Platzgummer's study. *See, e.g.*, *Airbus Corruption Scandal May Lead Straight to the Top*, Spiegel Online Int'l (Oct. 9, 2017), https://www.spiegel.de/international/business/airbus-corruption-scandal-threatens-ceo-tom-enders-a-1171533.html.

[69] *See* Balakrishnan, *supra* note 14, at 120 (noting that despite widespread allegations of corruption, evidence is lacking); Matthews & Ansari, *supra* note 4, at 383 (observing that allegations are

concern about offsets may be an obstacle to understanding the practice and whether or to what extent it poses genuine risks.[70]

A third problem with allegations of corruption is that of correlation and causation. It is not clear that offsets are *the* drivers of corruption.[71] Certain features are said to make offsets susceptible to corruption: they are capital intensive, involve high-technology industries, they lack transparency, and so forth.[72] Yet there is substantial overlap between these characteristics and risk factors common to the defense industry as a whole.[73] This suggests that offsets do not increase the risk of corruption so much as they reflect an industry that is inherently plagued by corruption.[74] It does not follow that risks connected with offsets should be ignored,

too harsh and based on "whiffs of intrigue"); Andy Irwin, Peter Jeydel & Christian Sylvain, *Offsets in International Defense Trade*, 15(8) Briefing Papers 1, 6 (July 2015) (noting that statistics about corruption as to offsets are not available). Industry insiders complain that despite the frequent allegations of corruption, many contracts are "clean" and convictions are few. *See* Offsets in the Aerospace and Defence Industry, Int'l F. on Bus. Ethical Conduct for Aerospace & Def. Industry (2015), http://www.global-kinetics.com/wp-content/uploads/2016/02/IFBEC-Offsets-Report.pdf.

70 *See, e.g.*, *Arms Trade Offsets and Cases of Corruption*, *supra* note 3, at 32 (describing a "negative prejudice"). Some say that defense is "hard wired" for corruption. Joe Roeber, *Hard-Wired for Corruption*, Prospect (Aug. 28, 2005), https://www.prospectmagazine.co.uk/magazine/hardwiredforcorruption (referencing a CIA report from the 1990s saying that the arms trade accounted for 40%–45% of corruption in world trade). *Cf.* Feinstein, Holden & Pace, *supra* note 39, at 13 (claiming that the arms trade is "infected" with corruption to a degree that is unique from and disproportionate with any other industry).

71 *See, e.g.*, Balakrishnan, *supra* note 14, at 120 (resisting a tendency to label offsets as inherently corrupt, saying this question is complex and multifaceted, and even noting that from her own experience in Malaysia that offsets can be a useful policy tool when formulated and executed properly); Matthews, *supra* note 2, at 90 (observing that perhaps unfairly, offsets have been categorized along with the defense industry as a whole, where corruption, bribery, shady deals, and nepotism are thought to be rife).

72 *See, e.g.*, TI Report, *supra* note 49, at 15–17.

73 *Compare id. with* Feinstein, Holden & Pace, *supra* note 39, at 17 (listing among the permanent features of the arms trade that it involves secrecy, technical specificity, and expensive items); OECD, Bribery in Public Procurement: Methods, Actors, and Countermeasures (2007), at 28, https://www.oecd.org/daf/anti-bribery/anti-briberyconvention/briberyinpublicprocurementmethodsactorsandcounter-measures.htm (explaining that defense is susceptible to corruption because it is a buyer's market and entails capital intensity, high technologies, and infrequent transactions). *But see* Mark Pyman, Transparency Int'l, Building Integrity and Countering Corruption in Defence and Security 62 (2016), https://ti-defence.org/publications/building-integrity-and-reducing-corruption-in-defence-security-20-practical-reforms/ (reporting that offsets received less scrutiny than the main defense contract, which suggests that offsets could present a greater corruption risk than the arms market as a whole).

74 *See* Balakrishnan, *supra* note 14, at 121–22 (observing that offsets should not be viewed in isolation but must be considered in the context of an industry that is prone to corruption); Matthews & Ansari, *supra* note 4, at 396 (finding "there is little evidence to suggest that offset is any more prone to corruption than defense procurement as a whole"); Shanson, *Behind the Shadows*, *supra* note 67, at 2 (citing Platzgummer, who had observed that underhanded behavior "is not necessarily directly related to offsets but to the overall tender process"). The author previously drew the same conclusion. *See Beyond Economic Efficiency*, *supra* note 6, at 127, 129–30. It is reassuring that several authors reached the same conclusion—seemingly independently, given that none of them referenced his work.

simply that perhaps the inference that offsets are a principal driver of corruption requires closer examination. Understanding whether offsets further corruption and if so, how they do so are crucial to crafting policies tailored to the problem.

Apart from these broader issues with allegations of offset corruption, there may also be problems with the TI Report. This matters because so much of the literature is derivative from that report.[75] The alleged problem lies with its methodology. This complaint has been made against a separate study by Transparency International,[76] which lamented that only 13 of 163 companies surveyed had exercised due diligence in their offset programs.[77] One of the principal authors of that study conceded that their method was not an exact science.[78] Further, Platzgummer was quoted in the report criticizing the second study, noting that often allegations of corruption are not borne out and questioning TI's use of the term "due diligence."[79] Perhaps similar complaints could be made about the original TI Report, which, though it acknowledged the limitations of the data,[80] still made recommendations that may seem too broadly drawn on the basis of scant evidence.[81] The problem with studies of offsets more generally is that we lack information and are left with intuitions and theories.[82] To the extent that the TI Report errs, its methodological failings are common to most studies of offsets. It is hard to study a subject whose basic facts remain unknown.

As with the discussion about problems with allegations of corruption risks, the point here is not to suggest that such risks do not exist or to minimize their

[75] *See, e.g.*, Lambrecht, *supra* note 59; Mark J. Nackman, *A Critical Examination of Offsets in International Defense Procurements: Policy Options for the United States*, 40 PUB. CONT. L.J. 511 (2011). The TI Report's wide influence is unsurprising because, as noted earlier, it was the first study of its kind. *See* BALAKRISHNAN, *supra* note 14, at 121.

[76] *See* Shanson, *Behind the Shadows*, *supra* note 67, at 2 (claiming TI had "landed another volley on the defence offset industry with a combination of poorly aimed punches"). He was criticizing not TI's original report about offsets but its annual anti-corruption index about defense companies generally. KATIE FISH, MICHELLE MAN, MICHAEL PETKOV & MARK PYMAN, TRANSPARENCY INT'L, DEFENCE COMPANIES ANTI-CORRUPTION INDEX 2015, TRANSPARENCY INTERNATIONAL UK (2016), https://ti-defence.org/publications/defence-companies-anti-corruption-index-2015-3/. This report was in part based on surveys asking defense companies 41 questions, only two of which were about offsets but from which the conclusions derived were far too broad. *See* Shanson, *Behind the Shadows*, *supra* note 67, at 1–2.

[77] FISH, MAN, PETKOV & PYMAN, *supra* note 76, at 20.

[78] Shanson, *Behind the Shadows*, *supra* note 67, at 1–2.

[79] *Id.* at 2 (reporting that Platzgummer saying "no one has any idea knows what due diligence is" and doubting whether the TI researchers had any better understanding).

[80] *See* TI REPORT, *supra* note 49, at 23 (acknowledging that most of the academic work on offsets has been based on anecdotal evidence rather than cross-sectional studies).

[81] *See id.* at 31–42 (making some specific policy recommending). Perhaps the problem lies not so much with the TI Report itself, which speaks mainly of corruption risks rather than certainties, and more the with authors who rely on the TI Report's findings and draw conclusions that are less circumscribed. *See generally* Lambrecht, *supra* note 59.

[82] *See* HELGE HVEEM, COUNTERTRADE: THE GLOBAL PERSPECTIVE 91 (1988) (suggesting that supposedly economic criticisms of offsets often rely on dubious "theoretical arguments"). *See also* *Second-Best Markets*, *supra* note 6, at 389–90; *Beyond Economic Efficiency*, *supra* note 6, at 115–16, 118.

significance; defense offsets undoubtedly present corruption risks, even if the extent of those risks and their exact workings are unknown. Yet further study is required. To reverse the cliché, policymakers should not just do something, they should *stand there*. Regulating offsets without understanding them may do more harm than good.[83]

3.2. Offsets and Exploitation

A second set of concerns about offsets arises from worries about a false advertising about their dubious economic benefits.[84] Taxpayers in developing countries pay a steep price for offsets that rarely deliver.[85] This line of argument seems to devolve into a sort of false dichotomy: either offsets are a good bargain economically or there can be no other legitimate rationale for them.[86] Evidence of failed offset policies is easy enough to find,[87] and—so the argument goes—offsets must serve only corrupt or other illegitimate motives. This is not without force. Yet economic benefits are not the only possible rationale. Other legitimate motives may be at work.[88]

One possibility is that purchasers may demand offsets not so much for development or near-term economic benefits but because they seek to deepen ties with the seller's government. When countries decide to buy arms from foreign suppliers, that decision is not a one-off but instead implies a commitment to provide technical assistance and entails dependencies between the two.[89] Buyers

[83] Matthews & Ansari, *supra* note 4, at 393, 396 (warning that restrictions could drive offsets underground and thereby create a subterfuge or informal offset regime wherein the corruption risks are even higher).

[84] *See* Arms Trade and Economic Development, *supra* note 2, at 1 (saying in the introduction to their collection that among the authors there is "near unanimous consensus that arms trade offsets do not work as advertised").

[85] *See id.* at 1–2 (describing the false promise of offsets to developing nations, which seek to "double dip," purchasing weapons from abroad and encouraging economic development at home); *Arms Trade Offsets*, *supra* note 41, at 254–55 (concluding that "virtually no evidence exists that general economic development goals are ever achieved via offsets").

[86] No one author makes her case precisely this way, and it is not the author's intention to attack a straw man; however, the general lines of this argument can be discerned from multiple sources. *See, e.g.*, TI Report, *supra* note 49, at 26–30; Lambrecht, *supra* note 59, at 77–87; Arms Trade and Economic Development, *supra* note 2, at 1–2.

[87] Few nations have successfully implemented offset policies. *See* E. Anders Eriksson et al., Final Report of 06-DIM-022, Study on the Effects of Offset on the Development of a European Defence Industry and Market 41–43 (2007) (summarizing various empirical studies).

[88] *See* Kogila Balakrishnan, *How to Measure Value from Defence Spending? The Malaysian Case Study*, 37(4) Def. & Sec. Analysis 387, 401 (2021) (arguing that offsets have been successfully employed for defense industry growth, economic diversification, and foreign investment).

[89] *See* María D.C. García-Alonso & Paul Levine, *Arms Trade and Arms Races: A Strategic Analysis*, *in* 2 Handbook of Defense Economics, *supra* note 9, at 941, 947.

and sellers thus form long-term commitments. This also "entangles" seller's governments, binding countries together politically, economically, and diplomatically.[90] Offsets may, in turn, deepen such entangling relationships between buyer and seller governments.[91] In some cases, the weapons are perhaps window dressing, and what purchasing nations really want is *relationships*.[92] This does not disprove that offsets are sometimes demanded for corrupt reasons, but it does suggest that the motives for desiring offsets are not always or necessarily suspect.[93] Because not all offsets are inefficient or unethical, each offset agreement should be judged separately on its own merits.[94]

3.3. Offsets and Instability

A third ethical concern about offsets is their relationship to destabilization. The argument goes like this: but for offsets, purchasing governments would spend less on weapons; greater defense spending increases the incidence of armed conflict among rivals; offsets, therefore, cause wars.[95] Allegations of such connections abound, but this question has not yet received robust treatment.[96]

[90] *See* Ethan B. Kapstein, *Allies and Armaments*, SURVIVAL, Summer 2002, at 141, 143–47.

[91] *See Beyond Economic Efficiency*, *supra* note 6, at 122–25. That article discussed mainly *economic* benefits may accrue from offsets that are distinct from the near-term benefits that purchasers may claim as justifications for offsets. However, this argument could also be extended to other non-economic benefits (political, diplomatic, or military) that may accrue from deepening the relationship with a foreign government that is influential, prosperous, and powerful.

[92] *See* Hall & Markowski, *supra* note 20, at 178–79.

[93] To be clear, the desire to deepen entangling relationships with certain allies is not the only alternative to corruption. Purchasing countries may demand offsets for technology transfers, to nurture infant industries, or for local employment. *Second-Best Markets*, *supra* note 6, at 391–95. Corruption is not the only possible explanation.

[94] *See* Hall & Markowski, *supra* note 20, 176, 188 (maintaining that there is no a priori reason to condemn all offsets and that offsets must be judge on a case-by-case basis); *Offsets as Industrial Policy*, *supra* note 11, at 161 (arguing that the assessment of the net welfare effect of offsets must be conducted on a case-by-case basis).

[95] *See, e.g.*, Steve Schooner, *Working Group 6: Reducing Corruption Risks in Defence Contracts: The Challenge of Offset Agreements*, *in* NATO CONFERENCE: BUILDING INTEGRITY AND DEFENSE INSTITUTION BUILDING, DRAFT CONFERENCE REPORT 97, 97 (2009) (arguing that offsets serve as inducements to purchasing governments that cause the proliferation of arms); Markusen, *supra* note 21, at 79–80, 85 (also arguing that offsets lead governments to spend more on defense than they otherwise would and warning of the destabilizing consequences of such arms proliferation); Matthews, *supra* note 2, at 367 (describing the opposition of groups like the Federation of American Scientists on the basis of offsets contribute to the proliferation of armaments and arms-making technologies); Hammond, *Role of Offsets*, *supra* note 23, at 211–13 (observing that through technology transfers, offsets sow "dragon's teeth").

[96] Some time ago, one student author suggested that studying what effect offsets may have on proliferation and regional unrest would be an interesting subject for future research. *See* Michael K. Woodward, An Analysis of the Impact of Offset Requirements on the U.S. and Defense Industry 90 (1995) (unpublished master's thesis, Naval Postgraduate School) (on file with NPS). It does not appear that anyone has undertaken this research question since then.

Just as questions about offsets are unanswered, there has been a similar neglect of the correlation between weapons proliferation and instability more broadly.[97] To the extent work has been done, the results have been ambiguous as to the relationship between arms transfers and war.[98] One school claims that the relationship between the arms trade and conflict is destabilizing, and the other that it is stabilizing.[99] So complex is this relationship[100] that it is too early to establish causality or make generalizations.[101] Those who make such generalizations about the arms trade and war "ignore the complex record."[102] Though the arms trade may have precipitant or deterrent effects,[103] much of the work in this field simply assumes that weapons proliferation would be destabilizing.[104]

More recently, there has been research that seems to prove a relationship between the proliferation of arms and the incidence of conflict, or at least that the effect of proliferation is not irrelevant.[105] Other researchers have also presented evidence that competitive arming does not prevent wars.[106] Yet this empirical research is still new and does not resolve the ethical questions that are at play. For example, Susan Sample's evidence of a statistically relevant relationship between arms races and armed conflict is evocative,[107] but we must take care to

[97] *See* Anderton, *supra* note 2, at 524–25, 527, 558 (reporting that surprising little theoretical and empirical work has been done on the economics of the arms trade and that this area is unexplored and ripe for foundational contributions); Dagobert L. Brito & Michael D. Intriligator, *Arms Races and Proliferation*, *in* 1 HANDBOOK OF DEFENSE ECONOMICS, *supra* note 2, at 109, 111 (saying that this area of economic research has been neglected); Douglas M. Gibler, Toby J. Rider & Marc L. Hutchison, *Taking Arms Against a Sea of Troubles: Conventional Arms Races During Periods of Rivalry*, 42(2) J. PEACE RES. 131, 131 (2005) (noting that "little conclusive social science evidence exists as to whether arms races deter, escalate, or are spurious to conflict").

[98] Anderton, *supra* note 2, at 548; Brito & Intriligator, *supra* note 97, at 151.

[99] Anderton, *supra* note 2, at 547–48.

[100] *Id.* at 550 (reviewing the studies and finding "there are enough exceptions to suggest that relationships between arms trade and conflict are not amenable to general statements"). This area is "exceedingly complex." *Id.* at 553.

[101] *See* R.E. Harkavy, *Arms Resupply During a Conflict: A Framework for Analysis*, *in* THE ECONOMICS OF MILITARY EXPENDITURES: MILITARY EXPENDITURES, ECONOMIC GROWTH, AND FLUCTUATIONS 239–82 (Christian Schmidt ed., 1987).

[102] "Often heard categorical statements—either that arms transfers are inherently conflict-enhancing or that, properly managed, they are a trustworthy instrument for stability—ignore the complex record." Frederic S. Pearson, Michael Brzoska & Christer Crantz, *The Effect of Arms Transfers on Wars and Peace Negotiations*, *in* SIPRI YEARBOOK 1992: WORLD ARMAMENTS AND DISARMAMENTS 399 (1992).

[103] *Id.*; *see also* Brito & Intriligator, *supra* note 97, at 151 (saying that proliferation may reduce the probability of war).

[104] *See Brito & Intriligator*, *supra* note 97, at 113.

[105] Recent studies have shown that the relationship between arms proliferation and conflict are not spurious. *See, e.g.*, Susan G. Sample, *Arms Races*, *in* WHAT DO WE KNOW ABOUT WAR? , 63, 71–73 (Sara McLaughlin Mitchell & John A. Vasquez eds., 2021); Gibler, Rider & Hutchison, *supra* note 97, at 144–45.

[106] *See, e.g.*, GREG CASHMAN & LEONARD C. ROBINSON, AN INTRODUCTION TO THE CAUSES OF WAR: PATTERNS OF INTERSTATE CONFLICT FROM WORLD WAR I TO IRAQ 26 (2021).

[107] Sample's pioneering work in this field has been called a major breakthrough. PAUL D. SENESE & JOHN A. VASQUEZ, THE STEPS TO WAR: AN EMPIRICAL STUDY 48 (2008).

avoid confirmation bias or to conclude too hastily that her research settles the matter. Sample relies on a data set from 1816 to 1945 and her findings do not hold true for the Cold War period.[108] So the evidence is inconclusive. Even if arms races can be blamed to some extent for increases in hostilities, that does not say how much offsets contribute to arms races. Further inquiry is required to determine how offsets affect proliferation, how proliferation affects the incidence of war, and what this means for ethical questions about offsets. So far, allegations that offsets induce armed conflict have been hasty, the evidence sparse, and the logic questionable.

4. Case Study: Corruption during the Execution Phase

As noted in the introduction, this case study does not fall into any of the three categories of ethical dilemmas discussed; it is not one that has been reviewed in the literature or noticed by the academy. This suggests that there may be a worrisome gulf between what we think we know about offsets from a theoretical perspective and how offsets work in practice. Even if the three alleged problems discussed previously are not so serious as some have supposed, perhaps there are other ethical dilemmas more deserving of scholarly treatment. This case study may present one such example. It is, therefore, perhaps this chapter's most important contribution.

Ethical questions about offsets have been neglected,[109] corruption even more so,[110] and corruption during the execution phase mostly ignored.[111] This section attempts to fill the gap by considering a dilemma in which U.S. contractors often find themselves during the execution phase. This problem was brought to the author's attention during a conversation with a prominent offset supplier at a 2016 conference sponsored by what was then called the Global Offsets and Countertrade Association (GOCA).[112] Though some background is required to explain this problem in full, here is the nub: buyers do not always honor the terms

[108] *See id.* at 48–49, 195.

[109] *See supra* note 3 and accompanying text.

[110] *See supra* note 48 and accompanying text (citing *Arms Trade Offsets and Cases of Corruption*, *supra* note 3, at 21, 24).

[111] *Id.* Though Platzgummer claims that corruption during the executive phase has been ignored, there has been some treatment of this subject. *See* Lambrecht, *supra* note 59, at 104–05; TI Report, *supra* note 48, at 2–3, 24–25, 31, 33.

[112] In 2020, GOCA renamed itself the Industrial Cooperation Association. Lindsey Shanson, *GOCA Is Gone, GICA Is Born*, 38(10) COUNTERTRADE & OFFSET, May 5, 2020, https://cto-offset.com/headline/goca-is-gone-gica-is-born/. One cannot help wondering whether the name change was due to offsets being associated with corrupt practices. As Platzgummer has comically observed, "the U.S. government use[s] the term 'offset' and 'corruption' in the same sentence as a matter of principle." *Arms Trade Offsets and Cases of Corruption*, *supra* note 3, at 31.

of the offset agreements and may seek to extract additional concessions during the contract execution phase, and U.S. defense contractors have little recourse.

Foreign governments can buy U.S. arms in two ways: either through Direct Commercial Sales (DCS) or the Foreign Military Sales (FMS) program.[113] The latter creates the dilemma in question. It is not clear what the share of sales is for each. One commentator has said that most transactions occur through FMS, noting that three decades ago, 90 percent of arms exports by value were government-to-government transactions.[114] More recently, publicly reported statistics indicate a major shift toward commercial sales, with about two-thirds going to DCS, the balance to FMS.[115] However, these numbers represent *deals* not deliveries, and not all deals are consummated. Thus, reliable figures have not been made available to the public.[116]

Whatever the exact figures, FMS still represent a sizeable share of U.S. arms exports, with almost $51 billion in new deals made in 2020.[117] Further, regardless of the program's share of total exports, FMS are important for another reason. Not all defense articles can be purchased through DCS.[118] Under the Arms Export Control Act (AECA) of 1976,[119] the president can designate certain items "FMS only."[120] The exact contents of this list are classified.[121] But from publicly available sources we know that items are listed there for technological and policy reasons[122] and to balance the protection of our defense technology with responsiveness to partners' needs.[123] The Security Assistance

113 DEF. SEC. COOPERATION UNIV., SECURITY COOPERATION MANAGEMENT 15-1 (2021) [hereinafter GREENBOOK].

114 ANTHONY J. PERFILIO, FOREIGN MILITARY SALES HANDBOOK, § 1.2 (Oct. 2021).

115 *See* NATHAN J. LUCAS & MICHAEL J. VASSALOTTI, CONG. RES. SERV., R46337, TRANSFER OF DEFENSE ARTICLES: SALE AND EXPORT OF U.S.-MADE ARMS TO FOREIGN ENTITIES 2–3 (2020) (comparing the DCS export license issued and with FMS totals for fiscal years 2016–18).

116 *See* Aaron Mehta, *America Sold $175 Billion in Weapons Abroad in FY20*, DEF. NEWS (Dec. 4, 2020), https://www.defensenews.com/pentagon/2020/12/04/american-sold-175-billion-in-weapons-abroad-in-fy20/. Although the exact value of DCS transactions is unavailable, estimates can be had from reports by the State Department's Directorate of Defense Trade Controls. *See* Jade C. Totman & Brian C. Baldrate, *International Defense Sales*, *in* THE CONTACTOR'S GUIDE TO INTERNATIONAL PROCUREMENT 9, 28 (Erin Felix & Marques O. Peterson eds., 2018).

117 Mehta, *supra* note 116.

118 Totman & Baldrate, *supra* note 116, at 10, 19.

119 22 U.S.C. §§ 2751, *et seq.*

120 SAMM C4.3.4 (explaining, "The AECA gives the President discretion to designate which military end-items must be sold exclusively through FMS channels.").

121 PERFILIO, *supra* note 114, at § 3.15.

122 *See Foreign Military Sales: Process and Policy: Hearing Before the H. Subcomm. on Terrorism, Nonproliferation and Trade*, 115th Cong. 115-35 (2017) (opening statement of Ambassador Tina S. Kaidanow, Acting Assistant Secretary, Bureau of Political-Military Affairs, U.S. Department of State), at 16 [hereinafter Kaidanow Statement].

123 *See* PERFILIO, *supra* note 114, at § 3.15. *See also* GREENBOOK, *supra* note 113, at 15-2 (suggesting four elements help explain the DoD and the military department policies on FMS-only items: political and military relationships with the end user, sale of new or complex items, diversion or exploitation of defense technologies, or feasibility of separating the components into separate FMS and DCS elements).

Management Manual (SAMM) provides an illustrative list of categories of the technologies on the FMS-only list. Thirty-two categories are listed, including attack helicopters, autonomous weapons, missile defense, fighter aircraft, and drones.[124] Notably, offsets are usually sought mainly for such high-end, major systems.[125] So even if the share of FMS compared to DCS has shrunk, FMS are still highly relevant to offsets. That is, because FMS are still the primary medium for selling major systems, offsets are more often connected with FMS than with DCS. This makes understanding the workings of the FMS program key. Its importance thus requires a digression to explain how FMS sales function in relation to offsets.

First a word about how the FMS program functions generally, setting aside the offsets question. It is best understood in contrast with DCS, where buyers and sellers are left to their own devices. Regulatory hurdles are significant.[126] Apart from the normal commercial negotiation process,[127] sellers must register with the State Department,[128] secure an export license,[129] and comply with the International Traffic in Arms Regulations.[130] The AECA requires congressional notification for larger transactions, and Congress retains authority to block sales.[131] U.S. government support is limited: *caveat emptor*.[132]

By contrast, FMS is a "total package approach."[133] For starters, it eliminates the complex export licensing requirements,[134] thus reducing time, cost, and uncertainty for the buyer.[135] FMS also leverages economies of scale, selling equipment at the same price that the Department of Defense (DoD) pays.[136] But it does

[124] SAMM C4.3.5.2.

[125] *See* GREENBOOK, *supra* note 113, at 9-19, 15-15.

[126] *See, e.g.*, LUCAS & VASSALOTTI, *supra* note 115, at 15–18; Totman & Baldrate, *supra* note 116, at 17–20.

[127] *See* Totman & Baldrate, *supra* note 116, at 18.

[128] LUCAS & VASSALOTTI, *supra* note 115, at 15.

[129] *See* GREENBOOK, *supra* note 113, at 7-8, 15-4, 15-6, 15-16 (explaining that contractors may have to apply for export license to both the State and Commerce Departments and that the DoD plays an integral role in this process.)

[130] 22 C.F.R. pts. 120–130. For a summary of these requirements, *see The International Traffic Arms (ITAR)*, U.S. DEP'T STATE DIRECTORATE FOR DEF. TRADE CONTROLS, https://www.pmddtc.state.gov/ddtc_public?id=ddtc_kb_article_page&sys_id=%2024d528fddbfc930044f9ff621f961987 (last visited Oct. 15, 2021).

[131] 22 U.S.C. § 2776(c). *See also* LUCAS & VASSALOTTI, *supra* note 115, at 15.

[132] The United States does not administer or facilitate DCS transactions. LUCAS & VASSALOTTI, *supra* note 115, at 17. At most, U.S. defense contractors can make complaints the local embassy's Security Cooperation Office (SCO) chief. *Id.* at 18. But the SCO chief can't actively work on behalf of any particular U.S. defense contractor. *Id.*

[133] *Id.* at 10. *See also* GREENBOOK, *supra* note 113, *passim*.

[134] SAMM C3.3.1. With this burden lifted, it is no wonder that FMS is by far the preference of defense contractors. *See, e.g.*, Matias Maloberti, *Foreign Military Sales*, LMDEFENSE, http://www.lmdefense.com/foreign-military-sales/ (last visited Oct. 16, 2021) (claiming that FMS is the "industry preferred method" for selling defense systems abroad).

[135] GREEN, *supra* note 10, at 113.

[136] *Id.* at 113, 120; DFARS 225.7303-2.

much more. The U.S. government not only brokers the deal but also provides support necessary to integrating, fielding, operating, and sustaining the equipment sold.[137] Further, because FMS contracts include the standard FAR[138] and DFARS[139] clauses used when the U.S. government purchases for its own use,[140] the purchasing government receives the same rights and protections.[141] Though the State Department is technically responsible for FMS, it is the DoD that implements the day-to-day management of the program through its existing logistics systems.[142] Apart from economies of scale and efficiencies that come from buying through FMS, there is another benefit. Buying directly from the U.S. government via FMS provides buyers with credible evidence that the transaction was done in a transparent fashion and that the purchase was corruption free.[143] The U.S. government's imprimatur is valuable to the purchasing government's domestic politics.

In terms of the actual mechanics of the process, FMS sales are made via contracts called Letters of Offer and Acceptance (LOAs).[144] The U.S. government and the foreign government are the parties. The AECA authorized the President to enter into such contracts for the procurement of arms with approved foreign countries, and this authority was delegated to the Secretary of State.[145] Payments are made not to the contractor but to a trust account managed by the U.S. Treasury,[146] from which the government is reimbursed for administrative costs and the defense contractor is paid.[147] Thus, in a standard LOA, no privity exists between the contractor and purchasing government.[148] Rather, privity of contract lies between the U.S. government and its foreign counterpart.[149] Federal courts have held that unsatisfied foreign governments lack standing to

137 Totman & Baldrate, *supra* note 116, at 15. *See also* LUCAS & VASSALOTTI, *supra* note 115, at 13 (also adding to that list logistics, transportation, training, financial management, oversight, coordination, and documentation).

138 Federal Acquisition Regulation (FAR), 48 C.F.R. ch. 1.

139 Defense Acquisition Regulation Supplement (DFARS), 48 C.F.R. ch. 2.

140 SAMM C4.3.9 (saying, "When procuring for a foreign Government, DoD will apply the same contract clauses and contract administration as it would use in procuring for itself, except where deviations are authorized in the DFARS.").

141 LUCAS & VASSALOTTI, *supra* note 115, at 10.

142 *Id.* at 10, 14.

143 Kaidanow Statement, *supra* note 122, at 20 (explaining that many countries appreciate the transparency that comes with the U.S. system and that evidence that the acquisition free from corruption is a major selling point for the public).

144 SAMM C5. *See also* GREENBOOK, *supra* note 113, at 5-1. Notably, although LOAs incorporate FAR clauses, they aren't procurement contracts, and their authority derives not from the FAR but instead from the AECA and SAMM. *See id.* at 8-1.

145 22 U.S.C. § 2762.

146 *In re Procurements Involving Foreign Military Sales*, 58 Comp. Gen. 81, 78-2, CPD para. 349, at 5 (1978).

147 GREEN, *supra* note 10, at 112–13.

148 PERFILIO, *supra* note 114, at § 3.1.

149 *Id.*

sue contractors for that reason.[150] So an impenetrable veil protects the defense contractor from foreign purchasers—unless, that is, the two enter into a separate offset agreement.[151]

When the FMS program and U.S. offsets policy are juxtaposed, it soon becomes clear that this is a complicated relationship, where the government tacitly facilitates offsets but denies doing so.[152] During most of the post–World War II era, the U.S. policy on offsets was laissez-faire.[153] For a brief period in the 1970s, it acted as a guarantor to ensure that offset obligations were met.[154] It stopped that practice in 1978, removing itself from the process and leaving the negotiation and implementation to the parties.[155] In 1990, the President issued a policy statement, further distancing the U.S. government from offsets.[156] It prohibited encouraging, entering directly into, or committing U.S. firms to such arrangements.[157] "The decision to engage in offsets, and the responsibility for negotiating and implementing offset arrangements," it held, "resides with the companies involved."[158] Three decades later, that remains the official policy.[159]

Given this generally aloof policy, the U.S. government does not directly regulate offsets; however, its laws, regulations, and procedures are not entirely silent.[160]

[150] *See, e.g.*, Sec'y of State v. Trimble Navigation Ltd., 484 F.3d 700, 709 (4th Cir. 2007) (affirming dismissal of a suit brought by the United Kingdom's Ministry of Defence claiming it was a third-party beneficiary of the contract).

[151] Totman & Baldrate, *supra* note 116, at 16.

[152] When the DoD's Defense Security Cooperation Agency gives notice of arms sales to Congress, such notice always contains this language: "There are no known offset agreements proposed in connection with this potential sale." *See, e.g.*, Arms Sale Notice, July 28, 2021, at 86 Fed. Reg. 42794 (Aug. 5, 2021) (providing notice of a $125 million sale to the Netherlands and using this boilerplate language to disavow knowledge of an offset). This language is worse than a polite fiction because the DoD is well aware of the existence of offset agreements associated with most arms sales. *See* Mark J. Nackman, *A Critical Examination of Offsets in International Defense Procurements: Policy Options for the United States*, 40 Pub. Cont. L.J. 511, 526–27 (2011) (recommending the elimination of the "no known offsets" policy and noting that offsets agreements are no secret given that they are reported in BIS's annual report to Congress).

[153] Lambrecht, *supra* note 59, at 92; Markusen, *supra* note 21, at 84; Hammond, *Role of Offsets*, *supra* note 23, at 217.

[154] *U.S. Offset Policy*, *supra* note 7, at 359–60 (recounting the U.S. government's backing of General Electric and Northrup with the F-5 sale to Switzerland and its later decision to refrain from underwriting U.S. firms).

[155] *See id.*; Markusen, *supra* note 153, at 84.

[156] *See* Presidential Policy Statement, *supra* note 35.

[157] *Id.*

[158] *Id.* Some argue that in the 1990s, there was a shift from restrictions based on concerns about proliferation toward a greater permissiveness in order to increase exports. *See, e.g.*, Markusen, *supra* note 153, at 66–67, 71–72, 79.

[159] Defense Product Act Amendments of 1992, Pub. L. 102-558, § 123. *See also* DFARS 225.7306 (establishing that the DoD "does not encourage, enter into, or commit U.S. firms to FMS offset arrangements" and that this decision about "whether to engage in offsets, and the responsibility for negotiating and implementing offset arrangements, resides with the companies involved"); DFARS 225.7302-2 (a)(3) (stating that offsets are "distinct and independent" from the FMS contract and stressing that the U.S. government bears no obligation to satisfy or administer the offset).

[160] *Compare* Butler, *supra* note 7, at 419 (favorably comparing the U.S. FMS rules, which at least provide *some* restraints on the use of offsets, with the European Union's Defence Directive, which

Though the government is not to encourage offsets,[161] Congress has mandated tracking and reporting offsets.[162] The United States is the only country to institute robust reporting requirements,[163] which is to be commended. But the rules do more that. They also encourage competition "to the maximum extent possible"[164] and establish that sole-source procurements must be justified.[165]

However much the FMS rules constrain offsets, they also encourage them by establishing clear standards for payment. First, offset costs are borne by the purchasing government.[166] Also, costs attributed to offsets are not subject to the same level scrutiny as other indirect costs;[167] to be deemed "reasonable" the contractor need only present evidence of an offset agreement.[168] If the purchaser approaches officials asking for a cost breakdown of the offset agreement, they will only be referred to the defense contractor.[169] Thus, by setting clear ground rules for payment, the FMS program at least tacitly endorses offsets.[170] This suggests a certain ambivalence.[171] This tension has been called an odd arrangement[172] and

provides none), *with* TRYBUS, *supra* note 16, at 490 (2014) (likewise criticizing the Defence Directive for its failure to address offsets directly); *see also* Lambrecht, *supra* note 59, at 92–94 (criticizing the DCS and FMS restrictions on offset agreements as broad and unsophisticated).

[161] DFARS 225.7306.

[162] *See* Owen E. Hernstadt, *Offsets and the Lack of Comprehensive U.S. Policy: What Do Other Countries Know That We Don't?*, ECON. POL'Y INST., Briefing Paper No. 201 (2008), at 9, 11 (criticizing the U.S. government for abdicating an active role in setting offsets policy and limiting itself to gathering data); *U.S. Offset Policy*, *supra* note 7, at 361 (observing that U.S. offset policy, such as it is, consists in data gathering and reporting requirements). Since 1984, contractors have been required to report offsets exceeding a certain threshold, which is currently set at $5 million. 15 C.F.R. § 701.3(a). Such reports must include the name of the purchasing country, a description of the sale, the industry classification code, the specific party to the agreement (e.g., the Ministry of Defense), the value, the length of time granted to fulfill the obligation, and any penalties established for nonperformance. 15 C.F.R. § 701.4(c)(1). This information is aggregated for BIS's report to Congress to ensure the protection of any proprietary information about how offsets obligations are fulfilled. *See, e.g.*, BIS REPORT 2021, *supra* note 10.

[163] *See* Matthews & Ansari, *supra* note 4, at 396 (advocating that Europe introduce something akin to the BIS report).

[164] SAMM C6.3.4, *citing* the Competition in Contracting Act of 1984, 10 U.S.C. § 2304.

[165] *Id.*

[166] SAMM Figure C5.F4, Standard Term 2.8.

[167] GREENBOOK, *supra* note 113, at 9-22.

[168] DFARS 225.7303-2 (a)(3)(iv) (providing that indirect costs are deemed reasonable provided that the contractor submits either a signed offset agreement or comparable documentation). Offset costs have been recoverable since 1991. *See U.S. Offset Policy*, *supra* note 7, at 368–69.

[169] SAMM Figure C5.F4, Standard Term 2.8 ("If the Purchaser wishes to obtain information regarding offset costs, the Purchaser should request information directly from the U.S. defense contractor."). *But compare* SAMM C6.3.9.3.

[170] Under the FMS rules, offsets are permissible, even though the government cannot be a party to or encourage them. *See* GREENBOOK, *supra* note 113, at 9-20.

[171] U.S. policy is to neither help nor hinder offsets. *See* Robert S. Metzger, *Offsets and Domestic Considerations*, *in* THE CONTACTOR'S GUIDE TO INTERNATIONAL PROCUREMENT 46, 50 (Erin Felix & Marques O. Peterson eds., 2018), *citing* Pub. L. No. 102-558, § 123(a), 106 Stat. 4198; DFARS 225.7306.

[172] GREENBOOK, *supra* note 113, at 9-20.

awkward.[173] It also reflects a pragmatic resolution of a vexing issue.[174] This is a buyer's market, and no matter how much the United States may wish it could ban offsets, it cannot impose that policy on other countries.[175]

This background about the FMS process was given to set up a certain problem. During execution, contractors sometimes encounter demands for compensation not contained in the offset agreement. Were this a question about the FMS contract, the U.S. contractor would enjoy a close relationship with the local Security Cooperation Office (SCO). One call to the embassy could resolve the problem through diplomatic channels; a U.S. government representative would help find a solution. But such a support system does not exist for offsets.

The absence of a support system creates several vexing problems. First, some foreign governments are well aware that the U.S. government will not answer contractors' complaints about offset contracts. They use that fact to leverage concessions. This behavior suggests a sophisticated understanding about the shortcomings of the FMS system and a willingness to exploit them. Second, additional offset costs are passed onto the buying government's taxpayers. To stand by idly, when U.S. contractors have alerted officials and sought the government's assistance, seems tantamount to aiding and abetting malfeasance. Third, this devalues the FMS's program's seal of approval. Worse, it may allow purchasers to hide behind that imprimatur, extracting additional concessions with impunity, ultimately at their own taxpayers' expense. That is because the FMS program conceals what share of the LOA goes to the primary contract and what share to satisfying the offset requirements.

What is the solution? One policy would be increased transparency; sunlight is often the best disinfectant. Yet sharing the composition of offset deals would be to give away valuable intellectual property. The better solution, though, may be not to unnecessarily reveal such information but to empower the SCOs and other officials so that they can assist contractors when they are duly warned about purchasers seeking concessions that exceed the terms of the offset agreement. The U.S. government need not become a full party to the offset, nor forfeit its neutrality about offsets as a general matter. But arguably, the government should investigate and, where appropriate, act when U.S. contractors warn about gamesmanship or other wrongdoing. The mere availability of relief would perhaps deter misconduct, making the need for interventions rare.

173 Butler, *supra* note 7, at 419.

174 *See* Greenbook, *supra* note 113, at 9-20, 9-26 (saying that the FMS policy reflects the reality of the marketplace).

175 *See* Hall & Markowski, *supra* note 20, at 177 (observing that a government's power to coerce is limited to domestic suppliers); *U.S. Offset Policy*, *supra* note 7, at 372 (noting that efforts to ban offsets have been stymied by the "troublesome fact" that the U.S. Congress lacks jurisdiction over foreign governments).

This case study is evocative. It describes a new problem that has gone unnoticed in the literature. It raises important questions. Have more ethical problems gone unnoticed? If so, how many and how serious are they? That is, how do they compare with the ethical challenges about offsets that have thus far occupied the attention of the academy? These questions in turn have important implications for debates about what policies ought to be adopted and what priority should be given. In short, this case study should give us pause and invite further investigation. We may know less about defense offsets than we think.

5. Conclusion

The debate about offsets has been too tendentious.[176] It seems they are neither an unalloyed good nor an inherently corrupt practice.[177] Engaging in offsets entails risks and opportunities.[178] Some lessons can be taken from the ethical challenges considered here. First, one of the salient risks for contractors is entering into a corrupt bargain. They hazard financial liability, criminal sanctions, lost business, and reputational damage.[179] So contractors must be cautious of terms that are at variance with international norms,[180] and when they are unsure, they should seek legal counsel.[181] Ethical traps for the unwary abound.[182] Purchasing governments should emulate the United States by publishing more statistics and should be more attentive to the cost-benefit analysis.[183] And governments of offset suppliers should perhaps become more involved when allegations are made that purchasing governments are leveraging the secrecy of offsets and attempting to alter the terms of the offset agreement.

Yet as noted at the outset, this chapter has not provided easy solutions to the ethical concerns associated with offsets. It has been suggested, instead, that we do not know enough about offsets to say for sure what the nature of these ethical challenges are, assuming that they do exist. Corruption risks exist, to be sure. Certainly too much about offsets is nontransparent. However, here is the true *dilemma* about offsets. We know little about them, and it seems unlikely that that will change anytime soon for two reasons. First, genuine concern about security

[176] *See* HVEEM, *supra* note 82, at 7 (suggesting that the debate about offsets has been too ideological and that defense offsets are not inherently good, bad, or even second best).

[177] *See* Matthews & Ansari, *supra* note 4, at 395 (discouraging a "blanket indictment" of offsets).

[178] GREEN, *supra* note 10, at 289.

[179] *See id.* at 289–90; Metzger, *supra* note 171, at 53–55.

[180] *See* Metzger, *supra* note 171, at 54.

[181] *See id.* at 52, 55–56 (observing that high-risk countries are often the largest purchasers of arms, making the assistance of experienced legal counsel essential).

[182] *Id.* at 53; GREEN, *supra* note 10, at 289–90.

[183] *See, e.g.*, Hartley, *supra* note 16, at 470 (reporting that offsets are not free gifts and may entail a 50 percentage cost premium).

of information means that purchasing governments will insist that the details about offsets be kept confidential.[184] Second, exactly how these obligations are satisfied is a valuable trade secret, and so the industry will understandably resist detailed reporting about the terms of offset agreements.[185] Good policymaking requires more data about offsets, but such data will be hard to come by for the foreseeable future. Hence the dilemma.

Meanwhile, perhaps the most that can be done is for researchers to continue making their best efforts to understand the mechanisms of defense offsets and the associated ethical challenges, despite the lack of detailed information about these often secretive transactions. To do more could make a bad problem worse—perhaps imposing solutions on problems that don't exist or ignoring actual problems that remain unknown. Before solutions are entertained, yeoman's work is still required.

References

Charles H. Anderton, *Economics of the Arms Trade*, *in* 1 HANDBOOK OF DEFENSE ECONOMICS 523 (Todd Sandler & Keith Hartley eds., 1995).

KOGILA BALAKRISHNAN, TECHNOLOGY OFFSETS IN INTERNATIONAL DEFENCE PROCUREMENT (2019).

Kogila Balakrishnan, *How to Measure Value from Defence Spending? The Malaysian Case Study*, 37(4) DEF. & SEC. ANALYSIS 387 (2021).

Kogila Balakrishnan, *Generating Value Through Offsets in International Defence Procurement*, *in* MANAGING SECURITY: CONCEPTS AND CHALLENGES 177 (Laura R. Cleary & Roger Darby eds., 2021).

JEFFREY P. BIALOS ET AL., FORTRESSES AND ICEBERGS: THE EVOLUTION OF THE TRANSATLANTIC DEFENSE MARKET AND THE IMPLICATIONS FOR THE U.S. NATIONAL SECURITY POLICY (2009).

RICHARD A. BITZINGER, THE MODERN DEFENSE INDUSTRY: POLITICAL, ECONOMIC, AND TECHNOLOGICAL ISSUES (2009).

Jurgen Brauer, *Arms Industries, Arms Trade, and Developing Countries*, *in* 2 HANDBOOK OF DEFENSE ECONOMICS 973 (Todd Sandler & Keith Hartley eds., 2007).

JURGEN BRAUER & J. PAUL DUNNE, ARMS TRADE AND ECONOMIC DEVELOPMENT (2004).

Jurgen Brauer & John Paul Dunne, *Arms Trade Offsets: What Do We Know?*, *in* THE HANDBOOK ON THE POLITICAL ECONOMY OF WAR 243 (Christopher J. Coyne & Rachel L. Mathers eds., 2011).

Dagobert L. Brito & Michael D. Intriligator, *Arms Races and Proliferation*, *in* 1 HANDBOOK OF DEFENSE ECONOMICS 109 (Todd Sandler & Keith Hartley eds., 1995).

[184] *Cf.* Michael Brzoska, *World Military Expenditures*, *in* 1 HANDBOOK OF DEFENSE ECONOMICS, *supra* note 2, at 46, 47 (observing that even in open societies figures on military spending are closely guarded secrets).

[185] Matthews & Ansari, *supra* note 4, at 383 (arguing that companies' secrecy often has nothing to do with corruption but rather is based on the imperative to protect the details of uniquely differentiated offset proposals from their rivals).

Michael Brzoska, *World Military Expenditures*, *in* 1 HANDBOOK OF DEFENSE ECONOMICS 46 (Todd Sandler & Keith Hartley eds., 1995).

BUREAU OF INDUS. & SEC., U.S. DEP'T OF COMMERCE, OFFSETS IN DEFENSE TRADE: TWENTY-FIFTH STUDY (2021).

LUKE R.A. BUTLER, TRANSATLANTIC DEFENCE PROCUREMENT: EU AND US DEFENCE PROCUREMENT REGULATION IN THE TRANSATLANTIC DEFENCE MARKET (2017).

GREG CASHMAN & LEONARD C. ROBINSON, AN INTRODUCTION TO THE CAUSES OF WAR: PATTERNS OF INTERSTATE CONFLICT FROM WORLD WAR I TO IRAQ (2021).

Marjorie Censer, *Contractors Refocus on Offsets as International Market Heats Up*, INSIDE DEF., June 3, 2015, https://insidedefense.com/daily-news/contractors-refocus-offsets-international-market-heats.

Concerns Over Offsets Generated Using U.S. Foreign Military Financing Program Funds: Hearing Before the H. Subcomm. on Commerce, Consumer Protection, and Competitiveness, Comm. on Energy and Commerce, 112th Cong. 4 (1994) (statement of Frank C. Conahan, Assistant Comptroller General, National Security and International Affairs Division).

Neil Davies, *Reducing Corruption Risks in Defence Contracts: The Challenge of Offset Agreements*, *in* NATO CONFERENCE: BUILDING INTEGRITY AND DEFENCE INSTITUTION BUILDING, DRAFT CONFERENCE REPORT 93 (2009).

DEF. SEC. COOPERATION UNIV., SECURITY COOPERATION MANAGEMENT (2021).

Kevin Dehoff et al., *Defense Offsets: From "Contractual Burden" to Competitive Weapon*, MCKINSEY & CO. (July 1, 2014), https://www.mckinsey.com/industries/public-and-social-sector/our-insights/defense-offsets-from-contractual-burden-to-competitive-weapon.

ROBERT B. DURHAM, SUPPLYING THE ENEMY: THE MODERN ARMS INDUSTRY & THE MILITARY–INDUSTRIAL COMPLEX (2015).

ANDREW FEINSTEIN, THE SHADOW WORLD: INSIDE THE GLOBAL ARMS TRADE (2012).

Andrew Feinstein, Paul Holden & Barnaby Pace, *Corruption and the Arms Trade: Sins of Commission*, *in* SIPRI YEARBOOK: ARMAMENTS, DISARMAMENT, AND INTERNATIONAL SECURITY (2011), https://www.sipriyearbook.org/view/9780199695522/sipri-9780199695522-chapter-2.xml.

KATIE FISH ET AL., TRANSPARENCY INT'L, DEFENCE COMPANIES ANTI-CORRUPTION INDEX 2015, TRANSPARENCY INTERNATIONAL UK (2016), https://ti-defence.org/publications/d efence-companies-anti-corruption-index-2015-3/.

Aude-Emmanuelle Fleurant & Yannick Quéau, *Defense Spending, Arms Production, and Transfers: The Political Economy of Defense in a Transitional Phase*, *in* PEACE AND CONFLICT 2016 79 (David Backer, Ravinder Bhavani & Paul Huth eds., 2016).

Foreign Military Sales: Process and Policy: Hearing Before the H. Subcomm. on Terrorism, Nonproliferation and Trade, 115th Cong. 115–35 (2017).

María D.C. García-Alonso & Paul Levine, *Arms Trade and Arms Races: A Strategic Analysis*, *in* 2 HANDBOOK OF DEFENSE ECONOMICS 941 (Todd Sandler & Keith Hartley eds., 2007).

Aris Georgopoulos, *Revisiting Offset Practices in European Defence Procurement: The European Defence Agency's Code of Conduct on Offsets*, 20 PUB. PROCUREMENT L. REV. 29 (2011).

Douglas M. Gibler, Toby J. Rider & Marc L. Hutchison, *Taking Arms Against a Sea of Troubles: Conventional Arms Races During Periods of Rivalry*, 42(2) J. PEACE RES. 131 (2005).

ALLEN B. GREEN, INTERNATIONAL GOVERNMENT CONTRACT LAW (2011).

Björn Hagelin et al., *International Arms Transfers*, *in* SIPRI YEARBOOK 2002: ARMAMENTS, DISARMAMENT, AND INTERNATIONAL SECURITY (2002).

Peter Hall & Stefan Markowski, *On the Normality and Abnormality of Offsets Obligations*, 5 DEF. & PEACE ECON. 173 (1993).

Grant T. Hammond, *Offsets, Arms, and Innovation*, 10 WASH. Q. 173 (1987).

GRANT T. HAMMOND, COUNTERTRADE, OFFSETS, AND BARTER IN INTERNATIONAL POLITICAL ECONOMY (1990).

Grant T. Hammond, *The Role of Offsets in Arms Collaboration*, *in* GLOBAL ARMS PRODUCTION: POLICY DILEMMAS FOR THE 1990S, at 205 (Ethan B. Kapstein ed., 1992).

R.E. Harkavy, *Arms Resupply During a Conflict: A Framework for Analysis*, *in* THE ECONOMICS OF MILITARY EXPENDITURES: MILITARY EXPENDITURES, ECONOMIC GROWTH, AND FLUCTUATIONS 239 (Christian Schmidt ed., 1987).

Keith Hartley, *Industrial Policies in the Defense Sector*, *in* 1 HANDBOOK OF DEFENSE ECONOMICS 459 (Todd Sandler & Keith Hartley eds., 1995).

Keith Hartley, *Arms Industry, Procurement, and Industrial Policies*, *in* 2 HANDBOOK OF DEFENSE ECONOMICS 1139 (Todd Sandler & Keith Hartley eds., 2007).

Owen E. Hernstadt, *Offsets and the Lack of Comprehensive U.S. Policy: What Do Other Countries Know That We Don't?*, Econ. Pol'y Inst. Briefing Paper No. 201 (2008).

Baudouin Heuninckx, *The EU Defence and Security Procurement Directive: Trick or Treat?*, 20 PUB. PROCUREMENT L. REV. 9 (2011).

Baudouin Heuninckx, *Security of Supply and Offsets in Defence Procurement: What's New in the EU?*, 23 PUB. PROCUREMENT L. REV. 33 (2014).

HELGE HVEEM, COUNTERTRADE: THE GLOBAL PERSPECTIVE (1988).

In re Procurements Involving Foreign Military Sales, 58 Comp. Gen. 81, 78–2, CPD para. 349 (1978).

Andy Irwin, Peter Jeydel & Christian Sylvain, *Offsets in International Defense Trade*, 15-18 BRIEFING PAPERS 1 (July 2015).

Joel L. Johnson, *The United States: Partnerships with Europe*, *in* GLOBAL ARMS PRODUCTION: POLICY DILEMMAS FOR THE 1990S, at 105 (Ethan B. Kapstein ed., 1992).

Aleksandar Jovovic & John Barney, *Survey of Defense Offsets, Global Partnerships, and Industrial Cooperation: Rising Awareness, Enduring Challenges and 7 Key Steps for Success*, AVASCENT, https://www.avascent.com/wp-content/uploads/2016/05/White_Paper_Survey_of_Defense_Offsets_05202016.pdf.

Ethan B. Kapstein, *Allies and Armaments*, SURVIVAL, Summer 2002, at 141.

Ryan J. Lambrecht, *The Big Payback: How Corruption Taints Agreements in International Trade*, 70 A.F. L. REV. 73 (2013).

Christopher Layne & Robert S. Metzger, *Reforming Post-Cold War US Arms Sales Policy: The Crucial Link Between Exports and the Defence Industrial Base*, 18(4) J. STRATEGIC STUD. 1 (1995).

NATHAN J. LUCAS & MICHAEL J. VASSALOTTI, CONG. RES. SERV., R46337, TRANSFER OF DEFENSE ARTICLES: SALE AND EXPORT OF U.S.-MADE ARMS TO FOREIGN ENTITIES (2020).

BEN MAGAHY ET AL., TRANSPARENCY INT'L, DEFENSE OFFSETS: ADDRESSING THE RISKS OF CORRUPTION & RAISING TRANSPARENCY (2016), https://ti-defence.org/publications/defence-offsets-addressing-the-risks-of-corruption-raising-transparency/.

Matias Maloberti, *Foreign Military Sales*, LMDEFENSE, http://www.lmdefense.com/foreign-military-sales/.

Ann Markusen, *Arms Trade as Illiberal Trade*, *in* ARMS TRADE AND ECONOMIC DEVELOPMENT: THEORY, POLICY, AND CASES IN ARMS TRADE OFFSETS 66 (Jurgen Brauer & J. Paul Dunne eds., 2004).

Shana Marshall, *The Modernization of Bribery: The Arms Trade in the Arab Gulf*, JADALIYYA (Dec. 22, 2010), https://www.jadaliyya.com/Details/23603/The-Modernization-of-Bribery-The-Arms-Trade-in-the-Arab-Gulf.

Ron Matthews, *Defense Offsets: Policy versus Pragmatism*, *in* ARMS TRADE AND ECONOMIC DEVELOPMENT: THEORY, POLICY, AND CASES IN ARMS TRADE OFFSETS 89 (Jurgen Brauer & J. Paul Dunne eds., 2004).

Ron Matthews & Irfan Ansari, *Economic Orthodoxy v. Market Pragmatism: A Case Study of Europe's "Abandonment" of Defense Offset*, 15(4) PUB. FIN. & MGMT. 378 (2015).

Aaron Mehta, *America Sold $175 Billion in Weapons Abroad in FY20*, DEF. NEWS (Dec. 4, 2020) https://www.defensenews.com/pentagon/2020/12/04/american-sold-175-billion-in-weapons-abroad-in-fy20/.

Robert S. Metzger, *Offsets and Domestic Considerations*, *in* THE CONTACTOR'S GUIDE TO INTERNATIONAL PROCUREMENT 46 (Erin Felix & Marques O. Peterson eds., 2018).

Mark J. Nackman, *A Critical Examination of Offsets in International Defense Procurements: Policy Options for the United States*, 40 PUB. CONT. L.J. 511 (2011).

JAMES F. NAGLE, HISTORY OF GOVERNMENT CONTRACTING (2d ed. 1999).

Stephanie G. Neuman, *Coproduction, Barter, and Countertrade: Offsets in the International Arms Market*, 29 ORBIS 183 (1985).

OFFSETS IN THE AEROSPACE AND DEFENCE INDUSTRY, INT'L F. ON BUS. ETHICAL CONDUCT FOR AEROSPACE & DEF. INDUSTRY (2016).

Frederic S. Pearson, Michael Brzoska, & Christer Crantz, *The Effect of Arms Transfers on Wars and Peace Negotiations*, *in* SIPRI YEARBOOK 1992: WORLD ARMAMENTS AND DISARMAMENTS 399 (1992).

ANTHONY J. PERFILIO, FOREIGN MILITARY SALES HANDBOOK (Oct. 2021).

Peter Platzgummer, *Arms Trade Offsets and Cases of Corruption: The Usage of Anti-Corruption Tools in Special Forms of Arms Acquisitions*, 14(2) INT'L PUB. MGMT. REV. 17 (2013).

Peter Platzgummer, *The EDA and Defence Offsets: Trailing After the Commission*, *in* THE EUROPEAN DEFENCE AGENCY: ARMING EUROPE 225 (Nikolaos Karampekios & Iraklis Oikonomou eds., 2015).

MARK PYMAN, TRANSPARENCY INT'L, BUILDING INTEGRITY AND COUNTERING CORRUPTION IN DEFENCE AND SECURITY (2016), https://ti-defence.org/publications/building-integrity-and-reducing-corruption-in-defence-security-20-practical-reforms/.

Joe Roeber, *Hard-Wired for Corruption*, PROSPECT (Aug. 28, 2005), https://www.prospectmagazine.co.uk/magazine/hardwiredforcorruption.

Susan G. Sample, *Arms Races*, *in* WHAT DO WE KNOW ABOUT WAR? 63 (Sara McLaughlin Mitchell & John A. Vasquez eds., 2021).

Susan R. Sandler, *Cross-Border Competition in the European Union: Public Procurement and the European Defence Equipment Market*, 7 WASH. U. GLOB. STUD. L. REV. 373 (2008).

MATT SCHAFFER, WINNING THE COUNTERTRADE WAR: NEW EXPORT STRATEGIES FOR AMERICA (1989).

Daniel E. Schoeni, *Second-Best Markets: On the Hidden Efficiency of Defense Offsets*, 44 PUB. CONT. L.J. 369 (2015).

Daniel E. Schoeni, *Defense Offsets and Public Policy: Beyond Economic Efficiency*, 76 A.F. L. Rev. 96 (2016).

Steve Schooner, *Working Group 6: Reducing Corruption Risks in Defence Contracts: The Challenge of Offset Agreements*, *in* NATO Conference: Building Integrity and Defense Institution Building, Draft Conference Report 97 (2009).

Paul D. Senese & John A. Vasquez, The Steps to War: An Empirical Study (2008).

Lindsey Shanson, *A Hundred Cases of Corruption Involving Corruption Are Not a Lot*, 6 Countertrade & Offsets 3 (Mar. 24, 2014).

Lindsey Shanson, *Behind the Shadows of Transparency International's Attack on Defence Offsets*, 33(9) Countertrade & Offset 1 (May 11, 2015).

Lindsey Shanson, *Transparency International Urges Defence Contractors to Respond to Intrusive Offset Questionnaire*, 36(24) Countertrade & Offset 1 (Dec. 17, 2018).

Lindsey Shanson, *GOCA Is Gone, GICA Is Born*, 38(10) Countertrade & Offset, May 5, 2020, https://cto-offset.com/headline/goca-is-gone-gica-is-born/.

Spiegel Online Int'l, *Airbus Corruption Scandal May Lead Straight to the Top* (Oct. 9, 2017), https://www.spiegel.de/international/business/airbus-corruption-scandal-threatens-ceo-tom-enders-a-1171533.html.

Murat Sumer & Jason Chuah, *Emerging Legal Challenges for Countertrade Techniques in International Trade*, 13(6) Int'l Trade 111 (2007).

Travis K. Taylor, *Modeling Offset Policy in Government Procurement*, 25 J. Pol'y Modeling 985 (2003).

Jade C. Totman & Brian C. Baldrate, *International Defense Sales*, *in* The Contactor's Guide to International Procurement 9 (Erin Felix & Marques O. Peterson eds., 2018).

Martin Trybus, Buying Defence and Security in Europe (2014).

Bernard Udis & Keith E. Maskus, *Offsets as Industrial Policy: Lessons from Aerospace*, 2 Def. & Peace Econ. 151 (1991).

Bernard Udis & Keith E. Maskus, *U.S. Offset Policy*, *in* The Economics of Offsets: Defence Procurement and Countertrade 357 (Stephen Martin ed., 1996).

U.S. Dep't State Directorate for Def. Trade Controls, *The International Traffic Arms (ITAR)*, https://www.pmddtc.state.gov/ddtc_public?id=ddtc_kb_article_page&sys_id=%2024d528fddbfc930044f9ff621f961987.

Leslie Wayne, *A Well-Kept Military Secret*, N.Y. Times (Feb. 16, 2003), https://www.nytimes.com/2003/02/16/business/a-well-kept-military-secret.html.

Oliver E. Williamson, The Economic Institution of Capitalism (1985).

PART IV

INNOVATIONS FOR IMPROVING ETHICS AND COMPLIANCE IN THE DEFENSE INDUSTRY

13

Ethical Issues in the Global Arms Industry

A Role for Engineers

Michael Davis[1]

1. Introduction

Most ethical issues concerning the global arms industry arise from the production and sales of lethal tools. The ethical issues inherent to this business field are not easy to grasp and manage, notably because of six underlying complexities: first, the defense industry does not only produce weapons. Second, customers of the global arms industry are oftentimes morally dubious regimes. Third, the industry is subject to cultural differences. Fourth, even if lawfully produced and procured, weapons may be used illegally. Fifth, weapons can fall into the wrong hands. Sixth, some weapons are relatively indiscriminate.

If the ethical issues and their inherent complexities are linked to the production of lethal tools, then there is also a link to those who design, develop, test, and manage the production of weapons and other military items. Indeed, engineers play a crucial part in the defense industry, and there is a role for engineers for addressing the ethical issues of the global arms industry. This chapter develops the role of engineers. It has four sections. The first two seek to clarify the subject of this volume, ethical issues in the global arms industry. The third sketches the role engineers have in much of the global arms industry. The last section considers one way that engineers might help with resolving some of the industry's ethical issues, namely, the adoption of engineering standards. While the first section of this chapter should contain few surprises, the last three will, I hope, contain more, especially for those who are unfamiliar with engineering.

[1] I presented the first version of this chapter to the Philosophy Colloquium, Illinois Institute of Technology, March 6, 2015, to which I owe several improvements. Thanks to the other participants in the conference out of which this volume grew and, most of all, to Lt. Col. U.S. Air Force Daniel Schoeni, for many later improvements.

Michael Davis, *Ethical Issues in the Global Arms Industry* In: *Ethical Dilemmas in the Global Defense Industry*.
Edited by: Daniel Schoeni and Tobias Vestner, Oxford University Press. © Daniel Schoeni and Tobias Vestner 2023.
DOI: 10.1093/oso/9780190675813.003.0014

2. Dilemmas and Defense

There are two differences between the official title of this volume and the title of this chapter. First, I have substituted "issues" for "dilemmas." Second, I have substituted "arms" for "defense." The purpose of these changes is to avoid unnecessary disputes rather than to change the subject.

According to most dictionaries, a "dilemma" is a situation in which a difficult choice has to be made between two equally undesirable alternatives. If there are three equally undesirable alternatives, the difficult choice is a trilemma; if four, a quadrilemma; and so on. The choice may be moral, for example, the choice the doctor in George Bernard Shaw's *Doctor's Dilemma* had to make between two potential patients when the one chosen to be his patient will live and the one not chosen will die—and the two potential patients are equally undeserving but in different ways. One is an artistic genius who appears to have little honor; the other, an honorable man but an average doctor. This is a moral dilemma, though some dilemmas are not, for example, the Prisoner's Dilemma (a problem of rational choice) or the Chess Player's Dilemma (grab pawns or develop one's position according to a strategy). To be a dilemma, the choice only needs to be between (seemingly) equally undesirable alternatives. If the alternatives were not *equally* undesirable, the choice would be easy: choose the less undesirable alternative. There is no dilemma (though the choice might, like most good choices, have its cost).[2]

My impression is that the main ethical issues, questions, problems, or quandaries posed by the global arms industry are not dilemmas (in this sense) but complex situations in which most of the choices on offer are hard to assess and many of the best choices have yet to be devised. Indeed, many of the issues, questions, problems, or quandaries are so ill-defined that we cannot say (with any exactness or realism) what a good choice would look like. We are dealing with a subject requiring the work philosophers typically do. We must understand the issues before we can state the choice as anything so tidy as a dilemma. Hence, my substitution of "issue" for "dilemma." I might have used "problem," "question," "quandary," or some other catch-all instead of "issue."

My substitution of "arms" for "defense" has a different rationale. I regard "defense" in such terms as "Defense Department," "defense forces," and "defensive weapons," as a misleading euphemism. The Department of Defense is the department of the U.S. government that oversees war-making, offensive as well as defensive—as its original name (1947) attested: "National Military Establishment." In most countries that call their military "Defense Forces," the

[2] "Dilemma" is today often used less precisely, wasting it as a mere synonym for "hard choice."

military still consists of an army, air force, navy, and so on, all of which can, and sometimes do, engage in offensive warfare. Much the same is true of weapons. Few, if any, are purely defensive. Even the shield, that epitome of defense, can be used offensively, for example, to crush the face of an opponent too focused on one's sword arm. Rather than try to sort out whether a particular piece of equipment, say, an anti-aircraft missile or landmine, is an offensive or defensive weapon (or both), I have substituted "arms" for "defense."

By "arms industry," I mean all those organizations, whether commercial or not, that design, build, sell, or service weapons or related equipment for military use, provide military research, training, or advice, or otherwise aid the military. The military is that technological system—a combination of people and things—the purpose of which is to kill, wound, disable, or destroy on a large scale. Though the military is typically an arm of government, it can also be an arm of nongovernmental agencies, such as a business corporation ("private army") or religious organization (the Knights Templar or the warrior monks of ancient Japan). What makes an armed force a military is not the armament as such but its purpose. A corporation's "security guards" are a military if their purpose is to kill, wound, disable, or destroy on a large scale; if that is not their purpose, the security guards, however well armed, are not a military. So though the Papacy's Swiss Guards might once have been a military force (say, in 1600), they are not now. They are the papacy's police or the Pope's bodyguards.[3]

"Arms industry" (as used here) does *not* include the design, construction, sale, or servicing of weapons for non-military use, whether use by police, hobbyists, or civilians intent on self-defense or mayhem, even if the nonmilitary weapon is indistinguishable from its military counterpart and manufactured in the same factory. The same is true for military equipment that is not itself a weapon. So while the manufacturer of ordinary bandages or backpackers' dinners is not, as such, part of the arms industry, the manufacturer of field dressings or combat rations is even if the two products are otherwise indistinguishable (and the same manufacturer makes both). Products of the arms industry include aircraft, ammunition, submarines, artillery, electronic systems, light weapons, operations support, software, research, and uniforms. While much of the arms industry is "domestic," that is, serves the "home country," a significant part is "international" or "global," that is, serves the military of other countries, rebellions outside the

[3] An independent armed unit, whether one of the "companies" of Renaissance Italy or bands of mercenaries available for hire today, is a military organization if hired to kill on a large scale but not a military organization if hired for some other purpose, such as keeping the peace or protecting a mine or factory.

home country, UN peacekeepers, and the like. In the following, I refer to the part of the arms industry that is not domestic.[4]

The distinction between the global arms industry and domestic is, of course, artificial in at least two respects. First, much of the domestic arms industry seeks foreign customers if they have a product that they can sell abroad (and permission of their home government to sell it abroad). Foreign sales can reduce the unit cost of a product, help tie foreign customers to the home country, and otherwise serve domestic interests. Much of the global arms industry is, in this respect, also part of the domestic arms industry.

Second, much of what even a strictly domestic arms industry produces may depend on raw materials, research, or subsystems produced outside the home country. Even a domestic arms industry may rely on international trade to provide much of what the military of the home country needs, everything from iron or rubber to computer chips or Kevlar. Much of the domestic arms industry is global in this respect—and has been for at least a century.

The distinction between the global arms industry and the domestic is nonetheless worth making. The patriotism that may justify producing arms for one's own country cannot justify producing arms for others, especially those not allied with the home country (officially or unofficially). The ethical issues of the global arms industry seem to differ in systematic ways from those of the domestic arms industry (however fuzzy the boundaries of the distinction may be). With this in mind, we can now turn to the ethical issues of the global arms industry.

[4] In defining "global" as that part of the arms industry that sells its wares abroad, I may seem to be departing from the original call for the conference out of which this volume grew. In that original call, Claire Finkelstein listed among the relevant "dilemmas" two that seem to apply to the domestic arms industry as much as to the global arms industry:

> Sometimes the industry can provide a necessary and ethically sound *national* security product only by using materials that are potentially legally problematic, such as "conflict minerals." Should the global defense industry be held to a higher standard than other industries given the sensitive and potentially controversial nature of its enterprise? Or perhaps a more relaxed standard, given the critical nature of its function and the overwhelming importance of a strong *national* defense. . . .
>
> Finally, many of the dilemmas that arise at the intersection of ethical and legal standards pertain to new technologies, such as surveillance equipment and cutting edge defensive weapons systems. Often there are objections to such technologies on ethical grounds: do advanced surveillance technologies violate privacy norms, especially when they [the technologies] can be used on civilian populations? Should the industry be responsive to objections to technological development in *national* defense, such as the frequent concerns expressed that smart weapons are replacing human judgment on the battle field?

E-mail from Claire Finkelstein to author (Dec. 5, 2014) (on file with author) (emphasis added). Concerns about *national* defense carry weight only when the nation in question is one's own—and, by the definition I proposed, the global arms industry is concerned (in part) with helping *other nations* make war; it is the domestic arms industry that is concerned with *the* national defense. I have therefore treated these two paragraphs as including "slips of the word processor" rather than as part of the definition of my subject.

3. Ethical Issues

"Ethics" has at least three uses potentially relevant here. First, it can be a synonym for ordinary morality, those standards of conduct that apply to all moral agents simply because they are moral agents—"Don't kill," "Keep your promises," "Help the needy," and so on. Second, "ethics" can refer to those morally binding standards of conduct that apply to members of a group simply because they are members of that group—"a group" being any number of moral agents that is more than one but less than all moral agents. Legal ethics applies to lawyers and no one else; business ethics to people in business and no one else; and so on. Third, "ethics" can refer to a field of philosophy, that is, the attempt to understand morality (including its group standards) as part of a reasonable undertaking. Other names for "ethics" in this third sense include "moral theory" and "ethical theory." I shall hereafter reserve "ethics" for the group-standards sense, using "morality" for the first sense and "moral theory" for the third.

Given this terminology, some "ethical issues" identified in the call for the conference out of which this volume grew seem at least in part moral (whether or not they are also ethical, that is, whether or not they concern an existing group standard or might lead to the adoption of such a standard). For example, the threat that drones pose to people's privacy is a moral issue (a violation of "privacy norms").[5] Every moral agent, even the agents of the global arms industry, should, all else equal, avoid contributing to the invasion of people's privacy. Other issues, such as what to do about "government officials [who] expect some form of quid pro quo for their cooperation,"[6] are not moral but ethical—because the standards in question, whether actual or proposed, apply only to the government officials, not to everyone. Of course, not all ethical issues are dilemmas. For example, bribery, though still an ethical issue in international trade, no longer poses a dilemma for most of the global arms industry. Most of the global arms industry have adopted a special standard resolving the dilemma. So, for example, the National Defense Industrial Association's "Statement of Defense Industry Ethics" says:

> When contemplating any international sale to a governmental or quasi-governmental buyer, it is imperative that effective measures be undertaken to ensure full compliance, not only with the letter, but also the spirit of the Foreign Corrupt Practices Act, as amended, and the FCPA's bar against improper payments to foreign officials.[7]

[5] *See id.* ("Often there are objections to such technologies on ethical grounds: do advanced surveillance technologies violate privacy norms, especially when they can be used on civilian populations?").

[6] *Id.*

[7] *Statement of Defense Industry Ethics*, NAT'L DEFENSE (Mar. 1, 2011), https://www.nationaldefensemagazine.org/Articles/2011/3/1/2011March%20Statement%20of%20Defense%20Industry%20Ethics (last visited Jan. 8, 2020). Lockheed Martin, a sponsor of the conference out of which this

Of course, we can debate whether a group standard prohibiting "improper payments" is wise, morally required, merely morally permitted, or even morally wrong. But that debate is likely to do little more than return us to ground that business ethics has worked over pretty well during the last forty years.[8]

By "business ethics," I here mean not only the philosophical study of morality in business but also the special standards of conduct that government agencies, such as those that produced the Foreign Corrupt Practices Act (FCPA), and businesses involved international trade, such as National Defense Industrial Association (NDIA) members, have adopted. I therefore propose to limit this chapter to moral issues that the global arms industry faces while ordinary businesses do not (or, at least, do not face in the same way), issues not much discussed in courses in business ethics or in the scholarly literature.[9] I have identified six. No doubt there are others.

3.1. Weapons versus Non-weapons

Much of what the global arms industry sells are weapons (artifacts designed to kill, wound, disable, or destroy) but much is not. For example, much of what the global arms industry sells consists of clothing, field kitchens, tents, and so on, artifacts relatively harmless in themselves even in military service. And some of what the global arms industry sells is neither clearly a weapon nor clearly not a weapon, for example, body armor, observation drones, communications equipment, circuit boards, reflective paint, software, and other nonlethal elements of a "weapons system." How morally significant, then, is the distinction between weapons and non-weapons? Should the global arms industry consider the sale of non-weapons less morally objectionable than the sale of weapons or

volume grew, has taken a similar position: "We have zero tolerance for corruption." LOCKHEED MARTIN CORP., SETTING THE STANDARD: CODE OF ETHICS AND BUSINESS CONDUCT 28 (2017), http://www.lockheedmartin.com/us/who-we-are/ethics/code-of-ethics.html. That web page includes enough explanation of what the standard means to make it clear that the *quid pro quo* in question is probably unethical.

[8] That is, since the Lockheed bribery scandal of the early 1970s. Interestingly, Lockheed is a corporate ancestor of today's Lockheed Martin. *See generally* Mike Koehler, *The Story of the Foreign Corrupt Practices Act*, 73(5) OH. ST. L.J. 929 (2012). *See also* Margo Cleveland, Christopher M. Favo & Thomas J. Frecka, *Trends in the International Fight Against Bribery and Corruption*, 90 J. BUS. ETHICS 199 (2009); Edmund F. Byrne, *Towards Enforceable Bans on Illicit Businesses: From Moral Relativism to Human Rights*, 119 J. BUS. ETHICS 119 (2013).

[9] *But see* Gavin Maitland, *The Ethics of the International Arms Trade*, 7 BUS. ETHICS: EUR. REV. 200 (1998); Edmund F. Byrne, *Assessing Arms Makers' Corporate Social Responsibility*, 74 J. BUS. ETHICS 201 (2007); Barton H. Halpern & Keith F. Snider, *Products That Kill and Corporate Social Responsibility: The Case of U.S. Defense Firms*, 38 ARMED FORCES & SOC'Y 604 (2012).

nonlethal elements of a weapons system? After all, every artifact embedded in the technological system we call "the military" is there to help the military do its job, which is (by definition) to kill, wound, or otherwise disable other human beings on a large scale or destroy property on a large scale, a morally dubious undertaking, especially if the regime directing the military is itself morally dubious. (A morally dubious undertaking can, of course, turn out, all things considered, to be morally justified, but the burden of proof must fall on those claiming justification.)

3.2. Morally Dubious Regimes

Customers of the global arms industry respect human rights, but many, to varying degrees, do not. Of those that do not, some may simply deny their people certain basic rights, such as self-government or decent medical care, but many actively harm those under their control by, for example, imprisoning, torturing, or killing them for political, religious, or other beliefs, for forming various kinds of peaceful voluntary associations, or for speaking a certain language, dressing in a certain way, or the like. How abusive must a regime be before the global arms industry should refuse to sell it weapons? How abusive before the global arms industry should have no dealings with it at all? How important is the argument that if "we" do not sell to them, others will? How important is it that what the regime is buying will not be used against the regime's subjects?

3.3. Cultural Differences

By "culture," I mean a distinctive way of doing something, including the beliefs and evaluations that accompany the doing. So, for example, eating with knife, fork, and spoon is a gastronomic culture (a distinctive way to eat), while eating as such is not (since everyone eats). There are military cultures. For example, some militaries "live off the land" on which they fight, while others routinely bring all their supplies with them. Some routinely take prisoners; some do not. Some militaries force young men to serve while others take only volunteers. Some allow "children" (adolescents under 18) to be soldiers; some do not. How important should such cultural differences be to the global arms industry, for example, should global arms industry act as if international standards preempt noncomplying military cultures? How much respect does the global arms industry owe the national culture of a military?

3.4. Lawful Artifacts Having Illegal Uses

Most weapons have illegal uses as well as legal ones. For example, the same rifle that is legally used to kill a soldier in combat can be used illegally to kill enemy soldiers who have surrendered. Something similar is true of many non-weapons. For example, the same small electric generator that can lawfully be used to power field radar can also be used illegally to deliver electric shocks to a prisoner's genitals. How important should the likelihood of illegal use of military equipment be to the decision to sell the equipment to a certain customer? Should military equipment be designed, as much as possible, to prevent illegal use?

3.5. Weapons that Can Fall into the Wrong Hands

Much of what the arms industry sells can be stolen, resold, transferred to another by capture, or otherwise "diverted." How much responsibility should the global arms industry take for preventing its products from falling into the wrong hands? For example, should the global arms industry refuse to sell to unstable regimes (regime likely to lose control of their military soon) or regimes (such as the current regime in Iraq) with a record of losing many of its weapons to its nonstate enemies? Should the products of the global arms industry be designed to make diversion of its products more difficult or less attractive (for example, by making rifles requiring unusual bullets or hard to replace parts)?

3.6. Relatively Indiscriminate Weapons

Some weapons are relatively indiscriminate, even when used by a sophisticated military. For example, landmines can as easily be set off by a civilian as by a soldier and even the U.S. military can fail to retrieve all its mines when it departs. Landmines may go on killing and maiming civilians for decades after the end of the war that justified their use. Something similar is true of conventional bombs. Lost "duds" can explode long after the end of hostilities, killing anyone who happens to be nearby. While some weapons are relatively indiscriminate even in sophisticated hands, some are indiscriminate only in unsophisticated hands. For example, without good record keeping, a military may lose track of the age of artillery shells. Past-date shells may explode when they should not, say, when being transported on a rough road. How much care should the global arms industry take to make weapons as discriminating as practical in the circumstances in which they are likely to be used? The classic indiscriminate weapons are, of course, nuclear bombs, biological devices, and deadly gases, weapons not currently part of the official global arms trade. I shall therefore ignore them here.[10]

4. Engineers in the Global Arms Industry

Engineers have had a significant role in the arms industry (home and international) since at least the 1700s. Their role has only increased as the products of the arms industry have become more sophisticated. Today one in 10 U.S. engineers works in military-related industry, including about 39,000 electrical engineers (just under 14% of all U.S. electrical engineers) and about 6,000 aerospace engineers (just under 19% of all aerospace engineers).[11] Engineers design weapons and other equipment the military needs, test them, sell them, and oversee their manufacture, delivery, maintenance, and even disposal. Indeed, it is hard to imagine today's arms industry without engineers, not only "bench engineers" but also technical managers up to, and often including, senior management.[12] So, for example, of 12 members of Lockheed Martin's current Board of Directors, five are engineers (by education and early practice).[13] There is no reason to think that engineers do not have a similar part with respect to most products of the global arms industry or, at least, with most of its most distinctive products.

Now let me illustrate: suppose that a certain large African country contacts a U.S. manufacturer of modern jet fighters in order to buy 20 for its air force. The sale is likely to be a long process, lasting months or even years. At an early stage, the U.S. manufacturer would have to send out engineers to assess the African country's airbases, maintenance practices, pilot training, local suppliers, and so on. A jet fighter requires a complex technological system to operate. The would-be customer may be surprised to learn that its runways are too short, that its fuel storage is inadequate, that its maintenance staff will have to be larger, better

[10] *But see* Jacque G. Richardson, *The Bane of "Inhumane" Weapons and Overkill: An Overview on Increasingly Lethal Arms and the Inadequacy of Regulatory Controls*, 10 Sci. & Eng'g Ethics 667 (2004).

[11] U.S. Chamber of Commerce, *Defense Trade: Keeping America Secure and Competitive* (Mar. 2007), 8, https://www.uschamber.com/sites/default/files/legacy/issues/defense/files/defensetrade.pdf (last visited Dec. 30, 2014); Department of Defense, "Defense-Related Employment of Skilled Labor: An Introduction to LDEPPS" (Mar. 2011), 4, www.economics.osd.mil/LDEPPS_Primer.pdf (last visited Dec. 30, 2014).

[12] *See also* Aaron Fichtelberg, *Applying the Rules of Just War Theory to Engineers in the Arms Industry*, 12 Sci. & Eng'g Ethics 685 (2006) (discussing engineers' critical importance to the defense industry).

[13] *See* biographies of James D. Taiclet (president and chief executive officer of Lockheed Martin Corporation); Daniel F. Akerson, James O. Ellis, Jr., Vicki A. Hollub, and Debra L. Reed-Klages, https://www.lockheedmartin.com/en-us/who-we-are/leadership-governance/board-of-directors.html#members (last visited July 26, 2020). Lockheed Martin no longer includes education in the corporate bios, but a quick web search using the director's name and "education" will provide that information.

trained, and provided with more sophisticated tools, and so on. While some of this information is typically public, some is not, being proprietary, classified, or just too technical to be easily available to the public. Much of it will, in any case, be in a form engineers are used to and others are not. The African country will need its own engineers to talk to those of the U.S. manufacturer.

The African country need not agree to all the conditions that the U.S. manufacturer seeks to impose as part of the sale. It may suggest changes in the design of the jet fighters so that, for example, they can use fuel that the African country is already using for other aircraft. Indeed, after a full assessment, the parties may agree on a less sophisticated fighter. In any case, the final specifications for the fighter, including training, support, munitions, replacement parts, and so on should be the result (in part) of extensive negotiations between the engineers of the U.S. manufacturer and the engineers of the African country.[14] Though the terms of such a sale are, in principle, entirely under the control of the U.S. manufacturer's senior management and the African country's senior government officials, in practice many of the decisions, perhaps most, will be made by engineers (American or African), some quite junior, no one else having the information, time, and skills to appreciate their import.

The involvement of engineers typically does not end with the writing of specifications or even with the signing of the sales contract. Engineers will oversee the manufacture of the planes, not only making sure that every part satisfies the specifications and the whole is constructed properly but also changing the specifications if, say, there is difficulty getting a specified part or a better part has become available. Given that there will typically be several years between the initial writing of specifications and the delivery of the last jet fighter, there may be many changes in the specifications, most quietly made by agreement among engineers. Some of these changes will, of course, be "no-brainers," but a substantial number may involve painful balancing of cost against reliability, timeliness, and so on. So, for example, a new part may be cheaper and, based on experience, as good as the old. But, since the part is new, experience with it must be short. The part may still fail long before it should. Who knows? The engineers will have to rely on experience with parts analogous in one way or another to the new part to forecast its probable life expectancy—and decide accordingly. There may be a good deal of discussion between the manufacturer's engineers and those of the African country.

The relationship between the engineers of the U.S. manufacturer and those of the African country should not end when the last fighter is delivered. The

[14] I write that the specifications should be "in part" the result extensive negotiations between the U.S. arms vendor-supplier and the African country to recognize that the U.S. government would normally have an important role in such a transaction, often through the Foreign Military Sales program.

U.S. engineers should keep the African engineers informed of problems identified in similar aircraft elsewhere in the world and the solutions devised. The African engineers in turn should advise the U.S. engineers of any problems they identify in the jets they purchased, anything from unusual wear on engine blades to difficulty getting ground crews to comply with required maintenance procedures. The purpose of this exchange of technical information between the manufacturer's engineers and those of the African country is not simply to maintain the fighters; it is in part to improve them where possible, not only the fighters that the African country has purchased but other fighters in that family, both those yet to be built and those already in use elsewhere in the world. In principle, this exchange of information should continue until the last fighter delivered has ceased to exist.[15] That is normal engineering. While much of this exchange of information will go on long distance, some of it may require "site visits," for example, to see the troublesome dust clouds possibly contributing to unusual engine wear or the conditions under which maintenance must actually be performed.

The relationship between a manufacturer's engineers and those of a customer can be both intimate and enduring. There is often a tension between the legal department's "arm's-length" conception of how information should be shared and the engineers' conception (something more like a long hug than a handshake). For example, engineers of a manufacturer can seldom do a good job of designing a sophisticated piece of equipment without knowing how it will be used, under what conditions, and for how long. Similarly, a customer purchasing such equipment cannot be as helpful in its design as it could be unless it knows the details of manufacture, including some trade secrets and (in the case of a fighter jet) even some highly classified information.

5. How Engineers Might Help Resolve Some Ethical Issues

Most engineers working in the global arms industry are civilians. Most who are not have nonetheless been trained in the same way as civilian engineers, work in much the same way as civilian engineers, and have little trouble communicating with civilian engineers. Engineering is (in this respect at least) a single occupation. It is also a global profession. Engineers in Brazil, China, Nigeria, or India are trained much as are engineers in Germany, Japan, or the United States. Engineers also share certain standards, whether formalized in a code of ethics or not. They are committed not simply to maintaining a certain technology but to

[15] I wrote "ceased to exist" not "ceased to operate" because engineers are now typically considered, all else equal, to be responsible for disposal.

improving it for the benefit of humanity. Their first loyalty is (or, at least, is supposed to be) not to their employer but to "the public health, safety, and welfare."[16]

Much of what engineers share are technical standards. Some of these are governmental, such as the safety standards issued by the Environmental Protection Agency or the Nuclear Regulatory Commission. But many technical standards, perhaps most, are not the work of government. Of these, some are the work of professional or technical associations, such as ASME (formerly, American Society of Mechanical Engineers), or the IEEE (formerly, the Institute of Electrical and Electronic Engineers). Others are the work of trade associations or other private groups, the best known of which today is probably the ISO (International Standards Organization).

Whatever the source of engineering's technical standards, they will, in large part, be the work of engineers. They will be the work of engineers because only engineers have the knowledge necessary to write them. Engineering standards are not now deduced from physics, chemistry, or any other natural science; nor are they simply common sense (though generally consistent with common sense). They are instead a product of engineering experience. Some of that experience derives from laboratory experiments, much like the experiments of natural science. The chief difference between the experiments of natural science and those of engineering (insofar as there is any) is that engineers typically experiment on artifacts (objects humans have made), not natural objects. However, much of the engineering experience on which the writing of standards depend is not experimental but "field experience," that is, experience with artifacts in use where the control necessary for experiment is absent, for example, when the left wing of a fighter jet falls off at 20,000 feet during combat training. Engineers try to learn as much as possible from every such "incident," but they have no interest in repeating the incident, especially if there was a loss of life or loss of an expensive piece of equipment. Unlike surgeons in the old joke, engineers do not bury their mistakes. Instead, they record them, study them, and try to learn from them, typically embedding what they learn in new technical standards. Will engineering ever be reducible to science, say, to some combination of natural and social science a thousand years from now? That's a question for philosophers interested in "the unity of the sciences." It's one we may pass over here.

The recent history of the global arms industry offers enough examples of unhappy experience with the products of engineering, such as the children killed or maimed by landmines in peace time, for engineers to begin to develop international standards for the global arms industry similar to engineering's other international standards, for example, the addition to many codes of engineering ethics of language concerning "sustainable development."[17] There are even a few

[16] *Statement of Defense Industry Ethics*, *supra* note 7.

[17] *See* CHARLES E. HARRIS ET AL., ENGINEERING ETHICS: CONCEPTS AND CASES 165–70 (2019).

signs that now is a good time to add to such standards for the global arms industry. I shall briefly describe three of those signs.

First, there is a U.S. statute, the Arms Export Control Act, as well as the International Traffic in Arms Regulations (ITAR) issued under it. Since 1976, these have governed what military information and artifacts may be shared with "non-U.S. persons." U.S. persons (including organizations) can face heavy fines if they have, without authorization or the use of an exemption, provided non-U.S. persons with access to ITAR-protected military articles, services, or technical data. Until the end of the Cold War, the focus of ITAR enforcement was preventing the Soviet Union from obtaining U.S. military technology. Since 1990, the focus has increasingly become preventing weapons and weapons technology slipping into the hands of terrorists, rogue states, and other potential wrongdoers.[18]

Second, in 2004, NDIA, a U.S. trade association, published a "Statement of Defense Industry Ethics" (cited earlier) and made several small revisions in 2009. Most of the larger U.S. participants in the arms industry have adopted a code of ethics including provisions similar to those in the Statement. The Statement seems to reject making ethics relative to geographical cultures: the arms industry is to "[i]mplement effective ethics programs for company activities at home or abroad." The Statement is, however, almost silent about the health, safety, and welfare of people outside the United States. The nearest the Statement comes to providing any guidance on that issue is the requirement that members of the arms industry "[e]stablish corporate integrity as a business asset, rather than a requirement to satisfy regulators, by making ethics compliance integral to all aspects of corporate life and culture, including employee appraisals and promotions, to foster an environment where employees aspire to do the right thing." For engineers at least, doing "the right thing" seems to include taking into account, for example, the welfare of non-U.S. children whom landmines might injure or kill. Such children are part of the "public" whose safety, health, and welfare engineers are supposed to hold "paramount."[19]

More important, the Statement does not treat ethical knowledge as proprietary. Instead, it urges members of the arms industry to "[c]ontribute to the common good of our industry and promote industry ethics whenever and wherever possible by sharing best practices in ethics and business conduct among NDIA members and including ethics training in NDIA sponsored events."[20]

[18] Arms Trade Treaty, Apr. 2, 2013, U.N. Doc. A/RES/67/234B, https://www.thearmstradetreaty.org/hyper-images/file/TheArmsTradeTreaty1/TheArmsTradeTreaty.pdf.

[19] *See generally* Michael Davis, *Thinking Like an Engineer: The Place of a Code of Ethics in the Practice of a Profession*, 20 PHIL. & PUB. AFF. 150 (1991).

[20] *Statement of Defense Industry Ethics*, *supra* note 7.

Third, there is the Arms Trade Treaty. Since its entry into force on December 24, 2014, 110 states have ratified it (with 31 more signing).[21] The Treaty is an important step in regulating the global arms industry. It certainly provides a starting point for writing global standards for engineers. The object of the Treaty is to (1) "establish the highest possible common international standards for regulating or improving the regulation of the international trade in conventional arms," and (2) "prevent and eradicate the illicit trade in conventional arms and prevent their diversion." The Treaty applies to all conventional arms. At the very least, it covers the following categories: battle tanks; armored combat vehicles; large-caliber artillery systems; combat aircraft; attack helicopters; warships; missiles and missile launchers; and small arms and light weapons.[22] The Treaty also covers ammunition/munitions as well as parts and components, although not all treaty provisions equally apply to these items. State parties issue national control lists, which delimit the exact scope of items that they consider covered under the Treaty.

How do these three documents provide a justification for engineering (or engineering's international allies) to begin developing standards for the global arms industry that might help to resolve the ethical issues identified earlier in this chapter? Let me give a simple example: if there were an international standard prohibiting engineers from involvement in the sale of complete weapons or parts of weapons of any sort to a regime likely to misuse them, the standard would simply echo the Treaty. If, in addition, the engineering standards contained criteria for identifying weapons likely to be misused and the sort of regime likely to misuse them, engineers might then inform an employer considering sale of such weapons or parts of such weapons to such a regime that the sale not only violates international standards but also is inconsistent with good engineering. Engineers can have no part in such a sale. Involvement would be unprofessional.

A source of engineering's standards, such as ASME, IEEE, or ISO, would have a justification for issuing such a standard. Article 7 of the Arms Trade Treaty specifically requires a state party to consider licensing an export to "assess the potential that the conventional arms or items [in question]" may be misused in various ways, for example, to "commit or facilitate a serious violation of international humanitarian law . . . [or] human rights law." While the Treaty's authors thought of the decision to license as primarily governmental and the Treaty's obligations only apply to states, there is nothing in that understanding to forbid a member of the global arms industry from deciding not to seek its government's permission, or for engineers working in the global arms industry from appealing to their own profession's ethical standards when asked to participate in such a

21 Arms Trade Treaty, https://thearmstradetreaty.org/ (last visited Oct. 3, 2020).
22 Arms Trade Treaty, *supra* note 18, arts. 1–2.

transaction. Their employer is (according to the NDIA Statement) supposed to want engineers to "do the right thing," and standing by (morally justified) engineering standards is, all else equal at least, doing just that.

Of course, engineers individually are not qualified to assess the likelihood that a particular regime will misuse a particular weapon, even though they are likely to know much about how the weapon can be misused. So any standard developed for the use of engineers would have to include the sort of information an engineer would need to make such an assessment. That information might come in a quite simple form, for example, in the form of a checklist asking (among other things) how this or that human rights group rates the regime, what uses the regime has made of weapons in the recent past, and so on. An individual engineer could then inform the appropriate superior, "We need to check out the following to be sure that this sale meets international engineering standards."

This sort of individual response may not seem like much help with the ethical issues identified earlier. After all, the engineer's superior might simply ignore the international standard and replace an engineer unwilling to participate in the sale with an engineer who is willing or, if no suitable engineer is willing, with a willing non-engineer.

While it is true that a superior might do that, there is good reason to think that, all things considered, that response is unlikely. Such a response can have substantial costs, especially when the manager most needs an engineer. There are at least three sources of that cost: first, engineers are not interchangeable. They are often quite specialized. The engineer first asked to participate in the sale is likely to be the most qualified. The replacement (assuming one can be found) is likely to be less qualified. Therefore, the substitution may increase the risk of bad decisions as the sale progresses. Second, the risk of bad decisions is even higher if the substitute for the engineer is a non-engineer. Engineers are generally brought into sales only when they are needed, only when they are likely to have knowledge or insight non-engineers lack. Third, overruling an engineer on a matter involving application of an engineering standard risks harm to the manager. If anything later goes wrong, the manager who overruled the engineer will be open to blame, even if he found another engineer or a "scientific expert" to replace the unwilling engineer. He was on notice that there might be a problem and he did not "do the right thing." If, on the other hand, he goes along with the engineer's recommendation, he can at least claim that he was acting on the best technical advice available.

These are all relatively short-term consequences of one manager's respecting or not respecting the engineering standard in question. There is also at least one long-term consequence worth considering if the organization makes a practice of overruling engineers on such issues. Widespread lack of respect for engineering standards may have a bad effect on the morale of the organization's engineers generally and so, on the ability of the organization to recruit and keep the most marketable engineers, not only the most marketable "bench engineers" but also the most marketable higher-ranking engineers (including senior management).

We have, of course, been assuming that the engineer's superior is unsympathetic to the appeal to engineering standards. That is a worst-case scenario. In practice, the superior is likely to be another engineer, one for whom engineering standards carry considerable weight, even if he is now acting as a manager rather than an engineer. And the organization in which these two engineers work is likely to have its own code of ethics, compliance procedures, and the like designed (as the NDIA Statement requires) to ensure, as much as possible, that organization employees, including engineers, "do the right thing." The ethical environment of the organization is likely to be far friendlier to engineering standards than we have tacitly been assuming in dealing with this example.[23]

This is, admittedly, a relatively simple example of a standard that might be adopted, one that does not look particularly technical. The standards actually adopted—for example, criteria for "safe landmines" requiring them to resist light touches, to disarm automatically after a certain period, and so on—are likely to look much more technical, making the overruling of the engineer look even more risky.

6. Conclusion

This chapter has analyzed significant ethical issues arising from the production and (international) sales of arms. It has also highlighted and discussed the complexities inherent in this business field. Building on three signs that now is a good time, this chapter developed how engineers can contribute to addressing the underlying ethical issues of the global arms industry. In particular, this chapter has argued that engineering standards for the global arms industry may help resolve some of the ethical issues. Indeed, engineers hold an important key for the ethical production and sales of arms in their hands.

Much of what I have said about engineers here may well be true of other professions important to the global arms industry, especially computer scientists. This is particularly relevant regarding the (future) development and use of cyber tools and artificial intelligence, for instance. When governments adopt technical standards less than a profession thinks proper, there is usually a way for the profession to adopt a higher standard—and make it stick. A good part of the regulation of the global arms industry is, or could be, the work of professions, such as engineering, or nongovernmental standard-setting bodies (like the IEEE or ISO).

[23] *But see* Harris et al., *supra* note 17, at 218–19, describing an engineer's duty to halt dangerous research projects.

References

Arms Trade Treaty, Apr. 2, 2013, U.N. Doc. A/RES/67/234B, https://www.thearmstradetreaty.or g/hyper-images/file/TheArmsTradeTreaty1/TheArmsTradeTreaty.pdf.

Edmund F. Byrne, *Assessing Arms Makers' Corporate Social Responsibility*, 74 J. Bus. Ethics 201 (2007).

Edmund F. Byrne, *Towards Enforceable Bans on Illicit Businesses: From Moral Relativism to Human Rights*, 119 J. Bus. Ethics 119 (2013).

Margo Cleveland, Christopher M. Favo & Thomas J. Frecka, *Trends in the International Fight Against Bribery and Corruption*, 90 J. Bus. Ethics 199 (2009).

Michael Davis, *Thinking Like an Engineer: The Place of a Code of Ethics in the Practice of a Profession*, 20 Phil. & Pub. Aff. 150 (1991).

Department of Defense, *Defense-Related Employment of Skilled Labor: An Introduction to LDEPPS* (Mar. 2011), 4, https://www.economics.osd.mil/LDEPPS_Primer.pdf.

Aaron Fichtelberg, *Applying the Rules of Just War Theory to Engineers in the Arms Industry*, 12 Sci. & Eng'g Ethics 685 (2006).

Barton H. Halpern & Keith F. Snider, *Products That Kill and Corporate Social Responsibility: The Case of US Defense Firms*, 38 Armed Forces & Soc'y 604 (2012).

Charles E. Harris et al., Engineering Ethics: Concepts and Cases 165–70 (2019).

Mike Koehler, *The Story of the Foreign Corrupt Practices Act*, 73(5) Oh. St. L.J. 929 (2012).

Lockheed Martin Corp., Setting the Standard: Code of Ethics and Business Conduct 28 (2017), http://www.lockheedmartin.com/us/who-we-are/ethics/code-of-ethics.html

Gavin Maitland, *The Ethics of the International Arms Trade*, 7 Bus. Ethics: Eur. Rev. 200 (1998).

Nat'l Defense, *Statement of Defense Industry Ethics*, (Mar. 1, 2011), https://www.nationaldefensemagazine.org/Articles/2011/3/1/2011March%20Statement%20of%20Defense%20Industry%20Ethics.

Jacque G. Richardson, *The Bane of "Inhumane" Weapons and Overkill: An Overview on Increasingly Lethal Arms and the Inadequacy of Regulatory Controls*, 10 Sci. & Eng'g Ethics 667 (2004).

U.S. Chamber of Commerce, *Defense Trade: Keeping America Secure and Competitive* (Mar. 2007), 8, https://www.uschamber.com/sites/default/files/legacy/issues/defense/files/defensetrade.pdf.

14

Mandatory Disclosure

How Anti-Corruption Measures Can Affect Competition in Defense Markets

Christopher R. Yukins

1. Introduction

In U.S. defense contracting, an increasingly important tool in fighting corruption is "mandatory disclosure"—the requirement that when a government contractor's managers discover that the firm has been engaged in certain wrongdoing, they must disclose that wrongdoing to the government.[1] Mandatory disclosure plays an especially prominent role in defense contracting, both because of the relative size of the defense spending in overall federal procurement and because a handful of very large prime contractors, with extraordinarily strong compliance and disclosure systems, dominate the U.S. defense marketplace. In part because those large contractors set a high standard for disclosure, which other

[1] The clause at Federal Acquisition Regulation (FAR) 52.203-13, 48 C.F.R. § 52.203-13, *Contractor Code of Business Ethics and Conduct*, requires that a contractor, as part of its system of internal controls, make:

> (F) Timely disclosure, in writing, to the agency OIG [Office of Inspector General], with a copy to the Contracting Officer, whenever, in connection with the award, performance, or closeout of any Government contract performed by the Contractor or a subcontractor thereunder, the Contractor has credible evidence that a principal, employee, agent or subcontractor of the Contractor has committed a violation of Federal criminal law involving fraud, conflict of interest, bribery, or gratuity violations found in Title 18 U.S.C. or a violation of the civil False Claims Act (31 U.S.C. 3729–3733).

Under FAR 9.406-2(b)(vi), 48 C.F.R. § 9.406-2(b)(vi), *Causes for Debarment*, a debarring official may debar a contractor, based upon a preponderance of the evidence, for:

> Knowing failure by a principal, until 3 years after final payment on any Government contract awarded to the contractor, to timely disclose to the Government, in connection with the award, performance, or closeout of the contract or a subcontract thereunder, credible evidence of—
>
> (A) Violation of Federal criminal law involving fraud, conflict of interest, bribery, or gratuity violations found in Title 18 of the United States Code;
> (B) Violation of the civil False Claims Act (31 U.S.C. 3729–3733); or
> (C) Significant overpayment(s) on the contract, other than overpayments resulting from contract financing payments.

Christopher R. Yukins, *Mandatory Disclosure* In: *Ethical Dilemmas in the Global Defense Industry*. Edited by: Daniel Schoeni and Tobias Vestner, Oxford University Press.
DOI: 10.1093/oso/9780190675813.003.0015

contractors have difficulty matching,[2] anti-corruption efforts in the U.S. defense market raise an interesting quandary: Does mandatory disclosure, an important anti-corruption tool, in effect dampen competition in a procurement market?

This chapter addresses that question in several steps. Section 2 of the chapter reviews the history of mandatory disclosure in federal contracting, and explains how mandatory disclosure is tied to broader compliance requirements in U.S. contracting. Sections 3–5 discuss some of the anti-competitive effects of mandatory disclosure, and Sections 6–11 assess possible remedies. The conclusion suggests that mandatory disclosure, like other anti-corruption efforts, should be carefully structured to reduce its negative effects on competition.

2. The Background of Mandatory Disclosure

Mandatory disclosure in federal contracting grew out of two separate initiatives: an effort to find a replacement for *voluntary* disclosures (which had largely failed in defense contracting) and a broader effort to establish *compliance systems* for federal contractors.[3]

The predecessor to mandatory disclosure—the Voluntary Disclosure Program—was launched by the federal government in July 1986,[4] shortly before the "Ill Wind" procurement scandals which swept up many major defense contractors.[5] The Voluntary Disclosure Program reflected an attempt to formalize and thus open to a broader set of contractors, a practice of informal, voluntary disclosures, which the major defense contractors were already making.[6]

Voluntary disclosure under the formal program was a very cumbersome process, with uncertain benefits for those that made disclosures; the Department of

[2] *See, e.g.*, Jessica Tillipman & Vijaya Surampudi, *The Compliance Mentoring Program: Improving Ethics and Compliance in Small Government Contractors*, 49 PUB. CONT. L.J. 217 (2020) (republished in Chapter 15 of this volume and based on the paper presented at conference "Ethical Dilemmas in the Global Defense Industry").

[3] For a widely cited monograph on the contractor compliance and mandatory disclosure requirements, *see* GUIDE TO THE MANDATORY DISCLOSURE RULE: ISSUES, GUIDELINES, AND BEST PRACTICES (Frederic M. Levy & Robert F. Huffman, eds., American Bar Association 2010).

[4] *See, e.g.*, Benjamin B. Klubes, *The Department of Defense Voluntary Disclosure Program*, 19 PUB. CONT. L.J. 504 (1990); U.S. DEP'T OF DEFENSE, THE DEPARTMENT OF DEFENSE VOLUNTARY DISCLOSURE PROGRAM: A DESCRIPTION OF THE PROCESS (Apr. 1990).

[5] *See, e.g.*, Timothy M. Cox, *Is the Procurement Integrity Act "Important" Enough for the Mandatory Disclosure Rule? A Case for Inclusion*, 40 PUB. CONT. L.J. 347, 371–74 (2011); *In re Search Warrant for Secretarial Area Outside Office of Gunn*, 855 F.2d 569, 570 (8th Cir. 1988) (discussing broadly the Operation Ill Wind investigation disclosed by search warrants executed on over 40 locations on June 14, 1988).

[6] *See* Letter of Deputy Secretary of Defense William H. Taft, IV, July 24, 1986 ("a number of major Defense contractors have adopted a policy of voluntarily disclosing problems affecting their corporate contractual relationship with the Department of Defense"), *reproduced in* THE DEPARTMENT OF DEFENSE VOLUNTARY DISCLOSURE PROGRAM, *supra* note 4, App. A.

Justice (DoJ), the Department of Defense (DoD), and other enforcement entities retained substantial discretion to decide what impact, if any, a voluntary disclosure would have on a contractor's eventual punishment, and voluntary disclosure risked triggering additional liability from whistleblowers (or "relators") under the federal False Claims Act.[7] The Voluntary Disclosure Program declined in popularity. When the mandatory disclosure rule was proposed at the DoJ's request in 2007, therefore, the DoJ's core goal was to replace the fraud and corruption cases which were no longer emerging through the Voluntary Disclosure Program.[8]

It should be stressed, however, that when the proposed rule requiring mandatory disclosure rule was published in November 2007, it came as something of a surprise to the federal contracting community.[9] The Federal Acquisition Regulation (FAR) councils had earlier published a proposed rule, in February 2007, which addressed contractor compliance requirements alone and built on earlier, agency-specific requirements for such compliance systems.[10] The requirement for a compliance system requirement was not a surprise; as many commentators outside the government had noted, corporate compliance systems were already called for by the U.S. Sentencing Commission's organizational sentencing guidelines, and so extending those requirements to contractors was a predictable next step.[11] In response to the request from the DoJ, however, the FAR councils in November 2007 published a broader proposed rule, which called for both contractor compliance systems *and* mandatory disclosure.[12] The mandatory disclosure requirement became part of the final combined rule in November 2008, which took effect on December 12, 2008.[13]

While it applied to contracts awarded by all agencies (not just the DoD), the new mandatory disclosure rule drew on many elements of the prior voluntary disclosure program. Disclosures under the mandatory compliance rule are typically to be processed through the contracting officer, who is to

[7] *See generally* Robert S. Ryland, *The Government Contractor's Dilemma: Voluntary Disclosures as the Source of Qui Tam Litigation*, 22 PUB. CONT. L.J. 764 (1993).

[8] 72 Fed. Reg. 64019, 64020 (Nov. 14, 2007) ("According to DoJ, the requirement for mandatory disclosure is necessary because few companies have actually responded to the invitation of DoD that they report or voluntarily disclose suspected instance of violations of Federal criminal law relating to the contract or subcontract.").

[9] For a discussion of how the mandatory disclosure rule emerged in the government's rulemaking process, *see, e.g.*, Brian D. Miller, *The Federal Acquisition Regulation Mandatory Disclosure Rule Program at the U.S. General Services Administration Office of Inspector General*, at 2–4 (updated June 2012), *available at* https://www.gsaig.gov/sites/default/files/misc-reports/FAR_MDR_JuneUpdate_Final.pdf; *see also* GUIDE TO THE MANDATORY DISCLOSURE RULE, *supra* note 3, at 9–10 (recounting the history of rule).

[10] 72 Fed. Reg. 7588 (Feb. 16, 2007).

[11] *See, e.g.*, Christopher R. Yukins, *Ethics in Procurement: New Challenges After a Decade of Reform*, PROCUREMENT LAW., Spring 2003, at 3.

[12] 72 Fed. Reg. 64019 (Nov. 14, 2007).

[13] 73 Fed. Reg. 67064 (Nov. 12, 2008).

coordinate a response with the agency inspector general.[14] As with the voluntary disclosure program, disclosures and enforcement are to turn on whether there is "credible evidence" of a bad act.[15] The mandatory disclosure rule calls for disclosures of *specific bad acts*, and the new rule leaves it to the *contractor*, after due investigation (potentially under an attorney-client privilege), to determine in the first instance whether there is credible evidence of the enumerated bad acts. The mandatory disclosure rule notably does *not* require disclosure of *other*, nonenumerated forms of bad acts, such as violations of the Procurement Integrity Act—even though that law was born of the same procurement scandals which emerged alongside the voluntary disclosure rule.[16]

The mandatory disclosure rule, unlike its predecessor, does not explicitly incentivize disclosure; a contractor will not necessarily win a reduced sentence by making a mandatory disclosure. But if a contractor *fails* to make a mandatory disclosure—that is, if a contractor's principals are aware of credible evidence of an enumerated bad act and the contractor fails to disclose that information—the contractor may be suspended or debarred on that ground alone.[17]

It is important to stress how mandatory disclosure is intertwined with the corporate compliance requirements, which were made part of the same rule. The mandatory disclosure rule assumes that a contractor's compliance system will survey for, and detect, bad acts and that those bad acts were will be reported up through the firm so that the bad acts can be assessed and then, as appropriate, reported to the government.[18] The mandatory disclosure rule thus arguably rests on an assumption that contractors will have an effective compliance system in place.[19]

Experience under the mandatory disclosure rule has been mixed. While some contractors have tried to mitigate risk by reporting many possible violations—from petty to major violations—other contractors have apparently taken a much narrower approach to disclosure under the rule.[20] What is clear,

[14] FAR 3.1003(b).

[15] *Compare* The Department of Defense Voluntary Disclosure Program, *supra* note 4, at 3, *with* 73 Fed. Reg. 67073 (discussion of adoption of "credible evidence" standard in final rule, per DoJ input).

[16] *See generally* Cox, *supra* note 5 (discussing the omission of the Procurement Integrity Act from the list of enumerated statutes).

[17] Applicable regulations are set forth in footnote 1, *supra*. The standards for potential suspension parallel those for debarment, which are set forth in the same footnote.

[18] *See, e.g.*, Guide to the Mandatory Disclosure Rule, *supra* note 3, at 97–113 (discussing techniques for ensuring adverse information regarding bad acts is "reported up" through the firm).

[19] *See id.* at 97.

[20] *See, e.g.*, David Robbins, *Embracing Mandatory Disclosure Can Save Contractors Time, Trouble and Legal Fees*, Nat'l Def. Mag., June 1, 2014, *available at* https://www.nationaldefensemagazine.org/articles/2014/6/1/2014june-embracing-mandatory-disclosure-can-save-contractors-time-trouble-and-legal-fees; Dietrich Knauth, *Contractors Overload Agencies by Reporting Smallest Frauds*, Law360, Apr. 20, 2012, *available at* http://www.law360.com/articles/326078/contractors-overload-agencies-by-reporting-smallest-frauds-?article_related_content=1 (subscription required).

however, is that mandatory disclosure is taken very seriously by mature defense contractors, including, especially, the handful of large prime contractors at the core of the defense market, and that those contractors cognizant of the requirement take careful steps to integrate disclosure into their broader compliance efforts.[21]

The mandatory disclosure requirements for contractors also can be read against the backdrop of disclosures required of publicly traded companies under the securities law reforms enacted in the early 1930s. The mandatory disclosures required by those laws were intended to reshape the balance of power between shareholders and managers in publicly traded firms, by forcing managers to open corporate governance by broadening shareholders' access to information. These disclosure requirements under the securities laws were born of unique cultural, historical, and political circumstances in the United States that favored disclosure to support the common investor in the wake of the financial crash of 1929.[22]

Viewed in this light, the mandatory disclosure requirements under the FAR can be seen as an analogous effort to redraw the agency relationship, not between managers and shareholders, but instead between the government and its contractors.[23] There is a natural asymmetry of information between the government and its contractors, which opens the door for strategic behavior—including, potentially, fraudulent and corrupt behavior—by the contractors. By forcing mandatory disclosure of information on bad acts, the government has mitigated that asymmetrical relationship, at least in part.

This leads, in turn, to a number of important questions. Why, for example, did the government choose *these* bad acts? Why not require disclosure, for example, of all production failures (even if they do not constitute fraud), or of violations of other important anti-corruption measures, such as the Procurement Integrity Act, the Anti-Kickback Act, or the covenant against contingent fees? More broadly for our purposes here, how and why does *this* system of mandatory disclosure affect competition in procurement markets (most specifically, the defense market), and what can be done to ease its potentially anti-competitive effects?

[21] For a practical discussion of developments that drive contractors' disclosure decisions, *see* Aron C. Beezley, *DOJ Signals Renewed Focus on "Mandatory Disclosure" Rule* (Mar. 2, 2020), *available at* https://www.buildsmartbradley.com/2020/03/doj-signals-renewed-focus-on-mandatory-disclosure-rule/.

[22] *See, e.g.*, James A. Fanto, *The Absence of Cross-Cultural Communication: SEC Mandatory Disclosure and Foreign Corporate Governance*, 17 Nw. J. Int'l L. & Bus. 119, 137–39 (1996) (citing Paul G. Mahoney, *Mandatory Disclosure as a Solution to Agency Problems*, 62 U. Chi. L. Rev. 1047 (1995)).

[23] *See generally* Christopher R. Yukins, *A Versatile Prism: Assessing Procurement Law Through the Principal-Agent Model*, 40 Pub. Cont. L.J. 63 (2010).

3. Anti-Competitive Effects of Mandatory Disclosure

As noted, changes to the securities laws of the 1930s forced new mandatory disclosures in financial markets, in order to *radically reshape* agency relationships between management and shareholders, by reducing the informational advantage that managers held. In contrast, as was described earlier, the mandatory disclosure rule imposed on contractors in 2008 was arguably an *evolutionary* measure, which did not reorder but instead reinforced existing competitive advantages held by the DoD's largest contractors and bolstered existing reputational bonds with those large firms. The following sections assess those practical effects of the mandatory disclosure rule and their potentially anti-competitive effects.

4. Mandatory Disclosures Depend on Effective Compliance Systems—Which the Largest Contractors Have Been Building for Decades

To understand mandatory disclosure's potential anti-competitive effect, it is important to stress that mandatory disclosure depends, first, on an *effective compliance system*. Without an effective compliance system, information on apparent violations—the stuff of mandatory disclosures—typically will not "bubble up" to management's attention, except by accident. Put another way, without an effective compliance system in place, a contractor runs a material risk of *not* being able to meet its mandatory disclosure obligation if, indeed, the firm engages in one of the enumerated prohibited acts (criminal or civil fraud, bribery, etc.).

The standards for compliance systems are remarkably uniform across borders,[24] both inside and outside procurement markets.[25] As the following chart illustrates, countries and standards-setting organizations across the world require the same basic elements—including a code of conduct, training, and so forth—in corporate compliance systems.

[24] For different perspectives on these common international standards, *see, e.g.*, Thomas Fox, *What Are the Essential Elements of a Corporate Compliance Program?*, *Corporate*, LexisNexis Legal NewsRoom, May 23, 2013, *available at* http://www.lexisnexis.com/legalnewsroom/corporate/b/fcpa-compliance/archive/2013/05/23/what-are-the-essential-elements-of-a-corporate-compliance-program.aspx (discussing a presentation by Paul McNulty and Stephen Martin of Baker & McKenzie).

[25] For a description of how to structure an effective ethics program within a defense contractor, *see* Def. Indus. Initiative on Bus. Ethics & Conduct, *Creating and Maintaining an Effective Ethics and Business Conduct Program*, *available at* https://www.dii.org/featured-tools (registration required) (last visited Aug. 29, 2020).

CORPORATE COMPLIANCE: INTERNATIONAL HARMONIZATION

Elements of Corporate Compliance Systems	U.S. Sentencing Commission: Organizational Sentencing Guidelines	U.S. Federal Acquisition Regulation: Contractor Compliance Requirements	UK Ministry of Justice: Compliance Under U.K. Bribery Act	Organisation for Economic Cooperation & Development	International Chamber of Commerce
Standards and procedures	√	√	√	√	√
Knowledgeable leadership	√		√	√	√
Exclude risky personnel	√	√	√	√	√
Training	√	√	√	√	√
Monitor, evaluate, reporting hotline	√	√	√	√	√
Incentives and discipline	√	√	√	√	√
Adjust program to risk	√	√	√	√	√

Although these harmonized standards mean that multinational firms bear lower costs of compliance across borders, the costs of *establishing* and *maintaining* an effective compliance and ethics system (however uniform) should not be underestimated.[26]

Though corporate compliance systems were first mandated in federal contracting in 2008, major contractors began to implement compliance systems (also known as corporate integrity systems) many years earlier, driven in important part by the defense industry's corruption scandals (laid bare by the DoJ's "Ill Wind" investigation) of the 1980s.[27] The large contractors that had embraced corporate compliance and ethics programs therefore were well prepared for the compliance requirements mandated in 2008, including mandatory disclosure.

[26] *See, e.g.*, *Cost of Compliance 2018 Report: Your Biggest Challenges Revealed*, THOMSON REUTERS, https://legal.thomsonreuters.com/en/insights/articles/cost-of-compliance-2018-report-your-biggest-challenges-revealed. *But see* Joseph E. Murphy, *A Compliance & Ethics Program on a Dollar a Day: How Small Companies Can Have Effective Programs*, CORP. COMPLIANCE (Aug. 2010), http://www.corporatecompliance.org/Portals/1/PDF/Resources/CEProgramDollarADay-Murphy.pdf (providing an interesting alternative viewpoint on how small businesses can establish ethics and compliance systems at almost no cost).

[27] *See, e.g.*, Nancy B. Kurland, *The Defense Industry Initiative: Ethics, Self-Regulation, and Accountability*, 12 J. BUS. ETHICS 137 (1993). A later report summarized the evolving efforts, through these years, to build compliance programs in the defense industry:

As a practical matter, however, it is widely believed in the federal procurement community that hundreds, if not thousands, of small and medium-sized defense contractors did not have (and do not have) effective compliance and ethics systems and thus cannot readily meet the mandatory disclosure requirements of the law.[28]

The risks of *not* having an effective compliance system are magnified by the unique anti-fraud/anti-corruption laws governing federal contracting—many of which trigger the mandatory disclosure rule. For example, when the rule requires disclosure of any violation of "Federal criminal law involving fraud, conflict of interest, bribery or gratuity violations found in Title 18 of the United States Code," this sweeps up personal conflicts of interest under 18 U.S.C. § 208, which can be highly technical and difficult to detect, with no de minimis exception[29] but with a complex set of regulatory safe harbors.[30]

Nor are the civil fraud requirements easy to meet: whereas common law fraud normally requires *intentional* fraud to trigger liability,[31] under the federal false claims act mere *recklessness* is enough.[32] Thus, a firm's aggressive recruiting of retiring government employees (which can be criminal under 18 U.S.C. § 208),[33] or sloppy accounting or production methods (which can constitute reckless fraud), all may trigger liability, and thus an obligation to report under the mandatory

> Large U.S. companies engaged as defense contractors with various branches of the U.S. military continued to be accused of fraudulent practices spawning federal government demands for a more comprehensive ethics and compliance program by many U.S. corporations. These firms revised their code of ethics, created employee ethics training programs and established internal processes for auditing employee practices, particularly with regards to pricing of products to the government. Many of these ethics and compliance program revisions or improvements were in response to the threats by the federal government to terminate all contracts in the future if changes were not made.

James Weber & David M. Wasieleski, *Corporate Ethics and Compliance Programs: A Report, Analysis and Critique*, 112 J. BUS. ETHICS 609, 611 (2012).

[28] Although contractors working under smaller contracts (under $5 million) are technically exempt from the compliance system requirements of the contract clause at FAR 52.203-13, *see* FAR 3.1004(a), 48 C.F.R. § 3.1004(a), if a contractor under such a small contract (typically a small business) fails to disclose the covered bad acts (including fraud and corruption), under FAR Subpart 9.4, that contractor risks potential suspension or debarment. In other words, while contractors on smaller procurements bear risk because they must disclose certain bad acts, under the terms of the rule itself those businesses may well *not* have a compliance system in place to screen for and identify those bad acts.

[29] *See* U.S. Office of Government Ethics, *18 U.S.C. § 208: Acts Affecting a Personal Financial Interest*, http://www.oge.gov/Laws-and-Regulations/Statutes/18-U-S-C-%C2%A7-208-Acts-affecting-a-personal-financial-interest/ (last visited Aug. 29, 2020) ("The criminal prohibition has no de minimis level. That is, it applies where any financial interest exists, no matter how small.").

[30] 5 C.F.R. pt. 2640.

[31] *See, e.g.*, Strategic Diversity, Inc. v. Alchemix Corp., 666 F.3d 1197, 1210 n.3 (9th Cir. 2012).

[32] *See, e.g.*, CLAIRE M. SYLVIA, THE FALSE CLAIMS ACT: FRAUD AGAINST THE GOVERNMENT § 4:38 (2014) (discussing authorities applying recklessness standard under False Claims Act).

[33] *See, e.g.*, *Former Boeing Exec Pleads to Conspiracy Charge*, 18 ANDREWS GOV'T CONT. LITIG. REP. 7 (2004).

disclosure rule. This means, in turn, that a firm without an effective compliance system in place—a firm, in other words, in the mass of unprepared defense contractors—is left exposed to potentially disastrous risks, both of substantive violations *and* of failing to make the mandated disclosure of those violations. In sum, the mandatory disclosure rule *exacerbates* the competitive disadvantages borne by small and medium-sized enterprises which have been slow to adopt corporate compliance systems.

5. Mandatory Disclosure Reinforces Reputational Bonds between Contractors and the Department of Defense

As the preceding discussion reflects, mandatory disclosure amplifies the competitive weaknesses borne by the many contractors—potentially thousands of firms—in the middle and lower tiers of the defense marketplace that do not have effective compliance systems. The mandatory disclosure rule hurts those small and midsized firms in another way: only the largest firms, with effective and highly public compliance and disclosure systems, can assure the DoD that the reputational capital that those firms share with the government will be carefully protected through internal enforcement and disclosure.

The U.S. defense industry has become much more concentrated over recent decades,[34] and now a handful of prime contractors dominate the market.[35] While previous studies have suggested that sophisticated contractors may structure themselves to reduce reputational risk to the government and the contractors,[36] there has been little, if any, specific assessment of the mandatory disclosure rule's role in this complex relationship between the DoD and its largest contractors.

The starting point for this discussion is a recognition that a government inevitably shares reputational capital with its contractors, especially those prime

[34] *See, e.g.*, F.G. Hayden, Elliot G. Campbell & Shannon Cummins, *The Ranking of Contractors to the U.S. Department of Defense According to Integrated Power Blocs Among the Contractors*, 44 J. Econ. Issues 411, 412–14 (2010) (providing a recent history of consolidation in defense history).

[35] *See, e.g.*, Erik Kopač, *Defense Industry Restructuring: Trends in European and U.S. Defense Companies*, 13 Transition Studs. Rev. 283–96 (2006).

[36] One study, by Chong Wang of the Naval Postgraduate School, suggested that the largest, most politically connected contractors may hire politically astute senior retirees from the military establishment so as to curb the contractor's own opportunistic (corrupt or rent-seeking) behavior that would undermine the government's reputation. *See* Chong Wang, *Political Connections of the Boards of Directors and Department of Defense Contractors' Excessive Profits*, 14 J. Pub. Proc. 96, 113 (2014) ("DoD contractors may hire . . . politically connected directors and use their experience to serve a benevolent role to the public. For instance, one legitimate use of the political experience is to keep DoD contractors from opportunistic profit-seeking behaviors that could reach or even cross federal government regulatory redlines.").

contractors under its direct control.[37] The debate over private military contractors (PMCs), for example, has highlighted that shared reputational capital, for those arguing for tighter regulation of PMCs have pointed out that the contractors' misconduct can also impair a government's reputation and legitimacy.[38]

Viewed in this light, the mandatory disclosure rule may be seen as a capstone on a broader government effort to force contractors, through ethics and compliance programs, to control the risks of fraud and corruption—especially reputational risks—on behalf of the government. The mandatory disclosure rule notably does *not* focus on performance risks; there is no requirement, for example, to report new obstacles which may slow a project.[39] Instead, as written and implemented, the mandatory disclosure rule serves more as an early warning device for fraud and corruption, to alert the government to potential egregious violations by contractors.[40] While contractors are expected to identify and initially investigate the violations, ultimate enforcement against those violations still rests with the government. From officials' perspective, the government leverages the contractors' compliance and ethics system to gain better visibility into violations, thus multiplying the government's enforcement capacity and—importantly—sharply reducing reputational risks from otherwise unpredictable and uncontrolled third-party reports of fraud and corruption (e.g., from the press and whistleblowers).

In practice, however, this mandatory disclosure model appears to be one which favors large, established contractors and which in effect bolsters barriers to entry in the defense market. The mandatory disclosure requirements are themselves idiosyncratic—some crimes are subject to mandatory disclosure, but many are not—and so demand time and sophistication to integrate into a

[37] *See, e.g.*, Douglas P. Beighle, *Defense Contractors—The Next Spotted Owl?*, 24 NAT. CONT. MAN. J. 1 (1991) (discussing Congress's and contractors' shared reputational loss due to negative studies and procurement scandals of the previous decade).

[38] *See, e.g.*, Zoe Salzman, *Private Military Contractors and the Taint of a Mercenary Reputation*, 40 N.Y.U. J. INT'L L. & POL. 853 (2007–2008). A study of the use of military law to address contractor criminal misconduct in combat areas pointed out that "[c]ontractor criminal activity can generate significant media interest, adversely impact strategic relationships with host nation governments, and require commanders to swiftly formulate a response when such incidents occur within their areas of operation." Charles T. Kirchmaier, *Command Authority over Contractors Serving With or Accompanying the Force*, 439 ARMY LAW., Dec. 1, 2009, at 35, 37. *See also* Nigel D. White & Sorcha MacLeod, *EU Operations and Private Military Contractors: Issues of Corporate and Institutional Responsibility*, 19 EUR. J. INT'L L. 965 (2008).

[39] Disclosure of those performance-based risks are typically dealt with separately, under contractual clauses which require, for example, that contractors report any extraordinary costs which may be chargeable to the government within 30 days.

[40] Guidance by the then-Inspector General for the General Services Administration, for example, explained that contractors should give early notification, even before an investigation is concluded, and that the agency would normally await conclusion of the contractor's investigation before taking any action. *See* Miller, *supra* note 9, at 10 ("We prefer early notification, and so long as the contractor keeps us informed of its progress, we do not intervene until the contractor has completed its internal review.").

broader compliance and ethics program. That foundation underlying mandatory disclosure, an effective compliance and ethics program, is also extremely expensive, and while some of those compliance costs may be allowable under cost-reimbursement contracts, a compliance program inevitably causes additional costs (including opportunity costs) that will *not* be absorbed by the government customer.

Nor do the costs end once mandatory disclosure has been integrated into an ethics and compliance program. The compliance system must remain active in gathering, processing, and assessing reports of possible violations. When violations may call for mandatory disclosure, those possible violations must be specially assessed, often with input from sophisticated outside counsel. The contractor may undertake an internal investigation, under the protection of an attorney-client privilege, and the contractor ultimately need only disclose those circumstances which present "credible evidence" of an enumerated bad act (bribery, fraud, etc.). Mandatory disclosure is, in other words, a long, costly process, one built on an already expensive system of ethics and compliance—not a process that favors those new to the market or short of resources. Mandatory disclosure is, in sum, a rule which can be readily implemented by large, established contractors, but which poses a daunting obstacle to those contemplating entering the defense market and which poses serious risks to competitors that cannot (or care not to) implement it properly.

6. Easing the Anti-Competitive Effects of Mandatory Disclosure

As the preceding discussion reflects, the mandatory disclosure rule creates substantial benefits for enforcement officials (by unearthing violations for enforcement) and, more broadly, for the government as a whole by reducing the costs and reputational risks of fraud and corruption. At the same time, though, the mandatory disclosure rule creates significant costs for contractors and tends to favor the largest, most deeply established contractors in the market. In a defense market that is already markedly concentrated, those anti-competitive forces are a cause for concern. The following sections assess possible ways to ease the rule's inherently anti-competitive effects.[41]

[41] For a general discussion of the legal and policy imperatives for assessing procurement rules' potentially anti-competitive effects, *see* Christopher R. Yukins & Jose Cora, *Feature Comment: Considering the Effects of Public Procurement Regulations on Competitive Markets*, 55 Gov. Contractor para. 64 (Mar. 6, 2013), *available at* http://ssrn.com/abstract=2230613.

7. Governments Should Facilitate Compliance and Ethics Systems

One obvious measure to enhance competition would be to reduce contractors' costs of administering the corporate compliance and ethics system upon which the mandatory disclosure requirement rests. This can be done, for example, by making model codes of ethics and training publicly available and by using common standards for compliance systems.[42] The important point is one of perspective: in mandating compliance systems among their contractors, governments should recognize that the goal is one of reducing *agency costs*—to ensure that the government's rules and principles are conveyed and efficiently complied with down through the supply chain. Doing so will reduce hiccups in the continuity of supply and expand the available competition. Viewed in this way, the government has every incentive to cooperate fully with its vendors, large and small, in establishing robust and effective compliance systems.

8. Harmonize Standards for Mandatory Disclosure

Governments' success in harmonizing the standards for compliance systems (discussed earlier) should be matched in mandatory disclosure requirements: to the extent a government decides to mandate disclosures, those requirements should be harmonized across regulatory regimes. Thus, for example, it makes little sense for the federal government to require:

- *federal contractors* to make mandatory disclosures once they have *credible evidence* of *enumerated crimes* (bribery or gratuity under Title 18, U.S. Code), civil or criminal fraud under the False Claims Act, or "significant overpayments," while at the same requiring,
- *federal grantees* to make mandatory disclosures of, "in a timely manner, in writing to the Federal awarding agency or pass-through entity[,] *all*

[42] Rather than simply adopt the organizational compliance standards promulgated by the U.S. Sentencing Commission—a sister federal agency, which maintains what are commonly referred to as the "gold standard" for corporate compliance standards, *see, e.g.*, Paul E. McGreal, *The Amended Organizational Sentencing Guidelines: Top Ten Things Attorneys Should Know*, HOUSTON LAW., Mar./Apr. 2005, *available at* http://www.thehoustonlawyer.com/aa_mar05/page10.htm, the drafters of the federal procurement rules insisted on creating their own, parallel standards. 73 Fed. Reg. at 67068. Because the FAR compliance standards are largely, but not perfectly, identical to the U.S. Sentencing Commission guidelines, the FAR regulators' insistence on drafting their own standards increased contractors' implementation costs, and may mean that the federal procurement standards will lag a step behind, as the U.S. Sentencing Commission's guidelines evolve over time.

> *violations of Federal criminal law involving fraud, bribery, or gratuity violations* potentially affecting the Federal award."[43]

Thus, while *contractors* must disclose both *criminal* (intentional) and *civil* (reckless) fraud, the covered grantees need only disclose *criminal* fraud; by the same token, it is not clear what other criminal statutes are covered in the grantees' requirements (is the Anti-Kickback Act, for example, a federal criminal law involving bribery?). There is no ready reason for these standards to differ, especially since federal contractors regularly serve as grantees as well,[44] and the federal grant rule was explicitly modeled on the mandatory disclosure rule for contractors.[45] Where, as here, mandatory disclosure requirements vary—apparently unnecessarily—private vendors must spend more to implement these varying standards, and other potential competitors are further discouraged from competing for federal contracts or grants.

9. Limit Scope: Target Violations for Which Contractors Have a Clear Informational Advantage, or Which Pose Most Severe Reputational Risks

Because of the costs and potentially anti-competitive effects of mandatory disclosure,[46] it is important that the scope of mandatory disclosure be carefully limited. In principle, because (as noted) regulators' goals here should be to level the informational imbalance between government and its contractors and to force early (and controlled) disclosures of violations which pose potentially severe reputational risk, logically regulators should craft the mandatory disclosure rule to force disclosure of bad acts:

[43] Section 200.113 of the Office of Management & Budget's "Super Circular" governing federal grants (now known as the "Omni Circular"), 78 Fed. Reg. 78590 (Dec. 26, 2013), codified at 2 C.F.R. § 200.113, which has been implemented by federal grantmaking agencies, provides as follows:

> *§ 200.113 Mandatory disclosures.* The non-Federal entity or applicant for a Federal award must disclose, in a timely manner, in writing to the Federal awarding agency or pass-through entity all violations of Federal criminal law involving fraud, bribery, or gratuity violations potentially affecting the Federal award. Failure to make required disclosures can result in any of the remedies described in § 200.338 Remedies for noncompliance, including suspension or debarment. (*See also* 2 CFR pt. 180 and 31 U.S.C. 3321).

[44] Data on federal funds received by grantees and contractors are available in a combined database, through https://www.USASpending.gov.

[45] *See* 78 Fed. Reg. 78595.

[46] Mandatory disclosure also may implicate broader issues of self-incrimination; these are potentially human rights issues beyond the scope of this chapter, which focuses instead on the economic costs and benefits of a mandatory disclosure regime. *See, e.g.*, Jeremy A. Goldman, Note, *New FAR Rule on Compliance Programs and Ethics: A Hidden Assault on the Corporate Attorney-Client Privilege*, 39 PUB. CONT. L.J. 71 (2009).

- for which contractors enjoy a clear informational advantage, and
- which pose the sharpest reputational risks to the government.

Although the federal mandatory disclosure rule apparently was not crafted with these goals in mind—instead, it appeared to reflect various enforcement agencies' efforts to include specific bad acts onto the mandatory disclosure list[47]—the final rule does, in rough terms, reflect these dual goals. The bad acts which must be disclosed are generally those which contractors have an easier time discerning than the government (e.g., bribes, gratuities, and fraud), and, again because of complicated reasons of agency,[48] these are precisely the bad acts that are most likely to have deeply corrosive reputational impacts on the government. In other words, although the federal rule is not perfect,[49] it does appear to accommodate these dual policy goals.

10. Allow Contractor Opportunity to Investigate, under Privilege

Another, relatively simple means of reducing the anti-competitive impact of a mandatory disclosure rule is to allow the contractor time, before making any disclosure, to assess the evidence under the protection of a privileged investigation.[50] The drafters of the federal rule prudently, and explicitly, decided to leave contractors this breathing space before making a mandatory disclosure.[51] Although critics may argue that the rule thus allows contractors time to

[47] For a detailed discussion of this aspect of the administrative history of the mandatory disclosure rule, *see, e.g.*, Miller, *supra* note 9, at 3–5.

[48] *See, e.g.*, Susan Rose-Ackerman, *The Law and Economics of Bribery and Extortion*, 6 ANN. REV. L. & SOC. SCI. 217, 218 (2010) ("Principal-agent relationships are at the heart of any corrupt transaction. An employee or another person acting as an agent for a government body or a private organization accepts a private benefit in return for acting in the payee's interest."); Nico Groenendijk, *A Principal-Agent Model of Corruption*, 27.3–4 CRIME, L. & SOC. CHANGE 207 (1997).

[49] The federal rule's open-ended requirement that contractors disclose "significant overpayments" remains uncertain. The provision also may be exploited by contractors which seek to make *some* disclosure, to ostensibly comply with the rule, but not to report more serious bad acts (such as fraud); these contractors instead may simply disclose a "significant overpayment," pending a more detailed internal review. *See* Miller, *supra* note 9, at 10.

[50] *See generally* GUIDE TO THE MANDATORY DISCLOSURE RULE, *supra* note 3, ch. 10 (on preserving confidentiality and privilege during an investigation).

[51] For example, 73 Fed. Reg. 67074 provides:

> [T]he [FAR] Councils believe that using the standard of "credible evidence" . . . will help clarify "timely" because it implies that the contractor will have the opportunity to take some time for preliminary examination of the evidence to determine its credibility before deciding to disclose to the Government. Until the contractor has determined the evidence to be credible, there can be no "knowing failure to timely disclose." This does not impose upon the contractor an obligation to carry out a complex investigation, but only to take reasonable steps that the contractor considers sufficient to determine that the evidence is credible.

"bury" troubling evidence, the alternative—to require contractors to disclose any apparent violation, without due investigation—would be highly inefficient. A rule demanding immediate disclosure could mean that the government would be flooded with reports which might prove, in the end, to be groundless. Furthermore, a rule which forced *immediate* disclosure of any bad act brought to light in a compliance system would, in effect, encourage contractors *not* to have effective corporate compliance systems, but instead to allow news of bad acts to drift into dark silence at the bottom of the firm.

11. Reinvigorate Voluntary Disclosure

The final proposed change to the mandatory disclosure regime may be the most radical, but the most useful: to recognize that mandatory disclosure will probably always be limited (for the reasons outlined earlier), so that the optimal policy choice instead may be to reinvigorate *voluntary* disclosure, by giving contractors positive incentives, perhaps through reduced enforcement penalties, to come forward with bad acts.[52]

A voluntary disclosure regime, unlike a mandatory one, could cover a much broader array of bad acts and crimes, for it would pose none of the risks that an overbroad mandatory regime carries, of inefficiently forcing disclosures of *too many* bad acts. A system of voluntary disclosure would reduce the costs of implementation, because a voluntary regime means that only those contractors that discover bad acts internally, and seek to make a voluntary disclosure to reduce their exposure, must study and abide by these rules. Finally, a voluntary disclosure regime would have a much less damaging effect on competition, for contractors that could not manage disclosure—the contractors at serious peril in a mandatory regime—would face no new risks of destruction in a voluntary regime; failing to make a disclosure would simply lose them the leniency they might otherwise enjoy under a voluntary regime.

As noted, several decades ago the federal government instituted a system of voluntary disclosure to handle fraud in defense procurement, a system which

[52] As Susan Rose-Ackerman noted, in discussing the importance of whistleblowing in addressing corruption:

> Successful detection of corruption depends upon insiders to report wrongdoing. Citizens and businesses victimized by extortion demands may report bribery attempts, but they may not be able to offer enough proof for prosecutors to act. Instead, effective law enforcement often requires officials to promise leniency to one of the participants. This creates an important paradox for law enforcement efforts. High expected punishments ought to deter corruption, but a high probability of detection may only be possible if some are promised low penalties.

Rose-Ackerman, *supra* note 48, at 222.

failed largely because of its own cumbersomeness and because it did not present defense contractors with sufficient incentives for disclosure. A renewed emphasis on voluntary disclosure, perhaps with clearer and stronger incentives for disclosure, and potentially modeled on the World Bank's reportedly successful system of voluntary disclosures for contractors,[53] might prove a useful way forward. In assessing a new voluntary disclosure system, though, policymakers might wish to weigh the increasingly important role that whistleblowers (often current or former employees) play in revealing fraud and corruption; a system of voluntary contractor disclosure should complement, not disrupt, existing systems to encourage and protect private whistleblowers.

12. Conclusion

The federal government's mandatory disclosure rule provides an interesting case study in how an anti-corruption tool, of good intent, can be quite costly and have anti-competitive effects in an already highly concentrated defense procurement market. To address those problems, a mandatory disclosure rule should be crafted to minimize transaction and opportunity costs and to focus on the problems at the core of a disclosure rule: the need to remedy the government's informational deficits regarding its contractors' bad acts, to redress fraud and corruption and the reputational damage they can cause the government. Recognizing these broader benefits of disclosure, and the inherent limitations of mandatory disclosure, policymakers may wish to revisit the benefits of incentivizing *voluntary* disclosures by contractors, as a complement to the information on bad acts gained through mandatory disclosures and whistleblowers.

References

Aron C. Beezley, *DOJ Signals Renewed Focus on "Mandatory Disclosure" Rule* (Mar. 2, 2020), *available at* https://www.buildsmartbradley.com/2020/03/doj-signals-renewed-focus-on-mandatory-disclosure-rule/.

Douglas P. Beighle, *Defense Contractors—The Next Spotted Owl?*, 24 NAT. CONT. MAN. J. 1 (1991).

[53] The World Bank publishes extensive materials on its Voluntary Disclosure Program, which incentivizes contractors on World Bank–funded projects to come forward with information on bad acts, to reduce or avoid the risk of sanctions (including potentially debarment) under the World Bank's sanctions system. *See generally* World Bank, *Voluntary Disclosure Program* (Aug. 18, 2006), *available at* https://www.worldbank.org/content/dam/documents/sanctions/other-documents/osd/VDPTermsandConditions.pdf.

Cost of Compliance 2018 Report: Your Biggest Challenges Revealed, Thomson Reuters, https://legal.thomsonreuters.com/en/insights/articles/cost-of-compliance-2018-report-your-biggest-challenges-revealed.

Timothy M. Cox, *Is the Procurement Integrity Act "Important" Enough for the Mandatory Disclosure Rule? A Case for Inclusion*, 40 Pub. Cont. L.J. 347 (2011).

Def. Indus. Initiative on Bus. Ethics & Conduct, *Creating and Maintaining an Effective Ethics and Business Conduct Program*, *available at* https://www.dii.org/featured-tools.

James A. Fanto, *The Absence of Cross-Cultural Communication: SEC Mandatory Disclosure and Foreign Corporate Governance*, 17 Nw. J. Int'l L. & Bus. 119 (1996).

Former Boeing Exec Pleads to Conspiracy Charge, 18 Andrews Gov't Cont. Litig. Rep. 7 (2004).

Thomas Fox, *What Are the Essential Elements of a Corporate Compliance Program?, Corporate*, LexisNexis Legal NewsRoom, May 23, 2013, *available at* http://www.lexisnexis.com/legalnewsroom/corporate/b/fcpa-compliance/archive/2013/05/23/what-are-the-essential-elements-of-a-corporate-compliance-program.aspx.

Jeremy A. Goldman, Note, *New FAR Rule on Compliance Programs and Ethics: A Hidden Assault on the Corporate Attorney-Client Privilege*, 39 Pub. Cont. L.J. 71 (2009).

Nico Groenendijk, *A Principal-Agent Model of Corruption*, 27.3–4 Crime, L. & Soc. Change 207 (1997).

Guide to the Mandatory Disclosure Rule: Issues, Guidelines, and Best Practices (Frederic M. Levy & Robert F. Huffman, eds., American Bar Association 2010).

F.G. Hayden, Elliot G. Campbell & Shannon Cummins, *The Ranking of Contractors to the U.S. Department of Defense According to Integrated Power Blocs Among the Contractors*, 44 J. Econ. Issues 411 (2010).

Charles T. Kirchmaier, *Command Authority over Contractors Serving with or Accompanying the Force*, 439 Army Law., Dec. 1, 2009, 35.

Dietrich Knauth, *Contractors Overload Agencies by Reporting Smallest Frauds*, Law360 (Apr. 20, 2012), *available at* http://www.law360.com/articles/326078/contractors-overload-agencies-by-reporting-smallest-frauds-?article_related_content=1 (subscription required).

Erik Kopač, *Defense Industry Restructuring: Trends in European and U.S. Defense Companies*, 13 Transition Studs. Rev. 283 (2006).

Nancy B. Kurland, *The Defense Industry Initiative: Ethics, Self-Regulation, and Accountability*, 12 J. Bus. Ethics 137 (1993).

Paul G. Mahoney, *Mandatory Disclosure as a Solution to Agency Problems*, 62 U. Chi. L. Rev. 1047 (1995).

Paul E. McGreal, *The Amended Organizational Sentencing Guidelines: Top Ten Things Attorneys Should Know*, Houston Law., Mar./Apr. 2005, http://www.thehoustonlawyer.com/aa_mar05/page10.htm.

Brian D. Miller, *The Federal Acquisition Regulation Mandatory Disclosure Rule Program at the U.S. General Services Administration Office of Inspector General* (updated June 2012), *available at* https://www.gsaig.gov/sites/default/files/misc-reports/FAR_MDR_JuneUpdate_Final.pdf.

Joseph E. Murphy, *A Compliance & Ethics Program on a Dollar a Day: How Small Companies Can Have Effective Programs*, Corp. Compliance (Aug. 2010), http://www.corporatecompliance.org/Portals/1/PDF/Resources/CEProgramDollarADay-Murphy.pdf.

David Robbins, *Embracing Mandatory Disclosure Can Save Contractors Time, Trouble and Legal Fees*, NAT'L DEF. MAG. (June 1, 2014), *available at* https://www.nationaldefensemagazine.org/articles/2014/6/1/2014june-embracing-mandatory-disclosure-can-save-contractors-time-trouble-and-legal-fees.

Susan Rose-Ackerman, *The Law and Economics of Bribery and Extortion*, 6 ANN. REV. L. & SOC. SCI. 217 (2010).

Robert S. Ryland, *The Government Contractor's Dilemma: Voluntary Disclosures as the Source of Qui Tam Litigation*, 22 PUB. CONT. L.J. 764 (1993).

Zoe Salzman, *Private Military Contractors and the Taint of a Mercenary Reputation*, 40 N.Y.U. J. INT'L L. & POL. 853 (2007–2008).

CLAIRE M. SYLVIA, THE FALSE CLAIMS ACT: FRAUD AGAINST THE GOVERNMENT § 4:38 (2014).

Jessica Tillipman & Vijaya Surampudi, *The Compliance Mentoring Program: Improving Ethics and Compliance in Small Government Contractors*, 49 PUB. CONT. L.J. 217 (2020).

U.S. DEP'T OF DEFENSE, THE DEPARTMENT OF DEFENSE VOLUNTARY DISCLOSURE PROGRAM: A DESCRIPTION OF THE PROCESS (Apr. 1990).

U.S. Office of Government Ethics, *18 U.S.C. § 208: Acts Affecting a Personal Financial Interest*, http://www.oge.gov/Laws-and-Regulations/Statutes/18-U-S-C-%C2%A7-208-Acts-affecting-a-personal-financial-interest/.

Chong Wang, *Political Connections of the Boards of Directors and Department of Defense Contractors' Excessive Profits*, 14 J. PUB. PROC. 96 (2014).

James Weber & David M. Wasieleski, *Corporate Ethics and Compliance Programs: A Report, Analysis and Critique*, 112 J. BUS. ETHICS 609 (2012).

Nigel D. White & Sorcha MacLeod, *EU Operations and Private Military Contractors: Issues of Corporate and Institutional Responsibility*, 19 EUR. J. INT'L L. 965 (2008).

WORLD BANK, *Voluntary Disclosure Program* (Aug. 18, 2006), *available at* https://www.worldbank.org/content/dam/documents/sanctions/other-documents/osd/VDPTermsandConditions.pdf.

Christopher R. Yukins, *Ethics in Procurement: New Challenges After A Decade of Reform*, PROCUREMENT LAW., Spring 2003.

Christopher R. Yukins, *A Versatile Prism: Assessing Procurement Law Through the Principal-Agent Model*, 40 PUB. CONT. L.J. 63 (2010), *available at* http://ssrn.com/abstract=1776295.

Christopher R. Yukins & Jose Cora, *Feature Comment: Considering the Effects of Public Procurement Regulations on Competitive Markets*, 55 GOV. CONTRACTOR ¶ 64 (Mar. 6, 2013), *available at* http://ssrn.com/abstract=2230613.

15

The Compliance Mentorship Program

Improving Ethics and Compliance in Small Government Contractors

*Jessica Tillipman and Vijaya Surampudi**

1. Introduction

Over the past decade, the anti-corruption, ethics, and compliance landscape has changed dramatically. This is a direct consequence of a global anti-corruption enforcement effort led by the United States through its enforcement of the Foreign Corrupt Practices Act.[1] The increase in enforcement has also been spurred by the adoption of several multilateral anti-corruption agreements, such as the Organization for Economic Co-operation and Development (OECD) Anti-Bribery Convention, and the UN Convention Against Corruption (UNCAC).[2] These agreements have spurred several countries to enact anti-corruption laws, such as the U.K. Bribery Act, Brazil's Clean Company Act, and France's Loi Sapin II.[3] The laws prohibit, among other things, the bribery of foreign government officials.[4] They also encourage companies to dedicate resources

[1] *See* Rachel Brewster & Samuel W. Buell, *The Market for Global Anticorruption Enforcement*, 80 L. & Contemp. Probs. 193, 193 (2017).

[2] *See id.* at 200; *see also* Elizabeth K. Spahn, *Implementing Global Anti-Bribery Norms: From the Foreign Corrupt Practices Act to the OECD Anti-Bribery Convention to the U.N. Convention Against Corruption*, 23 Ind. Int'l & Comp. L. Rev. 1, 1, 31 (2013).

[3] *See* Brewster & Buell, *supra* note 1, at 212–13; *see also* Pamela Davis & Lily Becker, Orrick, Herrington & Sutcliffe, The Ever-Changing Compliance Landscape: What Is the Next Wave? 13 (2016).

[4] *See* Foreign Corrupt Practices Act, 15 U.S.C. § 78dd-1(a) (2012); Decreto No. 12.846, de 1 de Agosto de 2013, Diário Oficial da União [D.O.U.] de 1.8.2013, art. 5 (Braz.); Loi 2016-1691 du 9 décembre 2016 relative à la transparence, à la lutte contre la corruption et à la modernisation de la vie économique [Law 2016-1691 of December 9, 2016 Relating to the Transparency, the Fight Against the Corruption and the Modernization of the Economic Life], Journal Officiel de la République Française [J.O.] [Official Gazette of France], Dec. 10, 2016, No. 0287 art. 3 (Fr.); Bribery Act 2010,

Jessica Tillipman and Vijaya Surampudi, *The Compliance Mentorship Program* In: *Ethical Dilemmas in the Global Defense Industry.* Edited by: Daniel Schoeni and Tobias Vestner, Oxford University Press. © Daniel Schoeni and Tobias Vestner 2023. DOI: 10.1093/oso/9780190675813.003.0016

to developing anti-corruption compliance programs and maintaining robust internal controls.[5]

The increase in anti-corruption enforcement has profoundly impacted large, multinational corporations. Many of these companies have responded to the enforcement increase by investing heavily in sophisticated compliance programs designed to prevent or mitigate liability for anti-corruption violations.[6] The development of rigorous internal compliance programs has been particularly pronounced in the defense industry, especially among large, U.S. defense contractors.[7]

Unlike their large counterparts, many small government contractors are largely unable to keep up with the rapidly evolving trends and best practices in ethics and compliance. Their inattention to this critical area leaves them at risk for compliance failures, fraud, and corruption.[8] As a result, small contractors are more likely than their large counterparts to be debarred from the U.S. procurement system.[9] Despite the harsh consequences of compliance deficiencies, few small contractors are likely to dedicate resources to the development of vital compliance policies and internal controls because of the reality of limited resources.[10] This has created a critical gap in the defense industry supply chain, as many large contractors may partner with small companies that lack the sophistication and resources necessary to ensure compliance with the many government contracts compliance requirements.[11]

One solution to this growing problem is to incentivize large government contractors to help their small subcontractors develop compliance programs. The incentives, of course, must be substantial enough to convince large

c. 23, § 6 (UK); United Nations Convention Against Corruption art. 16, Oct. 31, 2003, 2349 U.N.T.S. 41 [hereinafter U.N. Convention Against Corruption]; Organisation for Economic Co-operation and Development, Convention on Combating Bribery of Foreign Public Officials in International Business Transactions art. 1.1, Dec. 17, 1997, 2802 U.N.T.S. 225 [hereinafter OECD Convention].

[5] *See* 15 U.S.C. § 78m(b)(2); Decreto No. 12.846, de 1 de Agosto de 2013, arts. 6–7; Loi 2016-1691 du 9 décembre 2016, art. 17; Bribery Act 2010 §§ 7, 9; U.N. Convention Against Corruption, *supra* note 4, art. 12; OECD Convention, *supra* note 4, art. 8.

[6] *See* Fritz Heimann et al., Transparency International, Verification of Anti-Corruption Compliance Programs 5 (2014).

[7] *See, e.g.*, Northrop Grumman, *Anti-Corruption Compliance*, https://www.northropgrumman.com/CorporateResponsibility/Pages/AntiCorruptionProgram.aspx [https://perma.cc/4HTM-4D48] (last visited Nov. 11, 2019); Boeing, *Ethics and Compliance*, https://www.boeing.com/principles/ethics-and-compliance.page [https://perma.cc/6GTX-3QGD] (last visited Nov. 11, 2019).

[8] *See* Peter Jeydel, *Yoking the Bull: How to Make the FCPA Work for U.S. Business*, 43 Geo. J. Int'l L. 523, 531–32 (2012).

[9] *See* Jessica Tillipman, *A House of Cards Falls: Why "Too Big to Debar" Is All Slogan and Little Substance*, 80 Fordham L. Rev. Res Gestae 49, 56 (2011) [hereinafter *A House of Cards Falls*].

[10] *See* Ryan Bolger, *Small Companies Face Tougher FCPA Scrutiny*, Int'l Fin. L. Rev., Nov. 2011, at 1.

[11] *Cf.* Howard Weissman, *Changes in Defense Industry Are Increasing FCPA Risks*, Law 360 (Dec. 18, 2014), https://www-law360-com.gwlaw.idm.oclc.org/articles/602964?scroll=1&related=1 [https://perma.cc/KZ4W-PZZV] (discussing the potential compliance risks of working with outside businesses).

contractors to share their confidential and proprietary compliance programs and best practices.

Fortunately, a model for this type of arrangement exists in the U.S. procurement system. The "mentor-protégé" program is designed to help small businesses navigate the immense government contracts regulatory system.[12] Under this program, generally a larger, more experienced contractor serves as a "mentor" to a smaller contractor (the "protégé").[13] The mentor, among other things, guides the protégé through the complex procurement regime by sharing expertise and resources.[14] In return, the mentor is provided with contractual opportunities and incentives by the U.S. government.[15] This model could benefit companies in the compliance space by providing a mechanism for contracting parties to exchange information and ensure transparency throughout all levels of the procurement process.

This chapter recommends incentivizing large businesses to utilize their vast resources to assist their small business partners with the development of internal ethics and compliance programs in order to improve the overall integrity of the government procurement system. Section 2 of this chapter analyzes the development of global anti-corruption compliance standards through an overview of noteworthy changes in laws, regulations, and enforcement. Section 3 analyzes the current compliance risks that large companies face when contracting with smaller companies who lack robust compliance systems and internal controls. Section 4 recommends the adoption of a corporate mentor-protégé program that incentivizes larger companies to dedicate resources to helping smaller contractors develop anti-corruption compliance programs. Section 5 offers some concluding thoughts.

2. Global Shift in Anti-Corruption Enforcement and Compliance

Over the past decade, there has been a global shift in perceptions and approaches toward public corruption. Enforcement has increased dramatically, the sharing of information and resources among governments has improved, and global best practices in corporate anti-corruption compliance have continued to evolve. In response, dozens of countries have made multilateral commitments to combat

[12] *See* Matthew Schoonover, *5 Things You Should Know: All Small Mentor-Protege Program*, SmallGovCon (Sept. 20, 2017), http://smallgovcon.com/five-things/asmpp [https://perma.cc/7VB5-XX2F] (discussing the 2016 SBA All Small Mentor-Protégé Program).

[13] *See id.*

[14] *See id.*

[15] *See id.*

corruption and have enacted anti-corruption legislation to fight bribery and foster a new era of corporate anti-corruption compliance.[16]

Anti-bribery enforcement agencies, nongovernmental organizations, and civil society organizations have developed compliance guidance to assist companies with the prevention and deterrence of corruption.[17] In addition, large, multinational companies are now incentivized to invest in ethics and compliance programs to avoid expensive anti-corruption enforcement actions and long-term reputational harm that may result from public knowledge of their misconduct.[18]

2.1. Relevant Anti-Corruption Laws, Treaties, and Conventions

Enacted in 1977, the Foreign Corrupt Practices Act (FCPA)[19] has provided the foundation for today's global anti-corruption enforcement activities.[20] The U.S. statute has two pillars: it criminalizes the bribery of foreign government officials, and it requires persons and entities to maintain accurate books and records and robust internal controls.[21] Working in tandem, these two pillars

[16] *See* Decreto No. 12.846, de 1 de Agosto de 2013, Diário Oficial da União [D.O.U.] de 7.8.2013 art. 5–7 (Braz.); Loi 2016-1691 du 9 décembre 2016 relative à la transparence, à la lutte contre la corruption et à la modernisation de la vie économique [Law 2016-1691 of December 9, 2016 Relating to the Transparency, the Fight Against the Corruption and the Modernization of the Economic Life], Journal Officiel de la République Française [J.O.] [Official Gazette of France], Dec. 10, 2016, No. 0287, art. 3, 17 (Fr.); Bribery Act 2010, c. 23, §§ 6–7, 9 (UK); U.N. Convention Against Corruption, *supra* note 4, arts. 12, 16; OECD Convention, *supra* note 4, arts. 1, 8 (detailing the anti-bribery commitments member states pledge to make).

[17] *See, e.g.*, Criminal Div., U.S. Dep't of Justice & Enf't Div., U.S. Secs. & Exch. Comm'n, A Resource Guide to the U.S. Foreign Corrupt Practices Act (2012) [hereinafter DOJ FCPA Guidance] (describing the general purpose of the guide); Org. for Econ. Co-operation and Dev. [OECD], Good Practice Guidance on Internal Controls, Ethics, and Compliance 2 (Feb. 18, 2010), https://www.oecd.org/daf/anti-bribery/44884389.pdf [https://perma.cc/5TU4-AFSL] [hereinafter OECD Good Practice Guidance]; U.K. Ministry of Justice, Bribery Act 2010: Guidance About Procedures Which Relevant Commercial Organisations Can Put into Place to Prevent Persons Associated with Them from Bribing 6 (2011) [hereinafter U.K. Bribery Act Guidance]; U.N. Office on Drugs and Crime, Technical Guide to the United Nations Convention Against Corruption 56–60 (July 2009), https://www.unodc.org/documents/treaties/UNCAC/Publications/TechnicalGuide/09-84395_Ebook.pdf [https://perma.cc/XZH8-QGBB] (providing guidance to state parties implementing anti-corruption measures).

[18] *See* Richard L. Cassin, *With MTS in the New Top Ten, Just One U.S. Company Remains*, FCPA Blog (Mar. 11, 2019), http://www.fcpablog.com/blog/2019/3/11/with-mts-in-the-new-top-ten-just-one-us-company-remains.html [https://perma.cc/XT8K-2QW9] (detailing enormous fines paid by corporations for Foreign Corrupt Practices Act violations).

[19] Foreign Corrupt Practices Act, 15 U.S.C. §§ 78dd-1, 78dd-3, 78ff, 78m (2012).

[20] *Cf.* Susan Rose-Ackerman, *International Anti-Corruption Policies and the U.S. National Interest*, 107 Am. Soc'y Int'l L. Proc. 252, 252–53 (2013) ("The United States remains the dominant actor in global international trade and can help to establish an international marketplace with strong standards against corruption [via the FCPA].").

[21] *See* 15 U.S.C. §§ 78dd-1(a), 78m(b)(2).

not only combat bribery but also ensure that companies and individuals do not hide bribes and improper transactions in off-book accounts and slush funds.[22] FCPA enforcement has increased dramatically over the past decade and a half, resulting in hundreds of enforcement actions—a significant increase from previous decades of enforcement.[23]

The FCPA is famous for its broad jurisdiction—often ensnaring both U.S. and foreign companies that run afoul of its prohibitions—and its broad knowledge standard, which has resulted in significant fines and penalties for companies that rely on third parties to help them develop business opportunities abroad.[24] "The statute's knowledge standard . . . is designed to ensure that companies do not hide behind their agents or other third parties to avoid liability for the bribery of foreign government officials."[25] "Indeed, the vast majority of FCPA cases have been [triggered by] third parties bribing government officials on behalf of a particular company."[26] "To reduce the risk of liability that may result from the actions" of third parties, companies have developed "robust due diligence and oversight procedures for the selection and monitoring of their third" parties.[27] Companies that ignore bribery "red flags"[28] in the vetting or monitoring of third parties proceed at their own peril. Although the United States remained alone for 25 years in its fight against the bribery of government officials in international business transactions, the anti-corruption landscape began to change in the late 1990s.[29]

> In less than a decade, dozens of countries [had] signed on to treaties requiring them to criminalize transnational bribery of foreign officials in similar terms to the anti-bribery prohibition of the FCPA, requiring criminalization of money laundering where the predicate offense is a corrupt practice, and requiring cooperation with other counties in investigations and enforcement.[30]

22 *See* DOJ FCPA Guidance, *supra* note 17, at 10, 39; *see also* 15 U.S.C. §§ 78dd-1(a), 78m(b)(2).

23 *See* Ctr. for Responsible Enterprise & Trade, *FCPA Enforcement Trends* (Apr. 26, 2017), https://create.org/news/fcpa-enforcement-trends [https://perma.cc/9PYE-LUYN].

24 *See* Kristen Savelle, *The FCPA's (Narrowing?) Extraterritorial Reach: Implications of United States v. Hoskins*, China L. Connect, Dec. 2018, at 1–2 (discussing Chinese companies caught in the FCPA's web); *see also* 15 U.S.C. § 78dd-1(f)(2) (providing the statute's knowledge standard).

25 Jessica Tillipman, *Gifts, Hospitality & the Government Contractor*, Briefing Papers, June 2014, at 15 [hereinafter *Gifts, Hospitality & the Government Contractor*].

26 *Id.*

27 *Id.*

28 *See* TRACE Int'l, TRACE Due Diligence Guidebook: Doing Business with Intermediaries Internationally 19 (2010) (containing a list of common instances of potential bribery that should signal the need for caution and additional investigation).

29 *See* Lucinda A. Low, *The United Nations Convention Against Corruption: The Globalization of Anticorruption Standards*, Steptoe & Johnson LLP (May 4, 2006), https://www.steptoe.com/assets/attachments/2599.pdf [https://perma.cc/KA3L-8CJV].

30 *Id.* (detailing the numerous regional anti-corruption treaties that were also passed during this time period).

Moreover, multilateral agreements, such as the OECD Anti-Bribery Convention and the UNCAC, have spawned implementing legislation across the globe designed to, among other things, combat bribery in international business.[31]

Signed in 1997, the OECD Anti-Bribery Convention is aimed at reducing corruption in developing countries by encouraging sanctions against bribery in international business transactions.[32] The Convention largely mirrors the provisions of the FCPA, prohibiting the bribery of foreign government officials and requiring companies to maintain stringent internal controls.[33] Thirty-six OECD member countries and eight nonmember countries have adopted the Convention.[34]

[31] The OECD Anti-Bribery Convention spawned implementing legislation across the globe, including in Australia, Japan, Peru, and South Africa. *See* Org. for Econ. Co-operation and Dev. [OECD], Australia: Review of Implementation of the Convention and 1997 Recommendation 1, http://www.oecd.org/daf/anti-bribery/anti-briberyconvention/2378916.pdf [https://perma.cc/7U6V-ZU8F] (last visited Nov. 11, 2019) (providing an overview of Australia's implementing legislation); Org. for Econ. Co-operation and Dev. [OECD], Japan: Review of Implementation of The Convention and 1997 Recommendation 1 (May 21, 2002), http:// www.oecd.org/daf/anti-bribery/anti-briberyconvention/2387870.pdf [https://perma.cc/FD5X-FFKS] (providing an overview of Japan's implementing legislation); Org. for Econ. Co-operation and Dev. [OECD], Implementing the OECD Anti-Bribery Convention: Phase 1 Report 4 (Mar. 6, 2019), http://www.oecd.org/corruption/anti-bribery/OECD-Phase-1-Report-Peru-ENG.pdf [https://perma.cc/MPT6-A2MV] (providing an overview of Peru's implementing legislation); Org. for Econ. Co-operation and Dev. [OECD], South Africa: Phase 1: Review of Implementation of the Convention and 1997 Revised Recommendation 2, 8 (June 20, 2008), http://www.oecd.org/daf/anti-bribery/anti-briberyconvention/40883135.pdf [https://perma.cc/PS6E-DGAN] (providing an overview of South Africa's implementing legislation). The UNCAC spawned implementing legislation across the globe, including in Ethiopia, Finland, Guatemala, and the United Kingdom. *See* U.N. Secretariat, Conference of the States Parties to the United Nations Convention Against Corruption: Executive Summary 2–3, U.N. Doc. CAC/COSP/IRG/I/4/1Add.21 (Sept. 16, 2015), https://www.unodc.org/documents/treaties/UNCAC/Work-ingGroups/ImplementationReviewGroup/ExecutiveSummaries/V1506566e.pdf [https://perma.cc/U468-FK8N] (providing an overview of Ethiopia's implementing legislation); U.N. Office on Drugs and Crime, Mechanism for the Review of Implementation of the United Nations Convention Against Corruption: Response of Finland to the Comprehensive Self-Assessment Checklist 2–3 (Oct. 1, 2010), https://www.unodc.org/documents/treaties/UNCAC/SA-Report/Self-Assessment_Report_-_UNCAC_-_Finland.pdf [https://perma.cc/KQ95-Q4SG] (providing an overview of Finland's implementing legislation); U.N. Secretariat, Conference of the States Parties to the United Nations Convention Against Corruption: Executive Summary 2, U.N. Doc. CAC/COSP/IRG/I/4/1/Add.33 (Nov. 19, 2015), https://undocs.org/en/CAC/COSP/IRG/I/4/1/Add.33 [https://perma.cc/NQ7H-C9F9] (providing an overview of Guatemala's implementing legislation); U.N. Office on Drugs and Crime, United Nations Convention Against Corruption: UK Second Cycle Review-20180108-134632, at 20 (Nov. 24, 2017), https://www.unodc.org/documents/treaties/UNCAC/SA-Report/2018_01_09_UK_SACL.pdf [https://perma.cc/5PTW-JL58] (providing an overview of the United Kingdom's existing and implementing legislation).

[32] *See* OECD Convention, *supra* note 4, pmbl., art. 3.

[33] *Compare id.*, arts. 1, 8, *with* Foreign Corrupt Practices Act, 15 U.S.C. §§ 78dd-1(a), 78m(b)(2) (2012).

[34] *See* OECD Convention on Combating Bribery of Foreign Public Officials in International Business Transactions, ORG. FOR ECON. COOPERATION & DEV., https://www.oecd.org/corruption/oecdantibriberyconvention.htm [https://perma.cc/Z98T-UMXD] (last visited July 14, 2019).

The OECD Working Group on Bribery monitors the implementation of anti-corruption legislation and assesses anti-corruption law enforcement efforts.[35] Over the past decade, active implementation of the OECD Anti-Bribery Convention has led to the criminal sanctioning of 560 individuals and 184 entities for foreign bribery.[36]

The UNCAC requires signatory states to implement a variety of anti-corruption measures, which affect their laws, institutions, and practices.[37] As of June 26, 2018, there are 186 parties to the Convention.[38] The UNCAC provides a holistic approach to combating corruption, focusing not only on traditional law enforcement techniques but also on methods of enhancing international cooperation and preventative measures directed at both the public and private sectors.[39] Similar to the OECD Anti-Bribery Convention, the UNCAC requires states to impose "civil, administrative or criminal penalties" on individuals or companies that engage in acts of corruption to dissuade other entities from propelling or encouraging similar patterns of corruption.[40] Through its "Conference of the States Parties," the UNCAC provides a mechanism designed to encourage cooperation among state parties and to promote the Convention's implementation.[41] Its provisions also address the "promotion of corporate codes of conduct, best practices, and compliance programs for business and the professions, [and] measures to promote corporate transparency."[42]

In recent years, numerous countries have implemented these multilateral agreements by enacting robust anti-corruption laws. These laws, such as the U.K. Bribery Act, Brazil's Clean Company Act, and France's Sapin II, not only prohibit bribery but also reinforce the importance of anti-corruption compliance programs.[43] As these countries (and others) ramp up the enforcement of their

[35] *See id.*

[36] *See* Org. for Econ. Co-operation and Dev. Working Grp. on Bribery [OECD], 2017 Enforcement of the Anti-Bribery Convention 3 (Nov. 2018), https://www.oecd.org/daf/anti-bribery/OECD-WGB-Enforcement-Data-2018-ENG.pdf [https://perma.cc/Q5Q7-T7KQ].

[37] *See* U.N. Convention Against Corruption, *supra* note 4, arts. 1, 16 (stating the purpose of the Convention and providing an example of anti-corruption measures signatory states are obliged to take).

[38] *See* U.N. Office on Drugs and Crime, Signature and Ratification Status (June 26, 2018), http://www.unodc.org/unodc/en/treaties/CAC/signatories.html [https://perma.cc/48ZJ-ZPEL].

[39] *See* U.N. Convention Against Corruption, *supra* note 4, arts. 5, 7, 12, 46.

[40] *See id.*, art. 12.

[41] *See* U.N. Office on Drugs and Crime, Conference of the States Parties to the United Nations Convention Against Corruption, https://www.unodc.org/unodc/en/treaties/CAC/CAC-COSP.html [https://perma.cc/LW36-3RAZ] (last visited Oct. 30, 2019).

[42] Low, *supra* note 29, at 6.

[43] *See* Decreto No. 12.846, de 1 de Agosto de 2013, Diário Oficial da União [D.O.U.] de 1.8.2013 arts. 5–7 (Braz.); Loi 2016-1691 du 9 décembre 2016 relative à la transparence, à la lutte contre la corruption et à la modernisation de la vie économique [Law 2016-1691 of December 9, 2016 Relating to the Transparency, the Fight Against the Corruption and the Modernization of the Economic Life], Journal Officiel de la République Française [J.O.] [Official Gazette of France], Dec. 10, 2016, No. 0287, arts. 3, 17 (Fr.); Bribery Act 2010, c. 23, §§ 6–7, 9 (UK).

new laws, companies will face greater pressure to ensure their anti-corruption compliance programs meet the emerging global compliance standards.

2.2. Robust Anti-Corruption Enforcement Ushers in a New Era of Compliance

The dramatic increase in anti-corruption enforcement by the United States and (increasingly) other countries demonstrates a growing global commitment to combating corruption. Many household company names have run afoul of the FCPA, resulting in time-consuming, expensive, and embarrassing enforcement actions.[44] For example, in 2019, Walmart, Inc. agreed to pay a combined total of $282.7 million to resolve a year-long investigation into the retail giant's FCPA violations for failing, despite numerous red flags, to ensure sufficient global anti-corruption internal controls.[45] Not only was Walmart required to pay both approximately $138 million in criminal penalties and approximately $144.7 million in civil penalties, it was compelled to hire an independent compliance monitor to assist the company for an additional two years.[46] Not surprisingly, the negative consequences stemming from similar enforcement actions have incentivized large, multinational companies to invest in compliance programs that will detect, prevent, and deter illicit activities.[47] Moreover, governments, international organizations, and civil society have also championed the role of ethics and compliance in helping to prevent and mitigate corporate corruption.[48]

[44] *Cf.* Richard L. Cassin, *With Alstom, Three French Companies Are Now in the FCPA Top Ten*, FCPA Blog (Dec. 23, 2014), https://www.fcpablog.com/blog/2014/12/23/with-alstom-three-french-companies-are-now-in-the-fcpa-top-t.html [https://perma.cc/LSH4-HC8Z] (establishing that many household companies settled FCPA violations with the DoJ, including Siemens ($800 million in 2008), Alstom ($772 million in 2014), KBR/Halliburton ($579 million in 2009), and BAE ($400 million in 2010)).

[45] *See* Letter from U.S. Dep't of Justice Criminal Div. to Karen P. Hewitt, Jones Day (June 20, 2019), https://www.justice.gov/opa/press-release/file/1175791/download [https://perma.cc/8ZCX-FPUX]); *see also* Press Release, U.S. Dep't of Justice Office of Pub. Affairs, Walmart and Brazil-Based Subsidiary Agree to Pay $137 Million to Resolve Foreign Corrupt Practices Act Case (June 20, 2019), https://www.justice.gov/opa/pr/walmart-inc-and-brazil-based-subsidiary-agree-pay-137-million-resolve-foreign-corrupt [https://perma.cc/R7JM-DKQM].

[46] *See* Letter to Karen P. Hewitt, *supra* note 45.

[47] *See* Heimann et al., *supra* note 6, at 5.

[48] *See, e.g.*, DOJ FCPA Guidance, *supra* note 17, at 60 (providing an example of an governmental organization that supports corporate ethics and compliance); OECD Good Practice Guidance, *supra* note 17, at 2; U.K. Bribery Act Guidance, *supra* note 17, at 20–31 (naming six key compliance principles to guide corporations); Peter Wilkinson, Transparency International UK, Global Anti-Bribery Guidance: Best Practice for Companies in The UK and Overseas 14 (2017); World Bank Grp. [WBG], Summary of World Bank Group Integrity Compliance Guidelines 1–2 (Sept. 2010), http://siteresources.worldbank.org/INTDOII/Resources/IntegrityComplianceGuidelines_2_1_11web.pdf [https://perma.cc/ZC9E-28R5] [hereinafter World Bank Compliance Guidelines Summary].

In fact, the U.S. Department of Justice (DoJ) has publicly recognized and rewarded companies that implement robust compliance programs even where allegations of corruption arise. For example, in 2011, Johnson & Johnson (J&J) entered into a deferred prosecution agreement with the DoJ to resolve corruption allegations.[49] The government made clear that it had reduced the company's criminal penalty to $21.4 million and did not require it to retain a corporate monitor "[d]ue to J&J's pre-existing compliance and ethics programs, extensive remediation and improvement of its compliance systems and internal controls."[50] In 2012, the DoJ took the unprecedented step of publicly announcing that it had declined to prosecute Morgan Stanley for the bribery of a Chinese government official because of the company's strong, preexisting compliance program.[51] Instead, the DoJ limited its prosecution to the rogue employee who committed the wrongdoing.[52]

In addition, since 2017, the DoJ has included a formal "FCPA Corporate Enforcement Policy" in its Attorneys' Manual,[53] which considers, among other things, the "implementation of an effective compliance and ethics program" as a key criterion in determining whether a company may receive a reduced fine or penalty (or even declination) when settling an FCPA matter.[54]

Moreover, an international consensus has developed regarding best practices in corporate ethics and compliance programs.[55] Several government enforcement agencies, nongovernmental anti-corruption organizations, industry groups, and civil society organizations have released compliance "best practices"

[49] *See* Press Release, U.S. Dep't of Justice Office of Pub. Affairs, Johnson & Johnson Agrees to Pay $21.4 Million Criminal Penalty to Resolve Foreign Corrupt Practices Act and Oil for Food Investigations (Apr. 8, 2011), https://www.justice.gov/opa/pr/johnson-johnson-agrees-pay-214-million-criminal-penalty-resolve-foreign-corrupt-practices-act [https://perma.cc/CKD8-ETTB].

[50] *See id.*

[51] *See* Press Release, U.S. Dep't of Justice Office of Pub. Affairs, Former Morgan Stanley Managing Director Pleads Guilty for Role in Evading Internal Controls Required by FCPA (Apr. 25, 2012), https://www.justice.gov/opa/pr/former-morgan-stanley-managing-director-pleads-guilty-role-evading-internal-controls-required [https://perma.cc/NK7C-NBZZ] ("After considering all the available facts and circumstances, including that Morgan Stanley constructed and maintained a system of internal controls, which provided reasonable assurances that its employees were not bribing government officials, the [DoJ] declined to bring any enforcement action.").

[52] *See id.* Additionally, the DoJ's public pronouncements regarding the importance of compliance are not just limited to FCPA enforcement. *See* Brent Snyder, Deputy Assistant Att'y Gen., Antitrust Div., U.S. Dep't of Justice, Remarks as Prepared for the International Chamber of Commerce/United States Council of International Business Joint Antitrust Compliance Workshop: Compliance Is a Culture, Not Just a Policy (Sept. 9, 2014) (extolling the importance of compliance, calling it the "cornerstone of good corporate citizenship").

[53] *See* Press Release, U.S. Dep't of Justice Office of Pub. Affairs, Deputy Attorney General Rosenstein Delivers Remarks at the 34th International Conference on the Foreign Corrupt Practices Act (Nov. 29, 2017), https://www.justice.gov/opa/speech/deputy-attorney-general-rosenstein-delivers-remarks-34th-international-conference-foreign [https://perma.cc/6GBP-NNJD].

[54] *See* U.S. DEP'T OF JUSTICE, JUSTICE MANUAL: FOREIGN CORRUPT PRACTICES ACT OF 1977 § 9-47.120 (2019).

[55] *See infra* text accompanying notes 41–45.

guides that provide proactive guidance to companies designing risk-based, anti-corruption compliance programs.[56] For example, in 2010, the OECD published a framework to help companies design their compliance programs entitled "Good Practice Guidance on Internal Controls, Ethics, and Compliance."[57] In 2012, the DoJ published "A Resource Guide to the U.S. Foreign Corrupt Practices Act," designed to outline both the government's policies regarding FCPA enforcement and "the hallmarks of an effective corporate compliance program."[58] In 2019, the DoJ updated its "Evaluation of Corporate Compliance Programs," a formal resource exploring significant factors and questions used by prosecutors in evaluating the effectiveness of corporate compliance programs.[59] Similarly, the UN Office on Drugs and Crime (UNODC), published "An Anti-Corruption Ethics and Compliance Programme for Business: A Practical Guide," which outlines preventative measures to detect and deter foreign bribery during international business transactions.[60]

In each guide, companies are encouraged to employ measures designed to prevent and detect misconduct.[61] Although the recommendations are designed to be flexible and are tailored to each company's particular risks and resources, they provide similar recommendations, applicable to all companies, regardless of size, industry, or risk.[62] For example, most guides consider the following to be necessary components of an effective ethics and compliance program: (1) visible commitments from senior management; (2) a clear corporate policy prohibiting bribery and misconduct; (3) a code of conduct; (4) risk-tailored compliance policies and procedures; (5) risk assessments; (6) robust due diligence and oversight of third parties; (7) confidential reporting and internal investigation procedures; (8) dedication of sufficient resources to the implementation and oversight of the compliance program; (9) ongoing training for employees and relevant third

[56] *See, e.g.*, DOJ FCPA GUIDANCE, *supra* note 17, at 63; OECD Good Practice Guidance, *supra* note 17, at 2; World Bank Compliance Guidelines Summary, *supra* note 48, at 2.

[57] *See* OECD Good Practice Guidance, *supra* note 17, at 2.

[58] *See* DOJ FCPA GUIDANCE, *supra* note 17, at iv.

[59] *See* CRIMINAL DIV., U.S. DEP'T OF JUSTICE, EVALUATION OF CORPORATE COMPLIANCE PROGRAMS GUIDANCE DOCUMENT 1 (2019) [hereinafter DOJ EVALUATION OF CORPORATE COMPLIANCE PROGRAMS]. Note that this guide was updated in 2019 to expand its application to the DoJ's entire Criminal Division to better harmonize the guidance with other DoJ standards. *See id.* at 1–18.

[60] *See* U.N. Office on Drugs and Crime, An Anti-Corruption Ethics and Compliance Programme for Business: A Practical Guide 8–9 (Sept. 2013), https://www.unodc.org/documents/corruption/Publications/2013/13-84498_Ebook.pdf [https://perma.cc/9X3A-4XA9] [hereinafter UNODC Practical Guide] (discussing the importance of combatting corruption and providing guidance on the processes of implementing a corporate compliance program).

[61] *See, e.g.*, DOJ FCPA GUIDANCE, *supra* note 17, at 56; OECD Good Practice Guidance, *supra* note 17, at 2; World Bank Compliance Guidelines Summary, *supra* note 48, at 2.

[62] *Compare* Heimann et al., *supra* note 6, at 11–14 (naming effective leadership, resource management, reporting procedures, and monitoring as key compliance hallmarks), *with* DOJ FCPA GUIDANCE, *supra* note 17, at 56–58 (naming management commitment, proper allocation of resources, and oversight as necessary elements of corporate compliance).

parties; (10) transparent financial and accounting procedures; (11) effective communication and documentation; (12) periodic review and testing of internal controls; and (13) incentives and disciplinary measures for violations of company policies and the law.[63]

In light of the numerous compliance resources available to companies, "government regulators and enforcement agencies have little sympathy for companies that claim ignorance about the necessity of an effective compliance program."[64] For example:

> They are equally harsh with companies that do compliance "on the cheap," such as downloading and adopting the policies and codes of conduct found on the internet, dedicating little to no resources to compliance activities, failing to provide ethics and compliance training to employees, or ignoring red flags of corruption or unethical behavior.[65]

The DoJ's own published guidance makes clear that there is little tolerance for companies that lack an effective program.[66] Companies that fail to invest in compliance or merely maintain a "paper" compliance program will eventually violate a law—resulting in huge fines, penalties, investigative costs, reputational damage, and other related consequences.[67]

2.3. Compliance Developments in the U.S. Government Procurement System

Although state-of-the-art compliance programs have grown recently in the commercial sector, as discussed earlier, robust compliance policies and procedures have always been critical for U.S. government contractors, given the myriad of

[63] *See* DOJ Evaluation of Corporate Compliance Programs, *supra* note 59, at 2–5, 6, 10–12, 14–15; DOJ FCPA Guidance, *supra* note 17, at 57–62; Org. for Econ. Co-operation and Dev. et al. [OECD], Anti-Corruption Ethics and Compliance Handbook for Business, 16, 18, 24, 28, 40, 47, 54, 61, 73, 98, 103, 111, 113, 117 (2013), https://www.oecd.org/corruption/AntiCorruptionEthicsComplianceHandbook.pdf [https://perma.cc/3N52-82NR] [hereinafter Anti-Corruption Ethics and Compliance Handbook for Business] (providing a compilation of international compliance rules); UNODC Practical Guide, *supra* note 60, at 14, 18–19, 21–22, 33, 35, 63, 65, 81, 86.

[64] *Gifts, Hospitality & the Government Contractor*, *supra* note 25, at 20.

[65] *Id.*

[66] *See* Robert Tompkins & Rodney Perry, *An Ethics and Compliance Punch List for Gov't Contractors*, Law 360 (June 19, 2019), https://www.law360.com/articles/1170586/print?section=aerospace [https://perma.cc/8DDA-CEGL]; *see also* DOJ Evaluation of Corporate Compliance Programs, *supra* note 59, at 1 (discussing potential prosecution or monetary penalties for noncompliant companies).

[67] *See* DOJ Evaluation of Corporate Compliance Programs, *supra* note 59, at 1, 9; *see also* Tompkins & Perry, *supra* note 66.

laws regulating government procurement activities.[68] Ensuring that compliance officers keep compliance programs consistent with regulations requires tracking and analyzing changes in regulations, which in turn requires significant technology and manpower.[69] Compliance officers must be knowledgeable and retain a skilled staff in order to maintain up-to-date policies and procedures.[70] A contractor's failure to comply with government requirements and obligations can devastate the company's reputation and government revenue streams.[71] Not only does a contractor risk the termination of its current contracts, it also faces a multitude of administrative remedies and civil or criminal penalties.[72] Given the staggering consequences of noncompliance, it is no surprise that the United States' largest contractors have invested heavily in developing robust and effective ethics and compliance programs.[73] Indeed, some of the country's largest contractors have been leaders in developing comprehensive and innovative anti-corruption policies and procedures.[74]

In light of their significant compliance obligations, the comprehensive compliance guides are a significant resource for contractors designing, implementing, and refining their internal compliance programs.[75] They are of particular importance because most government contractors are legally obligated to implement a "Contractor Code of Business Ethics and Conduct."[76] This requirement is designed to ensure contractors "conduct themselves with the highest degree of integrity and honesty" and maintain a "written code of business ethics and conduct."[77] To promote compliance with these policies, the Federal Acquisition Regulation (FAR) requires contractors to employ an "ethics and compliance training program and an internal control system" that: "(1) [is] suitable to the

[68] *Cf.* John D. Altenburg, *Winding Down War Zone Contracts*, NAT'L DEF. MAG. (Nov. 1, 2013), https://www.nationaldefensemagazine.org/archive/2013/November/Pages/WindingDownWarZoneContracts.aspx [https://perma.cc/2C93-UZYJ] (discussing the importance of compliance programs for defense contractors operating in Afghanistan, given FAR requirements and legislative scrutiny).

[69] *See* STACEY ENGLISH & SUSANNAH HAMMOND, COST OF COMPLIANCE 2015, THOMPSON REUTERS 8 (2015).

[70] *See id.* at 3, 9, 15.

[71] *See* Fred Geldon, *Special Compliance Requirements for Government Contractors*, CORP. COMPLIANCE INSIGHTS (Oct. 14, 2019), https://www.corporatecomplianceinsights.com/compliance-requirements-government-contractors [https://perma.cc/9Q9V-BMN6].

[72] *See* FAR 9.406, 9.407 (describing suspension and debarment procedures for contractors); *see also* FCPA & Anti-Corruption Task Force, Morrison & Foerster LLP, The Foreign Corrupt Practices Act and Global Anti-Corruption Law 61, 68, 71 (2010).

[73] *See* Heimann et al., *supra* note 6, at 5.

[74] U.S. GOV'T ACCOUNTABILITY OFF., GAO-09-591, DEFENSE CONTRACTING INTEGRITY: OPPORTUNITIES EXIST TO IMPROVE DOD'S OVERSIGHT OF CONTRACTOR ETHICS PROGRAMS 8, 30 (2009) (finding that 55 out of 57 defense contractors that participated in a GAO survey had FAR-compliant ethics programs, even prior to the promulgation of the FAR rules).

[75] *See* DOJ FCPA GUIDANCE, *supra* note 17, at 57–58; OECD Good Practice Guidance, *supra* note 17, at 2; World Bank Compliance Guidelines Summary, *supra* note 48, at 2–3.

[76] *See* FAR 3.1000, 3.1002; *see also* FAR 52.203-13(b).

[77] *See* FAR 3.1002(a)-(b).

size of the company and extent of its involvement in [g]overnment contracting; (2) [f]acilitate[s] timely discovery and disclosure of improper conduct in connection with [g]overnment contracts; and (3) [e]nsure[s] corrective measures are promptly instituted and carried out."[78]

Implementing these "best practices" guidelines and ensuring a comprehensive compliance and ethics program requires substantial integration throughout all levels of a company. Large contractors often have a dedicated ethics and compliance staff that can oversee internal investigations and ensure that internal controls are functioning properly.[79] Firms are under significant pressure to ensure that they dedicate ample resources and staffing to their compliance department or face tough questions from regulators.[80] Further, companies must invest a significant number of hours providing ethics training to employees to ensure that all employees understand the company's legal obligations, as well as its commitment to ethics and compliance. For example, a "typical aerospace and defense employee receives several hours of training each year on ethics and compliance with government contract requirements"—beyond what is typically required of government employees.[81] The cost of training alone can easily result in any defense contractor spending "tens of millions of dollars annually" to ensure that all employees have a sufficient understanding of the interplay between government regulations and the daily operations of the business.[82]

Although many of the U.S. government's largest contractors have invested heavily in developing robust and sophisticated compliance programs, the smallest contractors lag far behind.[83] Small businesses may be contractually required by FAR 52.203-13 to maintain a "code of business ethics and conduct" but are exempt from establishing a compliance program and an internal controls system.[84] Although it is recommended that small businesses invest in these important compliance and internal control systems, the small business exemption is a recognition of the burden this requirement places on small businesses.[85] Specifically, unlike larger companies, small businesses "lack the financial resources or the market power to enforce their zero tolerance policies" toward

[78] *See* FAR 3.1002(b).

[79] *See* John T. Jones & Greg Bingham, Costs of Mandatory Ethics and Compliance Programs 5–6 (2009).

[80] *See* English & Hammond, *supra* note 69, at 3–4, 15.

[81] *See* Jones & Bingham, *supra* note 79, at 6.

[82] *See id.*

[83] *See* Kroll, 2014 Anti-Bribery and Corruption Benchmarking Report: Untangling the Web of Risk and Compliance 7 (2014) [hereinafter Kroll Anti-Bribery and Corruption Benchmarking Report].

[84] *See* FAR 52.203-13(b)(2), 52.203-13(c). Should a business represent itself to be a small business concern pursuant to the solicitation, it is exempt from establishing a compliance and internal control system. *See* FAR 52.203-13(c); *see also* Joseph D. West et al., *Contractor Business Ethics Compliance Program & Disclosure Requirements*, Briefing Papers, Apr. 2009, at 4, 9.

[85] *See* Joseph D. West et al., *supra* note 84, at 6, 9.

corruption.[86] Small businesses have less capital and smaller profit margins to implement and maintain robust compliance programs and thus may feel more pressure to take shortcuts or engage in corrupt practices to obtain greater profit margins.[87] Although the exemption of small businesses from a legally required compliance obligation is understandable (given the resources required to comply with this requirement), the exclusion continues to perpetuate weaknesses in the procurement system.

Small businesses' difficulty in complying with compliance regulations, and the effects of that difficulty, are well documented. A 2012 report by UNODC found that the failure of small and medium-sized enterprises (SMEs) to invest in ethics and compliance signals a significant failure in the system,[88] and a 2018 OECD report found that SMEs typically struggle more than large firms with handling many regulatory norms.[89] In contrast to their larger counterparts, SMEs have been much slower to implement or even acknowledge growing best practices in anti-corruption ethics and compliance programs.[90] The most common (and obvious) reason for the lack of SME commitment to compliance is cost.[91] Most small businesses spend their resources just trying to survive and view compliance as a luxury—not as an essential aspect of doing business.[92] In 2010, a report compiled for the Small Business Administration (SBA) reported that small firms with less than 20 employees paid $10,585 per employee to comply with all federal regulations, while firms with between 20 and 499 employees paid $7,454 per employee.[93] Given the high cost of compliance, many small businesses have found working outside regulatory requirements to be more profitable.[94] Indeed, "corruption in business is an economic issue, and it will continue as long as the

[86] *See* U.N. Indus. Dev. Org. & U.N. Office on Drugs and 2 Crime, Corruption Prevention to Foster Small and Medium-Sized Enterprise Development vii (2012), https://www.unodc.org/documents/corruption/Publications/2012/Corruption_prevention_to_foster_small_and_medium_size_enterprise_development_Vol_2.pdf [https://perma.cc/2FTV-2URM] [hereinafter Corruption Prevention Report Vol. II].

[87] *See id.* at 2.

[88] *Cf. id.* at v, 35 (discussing how the current failings in global anti-corruption systems have especially negative consequences for SMEs).

[89] *See* Org. for Econ. Co-operation and Dev. [OECD], Improving the Business Environment for SMEs Through Effective Regulation 3 (Feb. 22–23, 2018), https://www.oecd.org/cfe/smes/ministerial/documents/2018-SME-Ministerial-Conference-Parallel-Session-1.pdf [https://perma.cc/YV4W-J6ME].

[90] *See* 2 Corruption Prevention Report, *supra* note 86, at vii, 35, 57.

[91] *See id.* at 4, 35.

[92] *See generally* Nicole V. Crain & W. Mark Crain, Small Bus. Admin. Office of Advocacy, The Impact of Regulatory Costs on Small Firms, at iv, 7 (2010) (discussing the high burden compliance costs place on small businesses, which might cause small businesses to forgo compliance in lieu of day-to-day business costs).

[93] *See id.* at iv, 7, 55 (explaining the disproportionate cost of compliance for small businesses).

[94] *See* Vartuhí Tonoyan et al., *Corruption and Entrepreneurship: How Formal and Informal Institutions Shape Small Firm Behavior in Transition and Mature Market Economies*, Entrepreneurship Theory & Prac. 806 (Sept. 2010).

gains from corrupt [behavior] exceed the expected losses that are, in turn, closely connected to the probability of being caught."[95]

The failure of small companies to design and implement successful compliance programs may also be attributed to the complexity of the current compliance guidelines.[96] The "hallmarks of effective compliance programs" are often designed with large, multinational companies in mind.[97] Although all the guides make clear that policies and procedures should be tailored to the risks and resources of each particular company,[98] the guidance can be overwhelming to resource-strapped SMEs. The guidance is also decidedly less helpful to small businesses that lack the resources and sophistication necessary to meet these aspirational standards.[99] Many best practices are simply not feasible because the costs required to implement them are too high for resource-constrained entities.[100] Regardless of the financial burden and infeasibility of implementing a robust compliance program, the legal risks remain the same. Thus, many small businesses face the same corruption and compliance risks as their large counterparts, but do so without the same level of protection.

Although these compliance deficiencies of small businesses are bound to create problems, the failure of small businesses to invest in ethics and compliance creates significant risks for large companies as well.[101] A vast majority of large companies rely heavily on third parties or vendors to perform contracts, which in turn creates new oversight and monitoring obligations to ensure compliance with the law.[102] This is particularly true in the defense industry, where large, multinational contractors depend on small businesses to perform

[95] U.N. Indus. Dev. Org. & U.N. Office on Drugs & Crime, 1 Corruption Prevention to Foster Small and Medium-Sized Enterprise Development 13 (2007), https://www.unodc.org/documents/corruption/Publications/2012/UNIDO-UNODC_Publication_on_Small_Business_Development_and_Corruption_Vol1.pdf [https://perma.cc/HKW6-PHQ3].

[96] *See* Jane W. Moscowitz, *Compliance Programs for Small Businesses*, Prac. Law., July 2002, at 25.

[97] *Cf.* Anti-Corruption Ethics and Compliance Handbook for Business, *supra* note 63, at 17, 22 (focusing its case studies on those involving multinational corporations); DOJ FCPA Guidance, *supra* note 17, at 57 (recognizing that small and medium-sized companies have different needs in terms of crafting compliance programs than large corporations); UNODC Practical Guide, *supra* note 60, at 21 (discussing compliance issues faced by senior management of large companies).

[98] *See* Anti-Corruption Ethics and Compliance Handbook for Business, *supra* note 63, at 14; DOJ FCPA Guidance, *supra* note 17, at 56; UNODC Practical Guide, *supra* note 60, at 10.

[99] *See* Kroll Anti-Bribery and Corruption Benchmarking Report, *supra* note 83, at 7, 21.

[100] *Cf.* Jones & Bingham, *supra* note 79, at 9 (finding that a robust compliance program, even for a small business, could amount to $2 million per year to ensure satisfactory ethics, training, and internal controls).

[101] *See* Kroll & Ethisphere, Anti-Bribery & Corruption Benchmarking Report—2017: Beyond Regulatory Enforcement: The Rise of Reputational Risk 14, 17 (2017) [hereinafter Beyond Regulatory Enforcement] (discussing compliance risks associated with third parties, which are often smaller businesses).

[102] *See* Kroll, How Do Companies Navigate Bribery and Corruption?: 2015 Anti-Bribery and Corruption Benchmarking Report 6 (2015) [hereinafter Kroll 2015 Anti-Bribery and Corruption Benchmarking Report]; *see also* Beyond Regulatory Enforcement, *supra* note 101, at 14, 17.

contracts. Although large companies may value and invest in expensive compliance programs, these efforts may be moot when a small company in their supply chain does not have the resources, knowledge, or even willingness to invest in compliance.[103]

3. The Risks of Contracting with Small Businesses

Although commercial companies may be inclined to avoid risky small businesses that do not invest in ethics and compliance, large government contractors do not have the same luxury.[104] The U.S. government has injected socioeconomic policies into its procurement system to help develop small businesses;[105] indeed, Congress has been clear it is the responsibility of the procurement system to protect and promote small business interests.[106] Through the Small Business Act of 1953, Congress dedicated an entire agency—the SBA—to implementing and encouraging policies that "aid, counsel, assist, and protect . . . the interests of small-business concerns in order to preserve free competitive enterprise, to insure that a fair proportion of the total purchases and contracts or subcontracts for property and services for the [g]overnment."[107] More importantly, Congress memorialized its support for small businesses by requiring agencies to meet small business contracting goals—targets designed to ensure that a fair proportion of federal contracts are issued to small businesses.[108] Specifically, federal law requires agencies to meet a 23 percent small business contracting goal each year.[109] To meet these goals, Contracting Officers (COs) are required to reserve a certain percentage of total contracts so only small businesses may bid on the opportunities.[110] Typically, a CO must determine whether two or more small businesses exist offering proposals that do not exceed the market price, quality,

[103] *Cf.* Beyond Regulatory Enforcement, *supra* note 101, at 5, 9, 14 (identifying third-party compliance violations, which necessarily are not directly controlled by the large companies themselves, as a top anti-corruption concern).

[104] *See infra* text accompanying notes 89–100.

[105] *See* Andrew George Sakallaris, *Questioning the Sacred Cow: Reexamining the Justifications for Small Business Set Asides*, 36 Pub. Cont. L.J. 685, 686–87 (2007); *see also* Major Patrick E. Tolan, Jr., *Government Contracting with Small Business in the Wake of the Federal Acquisition Streamlining Act, the Federal Acquisition Reform Act, and* Adarand: *Small Business as Usual?*, 44 A.F. L. Rev. 75, 104 (1998).

[106] *See* Small Business Act of 1953, Pub. L. No. 83-163, § 202, 67 Stat. 232, 232 (1953); *see also* Mirit Eyal-Cohen, *Why Is Small Business the Chief Business of Congress*, 43 Rutgers L.J. 1, 3–4, 30–31 (2011).

[107] *See* 15 U.S.C. § 631(a)–(c) (2012).

[108] *See* Arthur Selwyn Miller & W. Theodore Pierson, Jr., *Observations on the Consistency of Federal Procurement Policies with Other Government Policies*, 29 L. & Contemp. Probs. 277, 295–96 (1964).

[109] *See* Small Bus. Admin., Fiscal Year 2018 Small Business Procurement Scorecard 5 (2018).

[110] *See* 15 U.S.C. §§ 644(g)(1), (j)(1).

and delivery.[111] If the CO determines that this is the case, he or she must "set aside" the contract for small businesses.[112]

In addition to prime contract set-asides, under certain circumstances, large prime contractors must also preference small businesses as their subcontractors.[113] Specifically, under certain circumstances, prime contractors "must agree in the contract that small business, veteran-owned small business, service-disabled veteran-owned small business, HUBZone [Historically Utilized] small business, small disadvantaged business, and women-owned small business concerns will have the maximum practicable opportunity to participate in contract performance consistent with its efficient performance."[114]

Defense contractors have enhanced small business obligations under the Defense Federal Acquisition Regulation Supplement (DFARS).[115] Further, the U.S. Department of Defense (DoD) is required to ensure that certain techniques such as "bundling,"[116] which may preclude small businesses from bidding on a particular contract, are minimized, or, when used, are supported by sufficient rationale.[117] Thus, although there is a perception that the defense industry excludes small business contractors from the market, in reality, the industry has an affirmative obligation to work with small firms.

3.1. Impact of Small Business Compliance Failures on the Supply Chain

Because of the important role small businesses play in the procurement system, their compliance failures can undermine the system's integrity, create liability for their large-contractor partners, and result in their exclusion from the

[111] *See* FAR 19.502-2(a).

[112] *See id.*

[113] *See* FAR 19.702.

[114] *Id.*

[115] *See* DFARS 219.502-2 (detailing mandatory set-asides for defense construction, dredging, and certain architect-engineer services).

[116] Bundling means consolidating "two or more requirements for supplies or services, previously provided or performed under separate smaller contracts . . . into a solicitation for a single contract . . . that is likely to be unsuitable for award to a small business concern." FAR 2.101(b).

[117] *See* DFARS 205.205-70(a) (requiring notice to be published when bundling is to be used); Acquisition Process: Task and Delivery Order Contracts, Bundling, Consolidation, 78 Fed. Reg. 61,114, 61,116 (Oct. 2, 2013) (to be codified at 13 C.F.R. pts. 121, 124, 125, 126, 127) (finding that new regulations are needed to ensure that small businesses as both prime and subcontractors can be considered rather than excluded from multiple award contracts and acquisitions that are consolidated through bundling); U.S. Gov't Accountability Off., GAO-14-36, Small Business Contracting: Updated Guidance and Reporting Needed for Consolidated Contracts 5–6 (2013); Matthew Weigelt, *DOD Now Required to Report Bundled Contracts, Sole-Source Awards*, Wash. Tech. (July 13, 2010), http://washingtontechnology.com/articles/2010/07/13/bundled-contract-sole-source-reporting.aspx [https://perma.cc/FVY2-XRP2].

procurement system. Although the U.S. government does not collect data on the number of small businesses excluded each year due to compliance failures, it is well known in the industry that small businesses are more susceptible to debarment because of their limited knowledge of regulatory requirements and "less-developed compliance and ethics programs."[118] Moreover, when misconduct is discovered, small businesses "often lack the resources to respond to and remediate harm."[119] When the U.S. government has attempted to reverse this trend by proposing enhancements to small business compliance programs and internal controls, the government contracts industry has pushed back vehemently, arguing that the costs would be too burdensome for the small companies.[120]

Small businesses have borne the brunt of the negative consequences of their compliance deficiencies, but those compliance deficiencies can also create significant risk for the large, prime contractors that partner with small supplier firms.[121] Thus, in an effort to minimize risks stemming from compliance deficiencies in their supply chains, many sophisticated contractors would do well to dedicate significant resources to the monitoring and oversight of their subcontractors.[122] Large contractors may also invest in ethics and compliance training for some of their small subcontractors or suppliers to ensure that their business partners throughout the supply chain are aware of the extensive compliance obligations required under their subcontracts.[123] Unfortunately, oversight and training is not enough to prevent compliance failures—especially where subcontractors have failed to invest time or resources in developing their own compliance programs. This is source of great concern for prime contractors, which could be held liable for the actions of their subcontractors.[124]

Although large contractors continue to work with small businesses in order to meet statutory goals, it is rare that a large company's commitment to small businesses extends beyond their minimum requirements.[125] Indeed, many

[118] *See* Dietrich Knauth, *5 Areas of Growing Debarment Risk for Contractors*, LAW 360 (Jan. 13, 2014), https://www.crowell.com/files/5-Areas-Of-Growing-Debarment-Risk-For-Contractors.pdf.

[119] *See A House of Cards Falls*, *supra* note 9, at 56.

[120] *See* Federal Acquisition Regulation: FAR Case 2007-006: Contractor Business Ethics Compliance Program and Disclosure Requirements, 73 Fed. Reg. 67,064, 67,064, 67,084–85 (Nov. 12, 2008) (to be codified at 48 C.F.R. pts. 2, 3, 9, 42, 52).

[121] *See* PRICEWATERHOUSECOOPERS, HOW TO FORTIFY YOUR SUPPLY CHAIN THROUGH COLLABORATIVE RISK MANAGEMENT 8, 12 (2009) ("A compliance failure at a supplier based anywhere in the world could become a major problem for a contractor.").

[122] *Cf.* Contractor Business Ethics Compliance Program and Disclosure Requirements, 73 Fed. Reg. at 67,069, 67,084 (discussing contractor resistance to mandatory subcontractor oversight and the government's response).

[123] *See* Aaron Grieser, *Defining the Outer Limits of Global Compliance Programs: Emerging Legal & Reputational Liability in Corporate Supply Chains*, 10 OR. REV. INT'L L. 285, 295, 303–04, 311–12 (2008).

[124] *See id.* at 301, 313, 315, 318.

[125] *See* MARK FOGGIN, CTR. FOR URBAN FUTURE, BREAKING INTO THE CORPORATE SUPPLY CHAIN 16 (2010) (discussing large contractors' hesitancy to partner with small firms).

large corporations have typically "shied away from small suppliers because of the sense that they are untested, less reliable and more likely to go out of business."[126] This not only undermines the government's long-term strategic goals of enhancing opportunities for small businesses, it handicaps opportunities for large businesses to partner with new and potentially more innovative firms.

3.2. Sharing Compliance Best Practices

The defense industry has made very visible commitments to elevating ethics and compliance in the industry. Many of the world's largest defense contractors are establishing global ethics and compliance standards by participating in organizations and forums dedicated to these issues.[127] For the past nine years, the aerospace and defense industries have held an annual conference attended by over 80 individuals from the industry, government entities, and nongovernmental organizations in an effort to share compliance "best practices" and to "promote trust and integrity."[128] Further, the Defense Industry Initiative (DII)[129] has fostered an annual forum of over 300 industry professionals and government officials to share best practices and discuss current issues related to ethics and compliance.[130] DII has developed a "Model Supplier Code of Conduct" designed to establish the "expectations" the Initiative holds for suppliers throughout the industry.[131] It also serves as a resource for small and medium-sized contractors "seeking to streamline the processes by which they agreed to individual contractors' codes of conduct when doing business with other DII members."[132] DII has also developed a "supplier toolkit" that is "designed to give SMEs the necessary guidance on creating effective ethics and compliance programs."[133]

126 *Id.*

127 *See, e.g.*, DEF. INDUSTRY INITIATIVE ON BUS. ETHICS & CONDUCT, *About DII*, https://www.dii.org/about/about-dii [https://perma.cc/35PT-362Y] (last visited Nov. 10, 2019) [hereinafter *About DII*]; INT'L F. ON BUS. ETHICAL CONDUCT FOR AEROSPACE & DEF. INDUSTRY, *What Is IFBEC?*, http://ifbec.info/about [https://perma.cc/F2Z9-TTLW] (last visited Nov. 11, 2019).

128 INT'L FORUM ON BUS. ETHICAL CONDUCT FOR THE AEROSPACE & DEF. INDUS., 5TH ANNUAL CONFERENCE REPORT 1 (2014) [hereinafter IFBEC Report].

129 The DII is a nonprofit organization with "seventy-seven signatory companies comprising the top U.S. defense and security companies." DGC INT'L, *DGC International Continues to Support the Defense Industry Initiative* (June 25, 2017), https://dgci.com/dgc-international-continues-to-support-the-defense-industry-initiative [https://perma.cc/P2CV-Z9HY]. The organization seeks the continued promotion and advancement of a "culture of ethical conduct" in companies that provide products and services to the government. *See About DII*, *supra* note 127.

130 *See* DEF. INDUSTRY INITIATIVE ON BUS. ETHICS & CONDUCT, *Membership*, https://www.dii.org/membership [https://perma.cc/3LBS-A4X2] (last visited Oct. 11, 2019).

131 *See* DEF. INDUS. INITIATIVE ON BUS. ETHICS AND CONDUCT, MODEL SUPPLIER CODE OF CONDUCT 1–2 (2019).

132 *See* IFBEC Report, *supra* note 129.

133 *See id.*

These examples make clear that the defense industry is actively collaborating with other industry leaders to share anti-corruption, ethics, and compliance best practices.

Although these forums and public initiatives certainly convey a willingness to share information about ethics and compliance practices, the specific details of company compliance programs are not always publicly available. A 2012 Transparency International study found that almost half of the companies involved provided little or no evidence of basic anti-corruption systems, and two-thirds provided inadequate levels of transparency in their systems.[134] By 2015, the same annual Transparency International study found some improvement—only about one quarter of companies provided absolutely no evidence of anti-corruption programs—but again found that two-thirds still provided only limited evidence of their anti-corruption systems.[135] Adding to these disclosure issues, these defense forums are closed events where only conference participants (typically industry members) are permitted to attend the discussions.[136]

The ongoing hesitancy to share this information publicly is understandable. Large contractors make significant investments in their ethics and compliance programs, and some view their programs as proprietary and confidential. Many contractors fear that competitors will exploit this information if they share it publicly. Yet by depriving small businesses access to this information and resources, the large contractors may ultimately be harmed if the suppliers suffer from compliance deficiencies or failures.

4. Incentivizing the Sharing of Resources and Guidance

The entire supply chain benefits when contractors at all tiers view ethics and compliance as a critical component of their business. Although enhanced supply chain integrity may incentivize some large businesses to share compliance best practices with their suppliers, many large contractors continue to keep this

[134] *See* Mark Pyman et al., Transparency International UK, Defence Companies Anti-Corruption Index 2012, at 4 (2012).

[135] *See* Katie Fish et al., Transparency International UK, Defence Companies Anti-Corruption Index 2015, at 4 (2015).

[136] *See, e.g.*, Def. Industry Initiative on Bus. Ethics & Conduct, *Member Connect*, https://connect.dii.org/home [https://perma.cc/MZ7X-E9TS] (stating that the forum is a "members-only community"). Although the DII forum is limited to industry members, the IFBEC has opened its annual conference to the general public. *See International Forum on Business Ethical Conduct (IFBEC) 2019 Annual Conference, Cvent*, http://www.cvent.com/events/international-forum-on-business-ethical-conduct-ifbec-2019-annual-conference/event-summary-9e77b6e4cae74c04a820daca8045f6f6.aspx [https://perma.cc/AYC6-EARY] (last visited Nov. 11, 2019).

information confidential.[137] The defense industry is increasingly committed to sharing guidance and resources with small business and suppliers; however, the amount and type of information shared varies greatly among industry members.[138]

Some large U.S. government contractors have invested resources into the ethics and compliance programs of their suppliers. For example, Lockheed Martin has created an "Ethics Supplier Mentoring Program," which includes a suite of self-serve resources, the evaluation of a supplier's existing ethics program, a live webinar series during which "Lockheed Martin Ethics staff walk participants through setup and implementation of each element of an effective [compliance] program," and the option for one-on-one mentoring by a Lockheed Martin Ethics Officer.[139] As of 2017, over 50 companies have participated in the program as mentees.[140]

Lockheed's effort to encourage the implementation of suppliers' ethics and compliance programs reduces the risk of a compliance failure in the supply chain and enhances the overall integrity of the procurement system. If other large and sophisticated contractors were to invest resources into improving their suppliers' ethics and compliance programs, it could strengthen the integrity of the U.S. government contracts regime. Unfortunately, not all contractors are willing to spend the time and resources necessary to mentor their suppliers on ethics and compliance best practices. It is clear that additional incentives are necessary to foster increased information sharing among the companies. Fortunately, a template for incentivized information sharing already exists in the U.S. procurement system: the "mentor-protégé program." If implemented in the ethics and compliance context, this model could provide lasting benefits to the entire procurement system.

137 *See* KROLL 2015 ANTI-BRIBERY AND CORRUPTION BENCHMARKING REPORT, *supra* note 102, at 6, 15.

138 *Compare* DEF. INDUS. INITIATIVE ON BUS. ETHICS AND CONDUCT, BUILDING AND MAINTAINING AN ETHICS AND COMPLIANCE PROGRAM—THE SMALL BUSINESS TOOLKIT 2 (2019) (explaining how the initiative's toolkit can provide a solution to compliance challenges through training, the utilization of sample codes of conduct, and self-audits), *with* LOCKHEED MARTIN, *Ethics Supplier Mentoring Program*, https://www.lockheedmartin.com/content/dam/lockheed-martin/eo/documents/ethics/ethics-supplier-mentoring-program-overview.pdf [https://perma.cc/N99L-F6PS] (last visited Nov. 11, 2019) [hereinafter *Lockheed 1*] (differing from DII's toolkit by explaining that the important elements of Lockheed's compliance program include self-assessment, working with an ethics officer, and learning how to build a compliance program via webinar instruction).

139 *See Lockheed 1*, *supra* note 138; *see also* LOCKHEED MARTIN, *Ethics*, https://www.lockheedmartin.com/en-us/suppliers/supplier-ethics.html [https://perma.cc/2ZAB-BEHC] (last visited Nov. 10, 2019) [hereinafter *Lockheed 2*].

140 *See* LOCKHEED MARTIN, *Ethics Supplier Mentoring Program: Participants in One-on-One Mentoring Program*, https://www.lockheedmartin.com/content/dam/lockheed-martin/eo/documents/ethics/supplier-ethics-mentees-list.pdf [https://perma.cc/4EVV-2WCJ] (last visited Nov. 11, 2019).

4.1. The Model: Federal Mentor-Protégé Programs

In 1991, the mentor-protégé assistance programs were created to provide small businesses with resources and support in the federal procurement sector.[141]

> A mentor-protégé program is an arrangement in which mentors—businesses, typically experienced prime contractors—provide technical, managerial, and other business development assistance to eligible small businesses, or protégés. In return, the programs provide incentives for mentor participation, such as credit toward subcontracting goals, additional evaluation points toward the awarding of contracts, an annual award to the mentor providing the most effective developmental support to a protégé and in some cases, cost reimbursement.[142]

Ideally, mentors and protégés work in conjunction to create a "developmental assistance" agreement.[143] The purpose of this agreement is to ensure that the large business trains the smaller business on industry specific subjects,[144] provides assistance in obtaining government and commercial contracts, advises on issues related to contract administration, and guides the smaller company on general business and organizational management skills.[145] Through these initiatives, the U.S. government hopes to develop and produce businesses that are able to function independently in the federal contracting system.[146]

Since the mentor-protégé program depends on the willingness of experienced and sophisticated contractors to serve as mentors to smaller companies, the government incentivizes large businesses to participate in the program.[147] These incentives are typically financial and contractual advantages that may be used to obtain or enhance procurement opportunities.[148] This may include credit[149]

[141] *See* U.S. GOV'T ACCOUNTABILITY OFF., GAO/NSAID-94-101, DEFENSE CONTRACTING: IMPLEMENTATION OF THE PILOT MENTOR-PROTEGE PROGRAM 1 (1994) [hereinafter GAO/NSIAD-94-101].

[142] U.S. GOV'T ACCOUNTABILITY OFF., GAO-11-548R, MENTOR-PROTÉGÉ PROGRAMS HAVE POLICIES THAT AIM TO BENEFIT PARTICIPANTS BUT DO NOT REQUIRE POSTAGREEMENT TRACKING 1 (2011) [hereinafter GAO-11-548R].

[143] *See id.* at 3.

[144] These subjects include "production, quality control, manufacturing, engineering, and computer hardware and software." *See id.*

[145] *See* GAO/NSIAD-94-101, *supra* note 141, at 1–2.

[146] *See* Keir X. Bancroft, *Regulating Information Security in the Government Contracting Industry: Will the Rising Tide Lift All the Boats?*, 62 AM. U. L. REV. 1145, 1194–95 (2013).

[147] *See* GAO-11-548R, *supra* note 142, at 1.

[148] *See id.*

[149] A credit allows prime contractors to count costs incurred during mentorship as if they were incurred in a subcontract awarded to their protégé. *See* NAT'L WOMEN'S BUS. COUNCIL, EVALUATING FEDERAL MENTOR-PROTÉGÉ PROGRAMS: ASSESSMENT, CASE STUDIES AND RECOMMENDATIONS 7, 9–10 (2011). This credit enables large contractors to meet their subcontracting goals. *See id.*

toward a prime contractor's mandatory subcontracting goals, additional evaluation points that increase a prime contractor's likelihood of winning a contract, or an annual monetary award to mentors that prove their support has benefited the protégé.[150]

Certain agencies may provide additional incentives. For example, the DoD allows prime contractor mentors to collect reimbursements for certain costs incurred while mentoring their protégés.[151] The U.S. Department of Energy, the U.S. Department of Veterans Affairs, and the National Aeronautics and Space Administration provide prime contractors with award fees[152] that recognize successful mentor protégé developments.[153] Additionally, the SBA's program permits large companies to work on contracts that are specifically set aside for small businesses if they serve as a mentor to the small business in the contract.[154] These incentives are designed to sweeten the deal for large companies assisting small businesses by providing prime contractors with opportunities normally barred by other federal contracting policies.[155] When the arrangements are executed properly, "[mentors benefit] from a strengthened cadre of subcontractors and [the agency benefits] from a resultant robust and competitive supplier base."[156]

4.2. The Compliance Mentorship Program

The existing mentor-protégé program template could meaningfully narrow the compliance gap that currently plagues the procurement system. This model of information sharing in exchange for financial and contractual incentives is a proven concept that could be implemented in the compliance context with modest effort and resources. The application of this program in the ethics and compliance setting could encourage the sharing of expertise and resources by large contractors with their small, less sophisticated counterparts.

[150] *See id.* at 7–9.

[151] *See* DFARS I-109(d) (permitting mentors to seek reimbursement of up to $1 million for costs associated with assistance provided to a protégé firm each fiscal year).

[152] An award fee is a monetary bonus for costs that are saved or for good performance and is used to motivate contractors to provide satisfactory and efficient performance. *See* FAR 16.401(a), (e)(2) (describing incentive contracts and guidelines for award fees).

[153] *See* DEAR 919.7006(a); NFS 1819.7201(b); VAAR 819.7105(d).

[154] *See* 13 C.F.R. § 124.513(a)–(b) (2019) (granting an SBA mentor and protégé relationship the authority to enter into a joint venture as a small business for a government prime contract or subcontract opportunity, including those set aside for companies who meet certain small business size standards).

[155] *See* Cong. Research Serv., R41722, Small Business Mentor-Protégé Programs 7–8 (Jan. 7, 2019).

[156] *See* U.S Gov't. Accountability Off., GAO-01-767, Contract Management: Benefits of the DOD Mentor-Protégé Program Are Not Conclusive 3 (2001).

The mentor-protégé template could benefit both small and large companies for several reasons. First, the protégé will benefit from the compliance guidance and resources shared by the mentor. By sharing resources and offering guidance, the mentor can elevate the protégé's ethics and compliance program to better reflect industry best practices. The partnership will also help the protégé self-identify potential areas of corruption risk, which will benefit the entire supply chain.

Although specific ethics and compliance goals would be established at the outset of the program, mentors would be expected to help the protégé do the following: (1) design a compliance program tailored to the protégé's specific size, industry, and risk profile; (2) develop a comprehensive and effective training program; and (3) draft tailored policies and procedures. Mentors would also be expected to share resources and guidance on an ongoing basis, thus eventually enabling the protégé to maintain an effective, internal compliance program.[157]

Although the small contractors would undoubtedly benefit from this program, mentors would also be rewarded for the time and energy spent guiding protégé firms. In addition to the incentives inherent in reducing supply chain risk, the program would provide mentors with significant financial and contractual incentives, such as award fees and access to certain set-aside contracts.[158] Large companies would benefit from additional contracting opportunities while simultaneously promoting a more ethical and compliant procurement process. Large companies in particular could benefit given the significant resources they already allocate to compliance functions: the costs of sharing best practices would be minimal and the financial incentives and enhanced market access could be quite lucrative.

Developments in the defense industry suggest that this approach could be embraced as a positive movement toward a more collaborative and transparent system. Organizations such as the DII and the International Forum on Business Ethical Conduct (IFBEC) provide resources to small businesses to encourage ethics and compliance, such as model supplier codes of conduct and information on how to implement an effective ethics program.[159] Moreover, as previously noted, Lockheed Martin offers ethics and compliance resources and optional

[157] To reduce any potential concerns mentor firms may have regarding liability for a protégé firm's actions, the mentor-protégé agreement (which will be approved by the government) should contain language making clear that neither party will be liable to the other for damages arising out of or relating to the development of the ethics compliance program in the context of the mentor-protégé relationship. Moreover, the agreement should also contain a standard mentor-protégé indemnification clause, designed to cover actions taken pursuant to the agreement.

[158] *See supra* text accompanying notes 154–57.

[159] *See* Def. Industry Initiative on Bus. Ethics & Conduct, *Featured Tools*, https://www.dii.org/featured-tools [https://perma.cc/68U5-HQMP] (last visited Oct. 18, 2019); *see also* Int'l F. on Bus. Ethical Conduct for Aerospace & Def. Industry, *Resources*, https://ifbec.info/resources [https://perma.cc/P878-3BR6] (last visited Oct. 7, 2019).

mentoring to its suppliers in order to ensure best practices are implemented throughout their supply chains.[160]

Significant strides could be made if large contractors regularly mentored small contractors to help them enhance their ethics and compliance programs. Mentoring could include: (1) comprehensive reviews of the small business's existing ethics and compliance programs; (2) recommendations for improvements; (3) assistance implementing compliance enhancements; (4) providing training to the protégé firms; (5) assistance evaluating and testing the programs; and (6) ongoing mentorship from the large companies' experienced ethics and compliance staff.

Of course, to maximize the proposed program's effectiveness, the government would need to dedicate resources to ensure that mentor firms provide sufficient guidance and assistance to protégés. It is also critical that mentors are properly screened to ensure they are joining the program to further the program's policy goals—not to exploit incentives at the expense of protégé firms. Although no government program is immune from abuse, safeguards like these will prevent and deter potential program manipulation.[161]

Fortunately, lessons can be drawn from audits of the existing mentor-protégé program. A 2007 audit of the DoD's mentor-protégé program found that some mentor firms benefited from the program's procurement and financial incentives, but failed to provide adequate procurement guidance to their protégés.[162] Dissatisfied protégé firms have pointed to a "lack of mentor commitment to the program, mentor failure to meet the objectives of mentor-protégé agreements, and costs to the protégés that exceeded the return from participation."[163] Although some concerns with the mentor-protégé program do exist, the audit found that the DoD's mentor-protégé program enhanced the overall capabilities

[160] *See* Lockheed 2, *supra* note 139.

[161] The SBA recently published proposed regulations, issued in November 2019, that respond to some of the criticisms of the Mentor-Protégé Program found in recent GAO and SBA audit reports. SBA has made clear in the proposed regulations that its focus is the protégé firm and the "business development assistance a proposed mentor can provide to a protégé to enable that firm to more effectively compete on its own in the future." *See* Consolidation of Mentor-Protégé Programs and Other Government Contracting Amendments, 84 Fed. Reg. 60,846, 60,859 (Nov. 8, 2019) (to be codified at 13 C.F.R. pts. 121, 124, 125, 126, 127, 134).

[162] *See* U.S. Gov't Accountability Off., GAO-07-151, Contract Management: Protégés Value DOD's Mentor Protégé Program, but Annual Reporting to Congress Needs Improvement 4, 7 (2007) [hereinafter GAO-07-151]. A 2011 audit by the U.S. Government Accountability Office also found that it was difficult to determine mentor-protégé program success because there was not enough annual reporting by federal agencies regarding protégés' progress after the conclusion of the mentor-protégé program. *See* GAO-11-548R, *supra* note 142, at 2, 7. The report found that ten of the thirteen agencies with mentor-protégé programs were not able to provide this kind of post-agreement analysis, which GAO determined could further assist agencies in modifying programs to better improve the protégés experience. *See id.* at 7–9.

[163] *See* GAO-07-151, *supra* note 162, at 7. *But see* GAO-11-548R, *supra* note 142, at 6 (noting that dissatisfied protégés may report dissatisfaction with mentors and suggesting that such reporting rarely occurs).

of 93 percent of the 48 protégés that were involved in the program and participated in the audit survey.[164] Similarly, Government Accountability Office (GAO) conducted an audit in 2017 of the DoD's pilot mentor-protégé program and found that while the program assisted participants during their participation, it was difficult to measure and track the effectiveness of the protégés when they left the program.[165] GAO determined that the DoD required additional measures to develop more concrete goals and indicators of program effectiveness during the protégé's participation.[166] The lessons learned from past experiences in the mentor-protégé program, coupled with contemporary developments in industry ethics and compliance mentoring programs, demonstrate that this model could be extremely beneficial in the ethics and compliance setting, so long as sufficient safeguards are put in place.[167] Not only would front-end screening of prospective participants be an essential component of the program, the government would need to install a back-end verification process to ensure all parties have maintained their commitments. With screening and oversight mechanisms in place, the impact of this program on small business compliance programs could be significant.

5. Conclusion

A "compliance mentorship program" could successfully foster the development of small business ethics and compliance programs. With appropriate safeguards in place, the potential improvements to the overall integrity of the procurement system could be significant. The program could greatly reduce supply chain risks and enhance the overall ethics and compliance practices of a chronically weak segment of the procurement system. By incentivizing ethics and compliance at all levels of the supply chain, a "compliance mentorship program" could substantially enhance the U.S. procurement system by ensuring that the government's business partners, large and small, are responsible, ethical, and compliant.

[164] *See* GAO-07-151, *supra* note 162, at 6. *See generally* GAO-11-548R, *supra* note 142, at 7 (discussing DoD successes with its mentor-protégé program in 2008 and 2009).

[165] *See* U.S. Gov't Accountability Office Report, GAO 17-172, Small Business Contracting: DOD Should Take Actions to Ensure That Its Pilot Mentor-Protégé Program Enhances the Capabilities of Protégé Firms 15–17 (2017).

[166] *Cf. id.* at 23 (recommending that the DoD develop improved systems to collect information from mentors on how the program enhances capabilities of protégées and noting that the DoD has already agreed to comply).

[167] *See generally* GAO-07-151, *supra* note 162, at 6–7 (discussing the relative success of the DoD's mentor-protégé program but also noting some dissatisfaction among protégés); *see generally* GAO-11-548R, *supra* note 142, at 6 (discussing mechanisms such as reporting requirements, reviews, and recourse for dissatisfaction used in mentor-protégé programs that could be beneficial to compliance programs).

References

John D. Altenburg, *Winding Down War Zone Contracts*, Nat'l Def. Mag. (Nov. 1, 2013), https://www.nationaldefensemagazine.org/archive/2013/November/Pages/WindingDownWarZoneContracts.aspx.

Keir X. Bancroft, *Regulating Information Security in the Government Contracting Industry*, 62 Am. U. L. Rev. 1145 (2013).

Boeing, *Ethics and Compliance*, https://www.boeing.com/principles/ethics-and-compliance.page.

Ryan Bolger, *Small Companies Face Tougher FCPA Scrutiny*, Int'l Fin. L. Rev., Nov. 2011, at 1.

Rachel Brewster & Samuel W. Buell, *The Market for Global Anticorruption Enforcement*, 80 L. & Contemp. Probs. 193 (2017).

Richard L. Cassin, *With Alstom, Three French Companies Are Now in the FCPA Top Ten*, FCPA Blog (Dec. 23, 2014), https://www.fcpablog.com/blog/2014/12/23/with-alstom-three-french-companies-are-now-in-the-fcpa-top-t.html.

Ctr. for Responsible Enterprise & Trade, *FCPA Enforcement Trends* (Apr. 26, 2017), https://create.org/news/fcpa-enforcement-trends.

Cong. Research Serv., R41722, Small Business Mentor-Protégé Programs (Jan. 7, 2019).

Nicole V. Crain & W. Mark Crain, Small Bus. Admin. Office of Advocacy, The Impact of Regulatory Costs on Small Firms (2010).

Criminal Div., U.S. Dep't of Justice & Enf't Div., U.S. Secs. & Exch. Comm'n, A Resource Guide to the U.S. Foreign Corrupt Practices Act (2012).

Pamela Davis & Lily Becker, Orrick, Herrington & Sutcliffe, The Ever-Changing Compliance Landscape: What Is the Next Wave? (2016).

DGC Int'l, *DGC International Continues to Support the Defense Industry Initiative* (June 25, 2017), https://dgci.com/dgc-international-continues-to-support-the-defense-industry-initiative.

Def. Industry Initiative on Bus. Ethics & Conduct, *Membership*, https://www.dii.org/membership.

Def. Industry Initiative on Bus. Ethics and Conduct, Building and Maintaining an Ethics and Compliance Program—The Small Business Toolkit (2019).

Def. Industry Initiative on Bus. Ethics & Conduct, *Featured Tools*, https://www.dii.org/featured-tools.

Def. Industry Initiative on Bus. Ethics & Conduct, *About DII*, https://www.dii.org/about/about-dii.

Stacey English & Susannah Hammond, Cost of Compliance 2015, Thompson Reuters (2015).

Mirit Eyal-Cohen, *Why Is Small Business the Chief Business of Congress*, 43 Rutgers L.J. 1, 3 (2011).

FCPA & Anti-Corruption Task Force, Morrison & Foerster LLP, The Foreign Corrupt Practices Act and Global Anti-Corruption Law (2010).

Katie Fish et al., Transparency International UK, Defence Companies Anti-Corruption Index 2015 (2015).

Mark Foggin, Ctr. For Urban Future, Breaking into the Corporate Supply Chain (2010).

Fred Geldon, *Special Compliance Requirements for Government Contractors*, Corp. Compliance Insights (Oct. 14, 2019), https://www.corporatecomplianceinsights.com/compliance-requirements-government-contractors.

Aaron Grieser, *The Outer Limit of Global Compliance Programs: Emerging Legal & Reputational Liability in Corporate Supply Chains*, 10 Or. Rev. Int'l L. 285 (2008).

Fritz Heimann et al., Transparency International, Verification of Anti-Corruption Compliance Programs (2014).

Int'l Forum on Bus. Ethical Conduct for the Aerospace & Def. Indus., 5th Annual Conference Report (2014).

Int'l Forum on Bus. Ethical Conduct for Aerospace & Def. Industry, *Resources*, https://ifbec.info/resources.

Peter Jeydel, *Yoking the Bull: How to Make the FCPA Work for U.S. Business*, 43 Geo. J. Int'l L. 523 (2012).

John T. Jones & Greg Bingham, Costs of Mandatory Ethics and Compliance Programs (2009).

Dietrich Knauth, *5 Areas of Growing Debarment Risk for Contractors*, Law360 (Jan. 13, 2014), http://www.crowell.com/files/5-Areas-Of-Growing-Debarment-Risk-For-Contractors.pdf.

Kroll, 2014 Anti-Bribery and Corruption Benchmarking Report: Untangling the Web of Risk and Compliance 7 (2014).

Kroll, How Do Companies Navigate Bribery and Corruption?: 2015 Anti-Bribery and Corruption Benchmarking Report (2015).

Kroll & Ethisphere, Anti-Bribery & Corruption Benchmarking Report—2017: Beyond Regulatory Enforcement: The Rise of Reputational Risk (2017).

Letter from U.S. Dep't of Justice Criminal Div. to Karen P. Hewitt, Jones Day (June 20, 2019), https://www.justice.gov/opa/press-release/file/1175791/download.

Lockheed Martin, *Ethics Supplier Mentoring Program*, https://www.lockheedmartin.com/content/dam/lockheed-martin/eo/documents/ethics/ethics-supplier-mentoring-program-overview.pdf.

Lockheed Martin, *Ethics*, https://www.lockheedmartin.com/en-us/suppliers/supplier-ethics.html.

Lockheed Martin, *Ethics Supplier Mentoring Program: Participants in One-on-One Mentoring Program*, https://www.lockheedmartin.com/content/dam/lockheed-martin/eo/documents/ethics/supplier-ethics-mentees-list.pdf.

Lucinda A. Low, *The United Nations Convention Against Corruption: The Globalization of Anticorruption Standards*, Steptoe & Johnson LLP (May 4, 2006), https://www.steptoe.com/assets/attachments/2599.pdf.

Arthur Selwyn Miller & W. Theodore Pierson, Jr., *Observations on the Consistency of Federal Procurement Policies with Other Government Policies*, 29 L. & Contemp. Probs. 277 (1964).

Nat'l Women's Bus. Council, Evaluating Federal Mentor-Protégé Programs: Assessment, Case Studies and Recommendations (2011).

Northrop Grumman, *Anti-Corruption Compliance*, https://www.northropgrumman.com/CorporateResponsibility/Pages/AntiCorruptionProgram.aspx [https://perma.cc/4HTM-4D48].

OECD Convention on Combating Bribery of Foreign Public Officials in International Business Transactions, Org. for Econ. Cooperation & Dev., https://perma.cc/Z98T-UMXD.

OECD, Good Practice Guidance on Internal Controls, Ethics, and Compliance (2010), https://www.oecd.org/investment/anti-bribery/anti-briberyconvention/44884389.pdf.

Org. for Econ. Co-operation and Dev. Working Grp. on Bribery [OECD], 2017 Enforcement of the Anti-Bribery Convention 3 (Nov. 2018), https://www.oecd.org/daf/anti-bribery/OECD-WGB-Enforcement-Data-2018-ENG.pdf.

Press Release, Department of Justice Office of Public Affairs, Press Release, Johnson & Johnson Agrees to Pay 21.4 Million Criminal Penalty to Resolve Foreign Corrupt Practices Act and Oil for Food Investigations, Department of Justice (Apr. 8, 2011), https://www.justice.gov/opa/pr/johnson-johnson-agrees-pay-214-million-criminal-penalty-resolve-foreign-corrupt-practices-act.

Press Release, Department of Justice Office of Public Affairs, Morgan Stanley Managing Director Pleads Guilty for Role in Evading Internal Controls Required by FCPA (Apr. 25, 2012), https://www.justice.gov/opa/pr/former-morgan-stanley-managing-director-pleads-guilty-role-evading-internal-controls-required.

Press Release, U.S. Dep't of Justice Office of Pub. Affairs, Deputy Attorney General Rosenstein Delivers Remarks at the 34th International Conference on the Foreign Corrupt Practices Act (Nov. 29, 2017), https://www.justice.gov/opa/speech/deputy-attorney-general-rosenstein-delivers-remarks-34th-international-conference-foreign.

Press Release, U.S. Dep't of Justice Office of Pub. Affairs, Walmart and Brazil-Based Subsidiary Agree to Pay $137 Million to Resolve Foreign Corrupt Practices Act Case (June 20, 2019), https://www.justice.gov/opa/pr/walmart-inc-and-brazil-based-subsidiary-agree-pay-137-million-resolve-foreign-corrupt.

PriceWaterhouseCoopers, How to Fortify Your Supply Chain Through Collaborative Risk Management (20009).

Mark Pyman et al., Transparency International UK, Defence Companies Anti-Corruption Index 2012 (2012).

Susan Rose-Ackerman, *International Anti-Corruption Policies and the U.S. National Interest*, 107 Am. Soc'y Int'l L. Proc. 252 (2013).

Andrew George Sakallaris, *Questioning the Sacred Cow: Reexamining the Justifications for Small Business Set Asides*, 36 Pub. Cont. L.J. 685 (2007).

Kristen Savelle, *The FCPA's (Narrowing?) Extraterritorial Reach: Implications of United States v. Hoskins*, China L. Connect, Dec. 2018, at 1.

Matthew Schoonover, *5 Things You Should Know: All Small Mentor-Protege Program*, SmallGovCon (Sept. 20, 2017), http://smallgovcon.com/five-things/asmpp.

Small Bus. Admin., Fiscal Year 2018 Small Business Procurement Scorecard (2018).

Brent Snyder, Deputy Assistant Att'y Gen., Antitrust Div., U.S. Dep't of Justice, Remarks as Prepared for the International Chamber of Commerce/United States Council of International Business Joint Antitrust Compliance Workshop: Compliance is a Culture, Not Just a Policy (Sept. 9, 2014).

Elizabeth K. Spahn, *Implementing Global Anti-Bribery Norms: From the Foreign Corrupt Practices Act to the OECD Anti-Bribery Convention to the U.N. Convention Against Corruption*, 23 Ind. Int'l & Comp. L. Rev. 1 (2013).

Jessica Tillipman, *A House of Cards Falls: Why "Too Big to Debar" Is All Slogan and Little Substance*, 80 Fordham L. Rev. Res Gestae 49 (2011).

Jessica Tillipman, *Gifts, Hospitality & the Government Contractor*, Briefing Papers, June 1, 2014.

Major Patrick E. Tolan, Jr., *Government Contracting with Small Business in the Wake of the Federal Acquisition Reform Act, and* Adarand: *Small Business as Usual?*, 44 A.F. L. Rev. 75 (1998).

Robert Tompkins & Rodney Perry, *An Ethics and Compliance Punch List for Gov't Contractors*, Law 360 (June 19, 2019), https://www.law360.com/articles/1170586/print?section=aerospace.

Vartuhí Tonoyan et al., *Corruption and Entrepreneurship: How Formal and Informal Institutions Shape Small Firm Behavior in Transition and Mature Market Economies*, Entrepreneurship Theory & Prac. (Sept. 2010).

Trace Int'l, TRACE Due Diligence Guidebook: Doing Business with Intermediaries Internationally (2010)

United Nations Convention Against Corruption art. 16, Oct. 31, 2003, 2349 U.N.T.S. 41.

U.N. Indus. Dev. Org. & U.N. Office on Drugs and Crime, 2 Corruption Prevention to Foster Small and Medium-Sized Enterprise Development (2012), https://www.unodc.org/documents/corruption/Publications/2012/Corruption_prevention_to_foster_small_and_medium_size_enterprise_development_Vol_2.pdf.

U.N. Office on Drugs and Crime, An Anti-Corruption Ethics and Compliance Programme for Business: A Practical Guide (Sept. 2013), https://www.unodc.org/documents/corruption/Publications/2013/13-84498_Ebook.pdf.

U.N. Office on Drugs and Crime, An Anti-Corruption Ethics and Compliance Programme for Business: A Practical Guide (Sept. 2013), https://www.unodc.org/documents/corruption/Publications/2013/13-84498_Ebook.pdf

U.N. Office on Drugs and Crime, Signature and Ratification Status (June 26, 2018), http://www.unodc.org/unodc/en/treaties/CAC/signatories.html.

U.N. Office on Drugs and Crime, Conference of the States Parties to the United Nations Convention Against Corruption, https://www.unodc.org/unodc/en/treaties/CAC/CAC-COSP.html.

U.S. Dep't of Justice, Justice Manual: Foreign Corrupt Practices Act of 1977 (2019).

U.S. Gov't Accountability Off., GAO/NSAID-94-101, Defense Contracting: Implementation of the Pilot Mentor-Protege Program (1994).

U.S Gov't. Accountability Off., GAO-01-767, Contract Management: Benefits of the DOD Mentor-Protégé Program Are Not Conclusive (2001).

U.S. Gov't Accountability Off., GAO-07-151, Contract Management: Protégés Value DOD's Mentor Protégé Program, but Annual Reporting to Congress Needs Improvement (2007).

U.S. Gov't Accountability Off., GAO-09-591, Defense Contracting Integrity: Opportunities Exist to Improve DOD's Oversight of Contractor Ethics Programs (2009).

U.S. Gov't Accountability Off., GAO-11-548R, Mentor-Protégé Programs Have Policies That Aim to Benefit Participants but Do Not Require Postagreement Tracking (2011).

U.S. Gov't Accountability Off., GAO-14-36, Small Business Contracting: Updated Guidance and Reporting Needed for Consolidated Contracts (2013).

U.S. Gov't Accountability Office Report, GAO 17-172, Small Business Contracting: DOD Should Take Actions to Ensure That Its Pilot Mentor-Protégé Program Enhances the Capabilities of Protégé Firms (2017).

Matthew Weigelt, *DOD Now Required to Report Bundled Contracts, Sole-Source Awards*, WASH. TECH. (July 13, 2010), http://washingtontechnology.com/articles/2010/07/13/bundled-contract-sole-source-reporting.aspx.

Howard Weissman, *Changes in Defense Industry Are Increasing FCPA Risks*, LAW 360 (Dec. 18, 2014), https://www-law360-com.gwlaw.idm.oclc.org/articles/602964?scroll=1&related=1.

Joseph D. West et al., *Contractor Business Ethics Compliance Program & Disclosure Requirements*, BRIEFING PAPERS, Apr. 2009.

WORLD BANK GRP., Summary of World Bank Group Integrity Compliance Guidelines (Sept. 2010), http://pubdocs.worldbank.org/en/489491449169632718/Integrity-Compliance-Guidelines-2-1-11.pdf.

16

Silo Mentalities, Dominant Logics, and Their Ethical Challenges in the Defense Industry

Patricia Werhane

1. Introduction

When there is wrongdoing in our society, whether on the individual, organizational, or systemic level, an individual, group of individuals, or an organization is or are often singled out for blame, and commonly it is assumed that the so-called culprits engaged in deliberate misdeeds. But sometimes, at least, these misdeeds occur not because of deliberate malfeasance but rather because of complex collective action that produced these negative outcomes. In this chapter, using the Challenger and Columbia space shuttle explosions and the Boeing 737 MAX aircraft crashes as examples, we will study types of collective action problems that are particularly acute in the defense industry: silo mentalities and a dominant logic.

"Silo mentality" is a widely occurring phenomenon wherein a profession, a particular division of an organization or an organization itself is so focused on their priorities or their expertise that they neglect or fail to perceive how those priorities affect or are affected by other professions, divisions in the organization, or others in their industry.

The term "dominant logic" defines another kind of organizational phenomenon. According to Prahalad and Bettis, who coined this term, a dominant logic refers to an organizational culture, a set of practices and habits that frame the organization's goals and modes of operation.[1] Dominant logics are vital for the coherent functioning of an organization as an organization. However, sometimes a dominant logic can become so ingrained that it creates blind spots or hinders change.

[1] *See generally* C.K. Prahalad & Richard A. Bettis, *The Dominant Logic: A New Linkage Between Diversity and Performance*, 7 STRATEGIC MGMT. J. 485 (1986).

Patricia Werhane, *Silo Mentalities, Dominant Logics, and Their Ethical Challenges in the Defense Industry* In: *Ethical Dilemmas in the Global Defense Industry*. Edited by: Daniel Schoeni and Tobias Vestner, Oxford University Press.
 DOI: 10.1093/oso/9780190675813.003.0017

These two ubiquitous organizational phenomena—silo mentalities and dominant logics—can result in organizational failures.[2] In the well-documented Challenger and Columbia shuttle explosions, I shall argue that despite a plethora of experts and the good intentions of all concerned, silo mentalities at NASA and its dominant culture played central roles in these disasters. As for the 737 MAX crashes, it will turn out that although pilot error as well as mechanical malfunctions were responsible, an outdated dominant logic at Boeing was also a contributing factor. These cases illustrate how these two organizational phenomena, when things go badly in an organization, can create untoward consequences and corresponding ethical dilemmas—especially when the consequences were avoidable and resulted from collective neglect within the organization. I shall conclude by suggesting how silo mentalities and dominant logics can cause similar ethical problems in the defense industry and offer some suggested remedies to this set of ongoing ethical issues.

2. A Social Constructivist Perspective

[T]he seemingly objective social world is constructed by human action and interaction.[3]

I shall begin reminding the reader of a commonly held presupposition. It is the acknowledgment that our minds are not merely absorbing mirrors of experiential data. Rather, human beings deal with and interpret their experiences through cognitive frames, mindsets, or mental models.[4] These models represent intuitive and unconscious methods of sense-making.[5] In addition to receiving sensory data, our minds continually interact with others. Through such shared interactions, we selectively filter and frame data through social learning processes. In the process of organizing, ordering, and discussing what we experience, we mentally bracket or omit data simply because we cannot observe or absorb all that we encounter through perception. Each person's mental model or set of models is finite because no one has the capacity to take in all of the data of one's experiences; to the contrary, we selectively focus on some aspects and

[2] *See generally* Dennis Moberg, *Ethical Blind Spots in Organizations*, 27 Org. Stud. 413 (2000); Max H. Bazerman & Ann E. Tenbrunsel, Blind Spots (2011); Patricia H. Werhane et al., Obstacles to Ethical Decision-Making (2013).

[3] Peter L. Berger & Thomas Luckmann, The Social Construction of Reality 1, 78 (1966)

[4] *See generally* Peter Senge, The Fifth Discipline (1990). *See also* Patricia H. Werhane, Moral Imagination and Management Decision-Making (1999); Ian Hacking, The Social Construction of What? (1999); Berger & Luckmann, *supra* note 3; Patricia H. Werhane, *Embedded Leadership*, *in* Leadership in the 21st Century (Joanne Ciulla, ed., forthcoming).

[5] *See generally* Karl E. Weick, Sensemaking in Organizations (1995).

necessarily must ignore others. Our cognitive framing exercises can and often do ignore important data.[6]

Social construction theory takes this idea one step further with the claim that our shared mental models or schemes frame *all* of our experiences in the sense that they guide the ways in which we recognize and organize what we then call the world. From this claim it follows that the categories that we apply to reality are socially structured.[7] Indeed, according to social constructionism, this is the only way in which human beings can understand *anything*. Notice this is not the claim that our minds construct reality or what we call experience or the data of experiences. Rather it is the contention that the incomplete and disparate ways in which we present and distill experiences are socially constructed, and thus finite. As a result, because we cannot take in nor frame all the data of our experiences, in sorting out we often omit or ignore important data that does not fit into our expectations. This phenomenon, called "bounded awareness," is unavoidable and common, but it can create what Moberg, Bazerman, and Tenbrunsel have called "blind spots," where we miss or ignore essential data.[8]

Often, too, we create habits that are reinforced internally or externally through social interactions. In new situations, these habits can reinforce choices and behavior that do not take into account bizarre or new situations as just that—new—and we tend to interpret these situations through our habits.

> The most serious problem . . . is not that we frame experiences, it is not that these mental models are incomplete, sometimes biased, and surely parochial. The larger problem is that most of us either individually or in organizations do not realize that we *are* framing, disregarding data, ignoring counterevidence, or not taking into account other points of view.[9]

This problem, wherein we do not recognize our framing and editing, is not merely descriptive. It raises ethical issues, because as human beings, and by analogy as organizations, we *can* become aware of this set of activities, albeit ubiquitous in all human perception and experience. If we can become aware of these issues and have the capacity to overcome or mitigate them, then, arguably, we may have a moral obligation to do so. How is that awareness possible?

Adam Smith, the eighteenth-century philosopher and political economist, worked out why we need not be trapped in one point of view, habit, or set of

[6] *See generally* WERHANE, *supra* note 4.

[7] *See generally* MICHAEL E. GORMAN, SIMULATING SCIENCE: HEURISTICS, MENTAL MODELS, AND TECHNOSCIENTIFIC THINKING (1992). *See also* WERHANE (1999), *supra* note 4; Werhane (2020), *supra* note 4.

[8] Moberg, *supra* note 2, at 413–15; BAZERMAN & TENBRUNSEL, *supra* note 2, ch. 2.

[9] Patricia H. Werhane, *A Place for Philosophers in Applied Ethics and the Role of Moral Reasoning in Moral Imagination: A Response to Richard Rorty*, 16 BUS. ETHICS Q. 401, 404 (2007).

mental models. In *The Theory of Moral Sentiments*, Smith argued that as conscious beings we have unique capacities. Not only are we aware of our surroundings, but we are also aware of ourselves as existing in these surroundings and of our capacity to change these circumstances and, if you like, redirect our lives and our histories. This self-conscious awareness comes from a uniquely human capacity Smith calls the "impartial spectator."[10] The impartial spectator describes our abilities to step back and study our surroundings, our friends and neighbors, and even our own and others' mindsets. It is, he argues, the source of conscience and moral judgment, whereby we can evaluate ourselves, our points of view, and others less subjectively. This capacity, he believes, explains how we can extricate ourselves from bad (or even good) habits, make choices, and revise our mental models, expectations, and lives. Smith claims that while we can never completely extricate ourselves to get a purely impartial "view from nowhere,"[11] by developing this capacity we can make better judgments and redirect our lives accordingly.[12]

If Smith's account of how it is that we can make choices and control our destinies is accurate, then, it explains how we can step back from a particular point of view and re-evaluate our focus and judgments. By analogy, organizations, too, can disengage from their dominant logics and evaluate those perspectives, although their capacity to do so may be limited by a corporate culture that is so ingrained as to block such inquiry.

3. Silo Mentalities and Dominant Logics

One dictionary defines a silo mentality as "an attitude within an organization when the different sections or departments do not share information properly because they do not want to share success with others, with the result that the organization is not efficient."[13] Another depicts it as "a mind-set present in some companies when certain departments or sectors do not wish to share information with others in the same company. This type of mentality will likely reduce the efficiency of the overall operation, reduce morale, and may contribute to the demise of a productive company culture."[14] In this context, I am defining this term not as an attitude or deliberate mindset but as an organizational phenomenon that can arise from various causes, the result of which is the insufficient

[10] Adam Smith, The Theory of Moral Sentiments, §§ III.1.1–7; III.2.1–10 (1759).

[11] *See generally* Thomas Nagel, The View from Nowhere (1986).

[12] Smith, *supra* note 10, at § III.1.1–3.

[13] *Silo mentality*, Macmillan Dictionary, https://www.macmillandictionary.com/dictionary/british/silo-mentality (last visited Nov. 26, 2019).

[14] *Silo mentality*, Business Dictionary, https://www.businessdictionary.com/definition/silo-mentality.html (last visited Nov. 26, 2019).

or lack of information sharing. This may or may not result from worries about corporate success or failure. Rather, silo mentalities can exist as outcomes of ingrown habits or narrow interpretations of organizational roles. An engineer may see herself as a scientist, not as a decision maker, while a manager might not fully appreciate the importance of negative data when other counterevidence was positive. Or silo mentalities can arise in an organizational structure that does not encourage dissent or cross-communications. This phenomenon is also sometimes described as tunnel vision or tribalism.[15] All of these sorts of phenomena can create a framing of expertise or organizational habits that focus on one area of expertise or model and ignore or do not take into account other areas that are pertinent to that organization and its decision-making.

In the defense industry—where there is a great deal of collaborative work between companies and between companies and government to develop and build a finished product—focusing only within one's silo can have dangerous consequences. Although NASA is not strictly speaking part of the defense industry, its connections to defense are indisputable, and, following the shuttle explosions in 1986 and 2003, its budget was mostly shifted to the U.S. Air Force.[16] In both the Challenger and the Columbia explosions, in brief, and for different reasons we shall outline in the next sections, not all of NASA's subcontractors communicated properly with each other or with NASA as to the risks entailed in their contributions to the constructing and evaluating the structure of the shuttle in question. And within NASA itself, it appears that many engineers and managers seemed each to have had different perceptions of the risks involved on those launches, and neither group understood the mindsets (and thus the risk analyses) of the other. Similarly, with the recent 737 MAX crashes, Boeing's worldwide sales and praise for its aircraft prevented management to recognize and address cultural and economic differences between their customer bases and pilot training in various countries.[17]

"Dominant logic" refers to the most prominent or overriding "logic" or mindset by which an organization operates: its customs, culture, habits of decision-making, and even organizational charts. But, as Prahalad and others have pointed out, a dominant logic can create blind spots by constantly reinforced sets of habits that preclude creative thinking and adaptability to change. Worse, Prahalad and Bettis maintain, "the more successful organizations have been, the more difficult unlearning becomes."[18] Firms' successes fortify their

[15] *See generally* Gillian Tett, The Silo Effect, ch. 2 (2015).

[16] Kimberly Amadeo, *NASA Budget, Current Funding, History, and Economic Impact*, U.S. Econ. & News (Jan. 20, 2020), https://www.thebalance.com/us-economy-4073968.

[17] Boeing is not strictly part of the defense industry, but a large share of its revenue comes from its military division and thus the lessons from the 737 MAX crashes apply with equal force to Boeing as supplier to the Department of Defense.

[18] Prahalad & Bettis, *supra* note 1, at 498.

theories of action and makes revisions more difficult.[19] "[T]he longer a dominant logic has been in place, the more difficult it is likely to be to unlearn."[20]

According to both the Challenger and Columbia government reports, because of its many successful launches, the culture at NASA was rooted in a basic conviction that they were immune from failure (despite the Apollo 1 fire in 1967 that killed three astronauts). Moreover, there was a dominant logic of strict hierarchy. Engineers assumed that managers were in charge of decision-making. Raising issues or questioning a decision was not encouraged, and genuine exchanges of ideas and suggestions were not a common practice. A third characteristic—and this was part of the invincibility mindset—was the belief that if something worked, and worked repeatedly, it should not be tampered with. The *Columbia Report* called this conviction the "normalization of deviance."[21] Cognitive dissonance precluded raising questions about early o-ring failures preceding the explosion, and the repeated loss of tiles on almost every flight, including Challenger, preceding Columbia's disaster. Let us consider these two examples in more detail as illustrating silo mentalities and unexamined dominant logics.

4. The Challenger Disaster

The details of the 1986 Challenger space shuttle explosion are well known. The causes of this explosion are complex, and all those involved were intelligent, well meaning, and cared deeply about the success of the program. And that highlights the problem in both examples: this was not a matter of a calculated or premediated evil that could easily be targeted and the culprits removed. There were no culprits.[22] This launch had an added complication: for the first time, a civilian, a teacher named Christa McAuliffe, would be on board, bringing national media attention to the launch, and some argued, added pressure to launch the shuttle on schedule.

As it is reported by the *Rogers Commission Report*, there were a number of contributing elements, which together, caused the explosion. The most famous is the failure of the shuttle's o-rings to properly seal the right Solid Rocket Motor during the launch "due to faulty design," exacerbated by frigid conditions on the

[19] *See generally* CHRIS ARGYRIS & DONALD A. SCHÖN, ORGANIZATIONAL LEARNING: THEORY, METHOD, AND PRACTICE, ch. 1 (1978); William H. Starbuck & Bo Hedberg, *Saving an Organization from a Stagnating Environment*, 2 STRATEGY + STRUCTURE = PERFORMANCE 45 (1977).

[20] *See generally* C.K. Prahalad, *The Blinders of Dominant Logic*, 37 (2) LONG RANGE PLANNING 171 (2004); R.A. Bettis & C.K. Prahalad, *The Dominant Logic: Retrospective and Extension*, 16 STRATEGIC MGMT. J. 11 (1995).

[21] NASA, 1 *Report of the Presidential Commission on the Space Shuttle Challenger Accident* 196 (1986) [hereinafter *Rogers Commission Report*].

[22] *Id.* at 40.

day of the launch.[23] But as early as the sixth shuttle launch there had been o-ring problems, documented problems reported by engineers, most famously, Roger Boisjoly. But his memos citing the possible risks to o-ring failure were by and large ignored. By the twenty-fifth launch, o-ring weaknesses were considered normal.[24] On the evening before the scheduled Challenger launch, a group of engineers led by one of the company's Thiokol's chief engineers, Allen MacDonald, objected to the launch for three reasons: first, the predicted bad weather would make a sea rescue of the module problematic; second, they were worried about ice on the launch pad; and third, the weather forecasts were worrisome because the engines had never been tested at such low temperatures and because the o-rings in particular had never been tested at temperatures below 53 degrees.[25]

An engineer's mentality is ordinarily to worry about safety first, and that is in the code of every engineer's professional organization.[26] Their mindset is usually based on the idea that if a mechanism cannot be proved to be safe, then one assumes it is not until there are more adequate testing and positive indicators. Describing the prelaunch meeting, Roger Lund, the head engineer said, "We had to prove to them [management] that we weren't ready, and so we got ourselves in the thought process that we were trying to find some way to prove to them it [the shuttle motor] wouldn't work, and we were unable to do that. We couldn't prove absolutely that the motor wouldn't work."[27] The project manager, Jerry Mason, told Lund to "take off your engineering hat and put on your management hat."[28] The thinking was that if the engineers could not prove that the o-rings would not work well under cold conditions, one would assume the launch was safe, a mindset in stark contrast to the engineering conclusion. Moreover, despite issues with the o-rings early on, all previous launches had been successful, thus leading to the managerial view that these alleged o-ring issues were normal and thus the o-rings would function adequately. From the management perspective, icing on the launch pad could be removed, a sea rescue even in high winds could be achieved based on previous rescues under similarly challenging conditions, and if the o-rings failed, the secondary seal would do the job.[29]

Conflicts between a managerial and an engineering mindset where each is operating from his or her role-based silo are obvious, but worse, neither understood

[23] *Id.* at 72.
[24] *Id.* at 92–93.
[25] *Id.* at 86ff.
[26] Paul Bailey, *Guidance for Institution Codes of Conduct*, ENGINEERING COUNCIL (July 21, 2016), https://www.engc.org.uk/engcdocuments/internet/website/Guidelines%20for%20Institution%20Codes%20of%20Conduct.pdf.
[27] *Rogers Commission Report*, *supra* note 21, at 94.
[28] *Id.* at 93, 94.
[29] *Id.* at 97.

that these were mindsets, points of view that deserved to be challenged and were not. The engineers thought of themselves as scientists, but succumbed to managerial decisions that went against their best judgment. Even Boisjoly, the most outspoken member of the engineering team, who had vehemently objected to the launch throughout the prelaunch meetings, said afterward, "I had my say, and I never [would] take [away] any management right to take the input of an engineer and then make a decision based upon that input . . . and so there was no point in me doing anything any further than I had already attempted to do."[30] This was partly due to the hierarchical almost military culture at NASA, where it was assumed that managers were the decision makers—the "bosses" who knew what they were doing and whose decisions were not to be questioned. Most engineers accepted managers' roles as decision makers even when those decisions were thought to be flawed. The engineers were in their silos, managers in theirs, and neither group challenged their roles or questioned the efficacy of the resulting decision-making process.

A second illustration of silo mentality is the various perceptions of risk. According to the physicist Richard Feynman, a member of the Rogers Commission team that studied the explosion in minute detail, estimates of the probability of failure varied considerably.[31] On the launch pad and at NASA the perception of the probability of an explosion was as little as one in 100,000, while engineers estimated the risk as high as one in 10.[32] Yet again, each group operated according to its own calculations and did not think to consult other engineers or managers.[33]

Similar corporate cultures were to be found in the private contractors supporting NASA. One of the important contractors for the Challenger was Morton Thiokol, where in 1986 there was a policy that anyone within the organization could "blow the whistle" at any time. But the engineers on this project did not step out of their assigned roles to do so. Whether speaking up would have made a difference in the decision to launch remains unknown. But the fact that no one either within NASA or among its contractors considered this possibility is disturbing.

Coupled with the silo mentalities at NASA was a dominant logic, a logic or ingrained belief, that managerial decisions were not to be questioned, and the siloed lack of communication and openness reinforced that. Because NASA had had so many successes and very few accidents, there was widespread belief both among managers and engineers that NASA was and could continue to be

[30] *Id.* at 93.
[31] *See generally* Richard Feynman, What Do You Care What Other People Think? Part 2 (1989).
[32] *Id.*
[33] *Id.*

virtually error-free. That dominant logic created an organizational silo that got in the way of carefully considering the business of NASA, the complexities of constructing space shuttles, the myriad contractors involved, and the inherent risks of each shuttle launch, orbit, and landing with experimental vehicles.[34]

5. The Columbia Shuttle Explosion

The Challenger explosion was a terrible tragedy and an enormous loss to NASA and the space program. There were lessons that should have been learned from the previous disaster. Unfortunately, one could almost do a "find and replace" between the two disaster reports—because of the many parallels between the two explosions and the events that precipitated them, each reinforced by an unchanged and unchallenged dominant logic. Like the Challenger explosion, whose occurrence was documented in the *Rogers Commission Report*, the Columbia explosion in 2003 was also carefully documented in the *Columbia Accident Investigation Board Report* (hereafter referred to as the *Columbia Report*).

The Columbia explosion was caused by a large piece of foam insulation from the Thermal Protection System that dislodged from the shuttle just after launch. That foam struck the left wing of the craft and penetrated its protective seal, thus allowing hot air at the shuttle's re-entry to penetrate the structure and break up the shuttle.[35] This same thing had happened in earlier Columbia missions. Indeed, according to the report, "[f]oam loss occurred in more than 80 percent of 79 missions for which imagery is available."[36] Still, despite some reporting to the contrary,[37] the *Columbia Report* concluded that "previous foam losses were in a small area and of little concern."[38] Nor was the foam material defective, having been tested numerous times and in various conditions. The report continues, "Negligence on the part of NASA, Lockheed Martin, or United Space Alliance workers does not appear to have been a factor."[39] Rather, the dramatic foam loss on this flight was due to a number of factors some of which are still undetermined. However, the report suggests that

> a combination of variable and pre-existing factors, such as insufficient testing and analysis [of the foam] in early design stages, resulted in a highly variable and complex foam material, defects induced by an imperfect and variable

34 *Rogers Commission Report*, *supra* note 21, at 2–9.
35 NASA, 1 *Columbia Accident Investigation Board Report* (2003) [hereinafter *Columbia Report*].
36 *Id.* at 53.
37 *See, e.g.*, William Langewiesche, *Columbia's Last Flight: The Inside Story and Investigation—And the Catastrophe It Laid Bare*, ATLANTIC, Nov. 2003, at 63.
38 Langewiesche, *supra* note 37, at 61.
39 *Columbia Report*, *supra* note 35, at 53.

application, and the results of that imperfect process, as well as severe load, thermal pressure vibration, acoustic, and structural launch and ascent conditions.[40]

Loose foam physically caused the explosion. But there were other contributing factors involving NASA's organizational culture, and these also played significant roles in the Challenger explosion. Although NASA allegedly reformed its organizational culture to some degree after Challenger, remnants of that hierarchical culture remained unchanged. According to William Langewiesche, dissenting opinions were discouraged throughout the organization, and as a result engineers saw themselves in a passive role and managers as the only decision makers.[41] When foam debris had hit the left wing during launch, the head of Mission Management, Linda Ham, dismissed it as "normal" and refused admit that there might be unique problems since foam loss had not created dangers on any of the previous flights. Thus, she did not approve a request for more photos of the wing to assess the damage and no one on the team questioned her authority.[42]

That engineers went along with management's decisions is not surprising. Numerous studies have documented that we naturally follow authority figures.[43] As children we learn to obey authority. This is reinforced in organizations where decision-making is hierarchical and "from the top." Sometimes then, those in the middle or bottom of the organization imagine that because of their positions, managerial decisions are correct or, at least, not to be questioned. In organizations such as the military, or in dictatorships, that assumption is rule-bound. Only in a flattened hierarchical culture where questioning is encouraged and disagreements are part of everyday communication can such habits be changed. NASA's successes have precluded considering such changes in their modes of operation. As one of the independent investigators, Hal Gehman, said:

> [NASA] is an incestuous hierarchical system with invisible rankings and a very strict informal chain of command. . . . [You hear,] "Well, I was afraid to speak up. . . . If I had spoken up, it would have been at the cost of my job." And if you're in the engineering department, you're a nobody.[44]

Part of this tragic result may be due to "normalized deviance," habits that build up because the many previous launches of the Columbia had experienced foam

[40] *Id.* at 53–54.

[41] *Id.* at 24.

[42] *Id.* at 145–147, 157; Langewiesche, *supra* note 37, at 58–82; Aine Donovan & Ronald M. Green, *Setup for Failure: The Columbia Disaster*, 4:1 TEACHING ETHICS 69 (2003).

[43] *See generally* STANLEY MILGRAM, OBEDIENCE TO AUTHORITY (2009); WERHANE ET AL., *supra* note 2, at ch. 3, 43–62 (2013).

[44] Langewiesche, *supra* note 37 at 76.

tile losses and damage on every shuttle launch. But because there were no fatalities, it became assumed that this phenomenon was "normal" or "acceptable risk," without imagining what would happen if a foam tile went astray and penetrated the shuttle.[45] (This parallels the normalization of the o-ring deterioration in the Challenger, which started as early as its sixth flight.)[46] Moreover, there was a dominant logic at NASA that the shuttle vehicle was tested and fully operational, when in fact the whole program and its vehicles were still experimental. Such mistaken beliefs led to flawed risk analysis of the inherent dangers of each launch and flight.[47]

Part of the neglect of the foam debris problem in this flight was also due to the lingering mindset of invincibility. Since the Challenger explosion in 1986 there had been 87 successful shuttle flights over the two decades between that explosion and Columbia.[48] No wonder NASA developed extraordinary confidence in their continued success in shuttle flights!

As the chair of the Debris Assessment Team and himself an engineer, Rodney Rocha wrote in an e-mail he shared with other engineers but did not send:

> [T]his is the wrong (and bordering on irresponsible) answer from the SSP [Space Station Program] and Orbiter not to request additional imaging help from an outside source. . . . [S]evere enough damage . . . combined with the heating and resulting damage to the underlying structure at the most critical locations . . . could present potentially grave hazards. The engineering team will admit it might not achieve definitive high confidence answers without additional images, but without . . . clarify[ing] the image visually, we will guarantee it will not.[49]

When asked why he did not send this e-mail, Rocha replied that he did not want to jump the chain of command. Having already raised the need to have the Orbiter imaged with a NASA manager, he deferred to management's judgment on obtaining imagery.[50]

This unsent memo has important implications. First, Rocha indicates that he did not send it because he feared questioning Ham's authority.[51] Second, as with Challenger, there was a disconnect between engineers and managers. As an engineer, Rocha would assume that the shuttle was unsafe unless evidence affirmatively proved otherwise. He sought for proof that the shuttle was not in danger,

45 *Columbia Report*, *supra* note 35, at 121.
46 *Rogers Commission Report*, *supra* note 21, at 136–40.
47 *Columbia Report*, *supra* note 35, at 196.
48 *Id.* at 101.
49 *Id.* at 157.
50 *Id.* at 157.
51 *Id.* at 157.

which might have been available through careful imaging of the shuttle's wing. Ham, like the Challenger managers, made the opposite assumption: despite dislodged foam debris, previous shuttles had not exploded and, therefore, neither would this one. Each group was functioning within its silo of expertise, and each was unwilling or unable to challenge its mindsets and groupthink. Moreover, the hierarchical structure did not welcome dissent; engineers felt that their place was to do the science and not to question managers' decisions. While stray foam was the immediate physical cause, the organizational culture was the ultimate cause. That culture precluded gathering evidence or taking safety measures while the shuttle was in orbit and the explosion still might have been prevented. The real tragedy, therefore, would be not to remember the organizational and physical causes of the previous explosions. Such forgetfulness could easily reoccur.

6. Analysis of These Explosions

Like the two reports, we can now step back and speculate about the causes of the two mishaps. This is second-guessing, but a great deal can be learned and generalized from such analysis. First, to repeat, there is absolutely no evidence that any of the participants at NASA or NASA's subcontractors had any but the best of intentions. And all the engineers, managers, and others involved in these scenarios were experts in their fields. As we noted earlier, there were no individual culprits.

However, there remain two sets of ethical issues, the outcomes of which could have been positive: in the case of Challenger, prior to the launch; in the case of Columbia, during the flight. The first issue has to do with silo mentalities. While we all tend to think and operate in silos, particularly if we are trained as professionals in a particular field, we need not. Not only would our lives be enriched if we broadened our perspectives, in some cases the failure to do so can have life or death consequences. For the Challenger and Columbia explosions, the fact that managers did not to understand an engineering point of view, particularly as to safety, seems more than an oversight. It rises to the level of an ethical question. It is engineering ingenuity that created the shuttles in the first place, and that expertise should not only be acknowledged but engineers' distinct perspectives as to safety needed to be better comprehended. If Adam Smith's arguments make sense, then this sort of comprehension is possible and, in these cases, even morally required. Similarly, engineers should realize that managers are not infallible and that they can make wrong choices, often because they lack full information or have bought into the myth that their judgments are generally sound.

My point is that in not questioning these sets of silos as *silos* that need to be acknowledged and dealt with, engineers and managers created blind spots that contributed to the explosions. Undue toleration of such blindness in organizations is unethical. This mindset fails to appreciate human beings' epistemic limitations and shows insufficient regard for expert opinion; such failings can have dire consequences.

A second set of reasons for the explosions was the hierarchical dominant logic or organizational culture at NASA. All organizations are at least semi-hierarchical, but in an open organization this does not create barriers to good judgment. At NASA, according to both shuttle explosion reports, there was a rigidness in the hierarchy such that questioning one's boss was impermissible or ignored. And engineers were treated as mere technicians, not stakeholders in managerial decision-making. Coupled with the growing myth of managerial invincibility, this led many at NASA to believe that the shuttles were fully vetted and to forget the shuttles were still experimental and that each launch entailed significant risks. That mindset enabled managers to ignore the growing dysfunction of the o-rings and the dangers of disengaged foam tiles. NASA's siloed thinking precluded appropriate risk analysis across the various sectors of the project. Interestingly, it was a Nobel Prize physicist, Roger Feynman, who worked outside of his field and unearthed the anomalies in the Challenger case. It is tragic that efforts to change NASA's culture after the Challenger explosion were insufficient and that some of the very same problems contributed to the Columbia explosion 17 years later.[52] Finally, in both scenarios no one at NASA blew the whistle to top management or outside the organization to signal the dangers of a possible disaster.

7. Some Possible Remedies at NASA

Silo mentalities and flawed dominant logics are evident in individuals, in organizations such as NASA and its subcontractors, and in our culture generally. They result from the ways in which individuals and organizations socially construct their experiences. As one commentator noted, "Institutional logics, once they become dominant, affect the decisions of organizations . . . by focusing the attention of executives toward the set of issues and solutions that are consistent with the dominant logic and away from those issues and solutions that are not."[53] Hierarchical structure and insufficient communication between engineers and managers reinforced silos of flawed decision-making at NASA. And the dominant logic, which the *Columbia Report* describes as a "culture of invincibility,"[54]

52 NASA, Executive Summary, *Actions to Implement the Rogers Commission Recommendations after the Challenger Accident* (July 14, 1986), https://www.hq.nasa.gov/office/pao/History/actions.html.

53 Patricia H. Thornton, Markets from Culture 12–13 (2004).

54 *Colombia Report*, at 199.

precluded an ongoing consideration of the risks of this experimental space shuttle. These organizational weaknesses are evidenced in both the Challenger and Columbia explosions, and such weaknesses are indicative of a pervasive mentality that was not seriously re-examined after the Challenger disaster.

How does one make changes to an organization to avoid some of these problems in the future? Adopting the model of the highly successful Navy Submarine and Reactor Safety Program, the *Columbia Report* proposes a series of recommendations. First and foremost, NASA must establish communication between all employees—engineers, managers, contractors, and administration—that are open, nonjudgmental, encourage minority opinions, and without fear of retaliation. These may seem to be obvious suggestions. Yet they ought to have been learned after the first shuttle disaster but were not.

Second, better training is essential, which is also obvious. Specifically, training must be provided to learn from the Challenger and Columbia accidents. This is best done through review of the reports to illustrate what can go wrong despite the good intentions of all those involved. This sort of training should be carried out in a cross-disciplinary way, bringing engineers, managers, subcontractors, and administrators together. Separate sessions would only reinforce the pervading silo culture. Emphasis should be on using these case studies as learning experiences, rather than faulting managers. This can also facilitate the development of institutional memory. Lessons learned are easily forgotten. Somehow, after 87 successful flights, the Challenger issues were forgotten, and dangerous foam debris was dismissed as normal. Perhaps collaborative training could have helped prevent that.

Third, additional training should be provided in risk analysis. This would include simulating worst-case scenarios. Such scenario-driven training, the U.S. Navy discovered, reinforced the dangerous and experimental nature of their program and reinvigorated risk analyses. Such worst-case scenarios better simulate reality than does everyday experience, which deceptively can underestimate true risks. Such analyses reinforce safety as a primary consideration. The *Colombia Report*, by contrast, found that safety was of secondary importance and that "a broken safety culture . . . of blind spots"[55] existed, created by many successful launches and a managerial conviction that the past would always predict the future.[56]

Finally, better systems analyses of the program and of the design and launch of each shuttle would have been required. This is only hinted at in the reports, probably because it seemed so obvious. The shuttle program was a massive systemic creation from a vast number of inputs from contractors, subcontractors,

[55] *Id.* at 184.
[56] *Id.* at 182–84.

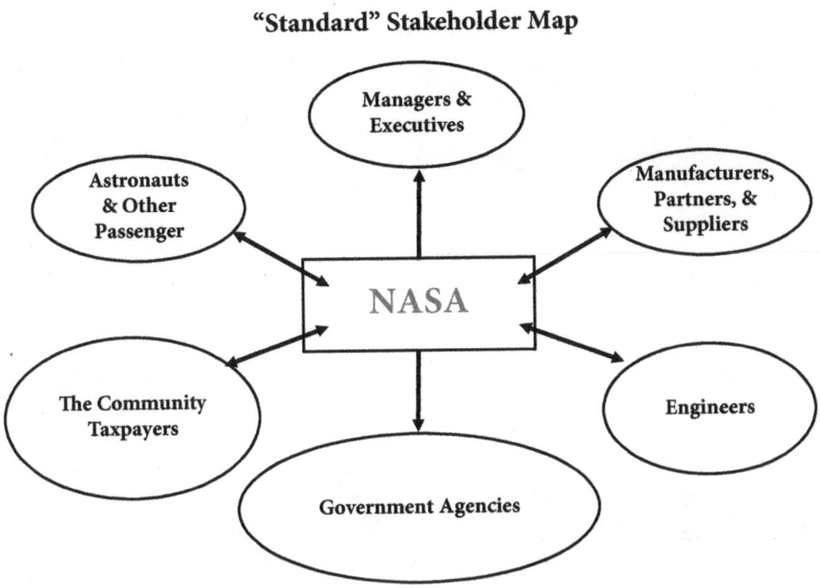

Figure 16.1

engineers, managers, suppliers, astronauts, bureaucrats, and the like. Such complex systems require rethinking the hierarchical structure or the organization. Figure 16.1 is one image of the organizational chart at NASA with arrows pointing to proposals for cross-sectional communication. Another way to encourage such rethinking is a graphic such as Figure 16.2, undetailed but demonstrative of the complex interrelationships (and this is simplified) at NASA. Figure 16.3 places the shuttle program in the center to emphasize that is what all of this is about. These are simple graphics, but they have been effective in other organizations. For example, Novo Nordisk's graphic of their organization (see Figure 16.4) places people with diabetes in the center, to emphasize that they are in the business of ameliorating disease and that that mission, rather than perpetuating the existence of the organization, is of primary importance. In the age of visual rather than written thinking, such graphics can be effective in revamping an organization's focus.

NASA's successes are admirable, and one would not want to interfere with the elements of an organization that produced so many successful shuttle launches. However, every launch had problems, problems that were not fully recognized as life-threatening or addressed. Going back again and again to these successful but flawed launches and simulating worst-case scenarios could be very effective in changing NASA's culture. More importantly, a realization that there were many "near misses" in every flight that need not have happened and that organizational

Stakeholder Networks

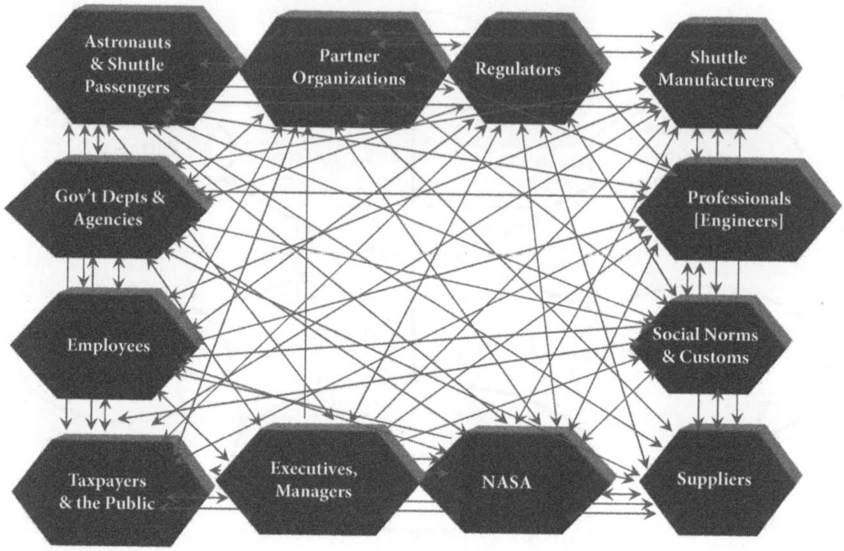

Figure 16.2

"Standard" Stakeholder Map

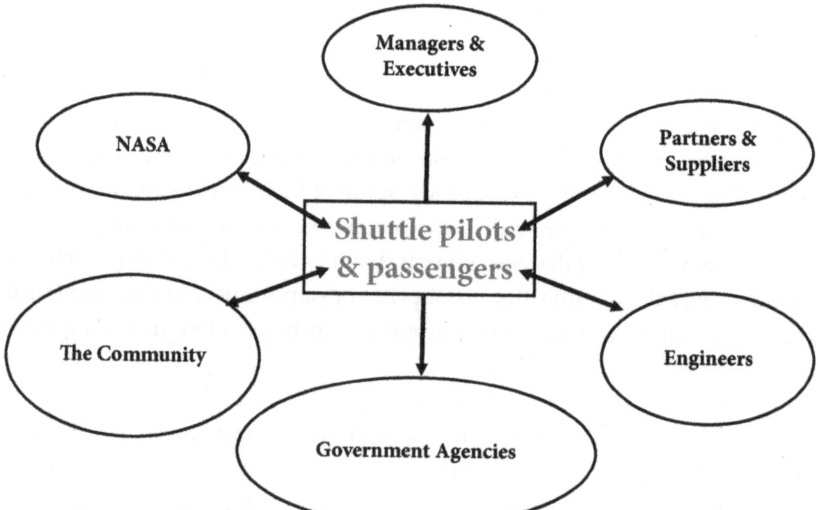

Figure 16.3

Repositioned Stakeholder Maps

Stakeholders at Novo Nordisk

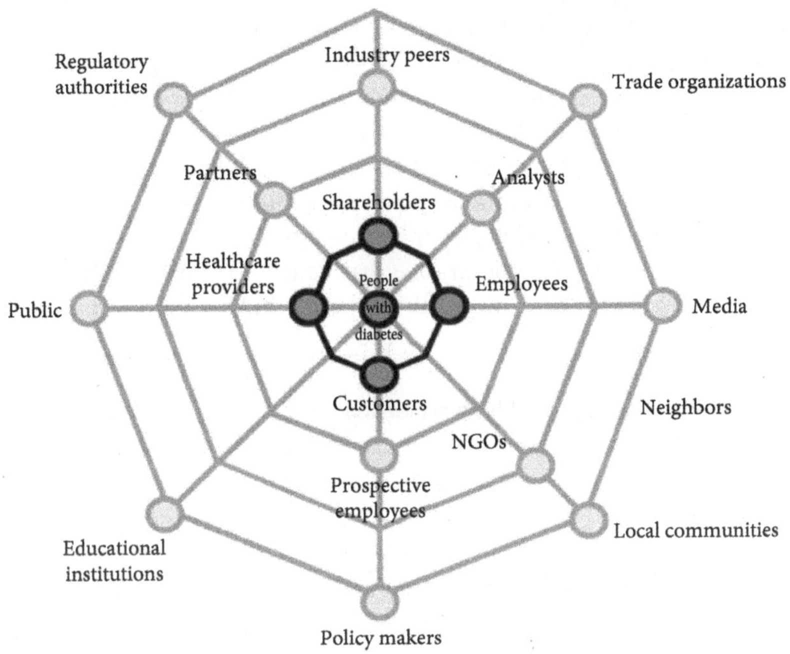

Figure 16.4

mindsets contributed to those near misses (which are all documented in the two reports) might help NASA to rethink itself. Lessons from the space shuttle program are valuable for its current and future structure and operations.

8. Application to Another Organization: Boeing and the 737 MAX Crashes

> *What we had in the two downed airplanes was a textbook failure of airmanship.*[57]

Let us look at another example of siloed mentality and a stale corporate culture that has most recently received media attention: the 2018 Boeing 737 MAX

[57] William Langewiesche, *System Crash*, N.Y. Times Mag., Sept. 29, 2019, at 66.

malfunctions that were the causes of two fatal air crashes in Indonesia and in Ethiopia. Boeing is one of America's largest defense contractors and is also one of the world's two largest aircraft manufacturers. It is known for reliable aircraft and the 737 models that have been the workhorse for short flights and for small airlines all over the world for more than 30 years. Recently, Boeing upgraded this plane with the 737 MAX model, and because of a stellar reputation and the reliability of the 737, it had orders for thousands of planes. Unfortunately, the 2018 crashes involving the Boeing 737 MAX caused the total loss of 346 lives. Subsequently, the FAA grounded all 737 MAX flights. Obviously, the crashes and the subsequent grounding of these aircraft are a financial blow to Boeing and a great loss to those airlines relying on these new aircraft.

Most of the blame for the crashes has fallen squarely on the aircraft's malfunctioning software. An article about the 737 MAX described the problem as follows:

> [T]he immediate culprit (of both accidents) was a sensor failure tied to a new and obscure control function that was unique to the 737 Max. . . . The system [called Maneuvering Characteristics Augmentation System—MCAS], an automated flight-control feature, applies double-speed impulses of nose-down trim, but only under circumstances so narrow that no regular airline pilot will ever experience its activation—unless a sensor fails. *Boeing believed the system so innocuous, even if it malfunctioned, that the company did not inform pilots of its existence or include a description of it in the airplane's flight manuals.*[58]

While there is no question about the occurrences of the malfunctions, the case is more complicated. Langewiesche writes in a *New York Times Magazine* article that "it was the decisions of the four pilots [in the two airplanes] more than the failure of a single obscure component, that led to the 346 deaths."[59] He argues persuasively that a well-trained pilot educated not merely on the mechanics and control panels of the aircraft but also a pilot experienced in what he calls "airmanship," learning how to react to unpredictable circumstances, could have flown these aircraft to safety, despite the malfunction. So, then, is the 737 MAX's flawed design only partly to blame?

To answer that question, we have to examine Boeing's corporate culture and dominant logic. Boeing has long built and preferred favored pilot-centric designs that depend as much on pilots' skills as on cockpit technology. Perhaps, as Langewiesche argues, skilled pilots could have dealt with the 737 MAX's

[58] *Id.* at 40 (emphasis added). *See also* Andy Pasztor, *Boeing Is Urged to Rethink Safety Tests*, Wall St. J., Sept. 27, 2019, at 1.

[59] Langewiesche, *supra* note 57, at 41.

difficulties simply by turning off a few switches. Boeing's rival, Airbus, on the other hand, has created planes with technologies that allow the aircraft to fly almost by themselves. According to Airbus's CEO, this technology has dramatically reduced the accidents resulting from pilot error.[60] Despite this competition, however, Boeing continues with its pilot-centric design approach.

That pilot-controlled approach works well when pilots are well trained and are familiar with the specific aircraft. Unfortunately, careful pilot training that is conducted in almost all developed nations is not well replicated in many emerging economies. The increasing demand for air transportation and stiff competition between airlines often result in hurried and rote training of pilots throughout the developing world. Such pilots can respond to routine instrument flying but are not always prepared for adverse flying conditions. Indeed, Lion Air has such a terrible safety record that in 2007 the European Union and the United States permanently banned all Indonesian airlines from flying in or over their air space.[61] Even the Indonesian government acknowledges that pilot error contributed to the Lion Air 737 MAX crash.[62] More specifically, it attributes the insufficient training to Boeing's failure to inform them of important changes to the 737 MAX's avionics software.

Boeing and Airbus have both been aware of the imperfect training and poor air safety records in many developing countries. They have engaged in pilot retraining, very successfully in China, which now has an impressive safety record. In other countries, however, Boeing's efforts were unsuccessful. Despite Boeing's awareness of its failed efforts with Indonesia's Lion Air pilot training, Boeing continued selling its planes to Lion Air, in 2011 accepting an order for 201 737 MAXes.[63]

Like the NASA disasters, this scenario illustrates silo mentalities at Boeing and a stale corporate culture or dominant logic. Boeing's expertise is in pilot-centric aircraft. They have not changed that view despite fierce competition from Airbus and even though many of their foreign customers' pilot training programs are not pilot-centric. This model resulted from a siloed engineering approach and assumption that their planes are the best. Given the longevity of Boeing's success and excellence of its aircraft, there was good reason for holding this view. But I would suggest that siloed thinking coupled with a dominant logic that Boeing is "the best" have created a twenty-first-century blind spot. Boeing depends on foreign orders to survive. But not all countries have the same commitment to excellence in pilot training and safety as in America. Therefore, as Pasztor writes, "the plane maker and the FAA [need to] pay more attention to interaction between

60 *Id.* at 44–45.
61 *Id.* at 42.
62 Pasztor, *supra* note 58, at 1.
63 Langewiesche, *supra* note 57, at 45.

humans and cockpit computers . . . average pilots who typically have less experience. . . . The pilots [of the Indonesian and Ethiopian planes that crashed] did not react in the ways that Boeing and the FAA assumed."[64]

The pilot errors in Ethiopia and Indonesia were not only the result of insufficient training but also had a cultural component. In the iPhone age, the internet and cell phones are nearly ubiquitous. This breeds a misplaced complacency about technology. Overreliance on seemingly reliable technology gives rise to expectations that automation is the norm and that machines are self-correcting. Long before the 737 MAX crashes, these pilots were unprepared for unanticipated malfunctions. Their complacency had conditioned them to think that malfunctions would rarely require human intervention. This was not what pilots expected from aircraft manufactured in America. Boeing's incongruity with its more automated rival in Europe exacerbated the problem. But rather than adjusting to its diverse customer base abroad and/or, like Airbus, building an airplane that could essentially fly itself, Boeing continued with a twentieth-century engineering approach. That decision would ultimately cost more than 300 lives.

Another problem was a specific design choice that undermined safety, and this highlights the close connection that existed between the defense and civilian divisions within Boeing. In the early 2000s, Boeing engineers developed the MCAS for their military tanker aircraft. That design had multiple redundant sensors serving as safeguards in case one malfunctioned. Another set of Boeing engineers designed the 737 MAX and adapted the MCAS system but with only one set of sensors. Whatever the reason—and evidence shows that installing multiple sensors increases the price of the 737 MAX—sadly, leaving out this duplication was likely critical because the original design afforded pilots and the airplane itself a better chance of reacting to and correcting malfunctions.[65]

Maureen Tkacik identified a third problem. She contends that the problem lies in the managerial structure at Boeing. Originally an engineering company with a focus on engineering excellence and safety, Boeing has now become preoccupied with profitability. Airplanes are considered commodities, and safety is secondary to efficiency of production and sales.[66] The division of engineering from managerial roles (as we saw at NASA) may have created silos and a corporate culture or dominant logic aimed at profitability and beating Airbus. Moreover, as difficulties surrounding the three-year late release of the 787 demonstrated,

[64] Pasztor, *supra* note 58, at 1. *See also* Andy Pasztor & Andrew Tangel, *Indonesia to Fault 737 MAX Design, U.S. Oversight in Lion Air Crash Report*, Wall St. J. (Sept. 23, 2019), https://www.wsj.com/articles/indonesia-to-fault-737-max-design-u-s-oversight-in-lion-air-crash-report-11569185664.

[65] Alison Sider & Andrew Tangel, *Boeing Omitted MAX Safeguards*, Wall. St. J., Sept. 30, 2019, at 1–2.

[66] Maureen Tkacik, *Crash Course: How Boeing's Managerial Revolution Created the 737 Max Disaster*, New Republic, Sept. 18, 2019, at 1, 9.

Boeing reduced its engineering staff by half, opting instead to outsource many components. This may have affected quality control that in the past might have picked up the design flaw on the 737 MAX.

According to an engineer at Boeing commenting on the 777 jet in the 1990s, "One of the things that we do in the basic design is the pilot always has the ultimate authority of control. There is no computer on the airplane that he cannot override or turn off."[67] This cardinal rule was forgotten in the design of the 737 MAX, since it was difficult, at best, to turn off the MCAS. Whether this was an oversight, an effort not to overburden the pilots with unnecessary information, or a budget issue remains to be seen. (Tkacik argues it is the latter, but the jury is still out on that question.)

Finally, there is the difficult question of corporate culture. Boeing has released a plethora of internal emails, internal communications between engineers, between managers, and sometimes between engineers and managers, many of which complained about the corporate culture at Boeing. The perception was that this culture was driven by cost-cutting and profitability that would sometimes override engineering quality and safety. Accordingly, in one email, an engineer wrote that he would not let his family fly in a MAX because of his safety concerns.[68] Another email described the MAX as "designed by clowns who in turn are supervised by monkeys."[69] Still another lamented:

> I don't know how to fix these things . . . its systemic. It's culture. It's the fact that we have a senior leadership team that understand very little about the business and yet are driving us to certain objectives.[70]

In summary, there are several unresolved questions in the 737 MAX crashes, and these all entail ethical issues. First, clearly the original malfunction was an avoidable design failure, and the technology existed at Boeing to correct this. Second, this airplane was designed for well-trained pilots; those unfamiliar with the MCAS were unprepared for a malfunction. That issue arose because of pilot error, apparently insufficient instruction on how to manipulate the MCAS, *and* an aggressive sales force that overlooked the weaknesses of pilot training in some countries where they were marketing the MAX. Third, and this is more speculative, Boeing's culture of developing pilot-dependent aircraft and what appear to

[67] *The 21st Century Jet: The Building of the Boeing 777* (1996), https://www.youtube.com/watch?v=0oyWZjdXxlw (last visited Nov. 26, 2019). *See also* Tkacik, *supra* note 66, at 7.

[68] *See* Andy Pasztor, *Boeing Workers Made Light of MAX Safety*, Wall St. J., Jan. 10, 2020, at 1–2.

[69] David Pinsen, *Boeing's 737 Max: An Airplane "Designed By Clowns Supervised By Monkeys"*, Seeking Alpha (Jan. 20, 2020), https://seekingalpha.com/article/4316381-go3intw-737-max-airplane-designed-clowns-superised-monkeys.

[70] Pasztor, *supra* note 68, at 2.

be silos both between two engineering teams (e.g., the tanker jet engineers versus the 737 MAX engineers) as well as between goals of management and the Boeing engineers was detrimental to creating a safe, reliable aircraft. Fourth, and this is also somewhat speculative, evidence from Boeing's internal culture suggests dysfunctions and poor communication as well as a leadership failure to instill a mission of safety and good quality throughout their organization. Boeing's mission states:

> Until the crashes, Boeing's corporate mission statement was "People working together as a global enterprise for aerospace industry leadership."
> 1. Improving people's lives
> 2. Global reach
> 3. High-quality products
> 4. People empowerment[71]

Somehow these grandiose ideas were not translated into the practice of organizational values and behaviors. For example, the emails quoted previously would suggest that high-quality products were perhaps not the priority that they once were and that "empowerment," at least insofar as the design engineers were concerned, was less a core value than an empty slogan. That Boeing updated its mission statement in 2020 with principles that are less lofty—including quality, safety, and integrity—suggests that its new leadership also considered the previous mission statement a bit lavish.

The tragedy is the neglected possibility that these crashes could have been avoided, but no one at Boeing, no engineer or manager or executive, was willing to blow the whistle to stop this.

9. Analysis of the Boeing Crashes

Returning to the argument made earlier in this chapter, namely, that even though our experiences are socially constructed, because they are incomplete representations or reconstructions of the data of our experiences, one can step back, re-examine a dominant mindset logic, and revise it. As human beings we do that all the time, and organizations do as well. To break out of a silo, to realize that one is in a role that overlaps with other functions, it is necessary to identify problems and to develop change agents. At Boeing, considering the mindsets and cultures of their customer countries seems obvious. Perhaps the marketing

[71] Boeing, *Boeing Mission Statement and Vision Statement Analysis*, https://mission-statement.com/boeing/ (last accessed Sept. 10, 2020).

team was unaware of Indonesia's bad safety record (a siloed view). Whatever the cause, Boeing's sales force outpaced its engineers. Yet everyone should have been aware of global safety issues, simply because they are in the aircraft business. Ignorance is not a good moral excuse in this industry. Barring some reasonable explanation, to design commercial aircraft without incorporating safety measures deemed necessary to the tanker model seems unacceptable. To market an aircraft that depends on pilot acuity to an air carrier or a country where such skill is uncommon is ethically unconscionable, particularly when Boeing (or at least some siloed few at Boeing) must have known full well of such pilot-driven safety risks.

To revise an organizational dominant logic, individuals in that organization, usually its leaders, and the organization itself have to realize that these silos exist, that the dominant logic of the organization is just one way to think about organizational decision-making and goals, and that its dominant logic, even if it is implicit, may be contributing to failure. Organizations must experiment with new logics, revise their goals, and be unafraid to change what seems to be "cemented" in place. Elsewhere I have called this developing a moral imagination coupled with courage to change.[72] Developing such courage is the most difficult thing to achieve in any organization. We are all creatures of habit, and when all seems to be going well, we loathe change. But today we live within and as part of an ever-evolving global economy and cultural, social, and economic particularities that often contrast with each other, even with our own culture. Boeing is part of this international community, yet it ignored customers' cultural and economic disparities. Awareness of such differences must be part of any twenty-first-century organization's mindset or else disasters such as the 737 MAX will reoccur. Worse, there will also be spillover into Boeing's various government contracts for the defense industry, an industry that itself exists in a global economy and for which the moral stakes are potentially even higher.

Borrowing from the analysis of the shuttle explosions, perhaps a stakeholder graphic for Boeing would help refocus their thinking on their twenty-first-century global customers. A systems perspective would create a stakeholder map that would look something like Figure 16.5. But what if global aircraft customers were the center of focus? As illustrated in Figure 16.6, such a simple graphic might jar Boeing's managers and engineers to think out of their silos, reconfigure their products and global approach to designs, and remind themselves of the diversity and humanity of the passengers and crew in these aircraft.

And the nagging question persists throughout all these scenarios: *why, why, why* didn't someone who knew the issues go to top management, the board, or

[72] WERHANE, MORAL IMAGINATION, *supra* note 4, at ch. 6.

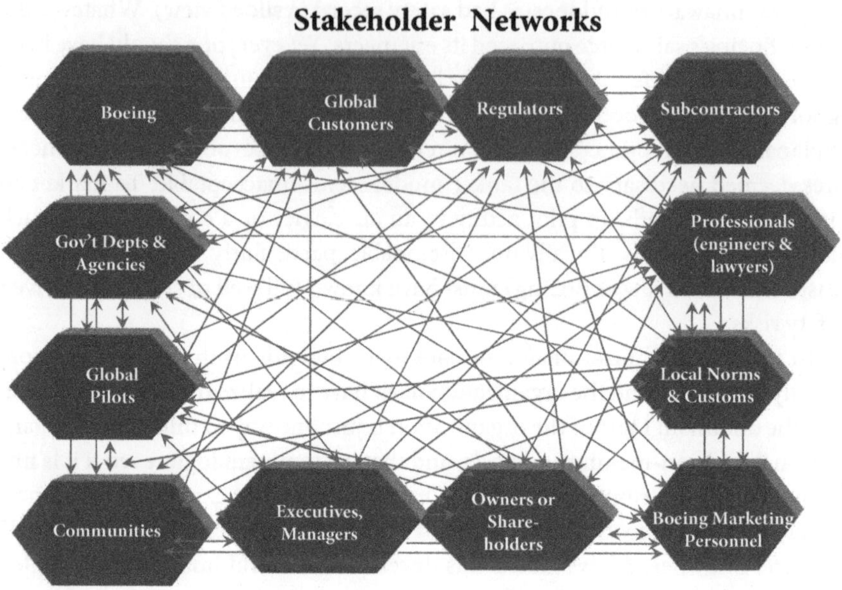

Figure 16.5

outside to blow the whistle on what were to be deadly but completely avoidable accidents? The tragic conclusion is that most of us are followers and afraid to step out of our comfort zones or we fear for our livelihoods. We seldom challenge our bosses or leaders, even when it is evident that they are mistaken or that their decisions are misleading. All of which, it often turns out, can cover up for disastrous consequences both for the company and for our roles in that disaster.

10. Conclusion

There are no simple solutions to discouraging silo mentalities or examining, evaluating, and revising ubiquitous dominant logics. Our schooling is, by and large, siloed. Managers do not know much about engineering, and engineers are rarely good managers. Organizations only function well if there is some of Adam Smith's prized division of labor. Yet specialization has limitations. Being cognizant of such limitations and re-examining the mindsets that dominate an organization from time to time are essential to avoid disasters. There is literature that argues that it takes a defining event (such as a shuttle explosion) to trigger these sorts of re-examinations. Isabella, Prahalad, and Bettis observe that changing a dominant logic requires a precipitating crisis. "In general it appears . . . that changes in the ways organizations solve significant new problems (i.e. change dominant logics)

"Standard" Stakeholder Map

Figure 16.6

are triggered by substantial problems or crises."[73] Another researcher notes, "Organizational unlearning [a precursor to developing a new dominant logic] is typically problem-triggered. . . . These triggers cause hesitancy and build up distrust in procedures and leaders. A turbulent period then frequently follows."[74]

Such a defining event is no panacea. It (a) does not always work—particularly in organizations with an ingrained culture such as NASA, which experienced a triggering event in 1986, and Boeing, which had experienced earlier 737 flaws. Both organizations still did nothing. And (b) some organizations can evaluate or re-examine their cultures and themselves without such a precipitating upheaval. In any case, the process of stepping back, which conscientious individuals often engage in—challenging standard operating procedures, ingrained habits, and rote decision processes—is also possible in organizations. This sort of thinking entails moral imagination and moral courage. NASA and Boeing are invaluable organizations in the defense industry in the United States and globally. Much of what they do is crucial to the safety and well-being of the United States and other

[73] Lynn A. Isabella, *Managing the Challenge of Trigger Events: The Mindsets Governing Adaptation to Change*, Bus. Horizons, Sept.–Oct., 1992, at 59–66; Prahalad & Bettis, *supra* note 1, at 498.

[74] Bo Hedberg, *How Organizations Learn and Unlearn*, *in* 1 Handbook of Organizational Design: Adapting Organizations to their Environments 19 (Paul C. Nystrom & William H. Starbuck eds., 1981).

countries. Thus, rethinking their organizational cultures, de-siloing engineers, managers, and other staff, and encouraging speaking out are vital to the future successes of such complex and worthwhile organizations in the defense industry and beyond.

References

Kimberly Amadeo, *NASA Budget, Current Funding, History, and Economic Impact*, U.S. Econ. & News (Jan. 20, 2020), https://www.thebalance.com/us-economy-4073968.

Chris Argyris & Donald A. Schön, Organizational Learning: Theory, Method, and Practice (1978).

Paul Bailey, *Guidance for Institution Codes of Conduct*, Engineering Council (July 21, 2016), https://www.engc.org.uk/engcdocuments/internet/website/Guidelines%20for%20Institution%20Codes%20of%20Conduct.pdf.

Max H. Bazerman & Ann E. Tenbrunsel, Blind Spots (2011).

Peter L. Berger & Thomas Luckmann, The Social Construction of Reality (1966).

R.A. Bettis & C.K. Prahalad, *The Dominant Logic: Retrospective and Extension*, 16 Strategic Mgmt. J. 11 (1995).

Business Dictionary, https://www.businessdictionary.com/definition/silo-mentality.html.

Aine Donovan & Ronald M. Green, *Setup for Failure: The Columbia Disaster*, 4(1) Teaching Ethics 69 (2003).

Richard Feynman, What Do You Care What Other People Think?, Part 2 (1989).

Michael E. Gorman, Simulating Science: Heuristics, Mental Models, and Technoscientific Thinking (1992).

Ian Hacking, The Social Construction of What? (1999).

Bo Hedberg, *How Organizations Learn and Unlearn*, *in* 1 Handbook of Organizational Design: Adapting Organizations to Their Environments (Paul C. Nystrom & William H. Starbuck eds., 1981).

Lynn A. Isabella, *Managing the Challenge of Trigger Events: The Mindsets Governing Adaptation to Change*, Bus. Horizons, Sept.–Oct. 1992, at 59.

William Langewiesche, *Columbia's Last Flight: The Inside Story and Investigation—And the Catastrophe It Laid Bare*, Atlantic, Nov. 2003, at 63.

William Langewiesche, *System Crash*, N.Y. Times Mag, Sept. 29, 2019, at 66.

Macmillan Dictionary, https://www.macmillandictionary.com/dictionary/british/silo-mentality.

Stanley Milgram, Obedience to Authority (2009).

Dennis Moberg, *Ethical Blind Spots in Organizations*, 27 Org. Stud. 413 (2000).

Thomas Nagel, The View from Nowhere (1986).

NASA, 1 *Report of the Presidential Commission on the Space Shuttle Challenger Accident* 196 (1986)

NASA, 1 *Columbia Accident Investigation Board Report* (2003).

Andy Pasztor & Andrew Tangel, *Indonesia to Fault 737 MAX Design, U.S. Oversight in Lion Air Crash Report*, Wall St. J. (Sept. 23, 2019), https://www.wsj.com/articles/indonesia-to-fault-737-max-design-u-s-oversight-in-lion-air-crash-report-11569185664.

Andy Pasztor, *Boeing Is Urged to Rethink Safety Tests*, WALL ST. J., Sept. 27, 2019, at 1.

Andy Pasztor, *Boeing Workers Made Light of MAX Safety*, WALL ST. J., Jan. 10, 2020, at 1.

David Pinsen, *Boeing's 737 Max: An Airplane "Designed By Clowns Supervised by Monkeys"*, SEEKING ALPHA (Jan. 20, 2020), https://seekingalpha.com/article/4316381-go3intw-737-max-airplane-designed-clowns-superised-monkeys.

C.K. Prahalad, *The Blinders of Dominant Logic*, 37(2) LONG RANGE PLANNING 171 (2004).

C.K. Prahalad & Richard A. Bettis, *The Dominant Logic: A New Linkage Between Diversity and Performance*, 7 STRATEGIC MGMT. J. 485 (1986).

PETER SENGE, THE FIFTH DISCIPLINE (1990).

Alison Sider & Andrew Tangel, *Boeing Omitted MAX Safeguards*, WALL. ST. J., Sept. 30, 2019, at 1.

ADAM SMITH, THE THEORY OF MORAL SENTIMENTS (1759).

William H. Starbuck & Bo Hedberg, *Saving an Organization from a Stagnating Environment*, 2 STRATEGY + STRUCTURE = PERFORMANCE 45 (1977).

GILLIAN TETT, THE SILO EFFECT, ch. 2 (2015).

PATRICIA H. THORNTON, MARKETS FROM CULTURE 12–13 (2004).

Maureen Tkacik, *Crash Course: How Boeing's Managerial Revolution Created the 737 Max Disaster*, NEW REPUBLIC, Sept. 18, 2019, at 1.

The 21st Century Jet: The Building of the Boeing 777 (1996), https://www.youtube.com/watch?v=0oyWZjdXxlw.

KARL E. WEICK, SENSEMAKING IN ORGANIZATIONS (1995).

PATRICIA H. WERHANE, MORAL IMAGINATION AND MANAGEMENT DECISION-MAKING (1999).

Patricia H. Werhane, *A Place for Philosophers in Applied Ethics and the Role of Moral Reasoning in Moral Imagination: A Response to Richard Rorty*, 16 BUS. ETHICS Q. 401 (2007).

Patricia H. Werhane, *Embedded Leadership*, *in* LEADERSHIP IN THE 21ST CENTURY (Joanne Ciulla ed., forthcoming).

PATRICIA H. WERHANE ET AL., OBSTACLES TO ETHICAL DECISION-MAKING (2013).

PART V

CONCLUSION

17

Strange Bedfellows? Representative Democracy and Academic Engagement with the Defense Industry

Steven L. Schooner and Evan Matsuda

1. Introduction: Gee, This Seems Important

"What gets measured gets managed" is a popular mantra among government performance management advocates.[1] In representative democracy, the converse might be "out of sight, out of mind." How did the United States come to be a government, originally created to be responsive to the will of its people, that boasts the world's most powerful military, spends more scarce resources on its military than any other, and exports the most kinetic capacity? How can such a public *not* study, research, analyze, think, and talk about the ethical aspects of its defense industry?

2. Ms. Frizzle Was Right: Question Everything

Get messy, take chances, make mistakes![2]

In his iconic piece, *Lighthouse No Good*,[3] William Prosser chronicled an intriguing, if slightly disorienting, career in legal education. Prosser begins:

[1] For an accessible example of the literature, *see* KATHERINE BARRETT & RICHARD GREENE, MAKING GOVERNMENT WORK: THE PROMISES AND PITFALLS OF PERFORMANCE-INFORMED MANAGEMENT (2020). For a critique of the mantra, *see* John Kamensky, *Does Performance Matter?*, IBM CTR. FOR BUS. GOV'T (Mar. 28, 2016) (citing Ed Gerrish, *The Impact of Performance Management in Public Organizations: A Meta-Analysis*, 76 PUB. ADMIN. REV. 48 (2015)), https://www.businessofgovernment.org/blog/does-performance-matter.

[2] Ms. Frizzle, voiced by the incomparable Lily Tomlin. *The Magic School Bus* (Scholastic 1994–1997).

[3] William L. Prosser, *Lighthouse No Good*, 1 J. LEGAL EDUC. 257, 257 (1948) (recounting a quotation reportedly "spoken by a West Coast Indian, sitting on a rock and looking out to sea"). When one of us left his procurement policy job to become a full-time academic, his spouse, who had previously joined the legal academy, recommended the Prosser piece. Regardless of whether or not either of us understood the piece, it did make us think.

Steven L. Schooner and Evan Matsuda, *Strange Bedfellows? Representative Democracy and Academic Engagement with the Defense Industry* In: *Ethical Dilemmas in the Global Defense Industry*. Edited by: Daniel Schoeni and Tobias Vestner, Oxford University Press. © Daniel Schoeni and Tobias Vestner 2023. DOI: 10.1093/oso/9780190675813.003.0018

Lighthouse, him no good for fog.
Lighthouse, him whistle, him blow,
him ring bell, him flash light, him raise hell;
but fog come in just the same.

He then meanders his way to an unnerving epiphany, in which an aging, truthful professor responds to the query: "How *do* you teach law?" as he was himself answered so many years before: "I don't know. None of us knows."[4]

But experience, at a minimum, reveals how *not* to teach law. For example, when teaching issues related to defense acquisition, government contracts, and the policies that animate "the business of government," it is a fool's errand to expect students to learn all of the relevant rules. Not only are there far too many, but Congress can—and frequently does—change (or supplement or delete or replace) them. Conversely, students benefit enormously if they learn how to interpret and implement rules. And they most rapidly ascend the learning curve if they can identify and understand the underlying policies that animate the rules.

This book offers students, the academy, defense industry professionals, and policymakers a wonderful opportunity to question many things we take for granted about the defense industry. Focusing on the underlying policies, and asking the *why* question, rather than simply *how* or *what*, is a valuable exercise because the military enterprise, the defense industry, and the market that binds private sector contractors with government customers are sprawling, impenetrable to the uninitiated, overwhelming to the casual observer, and riddled with inconsistent policies. For example, in our classrooms, students learn that:

- On one hand, statute and regulation demand that government contractors maintain complex, sophisticated, and costly compliance regimes. On the other hand, Congress mandates that nearly a quarter of all procurement dollars be funneled to small businesses that frequently lack the resources to establish effective compliance programs or the wherewithal to appreciate the risk of doing business without them.[5]

[4] *Id.* at 264 (emphasis added).

[5] *See generally* FAR Subpart 9.1 for the premise that the government should only do business with "responsible" contractors and Subpart 9.4, which discusses debarment, suspension, and ineligibility. Not surprisingly, a generation of empirical data demonstrates that, while large, important contractors are almost never blacklisted or excluded from competing for government work, staggering numbers of small (and, apparently, dispensable) small businesses are routinely suspended, proposed for debarment, and debarred. In Chapter 14 of this volume, Christopher R. Yukins eloquently demonstrates this asymmetry: "[A] firm without an effective compliance system in place . . . is left exposed to potentially disastrous risks, both of substantive violations *and* of failing to make the mandated disclosure of those violations. In sum, the mandatory disclosure rule *exacerbates* the competitive disadvantages borne by small and medium-sized enterprises." Yukins at 395. In Chapter 15 of this volume, Jessica Tillipman and Vijaya Surampudi remind us that, while some of these disparities can be reduced, it is unrealistic to assume them away: "Large contractors make significant investments in their ethics and compliance programs, and some view their programs as proprietary and confidential. Many

- The primary regulatory guidance makes clear that "[b]oth the Government and contractors should be concerned with profit as a motivator of efficient and effective contract performance."[6] However, congressional rhetoric and long-standing norms celebrate *minimizing* contractor profit, and contractors supporting the military in the battlefield are described pejoratively as "profiteers."[7]
- It is government policy to consolidate its purchasing requirements to achieve the benefits of economies of scale, but at the same time it is prohibited by law to aggregate or consolidate or "bundle" purchases that would make it impossible for small business to compete for the government's business.[8]

Complexity is a given in the defense industry,[9] and that complexity gives rise to fascinating, frustrating, difficult, and nuanced questions. But complexity and

contractors fear that competitors will exploit this information if they share it publicly. Yet by depriving small businesses access to this information and resources, the large contractors may ultimately be harmed if the suppliers suffer from compliance deficiencies or failures." Tillipman & Surampudi at 424; *see also infra* text accompanying notes 61–63 regarding these compliance programs.

6 FAR 15.404-4(a)(3). Many find this medicine difficult to swallow. For example, in Chapter 1 of this volume, Tobias Vestner asserts that "contribution to national security by the defense industry becomes a serious ethical issue because of its product: weapons and military technologies are tools to kill people. Making profits from this activity is problematic as a matter of principle." Vestner at 38. Putting aside how this perspective might apply to the (admittedly dubious) ethics of the National Rifle Association and its members, including the domestic handgun and rifle manufacturers, which are beyond the scope of this chapter and book, severing the profit motive from defense contracting feels analogous to the increasingly quaint aspiration that the government maintain a monopoly over the use of force but, alas, runs contrary to the conventional incentives underlying outsourcing, reliance on the private sector and, ultimately, capitalism.

7 Indeed, for nearly a quarter of the twentieth century, Congress created and sustained a "Renegotiation Board," which retroactively clawed back "excessive" contractor profits. The board plied its trade from 1951 until 1979. *Senate Vote Means End of Renegotiation Board*, N.Y. Times (Apr. 3, 1979), https://www.nytimes.com/1979/04/03/archives/senate-vote-means-end-of-renegotiation-board.html; Renegotiation Board—Reporting Requirement (50 U.S.C. App. § 1215)—Effect of Absence of an Appropriation—Repeals by Implication, 3 Op. O.L.C. 318 (1979), https://www.justice.gov/file/22096/download. *See also* Tobias Vestner's Chapter 1 riff on defense contractor profits, *supra* note 6. Although the rationale for this phenomenon is beyond the scope of this chapter, we would be remiss if we failed to mention than many significant government contractors—for example, most academic institutions—are not-for-profit entities.

8 *See, e.g.*, FAR 2.101 (defining "bundling" as "a subset of consolidation that combines two or more requirements for supplies or services, previously provided or performed under separate smaller contracts . . . into a solicitation for a single contract . . . or . . . order that is likely to be unsuitable for award to a small business concern"). *But see* FAR 7.107-2 ("Consolidation may provide substantial benefits to the Government.").

9 Indeed, we might fill another book with debate surrounding the definition and scope of "the defense industry." Tobias Vestner, in Chapter 1 of this volume, helpfully informs a potential, thematic definition by focusing on the defense industry's contribution to national security. We gravitate toward (and write in the context of) a broad and inclusive definition of the terms "military industrial base" or "defense industrial base sector," the latter of which "provides products *and services* that are essential to mobilize, deploy, and sustain military operations." *Critical Infrastructure Sectors*, Cybersecurity & Infrastructure Sec. Agency (emphasis added), https://www.cisa.gov/defense-industrial-base-sector (last visited Jan. 9, 2022); *see also* Heidi M. Peters, Cong. Rsch. Serv., IF10548, Defense Primer: U.S. Defense Industrial Base (2021), https://crsreports.congress.gov/

conflicting priorities afford no justification for avoiding academic discourse. To the contrary, when the U.S. government maintains such a massive kinetic arsenal, boasts the world's largest military budget, sustains the world's largest defense industry, and leads the world in arms exports,[10] the policy puzzles that pervade nearly every aspect of the defense industry take on even greater import. It would be imprudent to ignore such an impactful sector of the economy.[11]

Moreover, as Daniel Schoeni and Tobias Vestner remind in their *Introduction*, the ethical issues that permeate the defense industry and stimulate thinking in this volume are like "mowing the grass"; they "require our constant vigilance."[12] The hard work and thought-provoking issues are endless. For these reasons, we are flummoxed when academic institutions attempt to keep the defense industry not just at arm's length but out of reach and out of mind. Or, in other words, Prosser's lighthouse might fail to burn away the fog, but it still reveals dangers to passing ships and, in so doing, serves a valuable purpose.

For the post–Cold War generation, Eisenhower's familiar Military Industrial Complex warning[13] evolved from harbinger to gospel. Academic opinion, informed by congressional oversight hearings, Government Accountability Office (GAO) and Inspector General (IG) reports, Department of Justice (DoJ) press releases, and media coverage, tended to counsel distance and detachment regarding the defense industry[14] long before the popularity of "cancel

product/pdf/IF/IF10548/10 (explaining that DoD "relies on a wide-ranging and complex industrial base for the products *and services* that enable the Department's warfighting capabilities" and that "[d]efinitions of what this industrial base encompasses vary in scope and emphasis" (emphasis added)). CRS further explains: "[T]hese entities provide a wide range of products and services to the DOD, encompassing everything from complex platforms unique to the military (e.g., aircraft carriers) and highly specialized services (such as launching military satellites), to all kinds of commercial products (e.g., laptop computers and semiconductors) and routine services (e.g., information technology (IT) support)." *Id.*

This broad and inclusive definition is critical to this book's themes to the extent that: (1) for decades, defense procurement of services has significantly exceeded purchases of goods or supplies, and (2) the modern realities of outsourced defense—and the integration of, and reliance upon, service contractors in the battlespace—have dramatically changed everything from how the military projects lethality to the nature of "sacrifice" and who makes "the ultimate sacrifice." *See, e.g., infra* text accompanying notes 18, 50, 52, 88–89.

[10] "The United States now spends more on defense than the next 11 spenders combined." HARVEY M. SAPOLSKY, EUGENE GHOLZ & CAITLIN TALMADGE, U.S DEFENSE POLITICS: THE ORIGINS OF NATIONAL SECURITY 5 (4th ed. 2021); *see also 2021 Power Rankings*, U.S. NEWS & WORLD REP., https://www.usnews.com/news/best-countries/power-rankings (last visited Aug. 22, 2021); Chiara Vercellone, *Who Were the Largest Major Arms Exporters in the Last 5 Years?*, DEF. NEWS (Mar. 9, 2020), https://www.defensenews.com/2020/03/09/who-were-the-largest-major-arms-exporters-in-the-last-5-years.

[11] *See generally infra* text accompanying note 35.

[12] Schoeni & Vestner at 3.

[13] Dwight D. Eisenhower, *Farewell Radio and Television Address to the American People (Jan. 17, 1961)*, *in* PUBLIC PAPERS OF THE PRESIDENT OF THE UNITED STATES: DWIGHT D. EISENHOWER 1960–61, at 1035 (1961).

[14] During the Vietnam era, colleges and universities drove ROTC programs off campus. *See* Jean Marbella, *ROTC Resurgent on College Campuses Where Once Scorned*, BALT. SUN (Nov. 18, 2001),

culture."[15] Historical analogies to the tobacco industry come to mind, just as, looking ahead, we expect the academy to increasingly distance and divest itself from the fossil fuel industry.[16]

Given the importance of the defense industry to so many aspects of our lives, this chapter applauds and encourages academic engagement with the defense industry and robust discussion of, inter alia, the industry's composition, behavior, economic footprint and impact (and, in that context, incentives and disincentives), and role (whether as the state's business partner or, all too often, as a state actor).[17] It is not just that these issues are ripe for debate or that they

https://www.baltimoresun.com/news/bs-xpm-2001-11-18-0111180052-story.html ("Many of the nation's elite universities, including Harvard, Yale, Columbia and Stanford, kicked ROTC off their campuses in protest of the Vietnam War."); Elizabeth Phelan, *"A Watershed Moment": Reflecting on the Burning of the ROTC Air Force Building—50 Years Later*, Student Life (May 5, 2020), https://www.studlife.com/scene/2020/05/05/a-watershed-moment-reflecting-on-the-burning-of-the-rotc-air-force-building-50-years-later. Indeed, when one of us arrived at Rice University in the 1970s courtesy of an Army ROTC scholarship, he was surprised to find the ROTC detachment housed in a concrete bunker underneath the Central Kitchen on the edge of campus. A generation later, for different reasons, many law schools barred military (Judge Advocate General Corps) recruiters from campus. *See generally* Doug Lederman, *Wrangling over Military Recruiting*, Inside Higher Ed (Feb. 3, 2005), https://www.insidehighered.com/news/2005/02/03/wrangling-over-military-recruiting.

[15] In reviewing our chapter, one of this volume's editors, Tobias Vestner, raised the specter of on-campus cancel culture. *See, e.g.*, Conor Friedersdorf, *The Destructiveness of Call-Out Culture on Campus*, Atlantic (May 8, 2017), https://www.theatlantic.com/politics/archive/2017/05/call-out-culture-is-stressing-out-college-students/524679; Pippa Norris, *Cancel Culture: Myth or Reality?*, Pol. Stud., July 16, 2021, at 1, https://journals-sagepub-com.proxygw.wrlc.org/doi/pdf/10.1177/00323217211037023 ("The evidence suggests that the cancel culture is not simply a rhetorical myth; scholars may be less willing to speak up to their moral beliefs if they believe their views are not widely shared by colleagues . . . ."). While we consider the procedural aspects of advocacy, disagreement, and debate, including the innumerable forms of protest, beyond the scope of this chapter, we recognize the concern. In that context, we hope that the strength of our work and, indeed, this book, is measured by its merits rather than its proponents' identities. To that end, we agree with Vestner that, "in the context of ethical dilemmas, just because someone believes [themselves] to be right (and the other to be wrong) does not mean that the person is objectively right. . . . [I]f we lose our ability to debate and respect each other's opinion, we lose what it takes for a well-functioning democracy." Our agreement, however, extends only to "informed opinions." In discussing critically important issues related to defense, or for that matter climate change or responses to a global pandemic, we see more harm than good in elevating, promoting, respecting, or even tolerating "opinions" that deny science, ignore facts, or derive exclusively from unfounded, easily debunked conspiracy theories. *See, e.g.*, Andy Norman, *The Cause of America's Post-Truth Predicament*, Sci. Am. (May 18, 2021), https://www.scientificamerican.com/article/the-cause-of-americas-post-truth-predicament ("When we affirm each other's 'right' to believe things—even things that fly in the face of evidence—we essentially decouple critical thinking and belief revision. This damages the norm that keeps minds tethered to reality. . . . [W]e must grasp that bad ideas *are* mind-parasites—entities that can proliferate and harm the very minds that host them. In fact, they can lay waste to delusion-tolerant cultures.").

[16] "The most successful instance of higher ed divestment arguably occurred during South African apartheid, . . . Today, colleges and universities face pressure to divest on a number of hot button issues, with recent efforts focused notably on fossil fuels and tobacco." Roger Riddell, *Can Higher Ed Really Affect Change Through Divestment?*, Higher Ed Dive (May 29, 2014), https://www.highereddive.com/news/can-higher-ed-really-affect-change-through-divestment/265675.

[17] No doubt, our biases are informed by our location (and a professional career, for one of us) in Washington, D.C. The business of government—and defense or, more broadly, national security—is fertile ground for research and study. Our classrooms and programming are enriched by connections to the national security and intelligence communities, the military, and the federal government in

provide innumerable research opportunities. Rather, they are a critically important component of the kind of practical knowledge that citizenship in a representative democracy requires. Far too many caricatures of a unitary military industrial base and its motivations are uninformed, inaccurate, and unhelpful. Among other things, unlike cigarettes, sugar-saturated carbonated beverages, and gasoline, national defense is critical to national security, public safety, and, indeed, our very existence as a nation-state. Meanwhile, we need to acknowledge the evolution of the "industry"—from weapons manufacturing to service providers[18]—and reimagine the critical role the academy can play in crafting the modern defense industry's behaviors, norms, standards, aspirations, and, ultimately, ethics.

3. A Sumptuous Menu

The universe of important, thought-provoking ethical issues inherent throughout the defense industry merits discussion and study. Nonetheless, in teaching law and policy, it is easy for ethics to recede to the background. But once you open and walk through that door, the path skews to labyrinthian. Where does one even begin? Like perspectives, it probably depends upon how you categorize ethics.

If "national security" is your starting point, *teleological* ethics grounded in maintaining the state—or, more broadly, keeping the marauding hordes at

general. Indeed, the epicenter of all things defense is housed in the world's largest office building, just across the Potomac River and a mere three METRO stops away. *Pentagon Facts*, U.S. Dep't of Def., https://pentagontours.osd.mil/Tours/facts.html; Michaila Hancock, *Pentagon: The World's Largest Office Building—In Infographics*, Architect's J. (Aug. 27, 2015), https://www.architectsjournal.co.uk/news/pentagon-the-worlds-largest-office-building-in-infographics.

[18] Today's "defense industry" would be unrecognizable to World War–, Korea-, and even Vietnam-era veterans, policy officials, and academics. For example, the Federal Acquisition Regulation, promulgated in 1984, proceeds from the assumption that federal procurement is dominated by supplies or goods, treating services as a poorly regulated afterthought (and primarily focusing on labor relations). *See generally* 48 C.F.R. Today, services dominate. Indeed, service providers Leidos, L-3, and Honeywell were recently listed among the world's twenty largest defense contractors. Samuel Stebbins & Evan Comen, *Military Spending: 20 Companies Profiting the Most from War*, USA Today (Feb. 21, 2019), https://www.usatoday.com/story/money/2019/02/21/military-spending-defense-contractors-profiting-from-war-weapons-sales/39092315. More broadly, "[d]ollars spent on services contracts grew steadily throughout the 1990s . . . until dipping slightly in 2008. Since then, . . . service contract spending rose in relation to overall DoD expenditures as spending on products decreased." Gregory Sanders et al., *Defense Contract Trends: U.S. Department of Defense Contract Spending and the Supporting Industrial Base*, Ctr. for Strategic & Int'l Stud. 8 (2011), https://www.csis.org/analysis/defense-contract-trends-0; *see also infra* notes 50, 52; Richard L. Dunn, *Defense Industry Needs New Way of Doing Business*, Nat'l Def. (Nov. 6, 2000), https://www.nationaldefensemagazine.org/articles/2020/11/6/defense-industry-needs-new-way-of-doing-business. *See also supra* note 9.

bay—is an end that justifies dramatic means.[19] The consequences of failing to fulfill the *duty* to defend the state dominate, suggesting a utilitarianism that excuses much (that, for example, a pacifist would neither condone nor stomach). For a simple litmus test, consider the U.S. government's resort to nuclear weapons to accelerate the end of World War II.[20] To what lengths can one go to confront that which is evil? Whether this starts us down the slippery slope to economics and cost-benefit analysis is beyond the scope of this chapter. We know we all have our limits, but why? And where, with regard to our ethics or values, do we draw the line?[21]

For better or worse, it seems that Kant held sway in one of our superficial college philosophy courses, which, in hazy recollection, centered on *deontological* theories of ethics, universal moral laws, categorical imperatives, and what often seemed to be more binary questions of right versus wrong. Sure, lying is bad, and telling the truth is good, but that "golden rule" of "do unto others as you would have them do unto you" offered a comfortable touchstone or centering device. How that can be reconciled with the evolution (or, increasingly, devolution) of capitalism's winner-take-all social construct, again, exceeds this chapter's scope.

We concede that *virtue*-based ethics, focusing primarily on moral character, seem too fluid to provide clarity or guidance. As much as we find the aspiration of the virtuous life appealing—who would not value self-control, moderation, intelligence, pursuit of knowledge, courage, and justice?—the thread frays once cleanliness or frugality or punctuality came into play. Sure, it is rude to make others wait, but we are confident that most people would distinguish that from other virtues that seem to carry greater moral weight. And let us not forget that, from the Homeric tradition to modern-day recruiting, military service (and

19 "Although modern Americans debate the legitimacy of many other ways that government may also contribute to the commonwealth, *essentially everyone agrees that providing for the common defense is its first obligation*. . . . But in practice the national interest is a very slippery concept, and different people with different personal values define the national interest in different ways." SAPOLSKY ET AL., *supra* note 10, at 1 (emphasis added).

20 If you happen to visit Albuquerque, New Mexico, we strongly recommend the National Museum of Nuclear Science & History and its powerful Hiroshima and Nagasaki exhibit. *Hiroshima and Nagasaki Exhibit*, NAT'L MUSEUM OF NUCLEAR SCI. & HIST., https://www.nuclearmuseum.org/see/exhibits/hiroshima-and-nagasaki (last visited Jan. 9, 2022).

21 Anecdotes can be powerful and helpful, but, ultimately, they remain, well, anecdotal. History will reflect that the U.S. Central Intelligence Agency (CIA) should not have paid Dr. Bruce Jessen and Dr. James Mitchell more than $81 million to devise rather brutal interrogation techniques, subsequently deemed to be illegal torture, yet, in pursuit of their perceived mission at the time, the CIA appeared to fully embrace the techniques. *See generally* Sheri Fink, *Settlement Reached in C.I.A. Torture Case*, N.Y. TIMES (Aug. 17, 2017), https://www.nytimes.com/2017/08/17/us/cia-torture-lawsuit-settlement.html. Still, anecdotes are helpful in discussing values. "The question . . . is a values question rather than a question with a technically 'correct' answer. . . . [H]ow much 'risk' should Americans tolerate, and how should they compare the importance of one risk (say, of a terrorist act against the United States) to another . . . ? . . . [T]he answer is more subjective than scientific." SAPOLSKY ET AL., *supra* note 10, at 12.

martial skill, nay excellence) is about as virtuous as it gets. Let us not confuse morality with character.

In another time, one might have expected America's two-decade military engagement in Afghanistan[22] to generate a relentless focus on the ethics surrounding (and the morality of) the military's role abroad at some point *prior* to the August 2021 withdrawal that dramatically thrust the conflict back into the public spotlight.[23] Nearly a half-century since the final military draft,[24] teenagers register with the U.S. Selective Service System without anxiety, and students—like most of the public today—are further distanced from military service and all things defense-related than at any time in the nation's history.[25] Indeed, college and graduate students today, the offspring and grandchildren of veterans of (or those who avoided service during) dubious military actions in Korea and Vietnam, grew up with little reason to pay attention to, understand, or ultimately *care* about the nation's "forever wars" in Afghanistan and Iraq. At the same time, current events—and the daily act of reading the news—offer frequent illustrations of the difference between what is right and wrong, what is legal and illegal,[26] or, in practice, what some people can and do get away with,[27] all of which provides valuable context for asking hard questions in the classroom.

[22] "[T]he war [in Afghanistan] has run more than 19 years, longer than World War I, World War II and the Korean War combined." *America's Longest War: A Visual History of 19 Years in Afghanistan*, WALL ST. J. (Apr. 18, 2021), https://www.wsj.com/articles/us-longest-war-afghanistan-11583010024.

[23] *See also infra* note 89.

[24] *Historical Timeline*, SELECTIVE SERV. SYS., https://www.sss.gov/history-and-records/timeline (last visited Jan. 9, 2022) ("The last man inducted entered the Army on June 30, 1973.").

[25] *See* David Zucchino & David S. Cloud, *Special Report: U.S. Military and Civilians Are Increasingly Divided*, L.A. TIMES (May 23, 2015), https://www.latimes.com/nation/la-na-warrior-main-20150524-story.html ("Most of the country has experienced little, if any, personal impact from the longest era of war in U.S. history."); Bruce Drake, *On Memorial Day, Public Pride in Veterans, but at a Distance*, PEW RSCH. CTR. (May 24, 2013), https://www.pewresearch.org/fact-tank/2013/05/24/on-memorial-day-public-pride-in-veterans-but-at-a-distance-2 ("[T]he public that will be observing [Memorial Day] is also one increasingly disconnected from the military and the wars it fought since 2001 compared to those who lived through the wars of 20th century."); Steven Aftergood, *The Costs of War: Obstacles to Public Understanding*, FED'N OF AM. SCIENTISTS (Nov. 14, 2018), https://fas.org/sgp/eprint/costs.pdf ("[P]ublic awareness of U.S. military operations [has been] diminished or eliminated rather than heightened. . . . '[F]eedback loops' that are at the heart of deliberative democracy [have been] disabled. The public is not being forced, as it should be, to make difficult choices among competing priorities.").

[26] Before law school, as an undergraduate, one of us was exposed to many related issues through ROTC or "military science" classes. Although the textbook spoke of "humane treatment of noncombatants," "human treatment of PW [or prisoners of war]," "humane treatment of civilians," and "criminal orders and individual responsibility" as legal mandates, the text also emphasized "the unwritten laws" also "known as the customary law of war[, the general purpose of which] . . . is to limit the suffering or destruction to military targets and to provide humane treatment for all persons who are taken out of the fight." *See generally* ROTCM 145-85, DEP'T OF ARMY, ROTC MANUAL, FUNDAMENTALS OF MILITARY LAW 82–104 (Oct. 1980). Even the hypotheticals (such as "the question of what to do if it seems to be a situation of 'my life or his' ") have nicely stood the test of time. *Id.* at 100.

[27] "The wealthy and powerful rarely go to jail, and, when they do, it is for relatively brief stays at 'Club Fed.' . . . The rich and the powerful become richer and more powerful, while the public loses trust in our institutions. The accumulation of wealth and power is divorced from the means and the

So, yes, at times we struggle with incorporating the complex world of *ethics*, morality, and values into the work of teaching, studying, discussing, and analyzing the defense industry. In the classroom, the far more mundane topic of *compliance*—discussed at length in several of the preceding chapters—resonates more clearly. No doubt, despite its lofty aspirations, compliance, upon closer examination, is more rule-based than ethics. In that context, Philip M. Nichols, in Chapter 9, makes a compelling case for why this book's work is so important:

> Legal responsibility . . . differs from moral duty. . . . [Distinguishing what is legal and what is moral] is not a frivolous exercise. Exploring the moral responsibility of defense firms provides insights into the relationship between those firms and the rest of society, into the nature of defense markets, and into justifications for anti-corruption legal regimes. . . .
>
> . . . [In that context, with its unique opportunities for corruption, most agree that] firms owe primary duties to society at large and to potential victims of harm caused by the weapons and weapon systems that they sell. . . . Society allows defense industry firms to accrue revenue for investors within this distorted market, but in exchange for society's forbearance, these firms must respect the basic human right to be safe.[28]

cost of that wealth generation, such as public ills ranging from degraded air and water quality, food poisoning, inflated consumer prices, reduced pension funds, opioid addition, poverty, social stratification and even suicide." Steven L. Schooner, *We Need to Talk About Corruption*, GOV'T EXEC. (Sept. 29, 2020) (reviewing JENNIFER TAUB, BIG DIRTY MONEY: THE SHOCKING INJUSTICE AND UNSEEN COST OF WHITE COLLAR CRIME (2020)), https://www.govexec.com/management/2020/09/we-need-talk-about-corruption/168857. The four years of the Trump administration introduced the American public to term "kleptocracy" and generated robust discussion of a never-ending succession of issues related to public service ethics. *See generally* SARAH KENDZIOR, HIDING IN PLAIN SIGHT: THE INVENTION OF DONALD TRUMP AND THE EROSION OF AMERICA (2020). Also, for a tip of the iceberg anecdote, *see* Steven L. Schooner, Kathleen Clark & Scott Amey, *Suspend the Trump Organization from Doing Business with Government*, GOV'T EXEC. (Jan. 27, 2020), https://www.govexec.com/management/2020/01/viewpoint-suspend-trump-organization-doing-business-government/162672. *See also* Letter from Noah Bookbinder, President, Citizens for Resp. & Ethics, et al., to Bill Schmidt, Suspension & Debarment Off., Gen. Servs. Admin., et al. (Oct. 12, 2021), https://www.citizensforethics.org/wp-content/uploads/2021/10/2021-10-12-Trump-Organization-Suspension-Referral.pdf ("[A]gencies routinely suspend contractors based on allegations of wrongdoing similar to (or less egregious than) those facing the Trump Organization, even when no criminal charges are pending.").

[28] Nichols at 239–40. As Jeffrey Biller and Timothy Goines eloquently explain in Chapter 7 of this volume, our digital livelihoods mean that our most fundamental understanding of the scope of human rights continues to evolve—in this case, rather rapidly. For a host of reasons, today, "digital data is a crucial component of most aspects of modern life and worthy of the highest levels of protection that [international humanitarian law] can provide." Biller & Goines at 206. For better or worse, one of the most challenging, vexing, and controversial topics in modern defense acquisition is the Defense Department's highly scrutinized effort to manage private sector cybersecurity. *See generally* U.S. GOV'T ACCOUNTABILITY OFF., GAO-22-104679, DEFENSE CONTRACTOR CYBERSECURITY: STAKEHOLDER COMMUNICATION AND PERFORMANCE GOALS COULD IMPROVE CERTIFICATION FRAMEWORK (2021), https://www.gao.gov/assets/gao-22-104679.pdf ("DOD Has Not Met Initial Implementation Goals

Maybe, as Richard W. Painter suggests in Chapter 3, before we discuss the responsibilities of defense contractors to comply with the U.S. arms export regime and ensure that the weapons they export meet the purchaser's quality control standards, we need to ask more fundamental questions: Is there a clear ethical or moral justification for selling powerful weapons abroad? If foreign military sales in the name of joint defense are justified, do the reciprocal barter and trade aspects (or offsets[29]) dilute the moral imperative?[30]

These economic or budgetary issues seem less value laden than the thorny issues associated with arms proliferation,[31] particularly when the consumer—no

or Sufficiently Communicated Key Decisions to Industry"); HEIDI M. PETERS, CONG. RSCH. SERV., R46643, DEFENSE ACQUISITIONS: DOD'S CYBERSECURITY MATURITY MODEL CERTIFICATION FRAMEWORK (2020) https://crsreports.congress.gov/product/pdf/R/R46643/2 (acknowledging criticism that, among other things, (1) "DOD efforts to mitigate cybersecurity risks and vulnerabilities [have been] fragmentary and reactive to specific issues or emerging concerns, with the potential to create 'confusion' within the defense industrial base as contractors attempt to meet 'ever-changing' requirements seen by some within the industry as costly and overly burdensome," and (2) "the current system, which largely turns on self-reporting . . . , has 'demonstrably failed' ").

[29] ROBERT WOODARD, BUREAU OF INDUS. & SEC., DEP'T OF COM., OFFSETS IN DEFENSE TRADE—FREQUENTLY ASKED QUESTIONS (2017), https://www.bis.doc.gov/index.php/documents/pdfs/1677-offsets-in-defense-trade-faqs-final/file; *see also* Arms Export Control Act, 22 U.S.C. § 2751, *et seq.*; International Traffic in Arms Regulations, 22 C.F.R. §§ 120–130; DFARS Subpart 225.73. *See also* Daniel Schoeni's thoughtful exposition in Chapter 12 of this volume on defense offsets, "a subject that has been presumed guilty without receiving a fair appraisal." Schoeni at 339. We find comfort in Schoeni's concession that "the ethical objections [to offsets] made thus far lack force," which "is not to say that ethical [or moral] hazards do not exist," though "what has been written has often been too dismissive." *Id.* at 340. Ultimately, however, the fact that offsets are not "an inherently corrupt practice" does little to dislodge the traditionally perceived yoke of moral hazard. *Id.* at 361.

[30] Although C. Edward Peartree, in Chapter 4 of this volume, adds to the chorus suggesting that the U.S. government "is justifiably proud of its reputation as the 'gold standard' of export controls"—a nod to a highly regulated or compliant set of transactions—it is easy to forget that, as a consumer, the U.S. Department of Defense enjoys reduced unit prices for many of its weapon systems because its vendors offer lower unit prices courtesy of the economies of scale associated with global arms sales. Peartree at 123. Yes, Peartree acknowledges that "[s]tates face continuous ethical dilemmas in their decisions whether or not to transfer arms." *Id.* But students will likely appreciate the oft-unstated but seemingly cynical bargain associated with permitting other states to directly and indirectly subsidize our weapons industry through arms proliferation. "Cost comparisons between [foreign military sales] and [direct commercial sales] are often not possible, . . . [but] the FMS sale will always benefit from the economies of scale and experience the U.S. government has with a system." *Foreign Military Sales FAQ*, DEF. SEC. COOP. AGENCY, https://www.dsca.mil/foreign-military-sales-faq (last visited Aug. 22, 2021). Yet at the same time, in Chapter 11 of this volume, Nancy Hite-Rubin starkly warns that "defense contractors face an ethical minefield when they seek lucrative contracts from less developed countries . . . [that represent] an important market that defense contractors must target to stay competitive." Hite-Rubin at 307. It is what it is: "[T]he global defense industry is propelled by demand from institutionally weak, developing nations." *Id.* And kudos to Michael Davis for acknowledging in Chapter 13 of this volume that "[m]uch of what the arms industry sells can be stolen, resold, transferred to another by capture, or otherwise 'diverted [into the wrong hands].'" Davis at 376.

[31] As Mark Pyman explains in Chapter 10 of this volume: "Tackling defense corruption is about much more than stopping dodgy commissions on arms sales. Civilians and soldiers die because of corruption in defense, insecurity rises, peace is compromised, and wars are extended." Pyman at 259.

matter how well aligned its interests—may be a less stable or, in the worst case, more aggressively hostile regime. As Nancy Hite-Rubin cautions in Chapter 11, arms sales do not exist in a vacuum: "The transfer of major arms into . . . politically risky markets creates major security concerns, as well as development concerns."[32]

Again, there is no shortage of ethical fodder for research and classroom banter. But do we risk a "whataboutism" response[33] when we focus on regulating or managing or marginally improving discrete aspects of the defense industry? Is it somehow wrong to do so without instead focusing exclusively on the overarching issue of whether our nation could exist (or even thrive) without a defense industry (or a less massive, expensive, expansive defense industry)?

4. Assume a Peaceful World . . .

Imagine there's no countries
It isn't hard to do
Nothing to kill or die for
And no religion, too
Imagine all the people
Livin' life in peace . . . .[34]

One of us vaguely recalls being amused the first time seeing the bumper sticker: *It Will Be a Great Day When Our Schools Get All the Money They Need and the Air Force Has to Hold a Bake Sale to Buy a Bomber.*[35] With time and experience in the

Moreover, while Pyman highlights the importance of "the drive and leadership of key individuals" to reform, the same can be said of the setbacks suffered, for example, when the head of Air Force procurement goes to jail or the president disregards and disrespects ethical statutes, regulations, policies, and norms. *See generally supra* note 27; *infra* note 49.

[32] Hite-Rubin at 306 (footnote omitted). While we appreciate Michael Davis's optimism, in Chapter 13 of this volume, that enhanced quality control—for example, safe landmines—serves the public interest and may be less "morally objectionable," we also appreciate his acknowledgement that "every artifact embedded in the technological system we call 'the military' is there to help the military do its job, which is (by definition) to kill, wound, or otherwise disable other human beings on a large scale or destroy property on a large scale, a morally dubious undertaking, especially if the regime directing the military is itself morally dubious." Davis at 375. To be fair, however, innumerable military institutions (such as the Coast Guard) and missions (such as humanitarian relief) alleviate suffering and avoid loss of life, but the underlying point's validity endures.

[33] *See* Danielle Kurtzleben, *Trump Embraces One of Russia's Favorite Propaganda Tactics—Whataboutism*, NPR (Mar. 17, 2017), https://www.npr.org/2017/03/17/520435073/trump-embraces-one-of-russias-favorite-propaganda-tactics-whataboutism (observing, "One big reason whataboutism is so attractive: it's a simple way to shrug off criticism or even responsibility for any wrongdoings.").

[34] John Lennon, *Imagine*, *on* IMAGINE (Apple Records 1971).

[35] Popular bumper sticker and poster, created between 1965 and 1980, attributed to Women's International League for Peace and Freedom. *It Will Be a Great Day When Our Schools Get All the*

industry, the powerful clarity of its message grew stronger, and the unflattering things it said about our priorities, our values, and, in this context, our ethics still gives cause for reflection.[36]

With special conviction for one of us in particular (as a veteran, and the son of a veteran currently resting in Arlington National Cemetery), we unapologetically affirm our desire to live in a peaceful world. And although the military and the defense industry funded—directly and indirectly—much of one of our lives,[37] we would still prefer to live in a state that did not spend such staggering sums of money, and far too much of its available capital, on the defense industry.

Even Switzerland, which is traditionally committed to (armed) neutrality and de facto protected by NATO member states, nevertheless invests in a large military where every male must serve as a reservist (and women may choose to serve). Across the pond, Costa Rica, often referred to as the Switzerland of Central America, does not maintain a standing military, but relies upon its police forces for what other states consider traditional or conventional defense. Moreover, while most states without armed forces are relatively small, with island states featuring prominently, many enjoy protection afforded by other states through formal and informal agreements.

Unfortunately, that peaceful world of bards and bumper stickers, desired by pacifists and, yes, soldiers, remains beyond our grasp. Nor do we expect to see the United States transformed into such a state in either of our lifetimes. The defense industry—and, for that matter, the military—*does* consume staggering sums of resources and *does* play a disproportionate role in the public policy space. We therefore cannot afford to focus solely on broader existential hypotheticals that might, if real, render this book's nuanced discussions irrelevant. At least at present, they are not real, so we have no choice but to walk the labyrinthian path and pay attention to the ethical complexities and peculiarities of the defense industry.

Money They Need and the Air Force Has to Hold a Bake Sale to Buy a Bomber, LIBR. OF CONG., https://www.loc.gov/resource/ds.13124 (last visited Jan. 9, 2022).

36 Paul Krugman, *The Bogus Bashing of Build Back Better*, N.Y. TIMES (Dec. 13, 2021), https://www.nytimes.com/2021/12/13/opinion/build-back-better.html (putting in context that "the bill's $1.75 trillion price tag is, on the surface, a lot of money. But that's spending over 10 years, which means that annual outlays would be far smaller than the $1.9 trillion rescue plan passed this year or, for that matter, the $768 billion annual defense bill the House passed [without flinching] last week.").

37 Schooner's father served on active duty in the military until Schooner was in college, which he attended on a full Army ROTC Scholarship. Even before college, he graduated from a Department of Defense high school in Europe, where he actively participated in Junior ROTC. His first (nontemporary) full-time job was as an officer in the U.S. Army, and he served in the Army Reserves for many years after leaving active duty. Much of his legal practice and, eventually, scholarship was dominated by defense contracting or defense acquisition. As one might say, with apologies to Minnie Minoso, Roberto Clemente, Sammy Sosa, and, of course, Chico Escuela, "the Army was very, very good to him."

5. If You're Gonna Fight, Win

In the spring of 1980, for the first time, one of us stepped out the door of a perfectly good airplane in flight without a care for the seemingly mundane but oh-so-critical topic of "quality assurance" in defense acquisition.[38] That moment resonated years later when reading about defense contracts for "man-rated items," so designated "because the lives of people are at risk in an emergency in the event of a failure of that system."[39] Exiting the relative safety of an inflight aircraft, a soldier enjoys neither the luxury nor the opportunity to formally express her fervent hope, as an "end user," that the contracting officer[40] was not satisfied with (an otherwise impressive) 95 percent, or even 99 percent, success rate in parachute testing.

It is easy to forget about the end user—the consumer of what the defense acquisition system delivers to the warfighter—at the proverbial tip of the spear. But pause for a moment and remember that, for the parent or spouse or relative of such an end user, the defense industry looks quite different; indeed, the concept of "customer satisfaction" takes on a whole new meaning. Consider, then, the juxtaposition in which the Iraqi population, and, over time, the American public, came to revile the name Blackwater, while innumerable State Department officials, members of Congress, and others returned home to their loved ones thankful for and appreciative of Blackwater's (admittedly heavy-handed and risk-averse) protection.[41] All of which brings to mind the sublime proverb: *Until the Lion writes history, the tale of the hunt will always glorify the hunter.*[42]

So long as we maintain a military, and until we lay down our arms, this perspective—the soldier's perspective—matters. In government contracting policy discussions, we like to emphasize the "end user," and defense acquisition experts refer to "the warfighter" as the ultimate customer. Is that perspective the highest ethical imperative? In Chapter 5 of this volume, Thomas E. Ayres, Kevin

[38] *See, e.g.*, FAR Part 46, 48 C.F.R. 46; John Cibinic, Jr., James F. Nagle & Ralph C. Nash, Jr., Administration of Government Contracts 697–790 (5th ed. 2016).

[39] Appeal of Astro Dynamics, Inc., ASBCA No. 28381, 88-3 BCA para. 20,832 (1988).

[40] The contracting officer, a creature of statute and regulation, is the appointed official with authority to (among other things) bind the government in contract. *See generally* FAR 1.102-3; FAR Subpart 1.6. *See also* FAR 1.602-1 ("Contracting officers have authority to enter into, administer, or terminate contracts and make related determinations and findings.").

[41] "I think on balance we felt that . . . the protective security operation has been highly effective." Special Briefing with Patrick F. Kennedy, Ambassador, Dept' of State, on the Report of the Secretary of State's Panel on Personal Protective Services in Iraq (Oct. 23, 2007), https://2001-2009.state.gov/r/pa/prs/ps/2007/oct/94019.htm.

[42] *See, e.g.*, Annalisa Quinn, *Chinua Achebe and the Bravery of Lions*, NPR (Mar. 23, 2013), https://www.npr.org/sections/thetwo-way/2013/03/22/175046327/chinua-achebe-and-the-bravery-of-lions. In more concrete terms, " '[s]ilo mentality' is a widely occurring phenomenon wherein a profession . . . or an organization itself is so focused on their priorities or their expertise that they neglect or fail to perceive how those priorities affect or are affected by other professions, divisions . . . , or others in their industry." Patricia Werhane at 437.

Govern, and Michael W. Meier suggest that "no one longs for peace like the experienced soldier. But, when war comes, no one longs for superior technology and weapons like a soldier."[43] Indeed, they go so far as to posit that the laws of armed conflict do "not require a fair fight, nor [do they] prohibit the use of superior offensive or protective weaponry."[44] Is military superiority, in and of itself, a worthy ethical pursuit? For an armed combatant, or the relative of an armed combatant, that likely sounds like music to anxious ears. Until our military force becomes fully automated,[45] we cannot ignore this perspective.

6. Not Your Grandparents' (Nor Eisenhower's) Defense Industry

One of this volume's great contributions is the organized fashion in which it discretely analyzes many of the pathologies spawned by our long-standing military-industrial complex.[46] Yes, problems remain. But we have also seen real progress, ranging from industry cognizance and commitment to the evolution of compliance regimes, adoption of codes of conduct, and proliferation of voluntary disclosure systems.[47] At the same time, *some* of those problems simply are not as problematic as they might seem, and others cannot be laid entirely at the feet of the defense industry. Again, it is complicated.

[43] Ayres, Govern, & Meier at 152.

[44] *Id.* at 480. We concede being far less sanguine with the more extreme position staked out by Duncan MacIntosh in Chapter 2 of this volume: "[B]eing a wealthy enough culture to be able to buy the best, most expensive weapons tends to go hand in hand with being a morally better culture." MacIntosh, p. 48. For us, that is a logical, philosophical, and, in this context, ethical bridge too far.

[45] In Chapter 8 of this volume, Blake Hereth and Nicholas G. Evans draw attention to the exploding potential and promise (and potential ethical problems) of artificial intelligence and the future of, among other things, lethal autonomous weapon systems. Hereth & Evans at 217–19. During the prior generation, advancements in unmanned vehicles, remote piloting, and, increasingly, robotics drastically altered and animated a battlefield far different from prior experience. *See generally* Steven L. Schooner & Nathaniel Castellano, *Dawn of the Intercontinental Sniper: The Drone's Cascading Contribution to the Modern Battlefield's Complexity*, 8 J. Nat'l Sec. L. & Pol'y 321 (2016) (reviewing Richard Whittle, Predator: The Secret Origins of the Drone Revolution (2014)). Looking ahead, the range of potential issues is bounded only by our imaginations. *See, e.g.*, Erico Guizzo, *How Boston Dynamics Is Redefining Robot Agility*, IEEE Spectrum (Nov. 27, 2019), https://spectrum.ieee.org/how-boston-dynamics-is-redefining-robot-agility. On a lighter (but nonetheless eye-opening) note, *see* Boston Dynamics, *Do You Love Me?*, YouTube (Dec. 29, 2020), https://www.youtube.com/watch?v=fn3KWM1kuAw.

[46] *Supra* note 13. Legislation, regulation, compliance regimes, self-regulation, professionalization, transparency, and innumerable other inputs have led us to where we are today, where defense acquisition is dominated by massive, sophisticated firms, supplemented by an ever-changing cast of new entrants and innovators. Nonetheless, given the stakes, it is "scholarly neglect" to not contemplate these issues more frequently, and "this book aims to contribute to a field of study whose significance has been underappreciated." Schoeni & Vestner at 3.

[47] *See infra* text accompany notes 54–62. *See also supra* note 18.

As frustrated as many of us have become with overreliance on the military-industrial complex trope,[48] it serves as a helpful reminder that many of the ethical issues that arise from the context—kinetic solutions to social problems, staggering sums of money spent in the gray area where ends justify the means, and so forth—do not conform to intellectually lazy categories. Not all public servants are inherently good, nor are all contractor personnel greedy profiteers and pigs at the trough.[49] From the end of the twentieth century and into the post-millennial outsourcing era,[50] what happens to our preconceptions of military culture and norms of behavior[51] when the U.S. military cannot see, move, fight,

[48] "[T]he 'military-industrial complex' is often the bogeyman of journalistic investigations and conspiracy theories." SAPOLSKY ET AL., *supra* note 10, at 4.

[49] In looking back over the last few decades, even taking into account Blackwater's notorious 2007 Nisour Square massacre, it is impossible to tilt the scales sufficiently to conclude, let alone empirically demonstrate, that private sector behavior in the government contracting marketplace has been in any way less ethical, virtuous, or compliant than that of government officials, including the (former) president. *See generally* Laurel Wamsely, *Shock and Dismay After Trump Pardons Blackwater Guards Who Killed 14 Iraqi Civilians*, NPR (Dec. 23, 2020), https://www.npr.org/2020/12/23/949679837/shock-and-dismay-after-trump-pardons-blackwater-guards-who-killed-14-iraqi-civil; Falih Hassan & Jane Arraf, *Blackwater's Bullets Scarred Iraqis. Trump's Pardon Renewed the Pain*, N.Y. TIMES (Dec. 23, 2020), https://www.nytimes.com/2020/12/23/world/middleeast/blackwater-trump-pardon.html ("For some survivors of the attack, President Trump's pardon of the Blackwater contractors was a bitter reminder of what Iraqis have always viewed as a lack of concern over Iraqi lives."). Consider, among other high-profile scandals, that while "Fat Leonard" animated the most pervasive postmillennial scandal, *hundreds* of military officers and personnel put the Navy's Seventh Fleet's culture on trial, top to bottom. Craig Whitlock & Kevin Uhrmacher, *Prostitutes, Vacations and Cash: The Navy Officials "Fat Leonard" Took Down*, WASH. POST (Sept. 20, 2018), https://www.washingtonpost.com/graphics/investigations/seducing-the-seventh-fleet/. Before that, the Darlene Druyun saga saw both the Air Force's senior procurement official and the chief financial officer of one of the nation's largest companies (and household names), Boeing, Michael M. Sears, spend time in the federal penitentiary. John A. Tirpak, *Druyun's Downfall*, AIR FORCE MAG.: WASH. WATCH (Nov. 1, 2004), https://www.airforcemag.com/article/1104watch.

[50] Even at the peak of the U.S. involvement in Iraq and Afghanistan, where an increasingly blended battlespace saw contractors performing tasks previously considered the domain of uniformed personnel, or inherently government (or military) functions, the discussion of these difficult issues was short-lived. *See* Rachel Augustine Potter, *Macro Outsourcing: Evaluating Government Reliance on the Private Sector*, J. POL. (forthcoming), https://ssrn.com/abstract=3907539 ("Today, state governments routinely offload . . . government functions to the private sector. This trend is replicated at the federal level, where contractors help fight wars, run prisons, collect taxes, write regulations, render benefit decisions, and shape policy."); *see also* ALLISON STANGER, ONE NATION UNDER CONTRACT: THE OUTSOURCING OF AMERICAN POWER AND THE FUTURE OF FOREIGN POLICY (2011); PAUL C. LIGHT, THE GOVERNMENT-INDUSTRIAL COMPLEX: THE TRUE SIZE OF THE FEDERAL GOVERNMENT, 1984–2018 (2019); Steven L. Schooner, *The Well-Reasoned Case for Reversing the Outsourcing Trend: A Review Essay of Jon Michaels'* CONSTITUTIONAL COUP: PRIVATIZATION'S THREAT TO THE AMERICAN REPUBLIC, 59 GOV'T CONTRACTOR para. 319 (2017); Rebecca R. Vernon, *Battlefield Contractors: Facing Tough Issues*, 33 PUB. CONT. L.J. 369 (2004); Michael Davis, *Ruck Up: An Introduction to the Legal Issues Associated with Civilian Contractors on the Battlefield*, 29 PUB. CONT. L.J. 233 (2000); Steven L. Schooner & Daniel S. Greenspahn, *Too Dependent on Contractors? Minimum Standards for Responsible Governance*, 6 J. CONT. MGMT. 9 (2008); Steven L. Schooner, *Contractor Atrocities at Abu Ghraib: Compromised Accountability in a Streamlined, Outsourced Government*, 16 STAN. L. & POL'Y REV. 549 (2005); SEAN MCFATE, THE MODERN MERCENARY: PRIVATE ARMIES AND WHAT THEY MEAN FOR WORLD ORDER (2015).

[51] For a fascinating historical perspective on how far we have come in this regard, *see, e.g.*, CHARLES EDWARD WHITE, THE ENLIGHTENED SOLDIER: SCHARNHORST AND THE MILITARISCHE GESELLSCHAFT IN BERLIN, 1801–1805 (1989). White's historical vignette chronicles the transition

communicate, or sustain itself without a fully integrated contractor presence?[52] Yet as exhaustive and as thought-provoking as this volume proves, it merely scratches the surface. But like any good academic exercise,[53] it makes us confront that which we fail to think about, that which we take for granted, and that which we must not ignore.

Problems remain, scandals occur, and it is perfectly reasonable to hold the defense industry, which, as Leo Mackay, Jr. reminds in his *Foreword*, "builds instruments of destruction and lethality, . . . [used] to maintain [the public's] way of life, even [its] very existence,"[54] to a higher standard than the general commercial marketplace.[55] Fortunately, as a number of the chapters in this book

from a feudal (or royal) monopoly over the arms-bearing "arts" to the more modern *profession* of citizen soldiers, selected on merit, educated (not only in combat-related skills, but also in critical thinking and problem solving), led (in battle) by a meritocracy rather than the worst byproduct of a monarchy: ever-diminishing, arrogant, insular, ill-prepared, and closed-minded bloodlines. *See also infra* note 85.

[52] *See* Sapolsky et al. *supra* note 10, at 8–9, 298–99 ("The question policy-makers need to ask is: What must be retained as governmental or public, in the acquisition of weapons, training of soldiers, and the conduct of war? What tasks must the government perform directly to ensure its monopoly on the legitimate use of force . . . ? . . . The public and the private blend in providing America's defense. Private firms develop America's most advanced weapons and deploy personnel along with the troops to help them fight more effectively."); *see also* Government by Contract: Outsourcing and American Democracy (Jody Freemen & Martha Minow eds., 2009); *supra* note 18.

[53] In Chapter 3 of this volume , Richard W. Painter's four-part thought experiment offers an excellent opportunity to unpack some of these issues. Painter at 80–84, 92–97. In addition to the broad legal principles addressed in Painter's chapter, students (or for that matter, scholars) might be asked to read, compare, and contrast the coverage and guidance found in some of the major defense contractors' (publicly disclosed) codes of conduct to see if they would inform, guide, or constrain the contractors' (or their C-suites' or directors') actions. For example, the world's largest defense contractor, Lockheed Martin, publishes (in more than a dozen languages) its code of ethics and business conduct, which "details the high expectations we set for employee behavior, from our commitment to good citizenship to our zero-tolerance policy on corruption, serving as the most basic building block for future success." *Code of Conduct*, Lockheed Martin, https://www.lockheedmartin.com/en-us/who-we-are/ethics/code-of-ethics.html (last visited Jan. 9, 2022).

[54] Mackay at X. In Chapter 4 of this volume, C. Edward Peartree reminds us that much of the weapons market involves international arms trafficking, of the legalized sort, which in the United States is sanctioned under the Foreign Military Sales (FMS) regime and cabined by the International Trafficking in Arms Regulations. *See* Peartree at 115 ("If you are a defense firm selling your products pursuant to FMS, all aspects of the sale are subject to a legally binding 'letter of offer and acceptance' between the United States and the foreign government recipient."). *See generally Directorate of Defense Trade Controls*, U.S. Dep't of State, https://www.pmddtc.state.gov/ddtc_public (last visited Jan. 9, 2022); AECA, 22 U.S.C. § 2778; ITAR, 22 C.F.R. 120–130.

[55] Again, in Chapter 3 of this volume, Richard W. Painter poses a thorny policy problem, juxtaposing a loyalty aspiration for profit-seeking defense contractors against a long-standing congressional bias in favor of maximizing competition. Although many readers might instinctively agree that "companies should only be allowed to compete for large-scale U.S. defense contracts if they certify . . . that a primary purpose of the enterprise is to strengthen the national security," Painter at 101, that approach runs contrary to more than two decades of congressional policy, nay, insistence, that the defense acquisition marketplace *not* be limited to conventional defense firms. *See, e.g.*, FAR 12.101, 48 C.F.R. 12.101 (mandating that agencies "[a]cquire commercial products, commercial

explain, the defense acquisition landscape is far more regulated, responsible, transparent, and compliant than when Eisenhower left the White House. On the one hand, while all may not share Mackay's optimism that "we have come a long way regarding the most salient ethical challenges in the defense industry," it does appear that "national laws and industrial standards are rising and becoming mainstream,"[56] and that trend is a source of optimism. The industry has taken massive strides, prodded and propelled by a broad range of inputs, including but by no means limited to:

- conventional oversight and law enforcement organizations, such as, in the United States, Congress, the GAO, the DoJ, the IG community, and the Interagency Suspension and Debarment Committee (ISDC);[57]
- governmental institutions abroad, such as the Organization for Economic Cooperation and Development (OECD)[58] and the Geneva Centre for Security Sector Governance (DCAF);[59]
- civil society, including Transparency International (TI);[60] and
- the industry itself, led by, among others, the Defense Industry Initiative on Business Ethics and Conduct (DII),[61] the International Forum on Business

services, or nondevelopmental items when they are available to meet the needs of the agency"); *see also* FAR 2.101, 48 C.F.R. 2.101 (defining "commercial product" in a manner that suggests a commercial product or service "is of a type customarily used by the general public or by nongovernmental entities for purposes *other than governmental purposes*" (emphasis added)).

[56] Mackay at xi, xiii. Credit should go to Norman Ralph Augustine, who served, among other roles, as Under Secretary of the U.S. Army and later as chairman and CEO of the Lockheed Martin Corporation, for his leadership on these issues. *See* Richard G. Weingardt, *Norman Ralph Augustine*, 9 Leadership & Mgmt. Eng'g 149 (2009). *But see* William D. Hartung, *Saint Augustine's Rules: Norman Augustine and the Future of the American Defense*, 13 World Pol'y J. 65 (1996) ("It is hard to fault Augustine for driving the best possible bargain for his company, but one has to question the process by which he achieved his goal.").

[57] *See generally Interagency Suspension and Debarment Committee (ISDC)*, Acquisition.gov, https://www.acquisition.gov/isdc-home (last visited Jan. 9, 2022); Exec. Order No. 12,549, 51 Fed. Reg. 6370 (Feb. 18, 1986).

[58] *Anti-Corruption & Integrity Hub*, OECD, https://www.oecd.org/corruption-integrity (last visited Aug. 22, 2021).

[59] *What Is DCAF*, Geneva Ctr. for Sec. Sector Governance, https://dcaf.ch/about-us (last visited Jan. 9, 2022); *see also Private Military and Security Companies: Implementation of Montreux Document*, Int'l Comm. of the Red Cross (Dec. 16, 2014), https://www.icrc.org/en/document/private-military-and-security-companies-implementation-montreux-document.

[60] Transparency International's priorities include defense and security, *see What Is Defence and Security and Corruption?*, Transparency Int'l, https://www.transparency.org/en/our-priorities/defence-and-security (last visited Aug. 22, 2021), and public procurement, *see Public Procurement*, Transparency Int'l, https://www.transparency.org/en/our-priorities/public-procurement (last visited Aug. 22, 2021).

[61] Def. Indus. Initiative on Bus. Ethics & Conduct, https://www.dii.org (last visited Aug. 22, 2021).

> Ethics and Conduct (IFBEC),[62] and the International Stability Operations Association (ISOA).[63]

Failure to acknowledge the significance of the change, and the dramatically improved state of affairs, is as inaccurate as it is unfair. Of course, that does not suggest our work is complete, and plenty of room for improvement and growth remains. To that end, it is unsurprising that, in a high-stakes market involving hundreds of billions of dollars flowing through tens of millions of contractual agreements, new scandals constantly reveal themselves. Nor should it surprise us that the oversight community publishes a steady stream of critiques, that contractors overpromise or find themselves stretched too thin, that individuals behave badly, or that mistakes are made.

History reminds us that it is easy (and popular) to criticize the defense industry and, more broadly, the military-industrial complex. If you read GAO's seemingly never-ending tsunami of reports on the defense industry,[64] you could be forgiven for concluding that the Department of Defense is adrift, defense acquisition is in tatters, and no one knows where far too much of the money has gone. To a hammer, everything is a nail. And while oversight is necessary, it does not tell the whole story. Not surprisingly, academic study and closer examination breeds familiarity with complex issues that may explain certain pathologies, but nonetheless fail to illuminate a path to better practices or outcomes.[65] Patricia Werhane, in Chapter 16, explains:

[62] *About*, INT'L FORUM ON BUS. ETHICS & CONDUCT FOR THE AEROSPACE & DEF. INDUS., https://ifbec.info/about (last visited Aug. 22, 2021).

[63] INT'L STABILITY OPERATIONS ASS'N, https://stability-operations.org (last visited Aug. 22, 2021). "ISOA was founded . . . as the International Peace Operations Association [IPOA]." *Id.* at https://stability-operations.org/page/History. In particular, *see* ISOA's "Code of Conduct, which represents a constructive effort towards better regulating private sector operations in conflict and postconflict environments and disaster relief. It reflects our belief that high standards will both benefit the industry and serve the greater causes of peace, development, and human security." *Id.* at https://stability-operations.org/page/Code.

[64] For a representative sample, *see* the annual *High Risk List*, U.S. GOV'T ACCOUNTABILITY OFF., https://www.gao.gov/high-risk-list (last visited Oct. 7, 2021) (heavily populated with defense-related topics) or visit the GAO's topical pages focused on, inter alia, *National Defense*, https://www.gao.gov/topics/national-defense (last visited Oct: 7, 2021), *Auditing and Financial Management*, https://www.gao.gov/topics/auditing-and-financial-management (last visited Oct. 7, 2021), *Budgeting and Spending*, https://www.gao.gov/topics/budget-and-spending (last visited Oct. 7, 2021), or *Veterans*, https://www.gao.gov/topics/veterans (last visited Oct. 7, 2021).

[65] Discussing the life cycle of a major weapon system, and the various (typically polarized) perceptions of their history and utility, can be understood by analogy to the parable of the blind men and the elephant, commonly attributed to the ancient Indian subcontinent. As a single anecdote, *see* Steven L. Schooner & Nathaniel E. Castellano, *Review Essay: Reading* THE DREAM MACHINE: THE UNTOLD STORY OF THE NOTORIOUS V-22 OSPREY, *by Richard Whittle, in Light of the Defense Acquisition Performance Study*, 43 PUB. CONT. L.J. 391 (2014).

> When there is wrongdoing in our society, . . . an individual, group of individuals, or an organization is or are often singled out for blame. . . . But sometimes, at least, these misdeeds occur not because of deliberate malfeasance but rather because of complex collective action that produced these negative outcomes.[66]

It is also intellectually lazy to focus criticism exclusively on "the defense industry" or on the private sector's (or, in other words, defense contractors') failures and shortcomings when: (1) Congress exercises complete control over the defense budget, (2) individual members of Congress aggressively endeavor to maximize defense spending that benefits their constituents, (3) contractors cannot sell what governments will not buy, and (4) government authorization (and, typically, facilitation) is a prerequisite for selling their wares abroad. Arguably, no better recent anecdote exposes the absurdity of congressional defense priorities than the military's inability to retire the A-10 from service.[67]

For more than a decade, Wisconsin Senator William Proxmire highlighted government waste with a monthly "Golden Fleece" award.[68] Although spread across government instrumentalities, the defense industry was criticized for investing (a relatively modest sum) in a study to determine whether umbrellas should be carried by uniformed personnel.[69] But history reminds us that one critic's waste is another's passion, priority, policy, pet project, or, well, "pork." For example, what is the economic utility of the federal government maintaining multiple undergraduate institutions to produce entry-level officers? How can the federal government tolerate its military academies loosening their academic standards and diverting (allegedly scarce) resources to groom potential athletes

66 Werhane at 437.

67 *See* Mike Stone, *The Warthog and the Senator: The Politics of Retiring a Warplane*, REUTERS (July 16, 2021), https://www.reuters.com/world/us/warthog-senator-politics-retiring-warplane-2021-07-16 ("The U.S. Air Force is desperate to get rid of some of its fleet of expensive, slow and outdated A-10 Warthog airplanes, but politicians have blocked the move, aiming to keep the local dollars flowing."); *see also* Derek O'Malley & Andrew Hill, *Close Air Support in 2030: Moving Beyond the A-10/F-35 Debate*, WAR ON THE ROCKS (May 28, 2015), https://warontherocks.com/2015/05/the-a-10-the-f-35-and-the-future-of-close-air-support-part-ii (elaborating upon the misplaced priorities in the debate to retire the A-10 and quoting former Air Force Chief of Staff—and former A-10 pilot—General Mark Welsh: "I find myself arguing to get rid of things that I don't want to get rid of to pay a bill we've been handed. And the people [that] tell me I can't give up anything to pay it, are the people who gave us the bill. It's a strange situation.").

68 *See, e.g.*, *Reestablish the Golden Fleece Award*, 161 Cong. Rec. H3397 (daily ed. May 20, 2015) (statement of Rep. Hill), https://www.congress.gov/congressional-record/2015/05/20/house-section/article/H3397-2.

69 The idea that, for generations, it was considered improper for uniformed personnel to carry umbrellas flummoxes us to this day. Ben Kesling, *Semper Dry: Now Marines Can Carry Umbrellas, Setting Off Stormy Debate*, WALL ST. J. (Nov. 11, 2019), https://www.wsj.com/articles/semper-dry-now-marines-can-carry-umbrellas-setting-off-stormy-debate-11573494284 (noting that "[f]emale Marines were given permission to use umbrellas back in 1972 . . . [while t]he Army, Navy and Air Force have long authorized umbrellas for use by both sexes").

for the purpose of competing against institutions of higher education funded by individual states or the private sector?[70] From either an ethical or a fiscal law standpoint,[71] it is a long, tortured path from publicly funding competitive collegiate sports to the social imperatives associated with the nation's safety and security.

At the same time, history reminds us that, although anecdotes of wasteful spending are a given and counting defense scandals is good sport, particularly in light of the military's massive scale and insatiable needs and desires, anecdotes can be deceiving.[72] Just as the familiar triad of "fraud, waste, and abuse" often clumps together different pathologies and proposed remedies, overemphasis on anecdotes of defense industry shortcomings potentially paints an inaccurate picture and distract us from fundamental, often intractable, issues.[73]

7. The Forest, . . . And the Trees

I've been living to see you
Dying to see you
But it shouldn't be like this
This was unexpected
What do I do now?

[70] Billy Witz, *How a Military Prep School Helped Army Improve in Football*, N.Y. TIMES (Sept. 22, 2019), https://www.nytimes.com/2019/09/09/sports/army-prep-school.html. The service academies originally formed prep schools to create opportunities for enlisted soldiers to become officers and to increase diversity; today they also use prep schools to be more competitive in Division I sports, primarily football and basketball, instituting a de facto redshirt year during which these athletes get bigger, stronger, and faster. And before you ask *how much* the academies lower their academic standards, assume you don't want to know. "The mean SAT score for this year's class at the prep school was about 130 points [or just over 10 percent] lower than that of the cadets who were admitted directly to the academy. . . . While Army won't be admitting anyone with a 2.0 grade-point average or an 800 SAT score, . . . the admissions committee ha[s] been encouraged to take a more inclusive view of an applicant's file, including community service, leadership, character and athletic traits." *Id.*

[71] One of the fundamental statutes dealing with the use of appropriated funds is 31 U.S.C. § 1301(a), also known as the *purpose* statute: "Appropriations shall be applied only to the objects for which the appropriations were made except as otherwise provided by law." U.S. GOV'T ACCOUNTABILITY OFF., GAO-17-797SP, *Availability of Appropriations: Purpose*, *in* PRINCIPLES OF FEDERAL APPROPRIATIONS LAW 3-1, 3-9 (4th ed. 2017) (quoting 31 U.S.C. § 1301(a)), https://www.gao.gov/assets/2019-11/687162.pdf.

[72] And, of course, historical events can generate multiple storylines and parables. For many, familiarity with the World War II sinking of the U.S.S. *Indianapolis* (which delivered one of the atomic bombs' components before becoming the last American ship sunk during the war) is limited to the iconic galley scene from the movie JAWS (Universal 1975), *available at* https://www.youtube.com/watch?v=u9S41Kplsbs. When the wreck was discovered in 2017, 18,000 feet below the surface, many of us learned, for the first time, that Navy Captain Charles B. McVay III, who had been court-martialed for the loss of his ship in a high-profile, but deeply flawed proceeding, was exonerated *after* he committed suicide. *See* DOUG STANTON, IN HARM'S WAY (2001), for a powerful case study in diffusion of responsibility, scapegoating, and a failure of military justice.

[73] *See, e.g.*, *supra* note 21.

Could we start again, please?
I've been very hopeful, so far
Now, for the first time
I think we're going wrong
Hurry up and tell me
This is just a dream
Or could we start again, please?[74]

In retrospect, we may fairly be criticized, in examining defense industry ethics, for focusing on the failings and tension points—or what we might consider implementation pathologies—that arise within a large, complicated military-industrial complex. As we isolate discrete issues, problems, and quandaries, our various topical tasks permit us to take for granted that the nation *needs* a large military-industrial complex. Although we acknowledge the harsh reality that we do not live in a peaceful world, we do not, as noted earlier, address *why* the United States should (or should not) be our allies', the region's, or even (at its most aspirational) democracy's protector and enforcer. We welcome that debate.

But even that issue is framed too narrowly. How carefully do we endeavor to quantify the externalities, effects,[75] or opportunity costs of our massive military-industrial complex, and, more broadly, our martial instincts, culture, and self-image? Maybe the most pernicious aspect of the centrality of a high-profile military extends far beyond the defense industry. For many non-Americans, one of the defining features of what it means to be an American is the pervasive and destructive gun culture.[76] The American Public Health Association (APHA) reminds us that gun violence is a "leading cause of premature death" in the United States: "Each year, more than 39,000 people in the United States die as a result of gun violence, and tens of thousands more suffer non-fatal gun injuries."[77] While APHA advocates that "[g]un violence is not inevitable," there

[74] Andrew Lloyd Webber & Tim Rice, *Could We Start Again Please?*, *on* Jesus Christ Superstar (MCA Records 1973).

[75] We encourage use of the term "effects" instead of "negative externalities." *See generally* Kate Raworth, Doughnut Economics 123 (2017). Let us "drop the economist's beloved notion of 'externalities,' those incidental effects felt by people who were not involved in the transaction that produced them. . . . Due to the scale and interconnectedness of the global economy, many economic effects that were treated as 'externalities' in the twentieth-century theory have turned into defining social and ecological crises in the twenty-first century." *Id.*

[76] In Ch. 2 of the present volume, MacIntosh frames the popular sentiment this way: "it is no coincidence that . . . the U.S. . . . is also a gun culture. For what is true in the large in this case is also true in the manner of fractals right down to the small. . . . [T]he cost is 39,000 lives per year in gun violence. But the cost buys you absolute immunity to invasion from without, and from certain kinds of tyranny within."

[77] *Gun Violence Is a Public Health Crisis*, Am. Pub. Health Ass'n, https://www.apha.org/-/media/Files/PDF/factsheets/200221_Gun_Violence_Fact_Sheet.ashx (last visited Jan. 9, 2022).

seems minimal political will to address "[t]he burden of gun violence in the United States[, which] vastly outpaces that in comparable countries."[78]

Baby boomers grew up inspired by the technological advances spawned from NASA's pursuit of a moon landing: from freeze-dried food to fire-retardant suits and integrated circuits. Today, as we look outward toward space, as Brian D. Green explains in Chapter 6, it is not only the next frontier, but it also raises a raft of additional, complex questions.[79] Meanwhile, many point to the militarization of police forces as the natural evolution of the defense industry's pursuit of broader markets.[80] These are not idle concerns. And if you are worried about the state of the planet that your children and their children will inherit and inhabit, it is disheartening that, beyond the public purview,[81] the U.S. military consumes more fossil fuels than any other institution in the world.[82] So be sure to add the

[78] *Id.* How much of that core value derives from a zealous extrapolation of a 1791 constitutional amendment asserting that "[a] well regulated Militia . . . [is] necessary to the security of a free State"? U.S. Const. amend. II. It is beyond the scope of this exercise to attempt to unpack how, in good faith, or through principles of interpretation, the first 13 words in a 27-word sentence can be so easily, broadly, and vociferously ignored.

[79] As "the exploration and use of the space domain have grown . . . , new threats have emerged that require ever more vigilant, well-equipped, and ready military forces to defend the vital space capabilities of the United States and its allies." Green at 157. It seems axiomatic that "[a]s the barriers to entry for having a military presence in space have lowered over time and more countries therefore enter this domain, a policy of self-restraint may not serve to resolve all ethical dilemmas that are international in nature." *Id.* at 177 (footnote omitted).

[80] "[T]he idea is the Pentagon bought this stuff originally for the military, doesn't need it anymore and can give it to local police departments." David Brancaccio, Rose Conlon & Candace Manriquez Wrenn, *How Police Departments Got Billions of Dollars of Tactical Military Equipment*, Marketplace (June 12, 2020), https://www.marketplace.org/2020/06/12/police-departments-1033-military-equipment-weapons; *see also* Michael Leo Owens, Tom Clark & Adam Glynn, *Where Do Police Departments Get Their Military-Style Gear? Here's What We Don't Know*, Wash. Post (July 20, 2020), https://www.washingtonpost.com/politics/2020/07/20/where-do-police-departments-get-their-military-style-gear-heres-what-we-dont-know; *1033 Program FAQs*, Def. Logistics Agency, https://www.dla.mil/DispositionServices/Offers/Reutilization/LawEnforcement/ProgramFAQs.aspx (last visited Aug. 22, 2021) (explaining that the 1997 National Defense Authorization Act "granted permanent authority to the Secretary of Defense to transfer defense material to federal, state and local law enforcement agencies").

[81] We consider it inane that military greenhouse gas emissions continue to be exempted from reporting and national commitments following COP26. *See, e.g.*, Tom Ambrose, *World's Militaries Avoiding Scrutiny over Emissions, Scientists Say*, Guardian (Nov. 11, 2021), https://www.theguardian.com/environment/2021/nov/11/worlds-militaries-avoiding-scrutiny-over-emissions ("Armed forces are among the biggest polluters on the planet but are avoiding scrutiny because countries do not have to include their emissions in their targets. . . . The world's militaries . . . are estimated to create 6% of all global emissions, according to Scientists for Global Responsibility (SGR)."). COP26, held in Glasgow from October 31 through November 13, 2021, refers to the 26th conference of the parties (COP) to the United Nations Framework Convention on Climate Change (UNFCCC). *See generally Glasgow Climate Change Conference*, U.N. Climate Change, https://unfccc.int (last visited Jan. 9, 2022).

[82] "The U.S. military is an energy guzzler—it is the institution that consumes the most fossil fuels in the world. In fact, its carbon emissions are greater than those of many countries." Leah C. Stokes, *A Field Guide for Transformation*, *in* All We Can Save: Truth, Courage, and Solutions for the Climate Crisis 337, 341 (Ayana Elizabeth Johnson & Katharine K. Wilkinson eds., 2020). On a more positive note, *see* Michael T. Klare, All Hell Breaking Loose: The Pentagon's Perspective on Climate Change (2019), which chronicles DoD's under-the-radar "steps to

climate crisis[83] to the list of ills exacerbated by our massive military expenditures and activities.

Acknowledging these broader issues and incorporating them into the debates of defense industry ethics requires us to step back and remember to notice *both* the forest *and* the trees. As Patricia Werhane reminds us in Chapter 16: "[T]he process of stepping back, which conscientious individuals often engage in—challenging standard operating procedures, ingrained habits, and rote decision processes—is also possible in organizations. This sort of thinking entails moral imagination and moral courage."[84]

Are we a moral state? One common refrain of the coronavirus pandemic is that we are a toxic (and, sadly, mean-spirited) collection of profoundly selfish individuals, lacking the goodwill that binds together healthy communities.[85] Are we capable of moral action, of acting in our own, or our children's, best interests?[86] During the peak of post–9/11 American military activity in Iraq and Afghanistan, we were constantly reminded that ethics and morality are neither as consistent nor as philosophical as the academic thinking in undergraduate classrooms. We

mitigate its contributions to global warming," despite then-President Trump's executive order "instruct[ing agencies] to abandon their efforts to enhance climate preparedness." *Id.* at 1–2; Exec. Order No. 13,783, 82 Fed. Reg. 16,093 (Mar. 31, 2017), https://www.federalregister.gov/documents/2017/03/31/2017-06576/promoting-energy-independence-and-economic-growth.

83 "It is unequivocal that human influence has warmed the atmosphere, ocean and land. . . . Human-induced climate change is already affecting many weather and climate extremes in every region across the globe. . . . Projected changes in extremes are larger in frequency and intensity with every additional increment of global warming[.]" Intergovernmental Panel on Climate Change, *Summary for Policymakers, in* Climate Change 2021: The Physical Science Basis 4, 8, 18 (2021), https://www.ipcc.ch/report/ar6/wg1/downloads/report/IPCC_AR6_WGI_SPM_final.pdf.

84 Werhane at 461.

85 *See, e.g.*, Paul Krugman, *The Cult of Selfishness Is Killing America*, N.Y. Times (July 27, 2020), https://www.nytimes.com/2020/07/27/opinion/us-republicans-coronavirus.html; *see also* Robin Givhan, *Americans Are Stubbornly Unmoved by Death*, Wash. Post (Mar. 23, 2021), https://www.washingtonpost.com/nation/2021/03/23/americans-are-stubbornly-unmoved-by-death ("Increasingly it seems that we simply do not care about the other person, that other family, someone else's child. The self is everything. It's freedom and liberty, whims and desires. Community doesn't extend beyond one's front door. Everything else is someone else's concern."); *infra* note 90. Against that backdrop, *see* Leo Mackay's implicit yet poignant reminder, in this volume's *Foreword*, that institutions—government and private, from military services to multinational defense contractors—are communities of individuals. *See* Mackay at xii. It is perfectly reasonable to expect those institutions, including Mackay's Lockheed Martin, to "hire ethical people and then train and mentor them on applying ethical principles when they face tough decisions," but it is naïve to suggest that process is the optimal starting point for any discussion of ethical leadership, decision-making, or problem-solving. *Id.* Rather, government institutions and private contractors "hope that new employees come with well-tuned moral compasses . . . [calibrated by] lessons . . . nurtured in childhood [and] instilled through the higher education system." *Id.* It is only as a last resort, "when all else fails, [that ethical norms must be] enforced by governments." *Id.*

86 *See, e.g.*, Ezra Klein, *What if American Democracy Fails the Climate Crisis?*, N.Y. Times (June 22, 2021), https://www.nytimes.com/2021/06/22/magazine/ezra-klein-climate-crisis.html; *see also supra* text accompanying notes 80–82.

publicly celebrate active-duty military but underinvest in veterans' health care and pay lip service to the scourge of post–9/11 veteran suicide.[87] No number of standing ovations at ball games and concerts compensate for this long-running tragedy.

Bear in mind that those horrific statistics do not include contractor personnel—the anthropomorphic manifestation of Eisenhower's ire—who, for much of the postmillennial era, have not only outnumbered uniformed military in the battlespace, but have paced their level of sacrifice—in terms of injuries and fatalities—as well.[88] Long before the overdue, brief, and grossly inadequate efforts undertaken by the Biden administration in the summer of 2021, our government (specifically the Departments of Defense and State) consistently hung out to dry and left behind the interpreters and other "battlefield allies, who often braved death threats and put their families at risk of retribution" in support of American military and diplomatic efforts.[89] Our failure to educate the public on these issues is, to our minds, an irresponsible, improvident, and shortsighted moral and ethical failure.[90] This is not to say that we are by nature a fundamentally amoral

[87] "The overall suicide rate for veterans is 1.5 times as much as the rate for civilians. Among post-Sept. 11 veterans between 18-years-old and 35-years-old, the rate is 2.5 times that of all civilians." Jennifer Steinhauer, *Suicides Among Post-9/11 Veterans Are Four Times as High as Combat Deaths, a New Study Finds*, N.Y. Times (June 22, 2021), https://www.nytimes.com/2021/06/22/us/911-suicide-rate-veterans.html. *See generally National Veteran Suicide Data and Reporting*, U.S. Dep't of Vet. Aff., https://www.mentalhealth.va.gov/suicide_prevention/data.asp (last visited Aug. 22, 2021); Sapolsky et al., *supra* note 10, at 288. *See also* Steven L. Schooner & Nathaniel E. Castellano, *The VA Grand Challenge: Looking for Love in the Wrong Places*, Gov. Exec. (May 20, 2020) https://www.govexec.com/management/2020/05/va-grand-challenge-looking-love-wrong-places/165527.

[88] Steven L. Schooner & Collin Swan, *Dead Contractors: The Un-Examined Effect of Surrogates on the Public's Casualty Sensitivity*, 6 J. Nat'l Sec. L. & Pol'y 11 (2012) (reporting that on the modern battlefield, contractor personnel die at rates similar to—and at times in excess of—soldiers); Steven L. Schooner, *Remember Them Too: Don't Contractors Count when We Calculate the Costs of War?*, Wash. Post, May 25, 2009, at A21. You are forgiven if this sounds familiar to the way that our Border Patrol callously treated and recklessly separated immigrant parents and children. U.S. Gov't Accountability Off., GAO-20-245, Southwest Border: Actions Needed to Improve DHS Processing of Families and Coordination Between DHS and HHS (2020), https://www.gao.gov/assets/gao-20-245.pdf (reporting that agents had not correctly recorded family separations and official were unsure of the extent of the problem).

[89] Editorial Board, *America Must Not Turn its Back on Battlefield Allies from Iraq and Afghanistan*, Wash. Post (Jan. 30, 2019), https://www.washingtonpost.com/opinions/global-opinions/america-must-not-turn-its-back-on-battlefield-allies-from-iraq-and-afghanistan/2019/01/30/a3c969f4-2317-11e9-81fd-b7b05d5bed90_story.html; Helene Cooper & Eric Schmitt, *U.S. to Move Afghans Who Aided Troops Outside the Country*, N.Y. Times (June 24, 2021), https://www.nytimes.com/2021/06/24/us/politics/afghan-interpreters-visas.html ("More than 18,000 Afghans who have worked as interpreters, drivers, engineers, security guards, fixers and embassy clerks for the United States during the war [and their 53,000 family members] have been trapped in bureaucratic limbo after applying for special immigrant visas, available to people who face threats because of work for the U.S. government."). On a slightly positive note, the controversy surrounding the 2021 removal of U.S. armed forces from Afghanistan served to ever so fleetingly insert some of these issues into the public consciousness. Mark Cancian, *In Afghanistan, Contractors Were Unsung Heroes of US Efforts*, Breaking Def. (Aug. 30, 2021), https://breakingdefense.com/2021/08/in-afghanistan-contractors-were-unsung-heroes-of-us-efforts.

[90] This critique applies across the policy spectrum. *See generally* Kayla Chadwick, *I Don't Know How to Explain to You that You Should Care About Other People: Our Disagreement Is Not Merely Political, but a Fundamental Divide on What It Means to Live in a Society*, HuffPost (June 26, 2017),

state or that we are incapable of moral action. But it does serve to remind us that, even if we can summon the appropriate levels of moral courage, none of these issues are easily resolved.

Defense policy is polarizing—not only when engaging in warfare but when preparing for or, hypothetically, avoiding it. But the state's power to wage war—its so-called monopoly over the use of force—plays an outsized role in many of our nation's policies. We are ill-served if we are not constantly thinking, discussing, and, yes, voting on relevant issues. To our minds, this was Eisenhower's ultimate plea: that an "alert and knowledgeable citizenry"[91] would influence our elected leadership to make ethical decisions for the public good. It may seem obvious that, "[i]n a representative democracy, few decisions are more significant or heavily scrutinized than the decision to engage in heavy, sustained, military action abroad."[92] But if we do not study and discuss the relevant issues and policies, how can we expect to rely on our citizenry to push leadership in the right direction?

All of this brings us back to where Schoeni and Vestner began in the *Introduction*, with a compelling analogy to the law of war:

> Consider how this relates to the law of war, which governs how wars are conducted (*jus in bello*). This volume assumes that wars will continue and that a large share of global wealth will be devoted to the manufacture of arms for

https://www.huffpost.com/entry/i-dont-know-how-to-explain-to-you-that-you-should_b_59519811e4b0f078efd98440.

[91] To place that quote in context, Eisenhower said: "In the councils of government, we must guard against the acquisition of unwarranted influence, whether sought or unsought, by the military-industrial complex. The potential for the disastrous rise of misplaced power exists and will persist. We must never let the weight of this combination endanger our liberties or democratic processes. . . . Only an alert and knowledgeable citizenry can compel the proper meshing of the huge industrial and military machinery of defense with our peaceful methods and goals, so that security and liberty may prosper together." Eisenhower, *supra* note 13, at 1035.

[92] Schooner & Swan, *supra* note 88, at 11. During this book's final editing stage, the 2021 withdrawal of armed forces from Afghanistan thrust these issues into the public domain. *See generally* Ted Van Green & Carroll Doherty, *Majority of U.S. Public Favors Afghanistan Troop Withdrawal; Biden Criticized for His Handling of Situation*, PEW RSCH. CTR. (Aug. 31, 2021), https://www.pewresearch.org/fact-tank/2021/08/31/majority-of-u-s-public-favors-afghanistan-troop-withdrawal-biden-criticized-for-his-handling-of-situation ("[T]here is notable agreement among members of both parties that the U.S. mostly failed in achieving its goals in Afghanistan. Nearly identical majorities of Republicans (70%) and Democrats (69%) say the U.S. failed to accomplish its goals there."). *See also* Catie Edmonson, *Lawmakers Unite in Bipartisan Fury over Afghanistan Withdrawal*, N.Y. TIMES (Aug. 16, 2021), https://www.nytimes.com/2021/08/16/us/politics/afghanistan-withdrawal-congress.html; Peter Nicholas, *Biden Is Betting Americans Will Forget About Afghanistan*, ATLANTIC (Aug. 20, 2021), https://www.theatlantic.com/politics/archive/2021/08/biden-afghanistan-midterms/619838 ("For all the intense focus in Washington on the Taliban's resurgence, the broader public seems more preoccupied with other issues, like the still-raging coronavirus pandemic. . . . One former Biden campaign aide [noted that], '. . . at the end of the day, voters care about things that affect them and their families.'").

> the foreseeable future. Though industry is temporally and physically removed from the battlefield, how and in what manner it equips forces are questions of great moral significance, effectively questions about *jus in bello*. Just as soldiers are judged for their conduct in battle, so also can industry be held to account for the acquittal of its duties. *Jus in bello* is designed to limit the suffering caused by war. In a similar fashion, studying the moral questions about the manufacture, sale, and distribution of arms may teach us how to curtail any unnecessary harm that this bloody industry causes. Such an industry must exist, but its ethical shortcomings can be identified, studied, and perhaps even mitigated.[93]

Just as the transparency community advocates that "sunlight is the best disinfectant,"[94] the academic community is well served to keep scholars and students talking and thinking about the defense industry, warts and all. The thorny issues discussed in this volume challenge us to think, force us to ask difficult questions, and evade simple resolution. But they are also far too important for a representative democracy—a government of the people—to take for granted. If academic institutions aspire to remain robust marketplaces of ideas, teachers, students, and scholars must keep the discussion going.

References

2021 Power Rankings, U.S. NEWS & WORLD REP., https://www.usnews.com/news/best-countries/power-rankings.

ACQUISITION.GOV, *Interagency Suspension and Debarment Committee (ISDC)*, https://www.acquisition.gov/isdc-home.

Steven Aftergood, *The Costs of War: Obstacles to Public Understanding*, FED'N OF AM. SCIENTISTS (Nov. 14, 2018), https://fas.org/sgp/eprint/costs.pdf.

Tom Ambrose, *World's Militaries Avoiding Scrutiny over Emissions, Scientists Say*, GUARDIAN (Nov. 11, 2021), https://www.theguardian.com/environment/2021/nov/11/worlds-militaries-avoiding-scrutiny-over-emissions.

America's Longest War: A Visual History of 19 Years in Afghanistan, WALL ST. J. (Apr. 18, 2021), https://www.wsj.com/articles/us-longest-war-afghanistan-11583010024.

AM. PUB. HEALTH ASS'N, *Gun Violence Is a Public Health Crisis*, https://www.apha.org/-/media/Files/PDF/factsheets/200221_Gun_Violence_Fact_Sheet.ashx.

KATHERINE BARRETT & RICHARD GREENE, MAKING GOVERNMENT WORK: THE PROMISES AND PITFALLS OF PERFORMANCE-INFORMED MANAGEMENT (2020).

Boston Dynamics, *Do You Love Me?*, YOUTUBE (Dec. 29, 2020), https://www.youtube.com/watch?v=fn3KWM1kuAw.

[93] Schoeni & Vestner at 3.

[94] One longs for the day when readers will have forgotten (or never knew) that it was during the Trump administration that the *Washington Post* added "*Democracy Dies in Darkness*" to its masthead. *See* WASH. POST, https://www.washingtonpost.com (last visited Jan. 9, 2022).

David Brancaccio, Rose Conlon & Candace Manriquez Wrenn, *How Police Departments Got Billions of Dollars of Tactical Military Equipment*, MARKETPLACE (June 12, 2020), https://www.marketplace.org/2020/06/12/police-departments-1033-military-equipment-weapons.

Mark Cancian, *In Afghanistan, Contractors Were Unsung Heroes of US Efforts*, BREAKING DEF. (Aug. 30, 2021), https://breakingdefense.com/2021/08/in-afghanistan-contractors-were-unsung-heroes-of-us-efforts.

Kayla Chadwick, *I Don't Know How to Explain to You that You Should Care About Other People: Our Disagreement Is Not Merely Political, but a Fundamental Divide on What it Means to Live in a Society*, HUFFPOST (June 26, 2017), https://www.huffpost.com/entry/i-dont-know-how-to-explain-to-you-that-you-should_b_59519811e4b0f078efd98440.

JOHN CIBINIC, JR., JAMES F. NAGLE & RALPH C. NASH, JR., ADMINISTRATION OF GOVERNMENT CONTRACTS 697–790 (5th ed. 2016).

Helene Cooper & Eric Schmitt, *U.S. to Move Afghans Who Aided Troops Outside the Country*, N.Y. TIMES (June 24, 2021), https://www.nytimes.com/2021/06/24/us/politics/afghan-interpreters-visas.html.

CYBERSECURITY & INFRASTRUCTURE SEC. AGENCY, *Critical Infrastructure Sectors*, https://www.cisa.gov/defense-industrial-base-sector.

Michael Davis, *Ruck Up: An Introduction to the Legal Issues Associated with Civilian Contractors on the Battlefield*, 29 PUB. CONT. L.J. 233 (2000).

DEF. INDUS. INITIATIVE ON BUS. ETHICS & CONDUCT, https://www.dii.org.

DEF. LOGISTICS AGENCY, *1033 Program FAQs*, https://www.dla.mil/DispositionServices/Offers/Reutilization/LawEnforcement/ProgramFAQs.aspx.

DEF. SEC. COOP. AGENCY, *Foreign Military Sales FAQ*, https://www.dsca.mil/foreign-military-sales-faq.

Bruce Drake, *On Memorial Day, Public Pride in Veterans, but at a Distance*, PEW RSCH. CTR. (May 24, 2013), https://www.pewresearch.org/fact-tank/2013/05/24/on-memorial-day-public-pride-in-veterans-but-at-a-distance-2/.

Richard L. Dunn, *Defense Industry Needs New Way of Doing Business*, NAT'L DEF. (Nov. 6, 2000), https://www.nationaldefensemagazine.org/articles/2020/11/6/defense-industry-needs-new-way-of-doing-business.

Editorial Board, *America Must Not Turn Its Back on Battlefield Allies from Iraq and Afghanistan*, WASH. POST (Jan. 30, 2019), https://www.washingtonpost.com/opinions/global-opinions/america-must-not-turn-its-back-on-battlefield-allies-from-iraq-and-afghanistan/2019/01/30/a3c969f4-2317-11e9-81fd-b7b05d5bed90_story.html.

Catie Edmonson, *Lawmakers Unite in Bipartisan Fury over Afghanistan Withdrawal*, N.Y. TIMES (Aug. 16, 2021), https://www.nytimes.com/2021/08/16/us/politics/afghanistan-withdrawal-congress.html.

Dwight D. Eisenhower, *Farewell Radio and Television Address to the American People (Jan. 17, 1961), in* PUBLIC PAPERS OF THE PRESIDENT OF THE UNITED STATES: DWIGHT D. EISENHOWER 1960–61, at 1035 (1961).

Sheri Fink, *Settlement Reached in C.I.A. Torture Case*, N.Y. TIMES (Aug. 17, 2017), https://www.nytimes.com/2017/08/17/us/cia-torture-lawsuit-settlement.html.

Conor Friedersdorf, *The Destructiveness of Call-Out Culture on Campus*, ATLANTIC (May 8, 2017), https://www.theatlantic.com/politics/archive/2017/05/call-out-culture-is-stressing-out-college-students/524679.

GENEVA CTR. FOR SEC. SECTOR GOVERNANCE, *What Is DCAF*, https://dcaf.ch/about-us.

Ed Gerrish, *The Impact of Performance Management in Public Organizations: A Meta-Analysis*, 76 PUB. ADMIN. REV. 48 (2015).

Robin Givhan, *Americans Are Stubbornly Unmoved by Death*, WASH. POST (Mar. 23, 2021), https://www.washingtonpost.com/nation/2021/03/23/americans-are-stubbornly-unmoved-by-death.

GOVERNMENT BY CONTRACT: OUTSOURCING AND AMERICAN DEMOCRACY (Jody Freemen & Martha Minow eds., 2009).

Erico Guizzo, *How Boston Dynamics Is Redefining Robot Agility*, IEEE SPECTRUM (Nov. 27, 2019), https://spectrum.ieee.org/how-boston-dynamics-is-redefining-robot-agility.

Michaila Hancock, *Pentagon: The World's Largest Office Building—in Infographics*, ARCHITECT'S J. (Aug. 27, 2015), https://www.architectsjournal.co.uk/news/pentagon-the-worlds-largest-office-building-in-infographics.

William D. Hartung, *Saint Augustine's Rules: Norman Augustine and the Future of the American Defense*, 13 WORLD POL'Y J. 65 (1996).

Falih Hassan & Jane Arraf, *Blackwater's Bullets Scarred Iraqis. Trump's Pardon Renewed the Pain*, N.Y. TIMES (Dec. 23, 2020), https://www.nytimes.com/2020/12/23/world/middleeast/blackwater-trump-pardon.html.

INTERGOVERNMENTAL PANEL ON CLIMATE CHANGE, *Summary for Policymakers, in* CLIMATE CHANGE 2021: THE PHYSICAL SCIENCE BASIS 4, 8, 18 (2021), https://www.ipcc.ch/report/ar6/wg1/downloads/report/IPCC_AR6_WGI_SPM_final.pdf.

INT'L COMM. OF THE RED CROSS, *Private Military and Security Companies: Implementation of Montreux Document*, (Dec. 16, 2014), https://www.icrc.org/en/document/private-military-and-security-companies-implementation-montreux-document.

INT'L FORUM ON BUS. ETHICS & CONDUCT FOR THE AEROSPACE & DEF. INDUS., *About*, https://ifbec.info/about.

INT'L STABILITY OPERATIONS ASS'N, https://stability-operations.org.

JAWS (Universal 1975), https://www.youtube.com/watch?v=u9S41Kplsbs.

John Kamensky, *Does Performance Matter?*, IBM CTR. FOR BUS. GOV'T (Mar. 28, 2016), https://www.businessofgovernment.org/blog/does-performance-matter.

SARAH KENDZIOR, HIDING IN PLAIN SIGHT: THE INVENTION OF DONALD TRUMP AND THE EROSION OF AMERICA (2020).

Ben Kesling, *Semper Dry: Now Marines Can Carry Umbrellas, Setting Off Stormy Debate*, WALL ST. J. (Nov. 11, 2019), https://www.wsj.com/articles/semper-dry-now-marines-can-carry-umbrellas-setting-off-stormy-debate-11573494284.

MICHAEL T. KLARE, ALL HELL BREAKING LOOSE: THE PENTAGON'S PERSPECTIVE ON CLIMATE CHANGE (2019).

Ezra Klein, *What if American Democracy Fails the Climate Crisis?*, N.Y. TIMES (June 22, 2021), https://www.nytimes.com/2021/06/22/magazine/ezra-klein-climate-crisis.html.

Paul Krugman, *The Bogus Bashing of Build Back Better*, N.Y. TIMES (Dec. 13, 2021), https://www.nytimes.com/2021/12/13/opinion/build-back-better.html.

Paul Krugman, *The Cult of Selfishness Is Killing America*, N.Y. TIMES (July 27, 2020), https://www.nytimes.com/2020/07/27/opinion/us-republicans-coronavirus.html.

Danielle Kurtzleben, *Trump Embraces One of Russia's Favorite Propaganda Tactics—Whataboutism*, NPR (Mar. 17, 2017), https://www.npr.org/2017/03/17/520435073/trump-embraces-one-of-russias-favorite-propaganda-tactics-whataboutism.

Doug Lederman, *Wrangling over Military Recruiting*, INSIDE HIGHER ED (Feb. 3, 2005), https://www.insidehighered.com/news/2005/02/03/wrangling-over-military-recruiting

JOHN LENNON, *Imagine*, *on* IMAGINE (Apple Records1971).

Letter from Noah Bookbinder, President, Citizens for Resp. & Ethics, et al., to Bill Schmidt, Suspension & Debarment Off., Gen. Servs. Admin., et al. (Oct. 12, 2021), https://www.citizensforethics.org/wp-content/uploads/2021/10/2021-10-12-Trump-Organization-Suspension-Referral.pdf.

LIBR. OF CONG., *It Will Be a Great Day When Our Schools Get All the Money They Need and the Air Force Has to Hold a Bake Sale to Buy a Bomber*, https://www.loc.gov/resource/ds.13124.

PAUL C. LIGHT, THE GOVERNMENT-INDUSTRIAL COMPLEX: THE TRUE SIZE OF THE FEDERAL GOVERNMENT, 1984–2018 (2019).

LOCKHEED MARTIN, *Code of Conduct*, https://www.lockheedmartin.com/en-us/who-we-are/ethics/code-of-ethics.html.

The Magic School Bus (Scholastic 1994–1997).

Jean Marbella, *ROTC Resurgent on College Campuses Where Once Scorned*, BALT. SUN, (Nov. 18, 2001), https://www.baltimoresun.com/news/bs-xpm-2001-11-18-0111180052-story.html.

SEAN MCFATE, THE MODERN MERCENARY: PRIVATE ARMIES AND WHAT THEY MEAN FOR WORLD ORDER (2015).

NAT'L MUSEUM OF NUCLEAR SCI. & HIST., *Hiroshima and Nagasaki Exhibit*, https://www.nuclearmuseum.org/see/exhibits/hiroshima-and-nagasaki.

Peter Nicholas, *Biden Is Betting Americans Will Forget About Afghanistan*, ATLANTIC (Aug. 20, 2021), https://www.theatlantic.com/politics/archive/2021/08/biden-afghanistan-midterms/619838.

Andy Norman, *The Cause of America's Post-Truth Predicament*, SCI. AM. (May 18, 2021), https://www.scientificamerican.com/article/the-cause-of-americas-post-truth-predicament.

Pippa Norris, *Cancel Culture: Myth or Reality?*, POL. STUD., July 16, 2021, at 1, https://journals-sagepub-com.proxygw.wrlc.org/doi/pdf/10.1177/00323217211037023.

OECD, *Anti-Corruption & Integrity Hub*, https://www.oecd.org/corruption-integrity.

Derek O'Malley & Andrew Hill, *Close Air Support in 2030: Moving Beyond the A-10/F-35 Debate*, WAR ON THE ROCKS (May 28, 2015), https://warontherocks.com/2015/05/the-a-10-the-f-35-and-the-future-of-close-air-support-part-ii.

Michael Leo Owens, Tom Clark & Adam Glynn, *Where Do Police Departments Get Their Military-Style Gear? Here's What We Don't Know*, WASH. POST (July 20, 2020), https://www.washingtonpost.com/politics/2020/07/20/where-do-police-departments-get-their-military-style-gear-heres-what-we-dont-know.

HEIDI M. PETERS, CONG. RSCH. SERV., IF10548, DEFENSE PRIMER: U.S. DEFENSE INDUSTRIAL BASE (2021), https://crsreports.congress.gov/product/pdf/IF/IF10548/10.

HEIDI M. PETERS, CONG. RSCH. SERV., R46643, DEFENSE ACQUISITIONS: DOD'S CYBERSECURITY MATURITY MODEL CERTIFICATION FRAMEWORK (2020), https://crsreports.congress.gov/product/pdf/R/R46643/2.

Elizabeth Phelan, *"A Watershed Moment": Reflecting on the Burning of the ROTC Air Force Building—50 Years Later*, STUDENT LIFE (May 5, 2020), https://www.studlife.com/scene/2020/05/05/a-watershed-moment-reflecting-on-the-burning-of-the-rotc-air-force-building-50-years-later.

Rachel Augustine Potter, *Macro Outsourcing: Evaluating Government Reliance on the Private Sector*, J. POL. (forthcoming), https://ssrn.com/abstract=3907539.

William L. Prosser, *Lighthouse No Good*, 1 J. LEGAL EDUC. 257, 257 (1948).

Annalisa Quinn, *Chinua Achebe and the Bravery of Lions*, NPR (Mar. 23, 2013), https://www.npr.org/sections/thetwo-way/2013/03/22/175046327/chinua-achebe-and-the-bravery-of-lions.

Kate Raworth, Doughnut Economics 123 (2017).

Reestablish the Golden Fleece Award, 161 Cong. Rec. H3397 (daily ed. May 20, 2015) (statement of Rep. Hill), https://www.congress.gov/congressional-record/2015/05/20/house-section/article/H3397-2.

Renegotiation Board—Reporting Requirement (50 U.S.C. App. § 1215)—Effect of Absence of an Appropriation—Repeals by Implication, 3 Op. O.L.C. 318 (1979), https://www.justice.gov/file/22096/download.

Roger Riddell, *Can Higher Ed Really Affect Change Through Divestment?*, Higher Ed Dive (May 29, 2014), https://www.highereddive.com/news/can-higher-ed-really-affect-change-through-divestment/265675.

ROTCM 145–85, Dep't of Army, ROTC Manual, Fundamentals of Military Law (Oct. 1980).

Gregory Sanders et al., *Defense Contract Trends: U.S. Department of Defense Contract Spending and the Supporting Industrial Base*, Ctr. for Strategic & Int'l Stud. (2011), https://www.csis.org/analysis/defense-contract-trends-0.

Harvey M. Sapolsky, Eugene Gholz & Caitlin Talmadge, U.S Defense Politics: The Origins of National Security (4th ed. 2021).

Steven L. Schooner, *Contractor Atrocities at Abu Ghraib: Compromised Accountability in a Streamlined, Outsourced Government*, 16 Stan. L. & Pol'y Rev. 549 (2005).

Steven L. Schooner, *Remember Them Too: Don't Contractors Count when We Calculate the Costs of War?*, Wash. Post, May 25, 2009, at A21.

Steven L. Schooner, *The Well-Reasoned Case for Reversing the Outsourcing Trend: A Review Essay of Jon Michaels' Constitutional Coup: Privatization's Threat to the American Republic*, 59 Gov't Contractor ¶ 319 (2017).

Steven L. Schooner, *We Need to Talk About Corruption*, Gov't Exec. (Sept. 29, 2020) (reviewing Jennifer Taub, Big Dirty Money: The Shocking Injustice and Unseen Cost of White Collar Crime (2020)), https://www.govexec.com/management/2020/09/we-need-talk-about-corruption/168857.

Steven L. Schooner & Nathaniel E. Castellano, *Review Essay: Reading* The Dream Machine: The Untold Story of the Notorious V-22 Osprey, *by Richard Whittle, in Light of the Defense Acquisition Performance Study*, 43 Pub. Cont. L.J. 391 (2014).

Steven L. Schooner & Nathaniel Castellano, *Dawn of the Intercontinental Sniper: The Drone's Cascading Contribution to the Modern Battlefield's Complexity*, 8 J. Nat'l Sec. L. & Pol'y 321 (2016) (reviewing Richard Whittle, Predator: The Secret Origins of the Drone Revolution (2014)).

Steven L. Schooner & Nathaniel E. Castellano, *The VA Grand Challenge: Looking for Love in the Wrong Places*, Gov. Exec. (May 20, 2020) https://www.govexec.com/management/2020/05/va-grand-challenge-looking-love-wrong-places/165527.

Steven L. Schooner, Kathleen Clark & Scott Amey, *Suspend the Trump Organization from Doing Business with Government*, Gov't Exec. (Jan. 27, 2020), https://www.govexec.com/management/2020/01/viewpoint-suspend-trump-organization-doing-business-government/162672.

Steven L. Schooner & Daniel S. Greenspahn, *Too Dependent on Contractors? Minimum Standards for Responsible Governance*, 6 J. Cont. Mgmt. 9 (2008).

Steven L. Schooner & Collin Swan, *Dead Contractors: The Un-Examined Effect of Surrogates on the Public's Casualty Sensitivity*, 6 J. NAT'L SEC. L. & POL'Y 11 (2012).

SELECTIVE SERV. SYS., *Historical Timeline*, https://www.sss.gov/history-and-records/timeline.

Senate Vote Means End of Renegotiation Board, N.Y. TIMES (Apr. 3, 1979), https://www.nytimes.com/1979/04/03/archives/senate-vote-means-end-of-renegotiation-board.html.

Special Briefing with Patrick F. Kennedy, Ambassador, Dep't of State, on the Report of the Secretary of State's Panel on Personal Protective Services in Iraq (Oct. 23, 2007), https://2001-2009.state.gov/r/pa/prs/ps/2007/oct/94019.htm.

ALLISON STANGER, ONE NATION UNDER CONTRACT: THE OUTSOURCING OF AMERICAN POWER AND THE FUTURE OF FOREIGN POLICY (2011).

DOUG STANTON, IN HARM'S WAY (2001).

Samuel Stebbins & Evan Comen, *Military Spending: 20 Companies Profiting the Most from War*, USA TODAY (Feb. 21, 2019), https://www.usatoday.com/story/money/2019/02/21/military-spending-defense-contractors-profiting-from-war-weapons-sales/39092315.

Jennifer Steinhauer, *Suicides Among Post-9/11 Veterans Are Four Times as High as Combat Deaths, a New Study Finds*, N.Y. TIMES (June 22, 2021), https://www.nytimes.com/2021/06/22/us/911-suicide-rate-veterans.html.

Leah C. Stokes, *A Field Guide for Transformation*, *in* ALL WE CAN SAVE: TRUTH, COURAGE, AND SOLUTIONS FOR THE CLIMATE CRISIS 337 (Ayana Elizabeth Johnson & Katharine K. Wilkinson eds., 2020).

Mike Stone, *The Warthog and the Senator: The Politics of Retiring a Warplane*, REUTERS (July 16, 2021), https://www.reuters.com/world/us/warthog-senator-politics-retiring-warplane-2021-07-16.

John A. Tirpak, *Druyun's Downfall*, AIR FORCE MAG.: WASH. WATCH (Nov. 1, 2004), https://www.airforcemag.com/article/1104watch.

TRANSPARENCY INT'L, *What Is Defence and Security and Corruption?*, https://www.transparency.org/en/our-priorities/defence-and-security.

TRANSPARENCY INT'L, *Public Procurement*, https://www.transparency.org/en/our-priorities/public-procurement.

U.N. CLIMATE CHANGE, *Glasgow Climate Change Conference*, https://unfccc.int.

U.S. GOV'T ACCOUNTABILITY OFF., GAO-17-797SP, *Availability of Appropriations: Purpose*, *in* PRINCIPLES OF FEDERAL APPROPRIATIONS LAW 3–1, 3–9 (4th ed. 2017) (quoting 31 U.S.C. § 1301(a)), https://www.gao.gov/assets/2019-11/687162.pdf.

U.S. GOV'T ACCOUNTABILITY OFF., GAO-20-245, SOUTHWEST BORDER: ACTIONS NEEDED TO IMPROVE DHS PROCESSING OF FAMILIES AND COORDINATION BETWEEN DHS AND HHS (2020), https://www.gao.gov/assets/gao-20-245.pdf.

U.S. GOV'T ACCOUNTABILITY OFF., GAO-22-104679, DEFENSE CONTRACTOR CYBERSECURITY: STAKEHOLDER COMMUNICATION AND PERFORMANCE GOALS COULD IMPROVE CERTIFICATION FRAMEWORK (2021), https://www.gao.gov/assets/gao-22-104679.pdf.

U.S. GOV'T ACCOUNTABILITY OFF., *Auditing and Financial Management*, https://www.gao.gov/topics/auditing-and-financial-management.

U.S. GOV'T ACCOUNTABILITY OFF., *Budgeting and Spending*, https://www.gao.gov/topics/budget-and-spending.

U.S. GOV'T ACCOUNTABILITY OFF., *High Risk List*, https://www.gao.gov/high-risk-list.

U.S. Gov't Accountability Off., *National Defense*, https://www.gao.gov/topics/national-defense.

U.S. Gov't Accountability Off., *Veterans*, https://www.gao.gov/topics/veterans.

U.S. Dep't of Def., *Pentagon Facts*, https://pentagontours.osd.mil/Tours/facts.html

U.S. Dep't of State, *Directorate of Defense Trade Controls*, https://www.pmddtc.state.gov/ddtc_public.

U.S. Dep't of Vet. Aff., *National Veteran Suicide Data and Reporting*, https://www.mentalhealth.va.gov/suicide_prevention/data.asp.

Ted Van Green & Carroll Doherty, *Majority of U.S. Public Favors Afghanistan Troop Withdrawal; Biden Criticized for His Handling of Situation*, Pew Rsch. Ctr. (Aug. 31, 2021), https://www.pewresearch.org/fact-tank/2021/08/31/majority-of-u-s-public-favors-afghanistan-troop-withdrawal-biden-criticized-for-his-handling-of-situation.

Chiara Vercellone, *Who Were the Largest Major Arms Exporters in the Last 5 Years?*, Def. News (Mar. 9, 2020), https://www.defensenews.com/2020/03/09/who-were-the-largest-major-arms-exporters-in-the-last-5-years.

Rebecca R. Vernon, *Battlefield Contractors: Facing Tough Issues*, 33 Pub. Cont. L.J. 369 (2004).

Laurel Wamsely, *Shock and Dismay After Trump Pardons Blackwater Guards Who Killed 14 Iraqi Civilians*, NPR (Dec. 23, 2020), https://www.npr.org/2020/12/23/949679837/shock-and-dismay-after-trump-pardons-blackwater-guards-who-killed-14-iraqi-civil.

Wash. Post, https://www.washingtonpost.com.

Andrew Lloyd Webber & Tim Rice, *Could We Start Again Please?*, *on* Jesus Christ Superstar (MCA Records 1973).

Richard G. Weingardt, *Norman Ralph Augustine*, 9 Leadership & Mgmt. Eng'g 149 (2009).

Charles Edward White, The Enlightened Soldier: Scharnhorst and the Militarische Gesellschaft in Berlin, 1801–1805 (1989).

Craig Whitlock & Kevin Uhrmacher, *Prostitutes, Vacations and Cash: The Navy Officials "Fat Leonard" Took Down*, Wash. Post (Sept. 20, 2018), https://www.washingtonpost.com/graphics/investigations/seducing-the-seventh-fleet/

Billy Witz, *How a Military Prep School Helped Army Improve in Football*, N.Y. Times (Sept. 22, 2019), https://www.nytimes.com/2019/09/09/sports/army-prep-school.html.

Robert Woodard, Bureau of Indus. & Sec., Dep't of Com., Offsets in Defense Trade—Frequently Asked Questions (2017), https://www.bis.doc.gov/index.php/documents/pdfs/1677-offsets-in-defense-trade-faqs-final/file.

David Zucchino & David S. Cloud, *Special Report: U.S. Military and Civilians Are Increasingly Divided*, L.A. Times (May 23, 2015), https://www.latimes.com/nation/la-na-warrior-main-20150524-story.html.

Index

For the benefit of digital users, indexed terms that span two pages (e.g., 52–53) may, on occasion, appear on only one of those pages.

Note: Figures are indicated by *f* following the page number